Aerial Warfare

Aerial Warfare

An Illustrated History

Foreword by
General Adolf Galland

Edited by
Anthony Robinson

ORBIS PUBLISHING · LONDON

First published in Great Britain by Orbis Publishing Limited,
London 1982
© Orbis Publishing Limited, London 1982

Printed in Hong Kong by the Toppan Printing Co. (HK)
Limited

ISBN: 0-85613-261-6

*Endpapers: Vickers Armstrong Wellington Mk ICs of No 311
Squadron, No 3 Group, RAF Bomber Command pictured in
March 1941.*

*Half title page: the versatile Bristol Beaufighter served the RAF
with distinction as a night fighter and shipping strike aircraft.*

*Page 6: Adolf Galland pictured when he was Oberstleutnant in
1940 with his dog and characteristic cigar. One of the young
Luftwaffe fighter leaders brought to prominence in the Battle of
Britain, Galland was appointed General of Fighters in 1941. He
held this onerous position with distinction until early 1945 when
he was dismissed from his post following confrontations with
Hitler and Goering over the aerial defence of the Reich. He then
assumed command of JV 44, a Messerschmitt Me 262 jet fighter
equipped unit which was composed of the elite of the surviving
Luftwaffe fighter pilots.*

Material in this book was previously published in *Wings*, the
encyclopedia of aviation.

Contents

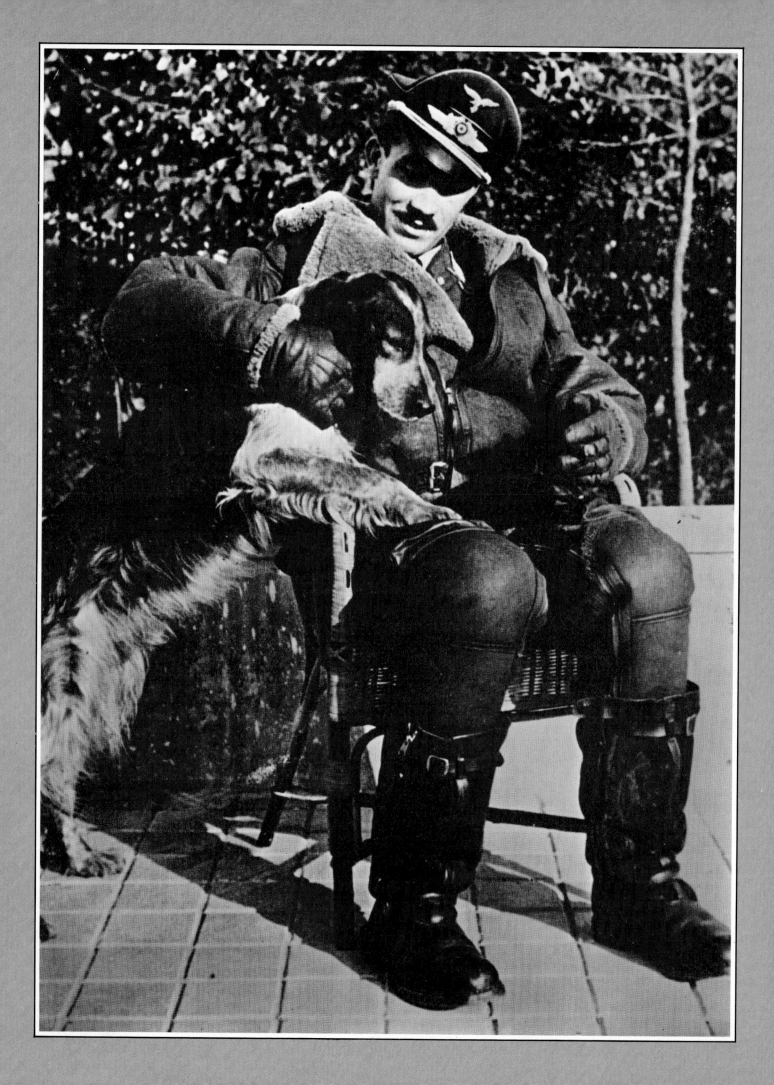

Foreword

The history of air warfare covers a period of less than seven decades, if one discounts the early use of observation balloons at the end of the eighteenth century. But in that short period enormous strides have been made in the development of weapons and in the evolution of tactics.

The first section of this book deals with the operational roles of the warplane. The development of tactics is described in such crucial roles as air fighting, bombing, reconnaissance, anti-submarine warfare and the lesser-known aspects of air warfare, such as electronic countermeasures, counter-insurgency and aerial propaganda.

However, warfare in any element is not just a matter of evolving the correct strategy and tactics to achieve one's aim. Combat is the acid test of any armed service and the section on air campaigns shows the part that air forces have played in the wars of the twentieth century. The air campaigns examined range from the hesitant beginnings of air warfare during the Italian war in Libya in 1911 to the jet age conflict waged over Vietnam between 1965 and 1972. Inevitably, though, it is the great air battles of World War II which dominate this section, including the Battle of Britain, the Defence of the Reich, the war over the Eastern Front and the fighting over the Pacific between the United States and Japan.

The first major air operation I prepared and successfully conducted was The Channel Dash of the German battleships *Scharnhorst*, *Gneisenau* and *Prinz Eugen*, a fleet movement involving some 80 ships through the English Channel on 12 February 1942. I was solely responsible for the complete fighter cover for this operation. Commander-in-Chief of Air Fleet 3, Feldmarschall Sperrle, was extremely happy not to be involved, because he and all the other High Commands were of the firm opinion, that this operation would be a complete disaster. I admit that I am proud of the successful part my fighters played in this operation.

The importance of the individual qualities of the airman is highlighted in the last section of this book, which deals with notable individual actions. In the annals of air warfare some feats of arms stand out from the ordinary and these are described in detail as a tribute to the courage and tenacity of the airmen of all nations.

GENERAL ADOLF GALLAND

Airborne Early Warning

Everyone knows that, on a clear day, you can see further if you raise yourself above the ground. This is, of course, due to the curvature of our near-spherical earth. Thus the further above its surface we can fly, the further round the curve we can see. For early warning systems in World War II this was of mainly academic interest and observers with binoculars at ground or roof level were chiefly relied upon to spot enemy aircraft. The resulting warning time of half a minute or less was ample to get workers under cover or a flak battery pointed at the target. One of the few early warning systems that did try to use height to see further was the earliest radar system, the British Chain Home (CH) radar fence around the east and south coastlines of the British Isles. It used large aerial arrays suspended between lattice towers 73 or 98 m (240 or 320 ft) high, often located on the highest available hill or cliff-top. Today virtually all early-warning radar stations, other than mobile ones, are located on the tops of hills or mountains, often accessible only by helicopter. This has two principal advantages: it allows the radar to 'see' further, and it helps to prevent low-fliers who streak in along low-lying valleys or behind woods from escaping detection behind obstructions.

Britain's CH 'picket fence' proved good enough in World War II to give adequate warning of attack, but since those almost prehistoric days in electronic air defence the differences in ground-based systems have been mainly in degree. In the 1950s the DEW-line (Distant Early Warning) was constructed in a vast belt across some of the toughest and least populated territory in the world from Alaska across northern Canada to Greenland. In the 1960s Western Europe at last got a single, integrated, instant-reaction computerised defence system in Nadge (NATO Air-Defence Ground Environment), which occupies most of the mountain peaks from North Cape (at the northern tip of Norway) through central Europe,

Italy and Greece to the easternmost mountains of Turkey that look far into the Soviet Union. Badge is a similar system defending Japan, as is Combat Grande in Spain. However, all suffer from the fact that modern attackers can approach faster than sound at treetop height, or at three times the speed of sound at high altitude and in either case, the warning time given by ground-based systems is barely long enough.

Fundamental limitations

As early as 1939 paper studies existed in Britain for a large aeroplane whose sole purpose was to carry a powerful search radar and thus give it the ability to see further over the low-altitude horizon and give longer warning of enemy raids. It was rightly thought of great importance to lift defending radars as high as possible to see enemy forces flying at low level, below the line-of-sight limit of radars even on hilltops, but the aircraft was never built.

In the early months of the war the need was for more established items. In the Battle of Britain the Luftwaffe obligingly sent its aircraft over in great high-altitude formations which could be detected by the CH stations as they formed up over their own airfields in northern France and the Low Countries, but this did not invalidate the basic concept of the AEW (Airborne Early Warning) aircraft. By mid-1943 the US Army and Navy had jointly formulated a study programme for such an aircraft, initially using either the B-17 or B-24 as carrier vehicle. Calculations showed that, in theory, such a 'radar picket airplane' could operate for long periods at an altitude of 8,230 m (27,000 ft), at which the radar horizon would be extended to about 330 km (205 miles). The US Navy also studied a radar-carrying blimp (non-rigid airship) for long-endurance protection of convoys and naval fleets.

Although the same radar could be used in both the aeroplane and the blimp, no suitable radar existed, and

Opposite: the Grumman E-2 Hawkeye was designed to meet a US Navy requirement of the mid-1950s for an airborne early-warning (AEW) picket aircraft capable of providing information on the disposition of friendly and hostile ships and aircraft to a Navy task force commander. The E-2 carries digital computers which interpret information from its long-range search radar and automatically select the best riposte to any given hostile move in the battle area

Right: a Grumman E-2 Hawkeye. The multiple-surface tail was decided upon to counteract the change in airflow over the large radome.
Below right: the Boeing E-3A AWACS can keep over 12·5 million cubic kilometres of air space under continuous surveillance

its development was not given high enough priority before VE-day. However, in the spring of 1945 the detailed specification was drawn up for Project Cadillac, the world's first AEW radar. Among the demands were the ability to discern individual aircraft in a close formation at ranges between 275–320 km (170–200 miles) determination of target height to an accuracy of 300 m (1,000 ft) at a range of 115 km (70 miles), and gapless surveillance in all weathers. On 8 August 1945, a week before the end of World War II, contracts for the Cadillac radar were awarded to General Electric and Hazeltine.

Never before had anyone set out to build a high-discrimination radar with so great a range and the two factors combined to produce many severe problems. One, the fundamental fact that at ranges of hundreds of kilometres radar signals, travelling at the great but finite speed of light, take a significant time to travel to the target and return. A basic characteristic of most radars is prf (pulse-repetition frequency). In order to obtain the maximum information about the target the prf has to be as high as possible, but at a range of 150 km (90 miles) each wave takes about one-thousandth of a second to make the return journey, so the maximum possible prf is only 1,000; at 300 km (180 miles) range the highest prf is a mere 500. This delay affected discrimination adversely. Another fundamental problem arose from the fact that the ranges associated with an AEW radar are many times greater than the heights. Although radar signals travel almost horizontally, it is for various reasons almost impossible to make a radar in which all the energy is sent out in a single straight beam to the target. Smaller beams at angles, called 'side lobes', emanate from the main beam and strike the Earth's surface or the atmosphere giving rise to echoes that were inevitably less controllable in 1945 than today and almost obliterated the useful target information on the radar screen.

The flying saucer

Nevertheless, the two cable American electronics companies doggedly pushed ahead with 'breadboard' and flight-test radar prototypes and finally flew the first flyable AEW radar on 13 November 1946. The installation was an ancestor of the widely used AN/APS-20, and it was installed in a remarkably small trials aircraft, a TBM-3W Avenger converted from a wartime torpedo bomber. Results were encouraging and by late 1946 the APS-20A was giving one megawatt of peak power in the S-band (wavelengths in the order of 10–15 cm). This was too much for the Avenger and flight development proceeded with a B-17, though by this time the unpressurised Fortress had been superseded as the planned operational

was a version of the incredibly versatile Douglas Skyraider. This US Navy carrier-based attack bomber appeared in 1947 as the XBT2D-1Q, the world's first electronic countermeasures aircraft and the following year as the XAD-1W, the first of several sub-types fitted with an APS-20A or related AEW radar with a vast belly radome covering the 2·5 metre rotating scanner. AD-3W and AD-4W Skyraiders, and various Avenger conversions followed, many of both types of aircraft serving with America's allies in the period 1953–65. Britain used 50 AD-4W Skyraiders, the radars from which were later

transferred to the specially designed Gannet AEW Mk 3, and still later removed and fitted to the current RAF AEW aircraft, the Shackleton AEW Mk 2. The extreme age of both the aircraft and the radar reflects the inadequacy of British defence funding in the late 1970s.

Other postwar AEW aircraft of the US Navy included the PB4Y Privateer, AF-2W Guardian, certain P4M Mercators and several sub-types of P2V (later P-2) Neptune. A unique experiment was the XHR2S-1, an AEW version of the Sikorsky S-56 helicopter for the US Marines, which with over 4,000 hp available could easily lift its radar installation and operators, but had low ceiling and limited endurance. Far more significant was the development in the mid-1950s of the APS-82 radar, with a new order of peak power, discrimination and range, and with an aerial (antenna) aperture nearly three times larger than that of the APS-20. The carrier aircraft chosen was the Grumman E-1B Tracer, a major redesign of the S-2 Tracker carrier-based ASW (anti-submarine warfare) aircraft. The aerodynamic prototype Tracer flew on 1 March 1957, sporting a radome measuring 10m (33ft) long by 6m (20ft) wide carried on pylons above the fuselage like a flying saucer. The first of 64 production Tracers flew in February 1958 and these were the world's most advanced seagoing AEW machines. For operation from land bases the Navy used extremely comprehensively equipped Super Constellations, renamed Warning Stars, originally designated PO-1W and later WV-1 and WV-2. Warning Stars used by the USAF were designated in the RC-121 series, today changed to EC-121. Several sub-types of EC-121 remain in use in various duties, with flight crews of up to 30 men. Many versions have a broad belly radome for the surveillance aerial and a dorsal radome, looking like the conning-tower fin of a submarine, housing a nodding heightfinder aerial. Similar above-and-below installations were used by US Navy blimps.

Above: a Grumman E-2C Hawkeye of the US Navy. The E-2C differs from earlier Hawkeyes in having a completely revised avionics system, an air data computer, uprated engines and a carrier aircraft inertial navigation system

aircraft. Various B-17H testbeds flew with an APS-20A in various installations, most having the enormous aerial radome under the former bomb-bay, but some having it on top immediately aft of where the dorsal turret had been installed. The first AEW aircraft in the world to see active service were 31 ex-USAAF Fortresses taken over by the US Navy as PB-IW radar pickets and fitted with the APS-20A (in several examples with the dorsal radome). They served in several theatres from mid-1947 until 1951. The Navy also used four converted B-29 Superfortresses, redesignated P2B-1S, which could fly at 10,000m (32,800 ft) for ten hours, with the crew comfortably accommodated in pressurised compartments.

One of the first aircraft specially designed for AEW

The Shackleton AEW Mk 2 entered service with the RAF in September 1971 as a replacement for the carrier-based Gannets of the Royal Navy

Airborne warning and control

Today's successor to the Tracer is the much more powerful Grumman E-2C Hawkeye. Powered by two 4,910hp Allison turboprops, this is a compact and extremely capable aircraft combining facilities for detection, tracking, threat assessment, reporting and control, which requires far more than just a radar. The PB-1W and TBF-3W presented a single radar display to a single operator, who had to track targets with a grease pencil. The later Tracer and Warning Star added video (TV) relays so that the radar picture could be studied as it was formed in the aircraft and also on the ground or in an aircraft carrier. The E-2C is filled from stem to stern with a completely automated ARPS (Advanced Radar Processing System), the APS-125, which can simultaneously track over 250 targets and control over 30 airborne intercepts. This concept of control, which calls for considerable computer capacity, is relatively new. In fact modern AWACS (Airborne Warning And Control System) aircraft can managed a whole war, involving all kinds of weapons. For example, it can tell attack aircraft the best route to fly to their target, where enemy radars are and how to jam or confuse them, and even guide a helicopter to rescue a downed pilot deep in enemy territory. All this can be done whilst detecting every kind of target, filtering out false alarms or other targets that need not be attended to, and then deciding which friendly force to use, which course they should take, which weapons they should use and numerous other quickly needed decisions. At all times the modern AEW or AWACS aircraft is totally integrated with surface or naval passive detection and ELINT (Electronic Intelligence) systems, air traffic control, tactical data systems and many other links, either airborne or ground-based.

Despite having to fit aboard an aircraft carrier, the volume of airspace that can be continuously kept under surveillance by an E-2C is 12·5 millioncukm. Yet even this can be surpassed by the Boeing E-3A AWACS, the largest aircraft in this category at present in use (though

the E-3A is just exceeded in wing span by the Soviet counterpart, the Tu-126 Moss). Based on the Boeing 707-320, and thus much larger and heavier than the KC-135 tanker and C-135 transport, the E-3A is the first result of one of the world's largest research programmes, ORT (Overland Radar Technology), of 1963–1975. The radar finally selected, the Westinghouse APY-1, is by a wide margin the cleverest and most advanced airborne radar to go into service. After extensive testing in modified EC-121 Warning Stars the APY-1 flew in an EC-137D test aircraft, externally resembling an E-3A, in March 1972, and the system entered initial service with the United States Air Force in September 1977.

Boeing E-3A trials

The USAF has a requirement for 34 aircraft at a unit price of some $60 million, all to be in service by 1982. The 3·5 tonne radar simultaneously operates in two modes, a high-prf pulse-doppler mode for operating against ground clutter and detecting moving targets as small and slow as a man on a bicycle at over 100km (60 mile) range, and a low-prf mode for BTH (beyond the horizon) operation at ranges out to 400km (245 miles).

NATO nations other than the United States have for several years been considering purchasing a fleet of 27 E-3A aircraft, but the plan has consistently failed to make progress. Impatient at the delay, Britain went ahead in 1977 with an AEW version of the Hawker Siddeley Nimrod ocean-patrol aircraft, equipped with completely new Marconi-Elliott radar and computers claimed to be superior even to the E-3A in some circumstances, especially in overwater operation. Design began in 1972, and in March 1977 the radar with underslung nose aerials was rolled out in a rebuilt Comet 4C test bed. Flight trials with a second aerial group in the tail will begin shortly. Eleven Nimrods are available for conversion for RAF AEW use, and there is an increasing likelihood that this outstanding early-warning and control aircraft will be the subject of new-build orders.

Air Control

'Air Control' was the term used for an effective method of peace-keeping in undeveloped colonial territories in which air power exercised the primary role, with ground forces being used in support of the air forces and under an air commander.

By 1920 the independence of the infant Royal Air Force was under threat from its sister services as post-war financial stringency resulted in cuts in defence budgets. The requirement for the capabilities which had brought the Royal Air Force into being – notably home air defence and long-range strategic bombing – had ended with World War I and a future need for them seemed remote. Meanwhile, the enduring task of policing the Empire had increased, as new territories formerly in enemy hands had come under mandate to Britain. The Army was suffering from that chronic Imperial condition, now known as 'over-stretch'. Colonial peacekeeping was, furthermore, a task in which, even friends of the RAF admitted, it was difficult to see an air force role, save as an auxiliary to either the Army or the Royal Navy.

The RAF's Imperial role

Then, at a ministerial conference in Cairo, Sir Hugh Trenchard, then Chief of Air Staff, put forward the unusual idea that air power alone could control unruly tribesmen, quell disturbances and safeguard remote frontiers in difficult terrain. Since the alternative was to abandon the

mandates of Iraq, Trans-Jordan and Palestine – thereby throwing the whole of the Middle East into renewed turmoil – the conference agreed to give the Trenchard proposal a trial. (It is, perhaps, not without significance that the conference was chaired by Winston Churchill, who was, at the time, temporarily Secretary of State for both War and Air.) Trenchard had not, of course, put forward his idea entirely without precedent. The RAF had already demonstrated its effectiveness in the late war against irregular troops both in support of Allenby and Lawrence in the Middle East and also in the rapid quelling of what became known as the Third Afghan War on the North-West Frontier of India in 1919.

The focus of the trial was Iraq, where there had recently

Above: the Bristol F2B played a notable part in the RAF's air control operations in the Middle East during the 1920s and early 1930s. A machine of No 208 Squadron in Palestine is illustrated. Below: No 1 Squadron, RAF formed part of the air policing force in Iraq between 1921 and 1926. Snipes of the Squadron are pictured near Baghdad

been a serious revolt which even two divisions of British and Indian troops had been hard-pressed to put down. As a result of the Cairo decision in 1922, all British troops, except one mixed brigade of British and Indian infantry, were withdrawn and the defence of Iraq and its internal security were entrusted to eight squadrons of the Royal Air Force under an Air Officer Commanding (Air Marshal Sir John Salmond), who commanded all the forces in the country. There were also some native levies and four squadrons of armoured cars manned by the RAF. Similar arrangements were made for Trans-Jordan.

Of the eight RAF squadrons, two squadrons of Vickers Vernon transports (Nos 45 and 70), two squadrons of DH 9A bombers (Nos 8 and 30) and one fighter squadron equipped with Sopwith Snipes (No 1) were stationed at the main airfield at Hinaidi six miles south of Baghdad. One squadron of DH 9As (No 84) was at Shaibah, near Basra, and another at Mosul in the north (No 55). There was also a squadron of Bristol Fighters (No 6) at Kirkuk on the Kurdish border. The airfields were defended by armoured cars and army detachments, with the bulk of the troops based with the transports at Hinaidi. In 1927 the Vernons were replaced by Vickers Victorias and later still, in 1935, by Valencias. The DH 9As and Bristol Fighters were succeeded first in 1928 by Westland Wapitis and in the thirties by Fairey IIIFs and Gordons.

Rebellion and raiding were part of the traditional way of life among Middle East tribesmen at the time. Just as on the North-West Frontier of India, the possession of a rifle was the badge of manhood and engagements with both feudal foes and the forces of law and order were virtually sporting occasions, with the added attraction of the opportunity of gaining more weapons and ammunition. Under the time-honoured system of army control, when local troubles proved too much for district police forces or militia, the nearest garrison sent a column of troops. Because this was inevitably an expensive exercise, the decision to send the troops was invariably delayed until the original dispute had got thoroughly out of hand and begun to spread. This meant that the troops met opposition from the very beginning of the march. In the first place, few tribesmen had clear consciences; in the second, infidel intruders were unwelcome on principle and thirdly, fighting was fun and nobody was going to let all those good Lee Enfield rifles pass through without at least an attempt to capture some of them. The tribesmen were also at home on their own very rugged ground.

Air blockade in Iraq

Air control could be applied rapidly to nip trouble in the bud. As soon as the police or the local political officer reported signs of unrest or some tribal outrage, a summons was sent to the offending chieftains to submit themselves for trial on specific charges in the law courts. If they refused or continued with their outrage a warning would be sent – or, to give it more point, dropped by aircraft – that on a certain date the village would be bombed and the tribesmen should evacuate their women and children and livestock to avoid casualties. Then, after a further warning immediately before the attack, bombs would be dropped on the village and the area surrounding it. The intention was not to inflict serious damage on the village but to institute an effective 'air blockade' to keep the villagers away from their homes and their crops and disrupt their normal way of life. This blockade was then sustained by the use of delayed action bombs and occasional machine-gunnings, together with the destruction of prominent buildings such as forts. Sooner or later the discomfort of living in caves

and the disruption of the harvest, plus the absence of an enemy they could hope to fight on equal terms, brought the offenders to heel.

As soon as the chieftains had surrendered, teams of police – only occasionally troops – were flown into the area to restore order, prevent looting and collect weapons. It was also usual to send in medical teams to treat wounds and deal with sickness and rehabilitate the area generally. Casualties on both sides were usually negligible and 'air control' seldom needed to be applied to the same village twice. Frequently the mere threat of air attack was enough. Surprisingly too, the use of bombing left no legacy of bitterness among the tribesmen. Baked mud and stone buildings were easily replaced and gave the tribesmen something useful to do. In Iraq the RAF first used air control methods to settle remaining pockets of disaffection and curb the activities of lawless sheikhs in remote areas who used the disturbed situation to indulge in acts of brigandage of all types. The same methods also dealt efficiently with raids by the Wahabis from Ibn Saud's territory in the south. In February 1923, however, a much more menacing threat developed in the north-east to give the new system its most severe test.

Aden and the North-West Frontier

Until the defeat of the Turkish armies by the British under Allenby in 1918, Iraq was for centuries a province of the Ottoman Empire. The Turks deeply resented the post-war settlement that had put the territory under mandate to the British and were particularly anxious to regain the northern province of Iraq, the Mosul Vilayet. Turkish regular troops infiltrated into the mountain villages of Kurdistan and distributed arms and ammunition to the

Left: a Bristol Fighter in flight over the Khyber Pass on India's North-West Frontier in 1925.
Above: a Hawker Hardy of No 30 Squadron is guarded by a member of the Iraq levies at Mosul, 1935.
Below: bombs drop from one of No 60 Squadron's Westland Wapitis. The Squadron was equipped with this type in India from 1930 until 1939

war-like Kurds who then, as they do today, wanted independence from Baghdad. The most influential of the Kurdish chieftains, Sheikh Mahmud, the rebellious governor of South Kurdistan, was persuaded by the Turks with promises of independence to advance on Kirkuk. The garrison consisted of No 6 Squadron equipped with Bristol Fighters, two platoons of Assyrian levies and half a squadron of armoured cars. It was quite inadequate to defend both the town and the airfield and, as the rebels began occupying the town, the RAF launched the first-ever air lift of troops. Vernons of Nos 45 and 70 Squadrons lifted some 480 officers and men of the 14th Sikhs, with stores and ammunition, in the course of about two days. The rebels, thinking that heavy rains had made the roads impassable for reinforcements were taken completely by surprise by the arrival of the Sikhs.

Mahmud was summoned to Baghdad but failed to show up. An ultimatum was therefore dropped on his headquarters at Sulaimaniya backed up with delayed action bombs outside the town. He agreed to parley but again broke his word and the RAF then demolished his house. He fled into the hills and continued to organise resistance. Eventually a strong force of troops was sent into the area with powerful RAF support. Sulaimaniya was occupied and Mahmud escaped into Persia. This was not, however, the end of him and he continued his 'holy war' against the British until well into the thirties. He was, nonetheless, 'bombed into retirement' on several occasions and operations against him both developed and proved the methods of air control.

One notable example of this was on the borders of the Aden Protectorate which for decades had suffered raids by fierce Zeidi tribesmen from the Yemen seeking to reap crops they had not sown. When the raids became particularly troublesome in 1925 it was estimated that to pacify the area would require at least one Army division with supporting air forces. A trial air control operation was carried out by 12 Bristol Fighters of Aden Flight led by Squadron Leader (later Air Marshal Sir Robert) Saundby. It soon had the tribesmen fleeing back into the Yemen and in 1928 full air control under RAF command was instituted and remained in being until Aden was evacuated in 1968.

The period of British air control in Iraq lasted ten years, when the Mandate was replaced by a treaty of peace and friendship. During that time the Turkish threat to the Mosul Vilayet was repulsed, minor rebellions in Kurdistan and the Euphrates region were put down and innumerable raids from Saudi Arabia were effectively dealt with by air control. Iraq had enjoyed a period of peace and security unknown for centuries. Her economy prospered as irrigation improved her agriculture and new roads her communications. Finally, came the discovery of oil. And all of this had been achieved at a fraction of the cost in lives and property – Iraqi as well as British – that any other method of peace-keeping would have exacted.

Air control proved equally effective in Trans-Jordan where the only major rebellion was dealt with by aircraft of No 14 Squadron in only two days. Attempts were also made from time to time to introduce the method into the perennially troubled North-West Frontier of India. There is little doubt that the method could have been made to work had the RAF been given a free hand and a reasonable share of the defence funds which were provided not by Whitehall but by the Government of India. As it was, the Army was far too well entrenched to put its long-standing privileges in jeopardy to the upstart RAF. Furthermore, there was no shortage of troops in India and the Frontier was an invaluable training ground.

Apart from the Army attitude, the reluctance of the Indian Government to buy aircraft spares from the British at what it regarded as extortionate prices meant that aircraft serviceability fell short of normal standards and the Army quickly jumped to the conclusion that the climate and conditions of the area made it unsuitable for aircraft. The RAF, though it did much sterling work, therefore remained in the support role. Even in 1937, when it was finally agreed that in the event of further trouble with Afghanistan or major tribal unrest the RAF would be committed to vigorous action while the Army played a defensive role, less than five per cent of the funds allocated to the defence forces was apportioned to the RAF.

French colonial policing

In the years between the wars both the French and the Italians were faced, in differing degrees, with problems of pacifying the inhabitants of overseas territories. With the exception of the Lebanon and Syria, where the French exercised a League of Nations mandate, however, military operations were on a much larger scale than those required merely for keeping the peace. Both countries—Italy in Libya and France in Morocco—were continuing against strong local opposition a process of colonial occupation begun before World War I. Both used a considerable number of aircraft in these operations—indeed the Italians had made the first-ever use of aerial bombing in Libya in 1911—but in support of their ground forces and under army control.

In such support operations, the establishment of powerful garrisons and the imposition of a colonial administration were well beyond the scope of the purely policing activities inherent in air control. The French used their 39th Regiment in Syria, however, in a very similar way to the British air control. With their Breguet 14s (a contemporary of the Brisfit and the DH 9A), the Regiment flew over 6,000 combat missions from 1925 to 1926 in helping to suppress a rising of the Jebel Druse and at one point kept the citadel of Soueïda supplied during a 61-day siege. But the French Armée de l'Air was at the time still the 'fifth arm' of the French Army and all its operations were subject to army control.

As a method of law enforcement, 'air control' in its primitive form had many limitations. In the first place it depended upon the rebels being clearly identifiable and providing static targets in the form of villages and settlements that could be located from the air. It could not be used against rebels who used infiltration tactics and urban guerrilla methods, as in Palestine in the 1930s and a host of similar situations since. Secondly, its economy depended upon the absence of effective anti-aircraft weapons in the hands of rebels; an immunity which could not last for long. Thirdly, comparatively bloodless though they were, the methods of air control which involved the bombing of 'innocent' primitive tribesmen became increasingly distasteful to local but influential elements of public opinion in the United Kingdom.

In the light of history, however, the experience served the Royal Air Force well. Many of those airmen who held high command during World War II—Harris, Saundby, Cochrane to name a few—were 'blooded' in Iraq. Furthermore, many of the principles established in Iraq in those pioneer days of air power were still valid in post-World War II colonial and 'limited' wars.

Air Defence

Since its inception air warfare has seen almost as many shifts in the balance between the offensive and the defensive as have the older forms of land and sea warfare over the centuries. There are many reasons for this: the innovatory nature of air warfare itself, with its particular emphasis on the offensive; the introduction of first a third – air – and, later, a fourth dimension – electronics – into the field of combat, and, above all, the immense public pressures upon governments to devote massive resources to protecting their civilian populations from direct attack from the skies.

Later, there was the need to develop counters to those same measures, to restore the power of the offensive. (In air warfare it has been argued that the best defence lies in the threat of counter-attack.) Indeed, it may be true to say that in no other field of human endeavour has there been as much rapid development, even in an era of advancing science and technology, as there has been in that of air defence. There is an immense technological span between a 1915 Cyclist Battalion taking pot-shots with rifles at Zeppelins and the current pre-occupation with the concept of knocking down hostile satellites many hundreds of miles out in space. Nevertheless the basic problems remain the same – how to know when an attack is imminent, how to identify the enemy, how to locate and intercept him and, having done so, how to destroy him.

The elements of defence

To be effective an air defence system needs to possess the current solution to all these problems. Warning is of little value unless it leads to interception, as the British learned from the early night *blitz* of World War II. Interception is pointless unless destruction follows, as the Japanese found against B-29s. Conversely, possession of a superb weapons system is of little value if it cannot be brought into engagement or if, unready, it sits on the ground when the attacker arrives, as in the Pearl Harbour attack of 1941. The short history of air warfare has many such examples of how failure in one aspect or another proved disastrous. First, however, it is of value to look in broad terms at the evolution of air defence since the early days of World War I.

The first phase was the evolution of what, in modern terms, we should call an air defence 'environment' – the institution of ground and air measures which not only forced the enemy to pay a high price for his attacks, but also minimised the effects of his attacks upon potential targets. It involved the setting up of a control and reporting system, using the best available means of locating and tracking enemy raiders and passing this information to the defending forces. The foundations were laid during World War I by the British, improved immeasurably by the development of radar and the advances made in radio communication in the inter-war years, and virtually perfected first by day and then by night in the early years of World War II.

By 1943 both the British and Germans had air defence systems of an efficiency that almost stultified strategic bombing. Then came the second phase – the inception of electronic warfare directed against components of the air defence environment; the confusion of radar and the jamming of communications. This phase is still with us and electronic counter-measures (ECM) and counter-counter-measures (ECCM) covering the whole emissive spectrum are as essential to effective air operations today as are bombs and bullets.

In the early stages there was no early warning (EW). The Zeppelins arrived, dropped their bombs and departed unscathed by the defences unless they were unlucky enough to blunder into a patrolling fighter or an area defended by guns. For the island British, even rudimentary tracking was impossible until the enemy crossed the coast and by that time it was frequently too late, especially when the faster-flying Gothas and Giants replaced the Zeppelins. In 1917 the Chief of the Imperial Staff explained: 'the distance in time from the Kent coast to important places like London is less than the time required by most of our present machines to ascend to the necessary height'.

A sound locator used to direct searchlights early in World War II. This primitive device was superseded by more accurate radar direction of guns and searchlights later in the war

(This perceptive statement of the fundamental air defence problem remains apt to this day.) When the Gothas were defeated in daylight by an elaborate and expensive system of standing patrols, they switched, as the Luftwaffe was to do twenty-three years later, to night attacks.

Tracking by sight from observer posts became unreliable and the first resort was made to sound location methods. The different engine notes provided a rough form of 'identification friend or foe' (IFF) and multiple sound bearings supplied a means of tracking. The results achieved were not significant, largely because there was no means of conveying the tracking information to the fighters, other than by searchlight. The incidental establish-

Above: the Supermarine Spitfire took 7 minutes to climb to 6,100m (20,000ft). During the Battle of Britain its qualities were exploited by RAF Fighter Command's highly developed radar-based fighter control system, the world's first integrated air defence system.
Right: the rocket propelled Me 163 entered Luftwaffe service in 1944, and represented a peak of interceptor development in World War II. It had an initial climb rate of 4,900m (16,000ft) a minute, but had a maximum endurance after climb to combat ceiling of only 2·5 minutes

ment, however, of a chain of observer reporting posts linked by telephone to local operations rooms and thence through the defence controller to airfields and gun-sites laid the foundations of a system that was to prove vital to national survival in 1940.

Early warning
In the years between the wars attempts were made to develop an early warning system based on sound location and one experiment involved building a 'sound mirror' 61m (200ft) long on Romney marshes. Even under ideal conditions its best range rarely exceeded 26 kilometres (16 miles)—much too short to get fighters to altitude. The solution came in 1935 when the first early warning station using the recently discovered radar technique was opened at Bawdsey. By 1938 there were five such stations operational with a range of about 110km (70 miles) against bombers at medium level—almost half a hour's warning, but little enough, even for Spitfires. Nonetheless, radar revolutionised the entire air defence system, establishing, after many years, the basis of a shift in the balance of advantage from offence to defence.

A few gaps in the warning system remained to be filled. The first fixed-aerial radar stations (CH) could not give warning of low-flying aircraft, and could not see inland to track aircraft which had already crossed the coast. A rotating beam radar planned originally for the detection of shipping (CHL) was adapted and fulfilled both functions. The introduction in 1940 of a small transponder in friendly aircraft, which showed up on radar screens, helped to solve the indentification problem. The defences could

then know with reasonable warning when the enemy was coming, what his position was, his height, his speed, how many there were of him and where the home defenders were. The next problem was to direct the fighters into an attacking position.

During World War I developments in ground-to-air radio communications were hamstrung by the Admiralty who, probably with good reason, thought that ship-to-shore had first priority regarding limited technical resources. Information about the enemy position could therefore only be communicated to patrolling aircraft by visual means—ground panels and searchlights. Of these, the latter were the more satisfactory, although both were vague and inaccurate, and interception inevitably depended upon the fighter pilot seeing his target—using the 'Mark 1 eyeball', still in service to this day. The 1930s, however, saw the development of high-frequency radio telephony, and by the outbreak of World War II interceptors throughout the West had been fitted with sets of varying adequacy. At the same time as radar was being developed for warning purposes, thought was being given to the problem of controlling interceptions from the ground, especially at night. The result, which had to await the invention of the PPI (Plan Position Indicator radar tube) and the rotating radar aerial, came to Britain in the form of GCI (Ground Control of Interception) and to the Germans as Würzburg.

German development of radar devices had parallelled

those in Britain. In Freya they had an EW radar with a 360 degree scan which was fully mobile and, working on a much higher frequency than the British CH, was shorter in range but gave better resolution. In Würzburg, initially an AA blind-fire system, they were also ahead of the early British GCI in range and accuracy. The Germans, however, believing with Goering that they were under no threat from Allied bombing, concentrated upon offensive bomber guidance systems like Knickebein and X-Gerat. As a result, they did not develop a ground-to-air control and communications system to match the British until the middle of the war. They also fell behind in the development of small radar sets which could be carried in aircraft, notably the night-fighter's AI (Airborne Interception) radar. Early British AI sets merely improved visibility with the naked eye from about 300 yards on a clear night to around a mile and a half in all conditions – a range somewhat below the margin of error of ground control to begin with.

Weaponry

The improvement in GCI, and later the introduction of the magnetron, in both AI and GCI saw the percentage of interceptions at night over the United Kingdom steadily increase until night fighters accounted for 70 per cent of enemy aircraft destroyed. Similarly, over Germany, once the formidable German technological machine had tackled the air defence problem, night fighters took the major toll of Bomber Command aircraft – from May 1942 to May 1945 flak claimed 1,345 enemy attackers and the night fighters 2,278.

Successful interception depends most upon an efficient ground environment but turning an interception into a kill calls for adequate armament – given the other crucial factors of aircraft performance and piloting skill. In World War I several interceptions of Zeppelins occurred where the aircraft armament of the day – 0·303 ball ammunition – failed to destroy the target. Then, in mid-1916 Brock and Pomeroy ammunition, which was both incendiary and explosive, was introduced. Its first success was the destruction of SL.11 – the Cuffley 'Zeppelin' – by

An RAF Hawker Hurricane being refuelled between sorties. Defending fighters were most vulnerable when on the ground replenishing fuel and ammunition

Messerschmitt Me 163 B/1 Komet

Second Lieutenant Leefe Robinson on 2/3 September 1916. The French also conducted experiments with rocket missiles but accuracy was poor and range was short. With improved ammunition the rifle-calibre machine gun was the most effective air-to-air weapon available until the arrival of the aircraft cannon. Multiple machine guns firing forward became standard installations on British fighters–the Spitfires and Hurricanes of the Battle of Britain era had eight each. But the use of armour plate and self-sealing tanks called for heavier calibre weapons. The Germans had fitted Oerlikon 20mm cannon to their Messerschmitt Bf 109s before World War II and the British first introduced the cannon in 1941.

Thereafter multiple installations of machine guns and cannon became the norm. These massive installations–the Beaufighter boasted four cannon and six machine guns– usually fired forward, but in a devastatingly effective installation called Schrage Musik, the Bf 110G night fighter fired two cannon obliquely upwards into the belly of a bomber above. Unguided air-to-air missiles were also used against bomber formations.

Apart from the area aspects of air defence–fighters and their control–there is also the question of what is now called 'point defence'–the defence of individual targets by guns or other missiles fired from the ground. World War I saw the introduction of the anti-aircraft gun but its use was confined to visual engagements below about 19,000 ft. At night AA guns were used to create a barrage of fire to deter attackers. There was no blind-fire capability and sound location could offer little more than a vague direction. It was estimated that 1,000 shells were needed to obtain one hit. There was little or no improvement in gun performance until the introduction of radar devices. Thereafter the accuracy of 'blind' AA fire improved steadily until by 1944 it approached that of visually-aimed fire. That year also saw the introduction of the first radar proximity-fused AA shell which enabled British gunners to knock down up to 74 per cent of the German V-1 flying bombs fired in a single week.

Electronic warfare

By 1943 air defence had evolved on both sides of the North Sea into a formidable and effective machine. It was to be improved and developed further but only in detail and the basic structure hammered out in World War II survives to this day. But 1943 also saw the systematic extension of air warfare into a new dimension with the setting up of No 100 Group, RAF. Its primary role was the jamming of the German night fighter force's communications channels and radar sets.

In the celebrated raids on Hamburg in July and August 1943 Bomber Command had used metallic strips, code-named 'Window', to saturate German early warning and control radars with devastating effect. No 100 Group's task was to expand and develop the whole technique of electronic counter-measures and from that time on the revolution which the introduction of radar had wrought in air defence effectiveness was under threat. It remains under threat to this day and the post-war history of air defence is largely that of significant developments in the ECM field. True, there have been immense technical improvements in the performance of early warning and control radars, in aircraft and their weapons systems and in air-to-air and ground-to-air missiles of every type. However, over every one has lain the threat that the value of new and expensive air defence equipment could be nullified or at least reduced by developments in the electronics field.

The devices used by No 100 Group were typical of those in use today, though lacking in the sophistication now possible. 'Window' played a major part in jamming operations, producing hosts of false targets that could obscure the real ones. Another device was Jostle, a high-powered transmitter which set up a raucous screech on German fighter control frequencies; others were Piperack and Mandrel which obscured the screens of airborne radars and ground radars with 'grass' through which

In the air defence role the McDonnell Douglas Phantom FGR MK 2 carries a maximum armament of four Sidewinder and four Sparrow missiles, plus a 20mm Vulcan rotary cannon in an external pod

into the use of airborne jammers and 'Chaff' (Window) to disrupt radars and communication links in order to reduce B-29 Superfortress losses. Then, in the late fifties, as surface-to-air and air-to-air guided missiles began to appear in the Soviet armoury, all the major air forces started to equip their jet-bombers with ECM equipment. One particularly powerful 'noise' jammer device which appeared about this time was a French invention, the carcinatron. As its name implies it is cancer-like in its penetrative effects upon radio frequencies and scanner cover. Use was also made of decoys to confuse early warning radars. One such was 'Quail' (carried by a B-52 bomber) which had a wing span of 1·5m (5ft) but gave a radar echo equivalent to that of a B-52–this carried jammers as well. Eventually, however, even with ECM equipment, it was clear that survival at high altitude

against sophisticated defences made a bomber-based deterrent less than completely credible. Consequently in 1963 low-altitude penetration tactics became the vogue. Since radio waves follow relatively straight lines and the earth is curved, there can always be a gap under radar cover–it was this that the new tactics sought to exploit. Then came the Vietnam War.

At first the Americans were able to operate at around 10,000ft because North Vietnamese defences comprised mostly small-calibre AA guns. Later, however, as the Russian-built SA-2 Guideline surface-to-air missile were deployed in increasing numbers, the USAF found it necessary to resort to tactics very similar to those employed by Bomber Command at the end of World War II. To ensure penetration and reduced casualties, every bombing sortie had to be accompanied by a specialist electronic countermeasures force in addition to the ECM devices carried in the bombers themselves.

The Yom-Kippur War of October 1973 gave the most recent demonstration of the state of air defence. The Israeli air force had reigned supreme over the Nile delta after their pre-emptive strike in the Six Day War in 1967. Egyptian air defences appeared virtually powerless against them. Yet, in the first week of the 1973 war, the Israelis lost more than 80 fighter-bombers to SA-6 guided missiles and ZSU-234 radar-controlled multiple cannon. The Israelis were not only surprised tactically, but electronically, for they had no counter-measures or jammers to cover the necessary frequencies and had to curtail their offensive operations until they acquired them.

A BAC Lightning F Mk 2A interceptor of No 19 Squadron RAF based at Gutersloh, Germany. The unit re-equipped with Phantoms in 1977

nothing could be seen. There were also more aggressive devices–Serrate, which made it possible to home in on a night fighter's radar, and Perfectos, which triggered off German IFF transponders and thus gave away the position of enemy fighters.

Between World War II and the Korean War development of electronic warfare suffered the same decline as did other defence activities. In the latter the growing strength of North Korean air defences at night forced the Americans

Air-Sea Rescue

Organised air-sea rescue began towards the end of World War I when engine failures over the English Channel increased with the number of aircraft which were being ferried across to France. Special fast launches were stationed at strategic points along the English and French coasts, close to the busiest air routes and were used to pick up airmen who had 'ditched' in the sea.

This limited rescue organisation was disbanded at the end of the war and cross-channel airlines had to develop their own rudimentary rescue systems. As flying boats became more popular it was found that they were vulnerable in rough water and the Royal Air Force's flying boats were fitted with inflatable dinghies. The US Coast Guard began using marine aircraft as 'airborne lifeboats' in the 1930s and the RAF received its first purpose-built rescue launch in August 1936. After trials, 15 more were ordered and put into service with general reconnaissance squadrons at home and abroad. Their purpose, however, was solely to assist their own units and there was still no centralised air-sea rescue organisation.

When World War II began, air-sea rescue in Britain became the responsibility of RAF Coastal Command, two of whose Sunderland flying boats were quickly in action. On 18 September 1939 the large Sunderlands landed in the Atlantic to rescue 34 survivors from the torpedoed *SS Kensington Court* who were in lifeboats. Heavy swell prevented a close approach but the crews of the two flying boats set up a shuttle service with their own rubber dinghies and took 21 people aboard one aircraft, 13 on the other. However, there were other less successful rescue attempts which resulted in unacceptable losses among the Sunderlands and necessitated a new look at organisation.

As RAF attacks increased, inevitably more airmen went down in the sea and in May 1940 a more comprehensive rescue service was created. This drew upon the RAF, Royal Navy, Merchant Navy, Lifeboat stations, Coastguards, Observer Corps and the Police. It used a collection of small craft and 12 Lysander army co-operation aircraft with small rubber dinghies which were dropped to the ditched airmen. The new service involved far greater liason between the various services and resulted in a higher success rate: in six months 30 Allied airmen were recovered from the English Channel.

Luftwaffe equipment

The Battle of Britain made further expansion of the service essential. In fact the Luftwaffe was better equipped at this time for rescue operations: large buoy-type floats with enclosed cabins, well stocked with food, water, first-aid equipment, bunks, blankets and distress signals, were placed half-way across the Channel. Painted bright yellow and with large red crosses on each side, they were used by Allied and German alike - often at the same time.

During the invasion of Norway the Germans used 30 Heinkel 59 'rescue' seaplanes, which were painted white with red crosses on their sides. But they were often used illegally for armed reconnaissance and as a result some were shot down in the Battle of Britain.

All German aircraft, including single-seat fighters, carried inflatable dinghies, as did all multi-engined RAF aircraft. But Allied Spitfire and Hurricane pilots had only Mae West lifebelts upon which to rely. The Luftwaffe also used another aid to guide its rescue services to airmen in the sea - fluorescein, a chemical marker which coloured the sea bright green.

The British High-Speed Rescue Launches, with their glaring orange decks, became one of the mainstays of the

Above: the turbine-engined Westland Whirlwind HAR Mk 10 of the present-day RAF. The type is to be superceded by more modern Wessex and Sea King helicopters
Opposite top: the Walrus amphibian was the mainstay of the Allies' Air-Sea Rescue Service between 1940 and 1945.
Opposite bottom: a German safety equipment section checks and repacks aircraft dinghies in World War II

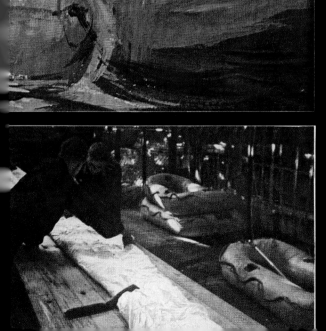

Allied Air-Sea Rescue Service. They were 22·2m (73ft) long and had a top speed of 38·6km/h (25mph) and room for 12 stretcher cases. Often the launches had to fight their way to or from a rescue point.

By 1941 the Rescue Service had 24 Lysanders and nine Supermarine Walrus single-engined amphibians to supplement the surface craft. In addition, 16 floats, based on the German type, had been placed off the British coast.

The small, robust Walrus often put down on the sea to rescue drifting aircrew and fly them off, or, if the load was too great or the weather unfavourable, taxy them back to shore. One Walrus taxied for no less than five hours, covering 50 miles to reach land; another took 3½ miles to get airborne. Sergeant Tom Fletcher taxied through a minefield to rescue six survivors from a German ship; his windshield was smashed by heavy seas and he had two feet of water swilling in the hull of the Walrus.

Dinghy lifesavers

By March 1942 the Rescue Service had been supplied with 50 Fairmile launches by the Admiralty. The K-type, self-inflatable dinghies, issued to fighter pilots, were equipped with sails as well as fluorescein dye and miniature waterproof radio transmitters, the idea for which had been copied from the Germans. Other dinghies made by P. B. Cow Ltd., founders of the Goldfish Club for rescued flyers, were the 'L', two-seater, 'M', three-seat, 'H', four or five, 'J', five or six, and 'Q', five to eight–for bomber crews.

By this time American aircrews were flying from Britain and in September 1942 a Combined Rescue Service was set up. On 9 October Air-Sea Rescue carried out its first rescue of Americans when a B-17 Flying Fortress crew of the 8th Air Force, returning from a mission over Lille, ditched off the North Foreland. One of the two dinghies had been damaged but a Spitfire spotted the position and radioed it home. The crew was rescued by launches.

The USAAF had its own Emergency Rescue Squadron by May 1943, with 25 P-47 Thunderbolt fighters each equipped with two four-man dinghies and four smoke-marker bombs. In July, as the US Air Force's daylight bombing offensive began its massive build-up, Air-Sea

Rescue saved 139 Fortress crewmen out of 196 from the sea and that figure included 78 of 80 brought down in one day.

In May of that year the new airborne lifeboat had first been used when a Hudson launched one to help survivors from a Halifax bomber which had come down off the Humber. The most widely used version, designed by Group Captain E. F. Waring, Deputy Director of Air-Sea Rescue and built by the famous British yachtsman and boat designer Uffa Fox, was 22 feet long and was fitted with two 4hp petrol engines and standby mast and sails. It could take ten men comfortably. Built of wood to a carvel (smooth) finish, it was floated down by seven parachutes–one yellow and six white. As it fell it set off a red rocket which released a sea anchor. The craft was self-rightable and had covered shelter fore and aft. Because of its size it had to be used by larger aircraft–most commonly the Vickers Warwick, though Lancasters also launched them in India.

Standard launch speed was 140 knots from 215·8m (700ft) and a careful drill using smoke markers–and later bomb sights–was carried out on launching. Their success rate was impressive enough to warrant their adaptation by the USAAF for use by B-17s.

The Lindholme

Before the introduction of the airborne lifeboat the main rescue equipment dropped to aircrew in the sea was the Lindholme device. This was a string of five cannisters–old bomb cases, in fact–linked by buoyant cord. In the centre cannister, a 1102kg (500lb) bomb case was an L-Type dinghy and in each of the others were life-support equipment and clothing. Typical contents would include a sleeping suit, ten four-ounce tins of water, seven seven-

An airborne lifeboat is carried by a Vickers Warwick of No. 282 Squadron in 1944

The Albatross was a reliable air-sea rescue aircraft for the USAF

ounce tins of condensed milk, two tins of Mark II emergency flying rations, two tins of cigarettes, two waterproof match containers and a Very light. Two or three Lindholmes would be dropped at one time, depending upon the number of people in the water. If they were likely to be there for some time, others were dropped later to replenish stocks.

Though D-Day, 6 June 1944, was relatively quiet for Air-Sea Rescue, the Arnhem offensive in September kept the service busy and it achieved a record of 181 airborne troops rescued from wrecked gliders.

In America the flying boats and seaplanes of the US Coast Guard carried out numerous missions to rescue victims of torpedoes or to relay their positions to rescue cutters standing by. A National Air-Sea Rescue Agency was established in Washington on 22 February 1944 under the administration of the Coast Guard. Its purpose was to ensure maximum co-operation between all the rescue services

Malta's Air-Sea Rescue Service saved 30 RAF pilots during the height of the Axis siege in the summer and autumn of 1941, some even being rescued by an Italian Cant Z506B seaplane which was captured by a Beaufort

crew rescued from the Ionian Sea and flown back to Malta. In the Mediterranean zone 1,114 American flyers were rescued up to the end of June 1945.

In Singapore the only High-Speed Rescue Launch retrieved 23 pilots in December 1941 and January 1942, before the Japanese captured the city. During the 1944-45 Burma campaign the Far Eastern Air-Sea Rescue Service also accomplished important work, using Sea Otter amphibians, while long-range Liberator bombers, stationed in India, carried out many successful sea searches.

US Navy, Coast Guard and Army aircraft co-operated in rescue work in the Pacific and again brought off some dramatic rescues.

The sturdy Catalinas were often used: a 'Dumbo', as the amphibian version of the Catalina was known, went right into Rabaul Harbour in the face of heavy fire from ships and shore to snatch a pilot from the water.

When the war ended the Air-Sea Rescue Service had saved 3,723 RAF and 1,998 American airmen from the waters around Britain and at least 3,200 aircrew and 4,665 soldiers, sailors and civilians in other theatres of war.

Helicopter role

Although of limited performance at this stage, the helicopter did useful work towards the end of the war and its potential was quickly appreciated. The USAAF Air Rescue Service had 17 Sikorsky helicopters, together with 13 SB-17 converted Fortresses with airborne lifeboats and 12 Catalinas, when it was formed on 19 May 1946 to cover the whole of the United States. Meantime, overseas detachments had to make do with equipment left over from the war.

United States helicopters saved many lives in the Korean war, setting down in terrain which would previously have been unapproachable from the air as well as carrying out the, by now, established routine of sea rescues.

The first really effective search and rescue helicopter was the Sikorsky S-51, known to the British as the Dragonfly. It led the way in being equipped with a winch for its rescue cable and was used by the British and American services. In February 1953 nine Dragonflies of 705 Squadron, Royal Navy, took part in the biggest SAR operation to date, rescuing more than 800 people from the heavy floods in Holland. The rescued included 64 winched up from housetops.

The Dragonfly was limited by its small payload: only one passenger could be carried, in addition to its two-man crew, unless fuel was dumped to allow for an extra passenger – thereby restricting its range.

Their own inventions

Much search and rescue equipment was invented by SAR aircrew, including the standard rescue strop, the double-lift harness for use in rescuing a disabled person, and the Sproule net, first used to recover a pilot from the English Channel on 8 March 1955. The Sproule net was developed at RNAS Ford in 1953 by Lt. Cdr. Sproule assisted by Chief Petty Officer Lock. It was originally designed for the recovery of bodies from the water but was quickly found to be a safer method of recovering disabled or injured people in the Dragonfly than the double-lift method which then used an unreliable winch telephone system. The net was first used operationally by its two designers to rescue the pilot of a ditched Firefly eight miles off Littlehampton. The net was later deomonstrated to the US Coast Guard and was probably the inspiration for the 'Willie Pugh' net,

Below: a Westland Lysander of No. 277 Squadron, which carried a dinghy pack for dropping to ditched aircrew.
Bottom: the Sproule net is demonstrated by a Fleet Air Arm Westland Dragonfly

During World War II a total of **3,723 RAF airmen and 1,998 US airmen** were rescued from the seas around the British Isles by the Air-Sea Rescue Service. In the Mediterranean and the Far East, **3,200 airmen and 4,665 other servicemen and civilians** were rescued. In the Pacific the US 5th Air Force rescued **1,841 persons.**

Sea King of 824 Squadron from HMS Ark Royal rescues an injured crewman from a US nuclear submarine off the Azores

The Whirlwind helicopter became a familiar sight as it carried out rescue operations round Britain's shores

which is practically identical and was used to recover astronauts.

For many years the Grumman Albatross amphibian was the mainstay of the American air-sea rescue services and was involved in numerous exploits. On 23 July 1954 Captain Jack Woodyard of 31st Air Rescue Squadron flew from Clark Air Force Base in the Philippines across the China Sea to rescue survivors from a Cathay Pacific Airlines DC-4 shot down by Communist fire. A Sunderland circled the raft on which the survivors were floating but could not land because of a ten-foot swell. The twin-engined Albatross had the advantage of reversible propellers which could stop it in a short distance.

After throwing out smoke markers, Woodyard flew parallel to the wave crests to check their bearings. 'Then,' he reported later, 'we used a stop-watch to time the crests as they passed the marker, dividing the number of swells into the time elapsed to get the period. The period squared, times five, gives the distance between the crests in feet. If you count five crests in 30 seconds, the period is six and when squared becomes 36; multiply this by five and you get 180 feet between crests.'

Woodyard stalled the aircraft on a crest, applied full reverse and slowed to almost a stop by the time the next crest arrived. The Albatross taxied for $2\frac{1}{2}$ miles from the lea of the island by which it had landed, towards the raft, guided by the marker and a circling French aircraft. The first to be taken aboard was a six-year-old girl from Texas.

Sikorsky S-55 helicopters, built under licence by Westland in England as the Whirlwind, superseded the S-51 in American and British service. It could carry eight passengers but lacked an Automatic Flight Control System and thus any real night or bad weather capability.

Co-ordination centres

The RAF is officially responsible for Search and Rescue in British territories. In Britain there are two Rescue Co-ordination Centres, at Plymouth, Devon, and Pitreavie Castle, Scotland. They control two helicopter SAR squadrons, long-range Shackletons of Coastal Command, RAF marine craft and Mountain Rescue teams and are closely linked with the Royal Navy, Royal National Lifeboat Institution, Coastguard, Army and the Police. Bright yellow RAF Search and Rescue Whirlwinds, with pilot, navigator and winchman, became familiar sights to holidaymakers on the coasts and rescue many from drifting boats, sandbanks and cliff faces.

By 1976 No 202 Squadron, SAR, had helicopters at four RAF stations along the east coast–Coltishall, Norfolk, Leconfield, Yorkshire, Boulmer, Northumberland and Lossiemouth, Scotland. The squadron was equipped with Whirlwinds, while another SAR Squadron, No 22, was scheduled to receive the larger Westland Wessex. The Sikorsky-designed Sea King added significantly to the SAR organisation and became particularly useful to the Royal Navy, with radar, sophisticated navigation equipment, seating for up to 27 people, a hoist capability of at least 273 kg (600 lb) and the ability to rescue 20 people out to a radius of 200 miles. SAR divers are available at all naval air stations and aboard carriers, their introduction having been hastened by the unneccessary death of an unharmed, fully-conscious pilot trapped in a ditched Scimitar aircraft which sank close to an aircraft carrier in 1960. Sea Kings were also used in commercial rescue services, such as the Helikopter Service in Norway, which supplemented the Norwegian Air Force's SAR organisation, and the British European Airways use of this jet helicopter in north-east Scotland.

The US Navy and Coast Guard also made use of Sea Kings, which, in fact, were intended primarily for anti-submarine duties but quickly proved themselves ideal as rescue craft. In 1973 the Danish Air Force also received Sea Kings for air-sea rescue and the Norwegian Air Force took delivery of a number in 1974.

From the early days of insubstantial rescue ware and hit-or-miss search tactics, air-sea rescue has grown into a highly sophisticated and continually developing technique making use of the most reliable equipment and aircraft and manned by specially trained crew who are responsible each year for saving thousands of lives, often at the risk of their own.

Air Superiority

"NEVER WAS SO MUCH OWED BY SO MANY TO SO FEW"
THE PRIME MINISTER

Air superiority is the domination of an area of airspace so that one's own air force is able to operate therein without sustaining unacceptable casualties. It follows from this that the enemy is denied the free use of the area for his air operations, which may be in support of ground forces, interdiction in the rear areas of a battlefield or air defence against a bombing offensive. The air superiority mission differs from that of air defence in that it has the positive aim of extending one's area of operations, whereas air defence seeks to protect national airspace from violation.

Offensive at any cost

British fighter operations over the Western Front during World War I offer a classic illustration of the process of seeking to gain command of the air over a battlefield and its rear supply areas. Hugh Trenchard, the commander of the Royal Flying Corps in France for much of the war, firmly adhered to an offensive air doctrine, seeking to cover the enemy battle area by continuous fighter patrols from dawn until dusk.

However, the air fighting during the spring of 1917 plainly showed that it was unrealistic to seek air superiority with a fighter force which was markedly inferior in technical quality to the defending fighters. 'Bloody April' of 1917 saw the highest British air losses in World War I and, during the period between March and May of that year, no fewer than 1,270 aeroplanes were destroyed. These losses were the result of applying Trenchard's doctrine of air offensive at any cost in the face of indisputable evidence of German air mastery. It was not until a new generation of British fighter aeroplanes reached the squadrons in quantity – such machines as the

Left: Sir Winston Churchill, Britain's wartime Prime Minister, eloquently summarised the unique importance of RAF Fighter Command's victory in the Battle of Britain, the first battle in history in which the outcome depended almost entirely upon the achievement or the denial of air superiority. Below: the German Albatros Scout was one of the finest of the fast, manoeuvrable fighters developed during World War I and was largely responsible for the heavy British losses during 'Bloody April' 1917

Bristol F2B Fighter, SE5a and Sopwith Camel – that the balance was redressed.

The shifts in advantage between the German and British air service continued over the Western Front up until the Armistice of November 1918, with neither side gaining a clear-cut decision. However, the advantages which accrued to the side which gained air superiority were plainly seen – albeit on a small scale – during the closing act of the Palestine Campaign. By September 1918 the Royal Air Force had gained air mastery through a combination of aggressive tactics and superiority of equipment. While British air reinforcements and supplies flowed smoothly into the Theatre by virtue of the Royal Navy's command of the sea, the Germans – on whom the Turks largely relied for air support of their armies – were starved of replacements and more modern equipment because of the shortcomings of their long overland supply route and the administrative inefficiency of the German airmen's Turkish allies.

Having neutralised the enemy air force, the RAF exploited its freedom in the skies by extensive air reconnaissance and bombing attacks on enemy ground forces. As the enemy was denied the benefits of air reconnaissance, General Sir Edmund Allenby was able to exploit their ignorance of his movements by highly-effective deception tactics during the Campaign which culminated in the capture of Jerusalem.

Blitzkrieg tactics

In Germany the lesson that an advancing army must enjoy some measure of air superiority was well-learned. The early successes of the *blitzkrieg* tactics were the outcome of German air mastery as much as the innovative use of armoured formations on land. In the Polish Campaign of September 1939, as in the German attack in the West the following year, the Luftwaffe's first objective was the elimination of the enemy's air arm. Given the technical superiority of the Messerschmitt Bf 109E over the PZL P-11, the outcome of the air battle was predictable.

The Poles had anticipated German air attacks on their airfields and had accordingly dispersed to concealed landing strips. However, such measures were of little use when the command and control of their squadrons broke down once they had left their regular bases. Furthermore, even when the Polish fighters could be brought into combat at the time and the place that they were needed, the gallantry of their pilots availed them little when confronted with the German fighters' advantages in performance and firepower. From the neutralisation of Poland's fighter force followed the German exploitation of air reconnaissance and the merciless air attacks on ground forces which were an integral feature of *blitzkrieg*.

The Luftwaffe's swiftly-gained air mastery during the assault in the West in May 1940 was not simply the result of the Germans possessing a superior fighter aircraft and

Right: a painting by J. McGilchrist depicting a Sopwith Camel attacking a Hannover CL-type on reconnaissance over the Western Front. Below: a superlative defensive interceptor in the Battle of Britain and over Malta, the Supermarine Spitfire undertook the role of air superiority fighter as the RAF moved onto the offensive over France, North Africa, Italy and Burma. Spitfire Mk VCs of No 417 Squadron in North Africa are illustrated

eliminate Britain and this was due in part to the high state of preparedness of the British air defences. In fact, the RAF's planners had been no more prescient than their continental counterparts, for RAF Fighter Command was intended to meet a bomber offensive against British cities mounted from Germany. The attack which came in the summer of 1940 was not a strategic offensive, but, in its early stages, an attempt by the Luftwaffe to gain command of the air over the Channel and southern England as a necessary preliminary to a seaborne invasion.

Unlike France and the Low Countries, Britain was protected from land attack by the waters of the English Channel and so the fight for air superiority was uncomplicated by a simultaneous land invasion, with its attendant disruption of supply services and catastrophic effect on morale. Furthermore, the RAF had in the Supermarine Spitfire a fighter that was a match for the Luftwaffe's Bf 109, although it equipped only a proportion of the defending force (19 out of 57 squadrons), unlike the German single-engined machine which flew with all *jagdgeschwader* on the Channel coast.

A further factor which greatly contributed to the RAF's victory was the superb system of command and control which included radar early warning. This ensured that the defenders' resources were concentrated on meeting enemy incursions, rather than being dissipated in standing patrols which would have only a problematic chance of

using it with greater tactical skill than their opponents, although these factors were of course important. The Allies lost command of their airspace by default, as they had not realised the crucial importance of securing their skies against enemy penetration and from this failure followed their shortcomings in *matériel* and tactics.

The first German defeat of the war was their failure to

meeting an enemy.

After Germany's decision to postpone (and eventually to abandon altogether) an invasion of Britain, which followed from her failure to gain air superiority over the invasion area, the bulk of the Luftwaffe's fighter force was moved eastward to support Hitler's ambitious invasion of the Soviet Union, which was launched in June 1941. The opening of Operation Barbarossa saw the decimation of the Soviet fighter force, which was largely equipped with obsolescent types–notably the Polikarpov I-16, which had been the most advanced design of its day when it first entered service in 1934. The Russians were also handicapped by mis-deployment of their squadrons, which were concentrated on forward airfields and thus easily fell prey to the marauding Łuftwaffe.

It was not until 1944 that the Soviet fighter force can be said to have gained air superiority. By this time it was equipped with such workmanlike designs as the Lavochkin La-5, Yakovlev Yak-9 and Yak-3. However, it was not by superiority of equipment that the Soviet air force overcame its opponent, but by sheer weight of numbers, amounting to a superiority of some five-to-one. The Luftwaffe's first priority by this time was defence of the homeland and the Eastern Front was starved both of modern fighters and of the numbers needed to re-establish air superiority.

The primary reason for the Luftwaffe's hard-pressed condition in 1944 was the massive air offensive by the USAAF's Eighth Air Force against Germany. This was not only an attack on industrial targets, but also a bid to wrest command of the air over Germany from the Luftwaffe by long-range escort fighters. At this time the North American P-51 Mustang was capable of sorties lasting up to seven hours, bringing Polish targets within range of their bases in Britain. Not only did the American fighters provide escort for the bombers, but they also sought out the Luftwaffe's fighters when parked on their bases, after take-off when they were assembling for an attack on the bomber boxes and–when they were most vulnerable–approaching their airfields to land, short of fuel and ammunition after engaging the bombers.

The jet age

When war broke out in Korea the USAF–as the US Army Air Force had then become–swiftly established air superiority, wiping out the small North Korean air force within weeks of the commencement of hostilities. However, due to politically-imposed restrictions on air action, which were to become a recurring feature of limited wars in the postwar era, the Communists were able to build up a fighter force of MiG-15 jets in Manchuria, where the airfields were safe from attack. Hence, the fight for air superiority over North Korea was restricted to air-to-air combat, with the Communists having the advantages of choosing the time and place of the encounter. However, this advantage and the MiG-15's superior altitude performance over the USAF's North American F-86 Sabre were not fully exploited and the Communist jets never seriously hampered USAF air operations.

This failure indicates a further factor which affects the outcome of the fight for air superiority–that of pilot morale and training. Throughout the Korean conflict the USAF's Sabre pilots displayed skill and efficiency which, combined with aggressive tactics, resulted in a kill-to-loss ratio of ten-to-one in their favour. In contrast, many of their opponents were inexperienced and prone to panic in combat. Indeed, there were many instances of pilots ejecting from their MiGs with little or no cause.

In the course of American air operations against North

Vietnam from 1965 until 1972, the USAF had to deal not only with North Vietnamese air defence fighters, but also with a formidable array of surface-to-air missiles (SAMs) and anti-aircraft guns defending key targets. Although defending MiG-17s and MiG-21s scored some successes, the attacking force was generally well-protected by combat air patrols of McDonnell Douglas F-4 Phantoms.

Surface-to-air missiles posed a serious threat to USAF bombers throughout the war; during the Linebacker II assault on the Hanoi-Haiphong area in late 1972, for example, no fewer than 15 Boeing B-52s fell to SAMs. Electronic countermeasures partly neutralised the SAM threat and special defence-suppression aircraft (code-named Wild Weasels) accompanied bombing forces to deal with the ground defences.

For the foreseeable future, air-to-air combat will not give place to the SAM, as is attested by the development of such fighters as the General Dynamics F-16 and the McDonnel Douglas F-15 Eagle. The latter is a highly-maneouvrable fighter capable of speeds in excess of Mach 2·5 and with an all-weather combat capability. Its operation in the air superiority role may well be in conjunction with the Boeing E-3 Sentry airborne-warning and control aircraft.

A North Vietnamese MiG-17 falls to the cannon fire of a Republic F-105D Thunderchief of the USAF's 388th Tactical Fighter Wing in June 1967

Anti-Submarine Warfare

The role of the aircraft in detecting and destroying submarines has been growing steadily over the last 40 years. From being no more than an aid, it graduated to being the potent and successful method of stalking and sinking submarines in World War II. Modern technology, particularly in the helicopter field, has made today's anti-submarine aircraft even more effective.

When World War II broke out in September 1939 the main force of anti-submarine aircraft was within the Royal Air Force's Coastal Command, formed in 1936, and charged with the task of combating the German Navy's U-boats as well as performing its main task of co-operating with the Royal Navy. The only other air force to maintain any proper anti-submarine capability was the airborne element of the United States Navy, but neither of these two groups could be described as well-equipped. Yet, the United States and Great Britain had been allies in World War I and although their aircraft had been crude, nearly all the fundamentals of anti-submarine warfare had been formulated and proved.

The first kill

The first submarine was sunk at sea by aircraft as early as September 1916, when two Austrian flying boats caught the French submarine *Foucault* running at periscope depth in the Adriatic. The clear visibility gave away the submarine's position; four bombs, aimed by eye, caused blast damage to the motors and the *Foucault* surfaced. When the craft's diesels would not function the commanding officer gave orders to scuttle and abandon ship. However simple this sinking sounded, it was only by the wildest chance that the four bombs fell close enough to damage the submarine; and had the *Foucault's* commander not thought that he had struck a mine his boat might have escaped.

In the North Sea British and Germans had been making sporadic and unco-ordinated attacks on submarines using heavier-than-air machines, 'rigid' airships (the German Zeppelins) and small 'non-rigid' airships (the British 'blimps'). The first attack on a submarine was in December 1914, when a Zeppelin, L-5, unsuccessfully tried to bomb the British *E11* off Norderney. The British quickly realised the value of patrolling aircraft. Submarines were far slower when submerged and, because their battery-power was limited, the mere fact of being forced beneath the surface restricted their freedom of action.

But the first problem to be overcome in submarine detection was the lack of suitable aircraft. In the Spring of 1915 the Royal Naval Air Service had only three airships which were powerful enough for patrols, and its seaplanes were considered too small and unreliable. The answer was the 'blimp' and by a remarkable spurt of productivity the Royal Navy produced a prototype in just three weeks, using a gas-bag from an obsolete airship and the fuselage of a BE2 aircraft. The 'Submarine Scout' airships which resulted from this ingenuity had the great virtue of being able to loiter over shipping in coastal waters, and led to much bigger craft. Curtiss twin-engined flying boats were brought over from America and although they were heavy and unreliable they proved their potential and later types were more effective. The Germans were well supplied with Zeppelins for submarine-hunting and reconnaissance and also made use of the small Friedrichshafen seaplanes.

When convoys were introduced in May 1917, the Allies made considerable use of aircraft to protect them. As often as possible a flying boat or a blimp met the incoming convoy in the South Western Approaches. By the end of 1917 the RNAS had more than 100 operational

The British Hawker Siddeley Nimrod, developed from the Comet 4 airliner, is one of today's most successful submarine hunters

A total of 892 German, Italian and Japanese submarines was sunk by the Allied anti-submarine forces in World War II. Of these, surface ships accounted for 394½ (30½ of them with the help of aircraft), other submarines destroyed 64 and aircraft sank 433½. The lion's share of the aircraft's score went to land-based patrol bombers, which sank 303½ submarines. The remainder was made up by 66 submarines sunk in port during raids by shore-based bomber aircraft and 64 sunk at sea by naval aircraft operating from carriers.

The British share of the total sinkings by aircraft was 281½ and the US share was 152. Of the victims, 396½ were German, 15½ Italian and 21½ Japanese.

blimps, in addition to flying boats. The slow blimps flew long, monotonous patrols and, because U-boats tended to stay clear of a convoy escorted by a blimp, airship crews hardly ever saw so much as a periscope. The flying boats were luckier: in April 1917 they started what were known as 'Spider Web' patrols, flying on octagonal track lines around a centre-point located in the southern part of the North Sea. During the first two weeks eight U-boats were sighted and three attacked.

During 1917 the policy of patrolling coastal shipping routes was extended and, in conjunction with the convoying of shipping, it played an important part in bringing down the average monthly total of shipping sunk from 834,000 tons in April to 340,000 tons in December. When the U-boats moved into coastal waters in search of easier pickings the idea of 'Scarecrow' patrols was suggested. This was the use of any aircraft, however slow or under-armed, to fly along shipping lanes, merely to make the U-boats 'keep their heads down'. Using some 200 obsolete DH6 aircraft, which had recently been superseded as trainers, the RNAS flew patrols which were as boring as those of the blimps. Yet in the last six months of the war the 'Scarecrow' squadrons sighted 16 submarines and attacked 11 times, but without success.

When the Armistice came several ideas for improving submarine search and attack techniques were being considered, including flying boats fitted with hydrophones, which would allow them to alight on the water to listen for a submerged U-boat. Another was the twin-engined Blackburn Kangaroo, a patrol bomber capable of the same endurance as a large flying boat, but carrying twice the bomb load. None of these ideas was developed to any significant degree, but what was more important was that the aircraft had proved its capabilities as a weapon against the submarine. Several valuable lessons were learned. First, any degree of air cover was better than none at all; second, observers had very little chance of spotting submerged submarines, and only a poor chance of sighting them in average weather and visibility conditions; third, a submarine had to be attacked quickly, and fourth, conventional bombs had to drop very close to inflict fatal damage.

Below: the twin-engined Blackburn Kangaroo patrol bomber of 1918 had the same endurance as contemporary flying-boats, but carried twice the weapons load.
Opposite: America's Consolidated Catalina flying-boat was one of the best anti-submarine warfare patrol aircraft at the start of World War II, but it was outranged by the later Liberator a land-based bomber produced by the same company

The fifth lesson was most important: that a single, long-endurance aircraft was more useful than several short-endurance aircraft. Next, and most important of all, was that convoys were considerably safer from submarine attack if aircraft as well as surface warships formed the escort. Between May 1917 and November 1918 some 84,000 voyages were made in convoy; only 257 ships were lost out of this total–and only two from convoys which had an aircraft present. One unfortunate lesson had been learned: the 'Spider Web' patrols which were thought to have sunk five U-boats, were, in fact, found to be virtually ineffective. The most effective use of aircraft had been in the vicinity of convoys, where they could not only be certain of finding targets but also of bringing direct help where it was needed.

Years of retrenchment

The long years of retrenchment which followed the end of World War I did much to ensure that nearly all these lessons were forgotten by 1939 and the parsimony of defence budgets prevented equipment from being tested and developed. The British phased out their blimps, although they still built flying boats; the Americans, on the other hand, liked the blimp and retained it in service. Everybody paid lip-service to the value of air patrols in protecting shipping, but in practice very little was done to develop new equipment to take advantage of the vast improvements in aircraft performance and reliability which had taken place since 1918. Although the British formed Coastal Command in 1936 and re-established an independent naval air arm a year later, the Navy's belief that the surface warship's new sonic underwater detector ASDIC (now called Sonar) had beaten the U-boat provided a good excuse to ignore anti-submarine work and Coastal Command remained the Cinderella of the RAF.

But there were straws in the wind. In July 1937 a Coastal Command Anson began flight trials of an air-borne radar set. In 1939 the Lockheed Hudson twin-engined bomber entered service, providing for the first time an aircraft well designed for anti-submarine patrols. Only the new Hudson had bomb-release gear to allow a 'stick' of bombs to be dropped in the most lethal pattern. The British, however, were far better equipped than their French allies, who had only a mixed bag of obsolete flying boats. The Germans and Italians had devoted very little thought to anti-submarine aircraft, apart from the provision of shore-based patrols over coastal waters. The United States had the best aircraft, including such advanced models as the long-endurance Catalina flying boat.

The early months of World War II did not inspire much confidence in anti-submarine aircraft. The British found that their bombs had very little effect against U-boats, and another disadvantage revealed itself: to compensate for the lack of a proper bomb-sight, Coastal Command pilots were going in at a height which exposed their aircraft to blast and splinters. To make matters worse the bombs tended to 'skip' off the surface of the water and back into the air. (It might be said that the British anti-submarine bomb accounted for more British aircraft than German U-boats.)

The Leigh Light

The problem was quickly identified and the solution adopted was to modify the standard naval depth-charge. Although crude, this makeshift aerial depth-charge was able to improve the attacking performance of aircraft against submarines until a properly designed depth-charge could be produced. By the end of 1940 other weaponry was on its way; the ASV Mark I (Air to Surface Vessel) radar set and the Leigh Light. The latter came about because of a limitation in the ASV radar sets–it could not detect a target *inside* a distance of less than a mile; unfortunately this distance was greater than the distance at which a U-boat could be seen at night, and so aircrew found it almost impossible to sink submarines

Ready for attack: depth bombs on a Sunderland's bomb racks are fused

even when they had been detected on radar. Of course, these sightings were not wasted, because they forced the submarine to submerge, but to the head of Coastal Command, Air Chief Marshal Sir Frederick Bowhill, there seemed little point in providing such sophisticated methods of detection if they did not sink U-boats. The Leigh Light was nothing more than a powerful searchlight mounted under the wing of an aircraft; it illuminated the U-boat during the last vital run-in, and enabled the bomb-aimer to see his target.

The prototype Leigh Light was fitted in a Wellington bomber in March 1941 but various problems kept it out of service for nearly the whole of that year. In the meantime a far-reaching decision had been made to set up an Operational Research Station for Coastal Command, under the direction of Professor Patrick Blackett. The concept, a new one, was that scientists should consider the problems almost in the abstract rather than simply design new and deadlier weapons. In effect certain scientists were allowed to study the results of operations to ascertain any pattern or weakness of equipment which could be rectified. One of the most important discoveries was that depth-charges were being set too deep to harm diving U-boats. Merely by altering the settings from an average of 125 feet to 20 feet (the hydrostatic pistol had to be redesigned to allow this) Coastal Command was able to turn what would previously have been near-misses into sinkings.

But the most pressing problem of all was the shortage

A Sunderland Mk I of 210 Squadron on patrol early in World War II

of long-range aircraft. In mid-1941 Coastal Command had 400 aircraft, of which only a relatively small number were the long-endurance Catalina and British Sunderland flying boats. The Hudson could patrol out to a distance of 500 miles from its shore base, the Sunderland could spend two hours at 600 miles and the Catalina could remain on patrol the same time but at the then staggering range of 800 miles. Beyond the range of these aircraft, operating from Halifax, in Nova Scotia, Iceland and Britain, lay the 'Black Gap' in mid-Atlantic, where ships had no air cover and the U-boats faced only the surface escorts. Although a very long range (VLR) conversion of the American four-engined Liberator bomber was already in hand, the best answer to the problem of air cover in mid-Atlantic was to take aircraft with the convoys.

The first escort carrier

The solution was reached in a typically roundabout fashion. The convoys from England to Gibraltar had been badly punished in 1940-41 by Focke-Wulf Condor maritime bombers operating from Bay of Biscay airfields, and initially some merchant ships had been fitted with catapult-launched Hurricane fighters. As an extension of this idea the Royal Navy commissioned a small 'escort carrier', HMS *Audacity*, in the summer of 1941. Using a wooden flight deck on top of her mercantile hull, the *Audacity* was intended to provide fighter escort against the Condors, but it was obvious that a similar conversion could carry anti-submarine aircraft all the way across the Atlantic. This was the genesis of the escort carrier, but some months were to elapse before ships and aircraft could be spared for more conversions.

The entry of the United States into the war in December 1941 should have made things easier for the British, but this was not immediately the case. So badly prepared were the Americans for the U-boats' onslaught against their East Coast shipping that both Allies had to devote their

A Sunderland of 10 Squadron, Royal Australian Air Force, banking round Eddystone Lighthouse

attention to remedying the situation before they could tackle wider issues. The US Army Air Force controlled nearly all shore-based aircraft, but personnel had received no training in co-operation with shipping; the US Navy knew what had to be done but had too few aircraft. By the time the U-boats had been checked on the Atlantic seaboard of the USA it was June 1942, but the delay had not prevented the introduction of new tactics and weapons. In that month five Wellingtons equipped with Leigh Lights became operational, but the most impressive addition to the strength was the VLR Liberator already mentioned. With 550 litres (2,500 gallons) of fuel on board, achieved by removing such items as armour plate and machine-guns,

Coastal Command Wellingtons at Gibraltar, which had the status of a Group within the command

A dramatic aerial shot of a Swordfish, an aircraft which repeatedly proved itself in attacks on submarines

the VLR could patrol for three hours up to 1,100 miles from base with a total flying time of 16 hours.

In the United States scientists were working on a radically new approach, the detection of variations in the earth's magnetic field caused by a submarine. Known as MAD (Magnetic Anomaly Detector) the device was carried in a 'sting' projecting from the tail of the aircraft, to remove it from magnetic influences in the airframe. Although MAD could detect a U-boat 300 feet below the surface of the sea it had a very short range and so the aircraft had to fly at no more than 100 feet, and there was thus very little warning when a submarine was detected. This called for a much faster reaction-time than was possible with a free-falling bomb or depth-charge, and so the scientists came up with the 'Retro-bomb'. This rocket-assisted bomb was fired backwards, inertia slowed it down to a dead stop, and it then fell in the normal way.

Another contribution from American scientists to help aircraft locate submarines was the sonobuoy, a small floating transmitter combined with a hydrophone (passive sonar). The sonobuoy was dropped into the water and relayed any underwater sounds within range of the sonar set for about four hours, until the batteries ran down. To prevent the buoy from being captured by an inquisitive submarine a soluble bung allowed it to flood and sink

when the batteries ran down. The sonobuoy was a big improvement in aerial anti-submarine warfare because it detected the position of a submerged submarine at up to three-and-a-half miles under good conditions, as long as the submarine was moving, and provided that the propellers were turning fast enough to cause cavitation (swirls and bubbles in the water). But these early sonobuoys were like the hydrophones used in 1916, and could only indicate that a submarine was there, without giving any distance or bearing.

Anti-submarine weapons

To match the new-found ability to locate submarines from the air, scientists introduced an acoustic target-seeking torpedo dropped from the air. Known officially as the Mark 24 Mine, its code-name was 'Fido' and its affectionate nickname 'Wandering Annie'. The purpose of Fido was to 'home' on the cavitation noise of a submarine diving rapidly and it could pick up the noise of rapid-running propellers from three-quarters of a mile. If U-boat commanders had known this they might have fooled Fido's acoustic head by slowing down after diving, but it was hoped that this would go against most U-boat captain's instincts.

The British had been dabbling in rocket-weapons since

The redoubtable Swordfish, here a Mk III fitted with Mk X ASV radar and rocket-assisted take-off equipment

A Liberator GR VI of Coastal Command returns to the Azores after patrol

the beginning of the War, and in 1942 they produced a 30kg (66lb) anti-submarine rocket. The advantages of this weapon were, first, its straight flight-path to the target, which made aiming simpler, and second, its ability to hit the underwater hull of a U-boat. Profiting by its experience with diving shells the Royal Navy suggested shaping the 11·3kg (25lb) semi-armour-piercing warhead, with the result that a rocket striking the water about 18m (20 yards) short of the target at an angle of 13 degrees would travel underwater on an upward curve, striking the U-boat's pressure hull *en route*.

It was fortunate for the Allies that such a fearsome array of airborne weapons was developed by the end of 1942, for in the Spring of 1943 the Battle of the Atlantic suddenly reached crisis point. A balance had been held with difficulty in the second half of 1942. Then, however, as the weather improved the U-boats seized their chance. Convoy losses rose alarmingly, and as they were already averaging 500,000 tons a month as the end of 1942 it was clear that the U-boat might win the war for Germany before the Allies could build up their strength. Fortunately the US Navy's anti-submarine requirements in the Pacific were not too demanding, since the Japanese proved remarkably inept at attacking American communications, and so the main effort was made in the Atlantic.

Unfortunately, in the Atlantic there were still conflicting priorities in the use of aircraft. RAF Bomber Command was firmly in the grip of the Trenchard doctrine of strategic bombing, and begrudged the use of four-engined bombers on anti-submarine duties. The question of how long the bombers could continue to batter Germany if the losses of tankers to U-boat attacks were not reduced does not seem to have been put by the exponents of strategic bombing and, in any case, post-war examination revealed that the bombing was not accurate enough to make any serious inroads into the U-boat production until 1944. It was estimated by Coastal Command that the provision of two extra squadrons of VLR Liberators sanctioned by Churchill and Roosevelt (in the teeth of bitter opposition from the bomber-chiefs) made the difference between defeat and victory in the Spring of 1943. Another point overlooked by the strategic bombing enthusiasts was the

The first escort carrier, HMS Audacity, converted from a captured German fruit carrier, Hannover

fact that the U-boats were now protected in harbour by giant 'pens' of massively reinforced concrete, which was practically impenetrable by normal bombs.

There were other factors in the equation, naturally, for the Battle of the Atlantic was not won merely by two squadrons of Liberators. First, the escort forces and, most important of all, their escort carriers, were released from covering the North African invasion. Flooding back into the battle, these long-overdue reinforcements had an immediate effect. Another important factor was the German failure to provide a defence against the Allies' new centimetric waveband radars, which provided very high definition and accurate bearings. The liaison between the U-boat Arm and its scientific advisors was poor, so it took a long time before anyone even suspected the use of centimetric radar, and longer still to design an efficient search-receiver which could give the U-boats warning of an approaching aircraft.

Victory conceded

The U-boats conceded victory in May 1943, when Admiral Dönitz withdrew them for 'regrouping', a euphemism for a desperately needed rest for the shattered flotillas to retrain and rebuild their strength. Although new weapons and tactics, and even revolutionary new fast U-boats, were under development, the U-boat Arm never regained the

initiative. With over a thousand aircraft now available in the Atlantic the Allies could take the offensive at last, and shore-based aircraft were henceforward to be used more and more in areas where the kill-rate was high. In the waters around the British Isles this meant primarily the routes through the Bay of Biscay used by U-boats on their way to the Atlantic.

For over a year, from mid-1942 until the Summer of 1943 RAF Coastal Command fought the 'Battle of the Bay' with increasing ferocity. Anti-submarine aircraft went out to hunt U-boats, so the Luftwaffe sent up long-range fighters to shoot them down; the RAF retaliated by sending out strong patrols of Beaufighters and Mosquitoes to protect the anti-submarine aircraft and the resulting encounters were sharp and bloody. In desperation Dönitz ordered his U-boats to fight it out with aircraft on the surface; some unwary Coastal Command aircraft were caught in this trap, but soon it was the U-boats which called an end to this particular game. The first part of the Biscay air campaign had yielded eight U-boats sunk and 16 damaged, but between the end of April and the beginning of August 1943 a further 26 were sunk and 17

A dramatic sequence showing successive attacks upon the U-boat U288 by Grumman Avengers from the escort carrier HMS Activity. The U-boat was destroyed

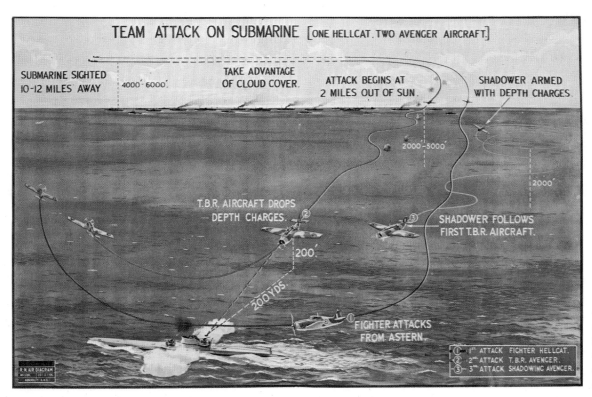

TEAM ATTACK ON SUBMARINE [ONE HELLCAT, TWO AVENGER AIRCRAFT]

SUBMARINE SIGHTED 10-12 MILES AWAY

4000'-6000'

TAKE ADVANTAGE OF CLOUD COVER.

ATTACK BEGINS AT 2 MILES OUT OF SUN.

SHADOWER ARMED WITH DEPTH CHARGES

2000'-5000'

2000'

T.B.R. AIRCRAFT DROPS DEPTH CHARGES.

SHADOWER FOLLOWS FIRST T.B.R. AIRCRAFT.

200'

200 YDS.

FIGHTER ATTACKS FROM ASTERN.

①— 1ˢᵀ ATTACK FIGHTER HELLCAT.
②— 2ᴺᴰ ATTACK T.B.R. AVENGER.
③— 3ᴿᴰ ATTACK SHADOWING AVENGER.

The approved tactics for a team attack on a U-boat are illustrated by this wartime diagram. Grumman Hellcats and Avengers flew from escort carriers during the latter years of World War II

damaged, an average of one sinking every 3·7 days. To put this in perspective against the rest of the anti-submarine war, a total of 118 German and Italian submarines were sunk during the same period, 78 to aircraft alone, 6 to aircraft co-operating with ships and 34 to surface escorts. Despite this the U-boat was not yet defeated; at the same time 600,000 tons of Allied shipping was sunk. Yet this staggering total was less than the current production from Allied shipyards.

The remainder of the war saw little refinement in the types of aircraft and their weaponry, but rather a ceaseless effort to find the U-boats wherever they might be. Most of the counter-measures adopted by U-boats were not very effective, and the new U-boats with high underwater speed were not ready until the moment of surrender. The only truly effective invention was the *schnorchel*, originally a Dutch-designed induction mast which allowed a U-boat to recharge her batteries while running at periscope depth. (Submarines used electric power at depth but relied upon diesels on or close to the surface). But the *schnorchel* merely enabled a U-Boat to evade detection and did nothing to help her sink ships. Its use caused extreme discomfort, and it did little to restore tactical freedom to the U-boats.

Protecting Normandy forces
Some indication of the weight of airpower which the Allies could bring to bear on the U-boats in 1944 is given by the arrangements to protect the Normandy invasion forces. Under the code-name 'Cork'–for the intention was to 'cork' the English Channel to prevent U-boats from getting into the invasion areas–a total of about 350 bombers, ranging from single-engined biplane Swordfish to four-engined Halifaxes, was allocated. Tests against friendly submarines showed that the density of air patrols made it almost impossible for a U-boat to operate, even if the aircraft themselves did not always sight the U-boat. Even the few U-boats fitted with *schnorchel* found that all they could manage was to survive, and concerted attacks on the slow invasion convoys was impossible. Admiral Krancke, commander of German naval forces in the West, noted with regret that the only

way for his U-boats to survive was to remain in their concrete pens. But in spite of these problems the U-boats did achieve some small successes, and torpedoed two warships and a tank-landing ship.

Strategic bombing had achieved very little in the fight against U-boats, but inevitably the enormous weight of bombs dropped on Germany began to tell. Mining of the Baltic took its toll of the U-boats training there, and bombing of the canals held up deliveries of prefabricated sections of the new fast U-boats. Aircraft were found to be very effective against the various types of midget submarine introduced late in 1944; whereas depth-charges simply bounced the midgets aside without sinking them, cannon-fire holed them easily. The final onslaught against U-boats took place in the Kattegat in April 1945, when rocket-firing Mosquitoes roamed at will, picking off a total of 26 U-boats.

The end of the war revealed to the Allies just how close the U-boat had come to beating them. Despite the slaughter of U-boats and the loss of 33,000 personnel, the U-boat Arm was almost ready to renew the battle. Ironically, the aircraft was back where it had started in 1939. The combination of high submerged speed and the *schnorchel* would have made the new Type XXI and Type XXIII U-boats very hard to detect, for radar sets could not pick up the *schnorchel* tube in anything but the calmest conditions. Only three Type XXI boats came into service, literally days before the unconditional surrender, but the smaller Type XXIII boats had already shown that they could repeatedly evade both air and surface patrols.

Helicopter ASW role
The Cold War which now developed between the major powers of the West and the Communist bloc countries meant no lull in the battle to find an antidote to the new type of submarine. All the victorious Allies, including the Soviet Union, possessed themselves of the latest German secrets and soon a series of improved Type XXI submarines began to appear. Post-war exercises showed just how lethal these fast submarines could be, but worse was to come. In 1954 the US Navy commissioned the world's

first nuclear-powered submarine, USS *Nautilus*, and the 'true submarine' capable of indefinite underwater travel came many steps closer to reality. Once nuclear propulsion was perfected and the design of submarines' life-support systems was improved to take advantage of its enormous power and endurance the anti-submarine aircraft seemed to be out of the race.

But, as always, a dominant weapon does not dominate for long. Passive detection had been improving steadily, and so had active sonar. Sonobuoys were made directional, so that a diamond-shaped pattern could give accurate bearings to the aircraft, and sonar sets capable of ultra-long range detection were developed. The growing reliability and potential of the helicopter suddenly provided an answer to the submarine's speed, for the helicopter could pursue an underwater target at roughly three times the speed of the fastest submarines in existence, and could also hover above a stationary, submerged one, which searching aircraft might 'over-shoot'.

To state the case so simply conceals the extent and nature of the revolution in anti-submarine warfare brought about by the helicopter. The first problem was to design equipment which the helicopter could use to detect a submarine, and the result was not dissimilar to the World War I flying boats and their dipping hydrophones. A 'dunking' sonar was produced to allow the helicopter to

patrol aircraft and the Americans the P2V Neptune in the post-1945 period, and both types are only just going into retirement after years of highly successful service. They carried radar, MAD and extensive plotting and communications gear, and could drop sonobuoys and homing torpedoes. An important advantage of the large anti-submarine aircraft is that it carries a crew large enough to be divided into watches.

Periscopes and *schnorchels* (now known as snorkels or

A Coastal Command Shackleton Mk 2 of 224 Squadron

An Avro Shackleton MR 3 of Coastal Command

hover while listening for propeller noises, and this concept has been developed to the point where the helicopter has a wealth of gear on board for classifying and processing the information. The homing torpedo proved an ideal weapon for the helicopter, for there is no risk of damage from the blast, as there would be with a depth-charge. The next step was to take the helicopter to sea to extend its range, and this called for radical redesign of warships. Now most escort vessels of any importance have a built-in capacity to operate helicopters, including re-fuelling, deck-lighting and workshops and hangar space. The vital point is to keep the helicopter operational as long as possible, and much effort has gone into improvements to helicopters' control equipment to enable them to operate in bad weather and at longer ranges.

The large anti-submarine aircraft has not been super-seded by the helicopter by any means, for they alone have the long range and the capacity to operate certain equipment. The British produced the Shackleton four-engined

snort masts) remain difficult radar targets, particularly in rough seas, but a snorkelling submarine emits diesel fumes through her air-mast. Detection equipment, known as 'Sniffer' in the US Navy and 'Autolycus' in the RAF, can detect the infra-red content of these fumes with sufficient accuracy to make a sonobuoy search worthwhile. Another development has been the discovery of the phenomenon known as the 'thermal scar', a trail of slightly warmer water left in the wake of a submarine for some minutes. Both infra-red emissions and exhaust trails are, of course, very easily dissipated and are likely to be saturated if surface ships are nearby.

Today's mainstay

Even though the role of the big fleet carrier and its fixed-wing strike aircraft is questioned by many naval pundits, nobody questions the value of the big helicopter carrier. Some years ago the French Navy built a helicopter-cruiser, the interesting hybrid *Jeanne d'Arc*, to operate

Super Frélon helicopters, and the idea has been taken a step further by the Royal Navy. Two 'command' cruisers to be called *Invincible* and *Illustrious* are on order, with a third ship to follow; they are to operate a mix of Sea King anti-submarine helicopters and Harrier VTOL/STOL aircraft. In 1976, just ten years after a political ruling

announced the death of the flat-topped carrier, three flat-topped vessels of 70,000 tons displacement were being planned, largely in order to get helicopters to sea to defend warships against submarine attack. The largely similar American 'sea command ship' was planned to do much the same job. The Russians built two helicopter-carriers, the *Leningrad* and *Moskva*, and recently completed the 40,000-ton *Kiev*. Like the British *Invincible* Class, the *Kiev* and her sisters were designed to screen task forces and squadrons, using VTOL/STOL aircraft to destroy reconnaissance aircraft, and helicopters to provide an anti-submarine screen.

Today the long-range aircraft and the helicopter are the mainstay of all front-line navies. The Anglo-French Lynx and the Russian Kamov 'Hormone' are typical of the light shipboard helicopters, whereas the bigger Sea King needs a big warship from which to operate. On the other hand the Sea King bridges the gap between the light helicopter and the long-range patrol aircraft by having much better facilities on board for classifying contacts and for control of flying operations. A big problem for the helicopter has been the relative ease with which it can get lost, and this has limited the range at which it can operate away from its parent ship. No such problem affects the long-range patrol aircraft, which is another reason why they are still so important. The British Hawker Siddeley Nimrod is a most successful aircraft, derived from the Comet 4 airliner's airframe but using a different power-plant to give long endurance. One of the most advanced pieces of equipment carried by the Nimrod uses a computer to classify the transmissions from sonobuoys.

The anti-submarine aircraft has come a long way from its crude beginnings. It undoubtedly played an important role in defeating the U-boat in World War I, but nothing could equal its achievements between 1939 and 1945. During the past 30 years the steady improvement of all types of anti-submarine aircraft and their tactics has been the only positive progress to set against the frightening growth in the power of the nuclear submarine. In any future conflict at sea the anti-submarine aircraft will be back in the front line.

Above: The Westland Sea King carries radar and sonar and is fitted with an automatic flight-control system.
Top and right: The mainstays of modern anti-submarine forces are the long-range aircraft and the helicopter. One of the most widely-used anti-submarine patrol aircraft is the Lockheed P-3C Orion.
Opposite: the Lockheed S-3A Viking carrier-based anti-submarine search and strike aircraft has a loiter endurance of 7·5 hours, and carries comprehensive avionics and internally stored weapons

Army Aviation

A Jaguar GR Mk 1 strike fighter of 14 Squadron, RAF Germany, an example of Britain's latest battlefield support aircraft

Army aviation is more than a century older than heavier-than-air flight. The first military air unit was formed to operate observation balloons with the French Revolutionary armies in 1794 and first saw action at the Battle of Fleurus in June that year. When aeroplanes were added to the armouries of the Great Powers, in the decade leading up to the outbreak of World War I in August 1914, they were primarily used, as were balloons, for reconnaissance.

In 1911 the Italian army despatched to conquer the Turks in Libya was accompanied by a small air component, equipped with Blériot, Nieuport and Etrich Taube monoplanes and Henri Farman biplanes. The unit's primary task was the location of Turkish forces, the first reconnaissance flight being undertaken by Captain Carlos Piazza, the unit's commanding officer, on 23 October. In addition, aerial photography, spotting and reporting the fall of artillery shells and bomb dropping were experimented with: all these techniques were to be perfected for the support of armies in the field during World War I.

It was during the opening months of World War I that the aeroplane established itself as an essential aid to military reconnaissance, for it was the information provided by the army air arms, together with that brought in by scouting cavalry patrols, which enabled the Allied armies to defeat the German plan for a quick and decisive victory in the West – the famous Schlieffen Plan – at the Battle of the Marne in September 1914. The intention of the Germans was to march through Belgium and, having crushed the relatively weak forces defending the Franco-

Belgian frontier, swing south of Paris and take the main French armies in the rear. The left wing of the Allied front (i.e. that facing the initial German assault) was held by the British Expeditionary Force, which included four squadrons (Nos. 2, 3, 4 and 5) of the Royal Flying Corps. These squadrons helped the Allies to discover a change in direction by the German attack and this vital information was exploited by the Allied counter-attack on the Marne. The German advance was halted and both sides began constructing the lines of trenches from which the war in the West was to be fought for the next four years.

Reconnaissance and spotting

These early flights of the war illustrate some of the difficulties faced by airmen, operating in open-cockpit aeroplanes, often without the help of a trained observer to navigate the machine and note the results of the reconnaissance. Lieutenant G. W. Mapplebeck, who flew the first British reconnaissance flight of the war on 19 August 1914, noted amongst his difficulties, the impossibility of navigating with the large-scale map provided – indeed it was not until after he had landed that he realised that a large town he had flown over was Brussels. The smaller map provided was much better for cross-country flying, but the larger was preferable for detailed observation over the area to be reconnoitred. However, these problems were soon overcome and the British airmen earned the praise of Sir John French, Commander of the British Expeditionary Force, who wrote: 'They have furnished me with the most complete and accurate information

An Etrich Taube, one of the most widely used German reconnaissance aeroplanes in 1914

which has been of incalculable value in the conduct of operations.' The German Commander on the Eastern Front, General Hindenburg, was even more fulsome in his praise of the infant air service, stating that without air reconnaissance, there could have been no German victory at Tannenberg (26-30 August 1914).

Trench warfare, in which movement, if it took place at all, was measured in yards rather than miles, removed the need for the kind of air reconnaissance which had proved so crucial in the early months of World War I. The aeroplane, nevertheless, continued to make an important contribution to the war on the ground. The need for accurate trench maps and for a means of corroborating the perforce fallible eye-witness reports from airmen resulted

in the rapid development of aerial photography. Consequently the camera became as much a part of the equipment of the observation aeroplane as the observer's notebook.

The extent to which ground troops came to rely on air reconnaissance photographs can be gauged by the British experience during the Battle of the Somme (July to November 1916), when no less than 19,000 photographs were taken of enemy positions. The increasing use of aerial reconnaissance had led to the camouflaging of important military installations. This in turn led to the development of the art of photographic interpretation, when it was realised that careful and expert scrutiny of reconnaissance photographs could reveal much that was not immediately apparent. The shadows cast by camouflaged buildings and well-worn tracks converging on dumps and headquarters were typical of the indications that could lead the interpreter to discover a hitherto unsuspected enemy offensive in the making.

A second development which closely followed the advent of trench warfare was the artillery spotting aeroplane. Great numbers of guns and howitzers were ranged behind the trench lines ready to fire off a prodigious weight of high explosive to halt an enemy's advance or in preparation for the assault of their own troops. It was soon found, however, that an indiscriminate artillery barrage did comparatively little harm to an enemy sheltering in well constructed trenches and dugouts. A means was therefore sought of directing the gunners' fire onto specific targets, such as enemy batteries, and for this the radio-equipped aeroplane proved ideal, although there were never enough of them to direct more than a small proportion of the available guns. The Germans were quick to realise the specialised nature of this work and in the latter half of 1915, 14 units (known as Artillerie Flieger Abteilungen) were formed exclusively for this task. It was intended that each front-line Division should have its own artillery spotting units and so rapid was the expansion of the Artillerie Flieger Abteilungen that by August 1916 they comprised over half of the German observation units (45 out of 81). The radio messages to a battery, logged by a British observer as early as September 1914, illustrate the method used in artillery ranging: 'A very little short. Fire. Fire. Fire again. Fire again. A little short; line O.K. Short. Over, over and a little left. You were just between two batteries. Search two hundred yards each side of your last shot. Range O.K. You have hit them.'

Reporting troop advances

Another problem of trench warfare for which the aeroplane provided a solution was that of finding out how far the troops had advanced during an offensive. Communications between forward troops and their rear headquarters were often completely severed once an attack went 'over the top' and even when information did filter back from the fighting area it was often hours out-of-date when received. The French airmen provided a solution to this problem during the Battle of Verdun (February to December 1916) and the British took up their method for the Somme offensive, which opened on 1 July 1916. The contact patrol system, as it was known, involved low-flying aeroplanes patrolling the fighting area and ordering friendly troops to fire flares from their forward positions by means of a pre-arranged klaxon signal. The information gained was then passed to rear headquarters. It was found that 'most information could be obtained by direct observation from a low height and that any uncertainty as to the nationality of the troops could usually be set at rest by going low enough to draw fire.'

Much of the aerial bombing of World War I was intended to be of direct help to ground forces, such targets as ammunition and supply dumps, railways and troop rest camps in the enemy's rear areas being attacked frequently. Similarly the fast-developing science of aerial fighting was stimulated by the need to keep the skies over one's front clear of enemy aeroplanes and to try to prevent him interfering with the work of one's own machines.

The culmination of the airmen's efforts to co-operate with their comrades in the trenches came with the development of tactics and machines which enabled the airmen to join in the ground battle itself. It had long been a point of honour for fighter, or as they were then known scout, pilots to empty their remaining ammunition into the enemy's reserve trenches when returning from patrol. With light bombs fitted in addition to machine gun armament, the fighter plane was well suited to ground-attack missions and British fighter squadrons flung into the desperate ground battle to halt the German offensive in March 1918 earned the respect of friend and foe alike. So important was this role by the final year of the war that the British developed the Sopwith Salamander (based on the Snipe fighter, but with armour protection for pilot and fuel tanks) specifically for ground attack.

The Germans, too, were well aware of the need for aeroplanes to support their infantry in battle and when they launched their great offensive in March 1918, 38 specially-trained units known as Schlachtstaffeln were given this task. By this time the Germans had a specially-

Right: the RE8, nicknamed 'Harry Tate' after a music hall star of the day, was widely-used for artillery observation in the last years of World War I. A machine of the Australian Flying Corps is pictured.
Inset below: the AEG J–1 carried twin Spandaus, angled downwards for trench strafing and was fitted with armour plate.
Inset bottom: an RFC NCO checks a reconnaissance camera fitted to a BE 2

Top: the all-metal Junkers
J–1 was an armoured ground
support aircraft, which went
into action during the
German offensive of 1918.
Above: the two-seat Junkers
CL–1 was a monoplane
successor to the same
company's J–1.

Left: Britain's armoured
trench strafer, the Sopwith
Salamander, was developed
from the Snipe fighter

*Above: the Westland
Lysander was the RAF's
main army co-operation type
at the start of World War II.
Below: Russian paratroops
jump from the dorsal hatch
of a Tupolev ANT-6*

designed ground-support aeroplane, the Junkers J.I, which, unlike the Salamander, which was too late for the war, went into action at the beginning of 1918. A two-seater, the J.I was an all-metal aeroplane at a time when most of its contemporaries were wooden structures with fabric covering, and its crew and engine were protected by 5 mm armour plate. As well as attacking enemy troops, J.Is radioed battlefield information to rear headquarters and dropped food and ammunition to troops in forward positions.

Lessons forgotten

By the end of World War I a great deal of valuable experience in the conduct of ground-support operations by air forces had been gained. Unfortunately, in the two decades of comparative peace which followed, Britain forgot many of these hard-earned lessons. Army co-operation between the wars centred on the succession of obscure, yet hard-fought campaigns against dissident Pathan tribesmen on the North-West Frontier of India. The aeroplanes which proved admirably designed for such warfare—Bristol Fighters, Westland Wapitis and Hawker Audaxes—were ill-suited to the very different conditions of a major European war, as their lineal descendant, the

some 50,000 men. However, shortage of transport aircraft and the fast-deteriorating situation at the front, forced the Soviet High Command to order these highly-trained forces into battle as ground troops.

The opening campaigns of World War II illustrate the impressive degree of co-operation between air and ground forces achieved by the German *blitzkrieg* (lightning war). Ground troops, spearheaded by tanks and motorised infantry, were supported by Luftflotten (Air Fleets) comprising a balanced force of fighters, bombers and reconnaissance aeroplanes. The first task of the bombers, assisted by escorting fighters, was to knock out the enemy air force and thereafter attack enemy strongpoints and troop concentrations. A potent new weapon in the Luftwaffe's armoury was the dive-bomber or Stuka–a term descriptive of all dive-bombers, but one especially associated with the Junkers 87 aeroplane. The Stukas were used as flying artillery, both against targets on the battlefield and against enemy rear areas. Aeroplanes for strategic and tactical reconnaissance were available to army commanders at all levels and airborne troops were used to attack especially important objectives.

Tactical air forces
The Western Allies were slow to follow Germany's lead in organising their army support air forces into commands made up of a mixture of modern fighter, bomber, close-

A GAL Hamilcar glider disgorges a light tank during unloading trials

Westland Lysander, found to its cost during the Battle of France (May to June 1940).

In Germany the story was different. Although she was forbidden an air arm under the terms of the Treaty of Versailles, a clandestine air force was maintained by the German army in the 1920s and early 1930s. When the Nazis began to build a strong air force in the later 1930s, it is hardly surprising that their Luftwaffe was primarily intended to support the army.

Before examining the Luftwaffe's contribution to the early German victories of World War II, an important development in army aviation which took place in the Soviet Union between the wars should be noted. This, the introduction of airborne troops, was heralded by the announcement that 'the parachute is no longer a lifebelt, but an offensive weapon of the future'. The first airborne units were formed in 1930 and by 1941 they numbered

support and reconnaissance units. The Desert Air Force, formed to provide the Eighth Army with air support, was the first truly effective unit of this type. However, by 1944 the Allies were fully committed to this system, the Normandy invasion force being accompanied by the RAF's 2nd Tactical Air Force and the USAAF's 9th Air Force, both of which were intended solely for the support of ground forces. Similarly, the 1st and 3rd Tactical Air Forces were providing support for troops fighting in Italy and Burma respectively. Soviet air units had always been primarily army support forces, but it was not until 1943 that they were able to make any appreciable impression on their German opponents. One of their most effective ground attack aeroplanes was the Ilyushin Il-2 Shturmovik, which was heavily protected by armour plate and was armed with cannon (a 23 mm or 37 mm weapon), bombs or rockets.

of No. 6 Squadron carry a 'flying can opener' emblem to commemorate the unit's anti-tank exploits. Germany also favoured the cannon as an airborne anti-tank weapon and two 37mm weapons were carried by the Junkers Ju 87G conversion of the famous dive-bomber. The Luftwaffe's virtuoso tank-buster, Hans-Ulrich Rudel, had knocked out a total of 519 enemy tanks by the close of the war. By June 1944, when the Allies landed in Normandy, their main anti-tank weapon was the rocket projectile. Hawker Typhoons of the 2nd Tactical Air Force, which each carried eight 60lb rocket projectiles, were considered the most effective answer to the latest German tanks.

The importance of air transport and supply of ground forces in World War II was most clearly shown during the Burma campaign. Air supply was by no means a new idea: it had been tried at the siege of Kut in 1915 and at the

The sturdy high-wing Beaver of 1946, designed for use in the Canadian north, proved ideal as an army co-operation aircraft. Three Beavers of 669 Squadron, Army Air Corps, (left) were among the last six of the type serving with the British Army of the Rhine in 1976

A de Havilland Canada DHC2 Beaver of the Army Air Corps with some of its equipment, including a stretcher and blankets

Airborne forces were used extensively and to good effect throughout World War II, although it was found that their intrinsic weakness was that they could not long survive against regular ground troops who had the heavy artillery and tanks that they lacked. German parachutists spearheaded the invasion of Norway in April 1940, seizing vital airfields into which Junkers Ju-52s flew reinforcing troops. Gliders made a dramatic debut during the invasion of the Low Countries in the following month, when they landed right on top of the seemingly impregnable Belgian fortress at Eben Emael and their troops quickly forced its surrender. Allied airborne units were used in the invasions of Sicily and Normandy and the successful crossing of the Rhine by the British 6th and US 17th Airborne Divisions in March 1945. Their record was marred by the tragedy of Arnhem, attributable to the failure of Allied ground forces to reach the airborne troops as quickly as planned.

'Tank-busters'

In view of the importance of armoured forces in World War II it is hardly surprising that aeroplanes soon added 'tank busting' to their ground support repertoire. The RAF's first anti-tank aeroplane was the Hawker Hurricane Mk IID, which carried two 40mm cannon. It first went into action with No. 6 Squadron in defence of Bir Hakim, in North Africa, in June 1942 and to this day the aeroplanes

siege of Stalingrad in the winter of 1942/1943 and neither operation had provided the besieged troops with sufficient supplies. However, on the Burma front, troops surrounded by the Japanese had been provided with sufficient supplies by air. In February 1944 the Japanese had cut off part of the 7th Indian Division at a position in the Arakan known as the 'Admin Box'. During the next month American and British transport aircraft dropped some 2,000 tons of supplies to the beleaguered garrison, which was able to hold out until relieved. The siege of Imphal was on an altogether larger scale and it proved to be the turning point of the war in the Burma Theatre. When the Japanese cut off the town in March 1944, they confidently expected that its garrison, whose daily requirements were estimated at 400 tons of supplies, would soon surrender. In the event, not only was the garrison adequately supplied by air, but it was also reinforced by an entire division which was flown in from the Arakan front and the Japanese besiegers were forced to retreat by lack of supplies.

In contrast to the years of stagnation between the two world wars, the post-war years have seen far-reaching changes in the sphere of army-air co-operation. They have seen the emergence of distinct army air arms, separate from air forces, although the latter continue to provide a large measure of the air support needed by ground forces. The soldiers' own air arms are usually predominantly helicopter-equipped and undertake battlefield reconnais-

Auster AOP 9 flies low round woodland in its spotting role

sance and liaison duties and operate specially-equipped anti-tank helicopters. Some army air arms, for instance that of the United States, provide helicopters for troop carrying and heavy lifting, whereas in Britain the RAF operates troop carrying helicopters (Britain has no heavy lift helicopters).

The nuclear age

Air support by conventional aeroplanes remains an air force responsibility. The aeroplanes involved may range from a twin-jet F-4 Phantom II armed with a tactical nuclear weapon to a piston-engined forward air control aircraft. (Forward air control is the technique whereby a slow, low-flying aeroplane identifies and marks targets for faster attack planes.) Recent important developments in air support include the introduction of the Hawker Siddeley Harrier V/STOL (Vertical/Short Take-off and Landing) fighter, which is able to operate from improvised airstrips just behind the fighting front, thus minimising the time taken to respond to a call for air support and greatly reducing the danger of the warplane being surprised and destroyed on the ground. Another important development is laser guidance, which enables weapons to be aimed with considerably greater accuracy than is possible with optical aiming. Perhaps the most interesting lesson of the Vietnam War was that sophisticated jet aeroplanes are not necessarily the best ground attack weapon. It was found that in South Vietnam, where there was, of course, no enemy air

opposition, elderly piston-engined types like the Douglas A-1 Skyraider and North American AT-28 were surprisingly effective. The comparatively slow Fairchild A-10 – maximum speed 806 km/h (449 mph) – has been developed for the USAF in the light of this experience.

The army helicopter is now used for a wide variety of combat, transport and liaison roles. The United States

Bell UH-1 helicopters of 82 Airborne come in to land at Fort Stewart, Georgia, USA in 1972

The US Army Air Force has 10,000 machines, 90% of them helicopters, the main types being the Bell UH-1, Bell AH-1, Hughes OH-6 and Bell OH-58. Britain's Army Air Corps has some 300 aircraft, its mainstays being the Westland Scout, Sioux and Gazelle helicopters. West Germany's 550 army helicopters include Alouette IIs and Bell UH-1s. The Soviet tactical air arm has 600 helicopters.

An SS-11 anti-tank missile is fired from a Westland Scout helicopter (left). The Scout is also used for casualty evacuation with an external stretcher fitted (below)

Harrier of No. 20 Sqn takes off during an exercise in North Rhine–Westphalia

Bell AH-1Q prototype TOW/Cobra anti-tank helicopter of the US Army. Eight missiles are carried, with four launching tubes beneath each stub wing

Army ranks as the world's largest user of helicopters, having some 9,000 machines on strength. Some 4,000 of these are stalwart Bell UH-1s, the standard American troop-carrying helicopter and mount of the Air Cavalry Divisions. About 3,600 helicopters are used for liaison and observation and a heavy lift capability—useful for transporting field guns and military engineering tasks—is provided by over 700 Boeing-Vertol CH-47 Chinooks and Sikorsky CH-54 Tarhes. Bell AH-1 gunship helicopters number nearly 1,000 and the latest versions carry TOW anti-tank missiles. The British Army Air Corps also has missile-equipped anti-tank helicopters—Westland Scout

AH Mk 1s, carrying Nord SS-11 missiles, which are to be replaced by Westland Lynx helicopters. Needless to say, the Soviet Union also has armed helicopters—Mil Mi-24s, code-named Hind by NATO—as well as troop-carrying and observation types.

Whatever the imponderables of warfare in the nuclear age, the large investment made by the major powers in the means to wage conventional war suggest that combat between ground forces is far from impossible in a future major war. It is certain that aeroplanes will play an important, and quite possibly a decisive, part in such a contest, as they have done in recent small-scale wars.

Counter-Insurgency

Since the end of World War II in 1945, the Western powers have been involved in five major military campaigns against guerrilla insurgencies. Three of them – Malaya, French Indo-China, and Vietnam – were Communist-inspired and took place in the dense jungles of South East Asia. The other two were nationalistic in character and occurred in rather more open country – the Mau-Mau rebellion in Kenya and the uprising in Algeria. In all of them air power was employed extensively in support of the ground forces, both in the search and strike role and as a means of improving communications and mobility in difficult terrain. In none of the counter-insurgency (COIN) campaigns, however, can air power be said to have exercised a decisive role since air forces, alone, cannot occupy and control ground.

The role of air power is restricted; firstly by political constraint and secondly by its necessary subordination to ground action. The inherent ability of air power to locate the guerrilla and engage him on the spot is only likely to be effective if it is backed up by ground action.

The first task is to hold the ground and deny the guerrilla sustenance and reinforcement – a job for the security forces. The second task – and a longer-term one – is to win back the allegiance and confidence of the local population by restoring peace; massive destruction from the air can have little place in this process. Furthermore, the defeat of the guerrillas themselves is best achieved not by massive sweeps and saturating the jungle with firepower, but by fighting them on their own ground with their own tactics of raid and ambush – small units against small units with the capability of rapid reinforcement if necessary. In this process air power frequently has as much to offer in the air-lift and supply roles as it has in that of fire-support. Furthermore, it has frequently been demonstrated that the smaller, less sophisticated aircraft is more effective in the COIN role than is the advanced combat type. Its slower speed and longer endurance make it a better observation and weapons platform; it is likely to be able to operate from forward airstrips.

It is important here, however, to stress that what we

A helicopter gunner pictured during a sortie over South Vietnam. The Vietnam War saw the extensive use of aircraft in the counter-insurgency role by the USAF

Above: Curtiss Helldivers are bombed-up on an airfield in French Indo-China for a sortie against the Viet Minh in April 1954.

Right: the North American Rockwell OV-10 was developed for forward air control duties in Vietnam

complete absence of modern navigation aids, made independent air operations very much hit-and-miss affairs. As the campaign against the insurgents developed, more and more aircraft types from all parts of the Commonwealth were employed against jungle targets—Brigands, Hornets, Vampires and Venoms, Lincoln heavy bombers from both the United Kingdom and Australia, Royal Australian Air Force supersonic F-86 Sabres 'booming' terrorists and RAF subsonic Sunderlands dropping fragmentation bombs on them. Altogether no fewer than 31 different types of aircraft in 36 versions eventually took part. A total of 375, 849 sorties was eventually flown throughout the emergency and thousands of tons of bombs were dropped into the jungle—on many occasions the crews had little or no idea of whether they had hit their target or whether indeed there was any target there at all.

The results of this massive expenditure of air force fire-power are difficult to assess, but there is no doubt that some insurgents were killed, some barracks were destroyed and some terrorist food crops were wiped out. The continuous harassment from the air also forced the terrorists to keep on the move and made it impossible

are concerned with is the guerrilla phase of what Marxists call the 'armed struggle'. This is the phase which was effectively dealt with by the British in Malaya and Kenya and by the French in Algeria. Given the right conditions—including 'safe' areas for training and adequate arms supplies—the guerrilla phase can escalate to the point at which the insurgents can embark upon a classic war of movement with the government forces. This occurred in French Indo-China and also in Vietnam—and all the time, guerrilla action continued behind the government lines. Air power has the inherent flexibility to operate in either situation, as was demonstrated in Vietnam.

The Malayan Emergency

The Malayan insurgency lasted from June 1948 to July 1960 and the seeds of the Communist guerrilla movement which inspired it were sown by the British themselves. During World War II they had landed 200 hand-picked Communists behind the Japanese lines in Malaya to set up the Malayan Peoples' Anti-Japanese Army. At the end of the war there were some 7,000 well-armed Marxist guerrillas in jungle hide-outs up and down the country. At first the Communists endeavoured to gain power from the newly-imposed British administration by their customary methods of strikes, subversion and selective terrorism. When these proved ineffective, the Communists went back to the jungle and re-activated the Peoples' Army. It concentrated its activities among the rural Chinese, a particularly deprived section of the community numbering about a million who lived for the most part as squatters along the jungle edge. Under the leadership of Chin Peng the guerrillas set up camps in the jungle with barracks, parade grounds and class-rooms. They usually operated in groups of 100 but in the early stages concentrated as many as 300 men at a time. For the most part their targets were rubber plantations and civil and military installations, coupled with the usual atrocities against civilians who were allegedly pro-British. The Royal Air Force began operations in support of the security forces in July 1948 with Spitfire FR 18s, Dakotas and Beaufighters. Although on occasions aerial photographs revealed the location of guerrilla camps in the jungle so that they could be bombed or strafed, the conditions of dense jungle, rugged hilly terrain and frequent low cloud, coupled with an almost

for them to establish the settled 'base areas' so necessary in the development of an effective guerrilla campaign. Insurgent morale was also affected by air action and to that extent the task of the ground forces and the politicians was made easier.

The successful conclusion of the Malayan Emergency was largely brought about by political means—notably the granting of self-government and the holding of free elections—but many lessons had been learned on the military front. The army abandoned large-scale jungle 'sweeps' in favour of small patrols—'ferret' forces—which took on the guerrillas at their own game of ambush and raid, effectively doubling their kill rate. The need for the closest co-operation between the ground and the air forces was clearly recognised. This was not only essential in the provision of air-dropped supplies and casualty evacuation but also in the forward air control of reconnaissance and strike. Experience demonstrated the value for these purposes of small aircraft like the Pioneer and the Auster, which could operate from small strips hacked out of the jungle and for aircraft that could 'loiter' in the target area while calling up ground or air support. Helicopters, too, first showed their value in Malaya not only as troop-carriers for *coup-de-main* raids but as an elementary form of gunship.

Mau-Mau and Viet Minh

Small aircraft also came into their own in the Mau-Mau emergency in Kenya, which began in October 1952 and lasted until June 1956. It was totally different in nature from the Malayan uprising, with none of the sophistication of weapons and technique of Chin Peng's well-trained Marxist followers. Members of Mau-Mau, a secret society of the Kikuyu tribe, became obsessed with the belief that their tribe should possess more of the Kenyan farm land. They set up forest hide-outs and started a reign of terror against European farmers, the government and those of their own people who opposed them. The army was reinforced and began counter-operations but lacked any form of air support. In Rhodesia, however, the RAF had a number of flying training schools using Harvards and flights of these aircraft, flown by instructors, were detached to Kenya. Armed with machine guns and 20lb fragmentation bombs, they played a major role over the next four years in helping the Army and the Kenya police hunt down and round up the terrorists. From time to time they were backed up by more orthodox combat aircraft detached from the United Kingdom, especially Lincolns. By September 1955 the security forces had accounted for 14,000 terrorists and early in 1956 the troubles were at an end.

The British successes in Malaya and Kenya, time-consuming and expensive though they had been, were in a large part due to the fact that the insurgents had been dealt with in the early, guerrilla phase of their uprising. They had not been able to establish sanctuaries or 'no-go' jungle base areas and achieve control of what the Marxists call 'popular' bases—villages supplying recruits and food. The French, when they attempted to re-assert their control over Indo-China in 1945, were not so fortunate. The Communist Viet Minh were solidly entrenched in Tongking province in northern Indo-China and strong enough to launch major attacks against French garrisons. These attacks were repulsed and driven back into the jungle, but the French lacked the strength both on ground and in the air to prevent the Viet Minh from building up 'liberated' areas and transforming their guerrilla formations into units of a mobile regular army. The French consistently attempted to bring these units to a decisive conventional battle by airborne operations behind Viet Minh lines similar to those of the British Chindits in Burma in 1944. They had some success but eventually, in November 1953, they over-reached themselves when they reinforced the beleaguered garrison at Dien Bien Phu. The vital airfield there was surrounded by a ring of hills packed with Viet Minh artillery and anti-aircraft guns and the French were short of transport aircraft. After a gallant but hopeless battle the garrison surrendered in May 1954. The Geneva Agreement which followed ended French hopes of remaining in Indo-China and effectively divided the country into four. Throughout the long struggle the French Air Force had done its best with inadequate equipment. It was forced to rely mainly upon Allied war-surplus types like Spitfire Mk 9s, Mosquito Mk 6s and, F6F Hellcats and F8F Bearcats with a sprinkling of captured aircraft—such as Nakajima Oscars. Many thousands of bombs, bullets and napalm tanks were hurled into the jungle—as they had been in Malaya—but with little effect. The war had, perhaps, been lost politically from the outset and from then on inept generalship and inadequate armament merely accelerated the relentless process of defeat.

But the French learned from that defeat. When guerrilla warfare broke out in Algeria in 1954, the military counter-measures they adopted were much more effective. The Algerian ALN (Army of National Liberation) never achieved a position in which it could meet the French in open battle and its operations were of the small unit raid-and-ambush type. The French eventually built the so-called Morice Line to isolate the ALN from its sanctuary in Tunisia and they employed small-scale units, notably the *commandos de chasse*, who went into the mountains and beat the guerrillas at their own game. Once again there was massive support from the air. In 1958, for example, there were 746 aircraft and 97 helicopters on the strength of the Armée de l'Air operating in North

Top: the Boeing-Vertol CH-47 Chinook was used in large numbers during the Vietnam War.
Above: a USAF Fairchild C-123 Provider sprays herbicides over a swath of Vietnamese forest

Africa. But the French had learned a lesson about air support of counter-insurgency operations too. Among their aircraft no fewer than 295 were T-6 Harvards and these were later reinforced by 135 North American T-28 Trojans converted to COIN duties. Extensive use was also made of helicopters, especially the Sikorsky S-58 (H-34) and the French were the pioneers of their use in the armed and 'air-cavalry' roles.

By 1960 the French had virtually won the military struggle in Algeria. It had, however, taken some 800,000 troops to do it and the war was costing the French taxpayer about £250 million a year, dividing the country internally. In 1962 de Gaulle decided to cut that particular Gordian knot and made Algeria independent.

The Vietnam War

The conclusion of the Geneva Agreements in 1954 did not put a stop to Communist attempts to control the whole of the Indo-China area – now divided into four countries, North and South Vietnam, Laos and Cambodia. What they now had was a sanctuary in which to train guerrilla units and a secure base from which to supply them. By 1960 they were carrying out guerrilla operations in Laos, Cambodia and South Vietnam. Of these operations, the most important were those in South Vietnam. Laos was important because the crucial 'Ho Chi Minh Trail' carrying supplies and reinforcements from North to South Vietnam and by-passing the well-guarded DMZ (de-militarised zone) border, ran along its eastern boundary. Similarly, Cambodia was important for the 'Sihanouk Trail' which ran from the port of Sihanoukville into the Mekong delta.

US involvement began first with the supply of obsolete combat aircraft to the three non-communist governments for COIN operations; it was increased when US Army and US Air Force 'advisers' were appointed and escalated rapidly after retaliatory bombing attacks on North Viet-

namese naval bases in August 1964. In their COIN operations against the Viet Cong in South Vietnam and their supply routes in Laos and Cambodia, the Americans from the outset endeavoured to use air power as a substitute for troops on the ground. The Viet Cong, however, unlike the dissident tribesmen of inter-war years, were not to be dissuaded from their purpose by even a torrent of well-aimed bullets, bombs and missiles and even less by a Niagara of random 'saturation fire support'. The jungle was the Viet Cong's greatest ally and they made full use of it. Kalashnikov AK-47 rifles fired from tree tops brought down American fighter-bombers and mortars hidden in the forest wrought havoc on crowded airfields.

The American solution was not to fight the Viet Cong on their own ground – their troops lacked training and experience – but to use technological methods of defeating the jungle itself. At first there was widespread use of herbicides to defoliate the forest and reveal ambushes and supply routes. Air-delivered herbicides, quite apart from

Above: the Bell UH-1 was the US Army's standard troop-carrying helicopter in Vietnam.
Right: USAF HH-53 helicopters were armed with three 7·62mm Miniguns for suppression of ground fire.
Below: a C-123 of the 19th Air Commando Squadron used for air transport and supply missions

the international furore their use created, defoliated crops as well as jungle and the rural economy of the area was threatened. Later in the war a multitude of ingenious sensors appeared. Sown broadcast over the jungle supply routes, these sensors responded to sound, pressure, magnetism, earth-shock and chemical stimuli and were designed to operate independently over long periods to locate the movements of men and vehicles through the jungle and transmit their information to searching aircraft or ground forces.

There were also a host of other innovations in the Vietnam conflict, which tended to serve as a weapons proving-ground, as most small wars do. The Americans perfected the helicopter gunship–the Bell AH-1 Huey Cobra with its 20mm gun turret, its TOW anti-tank missiles and its armour plate is a prime example–and developed the use of helicopter-borne 'air cavalry' on the French Algerian model. They also found out the hard way the extreme vulnerability of helicopters to ground fire and lost more than 3,000. The US also produced a number of fixed-wing aircraft specifically designed for the COIN role. Outstanding among them was the Marines' turboprop North American Rockwell OV-10A Bronco, with 1,630kg (3,600lb) of ordnance, four 7·62mm machine-guns and Sidewinder missiles; it had an endurance of $4\frac{1}{2}$ hours and ability to take off and land in 640 metres (700 yards).

Once again, however, military endeavour was defeated not on the battlefield but in the political arena. In March 1965 the United States began a strategic bombing campaign against North Vietnam intended to force the North Vietnamese to negotiate and this continued, with some politically motivated 'pauses' until the cease-fire in 1973. While it had a considerable influence on the counter-insurgency struggle in South Vietnam itself, and achieved its primary military objective, its political ramifications throughout the world and especially within the United States itself were eventually self-defeating. As Mao himself put it: 'War cannot for a single moment be separated from politics. Politics are bloodless war, war is the politics of bloodshed.'

Electronic Countermeasures

Whereas World War I was the first conflict in which mechanisation was important, World War II was the first to make use of what is commonly termed advanced technology. Far and away the most important of the new technologies was electronics and by 1945 this had come to dominate all warfare between developed countries. Electronics had come to rule almost all communications over distances greater than a few hundred metres, most of the navigation and guidance (especially in bad weather) and the most important methods of detecting enemies. However, to every new development in war there soon arise countermeasures, and ECM (Electronic Countermeasures) was a familiar term as early as 1943.

In the earliest days of radio detection and ranging–the initial letters of the word radar–little attention was paid to ways of countering its use. Britain, Germany and the United States all thought they were far ahead of other nations in such research and this coloured their thinking. Before 1939 research workers in all three countries had considered both active and passive ECM, but regarded such ideas merely in terms of ways of defeating their own countries' efforts. They did not realise they would soon be urgently needed.

Active ECM covers all forms of countermeasures that send out radio emissions (usually on the same wavelengths as enemy radars). Passive ECM sends out no signals at all, but serves as a screen. Other countermeasures clearly illustrate this distinction. With visible light, for example, an active countermeasure would be a false enemy in the wrong location such as a decoy model aircraft on a dummy airfield, while a passive one would be a smoke-screen. With IR (infra-red, or heat) an active countermeasure would be a flare giving a heat output resembling a fighter jet engine or other important source; flare payloads are an important part of the defensive kit of every warplane that attempts to penetrate hostile airspace. A passive countermeasure might be an exhaust shroud to conceal an aircraft's heat emission.

Foiling radar

By far the most important passive electronic counter-measures are small strips of electrically-conductive material, which, when allowed to float down through the atmosphere, behave as miniature dipole aerials and thus give reflections on a radar screen similar to aircraft or ships. Each strip should ideally be cut to the same length as the wavelength of the radar, or to a simple fraction or multiple of it, to have the greatest effect. Usually, the strip should be as light as possible, so that it will sink very slowly through the air and thus be in view of the enemy radar for the maximum time. At first researchers tried aluminium foil, aluminium wire and, most often, foil backed with lightweight paper. In the 1950s, when ECM research was consuming funds more quickly than during World War II, the best answer was found to be fine threads or 'rovings' of glass-fibre on which a metal film only a molecule or two thick has been deposited. As in the mirror of an astronomical telescope, the glass provides

the structural base and the thin film of metal provides the reflective property.

In Britain, Germany and the United States the basic mathematics of this passive ECM had been worked out before World War II, but it was 1941 before large-scale tests began. The British called the concept and the material Window–though it behaved more like a window with the blinds drawn–while the Germans called it Düppel after a country estate near Berlin where the first tests were made. From the start it was obvious that the idea worked. Foil strips were put into production by the ton, and soon scores of billions were stored in neat piles of boxes in warehouses and hangers–but nobody dared to use them, and their existence was kept a closely guarded secret. By 1942 the United States, having been told of the idea the previous year, added its own quota, calling it Chaff because it was to be scattered to the four winds. Today the American name is most commonly used to denote the most important single type of ECM.

Window's delayed introduction

But for how long can participants, locked in total war, fail to use something for fear of retaliation? In 1942–1943 the situation over Europe was most unequal. The RAF,

increasingly backed up by the US Army Air Force (Eighth Bomber Command), were mounting ever greater and more costly attacks on Germany and occupied Europe. The Luftwaffe, however, hardly ever dared visit Britain, had virtually no heavy strategic bombers and, in any case, had few forces to spare for offensive bombing apart from hit and run fighter-bombers to which radar and thus ECM was seldom relevant. Night after night enemy fire claimed the lives of RAF crews, while some who were party to the secret said Window could save many lives. In May 1943 the Japanese, who had done the obvious and used the idea as soon as they heard of it, filled the sky over

An Avro Canada Canuck of the Electronic Warfare Unit flies over a radar station. The aircraft is used for training and practice jamming missions against Canada's air defences

A T Mk 17 Canberra used for electronic counter-measures training with No 360 Squadron. The unit is manned by both RAF and Royal Navy personnel

the Solomon Islands with Giman-Shi (deceiving paper) strewn from both Army and Navy bombers, causing complete failure of the American radar-predicted flak and cutting Japanese losses by roughly three-quarters– but the news apparently never reached Air Marshal 'Bert' Harris, AOC RAF Bomber Command. Most informed opinion today does not blame Harris, who took his orders from the British War Cabinet, for holding back so long on Window in the face of mounting pressure. At least the dramatic new weapon was not disclosed half-heartedly, but used to crippling effect in the most damag-ing raids ever seen up to that time.

The Hamburg raid

The date was 24 July 1943. That afternoon over 800 RAF and Commonwealth bomber crews were at last told about Window, and that night the 746 heavies that bombed Hamburg released some 92,000,000 Window strips. The result was that the German defences were thrown into chaos. Though the Luftwaffe reacted speedily, with the first ECCM (electronic counter-countermeasures) of which the simplest was to ignore radar and search with unaided eyesight, the city of Hamburg was devastated in a series of attacks with relatively little loss to the RAF. From that date, ECM has been central to all air warfare.

Today there are many kinds of chaff and many dispensing systems. The simplest techniques are to feed it out through a chute or blow it out inside a cartridge which then bursts. Most chaff is carried by the attacking aircraft, but some is dispensed by special EW (electronic warfare) aircraft which either fly with the attacking force or seed the path the attackers will follow. Some chaff is dispensed in a steady stream, forming a kind of smokescreen which envelops subsequent aircraft and hides them from the enemy. Most modern radars can detect the moving aircraft against the almost stationary chaff, so a more common technique is to release it in a succession of bursts, each of which has an RCS (radar cross-section) resembling that of an attacking aircraft.

In one method tactical aircraft such as the A-7 Corsair,

Jaguar, Harrier or Su-19, carry dispensers either on or beside a pylon or built into the fuselage. Each discharges flare or chaff payloads in timed and controlled sequences, shooting each load out by a pyrotechnic squib like a large shotgun breech. The RBC (rapid-bloom chaff) bursts almost instantly. Within two seconds each burst has bloomed to give an RCS so attractive that enemy radars, previously tracking the aircraft, 'break lock' and instead look at the chaff cloud. Modern radar is clever enough to notice its error and switch back to the speeding aircraft, but a second chaff cloud then appears. This repeated breaking of the radar lock can make it impossible to launch a missile at the attacking aircraft. Of course, flare payloads can do the same to confuse infra-red-homing defence weapons.

Above and inset: the Grumman EA-6B Prowler carries its jamming equipment, consisting of high-power transmitters and tracking device, in pods – two under each wing and one beneath the fuselage

Other important ECM dispenser and payload suppliers are Tracor and Goodyear.

A few dispensed payloads are active jammers and in 1977 these were becoming important in attack squadrons. All the earliest active ECM took the form of large radio transmitters which simply blotted out hostile radar screens in the same way that radio jammers can blot out broadcasts or military communications. The technique does, in fact, include disruption of enemy communications, especially where fighters are directed by a ground controller. As early as 1941 the RAF had experimented with Tinsel, a plain noise broadcast using a bomber's ordinary radio transmitter connected to a microphone in an engine nacelle, and Mandrel, a much more powerful transmitter carried in special aircraft such as Defiants or Wellingtons. By 1943 noise jamming was being supplemented by false directions being broadcast to enemy fighters. Often, heavy bombers flying with the attacking force were equipped solely as flying radio stations to cause chaos by active ECM. A few companies have even packaged active ECM into miniature aircraft launched as decoys. The best-known example is the McDonnell Quail once carried by B-52 bombers.

Biggest active-ECM companies, again all American, are General Electric, AIL and Westinghouse, the leader in pod systems. Powerful emitters need much more electric power to drive them than ordinary aircraft can supply. One solution is to fit an external active-ECM pod drawing current from a self-contained electrical system with an alternator driven by a ram-air turbine or windmill. Four such pods are carried under the wings of the EA-6B Prowler, each housing two high-power transmitters, a tracking receiver and the associated aerial system. The Soviet Union, on the other hand, has sometimes used much larger aircraft as ECM platforms and fitted them not only with several tonnes of electronics, but also with the very large electric power supplies necessary. Most of these Soviet ECM machines are converted bombers, but one is based on the Antonov An-12 transport. Inside the extremely capacious fuselage of this aircraft are installed more that 200 separate items of receiving and transmitting electronics, computers and operator consoles, together with large power-generation systems. The main aerial systems are recessed into large fairings on the underside.

Today only a few attack aircraft carry active ECM, except low-power jammers packaged as expendable payloads shot out along with flare and chaff payloads. Generally, active jammers are used sparingly and are fired only when absolutely necessary. But special EW aircraft, such as the EA-6B Prowler, EF-4E Phantom and EF-111A, carry not only dispensed jammer payloads, but also large inbuilt installations or externally carried pods. Smaller pods are carried by attack aircraft, either on the weapon pylons (which reduces the ordnance load), or mounted flush against the fuselage or recessed into a missile channel. Basically, active ECM can be divided into noise or barrage jammers, which just blot out a particular set of wavelengths and the much costlier deception jammers, which try to make the enemy believe there are many attacking aircraft where in fact there are none. In all cases, the ECM system must first detect, locate and measure the hostile signal source and computers are needed to use the on-board electrical power only against the most dangerous threats instead of wasting it on other emitters. Perhaps a million calculations per second must be made in heavily-defended airspace, to make sure that every piece of active ECM – on a split-second basis – is exactly tailored to the immediate task.

Misleading orders
Larger bombers, or special EW aircraft, can do slightly better than merely dispense factory-made cartridges. They can carry sensors which continuously monitor all hostile transmissions, measure the exact signal characteristics of the defending radars and then make chaff the right length to defeat them. The chaff is carried in the form of thousands of kilometres of continuous roving, fed out from drums along parallel tracks. High-speed rotary cutters chop off the chaff in the required lengths, which are blown out in clouds by ram air through a divergent nozzle. Typical of these tailor-made chaff cutter/dispenser systems are those supplied by Lundy Electronics for various models of B-52 bomber, and the recently developed ALE-43 pod which can be carried on an external pylon.

Badges of some of the US Navy's tactical electronics squadrons which fly the Grumman EA-6B Prowler. The designs of the badges reflect the units' roles, which are to support strike aircraft and defend the Navy at sea by jamming enemy defence systems

Fighter Tactics

Left: the McDonnell Douglas Phantom II has been proven in fighter combat with the USAF in Vietnam and with the Israeli air force. Although modern jet fighters are highly complex supersonic weapons systems, and guided missiles have replaced guns as their main weapons, fighter tactics remain essentially similar to those of World War II. The Phantom II can carry four Sparrow and four smaller Sidewinder missiles. An RAF GR Mark 1 is illustrated. Below right: the German observer's view of the British Sopwith Camel is obscured by the tail of his own aeroplane, a Hannover two-seat fighter

In April 1915 Lieutenant Roland Garros, flying a Morane-Saulnier Type L parasol monoplane, shot down a two-seat Albatros, thereby opening the era of the true fighter aeroplane. On 1 August Leutnant Max Immelmann forced down Lieutenant William Reid RFC behind the German lines – the first of many Allied pilots to fall to the guns of the Fokker monoplane fighters. Immelmann was awarded the Iron Cross First Class for this victory. The Morane and Fokker had in common a significantly new feature: their gun armament fired along the axis of flight enabling the pilot to aim his aircraft and thus his gun at his opponent in combat.

The Fokker myth

Before this, air fighting had been conducted with all manner of hand-held ordnance – and other objects – discharged in the general direction of the foe. The French, German, Russian and British aircraft engineers all set to work to overcome the problem of effectively mounting guns on aircraft. An early solution, that of Raymond Saulnier, employed deflector plates on the tractor propeller blades to withstand strikes by rounds from a gun firing forward which happened to coincide with the passage of the blades. Garros succeeded in shooting down five German aircraft before he was forced down on 19 April 1915 and his deflector gear was examined by the Germans. The Fokker monoplane however used a true gun-interrupter gear which mechanically prevented the gun from firing a round at the moment the propeller blade passed the muzzle. Probably designed by the German engineers Heber, Leimberger and Luebbe, this invention owed much to a pre-war patent filed by Franz Schneider.

The first airman to advocate the use of whole squadrons of aircraft specialising in air combat was the German, Hauptmann Oswald Boelcke, then and ever since

revered as the father of air fighting. This advocacy coincided with the introduction of the Fokker monoplane. The mount of such pilots as Boelcke, Immelmann, von Althaus, Buddecke and Parschau, the Fokker created a legend within a few months of its introduction in the latter half of 1915. The pilots, usually flying alone were able to pick off Allied reconnaissance aircraft which were usually unarmed. Their tactics were simple. Given a slender speed margin the German needed only to dive on the victim from above and behind, aim their aircraft and fire a short burst. In the absence of any comparable Allied aircraft it was hardly surprising that the myth of Fokker invincibility was born.

The initial British formula, typified by the DH 2 consisted of placing the pilot, armed with a flexibly-mounted machine gun, in the front of a short fuselage nacelle with a 'pusher' engine behind, the tail being mounted on booms. The pilot had an excellent field of vision and fire, but the array of drag inducing struts and tail booms somewhat reduced the speed and thus the effectiveness of an excellent expedient. No 24 Squadron, commanded by Captain (later Major) Lanoe Hawker VC DSO, was the first to receive the DH 2, beginning on 10 January 1916. From April to May that year the Squadron destroyed or captured forty-four enemy aircraft. The arrival of the DH 2 went far towards laying the Fokker Eindekker spectre. No one did more to champion the DH 2 than Major Hawker himself who shot down nine aircraft before being killed on 23 November 1916 after a prolonged dogfight with a rising star in the German air force, Rittmeister Manfred, Freiherr von Richthofen.

In England several engineers had been striving to perfect gun interruptor gears, among them Harry Kauper at Sopwiths, Warrant Officer F. W. Scarff at the Admiralty, an immigrant Pole, Lt Cdr V. V. Dibovski, and Gogu

Constaninesco, a Romanian rock drill engineer. The Kauper and Challenger designs were among the earliest British gun interruptor gears but, like the earlier Fokker type, were unwieldy and in spring 1917 the more efficient and reliable Constaninesco hydraulically-operated synchronising gear was introduced.

The dogfight

By 1917, therefore, the problem of forward-firing guns had been overcome and the definitive pattern of fighting aeroplanes was established with pilot-operated guns firing forward along the line of flight. Also firmly established was the fighter squadron, given the duties of seeking and destroying enemy aircraft, and escorting the slower bombing and reconnaissance aeroplanes.

From solo combats involving individual pilots the 'dogfight' had developed, involving groups of aircraft. After the successes achieved by pilots on both sides towards the end of 1916, the number of aircraft in the groups escalated, especially in the big air battles of bloody April 1917. Eventually the Germans employed circuses of up to fifty fighters which roamed the front line area, only

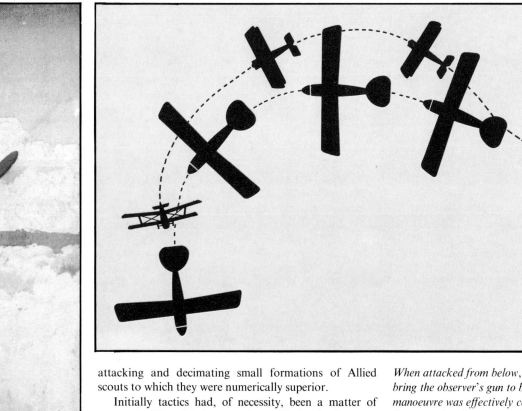

Above: a Sopwith Dolphin attacking a Fokker D VII (left). The fighter with the advantage of superior height could usually dictate the terms of the ensuing combat.
Left: a Bristol F2B's gunner engages an Albatros scout, whilst a Fokker Dr I swoops unnoticed from the eye of the sun

attacking and decimating small formations of Allied scouts to which they were numerically superior.

Initially tactics had, of necessity, been a matter of personal skill and judgement, but with the development of the dogfight and formation fighting the elements and cardinal rules of air fighting became recognised. An advantage of height had given an advantage of speed, and an attack 'out of the sun' achieved the maximum degree of surprise. Thus at first speed was regarded as vital for both attack and escape, but soon heavier armament was required and was widely increased from one to two or more guns. Moreover, as the dogfight and squadron battles developed, manoeuvrability as well as speed was recognised as being of prime importance in air fighting. Thus on the British side the highly manoeuvrable single gun Sopwith Pup was superseded by the more potent, powerful and faster two gun Sopwith Camel. Aircraft, operated in groups controlled by a leader, were becoming capable of a wider variety of offensive and defensive tactics, and the key was a combination of manoeuvrability and adequate engine power.

The manoeuvrability of the interceptor fighter was displayed by its ability to perform sequences of aerobatics while providing a means of perfecting a pilot's coordination of reflexes, senses and feeling for his mount, such manoeuvres as barrel and slow rolls, hammer stalls and wing-overs were of little value in themselves in combat, which originally involved only simple turning and relatively gentle diving and climbing. However during World War I attributes like steadiness and stability of flight improved with increased understanding of aerodynamics and the characteristics of aerofoils, but with the improvement in aircraft stressing and performance, the manoeuvrability of a fighter became an expression in terms of turning radius, the possible tightness of a turn without buffeting and stalling. Gradually the best pilots learned to fly their aircraft by sensing the limits of performance and strength.

The early pilots probably learned the flick roll before the slow roll which was almost impossible to achieve with the limited power of the engines. Once the spin and recovery were mastered, the experts tended to use it to escape from a dangerous situation, knowing that the

When attacked from below, a two-seater usually turned to bring the observer's gun to bear on the attacker. This manoeuvre was effectively countered if the attacking scout first turned in the opposite direction to his quarry. The former then used his superior speed and agility to regain an attacking position in the two-seater's blind spot

combination of pitching, yawing and rolling in a spin rendered the aircraft virtually impossible to hit or follow.

From 1917 the dogfight developed from a succession of tail chases, involving little more than aiming at a stable target ahead, and, gradually the fighter pilot developed rudimentary deflection aiming. The simple tube or ring-and-bead gun-sights in use, involved no more than an instinctive mental solution of a triangle of velocities: the greater the angle between the flight paths of attacker and attacked, the greater the aim-off angle required to hit. The legendary French pilot and highest-scoring Allied airman of World War I, Capitaine René Fonck, developed this instinctive marksmanship from his unmatched prowess with sporting guns. His skill in air fighting was such that he frequently fired no more than five or six rounds to down an enemy aircraft, placed, in his own words *comme avec la main*. Fonck was unequalled by any pilot of the war and was able to destroy as many as six enemy aircraft in a single day.

Fighting Area tactics
By 1918 the air forces of Britain, France and Germany had established a design formula for fighter aircraft that survived two decades. The German air force was to all intents abolished and demobilised, but the RAF, although much reduced in strength, continued to exist as an independent British service. Fighter equipment in the RAF consisted of a small number of squadrons equipped with the Sopwith Snipe, followed in turn by the Gloster Grebe and Gamecock, and the Bristol Bulldog. All were armed with two Vickers machine guns, synchronised to fire through the propeller disc and powered by bulky radial engines incapable of producing top speeds of over 270km/h (170mph).

Apart from a multitude of duties overseas, the fighter squadrons of the RAF were charged with the defence of

Britain against any overseas bombing force. By implication of range the only such foreign power was France and the fighter squadrons were accordingly deployed on airfields facing the Channel. However, without any means of providing warning of the approach of a bomber force, interception could only be achieved over land. This was termed the 'Fighting Area' – a strip of land 80 km (50 miles) wide in Southern England, stretching from Dorset in the west to Kent in the east.

On this assumption the operation of RAF fighters were, from 1926, based upon tactics considered appropriate for squadrons based on airfields on the inner edge of the fighting area. In every case it was assumed that whole squadrons would be ordered off against incoming raids, would have time to climb in formation and would be most effectively handled in a series of established formation attacks on the approaching bombers. These attacks took the form of set variations of line abreast, line astern, beam, tail or head-on attacks by the squadron, signalled physically by the squadron leader's hand, referred to as Fighting Area Attacks, No 1, 2, 3 and so on. Reminiscent of a parade ground drill movement, it was not unknown for a squadron commander to train his pilots in these manoeuvres on bicycles ridden round the drill square at

Bristol F2B Fighters served with the British over the Western Front in 1917–18. The pilot of this classic two-seat fighter attacked with his fixed forward-firing gun, while the observer protected the tail with his hand-held machine gun

Hawkinge! Such tactics took no account of different tactical situations, such as escorting fighters, bombers which fired back or the time required to regain squadron formation before a new attack was launched.

The progress being made in bomber design brought about major rethinking of fighter design early in the 1930s. As bomber speeds increased, the time during which the fighter's guns could fire an effective burst decreased. Moreover, the standard synchronised gun used by the RAF was still the unreliable Vickers of World War I – so unreliable that the gun bodies had to lie within reach of the pilot to allow him to clear stoppages. Negotiations to build the reliable Colt machine guns under licence went forward in the mid-1930s coinciding with the concept of the eight-gun fighter, intended to replace the Bristol Bulldogs and interim four-gun Gloster Gladiator. The result was the Spitfire and Hurricane.

With the re-emergence as a first-rate military power of Germany in the mid-1930s the organisation of the RAF underwent radical change. In 1936 the fighter defence, bomber and coastal forces were re-organised on a Command basis. Fighter Command came into existence, divided into areas designated for subordinate Group responsibility. This new concept was facilitated by the

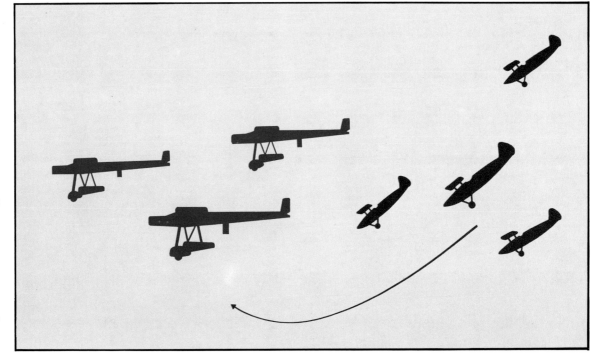

Right: British fighter tactics in the inter-war years were codified into the inflexible and cumbrous 'Fighter Area Attacks'. Below right: the Germans, with combat experience in Spain to guide them, evolved the flexible 'schwarm' formation, which proved well-suited to the combat conditions of World War II

creation of a radio-location chain – later termed radar – which promised to enable interception of enemy bombers while over the sea. It might be thought that this was the logical time to scrap the old, unwieldy Fighting Area tactics, but they were perpetuated. Two conflicting and deep-rooted tactical concepts provoked this anomaly and came to a head during the Battle of Britain. Trafford Leigh-Mallory, commanding the northern No 12 Group in the battle, had been steeped in the traditional concept of assembling set groups of fighter squadrons which, because of the time involved, were only able to intercept once the enemy had crossed the coast. It is interesting to note that the early flying career of one advocate of this Wing philosophy, Douglas Bader, had been between 1929 and 1933 – the heyday of the Fighting Area.

The finger four

Several other circumstances aided in perpetuating the Fighting Area tactics, among them the expansion of the RAF, the strain on the flying training schools and the operational squadrons themselves. In a relatively young Service, with hard-won traditions, only the reality of battle would decide what the new tactics would be. Germany, on the other hand, with an effective vacuum created by the abolition of her military air force after World War I, possessed no such preconceived ideas in the mid-1930s. True, her first generation of interceptors, the Arado Ar 68 and the Heinkel He 51, had followed the same formula as the contemporary Gloster Gauntlet, but the appearance of the monoplane Bf 109 brought about a rapid reappraisal based on a realisation of the virtues of the new operation of interceptors. Moreover, the air fighting philosophies of Germany were totally different from those of Britain; air defence of the Reich was hardly envisaged. The Luftwaffe was conceived as a support force for the Wehrmacht. Defence of the skies over a battlefield was of paramount importance, conforming to the radical concepts of *blitzkrieg*. In the skies over Spain the Luftwaffe was able to evolve tactics realistic to the modern fighter and fast-moving warfare; unfettered by traditions inherited from a cavalry-staffed air force.

The nature of the air fighting in the Spansh Civil War, involving relatively small numbers of aircraft in any one

area of the front, emphasised the abilities of the individual pilots who tended to fly and fight in very small formations. The lineal establishment of the Condor Legion emphasised the importance of the *staffel* as the largest tactical group of aircraft consisting of eight aircraft divided into two sections of four aircraft, the *schwarm*, consisting of two leading pilots with their wingmen, the *rotte*. The *staffel* would normally fly as two distinct sections, breaking into pairs on being engaged. The cardinal rule, observed then and ever since, was that the leader's tail was protected by his number two, and the success of the pair was largely dependent on the number two's ability to stick rigidly to his leader. It was men like Werner Mölders and Boelcke before him who were regarded as the fathers of these tactics and were responsible for their adoption by the *jagdflieger* in World War II. These tactics are the foundation upon which all subsequent air fighting has fundamentally been based.

On the other hand, the RAF Hurricane pilots in the Battle of France clung to the formation tactics and suffered for the lack of flexibility caused by attempting to hold formation position under combat conditions. The survivors adopted the tactics of the German fighter pilots

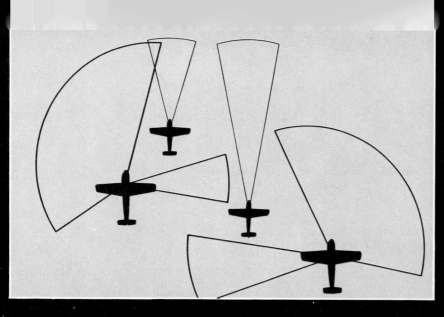

mand introduced a tactical formation known as the 'finger four'. For non-combat flying this was referred to as 'battle formation' but in combat broke into two close-flying pairs. The finger four combined a maximum of flexibility with a maximum of mutual protection.

The missile age

The quickening tempo of air fighting in the early 1930s fostered the eight-gun fighter, and increasing speeds in World War II brought about heavier armament. The RAF remained ahead of the Luftwaffe in fighter armament for many months with the standardisation of two Hispano 20 mm gun armament in many of its fighters. When the Germans introduced four 30 mm cannon, the RAF riposted by the introduction of four 20 mm batteries in RAF fighters. Ten years after the war, the Hawker Hunter jet fighter – intended as an interceptor, but soon relegated to ground attack – featured four 30 mm guns, although developments were rapidly overtaking guns as primary armament, and thus outmoding the pure dog-fighter type.

However, because of the increased speeds of combat greater hitting power is demanded to compensate for the shorter spaces of firing time available. Inevitably, radar-ranging gun-sights and rapid fire weapons such as the American Gatling gun had to be introduced, but the guided missile has increasingly dominated air fighting tactics from after the Korean War. The missile, which is largely independent of accurate aiming by the pilot is usually infra-red seeking, being guided by sensors to the heat cone immediately behind the target's turbojets. Notwithstanding these developments, the tactical funda-mentals established by Boelcke, Immelmann, Hawker, von Richthofen, Mölders and others remain unassailable foundations for future aerial combat.

Above: essentially an RAF adaptation of German tactics, the 'finger four' formation was not generally adopted by Fighter Command until 1941.
Below: the Convair F-102 of the USAF's Aerospace Defence Command relies on its powerful radar and missile armament for successful interception

and, on returning home, tried desperately to convince their colleagues that the Fighting Area attacks were likely to prove suicidal. By the time the Battle of Britain began, most Hurricane squadrons were operating tactical units based on the three-aircraft section, the vic, although newcomers among the Spitfire squadrons persisted in larger formations. However, squadrons such as No 152 were beginning to experiment with paired fighting and by degrees tactics were formalised when battle-experienced pilots were posted to operational training units as in-structors in 1941.

Thereafter the leader and his wingman came to be regarded, not only in the RAF and Luftwaffe, but through-out every air force in the world, as the basic air fighting element. Indeed, like the Luftwaffe, RAF Fighter Com-

Intruding

An intruder aircraft was one penetrating enemy airspace whose crew, not briefed for any special objective, sought targets of opportunity. In World War I the Germans regularly used their heavy bombers for intrusion behind the British and French lines, looking for lights betraying troop billets, or headlights of transport. French and British bombers searched for more specific targets in industrial Germany.

In World War II, during mid-1940, Luftwaffe bombers roamed over Britain at night probing the defences. This led to Bristol Blenheims of No 604 Squadron seeking out their airfields to attack and intruder-type operations evolved. RAF Fighter Command, recovering quickly from the Battle of Britain, went on the offensive with daylight fighter sweeps and night intrusion over enemy-occupied territory. Operational Instruction No 56 titled 'Operation Intruder', issued on 12 December 1940, defined intruders as aircraft sent to intercept the enemy over or in the vicinity of their airfields. They were instructed to attack enemy aircraft landing and taking off, personnel and buildings on the ground. They were to remain in the vicinity of the airfields, in order to inflict maximum damage and to create as much nuisance as possible, for as long as fuel supplies permitted.

Left: Flt Lt Karel Kuttelwascher, a Czech in the RAF, was credited with destroying 22 enemy bombers and six ships on intruder operations.
Below left: Sqn Ldr J. A. F. MacLachlan, who had lost an arm while fighting over Malta, led No 1 Squadron to many successes on night intruder patrols over France between July 1941 and July 1942.
Below: Hawker Hurricane Mk IIBs of No 3 Squadron. Although short on range, the Hurricane was very effective as an intruder

Early intruders

The Blenheim Ifs of No 23 Squadron made the first of the true intruder sorties in December 1940 and in early 1941 Blenheims, Boulton Paul Defiants and Hawker Hurricanes of night fighter squadrons were intruding on occasions at night over enemy-occupied territory. In the spring of 1941 the intruder specialists, No 23 Squadron, introduced the longer-ranged Douglas Havoc to this role.

Meanwhile the Luftwaffe, apart from conducting its nightly *blitz*, used I Gruppe of Nachtjagdgeschwader 2 (I/NJG 2), equipped with some 40 Junkers Ju 88s and a few Dornier Do 17s, for intrusion over Britain. They shot up a Defiant on night-flying training from No 54 Operational Training Unit (OTU) on 16 January 1941, igniting a parachute flare and causing the pilot to crash-land. On the evening of 25 February two Avro Ansons of No 12 Flying Training School (FTS) were both fired upon while circling Harlaxton relief landing ground. The following night an Airspeed Oxford was shot down near Fulbeck and another of the RAF College was attacked as it made a night landing at Barkston.

While the Luftwaffe used bombers for intruder operations, the RAF used mainly fighters. Typical are the operations of 12 April 1941, a day of thick cloud with intermittent rain. When the cloudbase rose around midday, giving better visibility yet affording cloud cover within easy reach, the conditions were ideal and six Hurricane pilots on standby were given the go-ahead. They took off in pairs at hourly intervals. The first pair, skimming the ground at Hazebrouck, machine gunned storage tanks and shot up a convoy of 20 military lorries. Then, as often happened, the pair lost contact with each other. Four Messerschmitt Bf 109s pounced on one of the Hurricanes and a fight at low-level ensued. The Hurricane

pilot tried to throw off his pursuers and succeeded, but grazed the ground with the aircraft's tail and broke through a high tension cable. However, both Hurricanes returned safely.

A second pair of Hurricanes, setting out as the others returned, found hangars in the Forêt de Crecy to attack, but the last pair wisely abandoned their mission as the sky had begun to clear. Later in the afternoon, the cloud thickened again and six Spitfires set out in pairs at intervals. Barracks, hangars and gun positions were attacked and a power station at Abbeville was damaged. At Berck, on the way out, a Spitfire was hit by anti-aircraft fire and came down in the sea 19 km (12 miles) off Dungeness.

Above: No 418 Squadron used the Douglas Boston Mk III primarily for night intruder operations over enemy airfields from March 1942 until March 1943, when it converted to the DH Mosquito Mk VI. Above right: No 23 Sqn operated the Mosquito Mk II from Malta on intrusions over airfields in Sicily and Italy

Hitler's intervention

For their part the Luftwaffe intruded mainly between dusk and dawn and RAF night flying training was being seriously hampered by I/NJG 2's activities. Two Ansons were attacked while circling Brackley on 12 June 1941 and on 28 July an Oxford was shot down, followed by another two nights later. Throughout the summer many training hours were lost due to night flying being suspended when intruders were reported and No 15 FTS had two of their Oxfords destroyed by intruders on 12 August. However, relief was at hand; I/NJG 2 was ordered to the Mediterranean area for other duties in September. Intrusion was then only by the occasional bomber – and by sheer chance one such aircraft collided with an Oxford over Grantham on 11 October, both machines crashing.

Hitler regarded intruding as a wasted effort and, when the British bombing offensive got underway, he demanded that night fighters should operate over the Reich or occupied territory to give the people tangible evidence of their successes. He did not appreciate that small numbers of aircraft, widely dispersed to cause disruption over a large area, could have a far more serious effect on a nation's war effort than concentrated raids on specific targets. During 1941 Britain lost 12,030 tons of steel production through damage to steel plants – but 234,678 tons of steel production was lost through stoppages during air raid warnings. These figures, compiled by the Ministry of Home Security, had a profound effect on the Air Staff and the RAF intruder force was ordered to be strengthened and their operations intensified.

Rangers

Responsibility for intruder operational planning, hitherto dealt with by No 11 Group, was passed to Fighter Command Headquarters in August 1942. The intruder force comprised Nos 23, 418 (RCAF) and 605 Squadrons, which were the intruder specialists, night fighter squadrons as detailed, light bombers of No 2 Group, Bomber Command, for mainly daylight intrusion and aircraft of Coastal and Army Co-operation Commands as available. The object was to operate over Germany and occupied territory, destroy enemy aircraft in the air and on the ground, disrupt German night flying organisation and destroy other targets on an opportunity basis.

Equipment and techniques were improved. The first DH Mosquitoes adapted for intrusion reached No 23 Squadron early in 1942 and later they replaced the night

Below: DH Mosquito Mk II night fighters of No 605 Squadron. This unit converted from the Douglas Boston Mk III to the Mosquito in February 1943 and was engaged in the intensive night intruder operations against Luftwaffe airfields during the period of resurgent bomber activity against Britain in 1944

flying Douglas Bostons in the other two full-time intruder squadrons. Strict radio silence was maintained over enemy territory, but special wireless/telegraphy reception sets were fitted. These received coastal signals to advise the intruders of areas of enemy activity noted by wireless interception stations, or to recall the aircraft in case of fog forming at bases. Airfields at Bradwell Bay, Essex, Manston, Kent and Ford in Sussex were made regular forward bases for intruder sorties, with Peterhead, Aberdeen, Coltishall, Norfolk, Warmwell, Dorset, and Exeter, Devonshire on standby as required. One shortcoming in the interception of enemy aircraft was that airborne radar was not carried in intruder aircraft at this time in case it fell into enemy hands.

Early in 1943 special intruder operations, known as Rangers, were introduced. They were flown by Mosquitoes, Bristol Beaufighters and North American Mustangs, which undertook long-range day and night sorties to compel the Luftwaffe to maintain a large and widely-dispersed fighter force in the west. This alleviated German pressure on the Russian Front. Pilots were ordered to destroy even training and communications aircraft as opportunity permitted. Those operating on Rangers had to be proficient night fighter aircrew, whether on day or night sorties. Special low-level navigation, cloud flying and beam approach training was given – Rangers were only for the *élite*.

Tip-and-run raids

The Luftwaffe tried a new form of shallow penetration by a series of tip-and-run raids along the South Coast of England. Some towns like Eastbourne bear the scars of these attacks to this day. Coastal towns were machine-gunned and bombed by fighters, mainly Focke Wulf Fw 190s, which would come in low over the sea to escape radar detection and quickly return in the same way.

Meanwhile on the Eastern Front the Red Air Force was utilising its obsolescent Polikarpov Po-2 and R-5 biplanes for attacks behind enemy lines. These light biplanes, carrying anti-personnel bombs, flew at between 400 and 1,000 metres (1,300 and 3,300 ft). Their pilots, including women, sought signs of campfires, headlights, or equipment revealed by moonlight. The Luftwaffe were stung into taking retaliatory action in late July 1943. They shot down four Po-2s in one night, but due to the wide front and the large number of light aircraft available this nuisance was not effectively countered.

Russian intrusion was shallow as the Soviets did not have aircraft with the range to reach eastern Germany. However, British-based aircraft were already operating east of Berlin. Additionally, from the night of 16/17 December 1943, RAF Bomber Command used their own intruder Mosquitoes and Beaufighters to attack enemy fighter airfields as part of the bomber support operations. Then in May 1944 the ban on using early marks of AI airborne radar over enemy territory was lifted and the force became even more potent.

The Luftwaffe's last effort

Intruder operations were not practicable in the Pacific area and the USAAF, with its precision day bombing policy, was untrained for such operations. Their Northrop P-61 Black Widow night fighter had the potential, but the closest the Americans came to regular intrusion was joining in Ranger-type operations over Germany with their Mustangs, Republic Thunderbolts and Lockheed Lightnings, mainly in connection with bomber support. On 22 April 1944 the USAAF became victims of a rare Luftwaffe intrusion. As the heavy bombers of the Eighth Air Force returned in the dusk from an attack on Hamm, they were followed by 15 Messerschmitt Me 410s, which shot down eight Consolidated B-24 Liberators and damaged others both in the air and on the ground. Another intrusion on the evening of 7 June caused the loss of three more American bombers near their bases in Britain.

On the night of 3/4 March 1945 Germany made another large-scale intrusion over Britain. Some 80 Ju 88s and Me 410s approached East Anglia in two waves. Sweeping over Norfolk they attacked airfields showing activity, shooting down aircraft in the air and bombing and machine-gunning aircraft landing and at dispersal. Flying northward, they caught Handley Page Halifaxes of No 6 Group RAF returning from a raid and wrought more havoc.

The operational order 'Scram' planned for just such an emergency, was given. The East Anglian airfields closed down and airborne aircraft made for fields in the Midlands. By then, however, the damage was done; 43 RAF aircraft had been attacked, 19 bombers were destroyed over Britain, three others were destroyed on the ground and eight were damaged.

Bedcheck Charlies

During the Korean War, following the tactics of the Red Air Force in World War II, the Russian-trained North Korean forces used light liaison aircraft in the night intruding role, or 'night heckling' as the Americans called it. The first major success was at 0300 hours on 28 November 1950, when Polikarpov Po-2s dropped fragmentation bombs over an American airfield, killing a sergeant, destroying three Mustangs and damaging eight others. Later, at Suwan, when vehicle headlights around perimeter tracks betrayed the airfield, a motor transport pool was hit, a North American F-86 Sabre was wrecked and others were damaged.

The Po-2s, joined by Lavochkin La-11s and Yakovlev Yak-18s, continued their nuisance raids, stinging the Americans into taking retaliatory measures. Extra anti-aircraft guns were brought in, but the light aircraft, flying low, made difficult targets. Major E. A. Van Grundy US Marine Corps, flying a Grumman F7F Tigercat, made the first radar interception in September 1951.

A lapse in intrusion followed, but these attacks were renewed with such regularity after dusk in the autumn of 1952 that the raiders came to be called 'Bedcheck Charlies'. A Lockheed F-94 Starfire made radar contact one night in October, but the light aircraft proved too elusive to destroy; the only American success that year was by a Douglas F3D Skynight.

Eventually the US Fifth Air Force solved the problem by calling in the Navy, who lent them four F4U-5N Corsairs from Task Force 77. They had both radar to detect the intruders and the capability of throttling down to relatively low speeds. Flying a Corsair, Lt Guy Bordelon destroyed two Yak-18s on 30 June 1953 and two more enemy aircraft the following night. His further success in downing another light aircraft made him the only naval ace of the Korean War.

In the Vietnam War the nearest types to approach true intruder aircraft were the 'gunships' – specially armed Douglas C-47s, Fairchild C-119 Boxcars, or Lockheed C-130 Hercules fitted with massed machine guns for ground saturation fire. From the trend of the short Arab-Israeli war of 1973, it would seem that surface-to-air missiles now make the role of an intruder extremely hazardous, if not impossible.

Minelaying

The laying of mines from the air was first investigated late in World War I by both the British and the Germans, by which time mine warfare had involved aircraft in other ways. The setting up of a chain of coastal flights of DH6s in 1918 was partly to discourage minelaying U-boat crews from operating around the shores of Britain, while coastal airships and towed kite balloons were employed in mine-spotting duties. After the Armistice the only German aircraft allowed to fly were those permitted by the Allied Control Commission to carry out mine-reporting duties.

When war clouds gathered again in the 1930s, serious consideration was given to aerial minelaying, for aircraft were the only means by which mines could safely be laid in waters already mined. During its formative years the Luftwaffe had shown little interest in aerial minelaying, but General Coeler, who had taken over command of the German naval air arm in August 1939, sent out his Heinkel He 59 floatplanes at night to lay mines in the Thames estuary and off the Kent coast. These outdated biplanes were soon replaced by Heinkel He 111s and Dornier Do 17s, which dropped mines fitted with parachutes to permit higher level drops to be made without subjecting the delicate detonating mechanisms to heavy impact with the water. With a sinker attached, the mines were brought to rest at pre-set depths.

Up until World War II, mines were mostly of the spherical contact type with horns which had to be depressed by collision with a ship for detonation. Both Britain and Germany had been working on a magnetic mine which would explode when a mass of metal, such as a ship, entered its magnetic field – the reason why today's mine-sweepers are built with non-metallic hulls. The Germans, unaware of British research along similar lines, estimated that it would take two years to find a countermeasure and started their magnetic mine dropping in November 1939. In three months they had sunk an impressive total of 250,000 tons of British shipping.

Gardening sorties

When one such mine fell into the mud flats at Shoeburyness on 22 November 1939, a brave and skilful team defused and salvaged the mine for examination and discovered that the magnetic technique was known to the Germans. There was, therefore, no point in withholding the British A Mk 1 magnetic mine and its large-scale production commenced. This mine was long and thin in shape like a torpedo, to enable its carriage by Fairey Swordfish biplanes of the

A painting by C. R. Fleming-Williams of a Short 184 floatplane of the Royal Naval Air Service exploding an enemy mine which lay in the path of a convoy. The main use of aircraft in mine warfare during World War I was detecting minelaying activities by enemy vessels

Fleet Air Arm or by Bristol Beauforts of Coastal Command. However, neither aircraft had the range to extend mining to Germany's Baltic seaboard. Handley Page Hampdens of RAF Bomber Command were given this task with mines fitted with tail parachutes to permit dropping from 600m (2,000ft). The Hampdens opened the British mining operations, known within the Service as Gardening, on the night of 13/14 April 1940, dropping their Vegetables–the code-name for mines–in Kiel Bay. They were joined by Beauforts mining the Ems and Jade-Weser estuaries, each area being designated by code-names of flowers and vegetables.

Meanwhile, Reichsmarschall Goering, interested in the German navy's mining successes, conferred with Coeler. As a result, a special Luftwaffe command, Flieger-division 9, was created in February 1940 as a minelaying force, absorbing the former naval element in this role. Focke Wulf Fw 200 Condors of 2/KG 40 were also employed as long-range minelayers, but these four-engined aircraft proved too vulnerable. Shortly after midnight on 20 July 1940 the Sunderland defence search-lights picked up an Fw 200 and the aircraft fell to the local anti-aircraft guns. within three hours another Fw 200 came down in the sea off Northern Ireland. In both cases two crew members were killed and two taken prisoner. The effect on KG 40 was profound, for the Fw 200 was promptly withdrawn from operations over the British Isles.

As German minelaying activity increased along the south and east coasts, so various steps were taken to minimise its effect. Bomber Command instituted night patrols over German seaplane bases in the North and East Friesian Islands to disrupt operations. Balloon Command extended its defences in the Thames, Humber and Mersey areas by having barrage balloons stationed on lighters and barges moored in the estuaries. Later, even Westland Lysanders of Army Co-operation Command were used for coastal and estuary mine-spotting.

The menace of the magnetic mines to ships was countered by degaussing, fitting current-bearing coils, or by magnetising the whole ship. As an alternative to sweeping the sensitive mines a means was found of exploding them from the air by fitting Vickers Wellington bombers with a 15m (48ft) hoop containing a magnetic coil fed by a 35 kilowatt Maudesley generator in the fuselage driven by a Ford V8 engine. Designated Wellington DWIs for directional wireless installation–a deliberately mis-leading name to confuse enemy intelligence–they flew low over the water exploding mines in their wake. The work of the DWIs was soon extended to the North African coastline and to the Suez Canal and its approaches as both German and Italian mining activity extended to the Mediterranean theatre of operations.

Aerial and land mines

Land mines were also developed to cause maximum blast, being dropped by parachute to prevent ground penetration; 127 such mines had been dropped by the Germans in their attack on Coventry on the night of 14/15 November 1940. An aerial mine, code-named Mutton, was tested by No 430 Flight RAF in 1940; this was suspended from a parachute by a great length of piano wire to provide an aerial curtain in which enemy bombers would tangle, exploding the mine on contact. However, the idea was abandoned as successes were limited.

While mining was a secondary role for British and German bombers, bombing was a secondary role for Russian minelaying DB-3f (Ilyushin Il-4) aircraft. The first Russian bombing attack on Berlin, during the night of 7/8 August 1941, was by Il-4s of the 1st Guards Mine/ Torpedo Bomber Aviation Regiment which operated against German shipping in the Baltic, while similar units operated in the Black Sea after German forces had reached Sebastopol.

British mining continued mainly by Bomber Command. As the Battle of the Atlantic took priority, mining was intensified between Cherbourg and Bordeaux in the hope of gaining success against U-boats. When the German warships *Scharnhorst*, *Gneisenau* and *Prinz Eugen* broke out of Brest on 12 February 1942 and sailed undetected through the Channel almost to the Straits of Dover, and then proceeded unscathed after repeated bombing and torpedo attacks, it was mines which caused them serious damage. These were not the mines which had been laid that night by Hampdens and Avro Manchesters in the presumed path of the ships, but the result of earlier air mining in the area. *Scharnhorst* exploded two mines and, shipping water, she limped into Wilhelmshaven for repair.

With four-engined bombers which could carry five mines each coming into service, Bomber Command, by the end of 1942, was laying more mines in a month than the entire RAF in 1940 and over far greater distances. The iron ore traffic between Scandinavia and Germany was delayed and reduced. Morale among German merchant crews declined and Swedish seamens' unions protested against the German charter of their ships. One of the most notable successes was the sinking of the 7,000-ton transport ship *Wuri* carrying 1,000 troops and 500 Luftwaffe ground personnel. Such sinkings engendered the German introduction of the *sperrbrecher*, a specially strengthened merchant ship to lead convoys and clear Allied mines in their path.

High-level operations

Mining had been mainly restricted to fairly low-level drops in moonlight to enable a visual navigational check on coastal landmarks to be made. With the introduction of radar aids, however, accurate dropping was possible in cloud and from heights of up to 4,500m (15,000ft). The first of the high-level mining operations was carried out on 4 January 1944 by six Halifaxes off Brest.

The Luftwaffe had formed six minesweeping squadrons or *minensuchstaffeln* using Junkers Ju 52/3m transports modified with a large ring, similar to the British Wellington DWI, or for dropping explosive charges to detonate acoustic mines. Along the Western European seaboard these aircraft were harried by RAF long-range fighters, including Mosquitoes, Beaufighters and Mustangs.

In mid-1944, at the time of the Allied invasion of Europe, the Germans started dropping a new type of mine actuated by pressure. Three American destroyers fell victim to this new weapon in quick succession, but its full effectiveness was reduced by gales that summer which caused many premature explosions. The Allies extended their mining to inland waterways. The Danube, rising in the Black Forest, provided the Third Reich with a vital communication link with the Romanian oil fields and Hungarian grain lands. Using Rhine-type barges, each carrying up to 1,000 tons, the river carried more supplies to Germany than the Balkan railway system, then under heavy attack by USAAF and RAF aircraft. From the night of 8/9 April 1944, bombers of No 205 Group RAF started mining along the Danube from Italian bases. The largest operation was on 1/2 July when 17 Consolidated Liberators and 57 Wellingtons laid 192 mines for the loss of four aircraft.

Above: sea mines await loading into the bomb-bay of an Avro Lancaster. The first operation by Lancasters was a minelaying operation in the Heligoland Bight on 3/4 March 1942. Right: a Consolidated Catalina of No 43 Squadron Royal Australian Air Force being prepared for a minelaying sortie at Darwin in May 1945

submarines. The Germans classified mines in a 250 to 1,000 kg range and British mines were in a 250 to 2,000 lb range, the smaller lightweight mines being used for mining particularly shallow waters.

America had displayed little interest in aerial mine-laying in the early war years. In the vast areas of the Pacific Ocean mining was used at first only tactically by the US Navy to deter interference by enemy surface vessels during amphibious operations. On the few occasions in which Grumman Avengers from carriers laid mines in the path of the Japanese navy, their own losses did not justify the result. The USAAF first made regular mining missions with their 7th Bombardment Group, based in India, whose Liberators sowed British and American mines in Indo-Chinese and Chinese waters. They were joined by RAF Liberator squadrons which, on occasion, set out from their bases in Ceylon (now Sri Lanka) to lay mines in the Singapore roads, involving a 21-hour round-trip of 5,390 km (3,350 miles). In the South-West Pacific, the Royal Australian Air Force conducted a mining campaign; in the closing months of the war Catalinas of Nos 20, 42 and 43 Squadrons were each averaging a mining sortie a day.

Operation Starvation

By early 1945 American strategic bombing had destroyed a quarter of Japan's rice reserves by bombing attacks on towns. To further demoralise the population, Operation Starvation was launched. This was an attempt to close the Shimonoseki Straits, dividing Kyushu from the main island, by mines and then to extend this threat around Japanese coastal waters. Boeing Superfortresses of the 313th Bombardment Wing, based at North Field, Tinian, were allotted this task and their attacks started on 27 March when 105 aircraft set out to drop mines in the straits. Some early losses to Japanese anti-aircraft fire caused the dropping height to be raised at the expense of accuracy of placement.

Japanese minesweepers were quickly brought to the area and were continuously employed in their task until the following August, when the country capitulated. In that time 21,389 mines of various types were dropped during 4,760 sorties for a loss of 55 aircraft. The mines sank or disabled 83 Japanese ships totalling 183,000 tons and caused 350 vessels and 20,000 men to be engaged on sweeping operations. Overall, in the Pacific area, the Japanese are estimated to have lost 266 ships to American and 21 to British mines.

During the Korean War, it was conventional contact mines of Russian design, laid by North Korean ships to hazard amphibious landings or inshore bombardment, which defied American airborne sweeping attempts. Thirty-nine aircraft from the carriers *Leyte Gulf* and *Philippine Sea*, dropping 50 tons of bombs on one field, failed to detonate the mines. The airborne dropping of depth charges also failed and surface sweeps had to be awaited. During the Vietnam War, American aircraft dropped mines in Vietnam waterways as part of their operations against Viet Cong transport systems. In 1973 they reversed the role by successfully sweeping mines from North Vietnamese ports and harbours with 50 specially modified Sikorsky CH-53 helicopters. This was followed in the mid-1970s by the delivery of 30 Sikorsky RH-53s specially built for airborne mine countermeasures, which can tow, stream, operate and retrieve equipment to detonate or neutralise mines. They were called in to help clear the Suez Canal of mines in 1974 – an operation which re-emphasised the fact that the mine can still be a menace in the missile age.

Above: a RH-53D of the US Navy using a Mark 105 magnetic minesweeping device to clear a section of the Suez Canal near Ismailia, Egypt in 1974. The Canal was temporarily closed as a result of minelaying during the Yom Kippur War of 1973.
Right: among the roles of the Grumman A-6 Intruder is minelaying, and the type contributed substantially to the effective minelaying of Haiphong harbour in the closing months of the Vietnam war

Mining inland waterways

Meanwhile, other waterways were being mined from bases in Britain. The Path Finder Force used their skill at marking and mining in the Kiel Canal and Mosquitoes laid mines in the Dortmund-Ems Canal. Control was exercised by the Admiralty and the mines for special operations were prepared at RAF stations by a detachment of the Womens Royal Naval Service. As in World War I, airships were introduced from September 1944 by the US Navy for mine-spotting duties along the liberated coasts of Southern France and to clear the North African coast. During World War II, 76,000 British mines were laid, 54,194 by RAF and Fleet Air Arm aircraft and the remainder by surface minelayers and submarines. A majority of 47,307 was dropped by Bomber Command aircraft which made 18,725 Gardening sorties for the loss of 468 aircraft on these missions.

During the war it was assumed that one vessel was sunk or damaged for every 50 mines laid. Postwar figures calculated by the Admiralty bore this out, claiming that 1,050 Axis warships and merchant ships were sunk and 540 damaged by British minelaying. The Germans had been even more prolific, with 120,000 mines laid in North-West Europe alone by aircraft, minelayers, E-boats and

Naval Aviation

The military aircraft is less than eighty years old, while the fighting ship of today has a pedigree of centuries, yet the newcomer has had an inordinate influence over the long-established weapon. Indeed, in living memory observers have claimed that the aircraft had made the oceans untenable by any surface warship. Yet today both forms of weaponry are still with us and neither has achieved dominance.

The earliest powered flights had virtually no more effect on the conduct of war at sea than the balloon flights made by pioneers of the eighteenth and nineteenth century. The reason is not hard to find, for they had such short range that they could do little more than fly over ships lying close inshore. Furthermore, the lack of radio communication prevented them from relaying a report until safely home again. There was certainly no possibility of an aircraft doing anything to damage a ship, as there were no weapons which could be carried.

Scouting airships

It was the dirigible airship which showed most promise, for it soon developed the power, range and payload needed for extended flights over the sea. An alternative was to fit landplanes with floats so that they could take off from the surface of the sea; in theory ships would be able to carry these seaplanes or 'hydro-aeroplanes' to the theatre of operations, hoist them over the side and recover them after alighting. In practice the Germans tended to specialise in the development of big airships under the aegis of their talented designer Graf Zeppelin, whereas the British and, more successfully, the Americans concentrated on producing seaplanes and flying boats–the latter being more solidly-built aircraft with boat-hulls.

By the outbreak of war in August 1914 the Royal Naval Air Service had 52 seaplanes and seven non-rigid airships, while the German Navy had 36 seaplanes, a rigid airship and three civilian airships available for requisition. The only other navies to show any interest in naval aviation had been the American, French and Italian, but although the Americans had managed to land on board a ship and the French had converted a ship into a seaplane carrier, the logical follow-on of a naval air force had not been achieved in these countries.

The first effect of these relatively untried air forces was to make naval warfare more difficult. The Royal Navy found to its chagrin that the Zeppelin airships as often as not sighted formations of British warships at sea, reported their position back to base and enabled the High Seas Fleet to avoid action. Indeed by the spring of 1915 Commodore R. Tyrwhitt of the Harwich Force was so

Below: shore-based flying boats, such as the US Navy Naval Aircraft Factory PN-9 illustrated, were used for maritime reconnaissance. Bottom: the Fairey IIIF served as a carrier-borne reconnaissance aircraft, an essential element of naval air power between the wars. Right: the Fairey Albacore was a carrier-borne strike aircraft of World War II

this sinking showed that aircraft might provide an answer to the menace. In fact the Royal Navy had already produced nearly 30 'blimps' (non-rigid airships) by the end of 1915; they were known as the 'SS' type as they were intended to scout for submarines.

Birth of the aircraft carrier

Under pressure of war the science of aviation was making big strides and all types of aircraft became more reliable and capable of carrying bigger loads of bombs and fuel. Nothing spectacular was achieved, but by the end of 1917 the technique of operating fast land aircraft such as the Sopwith Pup fighter from ships had been perfected. In June that year Flight-Commander F. J. Rutland flew a Pup off a 6m (20ft) platform on the forecastle of the light cruiser HMS *Yarmouth*. From there it was an obvious step to provide cruisers and capital ships with similar platforms, to allow them to fly off aircraft for reconnaissance or to drive off Zeppelins as and when required. Battleships were given platforms on two gun turrets and usually carried one Pup fighter and one Sopwith 1½-Strutter for scouting.

As far as the Royal Navy was concerned, the implications of air power at sea had been fully grasped and work proceeded rapidly on the provision of ships capable of exploiting the new developments. The large light cruiser *Furious* had been earmarked for conversion to an aircraft carrier and after an interim period she was given a landing deck as well as a flying-off deck. In addition the hulls of a Chilean battleship and an Italian liner were requisitioned and, although only one was ready by the Armistice, these were true aircraft carriers—floating airfields capable of supporting aircraft as well as flying them. The growing confidence of the RNAS was reflected in an ambitious plan drawn up for a torpedo bomber raid on the German fleet early in 1919. The surface fleet had spent four years trying to search out and destroy the enemy and it was at last recognised that an air attack on his bases promised far more positive results. The raid never took place, but it foreshadowed the highly successful Fleet Air Arm attack on Taranto in 1940 and could have produced equally spectacular results.

Against submarines, aircraft had not achieved anything like the results claimed. For example, only one U-boat was sunk by British aircraft acting independently and another four by aircraft operating with ships. However, what was proved was that the presence of aircraft was a strong deterrent to submarines and in this respect the blimps and flying boats were a powerful ingredient in the success of the convoy system, which administered a heavy defeat to the U-boats in 1918. During the last 18 months of the war, merchant ships made about 84,000 voyages in convoy, during which only 257 ships were sunk; of these only two were lost when the convoy was provided with any sort of escort.

Bombers versus battleships

The lessons of the war were not wasted on other navies and the Japanese and Americans immediately took steps to equip themselves with naval air forces equally as effective as the British. The Washington Naval Disarmament Conference of 1921 acted as a spur, for it concerned itself with cutting down the number of heavy cruisers and battleships to be built by each navy and paid much less attention to the aircraft carrier. The British, Americans and Japanese were all permitted to convert existing hulls to carriers and, in the case of the American and Japanese, they used very large hulls of cancelled capital ships, resulting in large, fast aircraft carriers with good aircraft capacity.

frustrated by the constant surveillance of his ships that he obtained permission to fit some of his cruisers with a launching platform over the forecastle. It was hoped to launch a fighter aircraft which would shoot down the spying Zeppelin, but the sad truth was that the aircraft could not climb to the altitude of the airships fast enough to intercept and destroy them.

Countering the Zeppelin

The British Grand Fleet found itself in the humiliating position of having overwhelming numerical superiority, but inferior reconnaissance. This led to an increasing clamour for some equivalent to the Zeppelins, or failing that, a countermeasure. A number of merchant ships were converted to seaplane carriers, including the famous ex-Cunard liner *Campania*. They performed many useful services and even carried out the first bombing raid on the Zeppelin sheds at Cuxhaven, but the aircraft were so unreliable that they could achieve little. The *Engadine* made history by getting one of her Short seaplanes airborne during the early stages of the Battle of Jutland; the observer sighted the German Fleet, but the radio was out of action and so the achievement had no effect on the course of the battle.

Results in the Mediterranean were rather more promising. The first seaplane carrier designed for the job, HMS *Ark Royal*, was sent to the Dardanelles to provide aerial reconnaissance for the landings on the Gallipoli peninsula. She provided good reconnaissance, but a converted Isle of Man packet, the *Ben-my-Chree* showed the way to the future when one of her Short 184s torpedoed a Turkish transport in the Narrows. At the end of 1915 her seaplanes carried out attacks on the Berlin-Constantinople railway line, but the puny 112lb bombs were unable to inflict any significant damage.

The Mediterranean was also the scene of another interesting development. In September 1916 two Austrian Lohner flying boats sighted the French submarine *Foucault* below the surface in the Adriatic and sank her with three bombs. Submarines were proving a far bigger menace to Allied control of the sea than battleships and

Above: capable of accommodating over 100 aircraft, USS Forrestal was the first of eight large conventionally-powered aircraft carriers to be built for the US Navy between 1955 and 1968.
Below: the DH Sea Hornet entered Fleet Air Arm service in 1947

The argument went on throughout the 1920s and 1930s, but in practice land-based air forces did little to test their theories, being content to claim that they could sink anything with ease. It could be claimed that one of the most costly errors made by air forces during the inter-war period was their failure to show their sister-services, in practical terms, how dangerous air attack could be. Thus the RAF, for example, did nothing to show the Royal Navy how to defend itself against dive bombing and high-level bombing, as it was obsessed with its over-riding mission of strategic bombing. Navies, for their part, continued to put their faith in anti-aircraft gunnery and were confident that ships would shoot down all attacking aircraft.

Triumph at Taranto

World War II soon showed how wrong both sides had been. Conventional bombing was far too inaccurate to hit ships easily and anti-aircraft gunnery seldom did more than distract and disrupt attacking formations. However, the Norwegian Campaign in April 1940 showed that shore-based dive bombers were a menace to ships operating without air cover off a hostile coast. No important British ships were sunk by bombs off Norway, but the constant harassment made fleet operations difficult and after the fall of France it was admitted by the Admiralty that big ships would not be able to operate in the confined waters of the English Channel.

Once again it was the Mediterranean which was the setting for the most impressive demonstration of air power at sea. In November 1940 the British Mediterranean Fleet attacked the Italians' main base at Taranto. Using only 21 slow Fairey Swordfish, the Fleet Air Arm was able to sink a battleship, damage two more and inflict serious

Unfortunately the development of naval aviation was hindered rather than helped by the efforts of extreme advocates of air power. The much-publicised trials by General Billy Mitchell in July 1921, when a collection of obsolete German and American warships was sunk by bombing, merely sparked off a sterile 'bomber versus battleship' argument. The trials were so unrealistic that they were seen by navy men as a dishonest means of attacking the very need for navies. Another deleterious effect was to leave airmen with an exaggerated belief in the accuracy and effectiveness of bombs against ships.

Above: the McDonnell F2H Banshee was the first jet fighter to enter large-scale US Navy service. Below: the Hawker Siddeley Buccaneer was designed for the Royal Navy as a carrier-based strike aircraft capable of sustained near-sonic flight at sea level

damage on the seaplane base and oil supplies. The material results were relatively small, for the damaged ships could be refloated within a year, but the strategic gains were immense. Despite having lost the help of the French navy in containing the Italians, the British had gained the initiative and had offset their numerical weakness in the Mediterranean. During the following months the carriers *Illustrious* and *Eagle* inflicted serious losses on Italian shipping and disrupted communications between Italy and North Africa.

The very scale of this success stung the Germans into

Submarine hunting

In the Battle of the Atlantic the lessons of 1914–18 had to be relearned at enormous cost. When the U-boats had the benefit of aerial reconnaissance undertaken by the Focke Wulf Condor four-engined bombers operating from French airfields, they were far more effective and to protect the convoys it was necessary to revert to the 1917 idea of flying off single fighters from ships. The first solution was to fire a Hurricane from a catapult on the forecastle of a merchantman – the Catapult Armed Merchantman, or CAM-ship. Then in 1941 it was decided to fit a captured German banana boat with a wooden flight deck to permit her to fly off and recover six fighters. This was the genesis of the escort carrier and in the following year more were built; they were sorely needed to bridge the so-called 'Black Gap' in mid-Atlantic, which was beyond the range of shore-based aircraft.

Although shore-based aircraft, particularly the uniquely-effective Very Long Range (VLR) Consolidated Liberator bomber, played an important role in defeating the U-boat, the provision of continuous air cover for a convoy proved the most effective method of protecting shipping from the catastrophic losses which had occurred in 1941. It is said that the arrival of two extra squadrons of VLR Liberators and half-a-dozen escort carriers in the spring of 1943 made the difference between defeat and victory for the Allies in the battle against the U-boats.

Meanwhile in the Pacific, the lesson of Taranto had not been lost on the Japanese, who were preparing for a pre-emptive strike against the American fleet. How well they learned can be judged by the fact that two strikes by 140 aircraft from six carriers sank four battleships and damaged the remaining three severely, as well as destroying

a bold counterstroke and in January 1941 a specially-trained force of dive bombers inflicted heavy damage on the carrier *Illustrious*. The loss of this single ship tilted the balance back in favour of the Axis in the Mediterranean and led to the grevious losses of the Battle of Crete. Only one redeeming point saved the British from disaster – good aerial reconnaissance. A bold torpedo attack on the battleship *Vittorio Veneto* led to the Battle of Cape Matapan, which blunted the Italian navy's enthusiasm for a trial of strength in the central Mediterranean.

The lack of adequate air cover exposed the British to terrible risks and made naval operations extremely expensive. Even as late as August 1942 a small convoy to relieve Malta needed battleships and aircraft carriers and the situation did not ease until German and Italian airfields in North Africa were eliminated.

164 landplanes, in a four-hour attack on Pearl Harbour. Three days later, on 10 December 1941, a force of land-based torpedo bombers sank the British capital ships *Prince of Wales* and *Repulse* off the coast of Malaya, completing the destruction of Western sea power with apparently ridiculous ease. With the main striking forces eliminated and with no serious opposition in the air, the Japanese land and sea forces were able to overrun Malaya and the East Indies, giving them the access to rubber, tin and oil which they so desperately needed.

Pacific Carrier battles

Pearl Harbour left the Japanese in command of much of the Pacific, but only six months later the Battle of Midway halted them and effectively marked the zenith of their fortunes. Both Midway and the indecisive Battle of the

Coral Sea the month before were remarkable in that they were fought entirely by carrier-borne aircraft, without the rival fleets sighting one another. This was proof that the battleship's guns no longer counted as the final arbiter of naval warfare, for air-launched bombs and torpedoes could strike decisive blows 320km (200 miles) away instead of the guns' 32km (20 mile) range. It was Midway which marked the end of the battleship, rather than Pearl Harbour or the loss of *Prince of Wales* and *Repulse*, and the influence of air power could no longer be denied. In the succeeding carrier battles across the Pacific the US Navy showed that pre-war predictions were wrong; a seaborne air force proved capable of taking on and defeating a land-based air force, and in the process the Japanese military empire was totally destroyed.

Until 1945 it seemed that the advantage in the duel between aircraft and ships was shifting against the aircraft, as radar-assisted gunfire became more and more effective, provided the fleet's outer screen was defended by friendly aircraft. However, the struggle for Okinawa introduced a new and deadly element, the *kamikaze* or suicide aircraft, which crashed onto its target in a desperate attempt to destroy it. The ships surrounding Okinawa suffered terrible losses from *kamikaze* attacks and the form of attack is now seen as the first use of guided weapons, with the human brain providing the guidance for the final dive onto the target.

The missile age

The lessons learned from World War II were that the aircraft and the submarine were far more deadly foes of the surface warship than had been imagined and were going to get even more deadly. On the other hand, the aircraft was also the prime enemy of the submarine. The massed batteries of anti-aircraft guns gave way to guided missile launchers and complex arrays of computers and electronic tracking and control equipment. Even the deadly torpedo was displaced by air-launched and surface-launched anti-ship missiles and, just as people had thought in the 1920s,

it was believed that the surface ship was doomed.

Today, nearly thirty-five years after the end of World War II, the situation is far from clear. The bomber is much less important as a carrier of anti-ship weapons, for the simple reason that it is vulnerable to guided weapons if it attacks from a high level and a torpedo attack would be suicidal. On the other hand, long-range maritime aircraft such as the Soviet Tupolev Tu-20 Bear, play a vital role in reconnoitring and providing data for the guidance of anti-ship missiles, but it is generally assumed that these will be launched by surface ships or submarines. The modern high-speed attack aircraft is not ideal for attacking small ship-targets, as it has to slow down for the attack and cannot cope with violent alterations of course. It is perhaps significant that a new range of sophisticated sensors and weapons has been developed for use in helicopters, whereas these relatively slow aircraft were originally thought of as quite defenceless.

Above right: a Vought F4U Corsair being bombed-up aboard a US Navy aircraft carrier during the Korean War. After Communist forces overran most airfields in South Korea, carriers provided mobile air bases.
Right: the versatile Douglas Skyraider attack bomber served on US Navy carriers into the jet-dominated 1970s.
Left: the McDonnell Douglas F-4 Phantom is one of the world's finest interceptors and tactical bombing aircraft.
Below: an F-4 being launched from a steam-catapult

It is ironic that the present trend towards equipping ships to operate helicopters brings the story around full circle. The big aircraft carrier, with its squadrons of heavy strike aircraft, is now felt to be too vulnerable to anti-ship missiles and submarine attack and there is a constant search for smaller hulls. The helicopter has become very important as a submarine hunter and, like the Sopwith Pup of 1917, it is often carried singly on board a small warship. It has even proved possible to operate a Hawker Siddeley/Harrier vertical take-off fighter from the flight deck of a destroyer and there is a temptation to try to build ships equipped with a single Harrier.

The capabilities of the air wing of a modern US Navy carrier are comprehensive. Aboard USS John F. Kennedy are: LTV A-7B Corsair II light attack bombers of VA-72 (right), Lockheed S-3A Viking anti-submarine aircraft of VS-21 (below) and Grumman F-14 Tomcat fleet defence and air superiority fighters of VF-14 (bottom). The air wing also undertakes all-weather attack, electronic warfare, airborne early warning and reconnaissance missions

Night Fighting

John Slessor–who was later to become RAF Chief of the Air Staff–could see Zeppelin L.15 clearly, seemingly not far away. Searchlights were hardly needed; the whole bulk of the monster was reflecting the lights of a London, which, in October 1915, was not blacked out. Yet the performance of his old BE was so inadequate that eventually, with tanks almost dry, he had to give up the chase and glide back to Sutton's Farm. There a combination of white mist and a helpful searchlight crew–who shone their light in his face–caused a crash.

It is hard today to imagine a world in which there was no organised scheme of air defence whatsoever and where combat aircraft–which is what the BE2c was supposed to be–could not overhaul or climb up to airships which could barely reach 113km/h (70mph). There were plenty of aircraft which could have intercepted Zeppelins– the first significant aerial threat at night–but they remained unused until, in September 1916, three brave airmen ventured forth by night in Sopwith Camel fighters. By late 1917, night fighting had gradually developed into

Below: a painting by Joseph A. Phelan titled 'Night Fighters against the Giants', depicting Sopwith Camel night fighters attacking Zeppelin Staaken bombers over England. British-based Sopwith Camel night fighter units included Nos 44, 78 and 112 Squadrons.
Bottom: a Voisin V-10 B2 bomber brought down at night on 20 September 1918 by a pilot of Jasta 73. Many German fighter units operated at night against Allied bombers in 1917–18

a practical proposition; No 151 Squadron Royal Flying Corps in France, the German Idflieg home-defence *jastas* and a few individual experts with other warring powers all had a fair measure of experience.

A little later No 151 Squadron RAF and the 185th Aero Squadron American Expeditionary Force acquired a reputation for night fighting, but the place where an organised system first grew up was south-east England. Here, ground defences and fighters had, by 1918, painfully constructed a crude method of detecting, tracking, plotting and shooting down at least some intruders. It did not greatly help the AA guns, unless the target was illuminated by searchlights, and even then nearly all the losses suffered by raiding airships and aircraft were due to fighter interception. Some RFC/RAF aircraft, notably the Camel, were modified so that they were easier to fly at night and their pilots' night vision was not impaired by the flash of their guns.

Blind-flying advances
Not much was done to advance the technology of night fighting between the wars, except for the fundamental development of blind-flying instruments, which made aircraft, of any kind, safer to fly with little or no visual reference outside the cockpit. A sprinkling of so-called night fighters was of little interest and these usually differed from others of their kind only in having dim lighting in the cockpit and releasable flares to illuminate the field for landing.

The really significant advance came about through a series of scarcely credible chances. A British radio expert, Robert Watson-Watt, was asked if in his opinion a so-called 'death ray' could bring down enemy bombers. He replied that it could not–but, as the first thing to do would be to find out where the target was in order to aim the ray, perhaps the Air Ministry would be interested in being told about radio methods of detection. Watson-Watt's offer promised to throw the first glimmer of hope into a scene which, in January 1935, looked implacably black to anyone trying to set up defences against the growing fleets of new high-performance bombers. What

followed is history: 'Wattie'–later Sir Robert Watson-Watt–master-minded RDF.1, the radio direction-finding system which assisted Fighter Command to win the Battle of Britain. The team he gathered also worked from 1937 to put a radar set in a fighter; the result of their efforts was designated RDF.2.

That the feat was accomplished was due to brilliance and luck by British 'boffins' and industry–notably the GEC, Pye, Metrovick and Cossor Companies. Called AI, for airborne interception, the new miniaturised radar was first flown in a Fairey Battle on 21 May 1939. In July 1939 AI Mk II was being fitted into Bristol Blenheim IF fighters; the first reached No 25 Squadron on 31 July. By early 1940 the first 21 Blenheims were being supplemented by a further 60 with improved AI Mk III radar. These clumsy sets could not then be fitted into single-seaters; furthermore, pilots of these fighters were usually inexperienced at night or in bad weather. For the next 20 years the British official view tended to be that night or bad-weather interceptions demanded a crew of two. In any case, the early AI radars were so fickle and hard to manage that nearly all the night interceptions achieved by the RAF prior to 1941 were by non-radar aircraft, several of them Hawker Hurricanes and Supermarine Spitfires boldly flown by men with skill and, in most cases, a burning hatred of the enemy. The first victory over enemy bombers by night was on 18/19 June 1940, when Sqn Ldr A. G. Malan brought down two Heinkel He 111s.

Left: the Lichtenstein radar installed in the Messerschmitt Bf 110G-4 necessitated a large and drag-inducing aerial array on the nose.
Right: the Germans' Würzburg mobile radar was used to direct night fighters, anti-aircraft guns and searchlights. The surrounding victory symbols attest to its operational success.
Below right: centimetric radar was introduced in the de Havilland Mosquito in late 1942. The cockpit of an aircraft with AI Mark VIII radar is pictured.
Bottom right: the Bristol Beaufighter claimed its first night victim with radar assistance in November 1940 and thereafter gained a formidable reputation as a defensive night fighter

First radar 'kill'

The first successful night interception using AI radar was made by Flg Off Ashfield, Plt Off Morris and Sgt Leyland in a Blenheim on the night of 22/23 July 1940, the victim being a Dornier Do 17. Such events were so rare, however, that until late 1943 the RAF experimented with such unlikely–and, it proved, futile–schemes as Turbinlite airborne searchlights, which, instead of shooting down the enemy, merely lit him up so that other aircraft could try to bring their guns to bear. The LAM, or long aerial mine, was an explosive device towed round the sky by night fighters (usually Douglas Havocs) in the hope that any aircraft they collided with would be hostile.

It took three years, from 1940 to 1942, to convince

everyone that the key to night fighting lay in teamwork, necessitating a skilled ground controller using clear VHF radio, radar beacons on the ground, a ground radar early-warning and plotting system, AI radar in the fighter and a good pilot/navigator team. It also needed a fighter with adequate performance and firepower; this was lacking until the Bristol Beaufighter entered service, at first without radar, in August 1940. For the remainder of World War II various radar-equipped Beaufighters were the dominant Allied night fighters, especially in theatres other than north-west Europe where, despite long and successful use by Wg Cdr Bob Braham's intruders of No 141 Squadron, the faster DH Mosquito gradually became more important. A Beaufighter was the first aircraft to fly with the revolutionary new centimetric AI, using the British-invented magnetron valve, in November 1941. This was a radical step forward which enabled a fighter to use a steerable dish-like scanner, which could send out a pencil beam like a searchlight to greater distances, with sharper definition and a much clearer cockpit display. By avoiding the problem of reflection from the ground below it removed the previously crippling problem of minimum range, enabling a fighter to close definitely within visual range. The first centimetric sets were designated AI Mk VII and VIII, with unusual spiral scanning and circular displays in which zero range was at the centre and target 'blips'–illuminated marks caused by the reflection off its airframe–were arcs, the position of which gave the required steering information.

In August 1940, long before Britain had assembled a centimetric set, the Tizard Mission disclosed the startling new technology to then-neutral America. With open-handed collaboration, a new fighter radar was begun at the Radiation Laboratory of the Massachusetts Institute of Technology. This eventually matured as SCR-720, with the British designation AI Mk X, and became standard in late-war Mosquitoes and a few Northrop P-61 Black Widows, the latter being the first totally new aircraft designed specifically as night fighters. But by 1944, when 640 km/h (400 mph) Mosquitoes with two-stage Merlin engines and AI Mk X and the vast and extremely complex P-61 were both operational, targets by day or night were beginning to become scarce. The US Navy deserve mention for pioneering AI radar working on the short wavelength of 3 cm (1·18 in) and small enough to fit single-seat carrier-based fighters such as the Grumman F6F Hellcat and Vought F4U Corsair.

Systems and sensors

Early Luftwaffe plans virtually ignored night fighting, but on 17 July 1940 Goering instructed Oberst Josef Kammhuber to form a force of night fighters. This became Nachtjagdgeschwader 1, with a nucleus of Messerschmitt Bf 110s, Junkers Ju 88C series and one or two examples of the Dornier Do 17Z-6 Kauz I, some of which had been experimenting with infra-red detection. The basic interception method was to construct a Kammhuber Line, officially called the Himmelbett (four-poster bed) system, which divided airspace through which RAF bombers had to fly into rectangular boxes in each of which were two ground radars. One tracked the bomber and another a night fighter, while harassed controllers strove to study the two sets of radar blips and bring the two together. One or two skilled or lucky pilots, notably Paul Gildner, Werner Baake and Ludwig Becker, managed to shoot down RAF 'heavies'. However, Luftwaffe night fighters became really effective only after Telefunken and other companies had developed the Lichtenstein series of AI radars and, very importantly, additional sensors which homed onto the strong emissions sent out by the RAF bombers and which betrayed their presence and location, even as they climbed away from their bases. Naxos Z, a simple and compact package with an aerial usually faired into a Ju 88G cabin roof, homed unerringly on to the H2S mapping radar, which was switched on continuously by most RAF bombers and served little purpose except to attract the deadly enemies. Flensburg, a box in the fuselage with two aerials near the wingtips, homed on the bombers' tail-warning radar (code-named Monica by the RAF), whose purpose had been intended to save them from enemy night fighters. Besides these high-technology methods, there grew up at the instigation of Hajo Herrmann – probably the most fearless and famed bomber pilot in the Luftwaffe – the Wilde Sau night fighting method. This utilised radarless single-seaters guided by ground directions and the pilot's eyesight, the bombers often being visible over burning cities. RAF bombers tried to survive by corkscrewing along horizontal spirals, but their blind and defenceless undersides were vulnerable to upward-firing Schräge Musik guns, and many *experten* (aces) ran up scores close to 100.

Jet night fighters

The first jet night fighters made no significant advance except in flight performance, but various new ideas were forthcoming in the United States. The first, which matured in 1949–50, matched a Hughes radar, an autopilot, a simple computer and an improved cockpit display with an automatically-triggered salvo of Mighty Mouse air-to-air rockets in the so-called collision-course technique. Ignoring the traditional curve of pursuit from astern, the fighter was steered automatically to aim its rockets so that, when they were fired in rapid succession, they would fly through a block of airspace in which the enemy would be at the same moment. This method was used in the Lockheed F-94C Starfire, Northrop F-89D Scorpion and single-seat North American F-86D Sabre. By 1953 Hughes was

nearing final success with a later MG-10 fire-control system in which the weapon was a guided missile, the first of the prolific Hughes Falcon family. In the subsequent MA-1 system the whole interception was made largely or entirely automatic, the carrier aircraft – the Convair F-106A Delta Dart – being 'slaved' to the SAGE ground environment system and the pilot going along in a monitoring capacity.

Modern night fighters, or more properly all-weather fighters, include such versatile aircraft as the McDonnell Douglas F-15 – claimed to have the best cockpit and avionics displays of any standard fighter – the Grumman F-14, with AWG-9 and Phoenix missiles giving over 160 km (100 miles) range capability and the RAF's forthcoming Panavia Tornado Air-Defence Variant (ADV), in which the art of night fighting will probably reach its highest pinnacle yet.

Below: pilots of a Royal Air Force Hawker Hurricane-equipped night fighter squadron are briefed in an operations tent. The unit flew night patrols and ground strafing missions in Central Burma. Bottom: depicted in a painting by Michael Turner, the Boulton Paul Defiant was designed as a day fighter. After heavy losses were sustained, the type was switched to night operations and served with some success

Reconnaissance

The idea of taking photographs from the air is almost as old as aviation itself and it inspired a number of early photographers and aeronauts to undertake experiments. Like so many aerial achievements the first aerial photographic 'sortie' took place in France, when, in the spring of 1856, a French photographer obtained some good views of the outskirts of Paris by fixing his camera to a balloon basket. He was Félix Tournachon (who used the pseudonym Nadar), a pioneer in his field, who went on to take many more photographs from the air.

Four years later J. W. Black, an American, successfully photographed Boston from a balloon. It is on record that the first military use of aerial photography took place in 1862 during the American Civil War. General McLellan commanding the Northern Army besieging Richmond, Virginia, used aerial photographs of the town to good effect. Two identical photographic prints were marked off into numbered squares. McLellan had one of them and two observers, 460m (1,500ft) above the battlefield, in a balloon, had the second. With a bird's-eye view of the area the observers telegraphed details of the movements and disposition of the enemy troops to the General, using the numbered squares as a reference.

A year later in England Henri Negretti and James Glaisher–who was a founder member of the Royal Aeronautical Society and a Fellow of the British Photographic Society–took successful photographs using free balloons flying at altitudes much higher than those of Tournachon or Black. Between 1880 and 1887 Major Elsdale, a pioneer of aerial photography in the British Army, performed a series of experiments of great subsequent importance using cameras in balloon baskets. These flights, plus the improved equipment then available to him, proved that there was great scope for the use and development of the airborne camera in military reconnaissance and mapping.

Aerial photography in war

The work of these few skilled men seemed to open the photographic floodgates; soon cameras were being carried aloft by balloons and kites in a number of countries, and well before the turn of the century balloon units for photographic and visual reconnaissance were being established in Europe and North America. Successful aerial reconnaissance by these means was carried out during the Franco-Prussian War (1870–71) and the Boer War (1899–1902).

Photographs from aeroplanes–with ciné surprisingly preceeding still photography–came on 24 April 1909, when Wilbur Wright took up a photographer from Centocelle near Rome, who took some air-to-ground ciné film. In December of the same year a Frenchman, named Meurisse, secured the first still photographs from an aeroplane. It was not until 1912 at Farnborough, Hampshire, that England emulated these successes, but a year later the Royal Flying Corps had a special air camera operating in a Farman aeroplane.

When war came in August 1914 aircraft were largely regarded as useful only for visual reconnaissance and not for the more militant role they very rapidly acquired. However, plans to use cameras to back up the human eye were already in hand; Lt J. T. C. Moore-Brabazon (later Lord Brabazon of Tara) was appointed to command a small aerial photographic unit, which he soon brought to a high state of efficiency. In March 1915 General Sir Douglas Haig's attack on Neuve Chapelle was undertaken with the aid of aerial photographs of the complex of trenches and gun emplacements of the enemy.

While there was an urgent and continuing need throughout the Front for photo-reconnaissance for recording enemy activities and for map-making, it was the pace

Below: an officer of the RAF Mobile Photographic Section shows the pilot of a BE12 the areas to be photographed on a map resting on the aerial camera. By 1918 the camera was a major instrument of tactical reconnaissance.
Bottom: a pilot reports to a photographic laboratory at Le Valdahon in 1918

Above: a camera-equipped Supermarine Spitfire PR Mk XIX. The Spitfire excelled in photo-reconnaissance duties and five specialised PR marks were built, four being unarmed variants.
Right: an observer/air gunner demonstrating his two roles. During World War II semi-automatic camera installations were introduced, activated by the pilot alone.
Opposite: a DH Mosquito PR Mk XVI of No 684 Squadron in Burma. The PR Mk XVI was the first pressurised high-altitude PR Mosquito. In 1944 No 684 Squadron made an aerial survey of the whole of Burma

of camera development and the operating range of the aircraft carrying them which dictated the advance in photo-reconnaissance techniques. Photo-reconnaissance also stimulated the development of armed aircraft to act as escorts for the all-important camera-carrying aeroplanes, which, of course, sparked off a new and never-ending trend in military aircraft design.

Understandably, the first Royal Flying Corps squadrons to be formed flew on reconnaissance duties until a more militant role could be undertaken. On 19 August 1914 Captain Joubert de la Ferté and Lt G. W. Mapplebeck of No 3 Squadron RFC, the oldest aeroplane-operating squadron in the Service, shared with pilots of No 4 Squadron the Royal Flying Corps' first visual reconnaissance in the field. Flying a variety of aircraft during those desperate days of the war, and later when the air offensive had built up, the reconnaissance crews ranged far and wide over the battlefields of France and above target towns. Often they combined their reconnaissance role with bombing, and air-to-ground photography was a feature of the overall planning and execution of the major battles from the Somme onwards.

For low-level fighter reconnaissance and photographic duties the Vickers FB5 was used with the RE5 and RE7

flying the higher level missions well behind enemy lines. On 31 July 1915 Captain J. A. Liddell of No 7 Squadron was awarded the third air Victoria Cross for bringing back to his Belgian airfield his heavily-damaged RE5 with information he had gathered from a photo-reconnaissance sortie over Ostend, Bruges and Ghent. During this flight he had been attacked by several enemy aircraft and received wounds from which he later died. The excellent photographic patrol work of No 15 Squadron and its BE2c aircraft assisted the Fifth Army attacks on the Ancre Salient in January 1917 and earned special recognition from Field Marshal Haig, then Commander-in-Chief of the British Expeditionary Force.

No 27 Squadron's Martinsyde Elephants, used for short-range reconnaissance over the German trench system, were fitted with a camera mounting on the starboard side of the fuselage beside the cockpit. It could carry an 18-plate semi-automatic all-metal P.7 camera, which changed the plate and reset the shutter automatically after each hand-operated exposure. Some excellent results were obtained with this camera during high-altitude photographic trials. They showed the practicability of obtaining good photographs from above 4,300m (14,000ft), which was twice the height normally flown by other reconnaissance units over the Western Front at that time.

while valleys and holes seem to recede into it.

Mosaics are made up from a series of still photographs obtained from an aircraft flying at a constant height on a straight course. Exposures are made at timed intervals to suit the height and to allow a 60 per cent fore-and-aft overlap and an overlap of about 20 per cent at the sides. Stereoscopic examination of the whole area makes for a more valuable and related interpretation of the region photographed.

It will be apparent that no matter how effective is the camera equipment, how accurately the PR sortie is flown, or how perfect the weather conditions, the entire operation will be wasted if the resulting photographic prints cannot be interpreted correctly. This need for skilled photo-interpreters, able to 'read' air-to-ground photographs, was not at first recognised, but the Army, RFC and later the RAF Intelligence Staff soon established special sections, whose members through practice, the application of common sense and a developed tactical knowledge, could 'read' photographs and produce an in-depth report of the activity – or lack of it – on the ground.

The camera was able to record information far more complete in detail than could be obtained by the keenest and most sharp-eyed observer with his sketch pad and pencil. Photographs were mainly used for the revision of trench maps, the plotting of enemy gun-positions and the

Photographic interpretation

As the war continued, various new techniques were being tried and evaluated to make each dangerous reconnaissance and mapping flight more valuable and rewarding. This work included the use of suitably-mounted cameras to obtain both vertical and oblique photographs. The vertical photographs showed the ground plan, revealing the correct shape of buildings, roads and waterways. The oblique photographs showed hill features, woods and contours and buildings in a way more familiar to the eye. From the use of single photographs of specific and, because of the type of equipment used, fairly limited areas, new photo-techniques and cameras made possible the production of pairs of prints for stereoscopic examination, and of mosaics.

Human vision is stereoscopic, a fact which enables a range-finder effect to be created. As with the two eyes, any stereoscopic effect is dependent upon the same object being observed from two different positions; this can be achieved by taking photographs of the same ground area from two positions several hundred yards apart. When viewed through a stereoscope objects which are common to the two photographs can be seen in relief with hills, buildings and trees appearing to rise out of the print

movement of troops, supplies and gun batteries.

By 1918 photo-reconnaissance was an established facet of military operations, even though the still-limited development of the camera equipment and the range of the aircraft involved caused it to be regarded as being of tactical value only. Nevertheless, camera development had reached a stage when film instead of plates was being used in automatic cameras, which were being used in single-seat aircraft – an omen for the future.

Between the wars the advances made were steady rather than spectacular with aerial mapping probably making the most headway. On 2 April 1933, for example, the Westland PV.3 and PV.6 aircraft of the Houston Mount Everest Expedition which overflew the mountain for the first time, also obtained a photographic mosaic of the range which was of great value to cartography. During 1930 a Gloster AS.31 had surveyed 163,200 sq km (63,000 sq miles) of Northern Rhodesia to enable this vast area to be mapped for the first time. On the military side in Britain sheer economics had spawned the general-purpose aeroplane which, while including reconnaissance in its duties, was not equipped for the specialist photo-reconnaissance role, and the World War I philosophy dominated until about 1938.

In Germany, however, photographic intelligence was an important part of the vast expansion of the Luftwaffe. It is said that General von Fritsch – who later fell both from favour with the Nazis and from office as Commander-in-Chief of the German Army – forecast that the side with the most effective photo-reconnaissance organisation would win the next war.

As the war clouds gathered over Europe during 1938, a British civilian aerial photographic unit, operating from Heston and controlled by Frederick Winterbotham and Sidney Cotton, obtained many photographs of important potential targets in Germany. Under the guise of a business-man dealing in colour film, Cotton flew his twin-engined Lockheed 12A to many capital and industrial cities of Europe – especially Berlin – while three hidden cameras in the Lockheed's belly produced excellent pictures of airfields, factories and defence systems far below.

Less than an hour after the declaration of war at 1100 hours on 3 September 1939, a Bristol Blenheim of No 139 Squadron Bomber Command, flown by Plt Off A. McPherson, took off from RAF Wyton, Huntingdon-shire, on the first official photo-reconnaissance sortie from Britain. It was to photograph the German fleet, lying at anchor at Wilhelmshaven, in preparation for an attack on these ships by Blenheims of Nos 107 and 110 Squadrons. The flight was to prove that the Blenheim was suitable neither for unescorted daylight attacks on heavily defended targets nor for photo-reconnaissance duties. The Blenheims then in service were vulnerable to fighters and anti-aircraft guns and, except when flown suicidally low, the cameras froze up, the lens frosted over and the film cracked with the intense cold.

Meanwhile Cotton's 'unofficial' but highly-effective work was attracting the attention of the Air Staff – so much

so that he joined the RAF in late September and with his team of experts established a special flight. The use of small, fast unarmed high-flying aircraft had always been Cotton's main aim; thus he battled hard with Fighter Command to get two Supermarine Spitfire fighters allocated to him – and won. On 18 November, with guns removed and cameras installed in the wing and, like the Lockheed 12A, painted to render them almost invisible when flying at high altitude, one of these Spitfires flown by Flt Lt Maurice 'Shorty' Longbottom, made an historic photo-reconnaissance flight at 10,000 m (33,000 ft) to obtain pictures of the French-German border.

Essential intelligence

The results of the Heston unit's work also came to the notice of the Royal Navy and the Army, and when Cotton was 'retired' from the Royal Air Force in June 1940 to hand over command of the unit to Wing Com-mander Geoffrey W. Tuttle, a regular RAF officer, it was a well-established organisation which had become 'regularised' as the Photographic Development Unit (later Photographic Reconnaissance Unit) in the previous January. As the war progressed, so did the equipment and the photographic techniques, particularly those concerned with producing prints rapidly in the field after the aircraft had landed from a sortie. The art of photo-interpretation was also developed and a major task of the unit was obtaining new and subsequent photographs – or 'covers' – of the same target so that a comparative analysis of the situation on the ground could be made. Aircraft were flown from British airfields at Benson, Mount Farm and Oakington, St Eval, Wick and Leuchars and overseas from Malta and a number of other bases. Blenheims, Spitfires and de Havilland Mosquitoes, together with

Above right: an aerial photograph of a devastated area of Cologne the day after the 1,000 Bomber Raid of 30 May 1942. Such photographs were used to assess a raid's success or failure. Right: RAF personnel locate aerial photographs on a map of Germany in World War II. Below: the camera of a Messerschmitt Bf 110F-3 being dismantled at a Luftwaffe base in the North African Theatre. Below left: a DH Mosquito PR Mk 34 in postwar service showing the camera ports in the aircraft's belly

Lockheed Lightnings and Martin Marylands of the RAF and the US Army Air Force systematically photographed the enemy and his equipment wherever they moved on land or at sea.

They photographed the success or failure of Allied bomber attacks, while photographs of enemy defences were essential to the planning of all special operations. Most notable were covers showing the breaching of the Dortmund-Ems canal by Handley Page Hampdens on 12/13 August 1940, of the harbour at Taranto before and after the epic attack on the Italian fleet by Fleet Air Arm Fairey Swordfishes and the discovery of the German battleship *Bismarck* in a Norwegian fjord.

Probably one of the most important pieces of photography and photo-interpretation teamwork was that by Sqn Ldr John Merrifield as pilot of a Mosquito which obtained the first photographs of a V1 flying bomb on its launching ramp at Peenemünde, and Flt Off Constance Babington Smith who correctly 'read' the prints and proved during November/December 1943 that the mystery 'ski-sites' in France were for launching Hitler's new revenge weapons on the United Kingdom.

The Luftwaffe was active over Britain too, with Junkers Ju 88P, Dornier Do 17 and Do 215 and Heinkel He 177 photo-reconnaissance aircraft and in other theatres with the short-range Henschel Hs 126 and with Heinkel He 115 floatplanes and Focke Wulf Fw 200 Condor aircraft over the sea routes. While the German photographic equipment and techniques were excellent and produced sharp pictures, they never used stereoscopic viewing or achieved the high level of photo-interpretation which was initiated and used to great effect by the RAF.

While both the Spitfire and the Mosquito were built in quantity for a variety of wartime operational roles, it

A painting by Michael Turner of an English Electric Canberra PR Mk 7 of No 13 Squadron flying over Gemona, Italy in May 1976 to photograph earthquake damage. The degree of need in stricken areas could be accurately assessed and relief hastened. Though developed under the impetus of war, aerial photography has aided in the swift alleviation of many natural disasters; it has been extensively used for mapping work and has played an important part in archaeology

was the PR variants which made the last operational postwar sorties, both by No 81 Squadron RAF in Malaya on 1 April 1954 and on 15 December 1955 respectively.

The nuclear age

The Mosquito and Spitfire were gradually succeeded in service during 1950–52 by the Meteor FR Mark 9 and PR Mark 10, the fighter reconnaissance version carrying armament and three cameras in the nose for oblique photography while the unarmed PR variant carried nose cameras plus two others in the fuselage for vertical photography. They served with six RAF squadrons in Germany and the Middle and Far East until they were replaced by three versions of the English Electric (BAC) Canberra, each carrying six oblique cameras plus one vertical camera. Squadrons of PR Mark 7 and PR Mark 9 Canberras continued to provide a tactical photo-reconnaissance service to the RAF in the late 1970s with Avro (Hawker Siddeley) Vulcans flying in the strategic reconnaissance role.

Republic Aviation of the United States built the graceful twin-engined XR-12 during 1945 to meet a USAF requirement for a very long-range photo-reconnaissance aircraft to provide covers of bomber operations in the Pacific Theatre. The war's end and the rapid advances in jet propulsion, however, killed USAF interest in this

aeroplane and it never entered production. Republic produced a modified version, the Rainbow, as a high speed 46-seat civil transport but this, too, failed to win orders. The first of Republic RF-84 Thunderflashes–the PR variant of the Thunderjet fighter–was completed in February 1952 to replace the ageing Lockheed RF-80. The Thunderflash served with the USAF until, in 1965, it was in turn replaced by the McDonnell RF-101 Voodoo. Other air forces were aware of the importance of photo-reconnaissance and no less than nine countries received Thunderflashes for their PR squadrons.

The USAF's FICON (Fighter Conveyor) project of the early 1950s involved carrying an F-84 Thunderjet fighter beneath the giant ten-engined Convair B-36 bomber to extend the fighter's operating range, but, in the event, it was the need to increase the effectiveness of the USAF's reconnaissance force which prompted the carriage of the Thunderflash. The first complete cycle of airborne launching and retrieving of an F-84E came on 23 April 1952; the 91st Strategic Reconnaissance Squadron based at Malmstrom, Montana, subsequently flew the GRB-36 motherships with RF-84K Thunderflash PR aircraft, extending their range from 1,350 km (840 miles) to nearly 8,000 km (5,000 miles).

With the advent of advanced photographic techniques and equipment, reconnaissance aircraft were able to obtain detailed photographs of the ground from very high altitude. Lockheed's U-2, officially owned and operated by the National Aeronautics and Space Administration, was described as a high-altitude atmospheric research aircraft. Its sailplane appearance with very high-aspect-ratio wings gave credence to this description. However, it was observed in 1956 to be flying from USAF bases in the United Kingdom, Japan and Germany. In May 1960, when a U-2B was shot down–reportedly by a ground-to-air missile–at 20,700 m (68,000 ft) over Sverdlovsk in Russia and its pilot F. Gary Powers was taken prisoner, the real spy-plane role of this aeroplane was revealed in a grave international incident.

The U-2 was used during the Cuban missile crisis and it is reported that production of the aircraft (in the TR-1 version) will continue well into the 1980s. The U-2 was joined in 1966 by the SR-71 Blackbird, a Mach 3.0 global reconnaissance platform built for the USAF Strategic Air Command.

The USSR has paid equal attention to strategic and tactical reconnaissance since the war, producing the twin-jet Badger, Brewer-D, Mandrake and Blinder-C, the four-jet Bison-C and the colossal turboprop-powered Bear. This latter aircraft is a regular intruder into the United Kingdom's airspace and its radar signature is well-known to the crews of RAF and USAF interceptors. Apart from its photo-reconnaissance duties, as with the U-2/TR-1 and the Blackbird, its role includes all forms of infra-red (IR) and radar reconnaissance, making it a formidable, if ageing tool of USSR intelligence.

With the development of advanced-technology airborne sensors of various types, able to record the presence and movement of surface forces, the importance of the traditional optical camera as the sole piece of reconnaissance equipment began to wane. All bodies radiate thermal energy in the infra-red waveband and IR reconnaissance is a new source of combat intelligence not obtainable by optical cameras or radar. As thermal energy is radiated by night and day, photographs can be obtained covertly in darkness without artificial illumination. A British infra-red detection device, called Linescan, can produce sharp, high-quality prints from

standard 70mm reconnaissance film using normal processing methods.

Intelligence gathering has, today, become a more
hazardous task than ever. Just as the need to obtain good
clear photographs in war sparked off the design of new
aircraft variants and equipment, the ever-increasing
vulnerability of manned aircraft to missile attack has
generated the creation of new vehicles to carry cameras
and a bewildering array of sensors. These are the RPVs,
remotely-piloted vehicles which can be launched and
controlled from wheeled or tracked carriers as small as a
Land Rover to photograph the immediate battlefield, and
the space satellites covering vast areas of the earth.

The United States and the USSR have launched
hundreds of satellites since the late 1950s which were, and
still are, of a secret nature. While nearly 75 per cent of all
earth satellites launched have had some military significance, they have not been weapons. Their task has been to
observe the earth with cameras, eavesdrop with electronic
listening devices on troop movements and missile sites
and send back the information to earth by telemetry for
interpretation. So far space has been a no-man's land for
the major powers, with both East and West accepting the
fact of being continually under surveillance. This situation
may be changed with the advent of killer satellites,
intended to attack and destroy those of other countries.

Shipping Strikes

RAF Bristol Blenheims flying low over Holland to strike the port of Rotterdam in July 1941. Strikes against enemy shipping at sea and in port became routine after the RAF began offensive operations over Europe in summer 1941. In that year a third of the total tonnage of bombs delivered on Europe by Bomber Command was expended against naval targets

Such is the nature of modern warfare that vast quantities of *matériel* are transported by sea and both world wars have been characterised by constant efforts by every belligerent nation to interrupt this flow of men and supplies both by naval action and from the air. Indeed it has been in the nature of modern war that Great Britain has faced her gravest dangers in the threat to her maritime lifelines by belligerent powers.

The air-launched torpedo

To destroy a ship at sea, be it a warship or merchant vessel, special tactics and weapons are called for and this is no more clearly emphasised than in the history of air attacks against shipping. The air-launched torpedo has remained the principal anti-shipping weapon and such are its shape and weight that special aircraft have usually been developed to deliver it. The first recorded success achieved by an aerial torpedo was the sinking of a 5,000 ton Turkish supply ship near the Dardanelles on 12 August 1915 by a torpedo dropped by Flt Cdr C. H. Edmonds in a Short 184 seaplane from HMS *Ben-my-Chree*. Unfortunately this claim was put in question when a British submarine commander claimed to have launched his torpedo simultaneously. However, five days later Edmonds torpedoed another Turkish supply ship and this time his claim was not disputed.

Very little success was achieved using bombs against ships during World War I and the 18 in naval torpedo remained the sole weapon in regular use by the land-based Royal Naval Air Service. Before the Armistice the

world's first flush-deck aircraft carrier, HMS *Argus*, was commissioned and embarked the first full squadron of torpedo-carrying aircraft – Sopwith Cuckoos – in October 1918; they were, however, too late to be used in action.

The widespread use of aircraft by naval air arms during World War I encouraged far-sighted officers in Britain and America to advocate development of specialised aircraft as vital anti-shipping weapon carriers, expounding a belief that in the presence of suitable bombing aircraft the days of the capital warship were drawing to an end. In the United States, Brigadier-General William Mitchell favoured the use of Army bombers in attack trials against warships, and succeeded in sinking several, including the 22,800 ton ex-German battleship *Ostfriesland* during a demonstration on 21 July 1921. Observers remained sceptical about the use of bombs dropped from medium altitude against moving targets, but were quick to notice that near-misses by heavy bombs frequently proved fatal.

Biplane bombers

In Britain the inter-war years witnessed a succession of biplane torpedo-carriers including the Blackburn Ripon and Shark and Hawker Horsley, culminating in the classic Fairey Swordfish, which was followed by the Albacore during World War II. It is perhaps interesting to note that anti-shipping attack training was the sole prerogative of the Fleet Air Arm and that shore-based RAF aircraft were almost totally excluded from this role. The result of this omission was that when, in the first days of World War II, Bomber Command aircrews of Nos 9, 107, 110 and

149 Squadrons were called upon to find and strike enemy shipping off the German coast, the raids were unsuccessful and seven bombers were lost. In further fruitless raids by Vickers Wellingtons of Nos 9, 37, 99 and 149 Squadrons in December 1939 losses proved so heavy that Bomber Command abandoned daylight attacks.

Indeed henceforth the whole offensive against enemy shipping at sea fell on the shoulders of Coastal Command and the Fleet Air Arm, with cross-Channel sweeps against enemy coastal traffic being undertaken by Fighter Command. Only once more did Bomber Command attempt to strike enemy warships at sea in daylight; after numerous attempts to hit the *Scharnhorst*, *Gneisenau* and *Prinz Eugen* while they lay in Brest, bomber crews were sent against the German warships as they escaped through the Straits of Dover on 11/12 February 1942. Not one bomb struck its target. The critics of Billy Mitchell's tests 21 years previously seemed to have been vindicated.

If the British had been caught short of suitable anti-shipping weapons at the beginning of World War II (Coastal Command aircraft only carried 250lb bombs) the Fleet Air Arm still pinned all its faith on the Swordfish torpedo aircraft. The Blackburn Skua had failed to match expectations as a dive bomber and was employed more as a fighter before being hurriedly withdrawn from service. The Swordfish, however, succeeded against all probability with outstanding victories at Tobruk in July 1940, Taranto on 11/12 November 1940, at Cape Matapan on 28 March 1941 and against the battleship *Bismarck* in the Atlantic on 26 May 1941. In the memorable attack against the *Scharnhorst*, *Gneisenau* and *Prinz Eugen* of 12 February 1942 all six Swordfish led by Lt-Cdr Eugene Esmonde were shot down without inflicting any damage. For all its success the 'Stringbag' was an anachronism; it was flown with gallantry but inevitably succumbed in the face of determined enemy air defence. The Albacore fared little better, and the Fairey Barracuda monoplane entered service too late in the war to see anything but limited combat. Although first flown as early as December 1940, few saw service in the European Theatre.

Enemy strikes

Although the Axis sea routes between Italy, Sicily and North Africa were under constant attack by Allied forces, the Allies, being largely maritime powers, depended upon sea routes and provided infinitely more targets on the high seas than the European Axis nations. The Germans accordingly applied much greater effort against these targets from the outset of World War II. On the one hand the Luftwaffe established specific *küstenfliegergruppen* manned principally by naval aircrews whose operational role it was to concentrate against shipping and naval shore establishments; on the other hand some emphasis was also laid upon aerial mining of Allied waters by *minensuchsgruppen* and these operations certainly gained some success.

The dive bomber also achieved much greater effect in the Luftwaffe than in the RAF and Stukas sank a total of three battleships, a battlecruiser and 15 cruisers during the war, in addition to more than 50 other naval vessels and countless merchant ships. German and Italian torpedo bombers (predominantly Heinkel He 111s and Savoia-Marchetti SM 79s) also gained numerous sinkings, particularly among the Allies' famous Mediterranean and Russian convoys.

Perhaps the most interesting anti-shipping weapons of World War II were the range of air-launched guided missiles developed by Germany. The rocket-powered Henschel Hs 293 was used with limited success during the last three years, when Allied invasion fleets offered such lucrative targets. The destroyers *Boadicea*, *Dulverton*, *Inglefield*, *Intrepid* and *Vasilissa Olga* were all sunk by Hs 293s. Another successful weapon was the Fritz X armour-piercing missile. Carried by Dornier Do 217K-2s of III/KG 100, these missiles sank the Italian battleship *Roma*, damaged the *Italia*, severely damaged the battleship HMS *Warspite*, and sank the cruiser HMS *Spartan* and the destroyer HMS *Janus*.

In the Far East the Japanese followed their treacherous air attack on Pearl Harbour (where the American ships were stationary targets in port) with the sinking of the British battleships HMS *Prince of Wales* and *Repulse* of

Right: Bristol Beaufighters attack an enemy ship with rockets and cannon. Formidably successful as a long-range anti-shipping fighter, the Beaufighter revolutionised air-sea warfare. By late 1943 the rocket had virtually replaced the torpedo as the main weapon against unarmoured ships

Above right: a painting by Richard Eurich depicting an attack on a British convoy by German Dornier Do 17 bombers.
Below: North American B-25J Mitchells of the 345th Bomb Group, US Army Air Force sank the Japanese destroyer Amatsukaze and two escorts (one illustrated) off Amoy on 6 April 1945 with 500 lb bombs

Force Z when torpedo bombers caught them 320 km (200 miles) north of Singapore without air cover. Japanese naval aircraft went on to sink the cruisers HMS *Cornwall* and *Dorsetshire* in the Indian Ocean on 5 April 1942. Off Ceylon HMS *Hermes* was the first aircraft carrier to be sunk by enemy carrier-borne aircraft.

Against this chapter of disasters in the Far East the Americans quickly responded with the successful employment of Douglas Dauntless and Douglas Devastator dive bombers (and later bomb-carrying fighters such as the Vought Corsair) and achieved a welcome success in the Battle of the Coral Sea on 7-9 May 1942 by sinking the Japanese carrier *Shoho*. In the decisive Battle of Midway on 4 June that year the Japanese suffered the loss of four fleet carriers, the *Agaki*, *Hiryu*, *Kaga* and *Soryu*–all victims of American carrier-based dive bombers.

Torbeau and Rockets

Yet it was the RAF that probably developed the most deadly shore-based anti-shipping strike tactics during the war. These stemmed partly from the successful use of low-flying, cannon-armed Hurricane fighters, which flew constant sweeps against enemy light coastal shipping in the English Channel during 1941 and 1942, and from the use of the purpose-designed Bristol Beaufort torpedo bomber of RAF Coastal Command. The latter performed a number of memorable attacks, including Flg Off Kenneth Campbell's torpedo hit on the *Gneisenau* in Brest harbour on 6 April 1941. As such attacks gained increasing successes against Axis shipping, the Germans deployed heavier and heavier air and surface defences to protect these targets, including flak ships and interceptor fighters, so that by mid-1942 such attacks had become fraught with extreme hazard and unescorted raids were invariably attended by heavy losses.

The Bristol Beaufighter was developed to carry a standard 18 in torpedo and later to mount three-inch rocket projectiles. Dubbed the Torbeau, the Beaufighter entered service with the first anti-shipping Strike Wing (consisting of Nos 143, 236 and 254 Squadrons) at North Coates in November 1942, gaining its first success on 18 April 1943. By the following year several such wings had been formed, each including rocket-armed 'Flakbeaus' and escorting Beaufighters on its strength.

Today the threat by potential enemy naval forces pose no small threat to the maritime nations. Consequently modern search and attack tactics and weapons are being constantly developed to a pitch undreamed of in the days of the Swordfish and the 250 lb bomb. Among modern anti-shipping aircraft, the Soviet Backfire bomber and the US Navy's Lockheed P-3 Orion, armed with Harpoon missiles, are especially noteworthy.

Special Duties

With their northern territories overrun by the German army in 1914, the French authorities sought the assistance of their countrymen in occupied territory to help by espionage and sabotage. Contact by passage through the enemy lines was fraught with danger from sentries posted in the trenches, so from 1915 the French army used their air arm to land agents behind the enemy lines. While other Allies indulged in the occasional dropping of agents by air, the Mission Speciale became a regular French aerial activity between 1915 and 1918.

Aerial saboteurs

As early as 1915, Italy landed an observer behind the Austrian lines. One of Italy's most successful spies was dropped by parachute in May 1918 from an SP4 biplane piloted by Major W. G. Barker with Captain Wedgwood Benn navigating. One of the most daring German air sabotage missions was by two officers, assisting the Turks in Palestine, landing behind the Allied lines to blow up water conduits supplying Imperial troops.

In World War II, after German Forces had overrun France and the Low Countries, there was a need in the United Kingdom for a special unit, equipped with short take-off and landing aircraft, to maintain liaison with clandestine anti-Nazi organisations in occupied territories. For this purpose No 419 Flight (later re-designated No 1419) was formed at North Weald, Essex in August

1940 equipped with Westland Lysanders. The unit was to operate under the Special Operations Executive (SOE), a branch of the British Secret Service, set up to initiate and co-ordinate subversive and sabotage activities in enemy territory. As resistance to occupation grew, so did the need increase for agents to be sent in to assist, others brought to safety, and for equipment to be supplied.

The Special Duty Flight expanded to form No 138 (Special Duty) Squadron at Newmarket, Suffolk, in April 1941. The work-load increased as the French partisan movement, the Maquis, expanded and contact was made with similar movements further afield in Czechoslovakia, Poland and Yugoslavia. A new Special Duties unit, No 161 Squadron, was raised at Newmarket early in 1942 from elements of the disbanded King's Flight. Both squadrons subsequently moved to Tempsford in Bedfordshire, a special station administered by Bomber Command but functionally controlled by the Air Ministry in co-operation with SOE.

Supply drops were made by Armstrong Whitworth Whitleys and Short Stirlings, and later supplemented by Handley Page Halifaxes, using special padded canisters attached to parachutes. Supplies dropped in this way included wireless transmitters, arms and ammunition, food and clothing, and specially-requested items. Lysanders initially made all the agent landing and collecting runs, a number of Mark IIIs being converted for this task. They

Subversive activities organised by indigenous resistance movements in occupied Europe were fostered by the supply of arms and equipment, often by parachute. Aircraft such as the Armstrong Whitworth Whitley, Handley Page Halifax (pictured) and Short Stirling were commonly used for this purpose

Above: aircrew of No 1585 (Polish) Flight, Royal Air Force which, operating from Italy, flew supplies to the beleaguered city of Warsaw in early August 1944. The aircraft is a Consolidated B-24.
Above left: parachutes stream from weapons containers in a daylight drop by the US Eighth Air Force over Warsaw. Despite large-scale air operations by the Allies, the city was eventually lost.
Left: Brigadier-General Frank Merrill, commander of Merrill's Marauders, superintends a supply drop to his men. Operating behind Japanese lines, they supported General Stilwell's advance towards Myitkyina, Burma in 1944

were fitted with a 680 litre (150 gallon) auxiliary fuel tank under the fuselage to increase their range. To compensate for the extra weight they were stripped of both armament and protective armour. The aircraft undersides were painted to give a sooty non-reflecting surface to searchlights, while their cockpit access ladder rungs were picked out in luminous paint to facilitate easy entry in the dark. They could carry two agents in reasonable comfort, three if necessary and four in a dire emergency.

While signal bonfires, or later the more sophisticated Eureka radio beacons, guided aircraft to a dropping zone, the technique for landing was more involved. The ground had to be surveyed by Resistance members who ap-appreciated the need for an even surface and no obstructions. On one early pick-up a Lysander rising from a field had struck high tension wires, a fact immediately obvious to the pilot by a blinding flash. Not until he had landed in England, however, did he also discover the wires wrapped around the undercarriage.

Expert navigation was needed to fly to the fields arranged by agents. Once in the vicinity, the field was marked by torches positioned in the shape of an 'L'–to denote the length and breadth of the landing strip. The Lysanders also brought in sabotage parties and special *matériel* such as plastic explosives.

Escalation of activities

Up until 1943, all the clandestine landings and pick-ups were made by Lysanders. However, with the need to remove fugitives from the Gestapo's sphere and the acceptance of approved personnel to join de Gaulle's Free French Forces, a larger aircraft was needed. Lockheed Hudsons were made available and in 1943 they brought 119 persons out of France–more than the Lysanders had flown out in three years. To assist in this work the United States Army Air Force assigned four Douglas C-47s to pick-up work. In all, SOE operations landed 293 passengers, 13 of them women, and brought out 554 men and 5 women for a loss of two agents and a pilot. Two Lysanders were lost on actual operations, but there was a higher toll of men and machines by accident during training.

A larger number of agents was sent in by parachute from aircraft of Nos 138 and 161 Squadron. As D-day drew near, additional help was given by the Stirlings and Armstrong Whitworth Albemarles of No 38 Group, responsible for lifting the airborne forces. At the same time massive help came from American aircraft. The US Office of Strategic Services (OSS) joined with SOE to set up a joint Special Force Headquarters in London.

The USAAF squadrons hitherto engaged on leaflet dropping and the occasional supply drop started large scale special duty work from the night of 4/5 January 1944, concentrating on the area north of the Loire. Four squadrons, the 856th to 859th, initially used on these 'Carpetbagger' sorties, were joined by the 788th and 850th Squadrons, all flying Consolidated B-24 Liberators. The aircraft were modified internally with seating for the 'Joes' and 'Janes' as the secret agents were known according to their sex. A hatch for paradropping was made in the fuselage floor and the ventral ball under-turret was removed to allow a clear exit. Rebecca homing devices were installed to respond to the Eureka transmitting beacons which, fitting into a standard kitbag, were among the initial items dropped to partisans.

The four-engined bomber types utilised for supply work normally carried twelve containers in their bomb-bays. Typical items carried by a single bomber would be 36 rifles, 27 Sten guns, 6 Bren guns, 5 pistols, 40 Mills bombs, plastic explosive with adhesive tape and over 20,000 rounds of 0·303in and 9mm ammunition. Over France alone, 53,725 containers were dropped by the RAF and 20,193 by the USAAF, plus over 10,000 packages by each Service. Over 316 million francs was delivered by air to pay for the subversive activities.

Activity intensified after the invasion; apart from the 16,000 Maquis already organised, the fighting taking place on French soil brought an additional 80,000 recruits. To deliver the large amount of arms required, main force bombers were called upon to assist: after a wait of several days for suitable weather, 180 Boeing B-17 Fortresses were loaded at night and took off at dawn on 25 June on Operation Zebra.

July 1944 proved a peak month for special operations. Not only did the special duty squadrons make 397 sorties, dropping 4,680 containers and 62 Joes, but another mass delivery, Operation Cadillac, was made. This involved nine bomber wings each of 36 B-17s with over 500 Republic P-47 and North American P-51 fighters escorting the bombers with their 500 tons of supplies for the Maquis. The final mass drop, Operation Buick, was made on 1 August. By this time much of France had been liberated and the USAAF was operating four C-47s for special work with agents in close touch with forward troops.

The OSS also used US Air Transport Services between July and September 1944, to drop 120 tons of supplies to the Norwegian resistance movement. Six black-painted Consolidated B-24 Liberators were used on these tasks and, although they were attacked on 15 of their 64 sorties, none were shot down. However, two Liberators with 12 crew members were lost due to crashes in bad weather.

Mediterranean operations

The need for special duty operations in the Mediterranean Theatre grew rapidly as the war progressed. Originally 'X' Flight, equipped with Liberators, flew supplies to partisans in the Balkans from Gambut in North Africa. This unit was raised on 14 March 1943 in status and strength to No 148 (Special Duty) Squadron for arms and supply-dropping in Albania, Greece and Yugoslavia. After moving to southern Italy in January 1944, the squadron re-equipped with Handley Page Halifaxes, plus a flight of Lysanders for landing and collecting agents and partisan representatives. Meanwhile No 624 Squadron had been formed and incorporated the Halifaxes of No 1575 Flight and moved to join No 148 Squadron at Blida, near Algiers. With the American 62nd Troop Carrier Group being co-opted on special operations and the Italian Co-Belligerent Air Force offering Savoia-Marchetti SM 82s and Cant 1007s for supply-dropping, these units were grouped into a new 334th (Special Duties) Wing.

Fleet Air Arm units in Malta became involved with clandestine operations in Vichy French North African territory, as their Fairey Swordfish biplanes had the necessary short take-off and landing capability. On one occasion Air Command Malta learned of two agents being taken by rail for execution. By wireless communication with agents, a message was smuggled to the condemned men to jump from the train as it slowed down at night to enter the coastal station of Enfidaville and run into the fields to seaward. There a Swordfish, having landed earlier in the evening, awaited.

In Poland, patriots who were hopeful that the seizing of control of Warsaw would hasten the Soviet approach from the east, rose up against their occupying power early in August 1944. While the Germans sought to crush the

fighter-bombers of the Desert Air Force, then in Italy, on urgent special drops. Overall, 6,500 tons of ordnance and equipment was dropped to Italian partisans alone.

Aircrew Rescue Unit No 1, formed in mid-1944, operated from the night of 2/3 August when its personnel were dropped some 80 km (50 miles) south-west of Belgrade, Yugoslavia to prepare a landing strip. The first collection was made precisely a week later when four C-47s landed to pick up Allied aircrew who had evaded capture. A total of 226 aircrew were to be picked up at this collecting strip, plus 42 refugees and partisan liaison personnel. Later, in September, during the hiatus caused by the German retreat and Balkan Governments torn between allegiance to the retreating Germans and the advancing Russians, the Allies seized the initiative and flew B-17 Fortresses to a Romanian airfield to collect Allied personnel. These were mainly American aircrew who had been shot down during raids on Ploesti.

In the Far East, SOE mounted special operations to Malaya (now Malasia) from bases in Ceylon (now Sri Lanka) using RAF Liberators for agent and supply dropping. The direct landing technique in this area was first tried on 31 October 1944 when Operation Oatmeal was mounted. An all-Malayan team of three was landed near an island off Trengganu. Unfortunately due to calm water the Consolidated Catalina could not take off; the aircraft's repeated water runs and revving engines evidently alerted the Japanese, as the agents were captured.

In North Burma the 101st Detachment OSS were using

Above: a pilot of No 148 Squadron RAF, a unit re-formed in March 1943 for operations in Albania, Greece and Yugoslavia. Above right: a special duty Westland Lysander flown by C Flight, No 357 Squadron from Drigh Road, Burma in mid-1945. Right: with a long-range tank and a side ladder, the Lysander Mark III (SCW) flew over 400 missions with Nos 138 and 161 Squadrons RAF between August 1941 and the end of 1944. Far right: French patriots at Châteaudun, Normandy collect arms previously dropped by parachute in the wake of the D-day landings

rising, the Russians slowed in their advance on the city and the plight of the isolated Poles became critical. Allied help was desperately needed and No 1585 (Polish) Flight, operating Halifaxes and Liberators dropped supplies from Italy on the night of 8/9 August 1944. Then, for three weeks, as weather and moonlight allowed, the 334th Wing aircraft flew the 2,800 km (1,750 mile) round trip. Flying in low at almost rooftop level to locate dropping zones identified by their position in relation to bridges or spires, the bombers dropped tons of supplies to the besieged partisans in the face of German anti-aircraft fire. Nos 31 (SAAF) and 178 (RAF) Squadrons were called in to help drop the containers of machine guns, rifles and British and German ammunition, the latter for captured weapons. However, the uprising failed and 13 aircraft were lost.

Provision for partisans
For special duty work in the Mediterranean area under OSS arrangements, the Twelfth Air Force detailed their 68th Reconnaissance Group as the occasion demanded. When an Allied Special Projects Operating Centre was set up in the Theatre, the 122nd Squadron (later re-designated the 885th) was assigned for full-time special duty, operating Liberators from Blida.

The Mediterranean Tactical Air Force was tasked in late November 1944 to supply Italian partisans with 550 tons of supplies monthly to encourage sabotage and harassing activities. At first, deteriorating weather limited these operations and when clearer conditions prevailed there were too few Dakotas available to meet all commitments. As a result, Mediterranean Strategic Air Forces carried out some of the long-range supply drops, helped by

the US Tenth Air Force bombers to organise a large body of Kachin rangers behind the enemy lines and over 1,000 agents and 10,000 tons of supplies were dropped. Further east in the South Pacific the Coastwatching Service, organised by Australia, was providing valuable intelligence from their remote positions in enemy controlled territory sustained at times by Catalinas and Liberators of the Royal Australian Air Force. Special operations came to a peak in August 1945 following the Japanese surrender, as agents made the initial contacts between the Allies and the Japanese in the field, pending formal surrender.

Strategic Bombing

On Christmas Eve 1914 a German seaplane dropped a high-explosive bomb in the garden of a house just outside Dover. Besides being the first aerial bomb to be dropped on the United Kingdom, it was almost certainly the first 'strategic' bomb in history, since it was not dropped in support of surface tactical operations but was aimed, in effect, directly at the 'will and ability of the British people to make war'. That it also fell on open ground, failed to explode, did little damage, injured no-one but frightened many was to anticipate the effectiveness of a great many strategic bombs dropped in successive wars over the next thirty years.

'Strategic bombing', ever since its conception in the years immediately preceding World War I, always had a single aim: to stop the enemy making war, not by the traditional method of defeating him in battle, but by striking directly at the source of his material and moral strength at home. There are two main ways of doing this. First, by destroying the enemy's material means of making war: his arms factories, his sources of supply and his means of transport. Second, by making life so frightening and horrible for his civilian population that it forces its rulers to give up the struggle. The first method calls for precision in selecting targets and in delivering attacks and is usually called 'precision bombing'. The second method, since it means the disruption of the entire way of life of the popula-

tion, demands destruction on a massive scale – what we would now call 'counter city bombing' which was once known as 'area bombing'. Although in theory the attacker has a choice, experience in war shows that this depends upon a number of factors, many of which are outside his control. The main ones are the nature of the enemy economy and society; the strength of his air and civil defences; the availability of intelligence both on the location of targets and the results of attacks. Above all, however, is the effectiveness in action of the bomber force itself. The story of strategic bombing was, until recent times, one of practice invariably falling short of the expectations of the theorists.

Smuts' prophecy

Before World War I, for example, the Germans evolved the Siegert Plan to bring the British to their knees by aerial bombing. Early in the war lack of aircraft range forced them to use airships – mostly Zeppelins. Although they possessed an impressive radius of action and could hover to drop their bombs, the Zeppelins were incapable of precision attacks. They tended to drop bombs at any lights they saw and what England lost in buildings it made up in new farm ponds. Casualties and damage were light and widely scattered. It took about ten bombs to kill one person and there was little effect on war production.

B-17 Fortress aircraft of 384th Bombardment Group, 8th Air Force, over their target, railway sidings in Dresden, in April 1945. Over 1,000 bombers of the 8th Air Force took part in this precision air attack on industrial centres in Germany and Czechoslovakia

Nor was there much effect on civilan morale.

Eventually heavy losses stopped the airship offensive and the Germans brought into use long-range heavy bombers–the Gothas and Giants. They attacked first by daylight, concentrating their attacks by flying in tight formation and dropping their bombs simultaneously. Their main target was London and civilian casualties were not only high and concentrated, but were also on the Government's doorstep. They also occurred in 1917, a low point for Allied fortunes in the war, and a worried War Cabinet took drastic action, the most important outcome of which was the creation of the independent Royal Air Force. As part of it, there were plans for a powerful strategic bomber force capable of carrying massive loads of bombs to Berlin : the Handley Page V/1500, for example, could carry 30 113kg (250lb) bombs. The War ended before the 'Independent Bomber Force', as it was called, went fully into action but it left behind it, in the person of Hugh Trenchard, a legacy of dedicated belief in the importance of strategic bombing. That belief is perhaps best summed up in the words of the report of the Smuts Committee which set up the Royal Air Force :

'... the day may not be far off when aerial operations with their devastation of enemy lands and destruction of industrial and populous centres on a vast scale may become the principal operations of war ...'

It was a remarkably prophetic passage and was to form the basis of the doctrine of strategic air power which was proclaimed between the wars by a variety of prophets in other lands, including Douhet in Italy and Mitchell in America. But Smuts' 'day' had certainly not arrived when World War II began in 1939.

Night area bombing

On the principle that 'the bomber will always get through', the British air staff in the late 1930s had worked on plans for a strategic air offensive involving precision air attacks in daylight against German industrial targets such as oil refineries and arms factories, marshalling yards and power stations. The effect of bombing upon civilian morale was also stressed but, largely on the experience of the Gotha raids on London and one or two 'lucky' hits, the Air Staff greatly exaggerated the casualties and damage likely to be caused by a given weight of bombs. Again, because the defensive fire-power of the formations of Gothas had been so effective against fighter attacks, they assumed that such tactics would succeed in the new conflict. They were soon proved wrong and before the war was six months old, Bomber Command was forced to resort to night bombing. With the primitive navigation equipment of the period, the Whitleys, Wellingtons and Hampdens could not hope to locate and bomb precision targets. The smallest targets they could locate with any degree of certainty were whole German towns–provided also that they were close to landmarks like rivers or coasts. Bomber Command in 1942, therefore, under Sir Arthur Harris, began its campaign of 'area bombing'. There was no alternative at the time–this was Britain's only way of striking directly at Germany.

Daylight precision attacks

In August 1942 the United States Eighth Air Force joined in the strategic offensive against Germany. Largely ignoring British experience, its leaders planned precision attacks at high altitude in daylight by large formations of Liberators and B-17 Fortresses, depending upon their own armament for defence against enemy fighters. During 1943 their attacks on a series of precision targets ranging from aircraft factories to ball-bearing works cost them unacceptable casualties.

Meanwhile RAF Bomber Command was steadily increasing its strength and effectiveness. New aircraft, especially Lancasters and Mosquitos, new navigation aids, notably Oboe and H2S airborne radar, coupled with new target marking techniques, improved the Command's accuracy, concentration and hitting power. The result was the catastrophic damage inflicted on Hamburg in July 1943, when nearly 50,000 people were killed. Even the German leadership was shaken and at the time, Speer, Hitler's Economics Minister, believed that six further attacks on the scale of Hamburg would have driven Germany out of the war. In the autumn of 1943, however, when Bomber Command began the great 'Battle of Berlin', it soon discovered that Berlin was a different prospect from Hamburg. Losses mounted and in the space of four months the Command lost over 1,000 aircraft. By the spring of 1944 Bomber Command, like the Eighth Air Force, was suffering casualty rates that could no longer be sustained.

The results of the Allied air offensive had also been disappointing. Not only had German war production been largely unaffected, it actually rose sharply between mid-1942 and mid-1944. There were many reasons for this, but the primary one was the effective dispersal of key industries supported by an efficient recovery and repair service. German civilian morale was severely affected in the devastated cities, but low morale had little effect upon behaviour. They did not rise in rebellion and they did not desert the towns. If strong patriotism were not enough to prevent either development, the Gestapo could offer alternatives less attractive than being bombed.

Decisive contribution to victory

Changes in the nature of the air offensive came early in 1944. First there was the diversion of effort on to the task of disrupting the French transportation system prior to the Normandy landings. Here the results achieved were so impressive that they pointed the way to more effective

The strategic bombing offensive mounted by RAF Bomber Command and the US 8th Air Force against German cities, particularly Hamburg and Berlin, resulted in thousands of civilian casualties

Above: Lancaster 'S for Sugar' of No 467 Squadron, RAF Bomber Command, after the completion of 100 operations. The Lancaster's normal bomb loas was some 14,000 lbs
Below: a comparison of the Allied and German strategic bombing offensives during World War II and the targets selected for attack

attacks upon the Reich itself. Then came the introduction of the long-range escort fighter–the P-51 Mustang–and the shortening of routes as a result of the Normandy bridgehead. But the most ominous development from the German point of view was the start of the Eighth Air Force's precision attacks on their synthetic oil industry. Production fell from 662,000 tons in May 1944 to 422,000 tons in June and to 80,000 tons in March 1945.

These attacks proved decisive and even if the Allied armies had not crossed the Rhine and the Oder, the Germans would have been forced to cease fighting by June 1945. Strategic bombing did not of itself win the war against Germany but its contribution to the victories of

the forces on the ground was, in the end, decisive. It will, however, always be a matter for conjecture whether or not such results might not have been achieved earlier by better target selection and more effective use of resources.

Dawn of the nuclear age
The strategic offensive against Japan was different in character and result. B-29 Superfortresses did not begin their assault until November 1944 and had not reached full momentum until March 1945. By this stage in the war Japan was on the very brink of defeat both militarily and economically. Her navy had been sunk and what remained of her merchant fleet was incapable of getting through the ever-tightening Allied blockade. War production had virtually ceased and food was getting short. Nonetheless, there seemed little possibility of the Japanese accepting the Allied demand for unconditional surrender unless their home islands were invaded and occupied. A plan was therefore made for a full-scale invasion in November 1945. After the experience of the landings on Iwo Jima and Okinawa, no-one on the Allied side was in any doubt that Japanese resistance would be suicidally fanatical. The cost in lives–Allied and Japanese–would be horrifying. The only possible alternative was to bomb the Japanese into surrender. Precision attacks were pointless–industry was already at a standstill. The area bombing of as many Japanese cities as possible was called for.

Japan was a different prospect for strategic bombing than Germany. It was much more urbanised and its cities were more vulnerable to fire. It also lacked the sophisticated air and civil defences built up by the Germans over the years. Furthermore, the Japanese civilian population was prone to panic and to evacuate bombed cities, spreading the message of despair throughout the islands. The American attack was heavy and concentrated. Sixty-six Japanese cities were attacked, all but six in the last three months of the war. Then came the two atomic bombs– at that time the ultimate in area bombing.

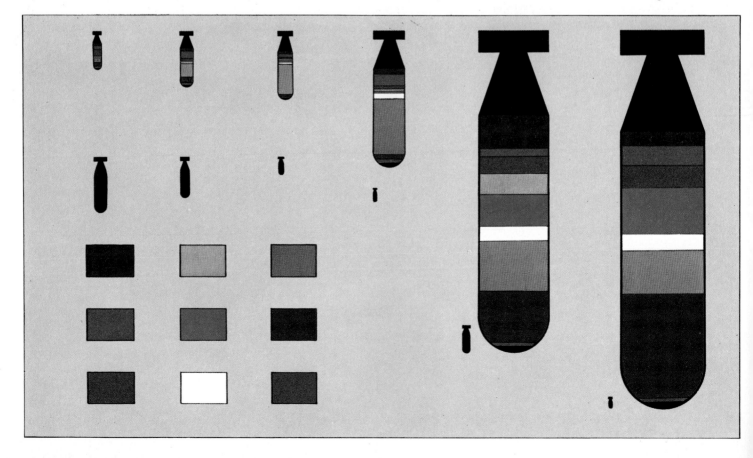

Boeing B-17 Flying Fortresses of the 91st Bomb Group, Eighth US Air Force, release their bombs 5,200m (17,000ft) over Avord, France, on 5 February 1944. The Eighth's daylight strategic bombing campaign contributed substantially to Germany's defeat. The campaign demonstrated that high-level precision bombing directed against selected strategic targets was highly effective in disrupting the enemy's war economy. However, the campaign again showed that air superiority over enemy territory was essential to the success of a strategic bombing campaign. The US Eighth Air Force's badge is illustrated at the left

Training

Today's military pilot or, indeed, any aircrew member will arrive at his operational squadron after many hours of instruction in the air, backed by months of ground school and background study to prepare him for the demands of the complex aircraft which equip the world's more advanced air arms. This contrasts with the situation that existed in the early days of World War I when men arrived in France or Belgium with little more than the handful of hours required to prove their general competence in handling an aeroplane. Tactics were largely learned in the heat of battle, which resulted in a high rate of attrition in both pilots and aircraft.

Although the Royal Flying Corps had been formed on 13 April 1912 with separate Military and Naval Wings—the latter becoming the Royal Naval Air Service on 1 July 1914–practical military flying in the United Kingdom can be said to have commenced with the formation of the Air Battalion, Royal Engineers on 1 April 1911. No 2 (Aeroplane) Company at Salisbury Plain was the first British military unit with heavier-than-air equipment. The pilots were recruited from officers who had learned to fly at their own expense at the embryonic civil schools and who subsequently received part repayment of their tuition fees from the government.

Central Flying School

The practice of recruiting holders of aviators' certificates issued by the Royal Aero Club continued well past the formation of the Central Flying School at Upavon, Wiltshire, although there were also novice pupils on the first course which commenced on 17 August 1912. Among the members of that course were Captain Hugh Trenchard, later to become the first Marshal of the Royal Air Force,

and Lieutenant Robert Smith-Barry, who was to found the School of Special Flying at Gosport.

Initial equipment at the School had included Maurice and Henry Farman designs, BE2s and Avro 500s; the latter type was the forerunner of the Avro 504, which was to remain in service with the Royal Air Force until as late as 1940. The characteristics of these types were such that trainees had variously to cope with the instability of aircraft with wing-warping for lateral control, the absence of a throttle–which necessitated the use of the ignition switch to 'blip' the engine–and the absence of dual controls for pilot and instructor.

The outbreak of World War I on 4 August 1914 led to the establishment of reserve squadrons, whose function was to train *ab initio* pilots before passing them on to either the CFS or an operational squadron for advanced training. As 1915 drew to a close, 18 reserve squadrons and eight front-line squadrons were operating flying training programmes. At this juncture the need for the establishment of specialised combat training schools became evident and the War Office set up a machine gun school (later designated No 1 School of Aerial Gunnery) at Hythe, in September 1915 and a school of wireless was established at Brooklands.

Central Flying School pilots were posted overseas with no more than 50 hours of flying time; they were, however, better trained than those of the less organised and less well-equipped flying training formations, at which the instructors were pilots 'resting' after tours at the front. They had not been trained to instruct, however, and many displayed little enthusiasm for the task. The results were reflected in the standard of pilots reaching front-line squadrons and Robert Smith-Barry, by then commanding

Above: the McDonnell Douglas TA-4J Skyhawk exemplifies the modern practice of adapting single-seat warplanes to accommodate a trainee pilot at the expense of fuel and armament.
Below right: pictured in Royal Naval service, the de Havilland Tiger Moth proved itself to be one of the world's most famous training aircraft. Nearly 9,000 examples of the type were built worldwide, many ending their lives with civilian flying schools

officer of No 60 Squadron, returned to England in 1916 to command No 1 Reserve Squadron at Gosport; here he was able to put to the test a new system of flying training evolved in the light of front-line experience in France.

His intention was to standardise training practice and raise the status of the instructor. Smith-Barry also wanted to reverse the practice of teaching pupils to avoid 'dangerous' manoeuvres such as spinning and aerobatics and to encourage them to understand the aerodynamic principles involved so that they could extricate themselves from difficult situations. The instructor was to fly in the front seat rather than the rear and pupils were to be taught from the outset on the Avro 504J, which was more representative of contemporary combat aircraft than the Farman Longhorns and Shorthorns then widely used for primary training. The aircraft were also to be equipped with the 'Gosport tube' inter-cockpit communication system; this consisted of earpieces for the pupil connected by a rubber tube to a mouthpiece for the instructor, allowing manoeuvres to be described as they were being demonstrated. Smith-Barry's methods were so successful that they were adopted throughout the service which was to become the Royal Air Force on 1 April 1918 and Gosport became an instructor's school, known as the School of Special Flying.

Inter-war innovations

After the Armistice the RAF was drastically reduced in strength, from 263 squadrons to 33, and all but a fraction of its 290,000 officers and men and 22,000 aircraft were demobilised. Flying training was drastically curtailed, but the Central Flying School at Upavon survived, assuming from the School of Special Flying the role of instructor training for which the CFS is still renowned today.

Below: the Valmet Vilma radial-engined biplane trainer was designed and built in Finland. While pictured in the markings of the Finnish air force, this example has been preserved in Britain.
Below left: selected in 1932 to succeed the venerable Avro 504 in the RAF's flying training schools, the Avro Tutor continued to serve until the outbreak of World War II

Technical advances in aircraft design during the inter-war period led to improved performance and the ability to carry greater offensive loads so that training programmes became more complex. Prolonged flying in cloud, however, was still an impractical art and instrument flight was not introduced to the RAF syllabus until 1930.

Flight Lieutenant W. E. P. Johnson of CFS had undertaken a course at the civil flying school operated by Farman at Toussus-le-Noble, near Versailles. This involved ten hours blind-flying in a Farman F.71 two-seat biplane with a metal hood over the pupil's cockpit, followed by a further hour in a twin-engined Goliath. Johnson, who completed his course in six days between 13 and 19 May 1930, was faced with a gyro turn indicator, a fore-and-aft spirit level, an airspeed indicator and a compass, which he had

to trust in preference to his senses. Back at Wittering, Northants–a new airfield to which CFS had moved in October 1926–Johnson compiled his report so effectively that, in July 1930, a decision was taken to run experimental instrument courses at CFS. The first of these commenced on 20 October 1930, using Avro 504N biplanes fitted with similar instrumentation to the Farman F.71 which Johnson had flown in France; folding canvas hoods designed and manufactured at Wittering covered the rear cockpits. The value of these courses, in terms of the military value of all-weather operations and a decrease in the RAF accident rate, was such that E Flight CFS was formed on 1 September 1931, specifically to teach instrument flying to both staff instructors and operational pilots; the subject was later included in the training programme at the elementary flying training schools.

The Avro 504N was later replaced by the Avro Tutor and the Hawker Tomtit; this pattern of flying training on biplanes, complemented by advanced work on Bristol Bulldog or Hawker Hart trainers was to remain RAF practice until 1937 when the first twin-engined monoplane advanced trainer, the Airspeed Oxford, was introduced. The Oxford entered service with CFS in November 1937 and, in its Mark I version, was used for gunnery training, having an Armstrong Whitworth dorsal turret which was deleted from the Mark II intended solely as a pilot training variant.

Although military flying had been banned in Germany following the nation's defeat in 1918, civilian training had continued on a restricted basis and provided a means for the clandestine training of a nucleus of pilots and observers for a revived air arm. Perhaps the most noteworthy of these

Deutsche Verkehrsfliegerschule bases were those at Berlin-Staaken, with its facilities for instrument flying and navigation training and at Munich-Schleissheim which, in the latter half of the 1920s, began to specialise in producing prospective fighter pilots.

Weapons training in Germany was out of the question but the German Government was able to persuade the Russians to permit the establishment of a suitable school in Soviet territory at Lipezk, near Moscow. Fifty Fokker D-XIII single-seat fighters, apparently diverted from a Spanish order, arrived in May 1925 and the school commenced operations the following month. Camera guns were employed in aerial combat training, probably representing the earliest large-scale use of this aid to gunnery proficiency. Heinkel HD 17s and HD 21s and Junkers K-47s were later added for observer training, which commenced in 1926. The school was closed in October 1933, less than two years before the existence of the Luftwaffe was revealed in March 1935.

Commonwealth Training Plan

Less than five years later Europe was at war again. To meet the urgent need for aircrew, Britain, Australia, New Zealand and Canada set up the British Commonwealth Air Training Plan after a meeting in Ottawa on 17 December 1939. Canada assumed prime responsibility for establishing facilities capable of producing monthly totals of 520 pilots to elementary standard and 544 to operational standard, together with 340 observers and 580 wireless operator/air gunners. With the advent of the large-crewed, four-engined heavy bombers the programme was enlarged to include bomb-aimers, flight engineers and navigators. Some idea of the size of the task can be gained from the fact that by the time the plan was terminated on 31 March 1945, a total of 131,552 aircrew members had been trained. This figure included 49,707 pilots who passed through 29 Elementary Flying Training Schools and a number of Service Flying Training Schools.

The Canadian civilian flying clubs were called upon to

Above left: a Fairchild PT-19 primary trainer is depicted in service with the Brazilian air force in a painting by Michael Turner. It was widely used by the USAAF and a version with an enclosed cockpit served in Canada.
Left and below: the Fleet Finch two-seat trainer served with the Royal Canadian Air Force in the 1930s

operate and manage the EFTS establishments, while the commercial and bush operators became involved in observer training. A total of 149 new airfields was built and 73 existing facilities enlarged and improved, all under the direction of the Department of Transport with the support of the provincial governments which made available their highway engineering resources. The first schools opened on schedule on 29 April 1940 and the first pilots graduated from No 1 SFTS, Camp Borden, on 30 September. The first trained observers left Trenton on 24 October and the first gunners from No 1 Bombing and Gunnery School at Jarvis on 28 October. They were the advance guard of 72,734 Canadians, 42,110 Britons, 9,706 Australians and 7,002 New Zealanders who were then to pass through Operational Training Units or direct to squadrons, both in their native lands or Britain.

Training of foreign aircrew recommenced in 1950; this time the pupils were from Canada's NATO partners in Europe and, with the revival of the Luftwaffe, German pilots began to arrive in mid-1957. The Canadian system continues to attract foreign students; the Royal Netherland Air Force, for example, has followed the basic Canadian Armed Forces programme since 1972.

Eight to ten hours or primary grading are flown in the single-engined Beech F33C of the Rijksluchtvaartschool at Eelde in Holland before pupils are transferred to No 3 FTS at Portage La Prairie, Manitoba. Here they fly an initial eight-week, 30 flying hour course in the Beech

P/O PRUNE SAYS - "A GOOD LANDING IS ONE YOU CAN WALK AWAY FROM"

Above left: an RAF pupil pilot and his instructor board a BAC Jet Provost T Mk 5A. The trainer serves alongside the earlier, unpressurised Jet Provost T Mk 3A with the RAF College at Cranwell, Nos 1, 3, and 6 FTS and the Central Flying School. Left: the misadventures of Pilot Officer Percy Prune drove home many valuable lessons to wartime aircrew in the RAF

Above: first flown in France in 1952, the Potez Magister twin-jet trainer has since seen service with the air arms of over a dozen countries. A licence-built Finnish example is pictured here.

Left: as with many training aircraft of the 1970s, the Hawker Siddeley Hawk performs a dual role as a weapons trainer. The aircraft illustrated from the RAF's Tactical Weapons Unit carries a Matra rocket launcher under the port wing, while the muzzle of a belly-mounted Aden cannon is visible

also initially trained in Canada, selection taking place at the completion of the CT-114 Tutor phase at Moose Jaw. They then return to Holland to fly a 100-hour course in the Aérospatiale Alouette IIIs of No 300 Squadron at Deelen.

A system has been in operation since 1977 under which 13 weeks are spent at Eelde with the Rijksluchtvaartschool. This spell is followed by 30 weeks at the NATO helicopter school at Fort Rucker, Alabama, flying the Hughes TH-55A and Bell UH-1 and a final 38 weeks at Deelen with the training element of No 300 Squadron.

The first course of Dutch fixed-wing pilots to be trained in the United States commenced in 1978 with an initial ten weeks at Eelde before leaving for Sheppard Air Force Base, Texas. During a 13-month stay students will fly the Cessna T-37 and Northrop T-38 on an all-jet course.

This Dutch programme follows the basic pattern of the Luftwaffe's scheme which is flown with similar aircraft at Williams AFB. The Germans own the T-37s and T-38s of 3525 Primary Training Wing, despite the fact that they bear USAF serials and markings. The two types are used

Musketeer, designated CT-134 in Canadian service. They then move on to No 2 FTS at Moose Jaw, Saskatchewan for 32 weeks, during which period they will fly some 200 hours in the Canadair CT-114 Tutor jet trainer. A further 100 hours of advanced training are flown with No 1 FTS at Cold Lake, using the Canadair CF-5B and culminating in the award of pilot's wings.

Although Canada's vast expanses of land and magnificent facilities are ideal for training, pilots returning to Europe must accustom themselves to local conditions, particularly to the problems of more restricted airspace. Operational conversion takes place at the Royal Netherlands Air Force base at Twenthe, utilising the NF-5 and two-seat NF-5B aircraft of No 313 Squadron, during a five-month period which precedes a posting to the NF-5 operational squadrons. Royal Netherlands Air Force pilots with in excess of 500 jet hours are eligible for conversion to the Lockheed F-104G Starfighter. If destined for the interceptor role, a pilot is posted to the Training and Conversion Unit All-Weather, at Leeuwarden. Equipment comprises the two-seat TF-104Gs of No 322 and 323 Squadrons which together form the Dutch all-weather fighter wing. Alternatively, he goes to the Conversion Unit at Volkel, also flying the TF-104G. Helicopter pilots are

for the basic and advanced training phases, of 132 hours and 130 hours respectively. At the end of this period, pilots for the Fiat G 91 squadrons return to Germany for 120 hours of operational conversion and acclimatisation with Waffenschule 50 at Fürstenfeldbruck. This unit will be the first to receive the Alpha Jet.

Prospective Starfighter pilots follow the 3525 PTW course by 58 hours in the TF-104G and 67 hours in the single-seat F-104G. Like the Primary Training Wing's equipment, the Starfighters were funded by Germany but operate in USAF markings. Following graduation, up to 40 hours are flown at the European Starfighter operational conversion unit, Waffenschule 10 based at Jever.

All-through training

Opinions are divided on the desirability of 'all-through' jet training, which was introduced by the RAF in 1955 when two courses of pupils were processed through No 2 FTS Hullavington, Wiltshire. One course utilised the standard Hunting (piston) Provost/de Havilland Vampire sequence, the other using the ten Jet Provost T Mark 1 jet trainers which had been acquired for comparative evaluation. The first course using the production Jet Provost T Mark 3 for *ab initio* training was to commence

Above: the TS-11 Iskra (Spark) has been Poland's standard basic jet trainer since its introduction to service in 1964. Seating trainee pilot and instructor in tandem, the aircraft has provision for underwing loads of light bombs or rockets to add to its versatility. Power plant is an OKL SO-1 turbojet exhausting under the tail

almost four years later on 7 October 1959.

Since then, there have been periods when there has been a piston content in the basic phase of the RAF scheme. The graduate entrants of the late 1970s will have flown approximately 85 hours in the University Air Squadrons' Scottish Aviation Bulldog T Mark 1 piston-engined trainers before arriving at the RAF College, Cranwell for 75 hours in the Jet Provost T Mark 3A and a further 60 hours of advanced work in the pressurised and more powerful T Mark 5A. Since 1974, however, direct entry students have been Jet Provost-trained from scratch, currently at No 1 FTS Linton-on-Ouse. Royal Navy pilots destined for helicopters fly the 75-hour Bulldog course with the Royal Navy Elementary Flying Training Squadron at No 3 FTS at Leeming in Yorkshire before receiving helicopter conversion training at RNAS Culdrose, Cornwall.

The most recent and, perhaps, the most interesting development in the training sphere has been the emphasis now being placed on air combat manoeuvring, arising primarily from experience in Vietnam. The US Navy Fighter Weapons School at NAS Miramar operates both the Northrop T-38 and F-5E to provide fighter crews experienced in all aspects of tactics, combat techniques and new weapons.

The US Air Force has its Aggressor Squadron which, as 527th TFTAS, bases more than a dozen Northrop F-5Es at RAF Alconbury, Cambridgeshire, to provide dogfighting experience for USAFE units and for RAF air defence squadrons. The colour schemes are varied, representing those observed on aircraft used by Warsaw Pact air arms, and the tactics on those of potential enemies. In the United States the Aggressors are based at Nellis AFB, Nevada.

Left: powered by a British Bristol Siddeley Viper turbojet, the Soko G2-A Galeb (Gull) first flew in 1961, with deliveries to the Yugoslav air force commencing two years later. A single-seat ground-attack derivative, the Jastreb (Hawk), was also built in quantity.
Below: the Aero L-39 Albatross is destined to become the Communist Bloc's standard trainer in the 1980s. The type is capable of operation from rough, unpaved strips and utilises a Czech-built Walter Titan turbojet

Transport

That aviation was more than 20 years old before serious attempts were made to exploit the aeroplane as a transport vehicle is clear evidence of mankind's preoccupation with the weapons of war at the time when the heavier-than-air machine had become relatively reliable. Indeed it was not until the last year of World War I that limited use was made of military aircraft to carry men and *matériel* from place to place other than on an *ad hoc* basis.

Bomber-transports

The Armistice of 1918 found the Royal Air Force on the threshold of a new age of the large bomber-transport with aircraft such as the Handley Page 0/400 and V/1500 and Vickers Vimy bombers. It was a development of the latter, the Vickers Vernon, which was the first aircraft specifically designed for troop-carrying to enter service. The type equipped No 45 Squadron RAF at Hinaidi in 1922 and No 70 Squadron soon after. These twin-engined biplanes gave sterling service in the troubled Middle East, and among their first duties was that of evacuating British soldiers to hospital from a remote area of Iraq when stricken by an outbreak of disease.

The Vernon, with accommodation for three crew members and 11 passengers, was replaced by the Vickers Victoria in 1926 which could carry 22 troops and remained in service until 1935 – again almost exclusively in India and the Middle East. It was the eight Victorias of No 70 Squadron which participated in the first-ever major airlift when, following the riots in Kabul, Afghanistan, no fewer than 586 civilians and over 10,880 kg (24,000 lb) of baggage were evacuated between 12 December 1928 and 25 February 1929. In addition King Inyatullah, his family and the British Minister, Sir Francis Humphreys were removed to safety. In 1932, when trouble erupted in Cyprus, Victorias of No 216 Squadron were employed to rush troops to the island from Egypt.

Humble though these origins of military air transport were, they were the manifestations of Britain's imperial responsibilities, having undertaken the role of peace-keeper in the Middle East and elsewhere after World War I. Up to this point she was virtually alone in the world in having a fleet of military transport aircraft capable of moving troops – albeit in relatively small numbers – from one trouble spot to another.

America on the other hand had little need for such aircraft and lagged years behind, preferring in the main to acquire small numbers of semi-experimental transports from Fokker and Ford. Russia pursued a policy, generated for propaganda purposes, which embraced the delivery of parachutists from large bomber-transports, although this

German paratroops board a Junkers Ju 52/3m, the main German transport type throughout World War II. First flown in April 1932, the Ju 52/3m served in every theatre of war in which the Luftwaffe was engaged. Production of the type continued until mid-1944, when an estimated 4,800 had been manufactured

tactic was never adequately backed by a competent military organisation, nor was it ever fully exploited in time of war.

Tante Ju

While the RAF continued along the road of established bomber-transports with such aircraft as the Bristol Bombay and Handley Page Harrow, designed in the mid-1930s, another development was taking place in Germany. As world commercial airlines struggled through the economic depression of 1929–32, the German state-supported Lufthansa had established an enviable reputation in Europe and serviced extensive routes both at home and abroad. With the clandestine decision to create a new military air force, Germany exploited Lufthansa to provide training and experience to potential aircrews of the bombers and transports of the future. Thus, when civil war broke out in Spain in 1936 and Hitler agreed to send men and aircraft to support General Franco, a ready-made bomber-transport force already existed. Twenty Junkers Ju 52/3m transports were quickly employed to bring 10,000 Moorish troops to Spain from Morocco; the Junkers then reverted to their bombing role.

Apart from its commercial applications, which spanned more than 20 years, the three-engined Junkers Ju 52/3m was, despite its rather crude, utilitarian appearance, one of the truly classic military transport aircraft of all time. During World War II it was employed by numerous *kampfgeschwader* and *kampfgruppen zur besonderen verwendung* (literally 'bomber units available for special operations') wherever troops and supplies were required to be moved by air. Campaigns in Poland, Norway, Denmark, Holland, Belgium, France, the Balkans, Crete, North Africa, Sicily and Italy all made heavy demands on

'Tante Ju', not to mention the prolonged, difficult requirements of the Russian Front. There, major airlifts and evacuations at Demyansk between February and May 1942, and at Stalingrad during the winter of 1942–43, were masterpieces of improvisation. In the former operation the Luftwaffe transport aircraft lifted 24,000 tons of supplies, delivered 15,000 troops into the encircled pocket and evacuated 20,000 wounded, all in 90 days.

Improvised transports

In spite of the early lead provided by the RAF between the wars, World War II showed that since the mid-1930s progress in military transport aircraft had been allowed to wither in Britain and the problem of moving troops by air had been largely ignored. Apart from small numbers of impressed commercial aircraft which were issued to transport squadrons, the main burden fell upon purpose-built Bristol Bombays which, having replaced the Vickers Valentia–a development of the Victoria–served with Nos 117, 216 and 267 Squadrons. Bombays were used to assist in evacuating British troops and supplies at the end of the disastrous Greek adventure in 1941.

If ever there was a need for an effective air transport organisation, it was in support of the Air Component and Advanced Air Striking Force in France during the first eight months of the war; such an organisation was sadly lacking. Few suitable transports existed and squadrons were moved and supplied by the most heterogeneous collection of aircraft ever assembled. It was not long before some of Imperial Airways' most modern airliners and flying boats were being employed to make up for the deficiency which existed in the armed forces.

As Britain moved towards the offensive in 1941 the limited demands for a paratroop transport were met by

The Douglas C-133 (above) could carry intercontinental missiles in its capacious hold. The Lockheed Hercules (below right) has flown with the air arms of over 40 nations, while the Antonov An-12 (bottom right) has served the Soviet Air Force since 1959. The world's first commercial jet transport, the de Havilland Comet (below left) also saw service with the Royal Air Force, as did the Short Belfast strategic freighter (bottom left)

small numbers of converted Armstrong Whitworth Whitley bombers. The first such action in which they were employed was the unsuccessful attack on the viaduct at Tragino in Italy on 10 February 1941 when Whitleys of Nos 51 and 78 Squadrons carried paratroops from Malta.

The ubiquitous Dakota

If Britain was lax in failing to maintain her early lead, America certainly repaired her shortcomings as events in Europe began to dominate world politics in the late 1930s. In April 1934 the Douglas DC-2 had flown; an example of this design, the XC-32, was the first aircraft procured by the US Army with its 1936 appropriations. Other variations, designated the C-32, C-33 and YC-34, followed. In 1939, they were joined by the first C-39, a military part-derivative of the DC-3, of which 35 were built. These were followed in turn by single examples of the C-41, C-41A and C-42.

In 1940 the first true military versions of the DC-3, known in the US Army Air Corps as the C-47 Skytrain, were ordered; no fewer than 10,123 production examples were built during the next six years. It entered service in 1941 and the following year was among the first American aircraft to be delivered by air to Britain across the Atlantic. The Dakota, as it was to become known in the RAF, could carry 27 troops or 4,540 kg (10,000 lb) of cargo.

To begin with, the C-47 entered service in 1942 in South-East Asia, ferrying war supplies to China over the Himilayas, which in due course resulted in more powerful engines being installed. The year 1942 also saw the formation of the US Troop Carrier Command, created to airlift American troops between the various war theatres. C-47s represented by far the greater proportion of troop carriers and glider tugs in the Allies' first major airborne invasion when, on 10 July 1943, 4,381 paratroops were dropped over Sicily. In the Far East they led the airborne invasion of Burma on 5 March 1944. In the massive Allied landings in Normandy of 6 June 1944 over 1,000 C-47s and Dakotas carried more than 60,000 men into action–and supported them–in the first 50 hours of the operation.

After the war many C-47s were sold to commercial operators or scrapped, but hundreds of others were retained by the USAF, and when the Military Air Transport Service (MATS) came into being on 1 June 1948, 239 C-47s were transferred to its inventory. Within eight weeks 105 of these were participating in the Berlin Airlift. The C-47 was also used in large numbers with Combat Cargo Command during the Korean War, as well as in a support capacity for Tactical and Strategic Air Commands. It was a measure of the particular aptitude of the C-47 as a military 'pack horse' that for 20 years no other aircraft matched it in rugged reliability, and not until the advent of the Lockheed Hercules in 1961 was another single military transport design widely adopted in the West.

Returning once more to the RAF during World War II, the Dakota certainly filled a wide gap in its military inventory, although deliveries were slow to accelerate. In all, nearly 1,900 Dakotas were supplied to British forces under Lease-Lend agreements, equipping 33 squadrons of the RAF. Some idea of the lack of an equivalent British design can be judged by the fact that when, in 1942, the Dakota joined No 31 Squadron in India, it replaced the Vickers Valentia biplane.

Converted bombers

As the strategic pattern of World War II became clear to the Allied war leaders in 1942, the need to produce larger military transport aircraft was recognised, a requirement partly satisfied by the adaptation of heavy bomber aircraft for troop-carrying and assault glider-towing duties. After the limited use of Whitleys already mentioned, the Halifax was developed for glider-towing and, in Operation Freshman, two Horsa gliders carrying commandos were towed to Norway on 19/20 November 1942 for an attack on a German heavy water plant. Halifaxes were also prominent in the invasions of Sicily and Normandy, the Arnhem operations and the Rhine Crossing. They also equipped the two Special Service Squadrons which dropped agents into enemy-occupied Europe. Later the Halifax came to be used as a transport in its own right, serving with twelve RAF transport squadrons until after the war. The Halifax was the only aircraft to tow the tank-carrying Hamilcar assault glider, the largest glider used by the Allies in the war. While the Halifax could carry up to 16 fully-armed paratroops, the Stirling, when adapted for use with the British airborne forces, could carry 20 paratroops or 40 armed soldiers.

The Avro Lancaster itself did not see formal service as a military transport during World War II, although immediately after VE-day large numbers of ex-POWs and other servicemen were brought out of Europe back home to Britain in the aircraft of Bomber Command. That is not to say that the Lancaster did not attract design attention as the basis of a transport aircraft. As early as 1942 the design started on what was to become the Avro York which utilised the wings and engines of the Lancaster, with a wholly new 'passenger fuselage' capable of accommodating 24 passengers. Such was the production priority afforded elsewhere that the York did not fully equip an RAF squadron, No 511, until 1945. There is no doubt that had the war with Japan been prolonged, the York would have seen widespread service in that theatre. As it was, its greatest contribution was in the Berlin Airlift, in which seven York squadrons took part.

Increasing airlift capabilities

The astronomical wartime expenditure on aircraft development had accelerated the development of aircraft and aero-engines of all types, not least in the design of transport aircraft. Britain persevered for many months with the wartime adaptations, but America, motivated by fear of unemployment, maintained a massive military aircraft programme and continued with the all-out development of transport aeroplanes. For many years Troop Carrier Command and Military Air Transport Service (MATS) supported large fleets of Curtiss C-46, Douglas C-54, Fairchild C-82 and Boeing C-97 aircraft. In the Korean

War, MATS mounted the Pacific Airlift to carry large numbers of American servicemen between the United States and Japan, largely with its own C-54s, which were joined by similar aircraft of Tactical Air Command.

The large Douglas C-124 Globemaster, which entered USAF service in 1950, was capable of carrying 30 tons of cargo or 200 passengers. Although it was periodically the subject of much-publicised air disasters – owing principally to the large number of casualties involved – the C-124 gave many years' service with squadrons of TAC, SAC, MATS, Air Materiel Command and the Far Eastern Air Force. In 1961 they joined the USAF Reserve.

In the RAF, Handley Page Hastings transports, followed by Bristol Britannias, provided the backbone of RAF Transport Command, the former being widely used with the airborne forces as a paratroop carrier. The post-war French air force staged a slow recovery and among its large military transports were the twin-deck Breguet Deux-Ponts which, ordered in 1956, could carry 146 fully-armed troops on two decks and the Nord Noratlas – a sturdy aircraft reminiscent of the American C-82. The Soviet air force developed such transports as the Antonov An-4 'Camp' during the 1950s, and this aircraft came to be widely used by nations of the Communist bloc.

Labours of Hercules

Military transport fleets today are mighty, sophisticated organisations employing high-cost developments of the finest airliners in service, although the workhorses remain relatively utilitarian. In the West the Lockheed C-130 Hercules four-turboprop aircraft forms the backbone of countless air forces, deliveries from the factory in Georgia extending over nearly 15 years.

Inevitably the introduction into commercial service of the turbojet-powered airliner (the Comet and Boeing 707) in 1957 was accompanied by parallel development for military use. RAF Transport Command deservedly acquired a new-found prestige with its adoption of the BAC Super VC 10 with which it operated a trooping service to the Far East with a regularity and reliability which was to become the envy of many a commercial airline. The American inventory, backing the worldwide responsibilities of US forces, is impressive, spearheaded by the enormous Lockheed C-5A Galaxy, the world's largest aeroplane. Intended primarily as a cargo transport, the Galaxy can carry such loads as two M-60 tanks.

There are also a large number of medium and light transport aircraft which complement a transport inventory and, in fact, perform the majority of everyday movements of military stores and personnel. Likewise only passing mention may be made of the transport and assault helicopters which today deliver line troops into combat in much the same way that the troop-carrying glider was used in World War II. However, aeroplanes like the Galaxy epitomise the importance placed by the world's major powers on the strategic flexibility of their forces, a flexibility foreshadowed by Britain's faltering efforts between the wars. What then occupied a squadron of transports for a month can now be accomplished by a single Galaxy in one day.

Libya 1911-12

The influence of World War I on the use of aeroplanes for military purposes has left a general impression that aerial warfare was originated during those fateful years. In fact, the true pioneers of air warfare in aeroplanes were a handful of courageous Italian airmen who served during the little-known Italo-Turkish war in Libya in 1911–12, almost three years before the commencement of the European conflict.

In August 1911 the Italian Army manoeuvres had shown a potential for aircraft in general reconnaissance roles, and on 25 September came an order to mobilise the Italian Special Army Corps and, more significantly,

an Air Flotilla. On that date the Flotilla comprised a total of nine aeroplanes–two Blériot XI monoplanes, two Henry Farman biplanes, three Nieuport monoplanes, and two Etrich Taubes–manned by five first-line pilots, six reserve pilots and 30 airmen for all forms of technical maintenance. All nine machines were immediately dismantled, crated and sent by sea to Libya, arriving in the Bay of Tripoli on 15 October. With minimum facilities available, the crated aircraft were put ashore and transported to a suitable flying ground nearby, where assembly commenced almost immediately. The first aeroplane was completed by 21 October.

A Blériot XI of the Italian Air Flotilla at Tobruk during the Italo-Turkish war in Libya. A reconnaissance flight by Capt Piazza, piloting a Blériot XI, on 23 October 1911 was the first use of an aeroplane in war

First wartime flight

On the morning of 23 October, Captain Carlos Piazza, commander of the Air Flotilla, took off at 0619 hours in his Blériot for an urgently-requested reconnaissance of an advancing body of Turkish and Arab troops and eventually landed back at base at 0720 hours. This was the first-ever war flight in an aeroplane. Shortly after Piazza left, his second-in-command, Captain Riccardo Moizo, piloting a Nieuport, also took off but returned after 40 minutes with little to report. Both men were airborne again on the following day, seeking the location of enemy troops and, in Moizo's case, being successful.

Next day, 25 October, Moizo was again in the air and sighted a large Arab encampment in the Ain Zara region. As he circled his objective, Moizo was greeted with a barrage of rifle fire and three bullets pierced his Nieuport's wings. Though these caused no serious damage, it was the first occasion on which an aeroplane had experienced hostile ground fire. Within the following three days two more aircraft had become available. These—an Etrich Taube, piloted by Second Lieutenant Giulio Gavotti, and a Henry Farman, by Lieutenant Ugo de Rossi—soon joined their seniors on scouting patrols over enemy camps and emplacements.

The Flotilla commander, Captain Piazza, quickly perceived further roles for his aircraft and, after several unsuccessful attempts, finally achieved a measure of air-to-ground co-operation with the local Italian artillery commander; Piazza dropped messages of correction or confirmation (in small tins) after observing the actual results of artillery fire. This presaged a major role for aeroplanes in the imminent European war. Piazza also envisaged the possibilities of aerial camera work and, on 11 November, sent an urgent request to his headquarters for provision of a Zeiss Bebe plate camera. After several weeks of waiting, Piazza took it upon himself to borrow a camera from the Engineer Corps in Tripoli and had this fixed to his Blériot, positioned just in front of his seat and pointing downwards. Manipulation of the controls and the plate camera at once meant that only one exposure could be made on each flight, but it was the birth of airborne photo-reconnaissance.

Aerial bombardment

Although there appears to be no evidence that any of the Flotilla's pilots ever attempted to take aloft and use any form of firearm, the concept of an offensive role for their aircraft was exemplified by the use of aerial bombs. The first-ever bombing sortie was that undertaken on 1 November 1911 by Second Lieutenant Gavotti, when he dropped three 2kg Cipelli bombs on the Taguira Oasis and a fourth bomb on Ain Zara. The relative success of Gavotti's sortie led to the use of modified Swedish Haasen hand grenades and these were replaced by a small cylindrical bomb, containing explosive and lead balls, designed by Lieutenant Bontempelli.

By February 1912, the Flotilla's machines had been modified to carry a large box (dubbed Campodonicos), each of which could hold ten Bontempelli bombs, which could then be released, simply by the pilot pulling a lever, in salvo or singly. The age of aerial bombardment had dawned. Nor was this form of aerial warfare confined to daylight sorties. Later in the campaign, on 2 May 1912, Captain Marengo, commander of a second air formation which arrived at Benghazi in late November 1911, made a 30-minute night reconnaissance as the first of several similar patrols. Then, on 11 June before dawn, Marengo dropped several bombs on a Turkish encampment, inaugurating the night bomber role.

During December 1911 and January 1912 the work of the Flotilla was severely hampered by atrocious weather conditions, including high winds and sudden storms. However, its aircraft continued to give direct tactical support to the ground troops by scouting ahead of advancing columns and locating enemy troops in the vicinity.

Below: a Maurice Farman is prepared for a sortie. Bottom: a Blériot XI in Libya. Piazza achieved two more 'firsts' on a Blériot XI: on 28 October 1911 he spotted for the battleship Sardegna, which was shelling the oasis at Zanzur, and on 23 February 1912 he made the first attempt at photo-reconnaissance

Fresh aircraft for the Libyan airmen began arriving in January, along with new pilots, including Lieutenant Oreste Salomone, later to gain honours and national fame as a bomber pilot during World War I. By the end of January, due to the eastward movements of the advancing Italian ground forces, it became necessary for the Libyan Flotilla to change its base airfield, and a move was made to Homs on 12 February. From here the aircraft flew in yet another new role: aerial propaganda. The pilots scattered thousands of specially prepared leaflets far and wide amongst Arab camps, with the result that large numbers of tribesmen were persuaded to become allied to the Italian cause.

Revolutionary tactics

By this time the value of the aircraft was being fully recognised by Italian Army commanders and the feats of the pilots were acclaimed in official dispatches. The overall commander of Italy's Air Battalion, Lt Col di Monte-zemolo, arrived in Libya in February 1912 to inspect the Air Flotilla and report on its activities and results. One item in his subsequent report was the recommendation

formation, Captain Marengo, instituted a series of night bombing and reconnaissance sorties between May and July. His only night-flying aid was an electric torch, fixed to his flying helmet and operated by a normal hand-switch, in order to read his few instrument dials. Tragically, it was a pilot of Marengo's formation who became the Italian Air Service's first-ever wartime casualty. On 25 August 1912 at 0610 hours Second Lieutenant Pietro Manzini took off for a reconnaissance patrol but almost immediately side-slipped into the sea and was killed.

With the end of the campaign, the Italian airmen won acclaim from the international Press. One particularly prophetic war correspondent, with the Turkish Army throughout the war, wrote, 'this war has clearly shown that air navigation provides a terrible means of destruction. These new weapons are destined to revolutionise modern strategy and tactics. What I have witnessed in Tripoli has convinced me that a great British air fleet must be created.' Certainly, by their skill, imagination and courage, the Italian Air Flotillas had inaugurated man's latest form of destruction, pioneering most of the military roles for the aeroplane.

Left: ground crew fit a 'bomb tube' for dropping Haasen bombs (grenades) to a Henry Farman biplane in Libya. The Italians were the first to make use of aerial bombardment, bombing behind Turkish lines both by day and night. Below: a Maurice Farman biplane after an accident in Libya

that Captain Piazza be repatriated to Italy, due to the commander's bouts of fever, and that he be succeeded by Captain Scapparo. Piazza, once fit again, should be employed in organising flying tuition.

The obvious success of the Libyan Air Flotilla soon led to a second, though smaller flotilla being dispatched to Cyrenaica and based at Benghazi. Once established, this formation's first war sortie – a reconnaissance patrol – was flown on 28 November by Second Lieutenant Lampugani. Though mainly restricted to the areas close to Benghazi, this formation had its full share of operational experiences. Most flights were met with fierce opposition from Turkish ground fire, including anti-aircraft artillery. This latter novelty was first experienced by Lieutenant Roberti on 15 December 1911 when flying over some Turkish trenches; his aircraft and propeller received several shrapnel strikes. As if to compliment the gunners on their accuracy, Roberti coolly dived across the enemy battery positions and dropped some of his personal visiting cards.

A terrible precedent

As recorded earlier, the commander of the Benghazi

Bloody April 1917

'Bloody April', the April of 1917, was what the Royal Flying Corps called the battle for aerial supremacy over Northern France. It was the second time in the war when the Germans gained the upper hand–the previous occasion had been with the introduction of the first Fokkers two years earlier.

Spring was traditionally a time for new offensives, and the Allied commanders had planned a huge 'push' for spring 1917, with the French attacking on the Aisne and the British at Arras. In the end the French attack failed, because the Germans had captured documents that gave away the French plans, and in time to move up

reinforcements to resist it. The British offensive at Arras, an action on the model of the Somme battle, was eventually a limited victory. The air campaign associated with it was, however, a disaster.

The British air offensive began on 4 April, which was five days before the land battle was to start. The aim was to drive German aircraft away from the battle area, leaving the skies clear for the Allied photographic and gunnery spotting aeroplanes. The air offensive was not helped by bad weather at its start, with low clouds and rain. In the first five days the British lost no fewer than 75 aircraft in combat and a further 56 in ordinary flying accidents, making a total of 131 machines down. Flying crews lost in action totalled 105; 19 were killed, 73 missing and 13 wounded. The RFC had been trying to introduce large numbers of new aircrew to service on the Western Front, and to do this had been cutting back dangerously on their training. The average flying experience of new pilots going into action was some 25 hours; today that would not be sufficient to qualify for a simple private pilot's licence, let alone produce a combat pilot.

The British were also introducing a new type of aircraft, the Bristol Fighter. There had been many training accidents with these 'Brisfits' in England, and the type had gained a reputation as a killer, with structural weaknesses that made it unsafe for it to be thrown about as was needed in combat. There were some small problems of the sort common with new military aircraft; little defects of the guns and engine, rather poor visibility from the pilot's cockpit, and so on; but these were quite quickly remedied. Much of its reputation was just gossip among young and inexperienced pilots–the kind of ill-informed talk that often affects the introduction of new aircraft types in wartime however good they are.

Mistaken tactics

The Brisfit crews also made a major mistake in tactics– probably the result of poor training. This was to assume that the observer's gun, mounted so it could be swivelled on a ring around his cockpit, but generally a rearward-firing defensive gun, was the important firing unit. They tended to neglect the pilot's fixed forward firing gun, perhaps because it was necessary to aim the whole aircraft at the enemy and not just the gun.

The Germans had new aircraft too; they had re-equipped with Albatros and Halberstadt aircraft earlier in the year, but by April had got used to them, and flew them without the hesitancy they had shown earlier. Such was

Pictured prior to take-off from its base at Bray-Dunes, this RE 8 of 52 Squadron was typical of the slow, vulnerable aircraft operated by the RFC in April 1917

the new German confidence that there were occasions in April when a single German scout attacked an entire Allied formation. The new German types were superb fighting machines. Before April the old Allied pushers such as the DH 2 had often been able to give a good account of themselves when attacked, but this was no longer the case. 'The hostile scouts with their superior speed and good handling were able throughout the fight to prevent the pilot from getting a single shot at any one of them,' reported one DH pilot in his combat report. No 57 Squadron, flying the powerful 250hp FE2d suffered very heavy casualties. On 5 April they lost five aeroplanes on a single patrol to a formation of German two-seaters. That same day four out of a patrol of six of the new Bristol Fighters from 48 Squadron, led by Captain W. Leefe-Robinson, VC, were shot down, and one of the two survivors returned having been badly shot up. This had been a dogfight with von Richthofen, no less, who personally got two of the Bristols. The Baron said that he thought his own aeroplane to be unquestionably superior to the new Bristols; this news got around among the German pilots and helped elevate their morale still further. In fact von Richthofen was misled; the Bristols, once their pilots had become accustomed to them and built up confidence in them, were fine machines.

One FE squadron, on almost its first sortie in France, was sent up as bait to lure von Richthofen and his men down to where they could be attacked by waiting British fighters. These fighters, however, never arrived. The bombers found that when the Red Baron attacked, over Douai, they were on their own. The pushers were led by Lieutenant Tim Morice, who led his men into a defensive circle. This forced von Richthofen to fly around the British pushers just out of range, shaking his fist at them and making rude gestures while he waited for a chance to attack. It came when a German two-seater droned past just underneath, and one of the RFC pilots left the circle and set off after it. Quick as a flash, von Richthofen was into the gap in the circle and the battle was on. Two FEs went quickly down, though Morice's observer managed to damage two German aircraft. Then the Baron appeared as if from nowhere, firing head-on, and the pusher's instrument panel was blown to bits. Morice and his observer were both unhurt, and managed to crash-land in the middle of a British gun emplacement.

Large formations

In the earlier period of German air supremacy, from the autumn of 1915 to the spring of 1916 when the Fokker Eindekkers ruled the skies over the front, the effect had been a huge shrinkage in the RFC's operational strength. A similar phenomenon occurred in 'Bloody April'. Reconnaissance formations could only be sent up with large fighter escorts; thus one single mission could involve more than a dozen aeroplanes. It was not unusual to see fifteen fighters escorting three observation aircraft. Bombing sorties had to be curtailed; 12 fighters–six two-seaters in close escort and six single-seaters above and behind–were needed to accompany just six BE bombers. The German pilots, because of their lower losses resulting from careful and economical employment of the German air strength, were more experienced than the average British pilot, as well as more confident, and better-mounted. The Germans also had the tactical initiative; they could dive in and dive out of combat at will, whereas the British had to stand and fight whatever the odds, and in the prevailing westerly wind that tended to blow them over the German lines the longer they fought. Many

damaged British aeroplanes that might otherwise have crawled back to British territory were in fact lost because they could not fight the headwinds to get back to the Allied side of the lines.

What it was like to be in the thick of the fight during 'Bloody April' was vividly described by a Royal Navy Sopwith Pup pilot of No 3 (Naval) Squadron, flying one day with some SPADs of No 23 Squadron as escort to a formation of BEs on a bombing raid. Over Cambrai they were attacked by German Halberstadts and Albatroses. 'I attacked an Albatros head on at about 8,000 feet. I saw many tracers go into his engine as we closed on one another. I half-looped to one side of him, and then the Albatros dived with a large trail of blue smoke. I dived down after him to about 4,000 feet and fired about fifty rounds when he went down absolutely out of control. I watched him spinning down to about 1,000 feet, the trail of smoke increasing. I was immediately attacked by three more Albatroses which drove me down to about 200 feet. We were firing at one another whenever possible, when at last I got into a good position and I attacked one from above and from the right. I closed on him, turning in behind him and got so close to him that the pilot's head filled the small ring in the Aldis sight. I saw three tracers actually go into the pilot's head; the German then simply heeled over and spun into the ground. The other two machines cleared off. I saw two other German aeroplanes spinning down out of control, and while fighting saw two BEs being attacked by German aircraft. Having lost sight of the other machines and being so low I decided to fly home at about that height, 200 feet. After about five minutes I was again attacked by a Halberstadt single-seater and as he closed on me I rocked my machine until he was within about 50 yards. I side-looped over him and fired a short burst at him. He seemed to clear off, and then attacked me again; these operations were repeated several times with a slight variation in the way I looped over him, until within about five minutes of crossing the lines (flying against a strong wind), when he was about 150 yards behind me, I looped straight over him, and coming out of the loop I dived at him and fired a good long burst. I saw nearly all the tracers go into the pilot's back, just on the edge of the cockpit. He immediately dived straight into the ground. I then went over German trenches filled with soldiers, and I was fired on by machine guns, rifles, and small field guns, in and out of range . . . I landed at the first Allied aerodrome I saw. My machine was badly shot about.'

In contrast to the mass fighting, two of the greatest

Right: defensive armament of this FE2 of 20 Squadron consisted of two 0·303 Lewis guns: one was situated in the front of the observer's cockpit, while the other could be fired back over the wing by means of a pillar mounting. Below: a comparison of the speeds and ceilings of four aircraft types operational in April 1917

fighter pilots of all time, Captain Albert Ball of 56 Squadron and Captain Billy Bishop of 60 Squadron, flew alone on 'roving commissions', going their own way, seeking combat where they found it. Ball's tactics against the German two-seaters were to dive from the half-rear, rather obviously, so that the observer swivelled his gun into position in that direction. Then Ball would dodge underneath the two-seater and fire at close range from below on the other side, before the enemy observer had time to reposition his gun. It was a most effective approach.

Flying circuses

Much of the credit for the German successes in 'Bloody April' must be due to their reorganisation into independent *jagdstaffeln*, fighter squadrons which were further grouped into *jagdgeschwadern*, wing-sized units. These wings could be moved as entire units, aircraft, equipment and all, in special trains. The Germans had always made exceptional use of their fine railway system in their war plans. *Jasta 11* was commanded by von Richthofen; he had recently been awarded the Pour le Merite, the coveted 'Blue Max' award, and was famous not only in the German press but in the British and French newspapers as well. Such prestige had military value; it inspired the pilots and men who served under him, and helped terrify the inexperienced British pilots he came up against. To aid the process he chose to have his aeroplane painted in an instantly recognisable blood red. He was not the first to try the idea of having a wildly distinctive machine; Oswald Boelcke, Richthofen's teacher in fighter tactics, had flown unusual all-white and all-black machines, and the French pilot Navarre had flown an all-red Nieuport over Verdun in the spring of 1916, when von Richthofen had been operating in that area as a two-seater pilot. Now von Richthofen took the idea of colour-coding aircraft to the limit, until not only he but his entire *jasta* flew gaudily-painted and patterned machines; in this way one pilot could recognise another in combat. The idea quickly spread to the rest of the German fighter service,

but was never generally adopted by the Allies.

In pre-war times travelling circuses had sometimes moved around by train, and the German *jastas* on the move in this way, with their brightly-painted aircraft dismantled to fit on the railway wagons, much resembled a circus travelling from one engagement to the next. Hence, the 'circus' nickname for the *jagdgeschwadern*.

The adoption of bright colour schemes helped ground observers' spaced at regular intervals along the German lines with field glasses and telephones to confirm the combat claims of individual pilots. Indeed, von Richthofen shot down no fewer than 20 Allied aircraft, a quarter of his total score at his death, during 'Bloody April'. With his total score now 43, he was for the first time the world's top-scoring fighter pilot.

On 1 May 1917 von Richthofen returned to Germany on leave, and his departure coincided with a slackening in the German effort in the air, which they had been sustaining to the limits of human endurance. In no other month of the war was the RFC so hard-pressed, or were its casualties so heavy. From the beginning of May, however, things began to improve for the British. They had learned much in April. They had gained confidence and experience in handling their machines. Their morale improved, and they had old scores to settle. The squadron mechanics had come to understand their new equipment and technical problems had been sorted out. It also became apparent that there were disadvantages to the new German tactics of grouping their fighters; it localised their efforts in limited areas, leaving the sky clearer elsewhere. The *jastas* were also seen to lack cohesion, being more loose collections of fighting individuals who tended to split up in combat rather than a cohesive and centrally-led unit.

With new equipment, fresh pilots and renewed confidence, the RFC squadrons began to exploit the flaws in the German operational procedures, and with each successive week their victories mounted and their losses dropped. They had registered the most disastrous month in the history of the service and the air war over France.

Developed from the earlier BE2c, the BE2e reconnaissance aircraft was in front-line service during Bloody April. Its 90 hp RAF 1a engine gave it a maximum speed of 132 km/h (82 mph), making it no match for German fighters nearly 32 km/h (20 mph) faster

Independent Force 1918

The concept of using aircraft for a sustained bombing offensive against the German homeland was seriously considered by both British and French air authorities from the outbreak of war in 1914. Isolated raids by Royal Naval Air Service and French pilots in the opening months of the conflict pointed the way to such an onslaught: however, the lack of aeroplanes capable of carrying a reasonable weight of bombs over a worthwhile range prevented any such force being assembled and operated. Nevertheless, the Allied air authorities continued to anticipate the day when this scheme might be feasible and the subject was discussed at many of their monthly meetings in 1915. By the spring of 1916 the Admiralty began receiving deliveries of the new Sopwith

Below: Major-General Sir Hugh Trenchard with the headquarters staff of the Independent Force. Taking command on 6 June 1918, Trenchard soon added five more squadrons to the five original units of the Force. Bottom: the Handley Page 0/400 heavy bomber entered squadron service in the spring of 1918 and soon became the backbone of the Independent Force

1½ Strutter and Short bomber; accordingly, the formation of a new bomber force was proposed, to be titled No 3 Wing RNAS, and used for 'long-range' attacks on German munitions and industrial centres. Captain W. L. Elder RN was appointed in command and he went to France in May 1916 to arrange facilities.

No 3 Wing was intended to reach an operational strength of 35 bombing aircraft by 1 July, but the start of the first Somme battle on the same day resulted on many aircraft earmarked for the Wing being diverted to the Royal Flying Corps for urgently-needed air support over the Somme front. Thus it was not until early October 1916 that No 3 Wing could commence its intended role, with a massed raid by 21 RNAS machines and 16 French bombers, escorted by Nieuport Scouts of the Lafayette Escadrille, against Oberndorf on 12 October. For the next six months, until the Wing's ultimate raid on 14 April 1917, its Sopwith and Handley Page 0/100 crews flew a series of sorties in varying strengths against strategic targets behind enemy lines. Notwithstanding these efforts, the fate of No 3 Wing was sealed by the ever-increasing needs of the RFC along the Western Front in terms of replacement aircraft and the pioneer Wing was eventually disbanded on 30 June 1917. Despite its early demise, No 3 Wing RNAS had demonstrated the clear possibilities for any future strategic bombing formation.

Bombers over Germany

In the same month that No 3 Wing was dissolved, London was subjected to its first daylight aeroplane raid on 13 June, resulting in an immediate outcry from the British public for reprisal raids against German cities. Such raids were not practicable with contemporary operational aircraft,

but Hugh Trenchard, General Officer Commanding the RFC in France, was officially requested to undertake a specific bombing campaign against targets 'deep' into Germany: he formed a special force for such a purpose, titled 41st Wing RFC. This comprised three units: No 100 Squadron, equipped with the FE2b, No 55 Squadron, flying the DH4 and No 16 Squadron RNAS with the Handley Page 0/100. Wing Headquarters was located at Bainville-sur-Madon with effect from 11 October 1917,

under the command of Lt Col Cyril Newall, while the three squadrons were grouped together at Ochey.

Despite severe winter weather, the three squadrons immediately commenced a series of bombing operations against German military installations. Their relative success led to expansion and on 1 February 1918 the Wing was retitled the VIII Brigade RFC, with Newall (then a Brigadier-General) still in command. In May two more squadrons joined VIII Brigade, Nos 99 and 104 Squadrons,

Below: a Handley Page 0/400 being refuelled. By September 1918 the Independent Force had four squadrons fully equipped with 0/400s and one with both 0/100s and 0/400s flying long distance night sorties

Right: the painting by Bertram Sandy shows DH4s of No 55 Squadron making the first British bombing raid on Mannheim on 24 December 1917. Below right: a map of the area of operations of the Independent Force

each equipped with DH9 two-seat day bombers. In the period from 11 October 1917 to 5 June 1918 the five squadrons of VIII Brigade completed a total of 142 sorties; 57 of these were flown against Germany, including day and night attacks on Cologne, Mannheim, Mainz, Coblenz and Stuttgart, while the remainder concentrated on enemy communication lines to the Western Front.

Independent Force forms

In May 1918 the newly-established Air Ministry in London decided to form an Independent Force for 'a specific and sustained air offensive' against German munition centres, communications and – significantly – population centres, the latter being cities and large towns of importance. Major-General Sir Hugh Trenchard, who had recently resigned his appointment as first Chief of Air Staff of the newly-constituted Royal Air Force, was given command of the Independent Force. He took up his new appointment on 6 June 1918, which became the effective date for official existence of the Force. His predecessor, Newall, had already prepared new aerodromes and facilities for additional units for VIII Brigade and Trenchard was able to use the formation as the basis for his new command.

Five more units were quickly added to the existing VIII Brigade; No 97 Squadron, which joined the Independent Force on 9 August was followed by No 215 Squadron on 19 August and No 115 Squadron on 31 August. All three units were equipped with Handley Page 0/100 and 0/400 heavy bombers, while No 110 Squadron, which also joined on 31 August, was equipped with the new DH9A two-seater. The fifth unit, No 45 Squadron, flew Sopwith Camels and became part of the Independent Force from 22 September 1918, having recently been withdrawn from the Italian Front. The role of the Camel unit was, ostensibly, fighter escort for the day bomber elements of the Independent Force, though in retrospect, it is difficult to see how a short-range fighter could be effective in such a role while escorting bombers with at least twice the type's endurance.

Fierce opposition

The urgent need for some form of fighter protection was all too obvious in view of the fierce and extensive opposition from German fighters to the day bombers. Exemplifying both this opposition and the superb morale and determination of the bomber crews, was a sortie undertaken by 12 DH9s of No 99 Squadron on 31 July 1918. Their target was Mainz and all 12 set out in the early morning. Before reaching the trenches three DH9s were forced to return with fractious engines. The remaining nine bombers were quickly beset by some 40 German fighters over Saarburg, which attacked from every direction. Closing into tight formation for mutual protection, the bombers eventually swung towards their alternative objective, Saarbrücken, but lost four DH9s to the wheeling Fokkers before reaching this target. The five surviving bombers duly released their bombs on Saarbrücken railway centre, but lost three more crews to the Fokkers as they turned for home. Only the appearance of two formations of No 104 Squadron aircraft prevented further losses and the two surviving DH9s of No 99 Squadron returned to base. In their sortie report both crews expressed the wish to return and 'finish the job'.

By night the trundling pusher FE2bs of No 100 Squadron pursued a series of low-level bombing and strafing raids against German air bases; 18 such attacks were made between 5 June and 31 August, with relative success.

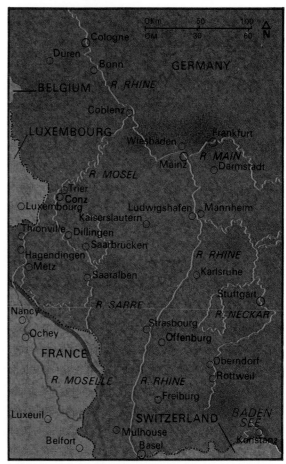

Ranging deeper into hostile country, the giant Handley Pages bombed munitions complexes, rail centres and such cities as Cologne. These raids included occasional use of the 1,650lb SN bomb – the largest bomb to be dropped in anger by Allied aircraft throughout World War I. Particularly distinguished were the DH4 crews of No 55 Squadron, whose long-distance daylight sorties, necessarily unescorted, meant running the gauntlet of defending

In September, October and the first ten days of November 1918 the five Handley Page-equipped bomber squadrons of the Independent Force dropped 350 tons of bombs. In one night five 0/400s of No 115 Squadron, making double trips, dropped 6½ tons of bombs on Morhange airfield

German fighters with consequent high casualties.

The Independent Force was ordered to co-operate with the combined French and American land offensive on 26 September; Nos 55 and 104 Squadrons duly attacked rail centres at Metz Sablon and Audun le Roman, scoring direct hits. Seven DH9s of No 99 Squadron set out simultaneously to bomb Thionville, but before reaching Metz they were set upon by some 40 German fighters. Deciding to bomb the alternative target Metz Sablon, the DH9s changed course but lost five aircraft in the continuing bitter fighting. A sixth DH9 managed to land near Ponta Mousson with a wounded pilot whose aircraft was shredded with bullet damage, while the seventh, carrying a dead observer, finally regained base.

Non-stop offensive
The ponderous Handley Page bombers were, perforce, employed on individual raids by night and their depredations ranged far and wide. On the night of 21/22 August, for example, two aircraft of No 216 Squadron – the former No 16 Squadron RNAS – dropped just over a ton of bombs on Cologne railway station. In all, this raid took seven hours of flying and was only one part of No 216 Squadron's extensive effort. During September 1918 this unit alone dropped 37·25 tons of bombs on enemy targets – the greatest bomb-weight delivered by any Independent Force unit in one month's operations. Similar audacious raids were flown by the Handley Page heavies of No 215 Squadron on 25/26 August, when two aircraft attacked the Badische Anilin und Soda Fabrik at Mannheim. The bombers skimmed across their target at a height of only 60m (200ft) despite intensive ground fire and obtained a string of direct hits.

The last bomber unit to join the Independent Force was No 110 Squadron. Exactly two weeks after arriving at Bettoncourt, France, with a full complement of DH9A two-seat bombers – all presentation aircraft from the Nizam of Hyderabad – operations began on 14 September

when 12 DH9As attempted to bomb Metz. Only six found their target, but these all returned safely to base. Eleven days later another dozen DH9As set out to raid Frankfurt, but five were shot down by German fighters. Four more bombers were lost on 5 October near Kaiserslautern, while on 21 October seven of a formation of 12 failed to return.

The central policy for the Independent Force – that of the sustained bombing of Germany, as opposed to a series of isolated raids – was maintained until the very eve of peace. The ultimate Independent Force sorties were flown by two Handley Pages of No 216 Squadron against Metz Sablon and Frescaty aerodrome on the night of 10/11 November 1918. This non-stop offensive had a great effect on German civil morale, apart from its constant interruption of enemy industrial output – an effect far greater than the physical damage and casualties resulting from actual bombing.

The Independent Force, including its 'parent' formations, operated from 11 October 1917 until 11 November 1918, a period of 390 days and nights. In that time Independent Force units had dropped a total of almost 666 tons of bombs during the course of 508 raids. Its air gunners and pilots claimed totals of 64 enemy fighters destroyed and a further 93 sent down 'out of control'. The Independent Force lost 138 aircraft in action, while another 320 aircraft had to be written off due to various other reasons. In human terms these losses were grievous, with a total of 439 pilots and observers killed, wounded, injured or missing – although several missing crew members survived as prisoners of war. If such statistics appear puny when compared with the huge casualty figures for bomber crews in 1939–45 operations, it should be remembered that the men of the Independent Force had been responsible for establishing the precepts for strategic bombing. These had been learned in the only way possible – by dint of sheer hard experience, without precedents, and with not a little sacrifice.

Spanish Civil War 1936-39

On 18 July 1936 insurrection broke out in Spain – the ultimate consequence of many months of political unrest, violence and murder. Leaders of the insurrection were right-wing army officers whose action achieved differing degrees of success in various parts of the country. The Socialist government failed in its attempts to restore order, however, and with alarming rapidity the country degenerated into one of the largest, bitterest and bloodiest civil wars in history.

In 1936 Spain's air force was, at best, equipped with obsolescent aircraft and had been about to embark on a programme of re-equipment and modernisation. Available in July were some 40 Nieuport-Delage NiD 52 sesquiplane fighters in three *grupos*, 60 Breguet 19 biplane reconnaissance-bombers in four metropolitan *grupos* and one African-based *grupo*, and 20 Vickers Vildebeeste torpedo bombers with the naval air force. There also existed a handful of miscellaneous landplanes, flying boats and three Hawker Fury biplane fighters, which had been intended for production to replace the NiD 52s.

Aid from abroad

While the greater number of aircraft was retained by the Republican government, most of the experienced officers joined the insurrection, the more junior pilots taking the opposite side. Initially the south became the critical area, and the success of the insurrection was seen to depend to a great extent on whether the tough, seasoned troops of the Army of Africa could be transferred swiftly to Spanish soil from Morocco by General Francisco Franco. While initial air activity by the insurgents – soon to be known as Nationalists – was concentrated here, appeals for aid were made to the sympathetic Fascist and Nazi regimes in Italy and Germany. This was forthcoming and on 27 July the first of a dozen Junkers Ju 52/3m trimotor bomber-transports from Germany arrived in Morocco to extend an airlift already begun with Douglas DC-2s and Fokker F-VII transports.

Meanwhile, the handful of NiD 52s which had reached the Nationalists was active, both in support of the airlift and the deployment of the newly-arrived troops in the south. The first aerial combat occurred as early as 23 July when Teniente Miguel Guerrero Garcia shot down a Republican NiD 52, adding a Dornier Wal flying boat on the 25th, Vildebeestes on the 29th and the 31st, and a Breguet 19 on 1 August.

Germany's initial aid was swiftly followed early in August by the arrival by ship of six Heinkel He 51 biplane fighters, pilot instructors and 20 anti-aircraft guns for airfield defence. By the end of the month a total of 20 Ju 52/3ms would also become available. The Italians were close behind, sending an initial 12 Savoia-Marchetti S 81 bombers in early August, followed in mid-month by 12 Fiat CR 32 biplane fighters, together with volunteer aircrew. The S 81s flew their first sorties on 5 August, bombing a Government cruiser attempting to interfere with the seaborne element of the movement of the Army of Africa. As soon as the bulk of the airlift had been

Spanish fighter pilots of a Nationalist unit equipped with the Fiat CR 32. Most of the experienced Spanish officers adhered to the Nationalists. Flying Italian and German aircraft and supported by the Condor Legion and the Aviazione Legionaire, the Nationalists had both a quantitative and a qualitative advantage

completed, the S 81s took over the remainder of the task, while the Ju 52/3ms were put into action as bombers in support of the army's advance northwards. The He 51s were also rapidly in action, flown by both Spanish and German pilots–the latter now permitted to fight as volunteers. The arrival of this initial foreign aid permitted some elements to be transferred north to assist the more hard-pressed Nationalist forces in that area.

International Brigades

The Government had been as quick as the Nationalists to appeal for help to sympathetic nations, and while much of the western world applied a strict arms embargo, the French initially responded quite generously. On 8 August the first seven of over 50 Potez 54 twin-engined bombers arrived, soon followed by 17 Dewoitine D.372 and ten D.371 fighters, five Loire-Nieuport LN 46s, seven Dewoitine D.501s and two D.510s, and 27 Blériot-Spad S.510s. Foreign volunteers also began to flock in, many drawn by the idealism of an anti-fascist crusade, others attracted by the adventure. On the ground, substantial International Brigades were formed, which played a major part in the early battles, while at least two International Escadrillas were formed in the air force. The Soviet Union also promised aid, to be paid for in gold. This included tanks, guns, aircraft, volunteer aircrew, technical advisers and a growing force of political advisers.

By September 1936 the French aircraft were coming into service and some quite substantial aerial combat ensued, both sides suffering losses. More aid was on the way, a second *squadriglia* of Italian-flown CR 32 fighters reaching the Nationalists, as did nine more He 51s and 20 Heinkel He 46 tactical reconnaissance aircraft. More CR 32s followed in October, together with a *squadriglia* of Meridionali Ro 37bis reconnaissance-bombers. October saw both the start of the Nationalist drive on Madrid and the arrival of the first Soviet war material at the front. The first aircraft into operation on 29 October were Tupolev SB-2 twin-engined bombers. These fast, modern monoplanes proved a great problem to the Nationalists for some time, as they outperformed all the biplane fighters then in service. However, by chance, a Spanish pilot, Angel Salas, was flying at high altitude in his CR 32 and was able to dive on this early raid and shoot one down. Five days later another Tupolev bomber was brought down in similar circumstances by an Italian pilot, Tenente Mantelli.

The Nationalists now deployed the remaining NiD 52s, together with the He 46s–which proved rather disappointing in action–and most of the remaining older aircraft to Aragon, while all other types were concentrated in support of the Madrid front. The Republican defences here were greatly strengthened during November by the introduction into action of the excellent Polikarpov I-15 biplane fighter, followed shortly after by the fast, modern Polikarpov I-16 monoplane–two units of which were also formed in the Biscay area to the north. Before the year was out 55 I-15s and 31 I-16s were to hand, and these were much in action during the desperate Nationalist attempts to take Madrid. Indeed, by early December the Government forces had attained a measure of air superiority over Madrid with their new equipment, and by mid-November the Nationalist offensive on the ground had become bogged down.

Now came some formalisation of foreign involvement, which was to continue on an expanding basis. In mid-November 1936 the Germans formed the Condor Legion under General Hugo Sperrle, a wholly-German volunteer force with three *staffeln* of Ju 52/3m transports, three of He 51 biplanes, one reconnaissance *staffeln* with He 70s and He 45s and a *seestaffel* with He 59 floatplanes, together with flak support and ground organisation. The Italian Aviazione del Tercio was formed into a full Aviazione Legionaria the following months, to include three CR 32 *squadriglie*, two of S 81s and one equipped with the Ro 37bis, while sufficient additional CR 32s were available for the formation of a full Spanish *escuadrilla* of these aircraft. The Germans were soon to send test batches of new aircraft for operational evaluation in Spain, the first arrivals during December being a few Henschel Hs 123 dive bombers and single examples of the experimental Heinkel He 112 and Messerschmitt Bf 109 fighters.

Following these tests, new equipment was to arrive in strength. First during February 1937 came 30 Heinkel He 111B bombers and 15 Dornier Do 17F reconnaissance-bombers, followed in March by 45 Bf 109Bs. The Italians also transferred two *gruppi* of new Savoia-Marchetti S 79 bombers to the Balearic Islands, to operate over Republican eastern territories and against shipping. The Russians also poured more aircraft and crews in to aid the Republic during this period, including Polikarpov R-5 and R-Z reconnaissance-bomber and ground-attack biplanes. Thus, by March, 62 more I-16s had joined a total of 31 SB-2s and 147 I-15s.

During February 1937 the Nationalists launched a new offensive on the River Jarama in an effort to cut the Madrid-Valencia road and break the deadlock on the main Madrid front. Both sides threw in their air power and very heavy fighting developed. A Republican counter-attack brought the offensive to a halt, convincing the Nationalist High Command that their forces could not break through here. Consequently the line was stabilised, much of the striking power of the land and air forces being transferred for an attack on the northern industrial areas of Vizcaya and the Asturias; this began with an attack on Bilbao on 31 March.

The Republican air strength in the north was much less than around Madrid. It totalled two *escuadrillas* of I-16s, one of I-15s, 27 Koolhoven FK-51 biplanes and a handful of older types referred to as the 'Krone Circus'. The Nationalists were backed on this front by the Condor Legion with its new equipment, and by growing numbers of indigenous Spanish units. Release by the Condor Legion of many of its He 51 and Ju 52/3m aircraft had allowed more units with both types to be formed by the Spaniards, and during early 1937 a full *grupo* each of CR 32s and He 51s was formed. Delivery of S 79s by the Italians also allowed the rather slow and vulnerable Ju 52/3m trimotors to be diverted mainly to night-bombing duties. Fifty-two ex-Czech Air Force Aero A-101 reconnaissance-bombers were on their way to the Republicans at this time, but one of the ships carrying 22 of these was captured and the aircraft put into Nationalist service. The Italian Aviazione Legionaria was reinforced during April by two more full *gruppi*–each of three *squadriglie*–of CR 32s, together with a test unit of Breda Ba 65 ground-attack monoplanes.

The Guernica bombing

The offensive in the north brought about the aerial operation for which the civil war is best known–the infamous bombing of Guernica by the Condor Legion on 26 April 1937. Whether this was a cynical test of terror bombing or a legitimate attack on a fortified front-line town remains a moot point to this day. Both sides were

Right: Fiat BR 20 Cicogna bombers were tested in combat in Spain by the 35º Gruppo Autonomo da Bombardamento of Italy's Aviazione Legionaria.
Centre right: the tail of a Republican Nieuport-Delage NiD-52 shot down in the first days of the civil war.
Below right and bottom: the Heinkel He 111B first went into action in Spain in March 1937 with the Condor Legion's Kampfgruppe 88

guilty of lapses, however, for during May Russian-flown SB-2s bombed international shipping in Palma harbour, Majorca, without orders from the Republican High Command. German warships were hit and lives lost, resulting in a retaliatory shelling by the German navy of the coastal town of Almeira.

At the end of May a Republican offensive, spearheaded by the International Brigades, was launched at Guadalajara with Segovia as its initial objective. The purpose was to draw off units from the hard-pressed north, and initially the Nationalist lines were breached. Much of the air power in the north was switched to this area and the thrust was held, no delay in the northern campaign resulting. Bilbao fell on 19 June, soon followed by Santander. A new Government effort was launched at Brunete on 6 July, this again enjoying initial success and driving a big salient into Nationalist territory. Once more, however, the Nationalists concentrated their highly-mobile air power in support, and by 11 July the Republicans were forced to dig in. Within a week a counter-offensive had been launched.

A third Republican offensive began late in August, this one at Belchite, with Saragosa as the target. Forty-nine more I-16s had arrived during July and equipment to hand now included improved I-152s and I-16 Type 10 fighters, which were in several ways superior to the CR 32 and Bf 109B respectively. Thirty-one more SB-2s were also coming to hand, together with ten Letov S-231s and the first of 40 Canadian-built Grumman FF-1 reconnaissance-fighters, obtained via Turkey. Licence-building of the I-15 was already in hand and a start had been made on a production line for the new I-16 Type 10. Many of the foreign volunteer pilots had by now gone, but were replaced by an adequate supply of Spaniards, many of them trained in Russia. As a result Republican air strength was still of the order of 470 aircraft against the Nationalists' 350; the Belchite offensive was directly supported by 150 of these, Saragosa being under serious threat by 26 August.

However, Santander had fallen on the 22nd and the Republican northern front now crumbled away. This allowed General Franco, who had by now become undisputed leader of the Nationalists, to regroup the greater part of his forces on the main front, which was now to

centre on Aragon and Catalonia for the rest of the war. With the industrial north in Franco's hands, the result of the war was a foregone conclusion from this time onwards, and the Nationalist strength on the ground and in the air was steadily to increase relative to that of the Republic.

The Republic was far from finished, however, and an assault on Teruel led to its capture from the Nationalists on 7 January 1938, although it was quite swiftly retaken. The Nationalists continued to receive more equipment as the Germans and Italians took advantage of the opportunity to use Spain as a testing ground for their latest military products. Late in 1937 more CR 32s and S 79s arrived from Italy, together with a test batch of half a dozen Fiat BR 20 bombers for the Legionaria. The Germans brought in three of their new Junkers Ju 87A Stukas, handing the Hs 123s on to the Spaniards.

While the Heinkel He 51 had been inferior both to the Russian fighters of the Republic and to its contemporary, the CR 32, the new Messerschmitt Bf 109 monoplane was achieving great success; during the Belchite battle the Condor Legion was to achieve its hundredth aerial victory. On 7 February 1938 over Teruel, Oberleutnant Wilhelm Balthasar, commander of 2 J/88, shot down no less than four SB-2 bombers while flying one of these fighters. A month later on 6 March the greatest naval battle of the war was fought off Cartagena, ending in a Republican victory. Next day the SB-2s were out in force, attacking the survivors. In retaliation 45 newly-arrived He 111Es of the Condor Legion bombed the main Republican naval bases, damaging and putting out of action the battleship *Jaime I*.

Ground support successes

Greatly heartened by their success in the north, the Nationalists attacked in Aragon on 9 March, pressing forward with great *élan*. By 5 April the spearhead troops could see the Mediterranean glittering in the distance and, while hard fighting was necessary to progress further, they reached the coast on the 15th, cutting the Republic in half between Barcelona and Valencia. Good progress was made in the north-east throughout April, the French frontier being reached by the end of the month. These advances were greatly aided by the very high level of ground support which the Nationalists were now receiving from their air force – particularly the He 51s and Ro 37bis units, known as *cadenas* because of their chain-like 'follow-my-leader' attacks. April also saw the introduction of the new Bf 109C to 3 Staffel of the Condor Legion's J88, replacing the last German-flown He 51s. The new commander of this unit was Oberleutnant Werner Mölders, later to become a leading Luftwaffe ace in World War II.

It was now obvious to the Soviet Union that a Nationalist victory was inevitable, and during the summer of 1938 the remaining Russian aircrews and advisers began to withdraw. The airmen had served well and suffered

Above: a few Czech Letov S-231 fighters were operated by the Republicans, who received aircraft from several friendly nations.
Right: the Fiat CR 32 (upper) equipped the XVIº Gruppo 'Cucaracha' (badge inset) of Italy's Aviazione Legionaria. The Heinkel He 51 (lower) was unequal to the Republicans' Russian fighters, but was highly successful in the ground-attack role. An He 51C-1 of 4 Staffel of the Condor Legion's is illustrated

Below: a Tupolev SB-2 bomber after capture by Nationalist forces.
Left: some 400 examples of the Polikarpov I-16 (upper) were flown by the Republicans, who dubbed the type Mosca (Fly). The badges of four units are inset. Three Hawker Fury biplanes (lower) on Republican strength saw extensive operational service

some heavy casualties. Successes had also been achieved and, amongst the leading fighter pilots, Anatoli Serov had been credited with 16 victories and P. K. Rychagov with 15. A final delivery of 99 more I-16s was made at this time, but despite occasional successes, as on 22 May when Republican fighters claimed 22 victories, losses were now very heavy as the inexperienced new Spanish pilots came up against the hardened veterans of the Nationalist side.

The summer of 1938 saw the last desperate Republican attempts to save the situation. In mid-July a southern offensive at Merida was held after a Nationalist counter-attack, while on the night of 24/25 July a major offensive was launched on the Ebro River front, again making good progress at first. By 2 August the advance had been

halted again, partly by air attack, and the Nationalist army counter-attacked throughout the rest of the month.

Meanwhile, He 111Bs and more CR 32s had been handed to the Nationalists together with 16 Caproni Ca 310 light bombers. The Italians had brought in more S 79s, and their bombers were very active, the remaining S 81s also going to the Nationalists. In addition, they introduced a special ground-attack unit of CR 32s. With the increased activity on the southern front following the Merida offensive, the Nationalists now moved down to Extremadura the Ju 52/3m bomber-transports, a *grupo* of He 51s, two of CR 32s, the Hs 123s, Aero A-101s and some He 70F and Ju 86D monoplanes which had been inherited from the Germans. The initial threat was ended swiftly and the CR 32s returned to the north, but within a few days they were rushed back when a new offensive on the River Zujar was launched by the Government. Heavy aerial fighting erupted here during late August and early September, culminating on 2 September when CR 32s escorting a bombing raid met SB-2 and I-16s over the front, claiming four bombers and five fighters shot down without loss. Three SB-2s and an I-16 were credited to Capt Angel Salas.

On the main front Republican losses to the German and Italian fighters were particularly heavy during the summer of 1938, and in the Condor Legion Oberleutnant Wolfgang Schellmann emerged as a new top-scorer with 12 victories. During October the International Brigades were disbanded, and in a gesture of de-escalation some Italian troops were also withdrawn. The Germans brought in five Ju 87Bs and six Arado Ar 95s, however, while in

the next month they provided the Nationalists direct with 17 He 112B monoplane fighters.

During November a major Nationalist offensive broke through the opposing defences and crossed the Ebro. On 23 December a drive on Barcelona was begun, the city falling on 25 January 1939. Following this, the northern segment of the Republic was swiftly rolled-up. On 19 January during the Barcelona operations, one of the new Spanish He 112Bs gained the only victory for this type, shooting down an I-16. On this same date the leading Nationalist pilot, Commandante Joaquin Garcia Morato, claimed his 40th and last victory. At this time came the last aerial reinforcements. The Condor Legion introduced six Henschel Hs 126A tactical-reconnaissance aircraft and 40 examples of the very latest cannon-armed Bf 109E, the fighter with which the Luftwaffe would fight the Battles of France and Britain in 1940. The Italians introduced a dozen of their new Fiat G 50 fighter monoplanes.

Even now the Republic tried again with an offensive in Extremadura early in January. This too failed, and the line in the south was stabilised by early February. All Nationalist units from the north now moved to the Madrid front, including the first Spanish-flown Bf 109B and C fighters, taken over from the re-equipped Condor Legion. On 5 March 1938 Oberleutnant Hubertus von Bonin, who had taken over 3 Staffel from Mölders after the latter had become German top-scorer of the war with 14 victories, shot down an I-15 for the last aerial victory. After abortive peace negotiations with a Republic in which factions were now fighting each other, a final advance from Toledo on 27 March penetrated to the heart of Madrid and brought the war to an end next day.

Many lessons had been learned by the Germans, Italians and Russians which would later be employed in World War II. The effectiveness of close air/ground support was to be put to good use, but the Italian belief in the desirability of retaining biplane fighters, together with the conviction of all three participants that lightly-armed, high-speed bombers could out-run defending fighters, was to prove disastrously wrong.

Top: Republican fighter pilots stand beside a Polikarpov I-15. The Soviet Union sent approximately 500 bombers and 1,000 fighters to Spain, of which over 500 were I-15s. Above: a Republican Polikarpov I-16 burnt out on a Catalonian airfield. The air war in north-east Spain diminished after the successful Nationalist offensive of April 1938. Left: Fiat CR 32s of the XVIº Gruppo escorting an Aviazione Legionaria Savoia-Marchetti S 81 on a bombing mission over Republican lines

Above: the Condor Legion's Jagdgruppe 88 re-equipped in April, 1937 with the Messerschmitt Bf 109, relinquishing their obsolete Heinkel He 51 fighters. The Bf 109 rapidly proved superior to the Republican fighters. A Bf 109E-1, a few of which saw combat near Madrid in the closing weeks of the Civil War with J88, is illustrated. The combat experience gained by the Luftwaffe's fighter pilots in the Spanish Civil War led to the formulation of tactics which gave the Luftwaffe a considerable advantage early in World War II.

Left: the Luftwaffe sent three Junkers Ju 87A-1 Stukas to Spain in late 1937 to test dive bombing techniques under combat conditions. They first saw action at Teruel in early 1938. Pilots from Germany were rotated, giving them valuable experience

Polish Campaign 1939

Formed at the end of World War I, Poland's air force (Lotnictwo Wojskowe) had originally been envisaged as an army co-operation force. While this was perhaps realistic for the light bomber units, being equipped since the late summer of 1936 with the PZL P-23 Karaś light bomber, the misuse of the fighter force over the battlefield left the key cities of Poland vulnerable to devastating air attack of the sort being rehearsed at that time by the German Condor Legion in Spain.

Last-minute re-deployment

By early 1938, 17 Karaś squadrons–each of about ten aircraft–had been formed, but a shortage of aircraft soon resulted in five of these being disbanded in order to keep the remaining 12 up to strength. However, acute though the national danger was seen to be, Poland continued to develop and export superior aircraft – mostly to Balkan neighbours–while highly-trained aircrews remained without aeroplanes to fly at home. In the spring of 1939, the Lotnictwo Wojskowe underwent further re-organisation; five Karaś squadrons, Nos 21, 22, 55, 64 and 65 (Polish Squadrons were numbered according to the Regiments to which they were attached and fighter squadrons were prefixed with the numeral '1' before the Air Regiment number) and four equipped with Los bombers were withdrawn and formed into an independent Bomber Brigade under the Polish Supreme Command. The remaining seven Karaś squadrons were distributed among the land armies for reconnaissance, No 24 to Army Krakow, No 31 to Army Karpaty, No 32 to Army Lodz, No 34 to Army Poznań, No 41 to Army Modlin, No 42 to Army Pomorze and No 51 to Operational Group 'Narew'.

Between 27 and 31 August these squadrons were moved to their combat airfields, four of which were unknown to the German tacticians.

In the fighter arm of the Lotnictwo Wojskowe matters were desperate. The Polish Government had failed to obtain deliveries of the Morane-Saulnier MS 406, Supermarine Spitfire and Hawker Hurricane (although the latter was exported to other countries), so that reliance rested almost entirely upon 30 obsolete PZL P-7s and 128 obsolescent P-11 Zedenastka fighters.

As early as July 1939 Dornier Do 17 reconnaissance aircraft of the German *fernaufklärungsgruppen* frequently violated Polish airspace to a depth of more than 160 km (100 miles) on clandestine photo-reconnaissance missions.

Below: PZL P-11 fighters and pilots of No 113 (Owl) Squadron, one of five units defending Warsaw. Bottom: Hitler (centre) with members of his General Staff in Poland including von Brauchitsch (to his right), C-in-C of the Army and von Reichenau (to his left), commander of the 10th Army. A Junkers Ju 52/3m stands in the background

Above: a painting by B. W. Linke entitled 'Luftwaffe', depicting the German Blitzkrieg of September 1939 and the consequent defiance of the Polish people

The blow falls

On the pretext of failure to negotiate free access to the Baltic port of Danzig, on the night of 31 August/1 September the Germans staged a macabre charade on the Polish frontier by attacking a border post and dressing dead Poles in German uniforms, thus seeking to suggest that the latter were the aggressors. At 0415 hours what was to be a text-book invasion according to the *blitzkrieg* philosophies commenced, but culminated in a campaign of barbarity only equalled five years later when the Germans fell back over the same ground in the face of the victorious Russian forces.

Spearheading the five Wehrmacht armies under General von Brauchitsch were seven Panzer Divisions whose armoured vehicles, though numerically and technically weak, were infinitely superior to anything possessed by the Poles. Overhead buzzed the inevitable Henschel Hs 126 reconnaissance aircraft, their crews watching for resistance and able to call on support from the dreaded Junkers Ju 87 Stuka. For the Campaign the Luftwaffe fielded nine *gruppen* of Junkers Ju 87s, a crushing total of 366 dive bombers. The heavy bomber force comprised the Heinkel He 111s of three *kampfgeschwader* the Dornier Do 17s of four *kampfgeschwader*, and a small number of aged Junkers Ju 86s. The Luftwaffe could call on large numbers of the Messerschmitt Bf 109 and Bf 110 aircraft, but deployed only 210 single and twin-engined fighters. The Polish air force, comprising fewer than 200 obsolescent fighters and roughly the same number of light bombers, thus faced a Luftwaffe which could field over 2,000 modern aircraft.

First casualties

On 1 September, as the 3rd and 4th Armies of the German Army Group North under General von Bock struck east and south-east towards Kutna and Warsaw, Army Group South under General von Rundstedt blasted its way towards Kutna from the south and eastwards past Krakow towards Lwow. That day 60 He 111s of I and III/KG 4 took off from Langenau to bomb an airfield at Krakow under an escort of 30 Bf 110s of I/ZG 76; 30 He 111s of II/KG 4, led by Oberstleutnant Erdmann, dropped 22 tons of bombs on Lemburg airfield, destroying six Polish fighters. In the north I/KG 1 struck the Polish naval base at Putzig-Rahmel.

More important was a series of heavy attacks on the Polish capital. II/LG 1, flying from Powunden, attacked Warsaw/Okecie airport, severely cratering the runways and also damaging the PZL factory. Ninety He 111Ps of KG 27 carried out the first of about 60 raids on the city in the next three weeks. The first German aircraft to fall in combat during World War II was a Junkers Ju 87 destroyed by Lieutenant W. Gnys of the 2nd Air Regiment near Olkusz at 0530 hours on that first day.

From the outset the situation facing General Edward Smigly-Rydz, commander-in-chief and virtual ruler of Poland, was hopeless. Planning to fall back to a concentration of forces in the south-east of the country around Lublin and Lwow, he suffered the loss of large groups of his forces, systematically encircled and destroyed by the swift-moving German armoured divisions.

During the first three days, despite extraordinary heroism by the Polish pilots, the Lotnictwo Wojskowe had been forced to abandon a defence based on its peacetime training and organisation. Squadrons flew from whatever airfield had escaped German bombs. Contrary to German propaganda reports – which were obviously designed to suggest that any resistance to *blitzkrieg* was futile – that the

There was nothing that the Polish fighters could do to prevent them, inferior as they were in both ceiling and speed. Indeed when war came, the only German combat aircraft that could be matched by Polish fighters were the Junkers Ju 87 dive bombers and the Henschel Hs 126 battlefield reconnaissance aircraft – both types which were usually covered in strength by escorting Messerschmitt Bf 109s and Bf 110s.

On the eve of war the fighter arm underwent a re-deployment similar to that of the bombers. Five units, Nos 111 (Kościuszko), 112 (Swallows), 113 (Owl), 114 (Fighting Cocks) and 123 Squadrons, were located around Warsaw under the Supreme Command for the defence of the capital and Nos 121 and 122 (Paper Horse) Squadrons were assigned to support Army Krakow. In addition Nos 131 and 132 (Raven) Squadrons were to support Army Poznań, Nos 141 and 142 (Wild Ducks) Squadrons went to Army Pomorze, No 152 to Army Modlin and No 161 (Turkeys) was attached to the Border Protection Corps at Sarny. By thus dividing the fighters' responsibilities between protection of the capital and support of the army, there were never more than about ten Polish fighters covering an area of 5,180 sq km (2,000 sq miles) in a situation where the initiative lay entirely with the enemy. The folly of these tactics soon became apparent.

Polish air force was totally destroyed on the ground, the Polish P-11 pilots were selling their lives dearly. Among the Poles who displayed great skill in a P-11 on 2 September was Stanislaw Skalski of No 142 (Wild Ducks) Squadron, who shot down two Dornier Do 17s. Later in the Campaign he added four more Luftwaffe aircraft to his score to become the Lotnictwo Wojskowe's highest-scoring pilot. Like so many other Poles he managed to escape to join the Royal Air Force to continue the fight against Germany.

Assault on Warsaw
By the evening of 3 September, Luftwaffe casualties had risen to 55 aircraft destroyed, 71 aircrew killed, 39 wounded and 94 missing. On that day alone the Germans suffered the loss of four Do 17s, three Bf 110s, two He 111s, three Ju 87s, two Bf 109s, three Hs 126s, two Fieseler Fi 156s, one Hs 123, one Ju 52/3m and one He 59. Polish losses by that date amounted to 46 P-11s and P-7s destroyed in the air and on the ground and about 60 Karaś light bombers. On the 2nd 18 Karaś bombers of Nos 64 and 65 Squadrons had successfully attacked German armoured columns, but suffered the loss of seven aircraft. On the following day, 28 Karaś attacked a Panzer concentration in the

Above: Luftwaffe personnel inspect a damaged Polish PZL P-11 fighter. The Polish air force was defeated by the superior numbers, aircraft and tactics of the Luftwaffe. Right: a painting by J. B. Stafford-Baker entitled 'Warsaw in Ruins'. Despite an heroic defence during which large areas of of Warsaw were devastated, the capital fell to the Germans after two weeks of fighting

The Polish PZL P-7 and P-11 fighters could make little impression upon the supremacy of the Messerschmitt Bf 109. During the campaign the Luftwaffe withdrew two of the five Bf 109 *gruppen* initially deployed, the remainder concentrating upon ground strafing. Insufficient in number, the obsolescent Polish fighters were inadequately supplied and deployed, split between army support and area defence and lacking either an advanced warning system or co-ordinated tactics. However, the highly-skilled Polish pilots transformed the P-7 and P-11 into both dreaded opponents and elusive targets, the aircraft's manoeuvrability and strength compensating for their lack of speed and heavy armament.

Radomski-Piotrków area, destroying more than a score of enemy vehicles, but again suffering crippling losses.

Despite all the Poles could do to counter the German armoured thrusts, even launching cavalry attacks on occasion, gaps were quickly found in the defences and the Panzers smashed their way through. By the 8th General

von Reichenau's armoured divisions had reached the outskirts of Warsaw. Another 61 German aircraft had been destroyed, but by now the P-11s were being used in the ground attack role, with attendant high losses and the result that no coherent defence could be given against German air attacks on towns and villages.

Attacks on places whose military importance was justified by the presence of an important railway bridge or road junction inevitably brought about that most tragic of all wartime phenomena, the hordes of pitiful refugees, wandering aimlessly about the countryside, hampering the movement of friend and foe alike. This was the element of the Polish campaign which was to become so indelibly stamped on the mind of the Western world. Inevitably the civilian casualties soared as Stuka and Panzer sought to force a passage to their objectives.

Valiant counter-attack

Among the Polish forces which had been bypassed by the Germans in their advance on Warsaw was a group near Kutno, and this, together with 12 other divisions, was thrown by General Kutrzeba into a valiant counter-attack on the 12th. By now the Polish air force was able to field no more than about 50 fighters and fewer bombers and the gallantry being displayed by its pilots was born of desperation. Lieutenant-Colonel Pamula, commanding the 'Fighting Cocks' shot down an He 111 and a Ju 87 before being attacked by the Bf 109 escort; he rammed one of the enemy fighters but managed to escape by parachute. Major Mieczyslaw Mümler, commanding the 'Ravens', shot down four enemy aircraft and shared another. His score was equalled by Czeslaw Glowczynski.

At about this time the one and only PZL P-24 to fight in the Polish campaign was operated by the Deblin Group. While flying the aircraft, Lieutenant Henryk Szczesny shot down a German aircraft on the 14th and another the following day. Szczesny then escaped from Poland and later joined the RAF but was shot down in 1942 and spent three years as a prisoner of war. Commanding this Deblin Group was Witold Urbanowicz who managed to escape from Poland to Romania with 50 cadets and, after a period in France, also joined the RAF to become Poland's highest-scoring pilot of the war with 17 victories.

German air force losses by the 13th had risen to 143 killed, 82 wounded and 150 aircraft destroyed, but during the following week Polish resistance in the air crumbled away to nothing. On the 17th the huge pincer movement, launched from north and south, closed at Brest-Litovsk, and two days later Kutrzeba's final counter-attack was smashed. When Russia's almost unopposed attack north and south of the Pripet Marshes was launched on the same day, Poland's fate was sealed.

Warsaw continued to hold out under constant air attack until the 27th, while occasional calls to surrender were made in leaflets dropped by the Heinkels of I/KG 4. Although isolated groups of Poles continued to hold out until 4 October, the capital's fall signalled the start of plans by Germans and Russians alike to divide and despoil the nation.

Against the total annihilation of the Polish air force, German Luftwaffe losses amounted to 203 aircraft destroyed, 221 aircrew killed, 132 wounded and 218 missing (of whom 49 returned to their units at the end of the Campaign). While the attack was by no means the walkover which has often since been suggested, the German losses must be seen in perspective, for they were substantially lower than those suffered in just one day when Hitler launched his attack on the West on 10 May 1940.

Norwegian Campaign 1940

The German forces had all the advantages of surprise in their Scandinavian venture in April 1940. While the 'Phoney War' period lulled the Allies into a false sense of security, the Germans decided to secure their northern flank and acquire bases from which to dominate the North Sea. Denmark could be crushed by sweeping across the border simultaneously with sea and airborne landings and Norway could be secured by putting a strangle-hold on ports and airfields. Plans had been made well in advance. Fliegerkorps X was allotted the air task and had nearly 300 Dornier Do 17, Heinkel He 111 and Junkers Ju 88 long range bombers, 40 Ju 87 dive bombers, 100 fighters and small numbers of coastal and reconnaissance aircraft. More significantly, the force had at its disposal nearly 500 transports–Ju 52/3ms and a few Ju 90s. Preparatory to the attack the Luftwaffe flew special reconnaissance missions over British naval bases while troops and aircraft moved into the Schleswig area, ready to attack at dawn on 9 April in co-ordination with landings from ships already at sea.

Denmark quickly fell, its border was crossed by ground troops while landings were made from the sea on Danish islands. Paratroops, seizing Aalborg East and West airfields, were followed by airborne troop landings; Vaerløse airfield was strafed by Messerschmitt Bf 110s concentrating on destroying the Danish fighters on the ground. The country was crushed in a day.

Token resistance

Simultaneously Norway was being invaded by sea and air. Oslo/Fornebu and Stavanger/Sola airfields suffered strafing by Bf 110s, followed by airborne landings. The Norwegian navy and army air services fought valiantly, but their outdated equipment permitted only token resistance. Still in their crates were 19 Curtiss Hawks recently delivered from America. Seven Gloster Gladiators from Fornebu shot down four of the attacking aircraft and damaged others, but, with their airfield captured and no alternative landing grounds, only one survived the forced landings by the end of the day. Some of the vulnerable Fokker C-V reconnaissance aircraft escaped northward with surviving communications aircraft.

The British had become aware of the movement of German ships following the RAF's watch on German ports and units of the Home Fleet steamed towards Norway. The Germans, sensitive to the presence of the Royal Navy, kept a close sea watch, located the ships and made heavy air attacks. The destroyer *Gurkha* was sunk, two cruisers suffered minor damage and the flagship, the battleship *Rodney*, received superficial damage from a direct hit on the foredeck.

Fully alerted to German intentions, the RAF kept the Norwegian coastline under surveillance, duly noting German cruisers and torpedo boats in Bergen harbour. That evening a strike was launched from Britain by Handley Page Hampdens and Vickers Wellingtons, but without success. This attack was followed up early next day by 15 Blackburn Skuas of the Fleet Air Arm flying at extreme range from Hatston in the Orkneys. Three hits were made on the cruiser *Königsberg* which slowly settled to the bottom–the first major warship to be sunk by air attack in World War II.

Further north, Norwegian resistance was more effective. Trondheim/Vaernes airfield held out the first day, but fell on the second when the Luftwaffe found an area nearby on which they could land troop-carrying aircraft. The airfield at Kristiansund, captured by a sea landing, was prepared as a fighter base for Messerschmitt Bf 109s staging forward from the airfields captured in the south.

Carrier-borne air strikes

The only British aircraft carrier available for Norwegian waters was *Furious*; her refit had been cut short when news of the invasion broke and she had sailed without her squadron of Skuas. The *Ark Royal* which was training aircrew off Gibraltar, was recalled to pick up her detached squadrons from Hatston and rendezvous with units of the Home Fleet off Norway. A third carrier, *Glorious*, was brought from the Mediterranean. Meanwhile, fleet air action devolved on *Furious*. On 11 April her Fairey Swordfish launched a torpedo attack against German destroyers at Trondheim, but without success.

German warships had already slipped past Home

Air attacks by both parachute and glider assault were important to the German forces' advance in Norway. One parachute battalion captured airfields at Oslo/Fornebu and Stavanger and those at Fornebu were successful in gaining control of the Norwegian capital

Top: Gloster Gladiator fighters burnt out during the German bombing attack on Lake Lesjaskog. Above: a camouflaged Gladiator of No 263 Squadron on a plateau near Aandalsnes. Opposite top: the Messerschmitt Bf 110 served with the zerstörergruppen, I/ZG 1 and I/ZG 76 in the Norwegian Campaign. Opposite below: Heinkel He 111s of KGr 100, which was initially based at Nordholz in Germany

Operations from frozen lakes

The Allies sorely needed local air support. RAF base personnel had landed at Aandalsnes on 22 April to prepare for the arrival of RAF fighters on the frozen Lake Vangsmjösa, where remanants of Norway's two air arms operated with ski undercarriages on a runway compacted by migrating reindeer. However, as this appeared to be in the path of German advances, the RAF was directed to Lake Lesjaskog which was cleared of thick snow by local civilians.

The incoming fighters were the Gloster Gladiator biplanes of No 263 Squadron RAF picked up in Britain by the *Glorious*, which, together with *Ark Royal*, approached Norwegian waters on 24 April. When 290 km (180 miles) offshore the Gladiators took off, led by a Skua to assist navigation. All the fighters landed safely and were dispersed around the lake. That night carburettors froze and ice blocked the wheels causing an early patrol to be postponed. By the time some aircraft had been made serviceable, they had been detected by German air reconnaissance and bombing attacks by He 111s and Ju 88s followed. By midday, as crews struggled to get more aircraft airborne, ten had already been destroyed. That afternoon such Gladiators as were able to fly were used continually by a relay of pilots who managed 30 sorties, but with continuing air attacks the ice was broken up and the surface was barely usable. To the north, off Narvik, *Furious* was attacked and a near miss damaged her turbines, forcing her to make for Scapa Flow.

Next morning the five remaining Gladiators flew to a plateau near Aandalsnes which also came under heavy air attack. In any case, the Gladiators were ineffectual against the high-level attacks which the Germans were making to avoid interception, as the British aircraft lacked oxygen equipment. By the end of the day only one Gladiator remained, so the surviving pilots were evacuated by merchant ship. With little hope of further local air support the decision was taken to evacuate the Allied forces from all but the Narvik area and the RAF mounted a series of bombing attacks to relieve pressure during the withdrawal. Flying at extreme range over the sea from bases in Britain, which allowed little time to locate targets in fjords, Bomber Command lost 27 aircraft in such attacks that month, facing appalling weather conditions and the German air and ground defences. The Luftwaffe also sank a British and French destroyer during the evacuation.

Fighter reinforcements

Meanwhile, Allied troops in the Narvik area were in desperate need of local air support. An RAF base party flew to Bodö early in May in two Short Empire flying boats, impressed from Imperial Airways and operated by No 119 Squadron. Such large craft were soon detected; the Luftwaffe sunk one within hours of landing and the other next day at its moorings. Suitable airfields took time to locate. Sites were selected at Bardufoss to the north, Bodö to the south and nearby Skaanland. While Skaanland, near the coast, was being prepared, fighters from *Ark Royal* and the anti-aircraft cruiser *Curlew* tried to give some air protection. However, the latter was sunk and, further out, the battleship *Resolution* had three decks pierced by a bomb, forcing her to retire.

A re-formed and re-equipped No 263 Squadron returned to Norway aboard *Glorious*, relieving *Ark Royal* as the carrier on station. At 0600 hours on 21 May the Gladiators took off in bad weather for Bardufoss, losing two of their number which crashed into mountain sides. No 11 Observer Screen was also landed, to set up a reporting

Fleet units to secure Narvik in the far north and Royal Navy ships sped northward in pursuit. Without prior reconnaissance, Swordfish from *Furious* set out twice to attack the German ships. However they only succeeded in sinking small harbour craft in the first attack and their second attempt was thwarted by a blinding snowstorm.

Britain and France made concerted efforts to stop the flow of German military might through Norway by preparing expeditionary forces. Meanwhile Bomber and Coastal Commands of the RAF waged a joint bombing campaign against bases already in German hands, Lockheed Hudsons attacked Bergen; Bristol Blenheims made regular airfield attacks from the middle of May onwards and Armstrong Whitworth Whitleys tried to destroy the airfield and seaplane base at Stavanger.

The Allied landings were made in the period 15–18 April near Narvik in the north, to the south at Namsos and still further south at Aandalsnes to contain the Germans at Trondheim and squeeze them out in a pincer movement. German air reaction was violent at Namsos, where the town was repeatedly bombed and largely destroyed. In the south the cruiser *Suffolk*, bombarded Sola airfield from offshore, evoking heavy reaction from dive bombing Ju 87 Stukas and high-level bombing attacks from He 111s. She was forced to retire to Scapa Flow in the Orkneys, low in the water and with many casualties as a result of the bombings.

organisation. Hawker Hurricanes of No 46 Squadron, awaiting the clearing of Skaanland, left *Glorious* five days later. However, three of the 11 Hurricanes tipped on their noses when landing on soggy ground; the remainder were re-directed to Bardufoss from where a detachment of three Gladiators had been sent to Bodö. During this time the Supermarine Walrus amphibians of No 701 Squadron Fleet Air Arm, based at the Norwegian military base at Harstad for patrol work, were used for their intended task of liaison and operationally on their crews initiative.

In the face of British preparations for a pincer movement on Narvik, the Germans tried desperately to re-inforce their sea landings from the air. However, with the launching of the offensive in France, both sides had limited resources. He 115 floatplanes infiltrated a small number of troops into the Narvik environs, but German attempts to fly in mountain artillery were thwarted.

Allied evacuation

On 28 May, with air cover from the local-based Gladiators and Hurricanes, Norwegian, British and French troops captured Narvik itself—only to find its harbour wrecked and the ore-handling plant destroyed. The Luftwaffe then started mining the fairway into Narvik, but unbeknown to them the Allied forces had already received orders to evacuate completely, in view of the pressures in France. There then came the difficult task of withdrawing and masking their intention from the Germans. The depleted fighter force was required to give cover and be last to leave.

Trondheim airfield had become a major Luftwaffe base for the conquest of northern Norway. Repeated attacks by up to a hundred bombers at a time had already laid waste to Bodö town, wrecked surviving Gladiators, damaged the Bofors anti-aircraft guns and rendered the runways unusable. The bombers then turned their attention to Bardufoss and plans were in hand for a glider-borne assault to capture the airfield and assist in the recapture of Narvik.

At Narvik 25,000 Allied troops were embarked on merchant ships and warships, screened by cloudy overcast

weather. *Ark Royal*, having returned to station off Norway, launched her aircraft to attack the Germans, who were clearing their own damage at Bodö. The RAF meanwhile continued attacks on German-occupied airfields in the south. This activity served to enhance the impression that Allied pressure was growing, instead of waning. With evacuation underway there was no longer any need to conserve fuel, ammunition and equipment. The fighters were patrolling and shooting down reconnoitring Do 26 flying boats and He 115 floatplanes and intercepting attacks by Ju 87Rs that had recently been switched to Norway as the only Stukas with the necessary range to menace Bardufoss.

Standing defensive patrols were maintained up to the end, on 7 June, and anti-aircraft guns were kept operative even though it meant abandoning them to the enemy. Shortly before midnight the ten surviving Gladiators flew out to *Glorious* led by a navigating Swordfish. They were followed by ten surviving Hurricanes, whose pilots had never before attempted a deck landing and had been given the alternative of destroying their aircraft: all landed safely.

Loss of the Glorious

Then came a sad twist of fate. As the *Glorious* was returning to Britain next day, she was intercepted by the German capital ships *Scharnhorst* and *Gneisenau*. The former opened fire, hitting the forward upper hanger, destroying the Hurricanes and starting a fire. A further salvo hit the

> **Luftwaffe units participating in the Norwegian Campaign included I Gruppe, Zestörergeschwader 1 and I/ZG 76 flying the Messerschmitt Bf 110, II Gruppe Jagdgeschwader 77 with the Bf 109, I Gruppe, Stukageschwader 1 with Junkers Ju 87, KG 30 with Ju 88 and KG 4, KG 26 and KGr 100 with He 111.**

bridge and subsequent damage below the waterline resulted in her sinking. A Norwegian vessel landed 39 survivors in the Faeroes and another took four back to Norway and captivity; another two were picked up by a German seaplane.

The Norwegian venture was over, but the air campaign lasted a little longer. *Scharnhorst*, damaged by a torpedo from a destroyer, made for Trondheim escorted by *Gneisenau*, which was also nursing a torpedo hit, but from a submarine. On 11 June, 12 Hudsons attacked the ships in harbour, but only scored near misses. Two days later while the RAF bombed Vaernes as a diversion, *Ark Royal* launched 15 Skuas to bomb the ships, but the defences were alert. Some of the Skuas were shot down and others failed to regain the carrier in the morning mist: a total of eight was lost. *Ark Royal* accompanied by elements of the Home Fleet, carrying the remnants from the evacuation of Norway, reached Scapa Flow on 15 June, the day after the fall of Paris. All attention was then focussed on the battle for France.

A Heinkel He 111 bomber shot down by Gloster Gladiator fighters near Aandalsnes in central Norway. In general, the Gloster biplanes were vulnerable in the icy conditions and were no match for the German aircraft, which flew high-level attacks to escape interception

Battle of France 1940

There can be few instances in history in which a major world power was more poorly equipped to defend herself from military disaster than that of France in 1940. The French army, with an impressive array of outdated armour, seemed to have learned few of the lessons taught in the Great War of just a quarter-century earlier and persisted in a fixed defence policy, pouring millions of francs and tons of concrete into one of the greatest defence 'white elephants' of all time, the Maginot Line.

In the matter of air defence, successive administrations had paid little but lip service, even after nationalisation, to an aircraft industry which for years had proved infertile. The Armée de l'Air had been formed in 1933 from the air units previously under army command. In 1939, not only were its aircraft of inferior and outdated design, but the whole French concept of aerial defence was inappropriate to modern warfare. The defence arrangements of France were organised on a geographical basis rather than that of function. Little heed was given to the capabilities of the modern bomber, although it was generally known that Germany possessed large numbers. The fighter forces were grouped around the larger areas of population and industry, with no provision for a warning system that could enable them to provide a peripheral defence of French airspace. Only a relatively small part of the fighter strength would be available to meet a major attack.

France stirred from its lethargy too late and as war loomed on the European horizon, went to America for the best aircraft available, ordering in particular the Curtiss Hawk 75A and Douglas DB-7. Both were inferior to the best European military aircraft, but were better than anything available in France in 1939.

France's order of battle

The aircraft equipment of the Armée de l'Air had not reached full strength by the eve of the German attack. Fewer than 300 American Curtiss Hawk 75As, with a maximum speed of 500 km/h (311 mph), and four 0·3 in guns, had been delivered by 10 May 1940. Only 36 Dewoitine D.520s—which had a maximum speed of 525 km/h (326 mph), and carried one 20 mm and two 0·3 in guns—had been delivered by that date, although aircraft for five further *groupes de chasse* were delivered during the Battle. The most numerous French fighter was the Morane-Saulnier MS.406. Armed with one 20 mm and two 0·3 in guns and with a maximum speed of 484 km/h (301 mph), it equipped 16 *groupes de chasse* and three *escadrilles* on 10 May. The Bloch 152, which had a maximum speed of 509 km/h (316 mph), was flown by nine *groupes* and three *escadrilles*. It was armed with one 20 mm cannon and two 0·5 in machine guns. The units which flew these four types of fighter lost about 680 aircraft and some 280 pilots in total—roughly half the aircraft were destroyed in attacks on French airfields. Other fighters, in use in smaller numbers, suffered proportionately.

It was probably among her bombers that France was most inadequately served, though more by inept application than by any lack of valour on the part of their crews.

The five-man Amiot 143M twin-engined bomber—with a maximum speed of 294 km/h (183 mph) and capable of carrying up to about 1,630 kg (3,600 lb) of bombs—flew with four *groupes* during the Battle of France, but early losses caused some amalgamation. The Bloch 175 bomber, with a top speed of about 515 km/h (320 mph), was the best available to the French Air Force but, although about 20 were available, none was used in combat. Of the American bombers on order only some 50 Douglas DB-7 aircraft had been delivered by mid-May 1940, but the two *groupes* of Martin 167Fs flew 400 sorties in action. The heaviest French bomber was the four-engined Farman 221/222 which, with a 325 km/h (202 mph) top speed, could carry over 19,840 kg (9,000 lb) of bombs. Only about a couple of dozen such aircraft, however, were available during the Battle of France, but these eventually flew a number of successful raids without suffering any casualties.

The bulk of French daylight bombing operations fell on units equipped with the Lioré et Olivier LeO 451, a 459 km/h (285 mph) four-man medium bomber capable of carrying about 1,270 kg (2,800 lb) of bombs. When the

Above: a Messerschmitt Bf 109E of II/JG54 brought down over France in December 1939.
Left: Major Werner Mölders (right), one of the Luftwaffe fighter force's rising stars in the Battle of France, talks with Hermann Goering

German attack in the west opened, only three *groupes* were fully operational with this aircraft but, despite being a difficult aircraft to fly, elements of seven further *groupes* were hurriedly classified as operational in the re-grouping of units after 26 May. About 130 of these aircraft were destroyed during the Battle of France.

Moreover, the RAF's contribution to the French defences in the north left much to be desired. The Fairey

Battle, ten squadrons of which made up the bulk of the Advanced Air Striking Force, was slow, poorly armed and able to carry only a puny bomb-load. The Bristol Blenheim, which equipped six squadrons as bomber and reconnaissance aircraft, was only marginally better. The Hawker Hurricanes, however, which accompanied the Air Component and AASF were unquestionably the best fighters available in France, although inferior to the Bf 109 of the Luftwaffe. The trouble lay in the fact that the majority of RAF aircraft in France were committed to support of the British Expeditionary Force, a job for which their crews were not trained and which effectively prevented them from being used for air defence. On the other hand substantially strengthening the RAF contingent in France was out of the question without further weakening the defence of the British Isles, which had already fallen below a level that could be considered safe.

The Blitzkrieg begins

The blow fell against the north-east of France. Striking at Holland, Belgium and Luxembourg on 10 May 1940, Germany launched a series of devastating attacks – in particular across the frontier of Belgium – and achieved almost total surprise. In outflanking the massive fortifications of the Maginot Line, the Germans were inducing the Allies to move forward into Belgium where, fighting on unfamiliar ground, they could be overwhelmed by *blitzkrieg* tactics.

The German tactics, for which the British and French

were quite unprepared, employed strong armoured thrusts supported by a highly integrated system of air support both over and beyond the immediate battle area. Short-range Henschel Hs 126 reconnaissance aircraft kept a constant watch over the land being covered by the ground armour; Junkers Ju 87 dive-bombers and Henschel Hs 123 assault aircraft attacked any sign of resistance, while Messerschmitt Bf 109 single-seat fighters swarmed over-

French fighter pilots stationed at a base on the Western Front don their flying clothing. Although outclassed by their opponents, many French airmen fought with great gallantry

Messerschmitt Bf 109E-1 of 8 Staffel, JG26

Curtiss Hawk 75 of Groupe de Chasse II/5

head to prevent interference from the RAF and the Armée de l'Air. Flying beyond the immediate battlefields, formations of Dornier Do 17s and Heinkel He 111s, with escorts of Bf 110s, bombed rail centres, troop concentrations, artillery and ammunition dumps and airfields.

Despite the most courageous resistance Holland capitulated on 14 May, a couple of hours after Rotterdam had in error been subjected to a catastrophic air attack which occurred in spite of efforts made by both Dutch and German commanders to avert it. The Luftwaffe suffered the loss of 470 aircraft during the invasion of Holland, a large proportion of them transports, although many were subsequently repaired.

Belgium, on the other hand, continued to resist for a further 12 days, partly due to the delays imposed on the invaders by the resistance of such strongpoints as Fort Eban Emael and successive canal defence lines. The remains of her army accompanied the Allied forces into the Dunkirk pocket until the King of the Belgians surrendered on 28 May. Many Dutch and Belgians, however, escaped to Britain to continue the fight against Germany.

An extraordinary state of affairs existed in the French High Command. No doubt disturbed by exaggerated reports of heavy bombing of provincial towns, the French Government had actually forbidden its bombers to attack German towns lest such attacks should prompt reprisal raids by the Luftwaffe. Indeed no orders were given on 10 May for any bombing attacks to be made on the German invasion convoys; on the following day authority was given only for 'offensive reconnaissance' by single aircraft over enemy territory. Thereafter the matter of attacking enemy territory was almost academic: the enemy columns were then on French and Belgian soil.

Formations of French and RAF bombers, sometimes with fighter escort, attempted to attack enemy ground forces but were invariably met by heavy flak and often by enemy fighters. Losses quickly mounted; attempts to destroy vital river and canal bridges in Belgium met with almost universal failure and cost the RAF more than 50 light and medium bombers, the Belgians six out of 12 Fairey Battles and the French about 15 aircraft. By the evening of 15 May the RAF alone had lost 248 aircraft.

Another phenomenon that contributed to the speed with which the German forces were able to move through

north-eastern France was the unwillingness or inability of the French High Command to believe the results of its own air reconnaissance. On 13 May the Panzers struck at Sedan, the key move in German success and a move that had been reported to be imminent by crews of Potez 637 reconnaissance aircraft but which took the defenders completely by surprise. Only one attack by seven Lioré et Olivier LeO 451s was made on the enemy columns and all these aircraft returned with severe damage.

A disastrous reprisal

On 14 May the Armée de l'Air staged a major bombing effort against the Sedan area in an effort to buy time for the French 2nd Army to counter-attack the two invading Panzer divisions. Breguet 693s, with an escort of Bloch 152s and AASF Hurricanes, made a low-level attack on German columns, escaping the attention of prowling enemy fighters. Thirteen antiquated Amiot 143 night bombers made a daylight attack but suffered badly at the hands of enemy flak: all the aircraft which returned were severely damaged. Groupement 6, based in the Soissons area with about 50 LeO 451s, was forbidden to make attacks by more than single or pairs of aircraft for fear of incurring heavy losses. Its airfields were without any anti-aircraft guns, and when on 19 May a dozen Heinkel He 111s attacked Persan-Beaumont they found the French bombers perfectly arrayed in a neat line as if for inspection. After the raid only ten bombers remained of the original 50.

The first phase of the Battle of France ended on 25 May. The first fortnight had cost the Armée de l'Air slightly more than 500 aircraft in the air and on the ground, of

Top: the cannon-armed Messerschmitt Bf 109E equipped ten jagdgeschwader at the time of the Luftwaffe's attack on France in May 1940. Among its opponents was the Curtiss Hawk 75A, which was armed with four or six machine guns. Above: Amiot 143 bombers carried out night attacks on German transport targets in May and June 1940

which 112 were bombers. There was now a comparative lull in the fighting on the Sedan front while the Germans threw their weight against the Dunkirk pocket and drew a large proportion of their air strength northwards. The German invasion had achieved its first aim: to drive an armoured thrust to the Channel Coast, thereby isolating the BEF and French 1st Army in the north from the remainder of the mainland of France.

The Dunkirk reprieve

Few French air units remained to contribute to the defence of the Dunkirk pocket; this responsibility now fell squarely on the RAF squadrons, virtually all home-based. On 26 May the great evacuation began. For eight days the Royal Navy and a huge fleet of small boats braved bombs and shells to bring back the remains of the BEF to England, while the bombers and dive-bombers of the Luftwaffe–launched by Goering's boast that his air force would destroy the Allied armies that Guderian's Panzers had not–strove to penetrate the squadrons of Hurricanes and Spitfires flying guard overhead. Assisted by a period of bad weather during the first day of June, no fewer than 338,226 men were brought back from the inferno of Dunkirk despite continuing heavy losses among the British fighter squadrons.

The Dunkirk evacuation ended on 3 June, but the previous day most of the Luftwaffe forces again turned south in preparation for a major assault on the Weygand Line and the Paris area. During the respite, effectively gained for the French by the fighting at Dunkirk, an attempt had been made to effect a major regrouping of surviving Armée de l'Air units. Indeed so far-reaching were the changes made at this late stage of the nation's agony that one can only wonder at the negligence that had persisted so long.

Right: a 'kette' (formation of three) Junkers Ju 87B Stuka dive bombers. Used as mobile flying artillery, these aircraft greatly assisted the rapid advance of the German ground forces. Below: the Luftwaffe's Henschel Hs 126 and the RAF's Westland Lysander were essentially similar designs evolved for reconnaissance over the battlefield

The second phase

Apparently warned of the impending air assault on the Paris area at the beginning of June, the French High Command hurriedly assembled the maximum available fighter defences in the area, their new deployment being completed by the early hours of 3 June. Groupements 21 and 23, flying Bloch 152s and Morane 406s, were based on a line centred on Melun about 32 km (20 miles) south-east of the capital and were ordered to intercept raiders before they reached Paris. The component units had an effective strength of about 120 fighters. To continue attacks on the raiders as they withdrew, Groupement 22 with Morane 406s, Dewoitine 520s and Curtiss Hawk was based over a large area 160 km (100 miles) east of Paris.

Henschel Hs 126A of 1 (Heeres) Staffel, Aufkl Gr 13

Westland Lysander of No 4 Squadron RAF

The German attacks duly opened at around midday on 3 June, launching Operation Paula – intended to be the death-blow to the Armée de l'Air – by the destruction of airfields and aircraft factories in the Paris region. Three formations, each of about one hundred bombers (He 111s, Do 17s and Junkers Ju 88s from seven *geschwader*), escorted by more than 200 fighters from JG 2, 53, 54 and 77 and ZG 76, were reported approaching from the north-east. German radio jamming of the French radio transmitter located in the Eiffel Tower prevented some of the defending fighters receiving their take-off orders and the German raiders were already in sight of the capital when the first aircraft became airborne.

For the French the German attack was a tragedy and a fiasco, although there were countless instances of matchless courage. In almost every instance that French fighters intercepted enemy bomber formations they were savagely engaged by the escorting fighters. A total of 31 Moranes and Blochs were shot down, but the Paris defenders managed to destroy four Do 17s, three Ju 88s and six Bf 109s. On their flight home the raiders had to contend with the fighters of Groupement 22 and in the combats that ensued the French fighters destroyed two Bf 109s, two Bf 110s and a Do 17 for the loss of only two Curtiss Hawks. From the German viewpoint the attack on Paris, the single attempt at strategic air warfare during the campaign, was a disappointment. There had been little damage and only a small proportion of the defence installations had been hit.

The collapse of resistance

Thereafter the fighters joined the bomber *groupes* in supporting the French ground forces struggling to hold the German offensive that now burst along the line of the Somme. Throughout 5 June von Bock's Army Group B, facing the French Seventh and Tenth Armies, attacked across the Somme, heavily supported by Luftflotte 2, including the Ju 87s of StG 1, 2, 3 and 77, the Ju 88s of LG 1, the Bf 109s of JG 3, 26, 27 and 51, the Hs 123s of II/LG 2 and the Bf 110s of ZG 26. The French Air Force, now assisted by the replenished Battle-equipped squadrons of the AASF, carried out repeated attacks on bridgehead targets at Amiens, Peronne and Chaulnes. Despite considerable success on this day, achieved with light losses, the French could not prevent the Germans building up their forces; within four days these managed to break through the Weygand Line near Rouen, Compiegne and Soissons. Not only did the French Army show all the signs of imminent collapse but the bomber units of the Armée de l'Air now began to crumble through losses among crews and the acute shortages of fuel resulting from the breakdown of transportation. On 6 June, for instance, 13 LeO 451s of Groupement 6 flew a sortie against the Somme crossing points but lost four aircraft to Messerschmitts; in six weeks this unit alone lost 71 bombers in the air and on the ground.

By 13 June the German armies were at the gates of Paris. The front, which stretched from the capital south-eastwards to Nogent and on to Verdun, was giving way. The following day all French bomber squadrons were ordered to start moving to bases in the South of France in preparation for evacuation to North Africa.

Meanwhile the French fighters had been in constant action. Between 5 and 10 June almost 100 aircraft had been lost, the majority in air combat. At the same time the RAF had sent a few Hurricane squadrons back to France to cover the western ports from which straggling British and French ground forces were being hurriedly withdrawn.

On 15 June there were still five squadrons, Nos 1, 17, 73, 242 and 501, patrolling Nantes, St Malo, Brest, St Nazaire and Cherbourg. The last squadrons to leave, Nos 1 and 73, which had been the first to arrive in France in September 1939 with the AASF, left French soil on 18 June.

Italy enters the war

Despite expectations that Mussolini's principal ambitions lay in North and East Africa, Italy entered the War on 10 June 1940 and made a token attack on the French Alpine Front, although there was no serious fighting for several days. Both sides were unprepared for the campaign, the French Air Force in particular being totally committed against the Luftwaffe in the north. Instead it fell to the Aéronavale to combat Italy's Regia Aeronautica. Early rounds clearly went to the Italians when on 12 June three elderly Lioré 70 flying boats were destroyed on their beaching trolleys in a bombing raid at Karouba. Three days later a formation of 38 Fiat BR 20 bombers and CR 42 escorts attacked Luc-en-Provence and four of the intercepting Bloch 151s were shot down.

Among the Aéronavale's inventory were 39 Chance-Vought 156 single-engined attack aircraft, manoeuvrable machines on which high hopes were pinned by the French. These, however, were not realised. Escadrille AB 3 lost 13 of its aircraft on the ground and, after re-forming in the South, lost six more in a ground strafing attack by Fiat CR 42s on Cuers. Occasionally the French Mediterranean fleet attacked Italian ports and on 17 June the French Navy bombarded Genoa under protection afforded by ten Dewoitine D.520s – but the Regia Aeronautica wisely failed to appear.

Postscript to defeat

One series of remarkable raids deserves special mention. Flown by a crew from Escadrille B 5, the huge but aged Farman 223.4, christened *Jules Verne*, took off during the afternoon of 7 June from Mérignac and set course to raid Berlin. Flying up the English Channel and along the North German coast to the Baltic, the great bomber then turned south to drop its bombs on the German capital, where it caused damage to a factory. Returning across the breadth of the German homeland *Jules Verne* landed at Orly the following day. Two days later the big aircraft flew all the way to Rostock where it dropped bombs on the Heinkel factory, returning home safely once more.

This supremely gallant episode was tragically characteristic of the whole French *débâcle*. The French pilots and aircrew displayed enormous courage with outmoded equipment until on 17 June the Pétain Government asked for an armistice. Even then units of the Armée de l'Air and Aéronavale sought escape from the Germans and made their way to North Africa, while others found bases in the unoccupied Vichy zone. All pretence of cohesion now disappeared as pilots and crews took their aircraft to the south. As late as 22 June Heinkels attacked a huge concentration of aircraft near the French west coast. The last sortie of the Battle of France was flown by Premier Maître Pivet in a Morane 406 over Royan, but even this last defiant act ended in tragedy when his aircraft was destroyed by flak.

Marshal Pétain signed the truce in the forest of Compiègne on 22 June 1940, ending this tragic phase of the war. The collapse of France marked a prelude to the Battle of Britain, the first check to Germany's fortunes. It was, for all that, a tragedy which could have been averted: the men were willing but the machinery was old and rusty.

Battle of Britain 1940

At 3 pm on Saturday 7 September 1940 the German Air Force launched what was at that time the greatest single bombing raid the world had ever witnessed. What is more, it overwhelmed the British defences, reached its target and created an inferno more devastating than any previous act of war. No one raid on Rotterdam or Warsaw came close to matching that made on the dockland of East London that evening. Moreover it sparked an air battle that involved more than 1,000 fighters and bombers.

Yet that raid was a vital turning point in the Battle of Britain; in shifting its aim from all-out attacks on the RAF to an assault on the British people, it marked a decisive admission by the Nazi leaders that they had been unable to defeat the RAF's all-important Fighter Com-

The Messerschmitt Bf 109E, the Luftwaffe's standard single-seat fighter in 1940, was equal to the RAF's Supermarine Spitfire and Hawker Hurricane.

mand. It represented, indeed, the first catastrophic check to Germany's territorial ambitions in Europe and can therefore be regarded as the first turning point in World War II.

The first principle in warfare is to select and maintain the aim. By shifting his aim in the Battle of Britain on 7 September 1940, Hermann Goering lost, and by the unforgiving rules of war, deserved to lose the battle to prepare the way for invasion. Britain therefore won the battle to survive. Her air force survived, and so long as it did there could be no invasion.

Germany's blitzkrieg

For nine months after the first German troops marched across the Polish border on 1 September 1939, Germany, as aggressor, had matters much her own way. Her whole belligerent philosophy was one of territorial seizure by *blitzkrieg* (lightning war) and, unfettered by moral responsibility towards the neutrality of uncommitted nations, she dictated the course of events by consideration only of her own military convenience. And Europe itself, slowly rousing from pacifist appeasement, was virtually powerless to interfere.

The confidence with which Germany pursued its aggression can be judged by the task it undertook on 10 May 1940 when, as the Blitzkrieg was turned westwards, the Wehrmacht and Luftwaffe took on the armies and air forces of Holland, Belgium, France and Britain simultaneously. And in six short weeks the first three of those nations were decisively beaten. Only the 'miracle' of Dunkirk saved the British Army from a similar fate. Only

the fact that Britain was not yet faced with an assault on her own shores saved her air force from decimation along with those of her continental Allies. Air Support for and defence of the British Army in France and Belgium had, however, cost the RAF dear, and the last three weeks of the Battle of France witnessed the almost complete destruction of at least two British fighter squadrons and heavy losses among men and machines in half a dozen others. At this early stage of the war almost all the RAF pilots who flew and fought in France were the peacetime-trained nucleus of the Service and their losses were thus the more keenly felt.

Ever since the sporadic raids by German airships and Gotha bombers of 1917–18 – whose novelty and assumed potential, rather than the damage and casualties they caused, had set in train events that led to the creation of the RAF itself – the organisation of an efficient air defence system had been pursued with a singleness of purpose that was rare among the world's peacetime air forces. And it must be said that even the great Lord Trenchard – rightly christened 'the Father of the Royal Air Force' – was a protagonist of the bomber as the decisive weapon in war, rather than the fighter.

The birth of radar

Those early air raids of the Kaiser's War furnished Britain with a priceless first-hand experience in setting out the design parameters of her air defence. They demonstrated the difficulties of fighter interception, of finding and following the enemy raiders, of deploying the defending fighters to meet the approaching bombers before they hit their

targets, and above all of creating a command structure of dedicated pilots and fostering squadron *esprit*. At first progress was slow. Parsimony in the British Treasury deprived the RAF of good fighter aircraft until 1930, when, thanks to the initiative of the British aircraft industry in concert with far-sighted men at the Air Ministry, the seeds of real technical progress were sown. They were soon to be harvested by men like Sydney Camm and Reginald Mitchell, who designed the Hawker Hurricane and Supermarine Spitfire fighters respectively.

British inventiveness was not confined to the field of aircraft design. Early efforts to produce a system of locating approaching raiders had depended on acoustic reflectors and had proved virtually useless. Almost by accident scientists, including Robert Watson-Watt, discovered that an aircraft passing through a beamed radio signal deflected the beam–and the deflection could be 'illustrated' on a cathode-ray oscilloscope. In only three years, between 1935 and 1938, this phenomenon was exploited to such an extent that a chain of radio location stations around the east and south coasts of England had been started and was being integrated into the operational air defence system.

These radio location (later called radar) stations surveyed the approaches from the sea but gave no satisfactory overland picture, and to provide this the nation called upon the services of civilian volunteers who manned a dense pattern of observer posts that covered the entire country. The Observer Corps (later given the prefix Royal for its wartime services) had its roots in the defence system to counter the Gotha raids of 1918.

Fighter Command

More than any other, one man was pre-eminent in the evolution of RAF Fighter Command as it was to fight in the Battle of Britain. Air Vice-Marshal Hugh Dowding had been appointed Air Member for Technical Development in 1931 and thereby came to the centre of efforts being made to introduce new fighters into the RAF, and

A Supermarine Spitfire of 72 Squadron flying over the coast. The Squadron was based at Biggin Hill and Croydon during August and September of 1940

Supermarine Spitfire Mk II of No 65 Squadron RAF

Dimensions
Span 11·23 m (36 ft 10 in)
Length 9·12 m (29 ft 11 in)

Engine
1,150 hp Rolls-Royce Merlin XII

Performance
Maximum speed 575 km/h (357 mph) at 5,180 m (17,000 ft)
Service ceiling 11,340 m (37,200 ft)
Range: 805 km (500 miles)

Armament
Eight 0·303 in Browning machine guns

later provided the stimulus needed to grasp the importance of radar and integrate it into the defence system. Furthermore, until 1934, British fighter defences, lacking the means to discover the approach of enemy bombers until they crossed the coast, expected and were organised to intercept incoming raids over a broad expanse of England, 80 km (50 miles) wide, extending from Dorset right round the south coast to Norfolk. The coming of radar promised the likelihood of interception *before* the enemy crossed the coast. In 1936 the RAF started a fundamental re-organisation whereby geographical defence responsibilities gave place to a new Command structure. Fighter Command was created and Dowding, then an Air Marshal, was appointed its leader – a position he was to occupy far beyond the normal period of tenure and beyond the age at which he expected to retire. His unique experience, the soundness of his judgement and the mutual respect that existed between him and his airmen represented assets no less priceless than those of Marlborough, Nelson and Wellington in previous ages of national danger.

During the inter-war years the air defences of Britain had faced across the English Channel towards France, as the only country with powerful military forces within striking range of her bomber aircraft – Germany having supposedly been disarmed after World War I. It had originally been calculated that to provide an adequate air defence against an aggressor the RAF required not less than 36 squadrons of fighter aircraft, but when Germany again emerged as a threat to European peace this estimate was increased to 52 squadrons, and this was still the RAF's expansion target when war was declared in September 1939. It must, however, be emphasised that in that month the German air force still occupied bases some 483 km (300 miles) from the nearest point on the English coast.

The fall of France

When France collapsed in June 1940 the German Luftwaffe was deployed on the French coast which, at its closest point, is only 32 km (20 miles) from England; furthermore, with bases in Scandinavia and the Low Countries, the enemy faced Britain from two directions.

As the Battle of France opened, Dowding had achieved his target of 52 fighter squadrons but losses in France had been very heavy and two further squadrons had been lost in Norway. Some squadrons were not yet fully operational and others were still equipped with the ineffectual Blenheim night fighter. His true 'order of battle' thus amounted to no more than 36 Hurricane and Spitfire Squadrons, equipped with about 450 Hurricanes and 250 Spitfires. Contrary to popular comment at the time and ever since, however, the Spitfire was not, in July 1940, wholly operational itself. Its stressed skin construction was still something of an innovation, and the repair of battle damage required base facilities that were in mid-1940 only available at five main fighter stations, namely Hornchurch, Biggin Hill, Duxford, Middle Wallop and Catterick. Moreover, the aircraft itself was still subject to operational ceiling limitations imposed by gun icing and by misting of the windscreen on descent from high altitude. There were also restrictions imposed on night flying by the Spitfire.

The Hurricane on the other hand had been in front line service almost a year longer than the Spitfire and was in effect constructed in much the same fashion as that of the biplanes of the previous ten years. Field experience in France, denied the Spitfire, had bestowed upon it a familiarity that rendered the Hurricane a 'go anywhere, do anything' fighter. The type's main weakness was that it was 48 km/h (30 mph) slower than the Spitfire.

Nevertheless, the fall of France posed numerous problems for the German air force and it was not immediately able to launch large scale attacks on the

Above: observers (right) took over from early-warning radar (left) after enemy raiders crossed the coast. Information was relayed to operations rooms (centre), which controlled defending fighters.
Below: Goering on the Channel coast in 1940

LOSSES IN JULY 1940				
Aircraft		**Pilots/Crew Members**		
Destroyed	**Damaged**	**Killed**	**Missing/ POW**	**Wounded**
Hurricane	33	17	23	—	11
Spitfire	34	24	25	—	9
Blenheim	4	1	9	—	1
Defiant	6	1	10	—	2
TOTAL	77	43	67	—	23
Dornier Do 17	39	13	30	74	19
Junkers Ju 87	13	11	10	12	3
Junkers Ju 88	39	11	52	67	11
Heinkel He 111	32	3	52	85	6
Messerschmitt Bf 109	48	14	17	14	13
Messerschmitt Bf 110	18	4	13	17	2
Other German aircraft	27	1	19	33	15
TOTAL	216	57	193	302	69

Inset below: Air Marshal Trafford Leigh-Mallory commanded 12 Group during the Battle. Below right: fighter ace Douglas Bader (centre, right) with Hugh Dowding who, as an Air Marshal, was appointed as Fighter Command's first commander in 1936

British Isles. This brief respite was both useful and unexpected to Dowding. His Command was divided into groups, each responsible for the defence of a large part of Britain. No 11 Group, commanded by Air Marshal Keith Park, covered the whole of Southern England. No 12 Group, under Air Marshal Trafford Leigh-Mallory, extended across the Midlands to the East Coast, while the North and Scotland were the defence responsibility of 13 Group under Air Vice-Marshal Richard Saul. It had for some time been realised that 11 Group, with London and the South-East, as well as important ports and industries (particularly aircraft factories), was too large for one command, and steps had already been taken to divide it again; thus, at an early stage in the Battle of Britain, a new group, No 10, came into being under Air Vice-Marshal Sir Christopher Quintin Brand – a brilliant commander and veteran night fighter pilot of World War

I, who had achieved fame with his historic flight to the Cape in 1920 with fellow South African Van Ryneveld.

Each fighter group was further divided into sectors, each containing a sector airfield and two or three advanced satellite aerodromes, usually near the coast. Not only was each sector airfield the main base for the two or three resident fighter squadrons allotted to the area, but also had the sector operations room, from which all orders were passed to the squadron pilots, whether they were in the air or on the ground.

Combat tactics

The process by which the fighter defences operated, had, under Dowding's scrutiny for four years, become a highly efficient weapon in the hands of an air force no more than tolerated by the pacifist administrations of the inter-war years, is outlined here.

First of all there were the CH (Chain Home) radar stations, located around the east and south coasts from the north of Scotland to Cornwall and South Wales. Manned round the clock by RAF personnel, these stations watched and reported to their respective sector, group and command operations rooms all incoming aircraft. Specialist officers at a filter room identified them as friendly, hostile or unknown (X-raids). Control of the defending fighters lay in the overall responsibility of the group commanders, who would bring squadrons to varying states of readiness according to the scale and direction of a threatening raid. These orders were passed to the respective sector operations rooms whose controller, often the station commander, would possess exact, up-to-date information of pilot and aircraft availability. Squadrons, which might be on the ground either at the sector station or one of the forward airfields, would be at one of the prescribed states, that is ten minutes on 'available', five minutes on 'readiness', or two minutes on 'standby', the latter with pilots in their machines with engines running.

Take-off orders were passed to the pilots by the sector controller by telephone or loudspeaker, and further instructions followed over the aircraft radio after take-

off. At the time of the Battle of Britain, information about enemy raids passed from the radar stations was fairly accurate in range and bearing, but height finding was still in its infancy and somewhat unreliable; in consequence the pilots tended to climb higher than ordered, to be more certain of gaining an advantage over the enemy raiders.

Combat tactics in use by the RAF in 1940 were undergoing radical changes. When British fighters met the Luftwaffe over Belgium and France during the Blitzkrieg most squadrons were still employing the formation attacks that had undergone little change since the previous war. The old 'fighting area attacks' involved a formation approach to the enemy raiders and, at a signal from the leader, would carry out a line astern or rigid formation attack. This procedure rendered the British fighters extremely vulnerable to enemy fighters, not to mention the defensive fire of the bombers, whose gunners could anticipate the approach of each attacker in turn. By the end of the Battle of France, the RAF fighter leaders were evolving new tactics employing the use of small sections of two or three aircraft; this size of fighting unit enabled the squadron leader to detach one flight or section to guard against enemy fighters while his other pilots carried out paired attacks on several bombers simultaneously. Similar tactics were being used by the German fighters and by the end of 1940 both air forces were established in the employment of paired sections (*rotte*), the 'finger four' (*schwarm*), and the flight (*staffel*).

Luftwaffe organisation

The Luftwaffe facing Britain in June 1940 was composed of three air fleets, Luftflotte 5 based in Scandinavia, Luftflotte 2 in Holland, Belgium and North-East France, and Luftflotte 3 in North-West France. Although under the overall direction of the OKL (*Oberkommando der Luftwaffe*, or Luftwaffe High Command), each *luftflotte* was an autonomous command, with its own bomber, fighter, reconnaissance and ancillary components. Additionally, Luftflotte 2 included dive-bomber units (*sturzkampffliegerverbände*)—the famous Stukas—and a special-

ist pathfinder group, Erprobungsgruppe 210. There were also minelaying groups, coastal bomber units and an efficient air-sea rescue organisation. The fighter arm was composed of the single-engined Messerschmitt Bf 109 and the long-range heavy fighter (Zerstörer), the Bf 110.

The basic operational command unit was the *geschwader* a large echelon of about 100 aircraft, divided between the staff (*stab*) flight and three groups (*gruppen*), each of about 30 aircraft. Each group was further divided into a staff flight (*stabschwarm*) and three *staffeln*, each of about ten aircraft. These formations were commanded respectively by a *geschwaderkommodore* (usually a colonel or lieutenant-colonel), a *gruppenkommandant* (a major), and a *staffelkapitan* (either a captain—*hauptmann*—or a senior lieutenant—an *oberleutnant*).

By the end of June 1940 the three air fleets consisted of 1,215 bombers, 280 dive-bombers, 755 single-engine

Above: the Junkers Ju 87 Stuka was operated against shipping and airfield targets.
Inset below: Feldmarschall Hugo Sperrle, who led Luftflotte 3 in 1940.
Below left: Goering visits a fighter squadron on the Channel coast in the Autumn of 1940

Right: Squadron Leader Douglas Bader with two pilots of 242 Squadron, Flt Lt Ball and Plt Off Knight. Flying Hurricanes, the squadron claimed over 60 victims during the Battle of Britain.
Below: Peter Townsend (second from right) with pilots of 43 Squadron in April 1940, when he was in command of 'B' Flight.

fighters, 225 heavy fighters and 70 reconnaissance aircraft ranged on 53 airfields facing Britain. While the Luftwaffe certainly lacked nothing in numerical superiority, it was, however, far from adequate for the task before it. Even the task itself, yet to be defined by the German High Command, was a nebulous continuation of German territorial domination. Clearly, if Britain would not sue for peace after the fall of France, then direct military action –even an invasion preceded by a devastating aerial assault–must be undertaken against the islands. When Hitler's call to the British on 16 July to surrender was summarily refused, the Germans laid plans to launch a cross-Channel invasion. Essential prerequisites of such an operation were first, the elimination of the RAF's capacity to resist an invasion, and second, denial of the use by the Royal Navy of ports in Southern England.

The Luftwaffe's ability to achieve these aims was never doubted by Goering or his senior commanders, yet a glance at the strategic philosophy behind the successful Blitzkrieg shows the entire composition of the German Air Force to have been designed to support a land battle. Even the much-vaunted Stukas were, in effect, merely long-range artillery, suitable for destroying pin-point targets but little else. The bomber arm, composed largely of medium bombers (the Heinkel He 111, Dornier Do 17 and Junkers Ju 88) was quite unsuited for a prolonged strategic offensive, especially in daylight, while the Messerschmitt Bf 109, when used as an escort fighter, could not accompany the bombers further than the south-east corner of England owing to a very limited range. Weaknesses in two other German weapons, the Stuka (Junkers Ju 87) and Zerstörer (Messerschmitt Bf 110) were to be exposed in the coming battle.

Skirmishing tactics

The Battle of Britain opened with a series of inconsequential sorties early in July. As already mentioned, no plan of campaign had yet been promulgated by OKL, but natural targets of opportunity, such as coastal shipping, would be attacked as a means of attracting RAF fighters into combat. These tactics would be formalised as the month advanced, and the *kampfgeschwader* (bomber wings) commenced sporadic training flights over British towns and cities at night by small numbers of aircraft.

The Battle of Britain can be considered to have started with the setting foot on sovereign British territory by the German Army (the occupation of the Channel Islands) on 30 June–1 July 1940, although the first month was spent by the opposing forces in skirmishing. The lack of an overall plan resulted in individual German units being committed to battle piecemeal, small formations of bombers being provided with fighter escorts which varied according to local availability. A deep-sea convoy, code-named 'Jumbo', was attacked on the first day of the month by Junkers Ju 87 dive-bombers in the Western Approaches, but the defending fighters only arrived on the scene after the bombs had fallen, and the Hurricane pilots were ordered to remain over the ships and not to pursue the raiders.

Another raid by the Stukas against the naval base at Portland occurred on the 4th in the hope of catching ships of the Royal Navy in port. Again the British fighters were too late, and the sole opposition to the raid was provided by ground fire and the guns of HMS *Foyle Bank*, a large anti-aircraft auxiliary vessel moored in Portland harbour. The ship was hit by a bomb and started to sink, but this did not deter a young naval rating who, mortally wounded,

remained at his gun and shot down one of the raiders. Leading Seaman Jack Mantle's gallantry earned him a posthumous Victoria Cross.

Both these raids had been carried out by Stukageschwader 51 (St G 51)–the first dive-bomber wing to deploy operationally after the fall of France–but another raid on Portland was launched six days later by 30 Stukas of St G 77. Forewarned by radar, British fighters were

Below: the Merlin-engined Hawker Hurricane bore the brunt of the early air fighting.
Bottom: a Spitfire II squadron scrambles. This mark flew only in the Battle's final months

quickly in action and, before the German escort could intervene. Spitfires of 609 Squadron shot down one of the dive-bombers flown by Hauptmann Freiherr von Dalwigk, holder of the Knight's Cross.

Target Fighter Command

If these and other scattered raids had been but a prelude to the great battle to come, those first nine days of July had cost the German air force 52 aircraft with their crews, compared with the loss of 11 Spitfires, five Hurricanes and a Blenheim. Twelve RAF pilots had been killed and seven wounded – the equivalent fighting strength of a single squadron. The pattern of the attacks – with raids on shipping and south coast ports – had been clear to Dowding and Park, although the aim was not. It was not yet obvious that the Luftwaffe's true target was Fighter Command: that by launching raids on coastal targets the Germans hoped to attract British fighters into the sky, where they could be destroyed, and to force the defences to maintain enervating and wasteful standing patrols over the convoys. On the other hand, what the Germans did not yet realise was the part being played by the coastal radar. They had known of its existence – 106 metre (350 ft) towers could scarcely be camouflaged – and were aware that the radar stations were for locating enemy raids, but they had no idea of the extent to which radar had been integrated into the fighter defences, or that direct control of fighters was being effected through an up-to-the-minute picture provided by radar.

On 10 July the weight of German attacks perceptibly increased. A large convoy, code-named 'Bread', sailed from the Thames Estuary round the Kent coast, and during the afternoon came under attack by escorted Dornier Do 17s of KG 2. The famous 111 – 'Treble One' – Hurricane Squadron went into action, shooting down three bombers and two fighters, but losing one of its number. Heavier attacks on another convoy the following day were co-ordinated with a raid by Heinkel He 111s on Portsmouth as well as further dive-bombing over the Channel: four Hurricanes and two Spitfires were lost, but casualties among Luftwaffe crews amounted to 49 dead.

By mid-July Luftflotten 2 and 3 had virtually completed their initial deployment against Britain, with 15 *gruppen* of bombers, six of dive-bombers, ten of heavy fighters and 12 of single-engine fighters now operational on the Channel coast, a combat strength of about 2,500 aircraft. These were to be joined by about 400 more in the coming month. In addition there were numerous support units including reconnaissance *gruppen*, air-sea rescue units and weather reporting *staffeln*.

Defiants withdrawn

A spell of poor weather in mid-July enabled Dowding to 'rotate' some of his squadrons, sending those that had been in action most to the north to rest and replenish with pilots and aircraft. Others which had been resting since Dunkirk were brought south to take their place. There were a few new squadrons which had not yet seen action and among these was the Defiant-equipped 141 Squadron which moved to the Biggin Hill sector at this time. Fighter Command's only other Defiant squadron, No 264, had achieved some success (much exaggerated at the time) over Dunkirk when enemy fighters evidently mistook the Defiants for Hurricanes and fell prey to the type's four turret-mounted guns. Misled by this momentary lapse on the part of the Luftwaffe, the RAF confidently committed this second squadron to combat, apparently satisfied that the aircraft could hold its own. Disaster struck on 19 July

Opposite: a map showing the main Luftwaffe airfields in France (additional units based in Norway also took part in the Battle). The RAF Fighter Command airfields and radar stations are also indicated, together with the boundaries between fighter sectors and groups

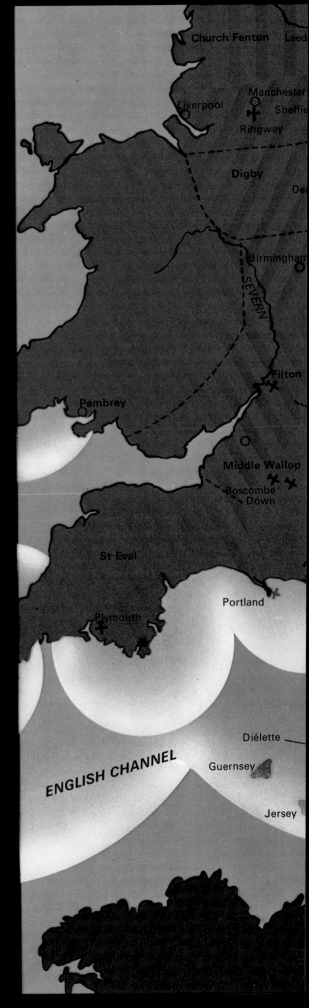

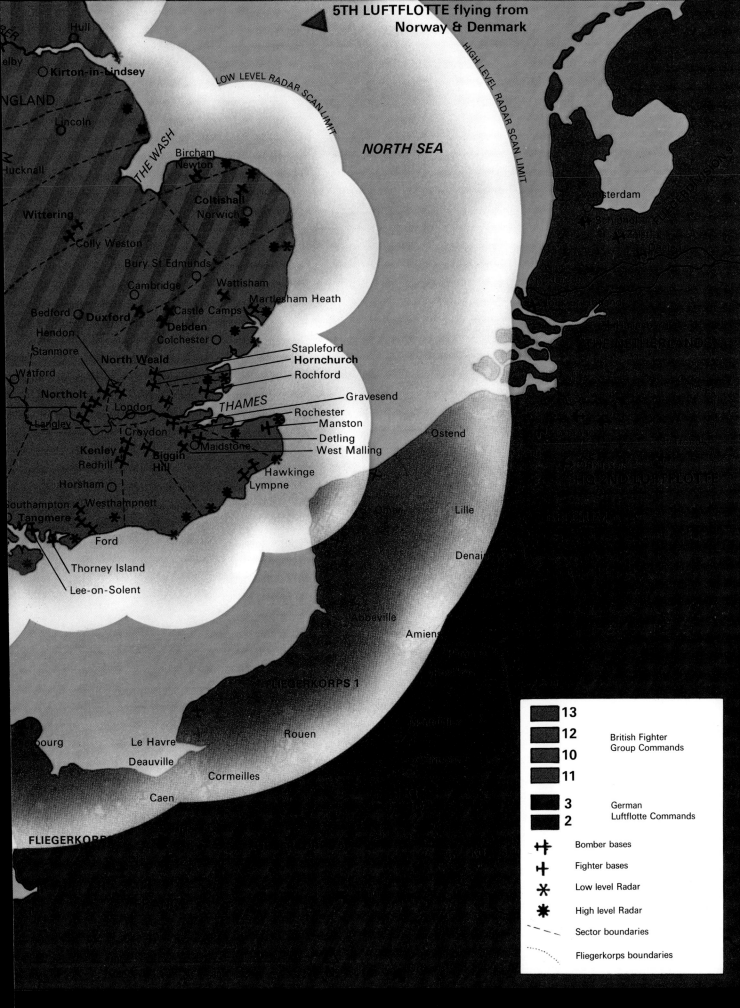

little significance in the Battle of Britain–that was to influence the entire pattern of future air defence. On the night of 22/23 July a lone Blenheim night fighter of the Fighter Development Unit apparently stumbled across a Dornier flying over the Channel and shot it down. In truth the Blenheim, flown by Flying Officer G. Ashfield, had been stalking the Dornier for some minutes using a small radar set–known as Airborne Interception (AI) Mark III–carried within the aircraft. For nine months a handful of these Blenheims had been equipped with rudimentary radar but combat success had eluded them. Ashfield's achievement was the world's first victory for a radar-equipped fighter.

Fighter sweeps

During the last week of July the Luftwaffe stepped up its attacks, particularly in the south-east. Attacks on convoys were noticeably better planned and a new German tactic emerged–one that was to cause Dowding and Park growing anxiety. This was the 'free chase' sweep, in which German fighter formations roamed the southern counties with orders to attack RAF fighters as they returned to base, low on fuel and ammunition. These sweeps were frequently timed to coincide with German attacks on convoys, and the tactics certainly paid quick dividends; during the last week in July RAF losses rose to 31 fighters destroyed and 18 others seriously damaged. Fifteen pilots were killed and six wounded. Yet it was the emergence of these tactics that served to clarify in the minds of British commanders the German aims and the methods by which they hoped to achieve them. Orders were immediately given to the squadrons to avoid combat with enemy fighters whenever possible, and particularly when no enemy bombers were in the immediate vicinity. These orders could, however, take no account of enemy fighters that lurked near RAF airfields, ready to pounce on returning Hurricanes and Spitfires, with the result that most station commanders detailed a single flight to be ready to guard against such attacks.

Round one also went to the German air force in its attacks on British shipping. Thirty-two convoys had sailed in the Channel during the month and all but seven had been attacked. The Royal Navy had lost 14 ships, including four destroyers, to air action, and it was now decided to move the Channel flotillas further afield, except

LOSSES IN AUGUST 1940					
Aircraft			*Pilots/Crew Members*		
				Missing/	
	Destroyed	*Damaged*	*Killed*	*POW*	*Wounded*
Hurricane	211	44	85	1	68
Spitfire	113	40	41	3	38
Blenheim	13	10	6	3	—
Defiant	7	3	7	—	4
Beaufighter	—	1	—	—	—
TOTAL	344	98	139	7	110
Dornier Do 17	71	30	70	129	57
Junkers Ju 87	57	16	35	58	19
Junkers Ju 88	89	32	94	182	19
Heinkel He 111	89	15	113	204	35
Messerschmitt Bf 109	217	45	54	91	39
Messerschmitt Bf 110	119	40	80	113	22
Other German aircraft	27	4	17	27	10
TOTAL	669	182	463	804	201

Opposite: the Messerschmitt Bf 109E (top) and Messerschmitt Bf 110 (bottom) were the main fighter types used by the Luftwaffe in the Battle of Britain

when nine Defiants were caught by a similar number of Messerschmitt Bf 109s off the Kent coast. Aware that the British fighters possessed no forward-firing guns, the Germans shot down six Defiants without loss and damaged another. The remaining aircraft of 141 Squadron were hurriedly moved out of the battle area.

Three nights later there occurred an event–itself of

Messerschmitt Bf 109E of Jagdgeschwader 27

Dimensions
Length 8·64 m (28 ft 4¼ in)
Span 9·87 m (32 ft 4½ in)
Height 2·5 m (8 ft 2⅓ in)

Engine
1,100 hp Daimler-Benz DB 601A

Performance
Maximum speed 570 km/h (350 mph) at 3,750 m (12,300 ft)
Rate of climb 954 m/min (3,300 ft/min)
Range 660 km (410 miles)

Armament
Two 7·9 mm MG 17 machine guns
Two 20 mm MG FF cannon

while escorting convoys. The frequency of the convoys themselves was much reduced and more were routed round the north of Scotland. Damage, though not yet heavy, had also been caused in the Channel ports.

By now the Germans had become aware, as a result of increased opposition over the convoys, that British radar was an integral part of the fighter defences. British and German air forces had parried each other's thrusts and each had learned a great deal about its opponent. Dowding could, however, feel satisfied that there appeared to be no serious gap in his defences. Only the Germans knew that July had been no more than the curtain going up.

Convoy Peewit
After the growing weight of attacks during the last week of July there followed a week-long lull in the fighting. The reasons for this inactivity were threefold. First, the frequency of convoy sailings being reduced deprived the Luftwaffe of targets whose defence would force Fighter Command into the air. Second, the weather deteriorated to some extent over northern France, although it remained relatively fine over Britain. Lastly, the Luftwaffe was itself preoccupied with final preparations for the all-out assault prior to the intended cross-Channel invasion. *Geschwader* and *gruppe* commanders attended briefing conferences at *fliegerkorps* headquarters, operational units moved to their forward bases and the opportunity was taken to bring combat strengths closer to their authorised establishment.

By the 8th most of the German preparations were complete, although an improvement in the weather proved only short-lived. The heavy air attacks on this day con-

stituted what was in effect, the battle of Convoy Peewit. This large convoy had sailed the previous day from the Medway and came under persistent attack by E-boats as it passed the Dover Straits; spotted and tracked by newly-installed German radar on the Calais shore, the convoy was heavily dive-bombed by more than 100 Stukas which kept up a series of strikes throughout the morning, culminating in a vicious air battle near the Isle of Wight in the afternoon. The convoy suffered badly, only four of the original 20 ships reaching Swanage. The Germans lost ten dive-bombers destroyed and six damaged; four Bf 110s and 11 Bf 109s were destroyed. RAF losses amounted to 13 Hurricanes and five Spitfires destroyed, with 15 pilots killed.

Coastal targets

Poor weather delayed further attacks until the 11th, when German tactics changed perceptibly, heralding a new phase in the battle. On that day the Luftwaffe divided its attention between south coast ports and coastal airfields–also throwing in a blistering attack by Erprobungsgruppe 210 on Convoy Booty near Harwich. Dover came in for a number of snap raids by strafing Bf 110s, but the day's major raid by 54 Ju 88s of KG 54 and 20 He 111s of KG 27, escorted by 61 Bf 110s and 30 Bf 109s, made for Portland and Weymouth. It was, however, well intercepted by 58 Hurricanes and 16 Spitfires, whose pilots downed 26 enemy aircraft and damaged seven others; 18 Hurricanes and four Spitfires were lost, 11 pilots were killed and four drowned. Elsewhere the Germans lost nine aircraft.

If there was one important outcome of the fighting on the 11th it was a realisation by the Germans of the manner in which the British pilots were being fed with up-to-the-minute information from the coastal radar. The raids on Weymouth and Portland had been met by large formations of RAF fighters–with dire effects. Following earnest demands by the signals branch of OKL, it was decided on the 12th to destroy this radar prior to the major attack–code-named Adlerangriff (Attack of the Eagle)–scheduled to start the following day. Once again the crack fighter-bomber strike unit Erprobungsgruppe 210 was sent into action, other raids being set up as feints and diversions. Led by the popular Swiss pilot, Walter Rubensdörffer, 16 Bf 110s flew westwards along the Kent coast, groups of four aircraft breaking inland to attack the CH stations at Dover, Rye and Pevensey, while the leader himself took four aircraft across country to hit Dunkirk CH on the north Kent coast. All the radars were damaged but none was out of action for more than 24 hours. Further west a large formation of almost 100 Ju 88s of KG 51 escorted by about 25 Bf 109s and 120 Bf 110s attacked Portsmouth and the Ventnor CH radar on the Isle of Wight. Among the casualties suffered in this raid was KG 51's commander, Oberst Dr Fisser. Other targets that attracted the Luftwaffe included the forward airfields at Manston, Lympne and Hawkinge–all of which were severely damaged during the temporary loss of radar early warning.

Although two small convoys, Agent and Arena, were dive-bombed off the Kent coast on the 12th, the fighting on this day represented a more serious shift in the enemy's pressure; the Luftwaffe was now ready to launch its major offensive against the fighter defence itself. No longer content with trailing its coat in the hope of attracting the fighters into the air, the Luftwaffe, using heavy escort forces, would henceforth strike all the fighter airfields in the south of England. Biggin Hill, Kenley, Croydon, Tangmere, Hornchurch, Middle Wallop, Debden–all

would feel the crushing weight of bombs, and some of them would be raided many times over.

Stronger fighter escorts

Yet herein lay serious weaknesses in the German plan. The very bitterness of the RAF's defence of the convoys and coastal targets had brought about unnecessarily high losses among German bombers–even before the main attack had opened. High casualties among officer crews now prompted Goering to issue orders limiting officers to not more than one per aircraft. Much more important, however, was his insistence on increased fighter protection of the bomber formations. Well over half the available Bf 109s were now committed to close escort, while the Bf 110 (which had been designed with escort duties in mind) was itself to be escorted by the single-seaters. These orders had two vital effects: they reduced the danger to RAF pilots posed by the free-chasing Bf 109s over Kent and Sussex, and the shackling of Bf 109s to the slow-flying bomber formations severely reduced the effectiveness of these otherwise excellent fighters. Moreover, the strictly limited range of the Bf 109 did not permit the fighter to accompany bomber formations beyond the southern fringes of Essex; there would be numerous instances when, after early interception, the Bf 109s would be forced, through shortage of fuel, to abandon their charges and return home–frequently seeking to avoid further combat.

Eagle Day

Goering's Adler Tag (Eagle Day) was planned for 13 August, but an extraordinary chain of events led to the bungling of the day's operations. Pre-dawn orders had been received by fighter and bomber units to open the assault, but a

Above: a Luftwaffe fighter pilot has his parachute harness adjusted before an offensive sweep.
Top right: tarpaulins are removed from the engines of a Heinkel He 111 medium bomber prior to take-off.
Above right: a wartime artist's impression of the air fighting over southern England

(of no importance to Fighter Command) was hit and a few bombs fell near Middle Wallop, but Tangmere escaped as did Weymouth and Portland; Southampton, however, was heavily raided. Over Kent, Ju 87s of von Brauchitsch's IV/LG 1 made a devastating attack on the airfield at Detling, destroying the hangars, messes and operations block and killing 67 men – including the station commander, Group Captain Edward Davis. Twenty-two aircraft were destroyed on the ground. However Detling, too, was not a fighter airfield.

The day's fighting cost the Luftwaffe 45 aircraft destroyed and 24 damaged, compared with the loss of 12 Hurricanes and two Spitfires, with three pilots killed and six wounded. It represented the first resounding defeat suffered by the Luftwaffe in the Battle of Britain – but worse was to follow two days later.

Sporadic raids were mounted on the 14th (during one of which KG 55's commander, Oberst Alois Stoeckl, was shot down and killed by Flt Lt D. M. Crook of 609 Squadron), but in the main this day was spent in recriminations over the previous day's fiasco, and in ensuring that there would be no repetition in the great raids planned for Thursday 15 August.

Raids on the north-east

Many exaggerated combat claims by his pilots led Goering to believe that continuing defence of the south of England was only being maintained by draining fighters from the north. Thus the planned operations of the 15th employed co-ordinated raids by Luftflotten 2 and 3 in the south, while two large set-piece raids by Scandinavian-based bombers of Luftflotte 5 on the north-east were expected to meet with little opposition. In the event a carefully planned raid by 63 He 111s escorted by 21 Bf 110s on the Newcastle and Sunderland area met 18 Hurricanes and 24 Spitfires from Drem, Acklington and Catterick, and lost eight bombers and seven fighters. No British fighters were lost. Shortly afterwards a force of 50 Ju 88s, flying from Denmark, swept in over the south Yorkshire coast to attack Driffield, Leconfield and Church Fenton, but were driven back by two fighter squadrons which destroyed eight of the raiders, again without loss. With casualties reaching almost 20 per cent, Luftflotte 5 never again attempted heavy raids against Britain in daylight.

In the south, however, the defences were hard pressed to meet the numerous raids which continued throughout the day. Portland was again heavily attacked by dive-bombers flying under heavy escort, and while Brand's fighters were busy dealing with this threat, Middle Wallop and Worthy Down were attacked by formations of Ju 88s. Lympne and Hawkinge were again dive-bombed, and British fighters were caught by some free chases which swept in over Kent at about mid-day. The hard-pressed Erpr Gr 210 carried out three raids, the first on Manston just after noon and the second on Martlesham Heath at 3 pm. Its last raid, carried out as part of a co-ordinated attack with Dorniers on Rochester, was intended to be mounted against the important sector airfield at Kenley at 6 pm. Led once more by Rubensdörffer, the Messerschmitts got off to a bad start when they missed their rendezvous with escorting fighters and then, owing to cloud cover, missed the airfield at Kenley and attacked Croydon just as two Hurricane squadrons were scrambling. Unable to extricate themselves in time, the German pilots were closely pursued all the way back to the south coast, losing almost every one of their staff machines, including that of Rubensdörffer. The raid on Croydon caused heavy damage and casualties, but it has been said

cancellation following adverse weather reports reached only the fighter units because of confusion over radio frequencies. Accordingly, a formation of 74 Do 17s of KG 2 took off from bases in north-east France and, without its scheduled escort, attacked the Coastal Command airfield at Eastchurch on the Isle of Sheppey, in the mistaken belief that it was a fighter base. Considerable damage was caused despite a spirited interception by 74 Squadron led by the famous South African, 'Sailor' Malan.

Elsewhere more confusion reigned. A raid by KG 54's Ju 88s took off without escort for a raid on Farnborough and the airfield at Odiham, but turned back when intercepted over the south coast. The Ju 88s' escort, provided by Bf 110s of ZG 2, had delayed its take-off while the cancellation order was queried. The aircraft eventually took off to cover a raid on Portland. Cancellation of the raid had not been notified to ZG 2 and the Bf 110s found two squadrons of fighters awaiting them!

Some semblance of order had been restored by the afternoon and it was Luftflotte 3 that mounted the day's major attack. Formations totalling 120 Ju 88s, 79 Ju 87s, 30 Bf 110s and about 100 Bf 109s advanced across the Channel from the Brest peninsula, their targets being the airfields at Middle Wallop, Warmwell and Tangmere, and the port facilities at Portland, Weymouth and Southampton. Given good warning by radar, Brand ordered up three Hurricane and three Spitfire squadrons, whose quick interceptions forced the Bf 109s to return home early, thereby depriving the vulnerable Stukas of their essential protection. The result was that small groups of dive bombers roamed the Hampshire countryside under constant attack by the British fighters. Andover airfield

that it had much wider significance. Orders were in force at the time prohibiting German crews from attacking targets in London and certainly few raids had been experienced by the metropolis up to that time; it was suggested that the casualties among civilians at Croydon prompted the Prime Minister, Winston Churchill, to authorise a reprisal raid on Berlin–a raid which was duly mounted nine nights later. This raid, in turn, so enraged the Nazi war leaders that it sparked the heavy retaliation by Goering on 7 September. Such a train of events must, however, be wholly discounted as it must have been seen that the original raid was clearly carried out against a legitimate military target in the Greater London area, and it was the very proximity of civilian factories to the airfield that brought about the casualties.

And so the great battles of 15 August eventually died away. The Germans had flown more than 2,000 sorties over Britain and suffered the total loss of 75 aircraft, or almost the equivalent of an entire *geschwader*. RAF losses were 18 Hurricanes and 11 Spitfires, with 11 pilots killed and 11 wounded. Two pilots landed in France and were taken prisoner. Seventeen other RAF aircraft were destroyed on the ground. But the defence had on the whole held firm; almost all the enemy raids had been intercepted and many of the targets attacked were nothing to do with the fighter defences. The very determination and effectiveness of the fighter opposition took the German aircrews by surprise and the day was, long after, referred to by the Luftwaffe as 'Black Thursday'.

Fighter Command's VC

Attacks on the following day were of much the same pattern, albeit without the participation of Luftflotte 5 in the north-east. On this day the airfield at Tangmere was attacked by dive-bombers and it was in this raid that the first American volunteer with the RAF, Pilot Officer W. M. L. Fiske, died in the defence of Britain. In a combat near Southampton another RAF pilot, Flt Lt John Nicolson of 249 Squadron, won the Victoria Cross when, suffering severe burns, he remained in his blazing Hurricane long enough to engage a Messerschmitt Bf 110 before baling out. His was the only VC ever won by a pilot of Fighter Command.

The next heavy attacks against England were launched on the 18th and this day was particularly significant as being the last occasion on which the Stuka was employed in any numbers against Britain. It has been suggested that the Stuka suffered defeat at the hands of British fighter pilots and certainly the losses sustained by the *stuka-geschwader* between 8 and 18 August were fairly severe. On the other hand one is left to question whether the Ju 87 should have been used in the Battle of Britain at all, so long as effective fighter opposition existed. The dive-bomber was, in all probability, simply withdrawn so as to conserve its numbers for the support of the invasion. Of the two types of targets for which the Stuka was the ideal weapon–shipping and airfields–only the fighter stations remained, and these were not healthy for the Ju 87. In any case it was already being shown that carpet bombing by conventional bombers was achieving sufficiently heavy damage.

The Battle's crisis

The beginning of the third and certainly the most critical phase of the Battle was 24 August. On this day the Luftwaffe stepped up its attacks against inland fighter stations, and co-ordinated these with widespread free chases over Kent, Surrey and Sussex. North Weald and Hornchurch

were both heavily hit during the day, and it was in the raid on the latter airfield that Defiants again featured. Inexplicably, in view of the previous tragedy suffered by 141 Squadron, 264 Squadron had been moved to Hornchurch and was ordered off against the approaching Ju 88s but was caught by the escorting Bf 109s, losing the squadron commander, who was last seen pursuing the bombers towards France. In the course of the next five days 264 Squadron was to lose no fewer than 12 aircraft before it was finally withdrawn from day fighting altogether. But it was the free-chasing Bf 109s, that on the 24th, were to strike down the majority of RAF fighters lost, 18 Hurricanes and Spitfires being shot down by marauding *staffeln* of enemy fighters. And it was during the night of 24/25 August that, while station personnel at Biggin Hill, Hornchurch and North Weald worked to repair the damage on their airfields, more than 100 German bombers carried out their first unopposed raid on London, although, unlike later raids, the bombing was scattered and posed no great difficulties for the fire and emergency services.

Climax of the daylight battle occurred during the eight-day period between 30 August and 6 September. This was the heyday of the free chase, and throughout the period RAF Fighter Command suffered losses equivalent to one whole squadron every day. From the outset, the Germans employed tactics designed to keep British pilots constantly in the air, assembling relatively small raids over the French coast and launching them at frequent intervals. By these tactics the Germans hoped to draw progressively more Hurricanes and Spitfires into the air, engage them and catch them with free chases as they returned to base short of fuel and ammunition. These tactics differed materially from those employed earlier in the numbers of fighters flying the free chases–whole *gruppen* frequently being used. On at least six known instances formations of nearly 100 Bf 109s were encountered over Kent. Pressure on the British pilots was exhausting, and it was frequently known for pilots to fly five or six sorties in a single day and be in combat three or four times.

Loss of experienced pilots

Notwithstanding the losses in aircraft by the RAF squadrons, it was the pilot casualties that were to cause Dowding the greatest anxiety at this time. The nature of interception fighting rendered Fighter Command an autonomous entity with only a strictly limited number of trained pilots available; the particular qualities of a fighter pilot were seldom to be found among other Command pilots, and it was with some misgivings that Dowding accepted the services of a small number of bomber and army co-operation pilot volunteers as replacements for his depleted ranks. At the same time he reluctantly decided to relegate some of his exhausted squadrons to a training role, simply retaining the most experienced and least tired survivors to provide the core of less experienced squadrons. Many of his veteran squadron and flight commanders had succumbed in battle, their places taken by relatively junior officers. On 41 Squadron, the squadron commander and a flight commander were killed, their places being taken by a flight lieutenant and pilot officer respectively. A fortnight later the latter frequently found himself leading the whole squadron (and incidentally shot down about nine enemy aircraft despite flying with fragments of an enemy shell lodged in his heel). New, inexperienced squadrons were being brought south into 11 Group only to suffer heavy losses in their very first encounter with the enemy. No 85

Below: the Bf 110 suffered appalling losses while operating as a fighter and was later switched to reconnaissance and fighter-bomber duties.
Below right: by 7 August 1940 a total of 2,309 Hurricanes had been delivered, equipping 32 squadrons.
Bottom: German forces deployed along the Channel coast in readiness for Operation Sealion. This planned invasion of Britain, scheduled for Summer 1940, was thwarted by the Luftwaffe's aerial defeat

LOSSES IN SEPTEMBER 1940

| | Aircraft | | Pilots/Crew Members | | |
	Destroyed	Damaged	Killed	Missing/ POW	Wounded
Hurricane	221	56	74	2	86
Spitfire	144	56	41	1	40
Blenheim	6	2	10	3	—
TOTAL	371	114	125	6	126
Dornier Do 17	43	23	76	57	29
Junkers Ju 87	1	1	1	—	—
Junkers Ju 88	101	39	170	148	40
Heinkel He 111	88	48	133	141	49
Messerschmitt Bf 109	207	54	50	99	25
Messerschmitt Bf 110	101	23	71	93	13
Other German aircraft	21	5	6	10	12
TOTAL	562	193	507	548	168

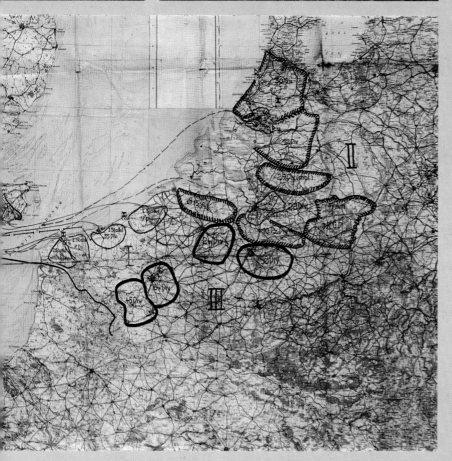

Squadron, led by Squadron Leader Peter Townsend, lost 14 Hurricanes in action between 26 August and 2 September when it was taken out of the line to re-equip and train new pilots. The top-scoring pilot on the squadron, 'Sammy' Allard, had been a sergeant pilot when the Battle of Britain started, had been commissioned as a pilot officer and by September was a flight lieutenant with the Distinguished Flying Cross and two Distinguished Flying Medals, having destroyed nine enemy aircraft and shared in the destruction of several others.

Valuable reinforcements were now arriving in Fighter Command in the shape of new Polish, Czechoslovakian and Canadian squadrons. Many of the Poles and Czechs were already veterans of air combat against the Luftwaffe, some of them having joined the French Air Force after the invasion of their own countries and subsequently been evacuated to Britain to continue the fight against Germany. Indeed it was a Free Czech, Josef František, who, flying with 303 (Polish) Squadron during September, destroyed the largest number of enemy aircraft by any RAF pilot during the Battle of Britain—being credited with 17 victories before he was killed on 8 October.

Goering's intervention

Apart from isolated instances, the Luftwaffe achieved little material damage to Fighter Command on the ground during that first week in September. Moreover the continued appearance of Hurricanes and Spitfires in the air over southern England gave rise to growing speculation in the minds of German airmen as to the accuracy of previous combat claims. According to their Intelligence sources Fighter Command should have ceased to exist by now, and heavy attacks on British fighter factories should have prevented the delivery of new aircraft. The long drawn-out battle was beginning to tell on German airmen; for too long the fighter pilots had struggled home, balancing their chances of survival against their slender fuel reserves. Bomber crews had started to calculate the odds on their surviving the summer as colleague after colleague plunged down to crash on the inhospitable island soil, to an unknown fate at the hands of a determined people.

Perhaps it was the exasperation that started at the lower echelons and spread upwards which brought Reichsmarschall Hermann Goering, resplendent in his foppish regalia and surrounded by fawning photographers, hotfoot to the Channel coast with a determination to deal a death blow to the British Isles. Playing scant heed to the achievements of his Luftwaffe in the past eight weeks and brushing aside the continued survival of Fighter Command, he simply formulated an all-out assault on London in the stated belief that, by so doing, he would crush the British will to continue waging war. With a strategic bomber force comparable with that of RAF Bomber Command three long years later, he might have achieved his goal. All that he did ensure in his attack on London (and later, other British cities) was the certain survival of the British defence system.

By the time Goering arrived in France, in early September, the Germans had assembled large numbers of invasion barges in many of the Channel ports, a fact that had not passed unnoticed by the RAF, whose bombers had paid frequent visits by night in attempts to destroy them before embarkation of the enemy army. Already warnings had been issued to British land forces that an invasion might be expected within a week; the very bitterness of that first week's air fighting over southern England seemed to confirm the defenders' fears that an enemy landing was imminent on the Kent or Sussex coasts.

When Saturday 7 September dawned with fine weather, the British radar screens were clear of enemy aircraft. Was this to be the calm before the storm? The morning passed with no more German activity than scattered reconnaissance flights, while Park moved his fighter squadrons as near the coast as he dared, keeping most of them at ten minutes readiness.

London attacked

It was not until mid-afternoon that the first indications appeared of German raid preparations. Initial raid plots of '50-plus' over the Pas de Calais quickly increased to several raids of '100-plus', and at 1616 hours the first visual sighting by an observer post reached the Maidstone plotting centre telling of 'many hundreds of enemy bombers and fighters' approaching the North Foreland coast. Reacting quickly, Park ordered 11 squadrons into the air over Kent and brought the remaining ten to two minutes standby, warning the neighbouring Groups to be ready to send reinforcements at a moment's notice. At first he kept the fighters in the vicinity of his airfields, but as the great raid continued westwards along the north Kent coast, realisation dawned on the British controllers that the enemy was making for London. At 1630 hours the first British fighters broke through the haze above the Isle of Sheppey to be confronted by a veritable armada of enemy aircraft—formation after formation of Dorniers, Junkers and Heinkels surrounded above and on either side by swarms of Messerschmitts stretching eastwards as far as the eye could see. As the pilots strove to penetrate the screens of fighters, Park ordered his remaining fighters into the air to make for the eastern outskirts of the capital.

The Battle's greatest combat

In the dockland of London the sound of gunfire grew louder by the minute. Soon in the east could be discerned a vast swarm of tiny specks approaching amidst a fantastic pattern of weaving vapour trails. The warning sirens had sounded ten minutes since, but only when the first bombs crashed down on the humble dockside dwellings did the Londoners realise that at last the Germans were dealing them the horrors of war with high explosive. As the Spitfires and Hurricanes fought to get at close quarters with the bombers above, the exploding bombs brought about a concentration of destruction in the London docks hitherto undreamed-of. A great pall of smoke rose from the leaping flames over the Surrey Docks when, after 30 minutes of death and destruction, the German bombers withdrew, some turning northwards and others south over Surrey and Sussex. A short lull followed while firemen fought to control the fires raging in the riverside warehouses. Fresh RAF fighters were beginning to join the great air battle over the Thames Estuary, some arriving from as far away as Dorset and Norfolk.

Then reports started to filter through to the operations rooms of a new wave of bombers approaching London. Once again Park frantically sought to assemble his forces over the Isle of Sheppey, and it was here that the greatest air combat of the entire Battle of Britain was fought as the retreating first raiders passed close to the advancing second wave and were attacked by more than twenty squadrons of RAF fighters in a 60 square mile area. But the British pilots were by now short of fuel and ammunition and the fight was shortlived. More than 50 Hurricanes and Spitfires were shot down (the exact number will probably never be known for certain owing to confusion in 12 Group's records), but only 12 German bombers were destroyed, in addition to 24 Messerschmitts.

Little could be done to prevent the second wave of bombers from reaching London, and throughout that night the Luftwaffe flew a constant stream of aircraft towards the great glow in the sky over the docks. At around midnight it was estimated that five separate conflagrations were out of control, and in the Surrey Docks there erupted the first man-made firestorm that, fed by showers of incendiary bombs, was abandoned by the fire services to consume all that was combustible before burning itself out. In the holocaust of the slum dwellings a land mine struck a school in which were sheltering more than 600 people, killing over 400 of them.

Yet what could this terrible raid achieve? Did Goering believe that by adopting the same course of war as at Warsaw and Rotterdam he would bring Great Britain to her knees? Had he truly ignored the fact that British fighters were still contesting the skies over Britain? Had no one told him that after 11 weeks of desperate fighting his air force had failed to destroy a single main fighter base, or that the German bombers had scarcely touched the bomber bases in England?

Invasion abandoned

The daylight phase of the Battle of Britain was, however, not yet over. The Luftwaffe continued throughout September to pound away at all manner of targets, only occasionally attempting to strike at the fighter bases. On the 15th the Luftwaffe again sent huge numbers of bombers against London by day, but the week's respite since the great raid of the 7th had given Fighter Command time to replenish its aircraft; six rested squadrons were brought south into 11 Group and two new squadrons (one Polish and one Czech) were declared operational. Repairs had been effected on Hornchurch, Kenley and Biggin Hill; three new radar stations had been brought 'on the air'. The result was that on the 15th the German Air Force suffered such a defeat that the invasion was seen to be too risky as long as Fighter Command remained in being, and was postponed and eventually abandoned. On that day the Germans lost 38 bombers and 24 fighters compared with 25 RAF fighters; 11 British pilots were lost.

During the last week of September, heavy attacks resumed in the south-west when Luftflotte 3 sent a number of raids against the aircraft factories in Southampton, Yeovil and Bristol. The old Spitfire factory at Southampton was very heavily damaged, but the main production line for the fighter had already been moved to the Midlands and the flow of new Spitfires was scarcely affected. The raids on the Westland works at Yeovil and the British factory at Filton met with only limited success and were attended by heavy losses at the hands of Brand's fighter squadrons.

One phase of the Battle of Britain remained to be fought. When seen in the context of the daylight battle, this phase has been ridiculed by historians as capable of achieving no purpose whatsoever. The German tactics employed high-flying Messerschmitt Bf 109s which flew over southeast England, scattering small numbers of bombs (usually of about 113 kg or 227 kg (250 lb or 500 lb size) over London and the Kentish towns. With only the most rudimentary aiming, these bombs did little significant damage anywhere and were considered to represent no more than nuisance value.

However, it should be remembered that the German air force had embarked on its night bombing campaign—London was fairly heavily raided on 57 consecutive nights,

Opposite: the Battle of Britain encapsulated in an example of British propaganda. Although the Battle, defined as the daylight fight for survival of Fighter Command, drew to a close at the end of October 1940, the Blitz had only just begun. It was to be some months before the Luftwaffe's large-scale forays over Britain were to end

THE BATTLE OF BRITAIN

Again and again the Luftwaffe attacked in every possible formation

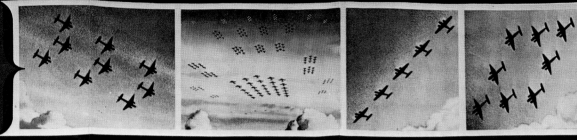

The full aerial might of Germany was hurled at Britain

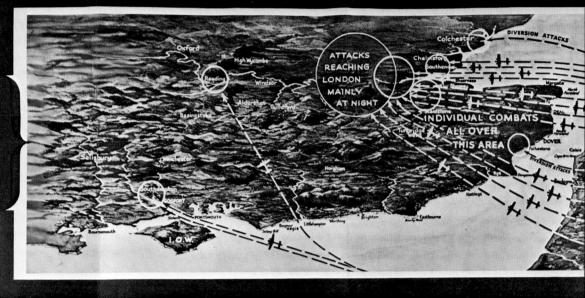

Again and again the British fighters ripped through the attacking hosts

And all over Southern England lay the German aircraft and the German hopes

LOSSES IN OCTOBER 1940

| | Aircraft | | Pilots/Crew Members | | |
	Destroyed	Damaged	Killed	Missing/ POW	Wounded
Hurricane	73	21	33	—	21
Spitfire	51	20	26	—	15
Blenheim	6	2	16	—	—
TOTAL	130	43	75	—	36
Dornier Do 17	39	13	71	37	21
Junkers Ju 87	—	2	—	—	—
Junkers Ju 88	74	46	81	79	34
Heinkel He 111	43	30	70	43	18
Messerschmitt Bf 109	119	42	27	60	11
Messerschmitt Bf 110	23	3	20	16	4
Other German aircraft	22	2	17	25	4
TOTAL	320	138	286	260	92

TOTAL LOSSES DURING THE BATTLE OF BRITAIN

British	922	298	406	13	295
German	1,767	570	1,449	1,914	530

The wreckage of a Dornier Do 17 lies in a Kentish field. By the end of the Battle of Britain, the Luftwaffe's bomber fleet was forced to operate under cover of night

and Birmingham, Liverpool and Coventry all received their first sharp night raids. Large areas of the country were subjected to raid warnings and there is no doubt that these raids served to disrupt all manner of community services, and the value of the fighter-bomber raids during daylight has probably been underestimated. The high-flying Messerschmitts were difficult to intercept by day, usually approaching above the ceiling of the Hurricane, while at night the RAF was virtually powerless to inflict any significant losses upon the raiding bombers.

The Luftwaffe's failure

The Battle of Britain, defined by the British as the daylight fight for survival by RAF Fighter Comand, drew to a close at the end of October 1940. It was not a conflict aimed at the destruction of the Luftwaffe; indeed at the end of the daylight phase the Luftwaffe remained very much a force in being.

However the whole aim of the attack on Britain had become blurred, while the reasons for victory and defeat in the daylight battle remain clearly defined. First, and most important, the German air force, although possessing considerable superiority in numbers, was ill-equipped and too badly directed to sustain a long drawn-out battle against a well-trained, well-equipped and dogged defence. In general, its bombers and heavy fighters were poorly matched against the British fighters, while the bombers could only reach one-tenth of the British Isles territory accompanied by effective fighter escort. The British defence system was designed in depth so that in daylight the German bomber losses rose steeply the further they tried to penetrate the British airspace. Failure by such aircraft as the Ju 87 dive-bomber and the Bf 110 heavy fighter to survive the attentions of Hurricanes and Spitfires threw a heavy strain on the Bf 109s whose pilots were, at a critical point in the battle, withdrawn from the very tactics which were causing the RAF most concern.

Second, it is almost certainly true that the Germans suffered a chronic lack of professional air commanders with unbroken tactical experience, who might otherwise have recognised exactly what tactics were damaging the RAF most. The German High Command was also badly served by its Intelligence branch, which seemed only vaguely aware of which were the vital airfields in Fighter Command. Goering himself was thoroughly inept in his understanding of the course of the battle; throughout the war the German fighter arm was to suffer unqualified interference from the supreme command, with morale-crushing results. So it was in the Battle of Britain. The strain on the German fighter pilots had been severe, but they had been winning the battle up to the very moment when Goering, like some medieval Ruritanian figure, descended on the Channel Coast in person and uncompromisingly redirected his cohorts away from the very prize that would have been his within a matter of weeks, if not days.

Above Left: Sqn Ldr R. Stanford Tuck leads a flight' of No 257 Squadron's Hawker Hurricanes from Coltishall, Norfolk, in January 1941. This squadron was involved in the early fighting of the Battle of Britain and suffered heavy losses.
Above: a Hurricane pilot adjusts his parachute harness.
Left: No 1 Squadron Hurricanes parked in a dispersal bay.
Below: No 56 Squadron's Hurricanes were heavily engaged in the defence on No 11 Group's airfields in July 1940

The Blitz 1940-41

The Blitz started as a phase of the Battle of Britain. After concentrated attacks on RAF airfields to destroy the British air defences had seemingly failed, the Luftwaffe turned their full weight on the British capital in an attempt to strike a mortal blow to British morale.

During Saturday 24 August 1940 the Luftwaffe's attacks had centred on airfields in the south-east protecting London, and dense smoke from burning fuel brought premature darkness to the area. The bombers continued coming over in the evening, making for London and bombs fell on Central London for the first time since 1918. A swift retaliatory strike by the RAF on Berlin the following night did nothing to deter German plans. While the RAF had to penetrate 960 km (600 miles), into mainly enemy territory, to reach the German capital, London was within 100 miles of many Luftwaffe bases.

This first attack was isolated, for the Luftwaffe was roaming at large over Britain at night seeking oil refineries, aircraft factories, railways and bridges to attack. But on 7 September there came a change of tactics. After a relatively quiet morning, Fighter Command became aware of intense activity across the Channel in the afternoon. At 1616 hours the Observer Corps reported a great aerial armada approaching. The massed formations made for London and made the banks of the Thames their target to cripple the London docks.

Fighter Command, in an all-out effort to stop the enemy reaching the capital, only succeeded in shooting down eight of the 348 bombers participating, which were closely escorted by 617 fighters. However, many others were crippled and eight crashed on landing at their bases in France and the Low Countries.

Defences doubled

The London anti-aircraft guns could claim only two

bombers–a small return for 28,000 shells expended. At the time there were only 92 heavy and AA guns for the defence of the capital, but within 48 hours they had been doubled by redeployment of some of the 1,220 available in the United Kingdom.

The docks were hard hit; along nine miles of waterfront blazing warehouses guided the bombers that continued the attack by night. Steamers were pressed into service as floating ambulances. The closely packed houses in dockland areas inevitably suffered and 306 people were killed in the London area in addition to 142 fatalities elsewhere and 1,337 people seriously injured.

Next day there were two smaller attacks on airfields and the London suburbs and at night London was again the target–as it was to be for 57 nights in succession. Many school-children who had been evacuated to country areas when war first came and had been trickling back were once more evacuated. But while London was the central target, the Luftwaffe continued to roam far and wide. The Ministry of Home Security, suspecting an attempt was being made to strangle the British lifelines of rail communication, which radiated from London, called for a report at the end of September showing hits on railways. The report showed that between 7 and 30 September there were 667 hits, excluding near misses, ranging from blind attacks on Crewe to a deliberate daylight mission against Reading, Berkshire.

German bomber force

Throughout October until the middle of November, attacks continued on London but on a less extensive scale and chiefly confined to night. Heavy attacks were delivered at other great cities–Birmingham, Coventry, Liverpool and Manchester all suffered several raids, but these were just a preliminary to intensified night attacks as the

St Paul's Cathedral ringed by fires at the height of the Blitz. London was the Luftwaffe's main target throughout the offensive, although Coventry, Liverpool, Birmingham and Manchester were also major targets

Luftwaffe readied themselves for the general shift from day to night operations. Although the attacks on RAF airfields were by now single aircraft or small formations, there were more frequent attacks on airfields in these six weeks, 131 attacks by day and 75 by night, than at the peak of the Battle of Britain.

The Luftwaffe's bombers for the assault were those used in the Battle of Britain daylight attacks, Dornier Do17s, Heinkel He111s and Junkers Ju88s, deployed in three air fleets – Luftflotten 2, 3 and 5 with headquarters at Brussels, Paris and Stavanger respectively. Some bombers were switched from Luftflotte 5 in Norway to France and Belgium, and some 90 bombers held in reserve in Germany were sent west as reinforcements. On paper the Luftwaffe had about 1,300 bombers in the west, but due to attrition in earlier daylight battles the effective operational strength was some 700 bombers. Although British guns and fighters rarely succeeded in shooting down more than 2 per cent of the bomber force engaged, there was a 5 per cent attrition rate. This was due to the inexperience of crews, improvised airfields and the winter weather.

Goering's directive

In spite of general lack of night flying experience the Luftwaffe had developed a night bombing aid – *Knickebein* – the projection of a radio beam that could be picked up by instruments in the bombers to guide pilots along the beam until an intersection by another beam indicated the point for releasing bombs. This beam, based on blind-landing techniques under development in both Britain and Ger-

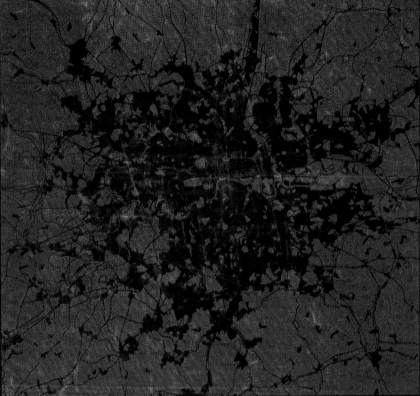

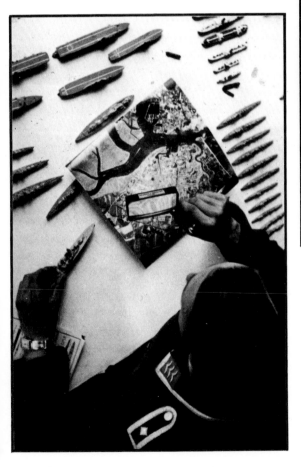

many, was in general Luftwaffe use. Two other types of beams, coded 'X' and 'Y', requiring special training for operation, were limited to specialist units for specific target attacks.

In November Goering gave a ten-point directive to the Luftwaffe, stating the following objectives:
1: London to be the main target, in daylight attacks by escorted fighter-bombers and when there is cloud cover by single bombers; in night attacks by equal forces of Luftflotten 2 & 3. 2: Attack the industrial centres of Coventry, Birmingham and Liverpool by small forces at night. 3: Mining of the Thames, Bristol Channel, Mersey and Manchester Ship Canal by Fliegerkorps IX. 4: Destruction of the Rolls-Royce Hillingdon aero engine factory by a Gruppe of KG26, using Y-beam. 5: Damaging of the enemy fighter arm by fighter sweeps. 6: Attacks on coastal convoys in the Channel and shipping assembly in the Thames, with fighter escort. 7: Destruction of the enemy aircraft by special crews of Luftflotten 2 & 3. 8: Attacks on enemy night-fighter bases. 9: Preparation for attacks on

Top: a Dornier 217 in flight over Holland. This type reached the Luftwaffe bomber units in the spring of 1941, II/KG 40 at Soesterberg, Holland, being the first to take it into action.
Above: a Luftwaffe map of London and its environs, especially produced for use at night.
Left: an intelligence officer identifies warships photographed at Portsmouth during a reconnaissance sortie

Coventry, Birmingham and Wolverhampton using X-beam. 10: Two large-scale attacks on London with bomb loads half high-explosive and half incendiary.

The devastating attack on Coventry on the night of 14/15 November heralded a new shift as point nine in the Goering directive was implemented. This was the first night attack of maximum intensity on a relatively small area. Incendiary bombs dropping on the city centre at the outset sealed the fate of the Cathedral and its environs. Apart from 500 people killed, 432 seriously injured and many homeless, large numbers had to be evacuated through the presence of 18 unexploded parachute mines.

Birmingham's turn came on the night of 19 November when 350 of the 500 sorties made over Britain were directed at the city. The bombing was widespread and scattered, killing 133 people, injuring 544 and disrupting public transport. This raid was repeated the following night, again two nights later and further attacks ensued in December. Attacks on a smaller scale were made against Liverpool in November with only one incident reported in the docks, but followed by attacks in December with the docks as key aiming points. Bristol, Portsmouth and Southampton, all with important dockyards, and the vital industrial centres of Manchester and Sheffield came under attack in November and December.

The City ablaze

The Great Fire of London 1666 had its sequel on the night of 29 December, and in much the same area. The City of London was set ablaze; yet strangely this was neither a

particularly heavy raid, nor did the bombers set out that evening with any special intent. It was a routine attack, with X-beams placed on the Charing Cross-Tottenham Court Road area; but a fresh wind, that was later to fan the flames, carried the markers from Kampfgeschwader 100's pathfinding bombers a mile to the east in the vicinity of St Paul's Cathedral.

Mercifully the weather over northern France deteriorated and the Germans cancelled take-offs from two hours before midnight. The damage was, nevertheless, extensive. Offices stacked with records, cellars stocked with spirits

Above: the aftermath of a night raid on London in 1941. Bomb damage and casualties were dealt with by numerous organisations, including Air Raid Precautions, Auxiliary Fire Service, Salvage Corps, Red Cross and St John's Ambulance.
Left: German pilots being briefed for a raid on England in January 1941, when Luftflotten 2 and 3 were operating from bases in France, Belgium and the Netherlands

and millions of stored books in underground galleries added to the conflagration. St Paul's Cathedral was ringed by fire, the Guildhall blazed and eight Wren churches were among the famous buildings destroyed. The fire services, called to deal with 1,469 fires, were hampered by the Thames being at a particularly low ebb and engineers were called in with explosives to make fire breaks. The ravages of this attack remain evident to this day.

The defences took a variety of forms that at times proved difficult to co-ordinate. Barrage balloons operated by the RAF, suspended by a loose fencing of cables, forced the bombers up where less accuracy by sighting was possible, and the same was true of the heavy anti-aircraft guns, operated by the Army, which had an operational height of around 25,000 feet. The smaller light Bofors guns, with a 6,000-foot ceiling, only occasionally came into action at night. London's anti-aircraft defences increased and, supplemented by naval ships in the Thames, made a heartening sound for those suffering under the bombing.

Night fighters, which had the ceiling to reach the bombers, appeared to offer better possibilities to grapple with the enemy. But the Spitfire had a high number of accidents in night landings and it was left to Blenheims, Hurricanes and Defiants to seek out the enemy in the darkness. Normal radar vectoring had relied on the pilot's vision after positioning him in the vicinity of the enemy. At night this was not possible, but the 4,000 searchlight posts scattered over Britain played a part in picking up the bombers, both for fighters and the guns.

their airfields and disrupt night flying.

During the early part of 1941, the Blitz became a phase of the Battle of the Atlantic. Merseyside, Teesside, Tyneside and Clydeside, Hull, Portsmouth, Plymouth, Swansea, Southampton, Bristol and Avonmouth figured largely in repeated major attacks. In mid-March the Luftwaffe flew north to deliver major attacks on Glasgow. Then, in attacks on Merseyside, the Gladstone and Hornby Docks were severely damaged, five merchant ships were sunk in dock and 11 others were damaged, together with many light craft. Out of a total of 144 berths, 69 were rendered unusable. Cardiff suffered six attacks, the heaviest causing 332 casualties. They were but a part of the overall Luftwaffe effort over Britain, including London, on these nights. The tempo of the Blitz was increasing.

Birmingham and Manchester continued to receive major attacks as the Luftwaffe attacks reached their peak. On 9/10 April the Luftwaffe attacked Birmingham, Bristol, Derby and Portsmouth among other towns. That night in Birmingham alone there were 758 casualties and 46 factories, three gas works and power stations were affected, a third of the city was without water and traffic was stopped on the Grand Union Canal which had been breached at Hay Mills.

London's darkest hour

On the night of 10 May, London suffered one of its most severe raids. Over 500 bomber sorties were flown: most bombers participating flew two sorties and some crews even flew three times. Among the 34 factories affected was R & J Beck's factory in Clerkenwell Road which was completely destroyed. The gutting of the Siebe Gorman factory in Westminster Bridge Road was the result of one of the 2,000 fires that caused not only the complete mobilisation of the whole of the London Fire Brigade, but an emergency call to the armed forces.

Londoners were not to know that this was the darkest hour before the dawn. The continued use of the capital as

A British 4·5-inch anti-aircraft battery in action, with predictor and rangefinder in the foreground. Anti-Aircraft Command was an Army formation which came under the operational control of RAF Fighter Command

Radio countermeasures

Research on airborne radar was continuing and from September 1940 Fighter Command converted from Blenheims to Beaufighters fitted with AI Mk IV, the first reliable airborne interception apparatus. Fighter Command also formed a number of special flights, using chiefly Bostons and Havocs, fitted with searchlights and suspended mines, but in spite of much effort this line of development brought little reward.

The formation of No 80 (Signals) Wing in October 1940 introduced radio countermeasures on an organised basis by jamming German beams and radio communications; Bomber Command assisted this operation by bombing German wireless stations from mid-November. One of the most significant defensive measures was the adoption of the control and reporting system for night raids. On 10 January 1941, Durrington, the first of the Ground Control Interception Stations, was taken over by the RAF, resulting in 23 night fighter attacks on bombers before the end of the month.

Passive countermeasures taken included the siting of smoke canisters to screen towns, which failed due to the German beam systems, and the introduction in early December of 'Starfish' – decoy fires to draw the German bombers from their real targets. More offensive countermeasures were the attacks on the German bomber bases in France and the Low Countries by Bomber Command, and intruder raids by Fighter Command to shoot the German bombers down over their own territory, strafe

an industrial and commercial centre was being questioned. Roads were blocked by rubble or hoses, and the railway system faced complete breakdown. Holborn Viaduct and Blackfriars were already closed from damage in April; Charing Cross and Broad Street could only run restricted services. Now other main line termini suffered – high explosive bombs between Nos 3 & 4 platforms at St Pancras pierced the Metropolitan railway tunnel and an unexploded bomb on No 2 platform hindered line repair. At Paddington lines were affected by a hit on No 13 platform. Liverpool Street offices and Kings Cross booking hall were on fire, and trains could not reach Fenchurch Street due to damage at Stepney. All lines, except for Marylebone, had to terminate some miles from central London. Businesses were also affected: the Siemens Bros premises at Woolwich escaped on this occasion with a slight fire from incendiary bombs – their buildings had been damaged 12 times in 1940 and on four occasions in 1941.

Business as usual

Morale in this difficult period had been maintained by a well-trained Air Raid Precaution organisation of part-time volunteers, an Auxiliary Fire Service and Salvage Corps, supported by the Red Cross, St John's Ambulance Brigade, and many other voluntary national and local organisations. The Services bomb disposal sections, Royal Engineers and Auxiliary Military Pioneer Corps all played their part in restoring public facilities. Local authority employees became key men in dealing with hundreds of broken water and gas mains, severed electric cables and the disruption in sewage disposal.

Much hardship was alleviated by the tenor of the times. The spirit of the British people was exemplified by shopkeepers who chalked 'Business as usual' on shattered premises, and the many who opened their doors to the thousands of homeless. The organisation of Reconstruction Committees, cutting through red tape, the official billeting of refugees and legislation such as the War Damage Reparation Act did much to give confidence to those who suffered most.

A great boost to morale was the success of the defences by improved control and the development of airborne radar; a total of 23 enemy aircraft destroyed, the highest number in one night so far achieved, was claimed on the last heavy London attack. But it was not this that caused the scaling down of the attacks from this time to mere isolated forays. The whole of Luftflotte 2 was ordered east for the attack on Russia, together with a large portion of Luftflotte 3, leaving a mere token force in France and the Low Countries by late May.

To allay suspicions of withdrawal German radio traffic was kept at a high level, to delude the British into thinking that their bombers remained deployed in the west. This was not successful, for these moves were one of the reasons why Britain warned the Russian ambassador in London of the signs of impending attack on his country. The Luftwaffe could still attack targets in Britain, but not to the extent of former months which had caused the British to give the raids the German word Blitz.

Despite the disruption to essential services caused by German raids, the morale of Londoners remained high. By the spring of 1941, the scale of attack was greatly reduced as the Germans redeployed for the attack on the Soviet Union

Left: the Heinkel He 111, despite being the heaviest bomber available to the Luftwaffe in 1940, was proved to have inadequate range, bomb-load and defensive armament during the daylight bombing raids on Britain in 1940. This was one of the reasons which forced the Luftwaffe to go over to night raids from October 1940.
Below: bomb damage from a night raid on London in January 1941 viewed from St Paul's Cathedral

Desert War 1940-43

The entry of Italy into World War II and the fall of France in June 1940 gave a significance to the territory surrounding the Mediterranean Sea which the area had not enjoyed previously. As long as no German invasion of the United Kingdom was launched and until a British invasion of Occupied Europe proved possible, it remained the one area where British troops could actually fight the Axis armies.

From the moment of the Italian declaration of war on 10 June 1940, the numerically strong Regia Aeronautica came into conflict with the Royal Air Force, both over Malta and in the skies of North Africa. It was along the Egyptian-Libyan coastal belt of infertile terrain – dubbed the Western Desert – that the major British war effort was concentrated during the following two and a half years.

The RAF in Egypt, though neither strong nor modern, was efficient and aggressively led. Three squadrons of Gloster Gladiator fighter biplanes, five of Bristol Blenheim light bombers, one of Westland Lysander army co-operation aircraft and one of Bristol Bombay bomber-transports, were available initially. The British were quick off the mark on the first morning of the war, striking at El Adem, the main Italian air base in the eastern Libyan province of Cyrenaica, before the Italians had even got their aircraft off the ground.

Although much larger than the RAF component in Africa, the Regia Aeronautica was not appreciably better equipped and its level of serviceability was undoubtedly much lower. The main fighter was the biplane Fiat CR 42 and the older CR 32 was still also retained in service in some quantities, mainly for ground attack duties. The modern tri-motor Savoia SM 79 was used for day bombing, while night bombing was undertaken by the older SM 81. The Meridionali Ro 37bis biplane undertook the army co-operation and tactical reconnaissance role. A new fast monoplane ground attack aircraft, the Breda Ba 65, was just beginning to enter service in Libya, but it was to prove a disappointment.

Initially the Italians made no move, while the British were not strong enough to do so. A little ground skirmishing by patrols took place, accompanied by some aerial patrolling over the front. This on occasions led to some fierce combats between the opposing fighters. Meanwhile formations of SM 79s raided the British base areas, particularly the Mediterranean Fleet base at Alexandria. Blenheims reciprocated, attacking Tobruk, Derna and other Libyan targets, joined at night by the Bombays and after a few weeks by newly-arrived Vickers Wellingtons.

Hurricane reinforcements
Both Blenheims and SM 79s proved difficult for the biplane fighters to intercept successfully and it was the RAF which first improved upon this. Only one modern Hawker Hurricane had been present in Egypt when war broke out, but before the fall of France more were flown out by air, together with numbers of Blenheim Mk IV bombers.

Below: the Bristol Bombay served as a bomber/transport with No 216 Squadron until 1942, flying night raids against Italian targets

With the closure of the route through France, an air reinforcement route across Africa from Takoradi on the Gold Coast was used. This route had been pioneered by the RAF some years earlier. As a result, a flight of Hurricanes was soon operating in defence of Alexandria and by the end of August sufficient had arrived to equip a complete squadron.

Finally on 13 September 1940 Marshal Graziani's army moved across the border into Egypt, supported by tanks, artillery and aircraft. The British had no option but to fall back. However, after reaching Sidi Barrani, the Italians halted and dug in. The arrival of British reinforcements was slow, as a campaign was also now developing in East Africa. Late in October an Italian invasion of Greece made further demands on the RAF, following a request for air reinforcements by the defenders.

The arrival of the 4th Indian Division, released from East Africa, allowed General Wavell to launch a reconnaissance in force under the tactical control of General O'Connor on 9 December 1940. Closely supported by Hurricanes, Blenheims and Gladiators, this achieved immediate success, and was extended into a full-scale offensive. The Italians were swiftly driven back into Libya with vast losses of men and equipment, most of which fell captive to the British forces. Strong air reinforcements of CR 42s and SM 79s were soon dispatched to the area and for a month there was quite severe fighting in the air, with losses on both sides. RAF attacks on Italian airfields proved particularly successful and large numbers of damaged and unserviceable aircraft were abandoned during the retreat. Bardia was taken early in January, Tobruk before the end of the month and Derna also fell.

The worn 7th Armoured Division now cut across the Cyrenaican 'bulge', following a desert track in order to cut off the retreating Italians south-west of Benghazi. This move was successful and on 6 February 1941 the Italian Tenth Army was destroyed at the Battle of Beda Fomm, all Cyrenaica then being in British hands. The victors were by then too weakened and overstretched to continue the advance on Tripoli and this was to prove their downfall.

German aid was, by this time, reaching Tripoli and German air attacks had rendered Malta temporarily inactive as an offensive base for the interception of Axis reinforcement convoys crossing to Africa. As a result, strong German and Italian reinforcements, including modern armour, were arriving, together with Luftwaffe Junkers Ju 87 dive-bombers (Stukas) and Messerschmitt Bf 110 twin-engined Zerstörer (destroyers). More Italian units also arrived, including some equipped with Fiat G50bis monoplane fighters.

The Luftwaffe's triumph

At the end of March the new German commander in Africa, Erwin Rommel, launched a reconnaissance in force, supported by strong Stuka attacks. The British forces – now almost non-existent – began to fold up at once, and Rommel pressed on. During early April the port of Tobruk was prepared for a prolonged siege, but the new 2nd Armoured Division was cut off and wiped out near Derna. By 10 April Tobruk was coming under siege and a number of severe air attacks began. For a time the Hurricanes of 73 Squadron operated from within the fortress perimeter, taking a steady toll, but on 19 April newly-arrived Messerschmitt Bf 109E fighters went into action, outclassing the British fighters.

During April the successful conclusion of the main East African campaign released forces for service elsewhere, but other demands still prevented worthwhile reinforcements from reaching the desert. In Greece the Germans had intervened early in April, driving the British out by the end of the month, while in May an airborne invasion of Crete brought further heavy fighting and severe British losses on land and sea, as well as in the air. That same month a rebellion in Iraq supported by the Axis required further diversion of strength. This was speedily pacified, but highlighted the desirability of oc-

Below: the Fiat CR42 was the main Italian fighter in Libya at the start of the Desert War in 1940. Bottom: Hawker Hurricane Mk IID tank busters, armed with two 40mm cannon, served with No 6 Squadron RAF and No 7 Squadron South African Air Force

Above: an RAF Lockheed Hudson flies over the pyramids. The type served as a transport aircraft over the desert, notably with Nos 117 and 216 Squadrons of the RAF

cupying and neutralising the neighbouring French colony of Syria. Begun in early June, this provoked severe resistance from the Vichy French, who considerably reinforced the air element of their defences, resulting in a hard-fought campaign lasting for over a month. Not until July 1941, therefore, could the British in the Middle East consider their flanks and rear secure and concentrate all efforts on building up the Libyan front.

Meanwhile, in Libya the British had been driven back to the Egyptian frontier, though Tobruk continued to hold out. On 12 May a large convoy reached Alexandria, carrying over 300 tanks and 50 Hurricanes and with these reinforcements a counter-offensive was launched three days later. This thrust was approaching Bardia when a strong German counter-attack threw it right back, the only gain retained being the Halfaya Pass.

'Battle-axe'

By the start of June the first US-built Curtiss Tomahawk fighters were available for action, and on 14 June a new British offensive was launched under the code name 'Battle-axe'. For this the RAF had three squadrons of Hurricanes immediately available, two of Tomahawks, two of Blenheims, two of Marylands and one tactical reconnaissance unit. Three squadrons of Wellingtons backed up this force by night, while more Hurricanes were on the way to Egypt from England, having been flown from an aircraft carrier to Malta in the first instance.

'Battle-axe' lasted three days, but the results were as before – the British were counter-attacked and driven back, suffering heavy losses. In the air fighting was heavy. Before the battle was over Italian Fiat G50bis fighters had appeared, and more RAF Hurricanes were thrown in. It was,

however, a victory for the German fighters.

There followed a long intermission which lasted until mid-November 1941, as both sides strove to build up their forces for an offensive. Tobruk slowed this process considerably, and much aerial fighting took place over convoys attempting to supply the port. The Germans had been alarmed by the improved performance of the new Tomahawks and were eager to introduce better equipment for their own fighter units. In September a second *gruppe* of Bf 109s arrived, but this time armed with the newer F model, which had a much improved performance. The *staffeln* of I/JG 27 also began re-equipping with these fighters. The Italians steadily replaced their units in Africa at this time, introducing more modern Macchi C200 and C202 fighters. By early November both sides had become far stronger, not least in the air.

Western Desert Air Force

The British attack began on 18 November 1941, Beaufighters making some telling early attacks on Axis airfields. A violent seesaw battle now began which was to last for nearly two months. In the air British numerical superiority, which had now been established, began to

sufficiently built up to strike again, but this time it was Rommel who acted first. On 26 May his infantry attacked the main Gazala defences whilst his armour began an outflanking sweep in the south, supported, as ever, by massed dive-bomber formations. For days the battle was in the balance, but by early June it had swung inexorably to the Axis as the British armour suffered crippling losses, and a retreat towards Egypt began.

The RAF formations–now the Western Desert Air Force (WDAF)–were thrown in to hold back the German advance, the fighters concentrating on ground attacks at the expense of air superiority operations. The results

tell. Fighting was intense and both sides suffered heavy losses. On 22 November the Luftwaffe fighters met the Tomahawks in a head-on battle for air superiority. While the Messerschmitts emerged with slightly more victories than losses, their percentage loss was at a level that could not, for long, be sustained. Thereafter the air war took on an entirely new complexion. No longer did the Germans attempt to challenge the British fighters directly in an effort to drive them from the skies. Instead they used the superior performance of their aircraft to sit high above and inflict maximum losses for minimum cost. As the British now had adequate fighters to escort their bomber formations, this resulted in losses of the protectors, rather than the protected. While painful, this in no way restricted maximum utilisation of tactical air power so long as the losses could be made good, and from this moment British tactical air power in Africa began to develop fast.

On 8 December the siege of Tobruk was at last raised, and thereafter the Axis began to fall back, their efforts seriously reduced by lack of fuel. Again, many of their aircraft were captured on the ground. The outbreak of war in the Far East resulted in the withdrawal of some British units and a reduction in the flow of reinforcements and supplies. Despite this, by 6 January 1942 the British were back to the line they had held a year earlier.

Then, however, a new Luftwaffe assault on Malta allowed supplies and reinforcements across the Mediterranean to reach Rommel and with his air support increased by a third *gruppe* of Bf 109Fs, he struck again on 21 January, driving the British back once more, though this time only as far as the Gazala Line, halfway across the Cyrenaican 'bulge'.

By the end of May 1942 the forces of both sides were

Above: Luftwaffe technicians load a reconnaissance camera onto a Messerschmitt Bf 110 on a desert landing ground.
Above right and right: the Bf 110 saw extensive service in North Africa as a heavy fighter and in the reconnaissance role

achieved in slowing down the Axis supply columns and convoys balanced the high number of casualties that were suffered from both ground fire and Messerschmitts, but there was no saving the Gazala position. A fighting retreat to prepared defences at El Alamein followed, the main factor in preventing a rout developing being the WDAF. Under the inspired leadership of Air Marshal Arthur Coningham, the bombers went out again and again under an umbrella of Kittyhawks and Tomahawks, which prevented German or Italian fighters interfering on almost every occasion. At lower level, Hurricanes and Beaufighters strafed constantly, while high overhead appeared the first few Spitfires to reach Africa. A diversion of effort during June to aid a convoy trying to fight its way through to beleaguered Malta from Alexandria did not help the situation, but the army was able to enter the Alamein defences in good order by the end of that month.

American aid

July saw continued heavy fighting as Rommel tried desperately to break through, while the British reinforced and counter-attacked to improve the line. By the latter part of the month both sides were exhausted, the Axis powers were desperately short of fuel again, and activity, both on the ground and in the air, continued at a much-reduced level. Then American help began to arrive in Africa, first in the shape of a few Boeing B-17 and Consolidated B-24 heavy bombers, followed by tactical units—one group of Curtiss P-40F Warhawks and another of North American B-25 Mitchell medium bombers. The RAF had now introduced its specialised Hurricane IID 'tank-buster' with a pair of underwing 40mm anti-tank guns, and more squadrons of Spitfires were becoming available. At night the first RAF four-engined 'heavies'– Halifaxes and Liberators–were entering operations.

The Eighth Army was now taken over by General Bernard Montgomery, who prepared for an expected Axis offensive at the south end of his line. He was proven correct when the assault commenced on 31 August 1942, resulting in the Battle of Alam el Halfa. The WDAF went in to attack at once, disrupting the German columns from the start, while British tanks from dug-in positions inflicted heavy losses on the Italo-German armour. The experienced German fighter pilots, now absolute masters of their art, inflicted huge losses on the British fighters, but failed on every occasion to prevent or inflict losses on the bombers which were so disrupting their colleagues on the ground. They also failed on numerous occasions to protect their own bombers, which were often rather harshly handled.

It was all to no avail, however, and during the rest of September and early October the Luftwaffe fighter units, whose losses to date had generally been extremely light, began to lose several of their greatest 'aces' to the Allied fighters, which were ever-growing in numbers and improving in quality. They found increasingly that they were prevented from achieving anything by the strength of the opposition, while growing weights of bombing and strafing attacks on their airfields and raids by daring commando groups steadily sapped their morale. On 30 September the great Marseille, credited with 158 aerial victories, 151 of them over Africa, and the most successful German 'ace' of the war in the West, was killed when baling out of his burning aircraft following an engine fire. Jagdgeschwader 27's morale was now so shaken that moves were made to replace the unit with JG 77 from Russia.

It was then that the British struck at El Alamein and on 24 October the last major battle in the desert began. Both air forces were now at their greatest strength to date, but this was of little comfort to the Axis. Their 347 fighters, 72 dive-bombers and 171 medium bombers were faced by 605 fighters, 254 light and medium bombers and 61 heavy bombers, which enjoyed better serviceability and far greater supplies of fuel and replacements.

Heavy aerial fighting continued throughout the long, hard Alamein slogging match, but once the Axis retreat got under way in November, harried the whole time by air attack, resistance almost disappeared. Montgomery followed at a steady rate and the Anglo-American landings in Algeria and Morocco on 8 November 1942 put paid to any major Axis recovery before Tripoli. Now the Hurricane units were left behind to protect the bases, only the Spitfires, Kittyhawks, USAAF P-40s, and the light bombers accompanying the Eighth Army. Still the marauding Messerschmitts, now mainly flown by the JG 77 veterans of the Russian Front, continued to take their toll, but Allied ground/air co-operation was reaching a high level of expertise–the Allied tactical air force had been well and truly born in the crucible of war.

There was some heavy fighting over Tripoli and the surrounding area during early January 1943 as the assault on this city was prepared. Despite the late introduction by the Germans of Henschel Hs 129 anti-tank aircraft and Me 210 Zerstörer, there was little they could do and as they retreated into Southern Tunisia at the end of that month, the fighting in the Western Desert at last came to an end. North Africa had seen the metamorphosis of the Royal Air Force as a tactical arm, and had seen the first really major Allied victories.

Right: a Curtiss Kittyhawk Mk IA of No 112 Sqn with distinctive shark mouth markings, pictured operating from a typically inhospitable desert airfield. In addition to the often heavy losses in action, units operating in the desert had to contend with the effects of the environment, upon engines in particular
Below: USAAF Douglas C-47 transports, together with North American Mitchell medium bombers and Curtiss Warhawk fighters, were a welcome addition to Allied air strength in 1942

Greek Campaign 1940-41

Left: a Bristol Bombay transport aircraft photographed at an airfield on Crete, when en route to Greece.
Below: the crew of an RAF Bristol Blenheim light bomber touch the bald pate of a Flight Sergeant for luck before taking off. The Blenheim squadrons suffered heavy losses in the campaign

As long ago as April 1939 Italy had staged an unopposed military occupation of Albania and, following her entry into the war on 10 June 1940, attacked Greece across the Albanian frontier on 28 October that year, supported by a numerically powerful force of aircraft.

At the time of the Italian attack, the Royal Hellenic Air Force possessed four fighter squadrons, equipped with 36 Polish PZL P-24F and nine French Bloch MB 151 aircraft and three light bomber squadrons. equipped with Bristol Blenheim Is, Fairey Battles and Potez 63s. In addition four ground support squadrons operated 16 Henschel Hs 126s and some antiquated Breguet 19A-2s and Potez 25s. Three naval co-operation squadrons flew ten Avro Ansons, ten Dornier Do 22s and nine old Fairey IIIF floatplanes. Against this puny force the Regia Aeronautica ranged one *gruppo* of Fiat CR 32s, two *gruppi* of Fiat·G 50s and one of Fiat CR 42s–a total of about 140 fighters–plus two *gruppi* of Savoia-Marchetti SM 79s and two of Fiat BR 20s, a bomber force of about fifty aircraft.

Despite these heavy odds the Greeks fought the Italians with great courage, even forcing the invaders back into Albania. Morale was high among the Greek aircrews, despite inadequate training. While their fighters were deployed in defence of the ports and airfields, the bombers struck at the Italian supply routes in Albania and the enemy airfields at Argyrocastro and Koritza.

The British forces under Wavell in North Africa meanwhile had been enjoying extraordinary success against the Italians under Marshal Graziani. It therefore came as a considerable disappointment to the RAF commander, Air Chief Marshal Sir Arthur Longmore, to be ordered by London to send some of his precious squadrons to the aid of the Greeks.

No 30 Squadron, equipped with Blenheims and one flight of No 33 Squadron with Gladiators, arrived in Greece at the beginning of November 1940. They were followed later that month by two more Blenheim squadrons, Nos 84 and 211, and another Gladiator squadron, No 80. At the beginning of December No 112 Squadron, re-equipping with Hurricanes, handed over its Gladiators to the RHAF. At the same time Wellington bombers carried out long-range night raids on targets in Albania and Southern Italy, flying from bases in Egypt and Malta. Command of the RAF forces in Greece was entrusted to Air Vice-Marshal John Henry d'Albiac.

Adverse conditions
The appalling weather conditions persisting in the battle areas during those winter months curtailed air operations.

During the 156 days which spanned the whole Greek campaign only 64 were fine enough to allow air operations. The combination of the weather conditions, poorly constructed Greek airfields and largely inadequate communications severely restricted RAF operations. Equally, the Regia Aeronautica was denied any form of air superiority. By the end of December, however, a number of vicious air combats had been fought and the Italians had suffered some heavy casualties.

No 80 Squadron was the first Gladiator unit to go into action over Greece with a sharp combat over Koritza against a mixed formation of Italian fighters on 19 November. Two CR 42s were shot down by a South African pilot, Flt Lt M.T.St J. Pattle, Plt Off 'Heimar' Stuckey shot down a G 50 and a CR 42, Flt Sgt Charles Casbolt destroyed a CR 42 and Plt Off W. 'Cherry' Vale another G 50.

On 28 November the Gladiators of Nos 33 and 80 Squadrons came across a formation of CR 42s over Delvinakion and shot down five, three falling to the guns of Flt Sgt D. S. Gregory of No 33 Squadron, and two to Flt Lt 'Tap' Jones of No 80 Squadron. On 4 December more Italian fighters were encountered by the two squadrons over Tepeleni. On this occasion six CR 42s and a G 50 were destroyed for certain and three enemy biplanes were credited to Pattle. On 20 December Pattle was leading Gladiators of No 80 Squadron on a patrol over the Albanian battleground when he spotted a formation of

enemy bombers, and himself destroyed an SM 79 and an SM 81; another SM 81 fell to Vale.

One further action was fought before the end of the year, again with Italian fighters over the Albanian front when eight CR 42s were shot down by Gladiators of both RAF squadrons; Vale claimed three of the biplanes, Gregory and Casbolt two each and Pattle one. Casualties among the Gladiator pilots had been comparatively light; five aircraft had been lost, three pilots killed and four

Below: one of the Luftwaffe's Junkers Ju 52 troop transports which took part in the successful assault on the Corinth Canal on 26 April 1941. This airborne coup hastened the end of the Greek campaign

wounded. Losses on the Blenheim squadrons had been heavier; a total of seven aircraft had been lost, but three of these losses had been caused by the atrocious weather conditions and all but two of the crews had been saved.

Ground and weather conditions during January 1941 brought the fighting to an almost complete standstill, with the Greek army held deep in Albania and only sporadic flying was possible. Apart from a fleeting brush with Italian bombers on 20 January, it was not until 28 January that an air battle was again fought when No 80 Squadron caught an unescorted formation of Cant Z 1007 bombers near Athens and destroyed three. Stuckey shot down one of these but his aircraft was damaged by enemy fire and he was killed while force-landing. 'Ape' Cullen took the second bomber and Pattle and Casbolt shared in the destruction of the third.

Germany intervenes

It was now becoming clear in London that Germany intended to intervene in the Balkans. A plan to move RAF squadrons into Turkey to threaten raids on the Romanian oilfields, upon which Germany depended heavily, had previously been dropped. The British then tried to persuade the Greeks to allow a British army to land in Greece to deter German moves through Yugoslavia and assist the Greeks in pushing the Italians out of Albania. These plans were turned down by the Greeks who were afraid of antagonising the Bulgarians, but it was agreed that should Germany make any move in the Balkans towards Greece, a British army would be welcomed. The delay in establishing British ground forces in the Balkans proved disastrous.

Moreover, German forces had begun to arrive in

North Africa, and by early January Fliegerkorps X was firmly established in Sicily, launching damaging raids on Malta. Longmore, therefore, delayed sending further air reinforcements to Greece: with resistance stiffening in North Africa, none could be spared.

February brought intensified air activity over Greece. In an effort to support a Greek attempt to capture Tepeleni, 48 km (30 miles) inside Albania, the Gladiators were flown in a number of patrols in that area on 9 February and attacked several formations of CR 42s. Casbolt, Cullen, Pattle and Vale each destroyed one biplane, while Flt Lt G. V. W. 'Jimmie' Kettlewell opened his score by

Above: an RAF airman examines bombs which have been unloaded at a port in Greece.
Below: Greek fighter units were equipped with the Polish-built PZL P-24F fighter. One of their opponents was the monoplane Fiat G 50bis, armed with two 12·7mm machine guns

PZL P-24F of the Royal Hellenic Air Force

Fiat G 50bis of the Regia Aeronautica

Gloster Gladiator II of No 80 Squadron RAF

Fiat CR 42 of the Regia Aeronautica

shooting down one CR 42 but was forced down, although he escaped unhurt. Flt Sgt Gregory of No 33 Squadron again shot down an enemy fighter, also over Tepeleni. On the following day the Italians made a number of determined raids across the Greek border which the Gladiators intercepted. Cullen shot down an SM 79 into Yanina lake and Vale a BR 20 about 24 km (15 miles) to the south-west.

Yanina airfield had been heavily attacked and damaged. The following morning 20 CR 42s carried out a strafing raid which destroyed or damaged several Greek Gladiators on the ground. On 13 February 'Tap' Jones, now commanding No 80 Squadron, led his Gladiators in a reprisal attack on Tepeleni while escorting a raid by Blenheims, but not one opposing Italian aircraft was sighted by the Gladiator pilots.

Longmore had been able to ferry a small number of Hurricanes to Greece; on 16 February six of these and some Wellingtons assembled at Paramythia. By then, however, the Gladiator biplanes were showing the strain of prolonged operations in Greece. Ground crews had performed miracles to keep them combat-ready but, flown for too long at full throttle to match the performance of enemy aircraft and with only limited spares available, they were, quite simply, worn out. While still a match for most Italian aircraft there was growing apprehension about the outcome of combat with the modern German aircraft at that time.

Combat over Albania

On 20 February D'Albiac decided to stage a maximum air operation to support Greek forces in Albania. Fighter cover of 17 Gladiators escorted two Wellingtons and a Greek Junkers Ju 52/3m, while the six Hurricanes covered nine Blenheims which were to bomb the bridge at Berat.

Eleven Greek PZL P-24s were to meet and escort the formations on their return flight. The raid was a complete success. Without Allied loss, 12 enemy aircraft were destroyed in a running battle with intercepting fighters. Casbolt, in a Hurricane, shot down two Macchi C.200s and another Hurricane pilot, Flt Lt 'Timber' Woods–recently posted from Malta to No 80 Squadron–accounted for a G 50. Four G 50s and a CR 42 were shot down by the Gladiators and four fighters by the PZL pilots.

An even more extraordinary and successful air battle followed. By 28 February No 112 Squadron had arrived in Greece with 12 Gladiators their replacement Hurricanes having been delayed. On 28 February together with No 33 Squadron, flying Hurricanes, and No 80 Squadron with one flight of Hurricanes and one of Gladiators, No 112 Squadron was ordered to patrol between Tepeleni and the Adriatic coast, as it was anticipated that a number of Italian aircraft would be operating in that area. Enemy formations, totalling about 50 aircraft, were sighted and engaged in a battle that lasted an hour and raged across the breadth of Albania. The pilots of No 80 Squadron gave a particularly fine performance, destroying no fewer than 17 aircraft. Pattle accounted for two BR 20s and three CR 42s and Ape Cullen two SM 79s, two CR 42s and a BR 20. No 112 Squadron shot down six Italian aircraft–all fighters–and No 33 Squadron four. The RAF's loss was one No 112 Squadron Gladiator, whose pilot, Flg Off 'Dicky' Abrahams, baled out unhurt. All the Italian aircraft fell within the Allied lines and were reliably confirmed destroyed, making this the most disastrous single defeat suffered by the Regia Aeronautica during the entire war.

The German invasion of Greece in March 1941 was undertaken by Hitler as an extension of Lebensraum and

The British Gloster Gladiator was pitted against Italy's highly-manoeuvrable Fiat CR 42, but in the hands of pilots such as the redoubtable 'Pat' Pattle the RAF fighter proved its worth time and again

RAF officers pose with a trophy taken from a downed Italian aircraft outside their mess tent in April 1941

Junkers Ju 88s of III/KG 30, a bomb dropped by Hauptmann Hajo Herrmann struck the freighter *Clan Frazer* in Piraeus harbour. The vessel, carrying 250 tons of high explosives, blew up with such force that ten other vessels were sunk and the port so devastated that it was rendered totally unusable for many weeks.

The Germans achieved in less than three weeks what the Italians had failed to achieve in more than four months. Successive British defence lines were overrun or outflanked. The Germans reached Salonika on 9 April and within five days had broken through a defence line in front of Mount Olympus. The abandoning of this line forced the evacuation of the airfield at Larissa, thus leaving the RAF no good landing ground between there and the Athens area. There were isolated acts of great gallantry and skill, as when Wellingtons smashed the key bridge at Veles during the night of the 14/15 April.

The following day retribution was exacted when German fighters swept over RAF airfields, destroying all the Blenheims of No 113 Squadron at Niamata. By the end of that day the total RAF strength had fallen to about 50 aircraft. At Paramythia, all 44 surviving aircraft of the Royal Yugoslav Air Force were destroyed or severely damaged in a lightning strike by German fighter-bombers. The following day an entire Greek Gladiator squadron was obliterated on the ground. By 19 April d'Albiac had ordered all surviving RAF units to retire to the capital. It was, by this time, only a matter of which army would be first in reaching the Athens area.

Masterly improvisation

The climax to the campaign came on 20 April. At dawn, following a total breakdown of the Greek raid reporting system, a formation of Messerschmitt Bf 110s penetrated unspotted to the airfield at Menidi and destroyed almost every one of a dozen Blenheims on the ground. In the afternoon the Germans mounted a raid by about 100 Junkers Ju 88s, Bf 110s and Bf 109s on the Athens area. The sole remaining Hurricanes, 15 in all, from Nos 33 and 80 Squadrons, engaged the enemy aircraft and shot down about 14, but among the five RAF pilots shot down was Pat Pattle. This most courageous South African had, in five months destroyed at least 36 enemy aircraft and 13 Germans had fallen to his guns in his last 14 days. His gallant friend, the giant 'Ape' Cullen, had already been killed, having destroyed more than 16 Italian aircraft.

During the next week more than 80 per cent of the British land forces in Greece were withdrawn either to Crete or Egypt, brought off, as at Dunkirk, by the Royal Navy. The remnants of Nos 33 and 80 Squadrons provided what air cover they could before they too were recalled to Crete.

The Greek campaign, fought so courageously by the Greeks when faced by the Italians, turned into a swift defeat for the Allies at the hands of the Germans largely as the result of the unwillingness by the Athens government to prepare against German intervention. As it was, the British involvement achieved no more than to delay Hitler's attack on Russia by four weeks.

The campaign in the air itself, like so many fought by the RAF during the first two years of the war, was a masterpiece of improvisation in appalling conditions of weather and bad communications. The air fighting, nevertheless, involving a handful of British squadrons for only five months, not only produced the highest-scoring RAF pilot at that time in the war but also the highest-scoring group of pilots commensurate with the number involved.

in preparation for his occupation or dominance of the entire Balkan area to secure his southern flank for his assault on Russia. In the short term, however, his advance through Yugoslavia into Greece was undertaken to relieve his Italian allies. Moreover, it was considered that German intervention in Greece would assist the Italians in North Africa. Although the Italian land forces had been held in check by the Greeks, their air forces had remained a strong threat. The RAF contingent, sent to bolster the small Greek and Yugoslav air forces against the Italians, aided as much as hindered by the weather conditions, frustrated the Regia Aeronautica and denied the Italians any success. The Germans attacked in more appropriate campaigning weather and their co-ordinated aerial onslaught was overwhelming.

On 1 March the Wehrmacht entered Bulgaria and seven days later a British Expeditionary Force began to disembark in Greece. Within one month the Germans had mustered 20 infantry divisions and seven Panzer divisions on the borders of Greece and Yugoslavia, in addition to about 15 Italian, Hungarian and Bulgarian divisions. In support of these ground forces the Luftwaffe assembled 1,200 aircraft of Luftflotte 4, and the Regia Aeronautica a further 300 in Albania and Italy. Against this force of about 500,000 men and 1,500 aircraft the Greeks, Yugoslavs and British ranged about 150,000 poorly equipped soldiers and about 300 aircraft.

With a savagery recalling Warsaw and Rotterdam, the German attack on Yugoslavia opened on the morning of 6 April with a series of devastating bombing raids on Belgrade, simultaneous with armoured thrusts across the Yugoslav borders. At the same time German forces struck from Bulgaria into Western Thrace and Eastern Macedonia towards Salonika through the Rupel Pass. Many Greek towns and ports suffered heavy air attacks in those first days. At 1800 hours on 6 April, in an attack by

Malta 1940-42

A tiny island no more than the size of the Isle of Wight, in World War II Malta occupied a strategic position in the Mediterranean second to none, lying as it did across the supply route from Italy and Sicily to North Africa. Between the two world wars Malta harboured units of the Royal Navy's Mediterranean Fleet and provided staging facilities for British ships passing between Gibraltar in the west and Alexandria in the east. When in the mid-1930s Mussolini's Italy displayed hostility, Malta's vulnerability to attack from Sicily – no more than 96 km (60 miles) distant – was emphasised and the Mediterranean Fleet was dispersed to Alexandria. However, it was realised that the island's value as a repair and staging post remained and in 1939 the Committee of Imperial Defence authorised the completion of three airfields at Hal Far, Luqa and Takali, maintenance of a flying boat base at Kalafrana and the establishment of a radar station. Four fighter squadrons were approved, together with 172 anti-aircraft guns.

Malta's Gladiators

The first priority was, however, for Britain to acquire modern fighter defences and in the first months of the war with Germany little could be done to provide Malta with these defences, other than to complete the airfields and radar station. When Italy entered the war on 10 June 1940 – at the height of the Battle of France – the island possessed a total of six assembled Gloster Sea Gladiators and six more in crates, five Swordfish and a naval radio-controlled target aircraft. There were also about 40 40 mm Bofors and ten 4·7 in naval anti-aircraft guns. The Sea Gladiators were not part of an established defence force, but were held as possible replacements for British aircraft carriers. However the senior RAF officer, Air Commodore Forster Maynard AFC, gained permission from Admiral Cunningham to create a defence flight at Hal Far using the Sea Gladiators, flown by staff pilots and those of an anti-aircraft co-operation unit. The flight was in action against the first Italian raid on the island on 11 June.

Early attacks by the Regia Aeronautica were half-hearted and it was a feature of the Sea Gladiators' tactics to break up the small Italian formations and upset their bombing aim, rather than to waste time concentrating on lengthy attempts to shoot down aircraft. Before long, however, the defending pilots had to contend with Fiat CR 42 escort fighters. It has often been suggested that there were only three Gladiators available and that these were referred to as *Faith*, *Hope* and *Charity*; this was in

A Bristol Beaufighter pictured over Malta. Beaufighters of No 252 Squadron began operating from Malta in May 1941

Right: the Junkers Ju 88
was the principal Luftwaffe
bomber used against Malta.
The strategic position of
the island rendered it a
prime Axis target. In late
1940 the Luftwaffe's
Fliegerkorps X was sent
to Sicily to lead a full scale
blitz on Malta.
Below: an RAF Martin
Baltimore takes off from
a Malta airfield. By
mid-1943 the Allies were
able to exploit fully Malta's
strategic position and
bombers were based on the
island in preparation for
the invasion of Sicily

fact a retrospective product of someone's vivid imagination. Air Marshal Maynard recalled only having heard these names first used when he was posted home to Britain in 1941.

When Italy entered the war, Hurricanes were already staging through Malta *en route* for the Middle East, the first four having passed through on 8 June. On the 22nd six more arrived and the same day Flt Lt George Burges achieved the island's first air victory when he shot down a reconnaissance Savoia Marchetti SM 79. Three of these Hurricanes were retained in Malta until 26 June, when the Gladiators destroyed a second SM 79. Two days later four Hurricanes arrived from North Africa to stay.

Fighter reinforcements

Early activity by Italian forces in North Africa quickly brought Malta's supreme value in the central Mediterranean to the attention of Whitehall. Six Fairey Swordfish of No 830 Squadron Fleet Air Arm arrived at the same time as the four Hurricanes and Short Sunderlands of Nos 228 and 230 Squadrons started flying from Kalafrana. One of these, flown by Flt Lt William Campbell of No 230 Squadron sank two Italian submarines during the first three days–returning with four prisoners. In the face of continuing Italian attacks, the overriding demand by the island was for fighters. Thus on 2 August the first major reinforcements arrived when a dozen Hurricane Mk Is flew off the carrier HMS *Argus* to land on Malta, forming No 261 Squadron. Three Martin Marylands of No 431 Flight arrived the following month.

The next reinforcements suffered tragedy. On 17 November, in the suspected presence of Italian warships, 12 Hurricanes and two Blackburn Skuas were flown off HMS *Argus* at the extreme limit of their range and, owing to inexperience, most of the pilots ran out of fuel and were lost at sea, only four Hurricanes and one Skua arriving.

Anticipating the arrival of further fighters, Maynard was authorised to form No 148 Squadron of 16 assorted Vickers Wellingtons on Malta and these bombers operated with telling effect both against Italian ports to the north and African supply targets to the south. It was one of Malta's Marylands whose crew brought back the all-important photographs of five Italian battleships, 14

cruisers and 27 destroyers lying in Taranto harbour on 10 November. The following day HMS *Illustrious* launched her Swordfish torpedo biplanes against the port in a brilliant raid which resulted in hits on three battleships and several other vessels.

Thus ended the first perilous chapter of Malta's war. Had Italy staged a determined assault against the island during those first weeks, when the defences were so slender, there could have been but one outcome. Thereafter Malta was either too strong, or there were inadequate forces immediately available to defeat the island fortress.

The Luftwaffe's arrival

The Italians' dismal performance in Cyrenaica and a suspicion that their navy was equally inept in the Mediterranean roused the Germans to send forces to Libya to bolster their allies. Moreover, the Regia Aeronautica had been almost totally eclipsed in the air. It was to safeguard his supply route to North Africa that Hitler persuaded Mussolini to accommodate Fliegerkorps X of the Luft-

the blitz on the *Illustrious* the Germans and Italians were able to call upon about 250 aircraft with which to attack the island, against which Maynard could muster but one squadron of Hurricanes. Four of the latter were lost in combat but six further Hurricanes arrived on 30 January.

Malta now faced its first period of serious privation. The assembly of Erwin Rommel's Afrika Korps, which was formally established on 18 February, and its offensive against Wavell's depleted desert forces deprived the RAF of forward airfields from which further fighters could be flown to the island. Continued pressure by Fliegerkorps X forced the withdrawal of No 148 Squadron from Malta. By the end of April stocks of food, aviation fuel and anti-aircraft ammunition on the island had dwindled to a dangerously low level. Fortunately, however, bad weather early in May enabled the Royal Navy to sail a large convoy through the Mediterranean to Alexandria with badly needed tanks and fighters, while another convoy, bringing food, fuel and ammunition, sailed into Grand Harbour from the east. At about this time 24 Hurricane Mk IIs

waffe in Sicily in late December 1940.

On 10 January the war in the Mediterranean entered a new and more deadly phase. A Malta-bound convoy from Gibraltar came under repeated air attack by about 60 Heinkel He 111s and Junkers Ju 87s as it passed through the Sicilian narrows. HMS *Illustrious* suffered six direct hits by bombs and three near misses and the next day the cruisers *Southampton* and *Gloucester* were severely damaged, the former being abandoned.

Illustrious limped into Valletta's Grand Harbour, where repair work was started, but the presence of this important ship only attracted the Luftwaffe bombers like moths to a flame. On 16 January a raid by 70 Ju 87s and Ju 88s caused heavy damage in the harbour besides scoring a further hit on HMS *Illustrious*. Three days later the carrier suffered yet another direct hit, but on the 23rd, by a miracle of effort, she slipped out under darkness and arrived safely at Alexandria two days later. At the time of

were flown to Malta from HMS *Ark Royal*, their pilots being formed into the island's second fighter squadron (No 185). No 431 Flight acquired more Marylands and was accordingly enlarged to become No 69 Squadron.

As enemy forces pushed forward to Tobruk in Cyrenaica, Fliegerkorps X was transferred from Sicily to Crete, Greece and the Dodecanese in June to carry out attacks against Alexandria, Cairo and the Suez Canal, leaving the Italians in Sicily to pursue their attacks on Malta. By October 1941 the Allied forces in the Western Desert were once more poised for an offensive in Cyrenaica, intended to relieve the besieged garrison at Tobruk, recapture Benghazi and sweep the Axis forces back to Tunisia. For this offensive known as Operation Crusader, forces were built up on Malta with which to attack the enemy's vital supply route, including three Hurricane Mk II squadrons, three of Bristol Blenheim IVs and one with Marylands. A detached flight of No 40 Squadron

arrived on the island with a dozen Wellingtons while two Fleet Air Arm squadrons flew in with Albacores and Swordfish torpedo aircraft.

The Malta squadrons now embarked on an all-out effort to prevent supplies from reaching North Africa with frequent attacks on ships at sea and raids on the ports of Brindisi, Naples and Tripoli and the airfield at Castel Benito. The Luftwaffe returned to Sicily in an effort to protect the shipping, but with little success, and the Italians had to admit the loss of 77 per cent of their available ships to air and submarine attack.

Faced with defeat in North Africa Hitler now ordered a substantial strengthening of the Luftwaffe in the Mediterranean with the transfer of Generalfeldmarschall Albert Kesselring's Luftflotte 2 from the Russian Front. By the end of the year the German and Italian air forces in Sicily alone could muster 250 bombers and 200 fighters, against which Air Vice-Marshal Hugh Pughe Lloyd (who had succeeded Maynard in May) could field no more than 70 fighters and 60 bombers.

Determined to suppress Malta and prevent convoys from reaching the island, Kesselring now launched a series of devastating raids whose targets were the all-important airfields. From a daily average of 12 sorties the Germans increased their efforts to almost 100. Though outclassed by the Messerschmitt Bf 109Fs, the Hurricanes managed to limit the enemy's bombing efficiency, but heavy rains soon reduced the crater-pitted fighter airfields at Hal Far and Takali to quagmires. Living conditions for airmen, soldiers and civilians had long since been reduced to a low level with acute shortages of food and fuel for heating, aggravated by the constant crash of bombs and whine of flying shrapnel. By February 1942 the bombers had to be withdrawn once more and the fighters were moved to the better-drained airfield at Luqa. To add to the island's misery the Luftwaffe destroyed the entire February convoy from Alexandria and on the 7th, Malta's air-raid sirens sounded no fewer than 16 times in 24 hours.

George Cross award

A new phase of attacks from the air started on 20 March when 143 Ju 88s attacked Takali. The following day the airfield was struck by 218 raiders and on the 22nd by half that number. On the 23rd the attack switched against four merchant ships approaching the island. One was sunk and although the others reached Grand Harbour all were destroyed by bombs within three days after only 5,000 tons of their vital cargoes had been unloaded.

In April the Germans attacked with redoubled determination, 200 sorties a day frequently being launched, and on two occasions–7 April and 20 April–more than 300 sorties. The proud city of Valletta had become a mass of rubble-choked streets with the docks and quays of Grand Harbour reduced to a shambles. Under this pressure the 'resident' destroyers and submarines were withdrawn. When Air Marshal Arthur Tedder visited the island in mid-April he found no more than six serviceable Hurricanes and the daily anti-aircraft ammunition rationed to fifteen rounds per gun. It was at this moment of extreme danger and fortitude that Britain, on 16 April 1942, expressed acknowledgement of Malta's supreme courage with the unusual award of a gallantry decoration to the island, the George Cross.

At this critical moment Lloyd received more tangible encouragement, when on 20 April, 47 Spitfire Vs were flown off the American carrier USS *Wasp* to replenish the defences. Unfortunately their arrival had been spotted by Luftwaffe pilots, who redoubled their efforts in an attempt to destroy the new fighters as they refuelled on the ground. By evening on the following day only 17 Spitfires were still serviceable.

At this nadir of her fortunes Malta became the focus of concern in Allied strategy. While Germany now faced growing and conflicting demands from the Russian Front and her cities cried out for improved air defence against RAF bombers, 62 more Spitfires reached the island from USS *Wasp* and HMS *Eagle* on 10 May–the same day that the fast minelayer HMS *Welshman* arrived in Grand Harbour with a full cargo of ammunition for Malta's guns. Within a week about a third of Kesselring's aircraft had been withdrawn from the Mediterranean.

With air defence bidding fair to provide cover over Malta, it was decided to risk the sailing of two convoys simultaneously from east and west in the hope of dividing and weakening enemy attentions. After the arrival of 59 further Spitfires from HMS *Eagle* at the end of May together with No 217 Squadron flying Bristol Beauforts and No 219 Squadron flying Bristol Beau-

fighters, and under far-reaching cover of African-based bombers (including the first RAF Consolidated Liberators), 11 merchantmen with cruiser and destroyer protection set out from Alexandria on 12 June at the same time as six merchantmen. They were escorted by a battleship and two aircraft carriers and numerous cruisers and destroyers sailed from Gibraltar. Under determined attack by the Luftwaffe and threatened by heavy units of the Italian fleet, the west-bound convoy was forced to turn

back after six merchant ships had been sunk. The Gibraltar convoy was subjected to constant air attack, but the Fleet Air Arm fighters limited its loss to one merchantman before the ships entered the Sicilian narrows. German dive bombers then sank another and damaged two more, so that by the morning of 16 June only two merchant ships survived to berth in Grand Harbour. The cost of fighting those two ships through to the island had been the loss of one cruiser, five destroyers, two minesweepers and six merchantmen, as well as damage to 15 other ships and 20 aircraft lost.

During the summer of 1942 the situation in the Western Desert stabilised. Allied and Axis armies faced each other across the line at El Alamein, both sides desperately gathering strength for the decisive battle in the North African campaign. Kesselring, as always, was anxious to protect the lifeline to Rommel and opened a new *blitz* against Malta on 1 July. However, within a fortnight, thanks to the efforts of the Spitfires and Beaufighters, he had lost 44 aircraft–losses Germany could ill afford–and the attacks dwindled. Hugh Lloyd was posted away for a much-earned rest and his place taken by that brilliant fighter commander, Air Marshal Keith Park, of Battle of Britain fame and by the end of July the number of aircraft on Malta had increased to 260. In August another pair of convoys were sailed under heavy naval escort. This time, for the loss of HMS *Eagle*, two cruisers and a destroyer, five merchantmen reached the island. The tide had turned.

Michael Cole's painting depicts Spitfires scrambling to defend their base. Malta's airfields became primary targets for Axis attacks in 1942. The Spitfire, unlike the Hawker Hurricane, was the equal of the Macchi MC 202 and Messerschmitt Bf 109F fighters encountered over the island

Eastern Front 1941-45

When Germany marched against Russia at 0315 hours on 22 June 1941 Hitler, conscious of his nation's traditional vulnerability in war on two fronts, gambled on a quick, decisive offensive, hoping to crush the Soviet Union before the onset of the hated 'General Winter'. Indeed the Führer's aspirations hung on this vain hope for, on paper, he knew that Russia was still years behind the modern world in military training and technology. In launching his offensive at numerous points between the Black Sea and the Baltic he aimed to strike simultaneously at the two major Russian cities, Moscow and Leningrad, at the huge industrial areas on the Central Front, at the great food-producing area of the Ukraine and, eventually, at the oil resources of the Caucasus. Had it been possible to deny these strategic centres to the Russians by the end of 1941, there is little doubt that Germany would not have had to fight through the dreaded winter. The fact that she was not able to do so in two years, let alone one, enabled the Russian industrial and manpower resources to be marshalled and flung against the failing German war machine.

Preparations for the launching of Operation Barbarossa (as the campaign was code-named) had preoccupied Hitler for almost eighteen months. Clandestine reconnaissance flights had been made over Russian territory since mid-1940 by the Aufkl. Ob.d.L. (the reconnaissance unit attached to the Luftwaffe High Command) under Oberstleutnant Theodor Rowehl, using such high-flying aircraft as the Junkers Ju 86P. These flights brought back vital information about the deployment of Russian air and ground forces. That these flights had continued unopposed and unremarked served to emphasise the impotence of the Soviet defences and seemed to confirm that German strength in the air would allow a swift and total victory.

German air power

On 22 June 1941 the German order of battle included no fewer than 145 divisions distributed between three army groups. As an example of the magnitude of German strength in the air it is interesting to note that Luftflotte 4 alone fielded a strength of 263 fighters, 421 bombers, 60 transports and more than 130 reconnaissance aircraft. The entire air force facing Russia on that day amounted to 680 fighters, 765 bombers, 317 dive bombers, more than 400 short-range reconnaissance aircraft, 180 transports and 60 long-range reconnaissance aircraft. Apart from a small number of dive bombers based in northern Norway, the Junkers Ju 87Bs of StG 1, StG 2 and StG 77 were divided between II Fliegerkorps. and VIII Fliegerkorps.

The fighter force was composed entirely of Messerschmitt Bf 109Es and Bf 109Fs. Every one of the fighter force units was a veteran of several hard-fought campaigns, not least the enervating Battle of Britain which had ended seven months earlier.

Deployed against the Luftwaffe was the huge, but incredibly ill-equipped and poorly trained Red Air Force, with large numbers of obsolete fighters and bombers. Foremost among these were the Polikarpov I-15 and I-16 fighters, while the bomber regiments still possessed large numbers of SB-2s, SB-3s, DB-3s and TB-3s. The assault squadrons were largely equipped with R-Z biplanes of 1934 vintage. Only one relatively effective, modern aircraft was beginning to appear in the Red Air Force, the Ilyushin Il-2 Shturmovik ground support attack bomber. This predominantly wooden aircraft – later versions were of all-metal construction – had entered production in March 1941 and within nine months only 249 examples had been completed It was just beginning to appear in service when the Germans attacked.

Copy-book blitzkrieg

The lack of training that quickly became evident in the Red Air Force was matched only by its lack of preparedness when the blow fell. The German assault was a copy-book repetition of the successful Blitzkrieg of the war's early campaigns. The initial air operations were launched by large forces of fighter-bombers and dive bombers against front-line targets, as formations of bombers attacked concentrations of armour and rail junctions immediately behind the front. The fighters, frequently carrying large numbers of 2 kg SD 2 fragmentation bombs, ranged over and behind the Russian lines, providing cover for the ground operations and shooting up enemy aircraft concentrated on about 60 airfields.

In truth the Russians had deployed their air force too far west at too low a state of readiness and were without any adequate system of raid warning. Few Soviet aircraft managed to take off to dispute the Luftwaffe's air mastery and the *jagdflieger* unquestionably fought a singularly one-sided battle. By the end of the first day German claims totalled an astonishing 1,811 Russian aircraft destroyed, for a loss of 32. A Russian communiqué later admitted the loss of 1,200 aircraft in the first nine hours.

The following day the Germans crossed the River Bug and occupied Brest-Litovsk in Eastern Poland. The Russians, now faced with overwhelming pressure along the entire front, started to react in the air. In almost suicidal circumstances, the ground support regiments attempted to attack the German tank columns under cover provided by the outdated I-16 fighters, only to be mown down by the ever watchful *jagdflieger*. As Russian opposition dwindled, the Luftwaffe mounted a raid on Moscow by 127 bombers. Opposed by about fifty I-16s, the raiders lost six of their numbers and returned to the capital on the following two days with raids of almost similar proportions.

In the south, the Russians launched a raid on the Ploesti oil field on the 26th by about fifty bombers, but suffered a loss of eight to the guns of JG 77. Deprived of adequate air cover on the Central Front the Russian armies suffered their first major defeat when, on 1 July, following a lightning encircling thrust by Guderian's armoured columns, 100,000 troops were forced to surrender in Poland. In the north, Riga in Latvia fell to the Germans. On the previous day Jagdgeschwader 52 shot down the fighter unit's 1,000th victim of the war.

Junkers Ju 87G-1 of SG 2

494193

Henschel Hs 129B-3 of IV.(Pz)/SG 9

0795

Henschel Hs 123A of II./SG 2

German fighter pilots were enjoying the finest sport in aerial history. Despite the suicidal courage of many Russian pilots in their antiquated fighters, the *jagdflieger* were daily destroying upwards of 100 enemy aircraft. The legendary Werner Mölders, who had brought his JG 51 from the Channel coast with a personal score of 68 victories, destroyed his 101st victim on 15 July–a total of 33 victories in 24 days. Shortly afterwards even this feat was surpassed when a young pilot of JG 52, Oblt Hermann Graf, shot down 47 Russian aircraft in 17 days, and soon after no fewer than 75 in 28 days.

Scorched earth

In one respect the Luftwaffe was sadly lacking in its balance of equipment; this was in transport aircraft. As the German advance continued the Russians quickly adopted a 'scorched earth' policy, destroying everything of any possible value to the enemy: railways, bridges, airfield facilities, road junctions and even whole towns and villages were annihilated. Such destruction threw considerable strain on the transport *gruppen* (only six of which had been deployed on the whole Russian Front), which were constantly called on to deliver prodigious quantities of fuel, ammunition and various other stores to the front line.

In an attempt to stem the flow of German tanks across the Pruth during August the air arm of the Russian Black Sea Fleet launched an attack on the Czernowicz bridge using the Zveno II technique. In this, two TB-2 bombers, each carrying two SPBs (I-16s equipped as dive-bombers) under the wings, approached the target, released their charges and returned safely. The SPBs then attacked the bridge and succeeded in destroying it, returning under their own power.

By the beginning of August 1941, Russian aircraft losses had risen to more than 4,000 out of the estimated 10,000 based in western Russia when the German attack opened. Survivors of the fighter force were now grouped

At the start of the war against Russia, German ground attack units were still equipped with elderly Hs 123 biplanes. However, these were soon joined by Hs 129s, which were specially-designed for close-support and anti-tank work, and anti-tank versions of the Ju 87 Stuka. Opposite: a German pilot lies dead beside the wreck of his Messerschmitt Bf 110, shot down during the Russian winter.

for the protection of the key towns and cities, particularly Moscow, Leningrad, Murmansk and Kiev. Early in August the Red Air Force twice attempted to raid Berlin using about sixty aircraft; on both occasions the Russians lost more than a quarter of the raiding aircraft, and neither caused any significant damage. On the 13th, while huge battles raged in the Ukraine, Smolensk on the Central Front was evacuated, and twelve days later Novgorod, south of Leningrad, was given up to the Germans.

Help from the West

Within hours of Hitler's attack on 22 June, Winston Churchill pledged to the world that everything within the capabilities of the Western Allies would be done to help their new Russian allies.

If Russia seemed powerless to prevent the advance of the German forces, Britain offered to redress the balance of arms quality by shipping large quantities of such supplies by the northern sea route to Murmansk. The first dozen convoys, which sailed during the autumn of 1941, arrived at Murmansk without serious interference. In March 1942, however, the convoy PQ 13 was attacked by Ju 88s of III/KG 30 from Banak, led by the indomitable Hajo Herrmann, and lost two ships. PQ 15 suffered the loss of three further ships to the Luftwaffe.

When PQ 16 sailed it was sighted on 25 April and shadowed by long-range reconnaissance aircraft, the pilots of which radioed the convoy's position to Banak. Thereafter more than 100 He 111s and Ju 88s from KG 26 at Bardufoss and KG 30 kept up a series of running attacks which caused the ships to scatter and brought them within range of the Ju 87s of I/StG 5. Seven ships were sunk.

Convoy PQ 17 was spotted and shadowed by Focke Wulf Fw 200s and the 34 ships soon came under devastating attack by the Ju 88s of KG 30. Prematurely dispersed by Admiralty order, no fewer than 23 vessels in the convoy were sunk. Such losses certainly dismayed the Allies, who delayed sailing the next convoy, PQ 18, until early September. Then the convoy was covered by a task force which included a light carrier with Sea Hurricane fighters aboard. This time the German attacks, which claimed thirteen ships, were met by determined resistance from the British pilots, who shot down five bombers. Recognising that the season of sinkings had come to an end, the Germans moved the Heinkels and Junkers to the Mediterranean. Subsequent convoys sailed along the Arctic route almost until the end of the war without interference from the Luftwaffe and huge quantities of war supplies reached the north Russian ports.

Among the cargoes carried in an early PQ convoy to Murmansk were the pilots and Hurricanes of No 151 Wing, RAF, under the command of Wg Cdr H. N. G. Ramsbottom-Isherwood, which reached Murmansk and Vaenga on 28 August 1941. After about eight weeks' fighting, during which Russian pilots were instructed in flying the Hurricanes, the RAF pilots shipped home, leaving their aircraft in the hands of the 72nd Regiment of the Red Naval Air Fleet. These were the first of 2,952 Hurricanes supplied to the Russians from British and Canadian factories.

The Russians also received 1,331 Spitfires, 4,743 Bell Airacobras, 2,400 Bell Kingcobras, 2,901 Douglas Havocs, 2,091 Curtiss P-40s, 195 Republic Thunderbolts, 862 North American Mitchells, 707 Douglas Dakotas, 81 North American AT-6 Harvards and 185 Consolidated Catalinas, as well as small numbers of de Havilland Mosquitoes and Armstrong Whitworth Albemarles. The supply of almost 20,000 modern aircraft to Russia must be judged, not just

in the light of her own dismally outdated indigenous equipment, but in the context of the tremendous sacrifices made by her peoples in the bloodiest and most protracted campaign of the whole war being waged against Germany.

The first winter

And so the first year's chapter of disasters for the Russians continued. While the RAF's 151 Wing was finding its feet in the far north early in September 1941, the Red Army abandoned Tallinn, capital of Estonia and heavy fighting moved closer to Leningrad which now came under repeated aerial attack by the Luftwaffe. In the south the great capital of the Ukraine, Kiev, fell to the invaders on 19 September.

At the Soviet naval base at Kronstadt at the head of the Gulf of Finland, lay the two great battleships *Marat* and *Oktyabrskaya Revolutsia* (October Revolution) together with a number of cruisers and other naval vessels. The large guns of the battleships constituted a flank threat to the German armies poised to surround Leningrad and dive bombing attacks were launched against them on 23 September by the Ju 87s of I and III/StG 2 based at Tyrkovo. One of the Stuka pilots attacked the *Marat* in a near vertical dive, his 1,000 kg bomb striking and sinking the great ship. The name of this pilot was Oblt Hans-Ulrich Rudel, then technical officer of III/StG 2 Immelmann. In further attacks on the same day Rudel succeeded in sinking a cruiser and a destroyer at Kronstadt.

The attacks on Kronstadt represented the climax of the Stukas' initial operations. For three months the dive bombers had operated from airstrips close up behind the advancing forces. Air control officers had ridden in the leading tanks and scout cars, calling down the dive bombers on pinpoint targets by radio link. The flying crews had flown continuously throughout the first twelve weeks of fighting, often completing eight combat sorties in a day.

As the German advance began to slow down before Moscow and Leningrad the most feared enemy, the Russian winter arrived. At first the rain, snow and mud effectively stopped all movement on the ground, while the poorly drained, hastily-prepared airships were quite inadequate to allow air support. To add to the Germans' discomfort, the Russians now embarked on nuisance tactics, flying old Po-2 biplanes at night over the German positions, cutting their engines for a silent approach, to shower the soldiers with grenades and petrol bombs. The Red Air Force also started glider operations to carry saboteurs behind the German lines. It was in this atmosphere of frustration, fear and privation among the personnel of both sides that the war in the East now plumbed new depths of horror and cruelty.

The turning tide

Winter was slower to take a grip in the south where the Germans continued their advance into the Crimea during November, capturing Kerch on the 16th. Then the German progress came to a full halt. Accustomed to operations in such weather conditions, the Russians counter-attacked and made some significant advances on all fronts (re-capturing Rostov-on-Don on 29 November) before they too were forced to abandon their efforts.

However, while the Luftwaffe struggled to protect their aircraft from the ravages of snow and frost and to replace the large numbers of worn out combat aircraft, the Russians were beginning to introduce new equipment into the Red Air Force. At first this merely amounted to summoning reserves from elsewhere in the Soviet Union, but soon the first of a new generation of fighters was to

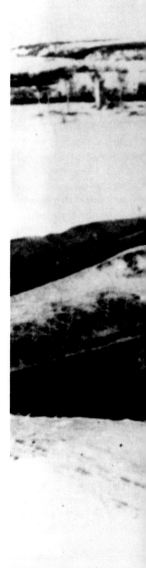

Above right: three Soviet pilots of British-built Hawker Hurricanes in September 1942. Left to right: Snr Lt Krikunov, Jnr Lt Volkov and Major Krondratiev. Far right: volunteer Spanish airmen of the Blue Division, which served alongside the German forces, re-arming a fighter on the Russian front in August 1943. Right: a Polikarpov I-15 of the Red Air Force destroyed on the ground in the summer of 1941. Although obsolete the I-15 and its derivatives were flown against the Germans in 1941. Below: the commander of a Russian light anti-aircraft battery scans the skies

emerge from the factories, beginning with the La-5 whose design had only started in earnest in October 1941.

If the Allies expected the Russians to maintain the initiative after the winter of 1941–42, they were to be sadly disappointed. Early in January 1942 a winter offensive by four Russian armies broke through the German front between the Northern and Central Army Groups and, within a month, six divisions of General Graf Brockdorff-Ahlefeldt's X Army Group had been surrounded at Demyansk. Immediately the Luftwaffe undertook to supply the trapped divisions by air. On 20 February the Ju 52/3ms of two transport *gruppen* started to land at Demyansk and within a week were joined by three more. Soon a second airstrip was in use at Pyesky inside the posket and the lumbering Junkers stepped up their efforts to reinforce and supply the forward troops. The Red Air Force took a heavy toll among the transports, which were soon forced to fly in compact formations under heavy fighter cover, but the operation was successful. In May the German land forces had smashed a corridor through and relieved the trapped divisions. During the three months' operation the transport aircraft had carried 24,300 tons of supplies and 15,446 troops into the pocket and evacuated more than 20,000 casualties. The cost to

Above: because of the intense cold of the Russian winter, the Germans were forced to use mobile heaters to maintain aircraft while on the ground

the Luftwaffe had been 262 aircraft and 385 men killed, including the leader of KGrzbV 172, Major Walter Hammer.

Pursuing the harsh organisational discipline peculiar to the German Army, the Wehrmacht and Luftwaffe seemed revitalised and ready to resume their offensive deeper into Russia by May 1942. Little progress could be made on the Northern and Central Fronts against determined Russian resistance, but in the Crimea the whole of the Kerch peninsula was overrun that month, and Sebastopol fell to the Germans on 1 July, an operation heavily supported by the Ju 87s of StG 77, which flew a total of 7,700 sorties in 12 days. May also brought a new Luftwaffe assault wing, Schlachtgeschwader 1, into action in support of the Kerch attack. Equipped with Bf 109F fighter-bombers, Henschel Hs 123 ground-support bi-planes and the new Henschel Hs 129, the *gruppen* and *staffeln* of this *geschwader* later went on to accompany the German operations at Sebastopol, in the Caucasus, on the Don River and at Stalingrad.

Russian reserves mobilised

While the Red Army maintained massive forces on the Northern Front, the Germans made rapid progress in the south during the summer of 1942, eventually occupy-

ing large areas of the Caucasus and reaching eastwards as far as the ill-fated city of Stalingrad. By the autumn of the year the whole character of the campaign had undergone a fundamental change. Already mobilisation of the huge Russian reserves of manpower was being felt, not only in the sheer weight of numbers, but also in the standard of training and discipline. Russian fighter pilots were now recognised as being of much better calibre than a year previously. Ground flak defences were now something to be feared by the Luftwaffe. The excellent Il-2, previously unable to penetrate German armour with its 20 mm guns, was now being armed with heavier guns well able to kill the Tiger tank. The La-5 and the Yak-9 fighters were beginning to appear over Leningrad, where they were more than a match for the Finns' Morane 406s, Brewster Buffaloes and Fokker DXXIs and, provided they met the Bf 109 below 4,600 m (15,000 ft), could certainly hold their own with that fighter. Among the pilots to achieve distinction was Hero of the Soviet Union Alexiey Meresyev, who had lost both legs when he was shot down in an I-16.

Even the reorganisation that occurred in the Luftwaffe combat echelons disclosed an anxiety that the Germans no longer possessed the initiative to maintain air superiority over the three fronts simultaneously. For the first time in the war there was a growing shortage of fighters, especially in the vicinity of Moscow and Leningrad – a situation further aggravated by Hitler's insistence on priority for bomber production.

The appearance of growing numbers of RAF and USAAF aircraft in German skies, the increasing demands of the Mediterranean theatre and operations in the West, such as the Dieppe landing, all inexorably eroded the strength of the Luftwaffe in the East. Moreover, factories at Irkutsk, Komsomolsk, Kazan, Novosibirsk and Semenovka were, by the end of 1942, beginning to deliver growing numbers of up-to-date fighter aircraft such as the MiG-3, LaGG-3 and La-5. The Yak-7 and Yak-9 would shortly arrive at the front. Production of the Petlyakov Pe-2 twin-engined bomber was increasing rapidly, as was that of the Pe-8 heavy bomber. The improved Il-2 was being joined by the Sukhoi Su-6 on the assault regiments. The Red Air Force had lost more than 8,000 aircraft in the

units. Henceforth much greater emphasis was laid upon the German fighter-bombers, which, if overwhelmed by Russian fighters, could jettison their bombs and fight.

Trapped army

The summer advance by the German Sixth Army had carried it far to the East, reaching the River Don at Stalingrad. However, a late autumn counter-attack by the Russians created a huge pincer movement which, on 23 November, closed behind the Sixth Army at Kalach. Remembering the success of his transport *gruppen* at Demyansk earlier that year, Goering rashly undertook to supply the trapped Army by air and, by so doing, effectively sealed the fate of General Paulus' forces. No fewer than 250,000 men had been surrounded at Stalingrad and the Luftwaffe possessed only 150 transports on that sector of the front.

Within a month, however, the Germans had managed to assemble a large fleet of heterogeneous aircraft, including Ju 52/3ms, Ju 86s, Heinkel He 111s and Fw 200 Condors. Eighteen Fw 200s of KGrzbV 200 under Major Hans-Jürgen Williers began by landing supplies, but as the airfields came under Russian attack they were forced to parachute their supply containers to the troops. A number

Left: German infantry reserves after landing near the Don front in March 1943. Some had been airlifted from other fronts.
Below: Russian Il-2s, known as 'flying tanks' were highly effective ground attack aircraft, and provided especially good armoured protection for the crew of two.
Bottom: among the unsophisticated, yet rugged and effective, Russian warplanes that wrested air superiority from the Luftwaffe in 1943–45 was the Lavochkin La-5 fighter and the Ilyushin Il-2 Shturmovik ground attack aircraft

first six months after the German attack, but by the end of 1942, with vastly improved equipment, its strength had risen to nearly 17,000 aircraft – of which roughly a third were of Western origin.

By the beginning of 1943 the Focke Wulf Fw 190 had appeared on the Russian Front, units so equipped including IV and 14/JG 5, I and III and 15/JG 51, and I, II and IV/JG 54. JG 51's Fifteenth Staffel was a component of the Spanish Blue Division, commanded by Major Mariano Cuadra; III/JG 54 and had been withdrawn from the East to join the air defence of Germany.

The appearance of fast-increasing numbers of modern Russian fighters no longer allowed German bombers and dive bombers to roam the battlefields without strong fighter protection and this imposed further strains on the depleted German reserves. This was the situation that resulted in a complete reorganisation of the ground attack

of Heinkel He 177A-3s of FKGr 2 were rushed south from their trials units to join the supply operations, but seven aircraft were lost owing to engine fires. An *ad hoc* transport unit, Viermotorige Transportstaffel (later designated LTS 290) was formed on 2 January and flew Ju 90Bs, Ju 290s and a Ju 252 over Stalingrad.

The winter now set in with a vengeance and flying conditions were so bad that full advantage could not be taken to employ the whole fleet. Three airfields were at the Germans' disposal at the beginning of the operation and 700 tons of supplies were flown in between 19 and 21 December, but on the 22nd, in thick fog, the Russians started shelling Tazinskaya; in scenes of utter chaos no fewer than 108 Ju 52s and Ju 86s took off and flew back to Novocherkassk and Rostov. Gradually the Russians closed in on the pocket; on 16 January the airfield at Pitomnik was overrun, and on the same day a Russian raid on Sverevo destroyed more than 50 Ju 52/3ms on the ground. On 3 February a Heinkel He 111 of I/KG 100 flew the last supply-dropping sortie over the doomed Army. General Paulus and his Staff had in fact surrendered two days earlier.

Apart from the losses among the transport *gruppen* at Stalingrad, which were grievous enough, it was the loss of 165 Heinkel He 111s from the *kampfgeschwadern* that was to be most keenly felt in the coming months. In more ways than one, Stalingrad was indeed one of the major turning points in the war.

A vital ingredient of the change in Russian fortunes was the sudden appearance of new armoured equipment, including the superb T-34 and KV-1 tanks whose armour could withstand all German aircraft guns so far introduced, including the 30 mm weapons. Realising that enemy superiority in armour threatened the entire Eastern adventure the Germans set spurs to the development of new anti-tank weapons both for the air and on the ground: 1943 was to be the year of the tank-killer.

Operation Citadel
It was on 5 July that the Germans mounted their last great offensive in the East. Operation Citadel was an attempt to wrest the initiative from the Russians on the Central Front by launching a massive pincer attack on the heavily defended Soviet salient at Kursk. To do so the Wehrmacht assembled almost a million men with 2,700 tanks and self-propelled guns, supported by 2,000 aircraft. Among the units specifically designated for anti-tank operations were nearly three hundred Ju 87Ds of StG 2, StG 77 and III/StG 3, the Fw 190s of 5 and 6/SchG 1, and about forty Henschel Hs 129Bs of 4 and 8/SchG 1 and 4 and 8/SchG 2.

In spite of enormous efforts and casualties in the tank battles that raged all round the Russian salient, the German forces could make little headway. On the first day, however, a single incident suggested that the new T-34 tanks were no longer invulnerable to air attack. Hans Rudel, by now a Hauptmann and holder of the Oak Leaves to the Knight's Cross, was flying the first Junkers Ju 87G in combat, armed with two 37 mm Flak anti-tank guns, over the battle area when he spotted a column of twelve T-34s and, aiming to hit their rear-mounted fuel containers, claimed the destruction of the entire column.

After three days of bitter fighting, the German armoured thrust had penetrated about 40 km (25 miles) into enemy-held country, but the southern flank of the pincer was itself in danger of being out-flanked by Russian armour. Hauptmann Bruno Meyer, leading a *staffel* of Hs 129Bs keeping an eye on the German flank, spotted

Russian tanks moving in a wood near Byelgorod. Realising that this was probably the feared flank attack developing, Meyer radioed his base at Mikoyanovka and within minutes further *staffeln* of Hs 129s were on their way to the target. By flying sortie relays the concentration of tanks was kept under constant attack for more than an hour, after which every Russian tank was either on fire or had withdrawn.

Notwithstanding the enormous efforts and sacrifices made by the Germans in this, the greatest tank battle of all time, the Soviet armoured reserves proved too strong and the offensive failed. Luftwaffe losses are estimated to have reached almost 600 (although losses by the Red Air Force, by then more easily sustained, are thought to have been at least twice this number). As German fighter pilots – particularly the survivors of 'the old guard' – continued to display superior skill and training and their individual victory scores soared to unprecedented totals, there began to emerge a new-found *esprit* and confidence among the Soviet pilots.

In the Kursk battles the La-5 was frequently used to launch rockets and hollow-charge bombs against the German tanks with considerable success, before climbing to provide top cover for the Shturmoviki. Already the first Russian aces were beginning to emerge. Ivan Kojedub, who later became the highest-scoring Soviet pilot, with 62 victories, flew his first combat sorties in a La-5 near Kursk. He was to be awarded no less than three Gold Stars of a Hero of the Soviet Union. Also in action at Kursk was the most famous of all Yak-9 pilots, Alexandr Pokryshin – also a three-time Hero – who went on to score 59 victories. The 586th Fighter Regiment of the Red Air Force was an all-women unit flying the Yak-9 on the Central Front.

On 5 August the Russians recaptured Orel and Byelgorod, and 18 days later Kharkov in the Ukraine. A week afterwards they entered Taganrog on the Sea of Azov. Smolensk fell on 25 September, followed by Kiev on 6 November. Yet at scarcely any time did the German loss of territory amount to anything like a retreat. Every mile gained by the Russian armies was bitterly contested and the Germans in turn completed the devastation begun during the Russian withdrawals 18 months earlier. In many instances a section of the front line remained 'fluid' for many days, the opposing armies moving back and forth as the fortunes of battle hung in the balance.

Bombing 'shuttles'
By mid-1944 the Russians had advanced sufficiently far to encourage the Western Allies to attempt bombing 'shuttles' between the United Kingdom and the Soviet Union. No doubt Russian propaganda suggested that the Red Air Force had also achieved adequate air superiority to render such missions feasible. Three bases, Mirgorod, Piryatin and Poltava – all near Kiev – were made ready for the arrival of the first American bombers, and on 2 June the first shuttle raid was flown without trouble by B-17s of the US Fifteenth Air Force. Preoccupied with support of the D-Day landings in Normandy, the Fortresses of the Eighth Air Force did not fly their first shuttle until 21 June when 163 B-17s, escorted by four squadrons of P-51s, bombed a synthetic oil plant south of Berlin and flew on to Russia, the 452nd Bomb Group's Fortresses landing at Poltava. Unknown to the American crews, their formation had been shadowed by a German aircraft whose pilot radioed the B-17s' destination. Five hours later two *gruppen* of Ju 88s and Heinkel He 111s swept over the airfield dropping flares and scatter-

Right: alone among the warring nations of World War II, the Soviet Union employed women in combat. Reconnaissance pilot Lieutenant Vera Feodorova stands beside her R-Z biplane.
Below: smashed German equipment near Kaluga

Left: the crew of a shot down Ju 88 being brought in under Russian guard in the Leningrad sector in January 1943

ing the dispersal areas with fragmentation and high explosive bombs. When dawn broke the Americans found the gutted remains of 44 Fortresses and 26 others badly damaged–out of 72 American aircraft that had landed the previous evening.

By the end of July 1944 the Red Army had not only recovered almost all the Russian territory previously occupied by German forces but had swept into Poland, capturing Przemysl, Brest-Litovsk and Yaroslav. In the south, progress into Romania was slower, although the Ploesti oilfields were overrun on 30 August.

Retreat from Warsaw

As the Russian armies closed in on the German frontier the diabolical treachery, to which warfare on the Eastern Front had descended, was manifest in the investment and reduction of the Polish capital. When the Red Army was still some miles short of Warsaw the Polish partisans were encouraged by the Russians to rise in armed revolt to assist in the liberation of their city. On 1 August the uprising burst upon the German garrison, which now employed all the terror weapons of gas grenade, flame-throwers and torture to put down the revolt. However, instead of pushing on towards Warsaw, the Russians, on the pretext of regrouping their forces, halted their advance. Indeed the Red Air Force did little or nothing to support the partisans from the air and it was left to RAF and USAAF bombers to make the long and hazardous flights from Britain and the Middle East to drop supplies to the supposed pockets of Polish resistance in Warsaw; not unnaturally much of this materiel fell into the hands of the Germans. Not until 17 January did the Red Army enter the city, more than three months after the last Polish partisan had been butchered by the Gestapo.

A measure of the frantic and ingenious expedients adopted by the Luftwaffe in attempts to stem the Russian advance from the East may be judged by the fortunes of the extraordinary Unternehmen Eisenhammer (Operation Iron Hammer), planned in November 1944 for the destruction of Russian power stations. The weapon employed was an unmanned bomber, usually a Ju 88, 'flown' by a piloted fighter, an Fw 190 or Bf 109, perched on top. Known as the Mistel (Mistletoe), the combination was flown under the power of both component aircraft towards the target, where the pilot released the bomber and, by radio control, aimed it at the enemy position. As the Russians held little radar coverage, the Germans considered the plan stood a fair chance of success. However, the advance of the Red Army rendered the attack on the power stations impossible, but Mistels achieved some notable successes elsewhere. On 9 March 1945 four Mistels were flown against the two bridges at Gorlitz over the River Neisse in Silesia. Each bridge was hit by one weapon and destroyed. By the end of March the total force of Mistels available approached 100 and many of these were used in bridge attacks–including some on bridges over the Rhine.

As with the Russian Zveno II bridge attacks of August 1941, the Mistels, though ingenious and often successful locally, could do little to slow the advance of the invading armies. However, in 1945 the Allies were backed by enormous reserves and could sustain losses that not even Germany could countenance four years earlier. Despite prodigious efforts in aircraft production during the last year of the war, all were to no avail when, deprived of her vital sources of fuel, her once-proud Luftwaffe lay scattered on the airfields of Germany at the mercy of British, American and Russian fighters and bombers.

Pacific War 1941-45

The air war in the Pacific actually began a decade before the Sunday morning attack in 1941 which initiated widespread hostilities between the Japanese Empire and the United States and her allies. After World War I there was increasing friction between expansion-minded Japanese militarists and the moderate government. Considering the European colonial powers to be too concerned with their own economic problems to exert strong influence in Asia, the Japanese expansionists saw an opportunity to create a Greater East Asia Co-Prosperity Sphere with Japan at the centre of political and economic power.

Japan's war plans

The expansionist mood – and contempt for the moderate government – was such that during the winter of 1931–1932 the Japanese Kwantung Army seized Manchuria with virtually no support from the Tokyo government. That independent military operation was a major event in a series of incidents which accurately foreshadowed the course of the coming war. Earlier, under the pretext of protecting Japanese nationals and their property, a force of Japanese troops began landing in Shanghai on 28 January 1931. The force received air support two days later, when

Below: Douglas SBD Dauntlesses return from a strike on the Marshalls on 22 November 1943. The SBD was the US Navy's principal strike bomber of the Pacific War.
Right: the battleship USS Pennsylvania pictured after the Japanese attack on Pearl Harbour

the aircraft carrier IJNS *Kaga* made its appearance off the coast. Two days after that, the 60-aircraft complement of *Kaga* was supplemented by 19 aircraft aboard the smaller aircraft carrier IJNS *Hosho*. The pattern was set: in the months and years ahead, Japanese ground forces, supported by land-based and ship-based aircraft, effectively expanded onto the Asian mainland.

By 1937, tired Chinese forces were bolstered by the arrival of four fighter squadrons and two bomber squadrons manned by 'volunteers' from the Soviet Union, as well as by an American group led by Claire L. Chennault. On one occasion in August 1937, elements of these so-called Chinese aircraft units shot down 11 of 12 raiders from IJNS *Kaga*. The lesson was quickly taken by the Japanese, who were continually improving their forces. Hence, when *Kaga* was next deployed to China, her biplane fighters had been replaced by new Mitsubishi A5M4 Claude aircraft, the world's first carrier-based monoplane fighters. They quickly proved to be superior to the Soviet-built Polikarpov I-16 fighters used by the Chinese. Three years later, the Japanese unveiled their Mitsubishi A6M series, later to gain renown as the Zeke

or Zero fighter. The A6M series gave Japanese army and navy pilots a marked advantage over their adversaries until 1943.

Indeed, it was the Japanese Empire's position of military superiority, enhanced by first-rate combat equipment, that contributed to the decision to execute a surprise attack on the primary American bases in the Pacific. After the Tokyo government fell completely under the influence of the militarists, Japanese strategists became convinced that their Pacific expansion put them on a collision course with American interests in the area. Assuming that war was inevitable, the Japanese felt it would be to their advantage to initiate such a war sooner, rather than later, when American military strength would be greater. The Japanese felt they could wage a three-year war against the United States, after which peace and boundary lines favourable to their empire could be negotiated.

During the early stage of World War II in Europe, the officially neutral United States had taken a number of steps to help Britain fend off the ever-increasing attacks by German forces that had sliced through France. Late to recognise the danger in the Pacific, the government of

The Japanese attack on Pearl Harbour was intended to cripple the American Pacific Fleet, but its carrier force escaped. Above: smoke from the battleship USS Arizona which sank after her forward magazine exploded.
Top: the battleships USS West Virginia and USS Tennessee ablaze.
Top left: bombs devastated the destroyer USS Shaw.
Top far left: most of the US ships were berthed, presenting easy targets.
Far left: few USAAF fighters became airborne.
Left: the initial attack focused on 'Battleship Row' on the far side of Ford Island.

President Franklin D. Roosevelt made a final effort in 1941 to reinforce its small Marine Corps outposts on Wake and Midway Islands. The two atolls were important points in the slender resupply network to American positions in the Philippines, which would certainly be the prime target of a Japanese military thrust ultimately aimed at Australia.

The situation had become so serious that in November 1941 US Marine Corps fighter squadron VMF-211 was transported to Wake Island aboard the aircraft carrier USS *Enterprise* (CV-6) under what were characterised as 'war conditions'. In fact, during that period, Vice-Admiral William F. 'Bull' Halsey instinctively kept his three Pacific-based aircraft carriers – *Enterprise*, *Lexington* (CV-2) and *Saratoga* (CV-3) – at sea. The main elements of the battleship fleet were anchored at Pearl Harbour naval base, Hawaii.

Pearl Harbour
While American and Japanese diplomats held a series of meetings intended to avert war between the two countries, a massive naval strike force commanded by Vice-Admiral Chuichi Nagumo was following a course in the northern Pacific away from normal commercial ocean traffic and

far from the target, or if American-Japanese negotiations turned out in the Tokyo government's favour. When neither of these conditions arose the attack was begun, even though the Japanese ambassador was still conferring with the US Secretary of State. At 0600 hours on 7 December 1941, Commander Mitsuo Fuchida led the first wave of 183 fighters, dive bombers and torpedo bombers to their assigned target. The 39-year-old squadron commander aboard *Akagi* was a veteran of the China War and a personal friend of Commander Minoru Genda, Yamamoto's aviation staff officer and primary architect of the attack.

For the American military forces on the island of Oahu, Sunday morning was a quiet time and the force was at its lowest level of preparedness when Commander Fuchida broke through the clouds and determined the element of surprise was completely his. He signalled for the attack to begin.

With great precision the A6M2 fighters, Aichi D3A1 Val dive bombers, and Nakajima B5N2 Kate horizontal and torpedo bombers headed for their targets. When the raiders struck, aircraft at the US Army's Wheeler Field and at the US Naval Air Station on Ford Island in the middle of Pearl Harbour were on the ground, and seven of the nine American battleships in the Pacific Fleet were neatly lined up along one side of Ford Island. The Japanese fighters and bombers attacked the airfields, while 49

Above: 16 squadrons of the Royal Australian Air Force flew the indigenous CAC Wirraway. Designed as an advanced trainer, the type served in a multiplicity of roles and was responsible for the destruction of a Japanese Zero fighter. Left: a US Army Air Force recruiting poster by aviation artist Clayton Knight depicting a Consolidated B-24 Liberator bomber in action over the Pacific Ocean

charted to bring the force to a point north-west of Hawaii. In addition to a support and screening force of battleships, cruisers and submarines, Admiral Nagumo had under his command the aircraft carriers *Akagi*, *Kaga*, *Hiryu*, *Soryu*, *Shokaku* and *Zuikaku*. The striking force carrier air groups were augmented by air crews from the light carrier *Zuiho* and escort carrier *Taiyo*, as well as additional aircraft and crews from the Imperial Japanese Navy's air training group and test unit.

Admiral Isoroku Yamamoto, commander in chief of the combined fleet, had instructed Vice-Admiral Nagumo to abandon the mission if the strike force was detected too

Above: the Bell P-39 Airacobra, together with the Curtiss P-40, formed the principal front-line equipment of USAAF fighter units in the Pacific during the early war years. Below: Douglas SBD Dauntless attack bombers take off from a Solomon Island airstrip during the Allied assault on Bougainville in late 1943

Kates attacked the ships with 800kg armour-piercing naval shells fitted with fins. By the time the last Japanese strike aircraft returned to the waiting carriers, they had devastated aircraft on the ground at Ewa Field, Hickam Field and Kaneohe Field. They had also sunk four battleships, damaged four others, sunk three destroyers and a minelayer and severely damaged two cruisers and a repair ship. There was some solace to be found in the fact that the battleships were caught at their berths. Had they been at sea when overwhelmed by the same force, they would have been sunk with their full crews aboard.

While Admiral Nagumo's strike force made a victorious withdrawal from Hawaiian waters, other Japanese military elements continued the offensive elsewhere. Midway Island was shelled by two Japanese destroyers and the Marine Corps outpost on Wake Island, which was within air range of the Japanese base on Kwajalein in the Marshall Islands, was attacked by Japanese bombers within five hours of the raid on Pearl Harbour. The first raid severely impaired the Marine air contingent of Grumman F4F-3 Wildcats, of which seven were destroyed straight away and one was damaged. That left four of VMF-211's serviceable aircraft to hold off an overwhelming enemy force.

The defenders of Wake Island held out for 16 days, during which the remaining aircraft sank two destroyers, damaged seven other ships and killed several hundred Japanese. For service both in the air and–when the last of the aircraft was destroyed–on the ground, Captain Henry T. Elrod became the first American naval airman of World War II to win the Congressional Medal of Honour, the highest American decoration. However, he was killed during the subsequent invasion of Wake.

Repulse and Prince of Wales
Since the Philippines lie on the other side of the International Date Line, it was Monday 8 December when Americans there received the first messages concerning the attack on Pearl Harbour. In response, Curtiss P-40E Warhawks of the US Army's 3rd Pursuit Squadron were ordered into the air. Shortly thereafter, Boeing B-17 Flying Fortress bombers at Clark Field were ordered into the air to avoid being destroyed on the ground. They were first ordered to patrol northern Luzon, then ordered back to Clark Field to be armed for a mission against the Japanese air bases on Formosa. While they were back on the ground, Japanese forces attacked the Philippines and caught the B-17 force when it was vulnerable; despite the efforts of American pursuit aircraft, the Japanese bombers hit most of the B-17s on the ground.

Five B-17s of the 14th Bombardment Squadron got away from Clark Field and proceeded to attack Japanese landing craft and transports which were part of the intended invasion fleet. One of the bombers, piloted by Captain Colin Kelly, scored a direct hit on a Japanese warship. Returning to Clark Field, however, Kelly's bomber was attacked by two Japanese fighters and, although Kelly held the stricken aircraft level to enable most of the crew to escape, he was unable to get out and perished in his aircraft.

The defence of the Philippines soon became little more than a holding action as American forces sought an orderly withdrawal to Australia. There they could regroup and assist in the defence of Australia and New Zealand. The Japanese forces were moving with decisive swiftness, seizing former French and Dutch colonies in the Pacific and converting them into their own advance bases.

If there was any doubt about the effectiveness of air power against surface ships with conventional protection, it was dispelled on 10 December 1941 when two British warships–the battleship HMS *Prince of Wales* and the battle-cruiser HMS *Repulse*–were spotted by Japanese air units based at Saigon in French Indo-China. A short time later twin-engined Mitsubishi G3M Nell bombers attacked the two ships with bombs and aerial torpedoes. The *Repulse* was hit by a 250kg bomb and five torpedoes, after which she abruptly capsized and sunk. Forty-five minutes later, *Prince of Wales* was struck by one or two 500kg bombs and six torpedoes, causing her to heel over and sink. Royal Air Force fighter aircraft based at Singapore arrived just after the battle was over. There was nothing these land-based aircraft could do for the survivors floating in the water. But the lesson was quite clear: without air cover no capital ship could withstand a concentrated aerial attack.

On the following day, 11 December, Germany and Italy declared war on the United States. The prospect of fighting a two-ocean war was a grim one for the United States, which had only just begun to mobilise and was not prepared for such a far-reaching commitment. To make best use of American resources, therefore, it was decided to place heavy emphasis on aircraft carriers to prosecute the Pacific War, with land-based heavy bombing to be used initially in the European Theatre of Operations. Japanese successes in China, Indo-China, Malaya and the Dutch East Indies–as well as their hard drive for the Philippines–inspired the formation of the American, British, Dutch, Australian (ABDA) area as a means of unifying various forces in Australia even before the carrier war began in earnest.

Advance on Australia

For the Japanese, however, aircraft carriers were the best means of bringing their air war to the retreating Allies. On 20 January 1942, the fleet carriers *Akagi, Kaga, Shokaku* and *Zuikaku* attacked Rabaul on the island of New Britain. They returned during the next two days and, on the 23rd, provided air support for the invasion of Rabaul and nearby Kavieng on New Ireland. The capture of those positions brought the Japanese within range of the strategically important Coral Sea, a clear ocean route to Australia. However, Java had first to be taken. Prior to the invasion of that island, four carriers of Vice-Admiral Nagumo's striking force attacked Darwin, Australia, on the morning of 19 February 1942. The strike, intended to cut communications to Java, was virtually a re-creation of Pearl Harbour, with Commander Mitsuo Fuchida leading 135 aircraft to the port, where they raided harbour traffic and airfields, leaving Darwin in a shambles.

As the Japanese pursued a course of eastward expansion, they posed a constant threat to Darwin, which was attacked on subsequent occasions. Thus, it fell to the US Army Air Corps and the Royal Australian Air Force to defend not only Australia, but also the important position of Port Moresby on the southern coast of New Guinea's Huon Peninsula. Port Moresby was within easy striking distance of Japanese bombers based at Rabaul and, had it fallen into enemy hands, its commanding position on the Coral Sea would have made it an excellent staging point for the invasion of Australia.

Some of the pressure on Australia was relieved by the presence of the American aircraft carriers USS *Yorktown* (CV-5), *Enterprise* and *Lexington*. Operating north-east of the point of Japanese expansion, the carrier air groups diverted attention from the main thrust toward Australia. The day after the first raid on Darwin, *Lexington* made an abortive attempt to attack Rabaul and, although the raid itself was not fully carried out, the carrier's presence drew

considerable Japanese fire-power. In the process, Lieutenant Edward H. 'Butch' O'Hare of fighter squadron VF-3 positioned his F4F-3 between *Lexington* and a flight of Japanese bombers heading for the carrier. In that single engagement, O'Hare shot down five of the bombers and damaged a sixth, for which he was awarded the Congressional Medal of Honour.

Lieutenant O'Hare was more than the first American naval ace of World War II. He was a hero at a time when the Allies needed victories to raise morale as much as they needed strategic and tactical success. Hence, the first Allied air raid over Tokyo two months later was another much-needed morale-booster, even though it did little to impair the effectiveness of the targets which were bombed.

The Doolittle raid

Lieutenant-Colonel James H. Doolittle, a well-known test pilot before the war and a pioneer in the field of aeronautical science, was to lead the raid. His 24 crews were chosen from the 34th, 89th and 95th squadrons of the 17th Bombardment Group, a part of the Eighth Air Force. After extensive training to take off in a North American B-25B Mitchell bomber in 140m (460ft), the aircrews and their specially-modified B-25s went to Alameda near San Francisco, California, where they were loaded aboard the aircraft carrier USS *Hornet* (CV-8).

The mission was to launch 16 of Doolittle's medium bombers from a point as close as the carrier could get to Japan. The B-25s were assigned military and industrial targets in and around Tokyo, after which they were to fly on to sites in China which were free of Japanese control. Early on the morning of 18 April 1942 the aircraft were launched, with Colonel Doolittle himself flying the first bomber off the carrier. The raiders swept over Tokyo, Kobe, Yokohama and Nagoya, surprising the Japanese, who felt the home islands were secure from Allied incursions. A bomb from the B-25 piloted by Lieutenant Edgar E. McElroy hit the light carrier IJNS *Ryuho* in the Yokosuka naval base dry dock where it was being converted from a submarine tender into an aircraft carrier.

Although the Tokyo raiders did not inflict any permanent damage and suffered serious losses of their own–eight men captured by the Japanese, three men who died

Left: a Kawanishi H6K5 Type 97 flying boat, code-named Mavis by the Allies, pictured after being shot down on 7 May 1944 by Lt J. D. Keeling of US Navy unit VB-109. Right: a Nakajima B5N Type 97 carrier-borne torpedo aircraft hit by anti-aircraft fire from the carrier USS Yorktown. Known to the Allies as Kate, the type was prominent in the attack on Pearl Harbour and later played a decisive part in sinking three American aircraft carriers

accidentally and five who were interned by the Soviets— they did have a certain effect on the war effort. The audacity of the raid was encouraging to the Allies and instilled a sense of caution in the Japanese which led to home island protection being increased at the cost of military equipment that might have been better used at the Battle of Midway and other future engagements.

The Doolittle raid on Tokyo made it all the more imperative for the Japanese to seize control of a wider area in the South Pacific and drive the Allies further east. Therefore, the Japanese high command ordered an offensive operation against the Solomon Islands and New Guinea. A key element of the plan was the occupation of Port Moresby, which, if successful, would eliminate the threat of Allied air strikes against Japanese bases in Rabaul and Kavieng. It would also open up the north-east Australian coast along the Coral Sea to attacks by Japanese land-based air elements.

The Japanese organised five separate naval groups to carry out Operation MO. Under the overall command of Vice-Admiral Shigeyoshi Inouye, the plan called for the use of the 25th Air Flotilla based at Rabaul, as well as a covering group which included the light carrier IJNS *Shoho* and a carrier strike force which included the two

Below: the attack on Nadzab, in north-east New Guinea on 5 September 1943: hidden by smokescreens, 96 Douglas C-47 transports flew in 1,700 paratroopers of the US 503rd Parachute Regiment and an artillery detachment of the 2/4th Australian Field Regiment. Cover was provided by 146 US fighters and the landings were preceded by bombardment by B-25 and A-20 medium bombers and B-17 and B-24 heavy bomber aircraft

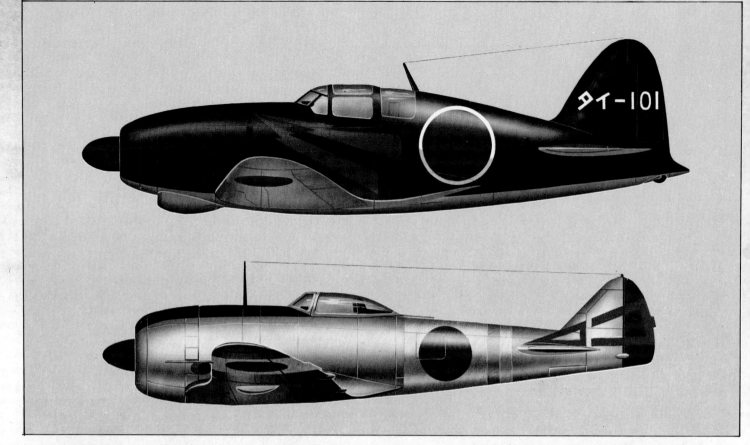

The unit insignia of US Navy bombing squadron VB-81 (top) and torpedo squadron VT-81 (above), aboard USS Wasp

fleet carriers *Shokaku* and *Zuikaku*. Details of the plan were known to the Americans, who had been breaking the Japanese naval code since the war began. However, they were at a loss to match the Japanese military strength being poured into Operation MO. Only the American aircraft carriers *Lexington* and *Yorktown* could be deployed to the Coral Sea in time, as the *Enterprise* and *Hornet* were *en route* to Pearl Harbour following the Doolittle raid on Tokyo.

Coral Sea carrier battle

During the first week of May the Allies moved their forces quickly to meet the enemy thrust. The two carrier task forces rendezvoused south of San Cristobal Island, while at Townsville, Australia, and at Port Moresby, New Guinea, the medium bombers of the USAAF's 13th and 90th squadrons, Douglas A-24s of the 8th Squadron, and Martin B-26s of the 22nd Group were readied for the expected strikes. Townsville-based B-17s of the 19th Bombardment Group covered Port Moresby and the sea lanes leading down from Rabaul.

The Battle of the Coral Sea began just before sunrise on 4 May 1942. Douglas SBD-2 and SBD-3 Dauntless dive bombers of bombing squadron VB-5 and scouting squadron VS-5 and Douglas TBD-1 Devastator torpedo

planes from VT-5 aboard the *Yorktown* were joined by F4F-3s from VF-43 in attacking Japanese ships off Tulagi, sinking several of them. The following morning *Yorktown* was joined in the Coral Sea by *Lexington*. That evening, north of the American task forces, the two Japanese fleet carriers *Shokaku* and *Zuikaku* entered Coral Sea. Although the two forces eventually closed to within 113 km (70 miles) of each other, neither was aware of the presence of the other.

It was not until the morning of 6 May that Japanese reconnaissance aircraft reported sighting the American vessels. On the following day 78 fighters, bombers and torpedo aircraft from *Shokaku* and *Zuikaku* went looking for the carriers. Instead they found the oil tanker USS *Neosho* and destroyer USS *Sims*. They sunk the destroyer and so disabled the oil tanker that it was later torpedoed by the Americans to keep it from falling into enemy hands. The next morning aircraft from USS *Lexington* spotted the Japanese covering group and were soon joined by *Yorktown*-based aircraft. The primary target was the light carrier IJNS *Shoho*, whose dozen fighters were no match for the combined air groups of the two American carriers. SBDs and TBDs put 13 bombs and seven torpedoes into the small carrier, sending it to the bottom of the Pacific within minutes. Only 200 of *Shoho's* 800 crewmen survived

the attack. Lieutenant-Commander Robert Dixon of VS-2 radioed back the jubilant message: 'Scratch one flat-top!'

The jubilation did not last long, however. Japanese reconnaissance aircraft were out before daybreak the next morning, 8 May, looking for the American carriers. They found the Americans some 320 km (200 miles) south of the Japanese carrier force and remained with their adversaries until aircraft from *Shokaku* and *Zuikaku* were on the way. A fierce attack followed and, by late morning, *Lexington* had taken two torpedo hits and a number of enemy bombs. An internal explosion, set off when a gasoline leak was ignited, sealed the carrier's fate.

As *Lexington* was sinking, her air group joined *Yorktown* aircraft in pursuing the two Japanese carriers and inflicting serious damage on each. In the final analysis, victory in the Battle of the Coral Sea is generally accorded to the Allies. Unique in the annals of warfare in that it was the first ship-versus-ship engagement in which the opposing vessels neither saw nor fired upon each other, the Battle of the Coral Sea did more than cost the Japanese the loss of the light carrier *Shoho*. The fleet carriers *Shokaku*

and *Zuikaku* and their air groups were damaged badly enough to keep them out of the Battle of Midway.

Despite the losses incurred during the Battle of the Coral Sea, Admiral Yamamoto felt he still had enough strength to follow up the thrust into New Guinea and the Solomon Islands by launching another major operation. Although his plan met with some resistance, Yamamoto argued that the capture of Midway Island and the occupation of the western portion of the Aleutian chain would give Japan a defence perimeter which would preclude further Allied raids on the home islands. Indeed, when such gains were consolidated, Yamamoto envisaged a thrust toward Hawaii to finish the movement initiated by the Pearl Harbour attack. His schedule of events called for Midway and the Aleutians to be taken in June and Oahu to be attacked before winter set in.

Decision at Midway
Every available warship was mustered for Operation MI, the assault on Midway and the Aleutians. To cripple the American fleet once and for all, Yamamoto knew he would have to mount a force that would draw heavy concentrations to Midway, while his initiative in the Aleutians would be enough to distract and divide the Americans long enough to ensure victory in both cam-

Above: the badge of VF-81, USS Wasp's fighter unit.
Opposite top: a Mitsubishi J2M2 Raiden (Jack).
Opposite above: a Nakajima Ki-44 Shoki.
Top: a Curtiss Kittyhawk of No 15 Squadron RNZAF.
Centre: a US Navy Douglas Devastator of VT-6.
Left: the USS Hornet under attack from a Nakajima B5N Kate

paigns. Yamamoto himself took charge of the operation from his flagship, the battleship *Yamoto*. Still viewing the battleship as the main naval combat vessel, he ordered 11 battleships to be readied. The carriers to be used included the Pearl Harbour veterans *Akagi*, *Kaga*, *Hiryu* and *Soryu*, as well as the light carriers *Hosho* and *Zuiho*. (The fleet carrier IJNS *Junyo* and the light carrier IJNS *Ryujo* were to be committed to the Aleutians campaign.)

To counter the overwhelming Japanese force, US Marine ground forces worked around the clock to bolster Midway's defences. Marine Aircraft Group 22 (MAG-22) was brought up to strength to include 19 SBD-2s, 17 Vought SB2U-3 Vindicators, 21 Brewster F2A-3 Buffaloes and seven F4F-3s. The 28 fighters were commanded by Major Floyd B. Parks and the 36 dive bombers by Major Lofton R. Henderson. US Army B-17s of the 26th, 31st, 72nd and 431st Bombardment Squadrons joined with B-26s to overcrowd the island with the type of aerial strength which would be needed to fend off the Japanese attack. On the afternoon of 3 June nine of the B-17s surprised the Japanese transport force 917 km (570 miles) west of Midway and bombed it with some success. However, the battle began in earnest on the following day. Just before sunrise, Vice-Admiral Nagumo's four fleet carriers launched a 108-aircraft strike against Midway. Scout aircraft were also sent out to look for the American carrier force, which consisted of *Enterprise*, *Hornet* and the hastily-repaired *Yorktown*.

While the Japanese carrier-based aircraft attacked Midway, meeting resistance from the outclassed US Marine Corps F2A-3s and F4F-3s, the bulk of American ship-based and land-based aircraft was engaged in locating the enemy carriers. Elements of that search force were detected by a Japanese reconnaissance aircraft, which was unable positively to identify a carrier among the group of American ships.

The first wave of Japanese aircraft was back aboard the carriers to be refuelled and rearmed and Nagumo deliberated whether to send the aircraft back to Midway loaded with bombs, or to arm them with torpedoes to counter the American naval force. He decided to have the aircraft armed with torpedoes. However, as this was being done, the fleet carrier IJNS *Hiryu* was attacked by 16 SB2U-3s of Marine scout bombing squadron VMSB-241. The attack inflicted no damage on the carrier and, in addition to causing the death of the squadron commander, Major Henderson, *Hiryu*'s defenders badly mauled the flight. Noting that the US Marine aircraft had been slaughtered without fighter coverage, Nagumo hesitated to send his own aircraft against the American ships without fighter cover. Hence, he decided to recover and refuel aircraft returning from Midway before launching the next strike.

When the American carrier-based aircraft spotted the Japanese carriers, the majority of Nagumo's aircraft were crowding the flight decks during pre-flight preparations. Japanese aircraft were launched as quickly as possible while the American torpedo aircraft and bombers attacked the vulnerable carriers. Initially, the Japanese defenders were successful. Almost all of torpedo squadron VT-8 from the *Hornet* was shot down before their TBD-1s could score a hit. The lone survivor was Ensign George Gay, who viewed the rest of the battle while holding onto a flotation cushion after his plane hit the water. A short time later eight of VT-6's 12 TBDs from *Enterprise* were shot down before any of their torpedoes found the mark and all 12 of VT-3's TBDs from *Yorktown* were knocked out by enemy fighters.

The three torpedo squadrons did not fall in vain, however. Their low, over-the-water torpedo runs brought enemy fighters down to very low levels, thus leaving the skies clear for Lieutenant-Commander C. Wade Mc-Clusky's 33 SBDs from *Enterprise*. Moreover, when Vice-Admiral Nagumo ordered torpedoes to be carried by the second wave of aircraft, the bombs originally intended for that strike were not returned to the ships' magazines. Instead, they were stacked in the carriers' hangar bays, thereby creating floating arsenals.

While McClusky's Dauntlesses went after *Akagi* and *Kaga*, Lieutenant-Commander Maxwell F. Leslie led VB-3's SBDs from *Yorktown* against IJNS *Soryu*. The three Japanese carriers were soon marked by towering pillars of smoke and the SBDs returned to their seagoing airfields. While aircraft from the three American carriers were destroying the three Japanese carriers, the remaining fleet carrier, IJNS *Hiryu*, launched aircraft which spotted and attacked USS *Yorktown*. Two waves of *Hiryu* aircraft caused enough damage for the *Yorktown* to be abandoned and subsequently sunk to stop it being seized by enemy vessels. *Yorktown* was avenged, however, when Lieutenant Wilmer E. Gallagher led a flight of *Enterprise*-based SBDs from VS-6 against *Hiryu* and set off a series of uncontrollable fires aboard the ship and US Army B-17s *en route* from Oahu to Midway also joined the attack on the sinking ship. If the Battle of the Coral Sea had been a close victory for the Allies, the Battle of Midway was decisive. In sinking four of the carriers which had launched the Pearl Harbour attack, the Allies broke the back of the Japanese carrier force and effectively turned the tide of the war against the Japanese.

The Japanese advance checked

The Japanese diversion into the Aleutians was also marked by a lack of success. It must have been a surprise to the Japanese to discover that the string of islands was defended by air elements of the US Army, US Navy and the Canadian Western Air Command. While aircraft from the carriers *Junyo* and *Ryujo* flew to the islands, US Army bombers spotted the ships. A B-26 launched a torpedo so close to the *Ryujo* that the missile skipped over the carrier and into the water on the other side of the ship. Other bombers went after the carrier, but with no success. In yet another attempted incursion, a cruiser-based Japanese floatplane was attacked and shot down by a pair of Curtiss P-40s flown by Lieutenants John B. Murphy and Jacob W. Dixon of the 11th Pursuit Squadron based on Unimak Island.

On 6 June Japanese forces landed on Kiska Island and on Attu the following day, creating a military presence on the most distant part of North America. The Japanese 'invasion' had no long-range effects on the war; it did not, for example, deter the transfer of American aircraft to the Soviet Union via the Alaska-Siberia route agreed upon by the two wartime partners. If anything, the campaign in the Aleutians gave the Americans an early look at Japanese fighter aircraft technology. A Mitsubishi A6M2 flown by Petty Officer Tadayoshi Koga from the light carrier *Ryujo* crash-landed on Akutan Island. The pilot was killed, but American forces discovered that the aeroplane was in good enough condition to be sent back to the United States. There it was repaired and test flown to provide a much-needed evaluation of a major adversary aircraft of the Pacific War.

A Vought OS2N-1 shipboard observation aircraft from the battleship USS Pennsylvania directing naval gunfire onto Japanese positions on Peleliu, September 1944

Although the Imperial Japanese Navy and its air elements had suffered badly during the battles of the Coral Sea and Midway, the army and its air units were still strong and posed a severe threat to Allied positions throughout the Pacific and on the Asian mainland. Hence, even though the Allies had obviously committed their resources to ending the war in Europe first, it was recognised that Japanese expansion had to be halted and some Allied advances begun. Having been checked in the Central and North Pacific, the Japanese pushed southward into the lower portion of the Solomon Islands as completion of a major airfield on Guadalcanal would give the Japanese Army Air Force a base to use in preventing all traffic between Hawaii and Australia. Since Guadalcanal was recognised as the second part of a potential

Douglas SBD Dauntless dive bombers about to take off from the aircraft carrier USS Yorktown in 1943. The Dauntless served with the US Navy throughout the Pacific War and also fought with the USAAF (as the A-24), US Marine Corps and Royal New Zealand Air Force

pincer movement aimed at Australia, the invasion of the Solomon Islands had to be a primary Allied objective.

While Allied naval and air forces sought to check the Japanese in the South-west Pacific, other pressure was being applied to the Japanese on the Asian mainland. The China-Burma-India (CBI) theatre of operations was aimed at supplying forces in the Far East – particularly in China – to combat the Japanese Army units in that area. The US Tenth Air Force in that area counted as one of its predecessors the American Volunteer Group (AVG), the 'Flying Tigers', who had taken their Curtiss P-40Bs into combat before any other American unit in Asia. The P-40Bs, which were provided to the AVG, even though they were regarded as obsolescent by the US Army and the RAF, were finally replaced by P-40Es in May 1942. Shortly thereafter, pilots of the US Army's 23rd Fighter Group arrived to bolster the AVG, which was eventually integrated into the American air arm.

To support further Allied operations in the Pacific, the aircraft carrier USS *Wasp* (CV-8) was transferred from the Atlantic Fleet to join *Enterprise, Saratoga* and *Hornet.* However, more air power was needed than could be provided by those carriers and in July 1942 a major airfield was worked into the plans for the next invasion. The island of Espiritu Santo in the New Hebrides group was designated as the site to reinforce air cover for the landings at Guadalcanal, some 893 km (555 miles) away. The Allies knew that the Japanese were constructing an

airfield on Guadalcanal and a key objective was to seize the airfield and use it against the Japanese. Initially, aircraft from the US Army Air Force and the RNZAF conducted aerial reconnaissance of the area. They were subsequently joined by reinforcements from US Navy and Marine Corps squadrons.

Cactus Air Force
Japanese land-based air units were scheduled to arrive at the newly completed Guadalcanal airfield on 7 August. Earlier that morning, however, the Americans launched an invasion during which effective control was gained of the airfield, which was named Henderson Field in honour of the commanding officer of VMSB-241, who was killed while attacking IJNS *Hiryu* during the Battle of Midway. The great challenge for the US Marines during the months ahead was to retain control of Guadalcanal, which the Japanese regarded as essential to their plans to cut off Australia. The first American aircraft to arrive at Henderson field were 19 F4Fs and 12 SBDs flown by Marines from USS *Long Island* (CVE-1), the first in a long line of merchant ships converted to escort carriers. They were also known as 'jeep carriers' (in honour of the ubiquitous four-wheel-drive vehicle) and 'baby flat-tops', but they served the US Navy and the Royal Navy well in both the Atlantic and Pacific.

Following the arrival of MAG-23 on 20 August, the Marines were ready to take on the Japanese invasion force originally intended to occupy Midway. Guadalcanal's code-name, Cactus, gave rise to the appellation 'Cactus Air Force' for the air units defending the island. They initially consisted of VMF-223's F4Fs, SBDs of VMF-231 and five Bell P-400 aircraft from the US Army Air Force's 67th Fighter Squadron, an unpopular export version of the P-39 Airacobra. After USS *Enterprise* was damaged during the first Japanese push to retake Guadalcanal, 11 of the carrier's SBDs flew to Guadalcanal and spent a month operating from the island airfield. During the engagement, on 24 August, aircraft from the *Saratoga* sunk the Japanese light carrier *Ryujo* while that ship's aircraft were pounding Guadalcanal.

A single US carrier
The Battle of the Eastern Solomons was the third carrier-against-carrier victory for the United States, a fact that no doubt steeled Japanese determination to go after the American aircraft carriers. They achieved a certain measure of success on the morning of 31 August, when the Japanese submarine *I-26* damaged USS *Saratoga* with a torpedo. The carrier was sent back to Hawaii for repairs. Japanese luck improved on the afternoon of 15 September, when their submarine *I-19* attacked USS *Wasp*, which was providing air cover for reinforcements landing at Guadalcanal. The torpedo attack set off uncontrollable fires aboard the carrier, which later sank. That left USS *Hornet* as the only Allied attack aircraft carrier in the Pacific Theatre.

Repair work on USS *Enterprise* was of the highest priority, but until she could return to the combat zone, the defence of Guadalcanal and the Solomon Islands was in question. Those defenders had to rely on whatever could be brought in. Allied combatants in somewhat better circumstances were the members of the Fifth Air Force, constituted on 3 September 1942 under Major-General George C. Kenney. His light bombardment group, two medium bombardment groups, two heavy bombardment groups and three fighter groups were augmented by Royal Australian Air Force units which included No 22 Squadron

The devastation wrought by US Navy dive bombers and torpedo bombers on Palau Island in March 1944. The damaged installations included a seaplane base, a phosphate plant and warehouses. Merchant ships and a naval tender were also hit

flying Douglas Bostons, No 30 Squadron flying Bristol Beaufighters, No 100 Squadron with Bristol Beauforts, and Nos 75 and 76 Squadrons equipped with Curtiss Kittyhawk fighters.

General Kenney also had another resource, his legendary 'special projects officer', Major Paul 'Pappy' Gunn, a retired US Navy enlisted pilot recalled to active duty as an army officer. Gunn's speciality was modifying A-20A and B-25 aircraft as powerful gunships loaded with machine guns whose concentrated fire-power could penetrate the thick jungle and blast Japanese troops in their hideaways. The Australians guarded their homeland from aerial assaults coming from the Dutch East Indies. With that perimeter secured, the Fifth Air Force ranged over eastern New Guinea and the Coral and Solomon Seas, as well as a future area of conflict, the Bismarck Sea.

Meanwhile, Admiral Yamamoto gave the army an ultimatum either to recapture Henderson Field or lose the support of his forces, which he threatened to withdraw to Truk to pick up supplies. The army agreed to an invasion attempt and Yamamoto offered a large task force which included three fleet aircraft carriers—*Junyo*, *Shokaku* and *Zuikaku*—and the light carrier IJNS *Zuiho*, with a total of over 200 aircraft. The ensuing Battle of the Santa Cruz Islands resulted in the destruction of the American carrier *Hornet*, but also cost the Japanese in terms of severe damage to *Shokaku* and *Zuiho*, which were forced to withdraw on 26 October.

Death of Yamamoto

Santa Cruz was a tactical victory for the Japanese, but their ability to rebuild their badly-damaged carrier fleet and aircraft squadrons did not match the resources of the United States. America was living up to President Roosevelt's promise to make the country 'the arsenal of democracy'. In addition to record numbers of aircraft being produced for the United States and its allies, a new fleet of aircraft carriers was in the making. In 1943 the first of the *Essex*-class carriers was to arrive in the Pacific. With a flight deck 250m (809ft) in length these carriers were to bring the war to the home islands of Japan and none of their number was ever to be sunk by the enemy. Augmenting the big, fast *Essex*-class ships were the new light carriers, built on a cruiser hull and equipped with a smaller air group. Conversely, the Japanese carrier replacement programme was largely devoted to converting existing hulls—seaplane tenders and ocean liners—to the aircraft carrier configuration. Thus it could never hope to match the American effort.

Late 1942 and early 1943 saw General George Kenney's air forces in a continual battle with Japanese forces from New Guinea to New Britain, culminating in the Battle of the Bismarck Sea in March 1943. Beginning in January 1943, B-24s, B-17s and Consolidated PBY Catalinas ranged over Rabaul and the Huon Gulf, off the New Guinea coast, shadowing Japanese resupply activities and intercepting convoys whenever possible. During the

January to March period, P-40s of the 49th Fighter Group accounted for 28 enemy aircraft destroyed in addition to numerous dive-bombing attacks made by the Curtiss fighters when armed with 300lb anti-shipping bombs. One member of the group, Lieutenant Richard I. Bong, flying a Lockheed P-38 Lightning, shot down three of the 40 enemy aircraft he was ultimately to be credited with as the leading American fighter ace. Other 49th Fighter Group P-38s accounted for 13 enemy aircraft destroyed. The group's victory was well over 50 aircraft, with their own losses standing at ten aircraft. The combined Allied air units laid the groundwork for the subsequent airborne and ship-based invasion of these strategically-important islands.

Allied air power was so effective in countering Japanese efforts to hold and expand their island bastions that it brought a fierce vengeance to airmen captured by their soldiers. One of the most successful low-level bombing pilots during this phase of the war was Flight Lieutenant W. E. Newton of No 22 Squadron RAAF. So angry were the Japanese at his proficiency, that, when he was shot down on 18 March 1943, he was beheaded by his captors. Flt Lt Newton was posthumously awarded the VC.

Left: Japanese artist S. Arai's impression of aircraft being serviced on the hangar deck of a carrier contrasts with T. Ishikara's painting (below left) of an air battle over the South Pacific between Japanese fighters escorting dive bombers and intercepting US Navy Grumman F4F Wildcats. Bottom left: wounded US Marines being evacuated by a Douglas C-47 from an airfield on Iwo Jima. Air transport was vital in the 'island hopping' war in the Pacific. Below: a Japanese dive bomber shot down by anti-aircraft fire from the aircraft carrier USS Wasp

During the first week of February 1943 the last Japanese troops were evacuated from Guadalcanal, thereby ending the major Japanese push to cut off Australia. With the island air base secured, the forthcoming battle for the central Solomon Islands was bolstered by the arrival of the first Vought F4U Corsairs. Major William E. Gise, commanding officer of VMF-124 led 12 of the gull-winged fighters to Henderson Field. Although not initially favoured for carrier-based flight operations, the Corsair eventually became standard equipment for all eight US Marine Corps fighter squadrons in the Pacific and proved to be particularly effective in the hands of such a top ace as Major Gregory 'Pappy' Boyington, who amassed 28 kills to his credit. Big and fast, the Corsair was far superior to the Mitsubishi A6M series that the Japanese had long used with much success.

Before and during World War II American cryptographers continued to crack various high-level codes used by the Japanese. This gave the Allies a tactical advantage to augment their growing strength in *matériel*. In at least one instance it offered the opportunity to wreak a personal form of vengeance upon the Japanese and thereby deprive them of one of their top military

planners. Having determined from decoded messages that Admiral Isoroku Yamamoto was scheduled to fly from Rabaul to Buin Island in the Solomons on an inspection tour, the Americans set in motion a plan to use their growing air strength to assassinate the Commander-in-Chief of the Imperial Japanese Navy's Combined Fleet. On the morning of 18 April 1943, 16 P-38s especially fitted for a long over-water flight went after two Mitsubishi G4M1 Betty bombers flying along the island of Bougainville. Captain Thomas G. Lanphier Jnr of the 70th Fighter Squadron shot down one (believed to be Admiral Yamamoto's transport) and First Lieutenant Rex T. Barber of the 339th Fighter Squadron shot down the other. This event took place one year to the day after the Doolittle raid on Tokyo.

The following month a Royal Navy aircraft carrier, HMS *Victorious*, arrived in the South-west Pacific to relieve USS *Enterprise*. The damaged American carrier returned to Hawaii for ten weeks' repair and modernisation while her air group operated from *Victorious*. The British carrier and USS *Saratoga* launched raids during the Solomon Islands campaign.

American carrier task force

Augmenting the US Army Air Force bombers during the Solomons campaign and other operations were the US Navy patrol bombers. One particularly successful type was the Consolidated PB4Y-1, a navalised version of the B-24 Liberator, and the PB4Y-2 Privateer, which was quite distinct from the earlier version. In one notable instance during the Solomons campaign, Lieutenant Commander Bruce A. Van Voorhis took off in the darkness on 6 July 1943 for an unescorted 1,130 km (700 mile) flight. Van Voorhis, commanding officer of patrol bombing squadron VPB-102, set out to prevent a sneak attack on American naval forces. His target was a series of well-guarded enemy emplacements. He was completely overwhelmed by enemy aircraft and anti-aircraft fire, but Van Voorhis and his crew continued to bomb and strafe the enemy position. Finally caught in one of his own low-level bomb blasts, Van Voorhis crashed into the water. Although Van Voorhis perished in the crash, his mission successfully deterred the Japanese attack and he was awarded the Congressional Medal of Honour.

What might be considered a second phase of the Pacific War began in the late summer of 1943, when the new *Essex*-class carriers began arriving. These ships were well-armed and could efficiently operate more than 100 aeroplanes. Indeed, their air groups were composed of a new generation of aircraft, including the Grumman F6F Hellcats to add to the growing superiority over existing Japanese fighters and Grumman TBF Avengers to attack surface targets.

First action for the new forces came on 1 September 1943, when the fleet carriers *Essex* (CV-9) and *Yorktown* (CV-10) and the first of the new light carriers, USS *Independence* (CVL-22), launched strikes against Marcus Island. Almost three weeks later, on 18 and 19 September, another three-carrier force struck. Seven strikes against enemy positions on Tawara and Makin were launched by USS *Lexington* (CV-16) and the light carriers *Princeton* (CVL-23) and *Belleau Wood* (CVL-24).

The carriers returned in force to the former American base at Wake Island. On 5 and 6 October the island was the object of intensive strafing and bombing by the first American carrier force equal in strength to the Japanese force that had attacked Pearl Harbour. The light carrier USS *Cowpens* (CVL-25) joined the battle-proven *Essex*,

Yorktown, *Lexington*, *Independence* and *Belleau Wood*. At Wake Island the carrier forces tested and refined the bombing and attacking techniques that would be used during the next two years.

Air assaults on the various atolls, followed by heavy naval shelling and landings by ground forces, started the Allies on a campaign of what one infantryman characterised as taking 'one damned island after another'. By mid-October, the Allies were ready for the final land phase of the Solomons campaign: the assault on Bougainville, the largest island in the Solomons group. For some months the island had been regularly attacked by Allied air units, including No 25 Squadron, Royal New Zealand Air Force, which began its existence earlier in the year with nine SBD-3 Dauntlesses 'borrowed' from the US Marines' MAG-14 based at Seagrove, New Zealand.

Land-based Allied air units continued to hit Rabaul and other targets that might reinforce Bougainville, while the newly organised Fast Carrier Task Force (TF 50) concentrated on that island and other potential troop landing spots. Beginning on 19 November, the Carrier Interceptor Group (TG 50.1), composed of *Yorktown*, *Lexington* and *Cowpens*, launched strikes against Jaluit and Mili in the Marshall Islands to keep forces there from reinforcing Tarawa and Makin. The Northern Carrier Group (TG 50.2), with *Enterprise*, *Belleau Wood* and USS *Monterey* (CVL-26), struck Makin, then being invaded by the US Army, and the Southern Carrier Group (TG 50.3), with *Essex*, *Bunker Hill* (CV-17) and *Independence*, sent their aircraft to attack Rabaul and New Britain. The fourth carrier unit, the Relief Carrier Group (TG 50.4), with the veteran *Saratoga* and the new light carrier *Princeton*, struck the northern Solomons. The type of fast, mobile carrier warfare that the Japanese had hoped to use in expanding their empire was now becoming the instrument of their defeat.

The American carrier task force kept moving, into the Marshall Islands, then back to Rabaul, hitting with such ferocity that the Japanese came to believe it was actually two forces. On 6 January 1944 Task Force 50 was redesignated Task Force 58 and placed under the command of Rear-Admiral Marc Mitscher, a pioneer naval aviator and commander of *Hornet* when the Tokyo raid was launched. Under Admiral Mitscher's command, TF 58 had a dozen carrier decks: six fleet carriers and six light carriers. Three of those ships covered the February landings on Truk atoll, later to become a key staging point for B-29 raids over Japan.

The Marianas turkey shoot

While the carriers provided air cover for operations over Tinian, Rota and Guam in the Marianas, the USAAF and other Allied units went into the final phase of their operations to drive the Japanese from New Guinea. Lockheed P-38J Lightnings were then being produced in the United States with 416 to 454 litre (92 to 100 gallon) fuel tanks added to the leading edges of the wings. The extra fuel extended the P-38's combat radius from 560 km (350 miles) to over 1,000 km (620 miles). Unable to wait for large numbers of the improved fighters to be shipped to the combat zone, the USAAF Air Service Command obtained modification kits and set to work on aircraft already committed to the fighting in New Guinea. Thus, the Fifth Air Force B-24s that pounded the Japanese regularly could now approach the more distant targets with a greater degree of security. The USAAF was applying the lessons learned in Europe, where it enjoyed the dominant air combat role, to operations in the Pacific.

American aircraft carriers were drawn into the Western Pacific in conjunction with the landings at Hollandia during the New Guinea campaign. This ultimately gave rise to another unique operation involving the Royal Navy and the US Navy. When the British carrier HMS *Illustrious* was transferred from the Mediterranean to the Pacific she joined USS *Saratoga* in operations in May 1944 off the eastern coast of Java. The pair of carriers launched two major strikes that achieved several objectives: they damaged the oil delivery system to Japan, thereby alerting the Japanese to their vulnerability in the East Indies, and they diverted the Japanese from Central Pacific. There, the Allies were preparing a devastating new campaign to seize the Mariana islands.

Following the death of Admiral Yamamoto, Admiral Mineichi Koga became Commander-in-Chief of the Combined Fleet. He shared his predecessor's desire to use his remaining carrier force to crack the Allied advance, but not by extending the force, as had been done at Pearl Harbour and Midway. Koga's plan was to draw the American carriers into his own territory, where his own land-based bombers could participate in the operation. However, with the death of Admiral Koga on 31 March 1944, a modified plan was carried out by his ultimate successor, Admiral Soemu Toyoda. The Allied venture into the Marianas–to capture Saipan, Guam and Tinian as further bases to use in striking Japan–provided the opportunity for Toyoda to strike.

On 11 June 1944, Marc Mitscher, then a vice-admiral, had the seven fleet carriers and eight light carriers of TF 58 launch sweeps to cover the opening phase of the battle for the Marianas. Mitscher's aircraft destroyed one-third of the defending air force. Bombing and strafing attacks on succeeding days prepared the way for the amphibious assault on Saipan and did much to deter a Japanese counter-offensive during the battle in the Philippine Sea.

During the early morning hours of 19 June, however, the last massive Japanese carrier force–five fleet carriers and four light carriers–was sent out to engage the large American force. The Japanese had correctly assumed that the American carrier task force would be covering the Saipan landings and not hitting airfields ashore. Hence,

Opposite: the light carrier Belleau Wood was hit by a kamikaze on 30 October during the Battle of Leyte Gulf. The resulting fire, which lasted for several hours, killed 92 of the crew and destroyed 12 aircraft. Opposite below: USAAF Boeing B-29 Superfortresses began bombing attacks on Japan in 1944, flying from bases in China and the Marianas. Below: a North American B-25C with modified nose armament. The later B-25G and H variants, which carried a 75 mm gun in the nose, were flown against shipping and land targets in the Pacific Theatre

land-based aircraft could be used to strike the carriers. As the sun rose that day, land-based Zeke fighters and carrier-launched Judy bombers spotted the first of the American carriers. Profiting from the lessons of Midway, the Japanese sent many aircraft to locate the American ships before their own were spotted.

The greater American force, however, had also learned from the Midway experience. Consequently, large numbers of American fighters, bombers and torpedo aircraft were launched once the enemy aircraft were spotted. The superior American naval aircraft tore into the attackers. By the end of the day the Americans had accounted for 402 Japanese aircraft destroyed, for a loss of only 23 US Navy aircraft. Indeed, the 'kill' ratio was so high, that this encounter has since become known as 'the Marianas turkey shoot'.

The tremendously high loss of aircraft was only part of the Japanese casualty situation. American aircraft and submarines combined on 19 July to sink the fleet carriers *Taiho* and *Shokaku*. The next day they sunk the *Hiyo* and two oilers and damaged four other carriers and several additional capital ships. The Marianas engagement was the biggest carrier battle in history and marked the end of the Japanese carrier fleet as a major offensive force. The only Allied regret was in not pursuing the remaining enemy ships and utterly destroying them. However, air operations on 20 June lasted so long into the night that it was a bold move on Vice-Admiral Mitscher's part to violate established procedures and turn on the lights to guide the victorious aircrews back to their ships.

The first kamikazes

While the carrier battle was going on, other air units moved in to consolidate gains made by the land forces. In fact, even before an airfield ashore was ready, US Navy seaplanes from patrol squadron VP-16 began operations from the open sea on 16 June. The next day US Marine observation aircraft from VMO-4 arrived and on 22 June Saipan's air cover was bolstered by the arrival of 22 Republic P-47 Thunderbolts of the USAAF 318th Fighter Group's 19th Fighter Squadron, which had been catapulted from the escort carriers *Manila Bay* (CVE-61) and *Natoma Bay* (CVE-62). Within two days the fighter strength was reinforced by the 73rd Fighter Squadron, a detachment of seven Northrop P-61 Black Widows from the 6th Night Fighter Squadron and the remainder of the 19th Fighter Squadron's P-47s.

Following up the Saipan victory, American forces hit Japanese bases at Guam and Tinian, as well as Iwo Jima. On 4 July 1944, however, the Japanese chose a unique way to strike back. A force of nine fighters and eight single-engine torpedo aircraft that had survived an intensive American attack was ordered to sacrifice itself to achieve victory by diving into its targets.

Undertaken four months before the Japanese Kamikaze Special Attack Corps was organised, the Iwo Jima-based mission was thwarted by heavy US Navy fighter protection. Only four fighters and one torpedo plane escaped the F6Fs and the carriers remained untouched for the time being.

The loss of the Marianas was recognised as the fateful blow to the Japanese war effort. Continued Allied victories in New Guinea ultimately led to attacks on the Philippine Islands in September and a further decline in oil supplies from the Dutch East Indies, the great prize whose possession was one of the principal reasons for initiating the war in the first place. Victory or an armistice were by then out of the picture. Hence, it remained for

Japanese planners to consider the best use of their resources in defending the home islands. Again, the plan was to lure the Allies into a position advantageous to shore-based aircraft acting in concert with the remnants of the Combined Fleet.

American carrier strikes against Formosa in October were met by heavy land-based opposition, which succeeded in crippling the cruisers *Canberra* and *Houston*, but which did not damage any of the carriers. The Japanese trap did not work. With the arrival of US Army Rangers on several small islands in Leyte Gulf, it was clear to the Japanese that extraordinary measures would have to be taken to block the major invasion that was surely in the offing. One such measure was the formation of the Kamikaze–the so-called 'divine wind'–force of suicide pilots in mid-October 1944.

While the modern day *samurai* warriors of the Kamikaze Special Attack Corps were undergoing training, massive American naval forces, reinforced by land-based USAAF aircraft, began the battles for Leyte Gulf that led to the liberation of the Philippine Islands. At dawn on 24 October, Admiral 'Bull' Halsey's Task Force 38 launched the first aircraft to engage the Japanese fleet that had been assembled to defend the Philippines.

Japanese forces were also in the air and, later that morning, a Judy bomber slipped through the anti-aircraft fire and delivered a lethal blow to the light carrier USS *Princeton* (CVL-23), which was sunk later that day. *Princeton* was the first of the fast carriers to be lost since *Hornet* went down almost two years to the day before in the Solomon Islands, but she was also the last of the bigger carriers to succumb to the Japanese. *Princeton* was avenged the following day, when TF 38 sunk four Japanese 'flat-tops': the light carriers *Chitose*, *Chiyoda* and *Zuiho*, as well as the fleet carrier *Zuikaku*, the last surviving carrier of the Pearl Harbour sneak attack.

The day after that, 25 October, the *kamikazes* went after the small–156m (512ft) long–escort carriers. From the time Lieutenant Yukio Seki hit the flight deck of USS *St. Lô* (CVE-63), it took less than three-quarters of an hour for the ship to sink. Six other escort carriers were damaged by *kamikazes*.

Next came the big fast carriers. On 28 October USS *Intrepid* (CV-11) suffered minor damage from a suicide plane. Two days later *kamikazes* slipped through the anti-aircraft defences and hit USS *Franklin* (CV-13) and USS *Belleau Wood* (CVL-24), damaging both ships to the extent that they had to return to the United States.

Island-hopping

The American Fast Carrier Force took a well deserved rest early in December 1944. In addition to replenishing supplies from its base at Ulithi in the Caroline Islands, the task force was reorganised to be better able to defend itself from future suicide attacks. Then Task Force 38 sailed back to the Philippines to conduct air strikes against Luzon in support of General Douglas MacArthur's impending invasion of Mindoro. First, however, the task force made an unprecedented cruise into the South China Sea to disrupt Japan's main shipping lane to the East Indies and to knock out potential surface opposition facing the forthcoming Mindoro landings. On 9 January 1945 the carriers began hitting their objectives.

Over a week later they were back off the Philippines, fighting the *kamikazes* before moving in February to the attack against Iwo Jima. That small island in the Bonins group was directly on the route taken by USAAF B-29s during their flights from Saipan to Tokyo and provided the Japanese with an effective early warning site. On 19 February, the Fast Carrier Force struck Iwo Jima and was itself struck by suicide planes. The venerable USS *Saratoga* (CV-3), oldest carrier in the US Navy at that point, took a hit on the flight deck that knocked her out of commission. Then, during the night of 21/22 February, the escort carrier USS *Bismarck Sea* (CVE-95) was hit by a bomb-laden Betty bomber and sank within three hours. The Japanese were defeated, however, and by 6 March USAAF fighters were able to fly from Iwo Jima.

The next logical target was the Ryukyu Islands, just south of Japan. The key island, Okinawa, was a prime target for the Allies. The carriers again took the lead, even attacking the home islands to reduce *kamikaze* activity, but the opening activity on 18 March was marked by several attempts to disable the carrier force. A Betty was shot down just before reaching USS *Intrepid*. The following day, while the carrier aircraft attacked the remnants of the Japanese fleet, enemy bombers hit the fleet carriers USS *Wasp* (CV-18) and *Franklin*. The latter was nearly lost and it is a tribute to Allied air superiority that, although *Franklin* was ablaze and immobilised, only 88km (55 miles) off the Japanese coast, enemy aircraft were unable to administer the *coup de grâce*. USS *Franklin* was saved and, though never put back into active duty, she returned to the United States under her own steam to prove that none of the *Essex*-class carriers had been totally defeated.

The Japanese defence of Okinawa was nearly a last ditch effort and the Japanese drew heavily on their disappearing resources. During some of the heaviest fighting, on 6/7 April, about 230 Navy aircraft and 125 Army aircraft were marked for use in suicide missions against American ships, while a further 341 aircraft were to undertake the conventional attack role.

The atom bomb

Upon the sudden death of President Franklin D. Roosevelt in 1945, the decision as to how to end the war was left to his successor, Harry S. Truman. At the Potsdam Conference that followed the defeat of Germany, President Truman made it clear to his wartime allies that he intended to demonstrate to the Japanese that his armed forces had the ability to annihilate them. He would use the atomic bomb on the Japanese homeland.

The USAAF Boeing B-29s that had regularly bombed Japan from island bases in the Pacific as well as airfields in China were chosen as the appropriate delivery system. The 509th Composite Group was chosen for the mission and made a practice run with a dummy bomb. On the morning of 6 August 1945 a B-29 bearing the name *Enola Gay* on its nose and commanded by Colonel Paul W. Tibbets left Tinian bound for Hiroshima. A little over six hours later, the atomic bomb was released.

Since the Japanese government ignored President Truman's ultimatum at Potsdam and did not respond to the bombing of Hiroshima, a second bombing was ordered on 9 August. This time the target was Nagasaki and the results just as terrible. However, it took the personal intervention of Emperor Hirohito to convince the government to sue for peace and to accept the unconditional surrender terms laid down by the Allies. Thus, the long and costly Pacific War, which had begun with one devastating air attack by one side and which had been ended by overpowering use of aerial weapons by the other side, was concluded on 2 September 1945 aboard the battleship USS *Missouri*. As the ship rode at anchor in Tokyo Bay, none of the participants failed to grasp the significance of the silver B-29s and dark blue Navy fighters which were patrolling overhead.

Burma War 1941-45

Japanese operations in South-East Asia dated from the late thirties, so that within two days of the Japanese striking at Pearl Harbour on 7 December 1941, their troops were able to enter Burma. Having infiltrated Thailand (Siam) they compelled the Thais to declare war on both the United States and the United Kingdom the following month. By this time they were in a position to deploy 7,000 men supported by 700 aircraft using 30 airfields in Thailand as a stepping-off base. Their initial objective was India, followed by a movement westward to link up with the Axis in the Middle East, but barring their path were a few hundred miles of sub-tropical jungle in Burma.

Communications in Burma relied on the limited railway system, a few trunk roads, jungle tracks and rivers. Both road and rail were susceptible to air attack and ambush, thus the broad rivers became highways, frequently the line of demarcation between friend and foe, an objective to be reached or a line to be defended.

Meagre air defence

The air defence of Burma in 1941 was the responsibility of No 221 Group, RAF, under Group Captain E. R. Manning, an Australian, who had already built up a chain of landing strips across the country with airfields at Akyab, Moulmein, Mergui and Myitkyina. But of the 280 aircraft planned for defence, there were only 16 RAF aircraft available – a flight of Buffaloes of No 67 Squadron at Mingaladon for the defence of Rangoon. They were quickly reinforced by 21 Curtiss P-40s of the American Volunteer Group, detached from Kunming in China because the port of Rangoon was essential for supplies to

that country. Additionally, this small force had the services of the light club aircraft of the Burmese Volunteer Air Force for liaison work.

From 23 December Rangoon was under heavy attack from the air, the Japanese using formations of up to 80 bombers escorted by fighters. Reinforcements were quickly sent: Hurricanes from India and Blenheims of No 113 Squadron, which flew in from the Middle East. Within hours of their arrival, the Blenheims were sent out to strike at the Japanese air base at Bangkok. This intensive flying combined with the lack of supporting ground crew and equipment put the aircraft out of operation until they were overhauled.

To co-operate with the troops on the ground, the Lysanders of No 1 Squadron Indian Air Force and No 28 Squadron RAF were called in from the North-West Frontier of India (now part of Pakistan), but their crews found difficulty in maintaining contact with the retreating troops. Moulmein was evacuated on the last day of January 1942 and four weeks later the Japanese crossed the Sittang River in force, cutting off the Rangoon-Mandalay railway. Rangoon was doomed and evacuation was inevitable. It says much for the few Allied fighters at Rangoon – rarely more than 45 at any one time – that they maintained control of the air. They destroyed over 100 Japanese aircraft and their protection permitted an orderly evacuation. The last RAF aircraft left Mingaladon on 7 March, flying northward to Magwe and Akyab to re-group and the P-40s went to Lashio.

A string of elephants pass a Hawker Hurricane parked on an Indian airfield. The Hurricane bore the brunt of the early fighting over the Burma front until replaced by Spitfires and Thunderbolts in 1944

British retreat

When RAF reconnaissance discovered that the Japanese Army Air Force (JAAF) was settling in at Mingaladon, a strike force of nine Blenheims, escorted by ten Hurricanes, set out from Magwe and destroyed 16 aircraft on the ground and 11 in the air, including that of an ace, Major Kato, who was shot down by a Blenheim gunner.

Thus challenged, the Japanese set out to smash the remnants of the RAF in Burma. A series of attacks on Magwe wrecked all but six Blenheims and 11 Hurricanes which limped to Akyab, where they were again attacked by the Japanese for three days, destroying seven Hurricanes and a Valentia.

The use of old Vickers Valentia biplane transports to bring in supplies and evacuate casualties introduced a technique which was to play a most significant part in the Burma Campaign. That same month, the survivors of the American 7th Bombardment Group flew their B-17 Fortresses from Java to India. These bombers were immediately used to ferry a battalion of British troops to Magwe. But reinforcement came too late and although the Fortresses evacuated 424 people, 350 RAF officers and men were cut off and were unable to retreat to India. Packing their radar station and remaining equipment on the 150 surviving vehicles, they moved out in convoy for China, where they set up a training camp for Chinese ground crews.

On the ground, the British and Indian troops under General Alexander retreated north-westward into India, while Chinese troops with American backing under General J. Stilwell (known as 'Vinegar Joe') protecting the western supply route to the East were driven back into China. The situation seemed desperate. No 221 Group re-organising in the Chittagong area could muster only five squadrons, including a transport squadron mainly composed of ex-American airliners. Reinforcements and supplies from Britain were being held up in the Middle East due to the opposition encountered in the Western Desert, and supplies from America took weeks to arrive.

Right: ground crew work on Thunderbolt Mk IIs at Wangjing, Burma, in 1944. The ugly Thunderbolt's role in the Burma jungle

Within India there was civil unrest and calls for independence. The Allies plainly needed time to regroup.

Fortunately the Japanese, too, required time: communications needed repairing, gains had to be consolidated and bases established in preparation for offensives against India and China. The Allies made good use of this respite. On 5 March 1942, United States Army Air Force, India-Burma, was activated at Delhi under Major General L. H. Brereton, followed on 10 May by Headquarters Tenth Air Force. At about the same time, while 221 Group was resting and refurbishing, No 224 Group was founded and took over control of the southern (Arakan) area, leaving 221 to control operations further north.

But the Allies had divergent aims. The American Forces were concerned with assisting China by keeping open supply routes, and the British with the defence of India and subsequently the re-conquest of Burma. However, in the emergency period up to 15 June 1942, the Allies worked in concert. The USAAF ferried in 733 tons of supplies and evacuated 4,499 people, while the RAF air-dropped 55 tons of supplies and brought out 4,117 civilian refugees and service casualties.

Allied reinforcements

By mid-1942 the RAF was three times as strong and a vast airfield building programme was in hand. Hurricane Is and Blenheim IVs, superseded in other theatres, arrived in India, followed by Blenheim Vs produced in Britain solely for overseas service. From America, under Lend-Lease, came Vultee Vengeance dive-bombers, Dakota transports, and Catalinas and Hudsons for maritime reconnaissance. Indian Air Force squadrons incorporated under overall RAF command made a valuable contribution using Hurricanes, Vengeances and Lysanders.

There was still little activity because Japanese expansion in other directions was calling heavily on their men and supplies and particularly their air power. The Allies were encouraged to attempt a limited offensive with close air support towards Akyab, one of the most important

Japanese air bases, but the monsoon brought this attack to a halt. During October the Japanese took the initiative, launching three large air attacks on American bases in Assam and receiving heavy losses at the hands of Curtiss P-40 pilots.

A night air offensive was then launched by the Japanese on Bengal, starting with an attack on Calcutta on 20 December 1942. The eight aircraft participating created havoc far out of proportion to the numbers involved. Military damage was slight, but as a result of civilian casualties over a million fled the densely-populated city. After further raids, rubble was left uncleared and bodies rotted unburied. There was a serious health hazard and a night fighter force was desperately needed. Beaufighters with airborne radar, hastily sent from Britain, started to shoot down the raiders from the night of 15 January, forcing the Japanese to limit their raiding and so encourage the refugees to return to their city. Later, more Beaufighters arrived for close support and earned the

Pilots of No 607 Squadron plough through the mud of a forward airstrip. The unit flew Supermarine Spitfire Mk VIIIs from March 1944 until it was disbanded in August 1945

The Vultee Vengeance dive-bomber was flown by Nos 45, 82, 84 and 110 Squadrons in Burma. It proved to be most effective in precision attacks on Japanese positions

A Hurribomber attacking a bridge on the Tiddim Road in 1944. At that time the Hurricane units were heavily committed to ground attack sorties in support of the fighting around Imphal

name 'Whispering Death' from the Japanese due to their quiet, fast and low approach.

Early in 1943 a force under Brigadier Orde Wingate made the first of a series of forays behind the enemy lines. At the same time the 14th Army started another limited offensive which was also halted by the monsoon. On 25 August 1943 Admiral Lord Louis Mountbatten was appointed Supreme Commander, South-East Asia. Under him an integrated Air Command, South-East Asia, was formed in November, headed by Air Chief Marshal Sir Richard Pierse and with headquarters at Delhi, which were moved to Kandy in Ceylon fairly soon afterwards. While headquarters was beyond the range of Japanese bombers, the great city of Calcutta was still suffering and had its first daylight attack on 5 December. Fortunately the first Spitfires had recently arrived, and by the end of January 1944 these Mk VC Spitfires had accounted for 44 of the raiders for a loss of seven–the pilots of two of these aircraft being saved.

Eastern Air Command
The airfield building programme had resulted in 140 airfields with two runways, a further 60 with a single runway and many fair weather and emergency strips.

Over 50 radar stations and filter units had been sited and a warning system instituted. Supplies increased and among aircraft coming into the theatre were Spitfire VIIIs, supplementing the earlier Mk VCs, promising air superiority in the battle area.

The Allies were ready to take the offensive and a joint Eastern Air Command under Pierse was formed on 15 December for the campaign. They had little to fear from the JAAF whose air strength in Burma at the beginning of 1944 was: 27 Sally (Mitsubishi Ki-21) medium bombers; 16 Lily (Kawasaki Ki-48) light bombers; nine Sonia (Mitsubishi Ki-51) ground attack/tactical reconnaissance aircraft; 14 Dinah (Mitsubishi Ki-46) long-distance reconnaissance aircraft; 58 Oscar (Nakajima Ki-43) and 30 Nick (Kawasaki Ki-45) fighters.

However, just as the British and Indian troops were making progress and re-entering Burma, the Japanese opened a large-scale offensive in the Arakan on 4 February 1944, trying to reach India along the coast via Cox's Bazaar and Chittagong. Enveloping the Commonwealth troops, they were amazed to find that they did not, as hitherto, retreat; instead they stood their ground, forming a defended perimeter. With command, control and supply in the centre, formations could be supplied with their essential ammunition, rations and equipment, from air drops–free-fall or parachute, depending on the commodity–or even by aircraft using strips within the perimeter formed by the troops.

Pierse had already concentrated forward supplies at Comilla for the planned offensive, which greatly reduced the length of supply hauls. But the amount required was beyond the capacity of RAF Dakotas, and the Americans had to help out by diverting Curtiss C-46 Commandos from the India/China Wing. On 6 February the JAAF reacted strongly to this air transport by sending up large formations of fighters. It was the chance the Spitfire pilots had been waiting for and in the ensuing dogfighting the JAAF were routed. Only rarely did the JAAF fly again over the battle area in large formations.

RAF and IAF Vengeances and Hurricanes used as light bombers gave valuable close support. They bombed enemy troops on the perimeters, at times using delayed-action bombs, so that the Japanese kept under cover for periods awaiting their explosion. Finally, when the time came for the Allied ground troops to attack, unfused

EASTERN AIR COMMAND OPERATIONAL ORGANISATION mid-1944

Strategic Air Force USAAF
  7th Bombardment Group (Liberators)
  490th Bombardment Squadron (Mitchells)
Tenth Air Force USAAF
  80th Fighter Group (Warhawks)
  311th Fighter-Bomber Group (Mustangs)
  443rd Troop Carrier Group (Dakotas)
Third Tactical Air Force
  No 177 (Transport) Wing RAF (Dakotas)
  3rd Combat Cargo Group USAAF (Dakotas)
  12th Bombardment Group (Mitchells)
Photographic Reconnaissance Force
  8th Photo Reconnaissance Group USAAF
    (Lightnings, Liberators, Warhawks)
  No 171 (PR) Wing RAF (Spitfires, Mosquitos,
    Mitchells)
No 221 Group RAF
  No 168 Wing RAF (Hurricanes, Spitfires,
    Vengeances)
  No 170 Wing RAF/IAF (Hurricanes, Spitfires)

  No 243 Wing RAF (Hurricanes)
No 224 Group RAF
  No 165 Wing IAF/RAF (Hurricanes, Spitfires)
  No 166 Wing RAF/USAAF (Spitfires, Lightnings)
  No 167 Wing IAF (Hurricanes, Vengeances)
  No 169 Wing RAF (Beaufighters)
No 231 Group RAF
  No 175 Wing RAF (Wellington, Warwicks)
  No 184 Wing RAF (Liberators)
  No 185 Wing RAF (Liberators)
No 293 Wing RAF (Spitfires, Beaufighters)
*No 222 Group RAF (Beaufighters, Beauforts,
  Catalinas, Spitfires, Sunderlands, Thunderbolts)
*No 225 Group RAF (Beaufighters, Catalinas,
  Hurricanes, Liberators, Wellingtons)
*No 229 Group RAF (Dakotas and Hudsons)

*Reporting direct to Air Command, South-East Asia
but with squadrons operating in conjunction with
Eastern Air Command.*

---

bombs were dropped and the Japanese, keeping under cover awaiting the explosions, were unaware of the troops advancing upon their positions.

Siege of Imphal

Thwarted in the Arakan, the Japanese crossed the Chindwin River in central Burma and opened a two-pronged attack against Imphal to cut communications on the night of 7/8 March. The 17th Indian Division, withdrawing from this threat, drew heavily on reserves and desperately needed reinforcement. Mountbatten decided again to divert aircraft on the China supply route and, together with No 194 Squadron RAF Dakotas, the 5th Indian Division was moved from the Arakan to Imphal by air, and reinforcements, including the 50th Parachute Brigade, were flown in from Indian bases. The Japanese advances, however, continued and on 31 March they succeeded in cutting the Dimapur-Kohima Road, isolating the main body of the 14th Army which then relied entirely on air supply.

Some of the fiercest fighting of the war then ensued. Within the besieged area were six airstrips and Air Vice-Marshal S. F. Vincent, commanding No 221 Group, concerned with close support, ruled that every airman would be armed and take his place with RAF Regiment personnel in repulsing Japanese raiding parties. Close support and air defence was maintained from these strips, while from outside the besieged area USAAF Lightnings and Mustangs, with their longer range, relieved the RAF by fighter sweeps. At the same time the strategic bombers concentrated on Japanese communications.

Air supply devolved mainly on the Third Tactical Air Force and for a time USAAF Mitchell bombers assisted with the airlift of ammunition, using the forward area Comilla airfield as a staging post. The diary of one of the Dakota airfields, Agartala, makes revealing reading, relating the hazards encountered and measures taken to raise morale. '5 May–Very heavy storm, destroyed about 25 per cent of the bashas (bamboo huts). One airman killed. 10 May–Miss Vera Lynn sang twice in the Station Cinema for approximately 30 minutes on each occasion. 21 May–The temperature on the station is now over the 100 mark (Fahrenheit) and the humidity makes conditions trying.

31 May–First night of ENSA show "The Brainwaves".'

Again the Japanese made a new thrust, this time in the Manipur Hills. Meanwhile, in Imphal they fell back before the 14th Army, which by 22 June had cleared the Kohima-Imphal road, so raising the siege of Imphal. On 19 August the Japanese were finally driven from Indian soil.

Battle for Myitkyina

Meanwhile two American-trained and equipped Chinese Divisions and an American regiment known as Merrill's Marauders, all under General Stilwell, were pushing the Japanese out of north Burma to re-open the supply routes. Their capture of Myitkyina airfield on 17 May was a turning point in the campaign. To this airfield the 36th (British) and 50th (Chinese) Divisions, totalling 35,000 men, were flown in and the 3rd (Indian) Division flown out. At peak this single unpaved strip was accepting 525 Dakota landings and take-offs a day. Casualties were flown in to this strip by Stinson L-5 Sentinels and transferred to Dakotas returning to their Assam bases.

An ENSA show for the entertainment of pilots and groundcrew of a Spitfire squadron. Living conditions in the Burma theatre were primitive, with few of the amenities enjoyed by airmen in Europe

The town adjacent to the airfield was fortified and still held by the Japanese; their positions were under continual attack and one pilot claimed a record for a fighter-bomber sortie of six minutes from take-off to landing. It was 3 August before the Japanese were finally dislodged from the vicinity of the airfield.

Offensive action by the JAAF was now only sporadic. On 3 September 12 enemy aircraft were seen dropping supplies in the Teng Chung area and their accompanying fighters shot up the nearest Allied airstrip before returning, destroying two L-5 Sentinels on the ground and shooting a third down. Later that month three Dinahs were intercepted reconnoitring the Imphal and Kebaw valleys and two were destroyed. Sporadic bomber attacks were made during October on Myitkyina, Cox's Bazaar and Ranga-

mati airfields, killing a civilian and superficially damaging three Spitfires and a few Thunderbolts.

Following the Allied offensive from Myitkyina towards Mandalay beginning on 15 October, 12 Oscars made a determined attack on a British battery, killing one soldier and wounding 14 on 8 November. That same day, Dakotas on supply missions were intercepted and one was shot down in the morning and three in the afternoon. The following day two Oscars and a Tojo jumped four Mosquitoes making a low-level strike on Meiktila, Headquarters of the 6th Air Regiment JAAF, causing one Mosquito to crash at Samon. This JAAF revival was quickly countered by fighter escorts, intensified fighter sweeps and attacks on airfields.

For the continuing operations, a large backing of transport aircraft was seen as indispensable and on 18 October a Combat Cargo Task Force was constituted for overall control of joint RAF/USAAF transport squadrons.

Bombing operations

The heavy bomber force, as well as striking at enemy ports as part of the strategic plan, supported the land battles by disrupting communications. Liberators bombing a Sittang bridge on 13 November were harassed by Japanese fighters, but, although two bombers were damaged, they all returned. In November USAAF B-29 Superfortresses of XXth Bomber Command brought into the theatre for strategic bombing, joined in 'Operation Eruption', a sustained attack on Japanese-held airfields, while the RAF and USAAF made supplementary striking attacks. From that time onwards, Allied air superiority became air supremacy.

RAF air strength at the beginning of 1945 was: 89 heavy bombers; 552 fighters/fighter-bombers; 110 transports and 36 reconnaissance aircraft. USAAF air strength was: 42 heavy bombers; 97 medium bombers; 226 fighters/fighter-bombers; 297 transports and 67 reconnaissance aircraft.

Rangoon was subjected to Allied raids, the heaviest of which was on 3/4 December, when Eastern Air Command joined XXth Bomber Command to attack the three main airfields, railway yards and locomotive sheds in the area. Over 200 heavy and medium bombers, plus fighter-bombers operating with auxiliary fuel tanks, participated. The ability of the Japanese to retaliate was waning and their Christmas Eve attack on Calcutta was their last on this heavily populated area. On Christmas night three Lilys attempted to raid the USAAF B-29 Superfortress base at Kharagpur and all three were shot down.

The year 1944 had seen the retirement from operations of the Hudson, Kittyhawk, Mohawk, Vengeance and Wellington, and the arrival of the P-47 Thunderbolt for the RAF under Lend-Lease. Hurricanes also arrived armed with rocket projectiles or 40mm guns for dealing with the tanks that the Japanese had brought on to the Imphal Plain. During that year the offensive against the enemy lines of communication had been extensive and not unsuccessful. The campaign amounted to 4,500 successful attacks against river craft, 350 locomotive strikes and about 1,000 on motor transport.

Amphibious operations

In the New Year, Akyab was occupied on 3 January by an Allied seaborne landing. Japanese reaction was so slow that it was six days before the waterfront was attacked, and then by only six Oscars. No damage was done on land, but a Sea Otter amphibian was shot down over the water. Spitfires, already settled in at Akyab airfield, were immediately scrambled and Thunderbolts took off shortly afterwards to strafe Meiktila airfield – the nearest Oscar base. But the Oscars returned next day and damaged landing craft, killing four sailors and wounding 19.

A landing by units of XV Corps on Ramree Island on 21 January was accompanied by large-scale Allied Air operations. Heavy bombers dropped 360 tons of bombs inland while fighter-bombers strafed the waterfront until

Opposite far left: Liberators from India attacking the railway sidings at Na Nien. Opposite left: a Japanese train under attack by a Beaufighter in 1945. Below: a bridge on the Burma-Siam railway, south of Thanbyuzayat, wrecked by Allied bombing. Bottom: No 30 Squadron's Thunderbolts on the prowl. The unit specialised in ground attack sorties

the foremost landing craft had beached. Air operations intensified as more aircraft and supplies poured into the theatre. As a measure of the scale of attack the following statistics relate to February 1945 alone: heavy bombers dropped 4,358 tons of bombs; medium bombers dropped 1,501 tons; light bombers, 124 tons and fighter-bombers, 3,646 tons.

Among aircrew claims were the destruction of five steamers and 566 smaller river craft, 13 railway and 12 road bridges, 100 items of rolling stock and numerous motor vehicles. That month 26,715 men and 66,230 tons of supplies were airlifted, mainly in support of 14th Army operations. Light aircraft on liaison and rescue duties made 16,293 sorties and altogether 9,883 casualties were brought out by air that month. Due to the much reduced strength of the JAAF, the Allies only claimed to have destroyed 11 aircraft and damaged 15 in that period.

Japanese aircraft withdrawn

As the Allies advanced towards the important communications centre of Meiktila, which fell on 3 March, Lilys, unable to operate by day in the face of overwhelming Allied air power, risked the more limited night fighter defence. On 1 February a Lily destroyed a Spitfire and damaged two others at Tabingaung. On the 7th, 20 signals personnel were injured at Akyab and their filter room was put out of action. On the 13th a Lily discovered Sinthe airfield through a flarepath which had been lit for a Curtiss C-46 to land; the subsequent bombing killed seven RAF personnel and injured 34.

Attacks continued on enemy bases so that by mid-March fewer than 25 Japanese operational aircraft remained serviceable in Burma. Other aircraft supporting the 30,000 Japanese troops had been forced back to Thai and Malayan bases, beyond reach of RAF close-support aircraft. But 40 USAAF P-51 Mustangs, based at Cox's Bazaar in India, flew across Burma to Thailand to strafe Don Mouang airfield 19 km (12 miles) north of Bangkok, on 15 March, destroying 26 Japanese aircraft and losing only one Mustang on the 2,575 km (1,600 mile) round trip.

The Japanese Army resorted to raiding parties on the ground searching for Allied airstrips. On the night of 12 March the RAF Regiment repulsed an attack on Onbauk satellite airstrip. The raid leader, Captain Inone, who was killed, was an expert in such tactics and had destroyed seven aircraft in a similar raid on the airfield at Palel the previous year.

Air supply operations

Following the defeat of the Japanese 15th Army in Central Burma early in April, the Allies advanced quickly, recapturing Magwe. To exploit this success it was essential to provide forward landing grounds and Meiktila airfield became a focal point. Here the aircraft of the 317th and 319th Troop Carrier Squadron USAAF, carrying 3 tons per trip, built up a reserve of 390,947 litres (86,000 gallons) of aviation fuel and towed in 55 gliders loaded with airfield building plant on 20 April. That afternoon Lewe airfield was found abandoned by the enemy and US Airborne Engineers, working with the advancing troops,

Above right: a USAAF Douglas C-47 with a Waco CG-4 Hadrian glider on tow. Many of the troops taking part in Wingate's second Chindit expedition were landed behind enemy lines in gliders.
Right: RAF Dakotas painted in Burma by the war artist Frank Wooton. Air supply was developed to a fine art in South East Asia Command

cleared a 732m × 137m (800 × 150 yard) glider strip and signalled Meiktila. At dawn next day supplies were coming in, the gliders carrying a tractor, scraper, two bulldozers, jeep and trailer, fuel and rations, an engineer and 19 men. The second glider to land ran off the track and was completely wrecked, but the crew and equipment it carried were unharmed.

The enemy troops put in a counter-attack and skirmishing went on all day, forcing work to stop before midnight. The JAAF made a surprise visit early next morning with eight Oscars which set five gliders on fire. But by noon the strip had been extended to 1,370m (1,500 yards) and the Dakotas of No 62 Squadron RAF were signalled to fly in troops and supplies. Just as the airfield was being completed, Toungoo fell to the 5th Indian Division and next day gliders were being flown to airfields in that area, and the equipment at Lewe was called forward.

But the monsoon came early, causing greater hardship for the troops and putting an increased burden on the air forces. At Meiktila the roads were too bad for a Casualty Clearing Station to move by road to Tennant, so on 25 April ten aircraft made 38 trips to move the 111 tons involved–doctors, nurses, orderlies, tents, beds, surgical equipment, mobile X-ray units, lighting sets, sterilisers, rations and baggage. At Lewe, by then a staging post, the ground became a morass in the continuous rain and aircraft continued to land with mud up to their wheel hubs.

Operation Dracula

Final plans for 'Operation Dracula', the assault on Rangoon, were formulated in late April while the aircraft concentrated at Akyab. On 1 May 800 Allied paratroopers, 221 parapacks and 18 door bundles dropped from

Dakotas, which were escorted by Mustangs. Meanwhile the three airfields in the vicinity, the radar station, gun positions and bunkers were attacked by 88 Liberators, escorted by 37 Thunderbolts, 50 Mitchells, 29 Mosquitoes, 24 Beaufighters and an additional 56 Thunderbolts operating in a strafing role. Next day the air attacks continued while an Allied landing force moved in from the broad river, and the paratroops closed in on land.

Japanese resistance was negligible and the reason for this became clear after photo-reconnaissance shots of a prisoner-of-war camp were studied, where the words 'Japs gone' had been set out in stones and, to remove any suspicion of a *ruse de guerre*, 'extract digit' had been added. Acting on this intelligence, Wing Commander A. E. Saunders of No 110 Squadron landed his Mosquito at Mingaladon airfield and walked into the city. After

Above: a photographic reconnaissance Mosquito Mk XVI of No 684 Squadron. Starting at the beginning of 1944, this unit covered the whole of Burma and by the end of the war had photographed targets as far distant as Singapore.
Below: a Dakota over the Sittang River, with supplies stacked in the doorway ready for dropping to troops in jungle clearings

A supply drop by US transport aircraft to Chinese troops between Myitkyina and Katha. In October 1944 the joint RAF/USAAF Combat Cargo Task Force was formed and during its brief 7½ month existence carried 330,000 tons of supplies

confirming that the Japanese had evacuated, he rowed a sampan out to the approaching Allied craft. That day Prome fell to the 14th Army, which continued its advance to Paungde, 209 km (130 miles) from Rangoon. Along a wide front fighter-bombers attacked in advance of the troops, supported by Spitfires operating in bombing roles, since they were rarely called upon to intercept enemy aircraft. The Americans at this time introduced the P-61 Black Widow, with armament including rocket projectiles, to Burma.

By mid-1945 the JAAF deemed it safer not to leave the ground; at the same time Allied pressure lessened as the monsoon reached its peak. Low cloud, heavy rain and thundery conditions, with cumulus clouds towering to 9,140 m (30,000 ft), made conditions extremely hazardous at times. A Dakota was turned upside-down in the air by the turbulence and during June seven transport aircraft crashed and five went missing over the jungle; in all, there were 72 air transport accident casualties that month. The weather was now a far graver menace than the JAAF. The Allies needed a respite to consolidate their gains and re-group. Such offensive operations as could be mounted were mainly to block the escape routes of the Japanese, now withdrawing on their own volition.

The Combat Cargo Task Force together with Eastern Air Command was disbanded on 31 May with the withdrawal of American units. During its brief existence, the Task Force had carried 330,000 tons of supplies. The British re-conquest of Burma and Malaya was a Commonwealth, not an Allied matter and No 232 Group RAF took over supply responsibilities in Burma.

Propaganda leaflets

In accordance with the axiom that the pen is mightier than the sword, leaflet-dropping had played its part; the Allies had dispensed over five million leaflets in October 1944 alone. For the demoralised Japanese, propaganda followed traditional lines: Leaflet SJ/45 showed a photo of smiling Japanese prisoners queuing for a hearty meal and adjured others to join them. For the Burmese, Leaflet SB/19 was typical and gave warnings not to help the Japanese, with assurances that the Allies were approaching. An unusual 'drop' was No XA/40, delivered seasonally over native villages; this was a bag containing cabbage, radish and bringal seeds with planting instructions in Burmese, Shan and Kachin.

Visual Control Posts (VCPs) were a successful introduction to jungle warfare. These consisted of an RAF officer and two wireless operators, using a Jeep or mules, according to terrain, working with troops and keeping in wireless contact with aircraft giving close support. They could call for attacks on pockets of resistance and get Army mortars or artillery to mark targets with smoke shells. A further step was to introduce the 'cab rank', which was being used successfully in Italy, whereby fighters circling over the battle area could be called up as required by VCPs to expend their bombs or rockets on targets as they were sighted.

Pockets of Japanese troops striving to break out of Burma still offered resistance in some areas, causing Allied troops to call for air action. On 12 and 13 August Spitfires and Thunderbolts descended upon such areas, attacking not only the obvious bunkers and trenches, but also camp fires and bashas. On the next two days bad weather grounded most of the aircraft, which was fortunate for all concerned, as the Japanese Emperor accepted Allied demands for unconditional surrender on the 14th. The following day the Allied Air Commander, receiving confirmation of the capitulation, signalled his units to suspend offensive operations forthwith.

Japanese surrender

For the next few weeks aerial activity continued unabated. There were supplies and medical teams to be dropped to prisoner-of-war camps as well as the maintenance of the troops in the field. A million leaflets were dropped by Thunderbolts alone, informing the Japanese of the surrender arrangements–and even to some isolated British troops patrolling in steep valleys that precluded wireless communication. There was brief action on 20 August at Shwegyin, where leaflets were greeted with machine-gun and mortar fire, to which a force of Mosquitoes, Spitfires and Thunderbolts quickly responded.

On 26 August Spitfires escorted a white-painted Topsy (Mitsubishi Ki-57) transport into Mingaladon, carrying the Japanese delegates who were to sign the surrender terms for the Burma area on the 28th. Allied forces in Burma quickly dispersed, the American units moving to bases in India and China and some of the RAF units southward to Malaya and Singapore which, but for the Japanese surrender, would have been invaded under 'Operation Zipper', which had been at an advanced planning stage. The jungles of Burma were left to the salvage units and War Graves teams, and the British forces gradually withdrew. Within three years, on 4 January 1948, the country attained full independence as the Union of Burma. Today the names of airfields of the Burmese Air Force have a familiar ring for many who participated in the air war over Burma–Akyab, Lashio, Mandalay, Meiktila, Mingaladon and Moulmein.

Tunisia 1942-43

At the beginning of October 1942 the situation in the Mediterranean area did not look particularly favourable for the Allies. The Eighth Army was entrenched at El Alamein following a disastrous defeat and long retreat during the summer. It was once again strong, well-equipped and well-led, and had just withstood a determined Axis offensive, which it had broken completely. It was, however, still further back in Egypt than it had ever been. On Malta a further major *blitz* was expected at any moment, although by then, the air defences had been increased to comprise five squadrons of Supermarine Spitfires and one of Bristol Beaufighter night fighters.

Within little more than a month, however, the situation had changed irrevocably to the Axis' disadvantage. Firstly, the renewed air assault on Malta had been decisively defeated; secondly, Montgomery's massive offensive at El Alamein was crushing the Afrika Korps and led to a precipitate retreat out of Egypt and right across Libya by early November. At sea, air power and submarines were proving most effective in preventing the flow of supplies from Italy to Libya, starving Rommel's desert forces of the means to replace their lost striking power in North Afrika.

Then on 8 November came the most unexpected and most devastating blow of all; Anglo-American forces landed in strength at three places in French North-West Africa. On the Atlantic coast of Morocco an all-American force, supported by a US Naval task force, landed at Casablanca, while on the country's Mediterranean coast a mixed Anglo-American force went in at Oran, backed up by the arrival of an airborne force flown direct from England in Douglas C-47 Dakota transports. Further east,

a mainly British force landed at Algiers; both the Oran and Algiers landings were supported by Royal Navy task forces, including strong carrier elements, and were swiftly reinforced by the arrival of air units of the Royal Air Force and US Army Air Force from Gibraltar.

At both Casablanca and Oran the Vichy French forces resisted fiercely and for the first day or two there was considerable fighting, particularly in the air. In Algeria, however, there was barely any resistance and the British forces were able to prepare at once for the move on their ultimate objective – Tunis. From this moment on, the war in the Mediterranean was to be concentrated on Tunisia, where for six months some of the most sustained and costly air fighting of the war swiftly developed.

Allied landings

To support the initial operations, a considerable fighter force had been moved in secret by ship to Gibraltar and the morning of 8 November found six USAAF squadrons of Spitfires, seven RAF squadrons of Spitfires, three of Hawker Hurricanes and a photographic reconnaissance unit being readied to take part. These units began flying in, the British to Algiers and the Americans to Oran, from the first day of the landings. The Axis in Sicily, under the direction of the German Supreme Commander, Luftwaffe Feldmarschall Albert Kesselring, reacted with commendable speed. All the bomber units which had so recently been engaged against Malta were in Sicily, while many Italian bombers were present on Sardinia and in the south of Italy. During the evening of 9 November some 30 German bombers approached Algiers. They were met by a strong force of Supermarine Spitfires and Hawker

Douglas Boston Mk III day-bombers over the desert. Flown by RAF and SAAF units, the type was used extensively in the later months of the Tunisian campaign in direct support of the army. Attacking troops, tanks and transport, the Boston significantly contributed to the Allied victory in Africa

Hurricanes, losing nearly half of their force to the defenders. Meanwhile, however, on the same date Kesselring had dispatched infantry to Tunis in Junkers Ju 52/3m transports, and these took over and secured the airport before the local Vichy French could decide whether to opt for the Allies or not. Before the day was out Messerschmitt Bf 109Gs of I/JG 53 and Ju 87Ds of II/StG 3 had also flown in. They were followed on the 11th by Macchi MC 202s of the Italian 155° Gruppo and, on the 12th, by more Bf 109s of III/JG 53.

The Allies too were moving fast; a small convoy sailed up the coast on 10 November to the little port of Bougie, where two fighter squadrons at once flew in. The next day units from Bougie headed towards Bône, while a paratroop force was flown up to this location, dropping just in time to forestall a similar operation by the Germans. Raids on Bougie and Bône began at once, and more RAF squadrons were flown up to the latter port and to an airfield at Souk el Arba, to provide cover both for the port itself and for the advancing forces.

Meanwhile more reinforcements were arriving; these consisted of four squadrons of Bristol Blenheim Mk V bombers of the RAF, two USAAF fighter groups with Lockheed P-38 Lightning fighters, two heavy bomber groups with Boeing B-17 Fortresses, a medium bomber group with Martin B-26 Marauders and an RAF night fighter squadron of Bristol Beaufighters (with their AI radar removed), all of which flew in from England during mid-November. Malta was also reinforced with a squadron of 'strike' Beaufighters from Egypt, these and the Spitfires achieving some considerable success against Axis transport aircraft which were being pressed into service in large numbers to aid in the supply and reinforcement of the forces both in Tunisia and Tripolitania.

The Allied bombers were first in action on 16 November, Blenheims of No 18 Squadron attacking targets in the Tunisian border area and demonstrating their vulnerability and obsolescence by losing four of their number, while B-17s of the 97th Bomb Group raided Sidi Ahmed airfield. It was at once evident to the Germans that aerial reinforcements would be necessary, and on 14 November II/JG 51 arrived from Russia with Bf 109Gs, followed later in the month by II/JG 2 from western France with

Focke Wulf Fw 190s, and the new III/ZG 2 from Germany with Bf 109E fighter-bombers. While the single-engined types provided cover, intercepted raids and made attacks in support of the army units arriving in Tunisia in growing numbers, great efforts were extended in attacks on the North African ports and airfields in Allied hands by the multi-engined bombers. Heinkel He 111s of KG 26, Ju 88s from elements of four *kampfgeschwader*, Italian Cant Z 1007s, Savoia-Marchetti S 79s and S 84s, even four-engined Piaggio P 108Bs were brought in, as were Sardinian-based Reggiane Re 2001 fighter-bombers. To aid in the vital air supply efforts Ju 52/3m and Savoia S 82 trimotors were joined by many other types–Blohm und Voss Bv 222 six-engined flying boats, Messerschmitt Me 323s and Fiat G 18s.

Radar-equipped defenders

During the night of 20/21 November a heavy raid on Maison Blanche airfield at Algiers destroyed many aircraft; the defending Beaufighters were almost helpless because of their lack of radar. While sets were being sent out from England and further squadrons were also dispatched, a flight of fully radar-equipped aircraft was detached from No 89 Squadron in Egypt as a temporary arrangement. This particularly heavy attack had been precipitated by the first appearance over Tunis on 19 November of B-17s with a fighter escort of P-38s of the 14th Fighter Group (FG). Next day the bombers had again attacked, this time accompanied by 1st Fighter Group aircraft. The two P-38 squadrons of the 14th FG moved to Youks-les-Bains on the Algerian-Tunisian border well to the south of Bône on 20 November, to give tactical support to US forces moving into the area on the British right flank. These were joined by French units, the French in North Africa having decided to throw in their lot with the Allies. The initial USAAF presence at the front was added to by the arrival at Youks of a single light bomber squadron equipped with the Douglas A-20.

However, by late November the Allies were in trouble. A very severe winter had begun; lines of communication were stretched to the limit and the Axis had poured forces into Tunisia much more rapidly than expected. A British attempt to take Djedeida airfield on 28 November, supported by a paratroop drop next day, failed, and the advance came to a halt in the mountains within sight of the Plain of Tunis. Here, stalemate was to exist for some months. Allied airfields were well back from the front line with poor radar early warning and control facilities and were much affected by adverse weather. The Axis were close to the lines on excellent all-weather airfields, and

Top right: a Messerschmitt Me 323 transport under attack by a Martin Marauder.
Above right: armourers work on a Messerschmitt Bf 109F.
Right: Michael Turner's painting depicts Hawker Hurricane Mk IIC aircraft of No 274 Squadron on take-off.
Below: Supermarine Spitfire Mk VBs parked on a forward airfield in Algeria shortly after the Torch landings

were soon gaining an upper hand. The RAF had Nos 322 and 324 Wings equipped with Spitfires at Bône and Souk el Arba, reinforced by one USAAF squadron of Spitfires. At Youks the 14th FG, after early losses, was reinforced by a squadron from the 1st FG; the rest of the 1st undertook escorts to the B-17s and B-26s, while the RAF's No 323 Wing flying Hurricanes provided base area defences and convoy patrols.

The experienced Luftwaffe fighter pilots proved a particularly unpleasant surprise for the US airmen, but both the RAF and USAAF suffered heavy losses to them at this time. On 3 December six P-38s of the 1st FG were lost on an escort mission over Tunis, while five more from the 14th were also lost on this date. Next day fighters of I and II/JG 53 and II/JG 2 caught a dozen unescorted Blenheim Mk Vs of Nos 18 and 614 Squadrons; the bombers did not waver from carrying out their raid, however, and the formation leader, Wg Cdr H. G. Malcolm, received a posthumous Victoria Cross. All the bombers were shot down and, following this disaster, the Blenheims had to be withdrawn from daylight operations. By the end of December the two P-38 units had lost a total of 31 aircraft to the enemy for a substantially smaller number of victories; US morale fell, but reinforcements were on the way. Curtiss P-40 Warhawks had been off-loaded from a carrier at Casablanca and on 6 December the first squadron of these from the 33rd FG arrived at Thelepte to support the Youks-based 14th FG.

In Algeria a force of RAF Vickers Wellington night bombers had arrived to carry out attacks on the Tunisian ports by dark, but during December the Luftwaffe brought in Ju 88C night fighters to counter these and soon a full-

Western Desert Air Force impinged upon operations in Tunisian skies. In the north the RAF had prepared a number of new airfields at Souk el Khemis and had moved up night fighters to the Bône area. The first Spitfire Mk IXs had also arrived to help redress the balance by day, going initially to No 81 Squadron in No 322 Wing, and then to No 72 Squadron in No 324 Wing.

The new forces in the south included on the Axis side all three *gruppen* of JG 77, I and III/StG 3, I/SG 2 equipped with the Bf 109E, and reconnaissance units, plus the Italian 3⁰ and 4⁰ Stormi with the MC 200 and MC 202. In Sicily the Luftwaffe had been reinforced by II/JG 27, re-equipped after operations over Libya and Egypt during 1942. Allied forces included No 239 Wing with five squadrons of P-40s, No 244 Wing with four squadrons of Spitfires, the USAAF's 57th FG with P-40s, several squadrons of Martin Baltimore and B-25 medium bombers and some reconnaissance units. Other elements of the force were further back, resting or awaiting introduction to operations. There were also two American groups of Consolidated B-24 Liberators and a force of RAF night bombers – mainly Wellingtons, but including both Liberators and Handley Page Halifaxes, together with some Beaufighter intruders.

On the central front, at Thelepte and Youks-les-Bains, the initial USAAF tactical support was on the way to being worn out. On 1 February the 33rd FG suffered the loss of five P-40s, with six more being shot down next day. The 14th FG was so demoralised that its pilots refused to fly any more, and it had to be withdrawn for re-formation. Early in February the Spitfire-equipped 52nd FG was sent to Thelepte, soon joined by the similarly-equipped 31st FG and by the first squadrons of P-39s – the latter to be used only as ground strafers as they were considered to be unsuitable for air combat.

Left: Douglas Bostons of No 24 Squadron SAAF being serviced at a desert dispersal point.
Opposite below: the crew of an RAF Bristol Blenheim leave their aircraft after a night raid on Tunis. The Blenheim was found to be vulnerable on operations in Tunisia and was replaced by the faster Boston.
Below: a Supermarine Spitfire Mk VB, equipped with a Vokes filter for desert operations. The Spitfire was flown by RAF, SAAF and USAAF units in the air superiority role over Tunisia

scale night air war had been added to that being under-taken by day. Further Italian reinforcements of Macchi MC 202s, MC 200s and Fiat G 50s were also brought in, but at this time USAAF strength was growing particularly fast – though much of it was not yet ready for action. During December a second B-26 group and one equipped with North American B-25 Mitchells were to arrive, together with the rest of the A-20 group. A third P-38 group flew in, although initially most of its aircraft and some of its pilots went to reinforce the two groups already operating. The 3rd Photographic Group was already available for reconnaissance work, but this was now joined by the 68th Observation Group for tactical work, while early in the new year two full groups of Bell P-39 Airacobras flew in from England in several formations.

The Mareth Line

The start of 1943 was marked by some very heavy air attacks on Bône while, on the ground, attacks on the US forces and the poorly-equipped French on the southern part of the front, drove them out of Pichon and off the Faid Pass. By now, Rommel's forces in Libya were close to the Tunisian border in the far south. Some raids on Tripoli were made by the B-17s, during which their escorts first met the Bf 109Gs of JG 77, which were moving back into Tunisia ahead of the ground forces. The US fighters were now beginning to enjoy some success and on one occasion P-40s of the 33rd FG shot down ten Ju 88s from a force raiding Thelepte.

By the end of January 1943 Rommel's forces had moved into Tunisia, taking up position behind the Mareth Line. Increasingly, his supporting air forces and those of the

Command reorganisation

Before the Eighth Army was ready to attack at Mareth, Rommel turned part of his force northwards to attack the US and French forces threatening his supply lines with northern Tunisia. These hardened veterans struck on 14 February, taking Sidi Bou Zid and thrusting into the Kasserine Pass. For a while it looked as if the Allied front would crack and Rommel's forces would stream into southern Algeria to attack the Allied base areas; bad weather prevented air involvement. There was, however, a lack of co-ordination between those Axis forces in the north and those in the south and, alarmed by the speed with which the Allies appeared to be reinforcing the threatened area, Rommel withdrew on 22 February to his original positions. Meanwhile the crisis had led to a reorganisation of the Allied air forces whereby all the tactical air forces in Africa including the US XII Air Support Command, came under the overall command of Air Marshal Coningham, the Western Desert Air Force (WDAF) Commander. The direction and control of all air power in the complete Mediterranean area was vested in Air Chief Marshal Sir Arthur Tedder, who also had control of a Strategic Air Force and Coastal Air Force.

Even as Rommel withdrew his forces from the Kasserine area, the softening-up of the Mareth defences began from the air with attacks by WDAF units. On 16 March he launched a spoiling attack towards Medenine, but it was utterly defeated. Sick and dispirited, he returned to Germany and the Italian General Messe took over in the south, while the commander in the north, General Jurgen von Arnim, became supreme commander in Africa. This period also saw the appearance of the first Spitfire Mk IX aircraft in the south, these going to No 145 Squadron. They were initially flown to a large extent by a special volunteer unit of experienced Polish pilots, the Polish Fighting Team, which was attached to the unit at this time.

During the night of 20/21 March 1943 the assault on the Mareth defences began, a frontal attack being coupled with a wide outflanking move to the south by the New Zealand division. When the frontal assault became bogged down, the outflanking forces were greatly reinforced, reaching the approaches to the heavily-defended Tebaga Gap. Here air power came into its own. On 25 March, after a preliminary artillery bombardment, wave after wave of Desert Air Force fighter-bombers swept in to attack German anti-tank gun positions, allowing the British armour to pour through almost unscathed. Losses of aircraft to ground fire were relatively heavy, but the results more than justified the cost. The Axis were forced to withdraw from Mareth, and next day Gabes was taken as they headed back to new positions on the Wadi Akarit river bed. These were to be assaulted on 6 April, quickly collapsing, and next day the first meeting between US troops from the central front with Eighth Army men took place at Gafsa. Meanwhile in the north, the British First Army launched an offensive, breaking through the Fondouk Pass on 10 April and advancing on Kairouan, where it too made contact with the Eighth Army. On 12 April the southern port of Sousse fell to the Allies.

Operation Flax

The position of the Axis was now becoming perilous. Sea communications had virtually been cut by the Allied sea and air forces and huge fleets of transport aircraft were providing the main means of resupply for fuel and ammunition. On 5 April the Allied air forces launched Operation Flax, designed to intercept and destroy these flights. Initially this chiefly involved US forces, the long-range P-38 fighters of the 1st and 82nd FGs being frequently employed. Within Tunisia, Axis airfields were now under constant air attack, but still continued to operate as best they could. On 13 March, for instance, Bf 109s of JG 77 had destroyed a complete formation of seven P-39s near Thelepte. During that month, however, the Fw 190s of II/JG 2 had left to return to France, although II/SG 2, partially equipped with these aircraft as fighter-bombers, had arrived. Other types introduced were Henschel Hs 129 'tank busters' and Messerschmitt Me 210 Zerstörer, but little could be achieved by any of these types in the face of growing Allied air supremacy. Early in April, the remaining Ju 87 Stukas of StG 3 suffered some very heavy losses to US Spitfires in the El Guettar area and were withdrawn. The same American fighters savaged a formation of Ju 88s on 9 April and thereafter Luftwaffe bombers were rarely seen over Tunisia by day.

Meanwhile, Operation Flax was achieving its aim. On 5 April P-38s claimed 31 transports shot down in two interceptions, adding 11 more on the 10th and 18 on the 11th. On 18 March–Palm Sunday–four squadrons of Desert Air Force P-40s, with a cover of RAF Spitfires, met a massive formation of Ju 52/3m transports in the evening and claimed 75 victories. Next day more Ju 52/3m transports fell to SAAF P-40 Kittyhawks, and on the 22nd the latter disposed of a whole formation of 16 Me 323s. The transports began operating under cover of darkness, but even then they continued to suffer heavily to patrolling Beaufighters.

During the night of 19/20 April, the Eighth Army attacked at Enfidaville, but finding the Axis now entrenched in mountainous country, were able to make little progress. Two days later, therefore, the First Army attacked and the noose round the remaining territory in Axis hands was drawn a little tighter. By now the Italians had withdrawn all their aircraft apart from a single *gruppo* of MC 202s, while the Luftwaffe moved II/JG 51 to Sardinia and withdrew I and II/JG 53 plus the remaining ground attack units to Sicily, leaving only JG 77 in Africa.

In an effort to delay the inevitable, the Axis launched a last counter-attack with all available forces on 28 April, but this was held by the 30th with most of their remaining armour destroyed. Some reorganisation of the Allied line followed, the US II Corps moving to the far north and some of the best Eighth Army divisions reinforcing the main First Army striking force for a direct drive on Tunis. The final offensive was spearheaded and supported by an extraordinary concentration of air power. Yet more USAAF bomber groups had been added, together with another fighter unit, while the Desert Air Force had brought up most of its remaining strength, British, American and Commonwealth, for this final push. Only a single unit of Hurricane Mk IID 'tank-busters' was omitted, due to the very heavy losses suffered during the Mareth and Wadi Akarit battles.

On 3 May 1943 Mateur fell to US armour, while on the 6th the First Army attack on Tunis itself was launched, tanks rolling into the city next day only minutes before US forces entered Bizerta. Remaining Axis resistance was concentrated onto the Cap Bon Peninsula, from where the last German and Italian fighters were withdrawn on 8 May. Units based in Sicily and Sardinia continued to operate over the area each day, refuelling on occasions at strips in the battle area, but there was little they could do. Allied fighters and fighter-bombers were everywhere, attacking pockets of resistance and preventing any attempts at evacuation. The final surrender took place on 13 May, with the loss of an estimated 250,000 men to the Axis cause.

Italy 1943-45

When Sicily fell to the Allies in mid-August 1943 the Axis air forces had suffered a calamitous defeat from which they were never fully to recover. Allied air power had reached a zenith and now represented the most decisive advantage possessed in the Mediterranean area. Immediately available on airfields in Sicily, Malta and northern

The German stormtroops who rescued the deposed Mussolini from his mountain top prison on 22 September 1943 landed in DFS 230C-1 gliders

Tunisia was the Allied Tactical Air Force, a combined Anglo-American force of fighters, fighter-bombers, light and medium bombers, and reconnaissance aircraft some 100 squadrons strong. This was backed by the Allied Strategic Air Force in North Africa, which had 24 squadrons of American heavy day bombers, joined by eight squadrons of RAF night bombers. In addition, a strong Coastal Air Force of fighters, bombers and maritime patrol aircraft was stationed along the North African coast, on Malta and in Sicily.

Facing this mighty force, which included 1,395 fighters, 703 medium and light bombers, 461 heavy bombers and 162 night bombers (backed up by 406 transport aircraft), were the tattered remnants of Italy's Regia Aeronautica and the Luftwaffe's much-weakened Luftflotte 2. This latter included six *gruppen* of fighters, four of fighter-bombers, and a few *gruppen* of Junkers Ju 88 bombers, plus reconnaissance units. Part of this strength was based on the island of Sardinia, but all units were operating below full strength. The only help immediately available was from bombers in Southern France.

At the start of September 1943, the B-17 and B-24 heavy bombers of the Strategic Air Force, together with North American B-25 and Martin B-26 medium bombers, were already raiding targets in southern Italy as far north as the Rome area – usually supported by an escort of

Savoia Marchetti SM 79-II Sparviero of 278° Squadriglia, 132° Gruppo Autonomo Aerosilurante, Regia Aeronautica

Lockheed P-38 Lightning fighters. The Tactical Air Force (TAC) was divided into two separate commands— Desert Air Force (DAF), to support Montgomery's Eighth Army, and the Twelfth Tactical Air Command to support Mark Clark's new US Fifth Army (an Anglo-American formation, despite its designation). Desert Air Force, while largely a British and South African organisation, included two US Curtiss P-40 fighter groups, while the Twelfth TAC incorporated two RAF Supermarine Spitfire wings alongside its American units.

Allied landings

Eighth Army troops crossed the Straits of Messina to land on the 'toe' of Italy in the Reggio Calabria area on 3 September, while next day landings were made at Taranto. DAF aircraft provided cover and support, but the only opposition came from a few Italian fighters and fighter-bombers. The German fighters were engaged against heavy US bombing raids, during which pitched battles were fought with escorting Lightnings by the Messerschmitt Bf 109Gs of JG 53 and JG 77. These combats brought the last major German fighter success in the area when 23 P-38s were shot down during two raids in early September.

Late on 8 September an armistice with Italy was announced by the Allies, and next morning a major Fifth Army landing was made at Salerno, on the west coast near Naples. Although no Italian resistance was met, the Germans reacted violently, and Luftwaffe units were thrown in with everything they had. While Royal Navy escort carriers were positioned offshore providing Supermarine Seafires for immediate local defence, P-38s, P-40s, North American. A-36s and Spitfires from Sicily patrolled in relays throughout the day, Bristol Beaufighters and DH Mosquitoes taking over from dusk to dawn. Repeated small-scale fighter-bomber attacks by Focke Wulf Fw 190s

from the Foggia area failed to achieve much, while Dornier Do 217s armed with Henschel Hs 293 glider bombs from the South of France, also failed to inflict any serious loss on the offshore shipping. They did, however, sink one battleship of the Italian navy as it made its way to Malta under the terms of the armistice.

Ashore German counter-attacks threatened to drive the Allied beachhead back into the sea. During the early hours of 14 September strong reinforcements of US paratroops were dropped into the area, however, with more being brought in the following night. Coupled with sustained fighter-bomber support and naval gunfire, this enabled the Fifth Army to hold its lines. Meanwhile Eighth Army forces from the south were approaching, and a link-up was made on the 16th. Thereafter the Germans rapidly withdrew northwards as the combined

Below: the painting by J. B. Stafford-Baker of Cassino. American bombers, diverted from strategic targets, bombed the German stronghold on 15 February and 15 March 1944, razing the monastery and town. Bottom and opposite below: the SM 79 was the Italians' most successful bomber and the MC 202 one of their best fighters. P-51s flew long range escorts from Italy

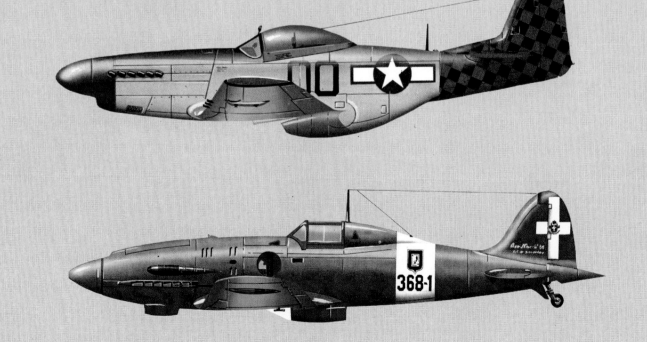

North American P-51D of the 317th Fighter Squadron, 325th Fighter Group, USAAF, Vicenzo, Italy

Macchi C202 Folgore of 368° Squadriglia, 152° Gruppo, Regia Aeronautica

Anglo-American front, now reaching from coast to coast of the peninsula, followed them. Naples was taken on 1 October, while during the night of 2/3rd landings were made at Termoli on the east coast. In this area the many airfields on the Foggia Plain–one of the prime Allied objectives–now fell into the hands of the Eighth Army. At once DAF fighter and fighter-bomber units moved in, soon followed by the light and medium bombers and then by increasing numbers of Strategic AF heavy bombers and their escorts. Squadrons from Coastal AF arrived here and at Naples to provide local air defence and to operate over the sea lanes.

Cab ranks

From Foggia, DAF fighter-bombers introduced new 'cab rank' operations in direct close support of the Eighth Army during its crossing of the Trigno River. Used only during periods of major ground activity, this system provided standing patrols of fighter-bombers overhead which could be directed immediately onto any desired targets by a forward controller with the troops.

In early November 1943 the US Fifteenth Air Force was formed in the Foggia area to control daylight strategic operations. While many attacks were still to be made on Italian targets, the bombers based here were increasingly sent further afield to bomb targets in Austria, southern Germany, France, Hungary, Romania and Bulgaria. Four fighter groups also became a permanent part of this air force for escort purposes–three equipped with P-38s and one with Republic P-47 Thunderbolts. The first of the latter were also introduced to the Tactical Air Force late in the year, joining the 57th Fighter Group which was operating with the DAF. Soon this type would become the standard US fighter-bomber in Italy.

Reduced Luftwaffe activity after the retreat from southern Italy allowed some reductions in Allied air strength to be made. Late in the year two RAF Spitfire squadrons were posted to India, while four more were sent to Syria for a rest. At the end of 1943 a reorganisation took place; North-West African Allied Air Forces became Mediterranean Allied Air Forces. Following this in January 1944, many of the Allied 'top brass' left to take command of the new invasion forces assembling in England, and an almost complete turn-over of army and air force leadership took place.

Having crossed the Trigno, Volturno and Sangro Rivers, the Allied armies now found themselves faced with formidable defences on the Gustav Line to the south of Rome, which were centred on the highly-defensible Monte Cassino. Here stiffening German resistance was accompanied by an increase in Luftwaffe fighter and fighter-bomber activity. Patrolling RAF Spitfires, many of them Mk VIIIs, saw considerable combat at this time, as did two American groups which were also flying Spitfires. Heavy losses were suffered by the Germans, particularly in the Fw 190-equipped *schlachtgruppen*.

Operation Shingle

In an effort to speed the collapse of the Gustav Line and the advance on Rome, a new Allied landing on the west coast was planned–'Operation Shingle'–to go ashore in the Anzio-Nettuno area, just to the south of the capital. Allied fighter patrols prevented Luftwaffe reconnaissance completely, and on 22 January 1944 the landings were made with complete tactical surprise. To support this venture, much of the DAF had moved to the west coast to join the Twelfth TAC, and some 850 aircraft were gathered in the Naples area.

Once again, bombers and torpedo bombers from southern France attacked desperately, but to no avail. Reinforcements of fighters and fighter-bombers were sent down to Rome, and some of the heaviest air fighting yet seen over Italy took place. The new fascist Italian government that had been formed in the German-controlled north had also formed a new Italian air force and elements from the first of two fighter *gruppi* were introduced to combat at this time.

Late in January the Fifth Army began an offensive over the Garigliano River and at Cassino, but made little progress. Massive bombing of Monte Cassino on 15 February achieved little, and the attacks which followed were held by the defenders. During February the Germans

counter-attacked at Anzio, but here air power did much to break up troop concentrations, restrict supplies and generally help the men on the ground to stand firm. Another massive bombing raid on Cassino during March, undertaken by both Strategic and Tactical Air Force bombers and fighter-bombers, once more failed to make the capture of the position possible. That month, however, a much more appropriate use of air power was made when Operation Strangle began. This was a massive interdiction effort by fighter-bombers, light and medium bombers, designed to cut bridges, railway lines and other communications, drastically reducing the movement of

Top: during a raid on Monfalcone, Italy, an RAF Consolidated Liberator was struck by bombs from another above: they did not explode, the crew was uninjured and the damaged bomber returned to base. Above: a painting by Stafford-Baker of a Lockheed Hudson covering the invasion of Sicily

bomber group were dispatched to India, while the two US Spitfire groups were both re-equipped with the first North American P-51 Mustangs to reach the area, and transferred to the Fifteenth Air Force for strategic duties. To make good this loss the RAF sent two wings of Spitfire Mk IXs from the Middle East to Corsica to operate as part of the Twelfth TAC. These were now joined by Spitfires and P-47s of the French Armée de l'Air from North African airfields.

Fall of Rome

On the east coast DAF units supporting the Eighth Army met less aerial resistance and operated increasingly over Yugoslavia, where partisan forces were becoming more active against the Germans. At this time several RAF light bomber units were changing their role from daylight formation bombing to night intruder sorties, as part of the overall interdiction effort. Four RAF and two USAAF night fighter units now provided night defence in Italy, against the depredations of the few Ju 88 units remaining in the north. They did not always prevent these getting through, however, and during the night of 2/3 December 1943, by the assiduous use of aluminium foil strips dropped to confuse the defence's radar, a force of Ju 88s from KG 54 and KG 76 bombed the east coast port of Bari: 14 ships were set on fire and there were many casualties.

A particularly successful Allied air attack was made on 5 May 1944, when Kittyhawk and Mustang fighter-bombers from the DAF's 239 Wing smashed the Pescara Dam without losing a single aircraft. On 11 May the Allied spring offensive began all along the front, backed by massive close air support. The Gustav Line was swiftly broken, while on the 18th the stubborn defences at Cassino at last fell to attack by Polish troops. Thereafter the advance progressed swiftly; a link-up with the beach-

Left: Italian streets renamed by the Germans after famous fighter pilots. Ironically, Luftwaffe fighter activity in Italy was minimal.
Above: Supermarine Spitfire Mk IXs of No 241 Squadron fly over Vesuvius. As Axis aerial activity diminished, RAF fighters were employed in the tactical support of ground forces.
Inset: propaganda was an effective weapon in Italy. The Italians suffered lightly from strategic bombing, but the ground fighting was among the bloodiest of the war and the Allied armies advanced slowly

supplies and munitions to the German units at the front.

Soon after the invasion of Italy began, the Germans had withdrawn from Sardinia and, before the end of 1943, Allied forces had landed on Corsica. This island was to become an increasingly important air base, many units moving here during the winter. Republic P-47s from Corsica were able to attack targets well to the north of Rome without overflying the front lines, and these were soon joined by most of the American medium bombers. The call of other fronts and the downgrading of Italy by the American High Command led to further reductions in strength. Two USAAF fighter groups and one medium

head at Anzio soon followed and Rome was taken on 5 June. Next day came the news of the landings in Normandy and at once the remaining German fighter and fighter-bomber units began to withdraw. Within a month only the new Italian fighter *gruppi* and a handful of Luftwaffe reconnaissance units remained, plus a single night ground attack unit NSGr 9.

The Allied advance continued north of Rome, but at a reduced speed as the Germans, fighting a number of rearguard actions, withdrew to formidable defences that were being prepared on the southern edge of the north Italian plain. The Gothic Line, anchored onto the northern Appennine mountains, was to prove very difficult to break with the forces available. As the Fifth and Eighth Armies approached the area, taking Florence on 4 August, the former was critically weakened. While the British wished to break through in northern Italy, and press on to the open plains of Hungary, the Americans were adamant in their wish to concentrate on the main assault in the West. To support this, they and the French were now planning to launch a large invasion of southern France and during July virtually all USAAF tactical units in Italy, plus one more wing of RAF Spitfires, moved to Corsica. While operations from here continued over Italy until mid-August, thereafter they were diverted almost exclusively over the new area. The DAF was left with the task of supporting the whole Italian front with depleted strength, as the first offensive against the Gothic Line was prepared.

Assault on the Gothic Line

The assault was begun in September 1944, but shortage of infantry and the onset of autumn weather prevented a breakthrough, although some ground was gained. During this fighting five US P-47 groups and the three RAF Spitfire wings returned to Italy from southern France, where the invasion had been well-established and had progressed far inland. USAAF medium bombers once again undertook raids on Italian targets as well, the new Twenty-

second TAC being set up to replace the Twelfth TAC, which was now permanently based in France. With virtually no worthwhile opposition in the air, all remaining DAF fighter units–even the air-superiority Spitfire Mk VIII squadrons–began carrying bombs and undertaking ground attack sorties as their main duties.

Throughout the winter interdiction behind the Gothic Line and up the Brenner Pass remained the primary Allied aerial task. Early in 1945 two of the US P-47 groups and the remaining Martin B-26 units were transferred for the last time to France, while several RAF units were disbanded. In April 1945, however, all was ready for a new assault on the Gothic Line. The Fifteenth Air Force now had few strategic targets remaining and was to take a part in this. First on the Eighth Army front, and then in the Fifth Army area, massive aerial bombardment and artillery barrages paved the way. The benefits of the long interdiction campaign now really paid dividends–the German defence proved to be no more than a hollow shell and total collapse followed swiftly. Allied troops raced through northern Italy, capturing city after city as two German armies retreated. On 2 May 1945 an unconditional surrender in the area was accepted.

Above: RAF Douglas Dakotas operated from Italy under the control of the Balkan Air Force in support of partisans in German-held Yugoslavia, dropping or landing supplies and evacuating casualties.
Left: Bristol Beaufighters sinking an enemy vessel in Port Vathy, Samos, in the Aegean. During 1944 the Beaufighters of No 46 Squadron, in particular, undertook strikes on shipping and islands and flew night intrusions in the Aegean area

Defence of the Reich 1944-45

As World War II reached its final stages in Europe, with the German defence perimeter shrinking round the Fatherland's historic frontiers, the air war entered a ferocious phase which was to represent the Luftwaffe's 'death rattle'. That the Allied air forces suffered so heavily–despite their superiority over the whole of Germany during the last six months of the war–was testimony to the bravery and ingenuity displayed by Luftwaffe airmen in their frantic efforts to protect their homes and families.

The all-out air offensive against the German war

Right: the headquarters of von Rundstedt, C-in-C Army West, destroyed by low-flying Allied bombers.
Below: the intense barrage of flak put up at the height of an Allied air raid on a German city

machine by day and night using the combined might of British and American air forces had formally stemmed from the directive formulated on 21 January 1943 at the Casablanca conference, which was addressed to the Allied Air Force commanders and stated: 'Your primary object will be the progressive destruction and dislocation of the German military, industrial and economic system, and the undermining of the morale of the German people to a point where their capacity for armed resistance is fatally weakened.'

The year 1943 saw the steady growth of Allied air attacks on German-occupied territories from bases in Britain and also from North Africa, and the introduction of 'shuttle' raids. In the latter operations, bomber formations left Britain to strike deep inside Germany and went on to land in the Near East, returning several days later.

By 1944 the combined weight of the Allied bomber forces was threatening to overwhelm the German air defences, particularly when the US Air Force was able to provide effective long-range fighter escorts for its daylight

bombers. Nevertheless, the European mainland, with the exception for Southern Italy, remained under German control during the first half of that year, providing a defensive perimeter which cushioned blows against Germany herself. However, although the collapse of Italy in September 1943 and the invasion of Normandy in June 1944 did not immediately provide the Allies with bomber bases close to Germany, the erosion of Festung Europa (Fortress Europe) had begun. Germany's defensive perimeter came increasingly under Allied control, depriving the Luftwaffe of the essential outer ring of radar stations and forward fighter airfields which would enable it to mount prolonged attacks against Allied bombers on their missions to targets deep in Europe.

After the initial assault in France, both in the north and the south, during which the Allied bomber effort was employed in support of the ground operations, the weight of bombing was switched back to Germany with devastating effect. During September Avro Lancasters and Handley Page Halifaxes of the Royal Air Force blasted Kiel, Munchen-Gladbach, Darmstadt, Berlin, Frankfurt, Stuttgart, Osnabrück, Munster, Bremerhaven, Karlsruhe, Kassel and Brunswick in numerous night raids. Meanwhile, American Boeing B-17s attacked Ludwighafen, Karlsruhe, Ulm, Mainz, Coblenz, Kassel, Bremen, Hamm, Bielefeld and Magdeburg by day, as well as other synthetic oil and railway targets throughout Germany. Such was the enormous damage wrought in these raids that the Germans were forced to make major re-dispositions of their fighter forces. September also brought the initial defeat of Hitler's retaliation weapons, the V1 flying bomb and the V2 long-range rocket, with the over-running of their launching sites.

These catastrophes finally induced Hitler to rescind his previous priorities for bomber production and to order priority for fighters, and the establishment of a massive concentration of *reichsverteidigunggeschwader* (Defence of the Reich Wings). The OKL (Luftwaffe High Command) ordered back to Germany every available day and night

fighter unit for the Defence of the Reich, leaving such *schlachtgeschwader* (ground attack) and *panzergruppen* (anti-tank) units as could be spared to support the ground forces in the West, on the Russian Front and in Italy.

Leaders of the Luftwaffe

Strategic command of the air defence facing the Western Allies was given to Generalleutnant Josef 'Beppo' Schmid, a man who had previously filled a number of staff appointments with indifferent success. His wartime career had ranged from the thoroughly inept occupation of a senior intelligence post at OKL during the Battle of Britain to a fairly capable management of I/Jagdkorps for home air defence after September 1943 in succession to Josef Kammhuber.

Alongside him at headquarters were three key Inspector Generals, of whom the most capable was Adolf Galland. As senior Inspector, Galland remained in charge of day fighters until the end of January 1945, when he was relieved of his post by Goering and replaced by Walther Dahl, who occupied the position until the end of the war.

Night fighters were the province of Oberst Werner Streib, a Messerschmitt Bf 110 veteran who, prior to March 1944, had shot down 65 night bombers and been awarded the Swords to the Knight's Cross. Third of the Inspectors was Oberstleutnant Wolfgang Schenk, who was responsible for the new jet fighters; Schenk had had a distinguished career both on operations as a *zerstörer* leader and as Inspector of Close Support Units, and had been in charge of bombing tests with the Messerschmitt Me 262 jet fighter-bomber in mid-1944.

As a means of speeding new aircraft into service for Germany's defence, Oberst Gordon Gollob had been given the job of leading the service test units which were releasing the Me 163 rocket fighter, the Me 262 and the diminutive Heinkel He 162 to operational *gruppen*. At Rechlin Hauptmann Bruno Stolle was ordered to clear the excellent Focke Wulf Ta 152 (a development of the Fw 190) for combat, while Major Diethelm von Eichel-Streiber, another veteran fighter pilot with 96 air victories, was given the job of organising the re-training of Me 262 bomber pilots for the fighter role.

Jagdgruppe 200, under Major Herbert Kroack, which fought over Southern France with the Messerschmitt Bf 109G and the Focke Wulf Fw 190A-7, was brought back to Wiesbaden where it was disbanded and its pilots distributed among the other home defence units. III/JG 54, led by Major 'Bazi' Weiss, with the new Fw 190D-9, was withdrawn to Achmer and Hesepe, to protect the Me 262 jet fighters of Kommando Nowotny then working up to operational status. I/JG 26, commanded by Major Karl Borris, was re-located at Furstenau and Handrup, near Osnabrück, also with 'Dora-Nines'. In addition the *sturmgruppen*, previously formed to counter the American daylight raids, were brought home and strengthened; to Hauptmann Wilhelm Moritz's IV(Sturm)/JG 3 were added *sturmgruppen* of JG 1 and JG 4.

By mid-October 1944 the air defence of Germany itself had grown to a total of 17 *nachtjagdgruppen* (476 aircraft, mostly Bf 110s, Ju 88Gs and He 219s) and 26 day *reichs-verteidigunggruppen* (613 Bf 109G and Fw 190A and D aircraft, plus a small number of Me 163 rocket fighters and Me 262 Schwalbe jets).

Above: a USAAF Martin B-26 Marauder engulfed by flame after a direct hit by flak during an attack on German front-line communications. Disrupting German supplies, reinforcements and communications was an essential but costly part of the Allied air offensive. Right: the remains of Junkers Ju 188s in a hangar at Leipzig-Mochau aerodrome after a raid by the USAAF

Mounting Allied losses

That the pilots of these fighters fought with skill and bravery is evidenced by the mounting Allied losses suffered in the course of one month's operations over Germany itself during the late autumn of 1944. By night the RAF suffered the loss of 570 heavy bombers and 312 other aircraft (a total of 3,216 trained aircrew), while the Eighth US Air Force lost 416 Boeing B-17s and 211 Consolidated B-24s (about 6,200 aircrew) and more than 180 fighters in the same period. Of the RAF losses an estimated 85 per cent fell to fighters and the remainder to flak; about 35 per cent of the American aircraft lost were victims of ground fire.

By comparison the losses of just nine *jagdgruppen* (JG 26, JG 27, III/JG 3 and IV/JG 54) during the latter half of December, flying Fw 190A-8, D-9 and Bf 109G-14 fighters, amounted to 103 pilots killed out of an established strength of about 300. German aircraft losses were said to be about 400 in the same period. Among those highly experienced Luftwaffe men shot down were Heinz Strüning and Paul Brandt–killed on 24 December by RAF fighters–and the great Walter Nowotny, commanding the first operational Me 262 jet fighter unit, who was killed during landing at Achmer on 8 November after combat with American bombers. Robert Weiss, who was in command of III/JG 54, was shot down and killed by Spitfires near Lingen on 29 December. These were the men on whom any hope of resistance in the air depended; all were highly experienced, highly decorated and demonstrably brave. Above all, they were respected as gifted leaders among the fledgling pilots being rushed to operational units in the hour of Germany's greatest peril.

While the Allies sought to crush German resistance by sheer weight of numbers and by persistent round-the-clock raids from the battlefronts all the way back to the hinterland of Germany, the Luftwaffe introduced new equipment and desperate tactics. The new long-nose Fw 190D-9 was at least a match for the RAF's Hawker Tempest and the USAAF's North American P-51D Mustang, while the Me 262 was clearly superior to both. The numerical odds were stacked heavily against the Germans, however, and while the Allied pilots operated from the comparative safety of airfields covered by strong fighter patrols, the Luftwaffe's airfields were constantly strafed by roving Republic P-47s, P-51s and Tempests whose pilots frequently pounced on the enemy fighters as they returned to base low on fuel and ammunition. Even when dispersed to such sites as the highways, or *auto-bahnen*, the German fighters were quickly spotted and mercilessly destroyed.

After Nowotny had been killed, the survivors of his unit were assembled into a regular *jagdgeschwader* designated JG 7, command of its I Gruppe being given to Theodor Weissenberger and the II Gruppe to Erich Rudörffer, the former assuming command of the whole Geschwader in January 1945. Command of JG 3 was given to Werner Schroer, JG 54 to Dietrich Hrabak, JG 104 to Reinhard Seiler and JG 10 Parchim to Georg Christl, while Anton Hackl took command of the Wild Boar unit, JG 300, during February until March when he became *kommodore* of the newly-formed JG 11.

It was on 1 January 1945 that the Luftwaffe staged its dramatic but forlorn attempt to wrest air superiority from the Allies. At dawn that day more than 800 German fighters and fighter-bombers attacked Allied airfields throughout Belgium and Holland in a series of co-ordinated low level strikes, guided along their prescribed routes by twin-engined aircraft such as the Junkers Ju

Above and top: two views of the aftermath of an RAF Bomber Command raid in the vicinity of Cologne in November 1943. The Royal Air Force's area bombing by night sought to destroy centres of industry and population, while the USAAF's day bombers attacked specific targets

88, Bf 110 and Messerschmitt Me 410. Great secrecy had been achieved by the Luftwaffe in the assembly of this force and there is no doubt that many Allied airfields were caught off-guard and considerable damage was done. The loss by the RAF of 149 aircraft destroyed and scores more by the Americans were, however, but a minor setback to the Allied air forces. The Luftwaffe, on the other hand, lost more than 200 aircraft and pilots, men who would otherwise have sold their lives dearly in the defence of their country. Many of them were certainly inexperienced, but others were irreplaceable–men like Oberstleutnant Günther Specht, commanding JG 11, who was shot down by flak near Brussels and Hauptmann Horst-Günther von Fassong, commanding JG 11's III Gruppe, shot down by American P-47s near Maastricht. Operation Bodenplatte, the Luftwaffe's folly of New Year's Day, was not only forlorn but proved disastrous to the long term Defence of the Reich.

There seemed little left to stem the inexorable advances by the Allies from west and east and the year 1945 commenced; the Ardennes offensive had crumbled and Bodenplatte had failed to blunt the Allied tactical strength. A deluge of bombs threatened to lay waste to German cities and, born of desperation, the Luftwaffe now threw its last reserves into the air battle. The indomitable Hajo

Herrmann, previously Inspector of Aerial Defence, a veteran bomber pilot of great distinction and originator of the radical Wild Boar night fighting tactics, now advocated the creation of a unit whose pilots would ram American bombers–named Rammkommando Elbe. Flying the Bf 109G, the pilots were mostly young student airmen, but it was never specifically intended that their tactics would be suicidal as such, it being deemed entirely practical to bale out before impact with the enemy bomber.

Only one massed ramming sortie was ever carried out by Rammkommando Elbe. On 7 April 1945 120 pilots took off to attack American bombers over Germany, their flight path being protected by Me 262 jets and marked by VHF beacons. The escorting American P-51s, however, evaded the jet fighters and shot down 59 of the Bf 109s. Only eight of the 18 American bombers brought down that day are known to have fallen to ramming tactics, while only 15 Rammkommando Elbe pilots returned to base. Employing more conventional tactics some German pilots had already amassed impressive scores of American heavy bombers shot down, the most successful of whom was probably Oberleutnant Herbert Rollwege with a personal tally of 44.

While strenuous efforts were being made to introduce more Me 262 fighters into front-line service (and the creation of Jagdverband 44, an assembly of crack pilots led by Galland, to fly the Me 262), the great bulk of responsibility for the Defence of the Reich continued for a time to be shouldered by the piston-engined Bf 109G and K and the Focke Wulf Fw 190D. These aircraft were identifiable during those last few months by broad coloured bands painted round their rear fuselages. Efforts to introduce the Heinkel He 162 jet fighter into service failed and, although mass production of this aircraft was in full swing at the end of the war in Europe, only I Gruppe, Jagdgeschwader 1, commanded by Oberleutnant Demuth, became operational with the He 162; it is not believed to have seen combat, however. When the Allies captured Leck, JG 1's base, they found 50 He 162 Salamanders neatly lined up on the airfield.

Crippling fuel shortage

The *reichsverteidigunggeschwader* were finally defeated by the Allied air forces, not in the air but rendered impotent on the ground through starvation of fuel. Constant attacks on Germany's synthetic fuel plants brought about

a catastrophic shortage of aviation fuel. Symptomatic of this disaster was the example of Major Gerhard Barkhorn's JG 6, based at Sorau which, with a healthy establishment of pilots and 150 brand-new Fw 190D-9 fighters from the nearby Focke Wulf factory, was unable to fly patrols of more than four aircraft at a time owing to a lack of fuel on the base. When small groups of aircraft did get airborne they were all too often 'jumped' by Allied fighters. Many great pilots who, when the odds had been more even, had acquitted themselves with distinction, were lost in Germany's final maelstrom.

The reality of the situation dawned on men like Galland when it was decided to divert most of the remaining fuel stocks to the Me 262 units, thereby starving the Bf 109s and Fw 190s. At the beginning of May 1945 all JG 7's surviving Me 262s joined JV 44 at Salzburg-Maxglam where almost 100 such aircraft were assembled. But now the 'old hands' had gone; Galland himself had been wounded and the survivors surrendered on 3 May. The organised defence of Germany was at an end.

Below: von Ribbentrop's Foreign Ministry buildings in Berlin in ruins after raids on the 'Big City' by US Eighth Air Force daylight bombers. Between August 1940 and April 1945 80,000 tons of bombs were dropped on Berlin. Lower: surrendered Junkers Ju 88s parked on Flensburg airfield await dismantling by the Allies after the collapse of the Third Reich. Starved of fuel, hundreds of Luftwaffe aircraft remained on the ground during the final phases of World War II in Europe

Above: a flight of North American P-51D Mustangs of the 375th Fighter Squadron, 361st Fighter Group pictured on an escort mission. The P-51 was primarily responsible for winning air superiority over Germany.
Left: a Handley Page Halifax B Mk III of RAF Bomber Command pictured over the target area in a daylight raid on a synthetic oil plant at Wanne-Eichel, the Ruhr. The Allied bombing offensive against German oil production was the main factor in causing the collapse of effective German resistance by starving the Luftwaffe and army of fuel

Berlin Airlift 1948-49

The first time that a complete military force was kept supplied by air communications alone was in 1944 during the Burma campaign when a whole division of the 'forgotten' army in the Arakan, cut off from all surface supply routes, had to rely totally on air support to fight off powerful Japanese assaults and did so for several weeks until relieved by other forces. Four years later one of the largest-scale airborne aid operations in aviation history came into effect. The Berlin Airlift, which took place over a 17-month period from 1948, was initiated to prevent the city of Berlin from falling into Russian hands after the USSR imposed a blockade on all supplies entering the city from the West by surface transport routes.

Although a complete Soviet blockade did not begin until 24 June 1948, as early as January of that year the Russians were harassing communications and travellers between the Soviet zone of the city and the other three sectors which were controlled (as a result of the agreement between the four powers) by the United States, Britain and France.

The situation had worsened considerably by the end of March and the United States authorities had been given an ultimatum by the USSR that they should submit all military shipments entering Berlin to Soviet investigation. The Americans refused to be browbeaten in this manner and defied the Russians for 11 days from 1 April by flying nearly 330 tons of supplies into the city. However, Soviet tactics continued to hinder the daily flow of around 12,000 tons of supplies which, under normal conditions, would have been sent into Berlin from the western zones of Germany by rail, road and waterway. By this time the British were seriously having to consider contingency plans in case the Russians introduced a complete surface blockade. By the middle of June that fear had been almost totally confirmed as waterborne transport was almost nil, the railways had ceased to operate and road transport had thinned out to just one route which entailed the use of a hand-operated ferry across the River Elbe.

The RAF joins operations

On 19 June 1948, five days before the total Russian obstruction of ground-transported supplies came into effect, the BAFO (British Air Forces of Occupation) began to organise the first of the British code-named airlift operations. Called Operation Knicker, it began in earnest on 28 June with 13 Douglas Dakotas from RAF Transport Command delivering around 44 tons of food over a 24-hour period to the 2¼-million citizens of Berlin.

Short Sunderland flying boats operating from the River Elbe to the Havel Lake carried over 4,800 tons of freight between July and December 1948, their loads including vital supplies of salt

Right: the fleet of Douglas C-47s, operational from the beginning of the Airlift, numbered 105 by July. The aircraft was withdrawn in September in favour of the more efficient C-54 Skymaster and the Fairchild C-82 Packet.
Below right: German civilians disembarking from a Douglas Dakota. The RAF evacuated 50,000 people, most of them children, on their return flights from Berlin to western Germany

Six days previously, on 22 June, the United States Air Force (Europe) had begun to fly in supplies to US personnel in the city.

On the day following their absolute ban on communications between Berlin and the West, the Russians then declared that they would not supply any food to West Berlin and food therefore became the immediate priority for the airlift forces. The official date for the start of the Berlin Airlift was 26 June and the daily tonnage of supplies entering the city by air planned to be a minimum of 4,500. Four days later the British effort had swelled to include more aircraft and crews brought in from British stations around the world and Operation Knicker was renamed Operation Carter Paterson.

The first day of July saw 54 Dakotas from 38 and 46 Groups and 40 Avro Yorks from 47 Group arrive in Germany as well as a fair number of civil aircraft, many of which were converted bombers. Also included in the RAF operation were Sunderland flying boats acquired from Coastal Command, which flew from the River Elbe near Hamburg to the Havel Lake near the British-controlled airfield at Gatow. Meanwhile the Americans were successfully running the US Airlift Task Force and soon both the British and American operations were renamed Plainfare and Vittles respectively.

Air traffic congestion
Three air corridors, each 20 miles wide and with a ceiling of up to 3050m (10,000 feet), led from Frankfurt in the south (US zone), Hannover in central Germany and Hamburg in the north (British zone) to airfields in the British, American and French sectors of the city. Along these overcrowded corridors flew an ever-increasing number of both military and civil transport aircraft and when the airlift was in full swing there was understandably a good deal of congestion at all operational airports, with take-offs and landings at Gatow, for example, every couple of minutes. Work went on round the clock unloading supplies from fully loaded and occasionally overloaded aircraft. Emergency lighting equipment was brought into use to facilitate easier night working and runways were extended to cope with aeroplanes and tonnages of cargo for which they had not been designed.

Although the British effort was nothing short of magnificent, it was the USAF which carried the greater amount of cargo because it possessed a considerably larger fleet of transport aircraft. As against the RAF's

quency of movements at the airfields. Less than 70 people were killed as a direct result of the airlift; the US forces lost 28 lives in 11 fatal crashes, the British forces had 25 fatalities in five crashes, five people were killed in ground accidents, plus some German personnel fatalities.

Operational airfields in the British zone of West Germany included the following: Fassberg, which was utilised by the RAF for Plainfare in July 1948 and later given over to the USAF, had a 1830 m (6,000 ft) concrete runway; Schleswigland, an ex-Luftwaffe fighter base with a 2010 m (6,600 ft) runway; Celle, formerly used by the Luftwaffe, which started with a pierced steel planking (PSP) runway and was rebuilt with a 1650 m (5,400 ft) concrete runway and had the additional facility of about 51250 m² (61,450 sq yd) of hard-standing area; Lübeck, a former Ju-88 night fighter station with a concrete runway of 1830 m (6,000 ft); Wunstorf, which was used by RAF fighters until 1948, when June of that year brought the arrival of the airlift Dakotas and where there were two 1830 m (6,000 ft) runways; Fühlsbuttel, Hamburg's civil

Dakotas, Yorks and Sunderlands, the USAF operated Douglas Dakota C-47s and C-54s and by September 1948 the C-47s were withdrawn to give prominence to the more efficient C-54 Skymaster and some Fairchild C-82 Packets. The US Navy also contributed to the effort, and between November 1948 and July 1949 its transport squadrons VR-6 and VR-8 airlifted nearly 130,000 tons. Reinforcements for the US Navy squadrons came from the Pacific and those for the USAF Task Force from areas like Alaska, Hawaii, Guam, Japan and Panama.

British-operated aircraft were frequently responsible for carrying the more awkward cargoes which took longer to manoeuvre and it was British civil aircraft which eventually carried all the liquid fuel – the first such delivery being made by a Lancastrian of Flight Refuelling which flew into Berlin on 27 July 1948 from its base at Tarrant Rushton, in Dorset, with a load of motor transport (MT) fuel. The liquid fuel carriers included 17 Haltons, 14 Lancastrians, seven Tudors and two Liberators.

On 15 October the Air Force of Britain and the United States joined up to form the Combined Air Lift Task Force (CALTF) which had an American, Major-General Tunner, as its supreme commander and an RAF officer, Air Commodore John Merer, as deputy commander. Air Commodore Merer was also commander of the RAF's Plainfare operation which carried a variety of cargoes including coal (which accounted for the highest tonnage), generators for power-stations, newsprint, food, clothing, main and oil. In order to save time after landing at one of the busy airports, crews would often radio ahead to inform those on the ground of the exact nature of the cargo they were carrying so that facilities and specialised unloading equipment could be made ready in advance for speedy handling.

Commonwealth participation

The RAF was backed up by crews from a Royal Australian Air Force squadron, a Royal New Zealand Air Force group and a squadron from the South African Air Force. The hard-working Dakotas and Yorks carried a total of over 26,400 tons during the operation while the Sunderland flying boats were only able to operate from July until December 1948 when the weather conditions worsened and the Havel Lake iced up. The RAF also operated the Handley Page Hastings, which joined the airlift in November 1948. The accident rate connected with airlift operations was not high considering the complexity and fre-

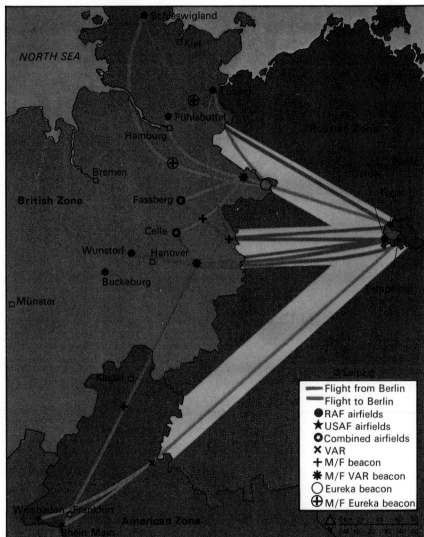

A map showing flight paths and airfields used during the Berlin Airlift, which began on 26 June 1948 and continued for 17 months. The airlift cost a total of $224,000,000 and over two million tons were airlifted into Berlin

airport and the last airfield to be acquired for airlift use (a 1830 m [6,000 ft] runway was completed by December 1948); and finally Finkenwerder, the flying-boat base on the River Elbe near Hamburg, where the conditions were not good enough to permit flying outside daylight hours.

Airfield development

One of the most famous West Berlin airlift airfields was Gatow in the British sector, close to the Havel Lake, which

Above: the US Navy Air Transport Squadron VR6 at Rhein/Main flew R5D Skymasters during the Airlift and are pictured above in the crew room on the day that the blockade was lifted. Below: seven squadrons of Yorks took part in the Airlift, flying nearly 230,000 tons of supplies to the city–about half of the RAF's total contribution

had a concrete runway extended to 1830m (6,000ft) and a PSP runway extended to the same length. Eight large underground tanks were used for storing liquid fuel discharged from incoming tanker aircraft and there was an unloading apron of about 7250m (8,670sq yd). The biggest and most important airfield used during the whole airlift operation was that at Rhein/Main near Frankfurt in the American zone. A former Luftwaffe base, it was once badly damaged by allied bombs but with a runway of 1830m (6,000ft) plus a brand new one of 2130m (7,000ft), it saw many departures of USAF aircraft on the direct run north to Berlin. One of the first bases to be pressed into airlift service by the USAF was Wiesbaden, the main Luftwaffe fighter station during the war, with a 1680m (5,500ft) runway. Wiesbaden's runway was later extended to 2130m (7,000ft).

The main US airfield in West Berlin was Tempelhof, which also served as the city's main airport. It was well endowed with facilities, including two parallel runways (constructed during the airlift) of 1750m (5,750ft) and 1875m (6,150ft) plus a 1520m (5,000ft) PSP runway, and a seven-storey underground administration and operations headquarters which, during the war, had been used as both a hospital and an aircraft factory. Tempelhof, however, had a hazard as regards airlift flying and this was a difficult approach due to the presence of high buildings nearby. When the traffic through Tempelhof

increased so much that another airport became necessary, the Americans set to work and within three months had cleared away a large wooded area at Tegel in the French sector and built a completely new airfield. Intended to receive parachute-dropped supplies, the Tegel base had a 1680m (5,500ft) runway completed in August 1948 and the airfield was operational by December of that year.

Many humorous stories and anecdotes have circulated around the activities connected with the airlift and a rather well-known one which shows the camaraderie between the British and US personnel is that of the American pilot who spotted a Bristol Wayfarer in the Hamburgh air corridor and radioed Gatow to find out what the ancient-looking contraption was. Told it was a Wayfarer, he misheard and jokingly suggested that by bringing in the *Mayflower* the British were well and truly throwing everything they had into the effort!

Total deliveries by the USAF amounted to 1,783,572·7 tons flown into Berlin between June 1948 and September 1949 with more than 500,000 flying hours; the RAF delivered 394,509·0 tons and 147,727·0 tons were carried by civil aircraft. Total tonnage amounted to 2,325,808·7.

Blockade lifted

The Berlin Airlift was remarkable in many ways, not least for the tremendous resolve, determination and energy shown by the British and Americans in delivering, at the operation's height, an average of 5,000 tons daily during the gruelling winter of 1948–49 which the Russians thought had doomed the whole exercise to failure. The development of radar scanning made considerable advances during the airlift and by the time the operation came to an end in October 1949 (the Russian blockade was lifted on 12 May 1949) much more was known about the use of radar for such purposes.

However, deficiencies also came to light, one of which, on the British side, was the fact that the UK aircraft industry had concentrated heavily during the war years on the production of bomber and fighter aircraft to the exclusion of transport aeroplanes. The US aircraft companies, however, had steadily manufactured long-range transports and were able to bridge the gap successfully when the occasion demanded. The US transport fleet, as demonstrated by the C-54 Skymaster, was able to carry standardised loads more easily, thus streamlining the US side of the lift by a fair margin. It is hardly surprising, therefore, that the variety and diversity of the aircraft employed in the British effort gave rise to comments like the friendly 'Mayflower' quip.

Korean War 1950-53

When Communist forces poured across the 38th Parallel into South Korea on 25 June 1950 they met with little opposition. The lightly-armed South Korean troops were quickly swept aside and the North Koreans pushed on towards the South's capital, Seoul.

The American airmen of the USAF's Fifth Air Force based in Japan were as unprepared for operations as their Korean allies. Three of the Fifth Air Force's units were armed with the Lockheed F-80C Shooting Star jet fighter –the 35th Fighter Interceptor Wing, the 8th Fighter Bomber Wing and the 49th Fighter-Bomber Wing. Also based in Japan were two all-weather fighter squadrons equipped with North American F-82 Twin Mustang fighters and two light bomber squadrons flying Douglas B-26 Invaders. The Fifth Air Force's order of battle was completed by a squadron of Lockheed RF-80A photographic reconnaissance jets and a troop carrier wing comprising two squadrons of Douglas C-54 transports. South Korea had no combat aircraft at the time.

First combats

The USAF's first task was to airlift American citizens from Seoul and to provide fighter cover for this operation and for a Norwegian merchantman which was evacuating refugees by sea. At noon on 27 June patrolling F-82s encountered North Korean Lavochkin La-7 and Yakovlev Yak-9 fighters and sent three of them flaming down. The distinction of destroying the first enemy aircraft of the conflict went to 1st Lt William 'Skeeter' Hudson and 1st Lt Charles 'Chalky' Moran of the 68th All-Weather Fighter Squadron and Major James Little of the 339th All-Weather Squadron. In the afternoon of the same day the American jets had their first combat, when F-80s from the 8th Fighter Bomber Group 'bounced' eight Ilyushin Il-10 ground-attack aircraft, destroying four of them and putting the remainder to flight.

On 28 June the Fifth Air Force went over to the offensive. General Douglas MacArthur, the overall commander of the United Nations forces opposed to the North Korean invasion, decided that the only chance of halting the Communist offensive in time for ground reinforcements to arrive was by launching air attacks against the advancing enemy. Accordingly B-26s went into action with bombs, rockets and machine-gun fire, to be joined later on the 28th by F-80s and F-82s. Towards the end of the day Boeing B-29 Superfortresses from Guam unloaded their bomb-loads onto road and rail targets north of Seoul.

The USAF's ground attack sorties assumed increasing importance during the days that followed, yet an even more significant target was the North Korean air force, which had made its presence felt in attacks on airfields in the South. MacArthur accordingly authorised the commander of Far East Air Forces, Lt Gen George Stratemeyer to attack airfields in North Korea. The first such attack was launched by B-26s of the 3rd Bombardment Group against Pyongyang on the afternoon of 29 June. It was estimated that the raid destroyed 25 enemy aircraft on the ground and the only North Korean fighter to intercept the raid, a Yak-3, fell to the guns of one of the raiders.

The situation on the ground grew progressively worse. The South Korean defences along the Han river were breached on 30 June and President Harry Truman decided to commit American ground forces to the defence of Korea's southernmost port at Pusan. The following day, the aircraft of the 374th Transport Wing began to fly troops of the US Army's 24th Infantry Division into Pusan. The operation was hampered by bad weather and by the poor state of repair of Pusan's runway, which was soon unable to operate the four-engined Douglas C-54 transports.

On 27 June the United Nations Security Council passed a resolution recommending that member nations provide South Korea with aid 'to repel the invasion and restore international peace and security within the area'. Although the bulk of this assistance was to come from the United States, other nations provided combat forces for service in Korea. The Royal Australian Air Force's No 77 Squadron, flying North American P-51 Mustangs, was in action in July. The unit later converted to Gloster Meteor jet fighters, with which it flew ground attack sorties and air combat missions. South Africa assigned No 2 Squadron to Korea, initially flying P-51s and later progressing to North American F-86F Sabre jets. Britain's main contribution to the air war was the Fleet Air Arm's carrier-based Hawker Sea Furies and Fairey Fireflies, which flew from HMS *Glory*, HMS *Ocean*, HMS *Theseus* and HMS *Triumph* in strikes against shore targets.

A Lockheed F-80 Shooting Star pulls away from a ground target which it has just attacked. F-80s began operations over Korea from bases in Japan, mainly in the tactical ground attack role. Air power was a critical factor in the Korean conflict. The Chinese defeat on the ground was largely attributable to their failure to appreciate the necessity of gaining air superiority

Carrier strikes

Throughout July the United Nation's tactical aircraft kept the fast-advancing North Korean forces under air attack. Most of these sorties were flown by F-80s, armed with machine guns, rockets and bombs, and the type proved to be highly-effective in this role. However, the jet fighter's one shortcoming was its inadequate endurance, for, when operating from Japanese bases, the F-80 could only remain over the target for some 15 minutes. This problem was partially solved by the improvisation of larger-capacity wingtip fuel tanks for the Shooting Stars. The piston-engined P-51 and B-26 also proved their worth and over 140 Mustangs were withdrawn from Air National Guard units in the United States and shipped out to Korea.

As the crucial battle for Pusan approached, land-based aircraft were joined by naval Vought F4U Corsairs and Douglas AD Skyraiders, flying from USS *Valley Forge* in the Yellow Sea. The naval fighters and attack aircraft took Communist airfields as their primary target and by the end of July (by which time USS *Valley Forge* had been joined by HMS *Triumph* from Hong Kong) the North Korean air arm had been virtually eliminated as an effective fighting force.

Although air strikes had done much to hamper the advance of the North Koreans, air power alone could not halt them. By the beginning of August the ground battle for the remaining South Korean port of Pusan was under-way. The air commanders then turned their thoughts to providing effective close air support for the troops in combat. Naval aircraft and fighter-bombers of the USAF's Fifth Air Force were directed over the battlefield by controllers flying in Stinson L-5s. These radio-equipped light observation aeroplanes, codenamed Mosquitoes, proved to be highly vulnerable to hostile ground fire and they were soon replaced with the faster American T-6.

Among the troop reinforcements which reached Pusan was the 1st Provisional Brigade of the US Marine Corps, which was accompanied by its own air support element, Marine Air Group 33. Two Corsair-equipped squadrons, VMF-214 and VMF-323, flying from the escort carriers USS *Sicily* and USS *Badoeng Strait*, undertook close air support for the Marines, while a Marine night-fighter squadron (VMF(N)-513), also flying Corsairs, flew night intruder sorties from Japan.

United Nations counter-attack

So critical was the fighting around Pusan in mid-August that the B-29 strategic bombers were thrown into the fray. A saturation attack by 98 B-29s on the area in which 40,000 enemy troops were reported to be concentrated was mounted on 16 August. The bomb-load dropped was equivalent in blast effect to a barrage of 30,000 heavy artillery shells, yet reconnaissance shortly after the attack could find no evidence of any enemy casualties. However, the B-29s were put to better use in an interdiction campaign against Communist supply routes further to the north, the principal targets being railway marshalling yards and bridges. Below the 38th Parallel, road and rail targets were attacked by the Fifth Air Force both by day and by night in an attempt to isolate the battlefield from North Korean supply centres.

By the first week in September, the North Korean offensive against Pusan had exhausted itself and the United Nations forces were ready to counter-attack. The breakout from the Pusan perimeter came on 19 September, assisted by fighter-bomber attacks and by a second B-29 raid, which on this occasion succeeded in finding an enemy troop concentration for its bombs. However,

indications of the rapid build-up of Chinese Communist forces necessitated rapid exploitation of the United Nations newly-won ascendency, if intervention by the Chinese was to be forestalled. MacArthur accordingly launched a daring amphibious assault on Inchon, with the South Korean capital at Seoul as its ultimate objective.

Within a week of the breakout from Pusan, the North Korean army was virtually annihilated. The fighter-bombers of the Fifth Air Force alone accounted for some 8,000 enemy troops in five days. As South Korean airfields were reoccupied, they were hastily repaired to receive the fighter-bomber units from Japan. The United Nations forces were then poised for the invasion of North Korea, which Communist intransigence made inevitable.

MiGs against Sabres

The advance into North Korea encountered no serious opposition in its early stages. An airborne assault on the northern approaches to Pyongyang was carried out by paratroops of the 187th Airborne Regimental Combat Team, dropping from Fairchild C-119s and Douglas C-47s of the Far East Air Force's Combat Cargo Command. Not until they approached the Yalu River, which divided North Korea from China, did United Nations forces come up against a determined opponent and it then soon became apparent that Communist China had entered the war.

American aircraft were forbidden to enter Chinese airspace and consequently their primary targets became the bridges over the Yalu over which all Chinese reinforcements must pass. As enemy fighters could no longer be attacked on their airfields, Communist air opposition again became a force to be reckoned with. Furthermore, the swept-wing MiG-15 jet fighter now made its operational debut, opposed to the technically inferior F-80. Yet in the first battle between two jets in the history of air warfare it was the F-80 which emerged as victor. The encounter took place on 7 November, and Lt Russell J. Brown of the 51st Fighter Interceptor Wing was the successful pilot.

It was not until 27 November 1950, when General Lin Piao flung his 18 divisions into battle, that the full impact of Chinese intervention was felt. The United Nations forces quickly broke under this sledgehammer blow and streamed southwards in a disorganised retreat. As in the opening phase of the war, the United Nations' air forces were the only means of slowing the enemy's headlong advance to enable ground defences to be organised.

The USAF wasted little time in providing the Communist MiG-15 with a worthy opponent. On 8 November the 4th Fighter Interceptor Wing, equipped with North American F-86A Sabres, was alerted for overseas duty. Within a week the aircraft were embarked on aircraft carriers for shipment from the United States to the theatre of war. On 17 December, four Sabres of the 4th Wing's 336th Fighter Interceptor Squadron took off from their Korean base at Kimpo and flew north. Approaching the Yalu, four MiG-15s were sighted and combat joined. The first of more than 790 MiG-15s to fall to the Sabre's guns went down under the fire of Lt Col Bruce Hinton. Five days later the first Sabre was lost, yet by the end of the month eight Communist fighters had been claimed as destroyed.

Ground attack sorties

The Chinese advance on the ground was also feeling the effects of American air power. The Far East Air Force estimated that by mid-December the enemy had lost 33,000 troops to air attack. Whatever the accuracy of this

Right: the Boeing B-29 was employed against a variety of targets over Korea, notably bases, communications and, latterly, strategic targets. With the advent of the MiG-15 the B-29 loss rate soared and the type was compelled to operate with heavy fighter escorts. Below: Vought F4U-4B Corsairs warm up aboard USS Philippine Sea (CV-47) before a strike on Korea in October 1950. Naval air power was of great importance to the United Nations forces throughout the war

figure, it is certain that at this time the Chinese changed their tactics—moving by night and lying-up in camouflaged positions during the daytime. The USAF countered by launching B-29 attacks against areas suspected of harbouring enemy troops.

Still further Chinese losses to air attack resulted from the New Year's offensive, which forced the United Nations forces to evacuate Seoul and led to the withdrawal of the 4th Fighter Interceptor Wing's Sabres to Japan. During the first five days of January 1951 the Fifth Air Force mounted 2,596 sorties against the advancing Chinese infantry. At night the harassment continued, as B-26s struck at enemy columns illuminated by flares dropped from patrolling C-47s. At the end of three weeks Chinese casualties were put at 38,000, air attack accounting for about half of the total, and by the end of January the enemy advance ground to a halt and the front stabilised south of Suwon and Wonju.

The Chinese air force had been conspicuous by its absence during the New Year offensive. Only the MiG-15s could hope to survive in the American-dominated airspace over the battlefield. Yet when operating from their sanctuary airfields in Manchuria (United Nations aircraft being forbidden to penetrate Chinese territory), the Communist jets had insufficient range to intervene in the ground fighting. However, by the end of January the MiGs were again harrying American fighter-bombers on interdiction missions over north-west Korea—an area soon to be christened 'MiG Alley'.

Right: a Fairchild C-119 transport drops ammunition to United Nations forces. Below: the Lockheed F-80 was superior to the early Russian types it met over Korea, but was inferior to the MiG-15 introduced in November 1950. The F-80 was used for tactical support duties whereas the Communists used the MiG-15 as an air superiority fighter to oppose the United Nations' tactical air operations

A United Nations ground offensive in February reoccupied Seoul, but it would be some time before the recaptured airfields there and at Suwon and Kimpo would be able to handle the USAF's Sabres. Meanwhile, a squadron of the 4th Fighter Interceptor Wing moved back to Korea, operating from Taegu, whence they could patrol as far north as Pyongyang, but not into MiG Alley. It was nevertheless decided to launch B-29 attacks in the area, escorted by F-80s. The first such mission narrowly avoided disaster, when the American bombers missed the rendezvous with their escort and where intercepted by nine MiG-15s. Ten B-29s were damaged, although all of them regained friendly territory.

First jet ace
By the second week in March the Sabres were able to rejoin the air battles in the north west, operating from a patched-up and barely adequate runway at Suwon. B-29 attacks against bridge, railway and airfield targets in MiG Alley continued and the Chinese fighters put up a

MiG-15 of the North Korean Air Force

Lockheed F-80C Shooting Star of the 51st Fighter Interceptor Wing, USAF

stiff fight against these incursions. On 12 April some 70 MiGs intercepted a B-29 force *en route* for Sinuiju. Close escort was provided by Republic F-84 Thunderjets of the 27th Fighter Escort Wing, which claimed three of the attackers as probably destroyed. The 4th Wing's Sabres, flying top cover, had better success and accounted for four MiG-15s destroyed and six damaged. Yet three B-29s had been destroyed and five badly damaged; an unacceptable loss rate that resulted in the B-29 attacks being suspended.

The aggressive and skilful tactics of the Communist fighter pilots was countered by the USAF sending out small patrols of Sabres, backed up by following flights, which could be called into action to support the first flight when it was attacked. The effectiveness of this strategem was illustrated on 20 May in a fight which produced the first jet ace of the conflict, Captain James Jabara. A flight of 12 Sabres was attacked by 50 MiGs on this occasion and they were swiftly reinforced by two more flights of Sabres, which took the Communists unawares and shot

Below: the Vought F4U Corsair was used mainly in the battlefield close-support role in Korea, operating from carriers and shore bases. Grumman F9F-2 Panthers, operating from USS Valley Forge, were the first US Navy jets used in combat, going into action over Korea on 3 July 1950. On 9 November 1950 an F9F pilot shot down a MiG-15, the Navy's first jet against jet victory

Vought F4U-4 Corsair of VMF-321, US Marine Corps

Grumman F9F-2 Panther of VF-51, US Navy

down three MiGs and damaged a further five.

In June 1951 the Communists began to mount nuisance raids by night, using the slow and antiquated Polikarpov Po-2 trainers which had proved so effective in this role on the Eastern Front in World War II. The damage inflicted by these attacks was often far from negligible, quite apart from their effect on the morale of United Nations forces. On the night of 16/17 June, for example, an attack by a Po-2 on the airfield at Suwon completely destroyed one Sabre and damaged a further eight. However, retribution was swift and US Marine Corps night fighter squadrons flying Grumman Tigercats and Vought Corsairs soon found the measure of these Bedcheck Charlies, as their victims christened the night raiders.

Operation Strangle

Although sorties against communications targets in North Korea was increasingly hampered by Communist interceptors and anti-aircraft fire during the early months of 1951, the interdiction campaign was nevertheless continued. However, with increasing losses of B-29s to the defences and the urgent need to concentrate their attacks on North Korean airfields, the responsibility for interdiction passed to the fighter-bombers of the Fifth Air Force.

At the end of May the Fifth Air Force, together with carrier-based aircraft of the US Navy and the 1st Marine Air Wing, inaugurated Operation Strangle. This offensive was intended to paralyse the enemy's road and rail systems by attacks on specially-selected choke points. Initially, the Operation worked well, yet once the initial surprise was over, the Communists responded to this threat to their communications with considerable ingenuity. Supply dumps were concealed in caves and tunnels, roads and railway tracks were quickly repaired after attacks and bombed bridges replaced, these repairs being cunningly camouflaged to discourage further attacks. Nor were defences restricted to such passive measures and in three months Communist anti-aircraft fire accounted for 81 United Nations aircraft destroyed.

United Nations pilots shot down in enemy territory benefited from the efforts of helicopter-equipped rescue squadrons. One such rescue was accomplished by Lieutenant David Daniels flying a Sikorsky H-5, who flew 145 km (90 miles) behind enemy lines to pick up a downed pilot on 10 October 1950. The rescued man was a Hawker Sea Fury pilot serving with No 807 Squadron of the Fleet Air Arm, who was able to hold off Communist troops with the help of relays of Sea Furies until help arrived. By the time the war ended, the rescue squadrons had recovered 254 United Nations airmen from behind enemy lines. Helicopters also proved useful as troop transports, for casualty evacuation and for observation.

Intense air fighting

By June 1951 it was apparent that the Communists were building up their jet fighter force in China. New airfields were being built across the Yalu and it was believed that the Chinese fighter units were being improved by an infusion of experienced Soviet pilots. Accordingly the USAF's newly-appointed commander of the Far East Air Force, General Otto P. Weyland, urgently demanded that his Sabre force be augmented and that the F-86A model be replaced by the improved F-86E.

The effects of the Communist air build-up began to be felt in September, when fighter-bombers operating in north-west Korea were frequently intercepted by marauding MiG-15s. The Fifth Air Force was forced to withdraw

its aircraft from this area, thus enabling the enemy to press ahead with airfield construction in the north-west. The implications of this programme were serious, for if the MiGs occupied the new airfields they would be able to dominate a greater area of Korean airspace than was possible when operating from Chinese bases.

The USAF's answer to this latest Communist threat was to increase the frequency of its patrols over MiG Alley and to bomb the new enemy airfields before they were ready to receive their fighters. These measures brought about some of the hardest-fought air battles of the conflict.

On 23 October eight B-29s escorted by more than 50 F-84 Thunderjets headed for the North Korean airfield at Namsi. Ahead of the formation was a defensive screen of 34 F-86 Sabres, which were intended to keep the MiGs away from the bombers. The Sabres were the first to engage the enemy when they were set upon by more than a hundred MiG-15s. While the F-86s were fighting off this formation, a second group of 50 MiGs headed for the bombers. For 20 minutes the B-29s and their Thunderjet escort were subjected to repeated attacks by fast-diving MiGs. Three bombers went down under their fire and the battered remainder regained their airfields with dead and wounded crewmen.

The long-awaited fighter reinforcements arrived in November and on 1 December the Sabre-equipped 51st Fighter Interceptor Wing, commanded by World War II ace Francis Gabreski, went into action. The first two months of 1952 saw sporadic combats between MiG and Sabre. In March the air war intensified and after eight weeks bitter fighting the USAF emerged as victors with a tally of 83 MiG-15s shot down for the loss of only six F-86s, two F-84s and a single F-80.

Railway interdiction

It was decided in December 1951 to continue the interdiction campaign as an extension of Operation Strangle, but to concentrate on the railway system. In March 1952 the tactics changed and, instead of ranging over the whole enemy railway system, the United Nations fighter-bombers concentrated on specific short stretches of track with the object of keeping them permanently out of use. Operation Saturate, as the new offensive was dubbed, succeeded in closing the railway between Sinanju and Sinuiju almost continuously between April and May, but it was found that to do so placed a heavy strain on the available fighter-bomber aircraft and their crews. Losses to enemy anti-aircraft fire were still serious, but by the end of May, Operation Saturate had resulted in 20,000 cuts in the North Korean rail network. Although supplies had not been prevented from reaching the battlefield, the enemy's lines of communication had been seriously disrupted and he had been prevented from launching a serious offensive.

While tactical bombing attacks continued, the Far East Air Force's planning staff were devising an offensive against targets of strategic importance in North Korea. It was hoped that ceasefire negotiations, which in the spring of 1952 were making little progress, would be facilitated by a convincing attack against a vital target system in North Korea. The country's hydro-electric power plants were considered to be such an objective and plans were co-ordinated between the USAF and US Navy for their destruction. Between 23 June and 27 June strikes by carrier-based bombers and the Far East Air Force's B-29s and fighter-bombers virtually obliterated the selected target system for the loss of only two aircraft.

Armistice talks dragged on through the winter of

Top left: North American F-86F Sabres of the 8th Fighter-Bomber Wing, Fifth Air Force in Korea. The F-86 achieved a kill-to-loss ratio of 14 to 1 and was the mount of all 39 USAF aces of the war. Above left: a Sikorsky H-5 operating in Korea in the casualty evacuation role. Helicopters were also used extensively to rescue aircrew brought down behind enemy lines or in the sea. Left: the Sinuiju bridge over the Yalu river on the Sino-Korean border after a raid on 18 November 1950 by the aircraft of USS Leyte (CV-32). Bridges were important targets in the campaign against Communist supply routes and communications. Below: a US Marine Corps Vought F4U Corsair pulls out after dropping napalm on a Communist position

USAF ACES IN KOREA	
Capt Joseph McConnell	16 victories
Lt Col James Jabara	15 victories
Capt Manuel Fernandez	$14\frac{1}{2}$ victories
Lt Col George Davis	14 victories
Col Royal Baker	13 victories
Maj Fredrick Blesse	10 victories
Capt Harold Fischer	10 victories
Col James Johnson	10 victories
Lt Col Vermont Garrison	10 victories
Maj Lonnie Moore	10 victories
Capt Ralph Parr	10 victories
Lt James Low	9 victories
Lt Cecil Foster	9 victories
Lt Col James Hagerstrom	$8\frac{1}{2}$ victories

1952–53 and in February North Korean industrial targets again felt the weight of the Far East Air Force's bombs. Attacks on bridges and supply routes continued unabated, but enemy air activity remained at a low level until early May. It was then noticed that the MiG-15 pilots had lost a great deal of their cunning and it was assumed that the Russian 'advisors' had been withdrawn. The Sabres notched up 56 kills during the month for the loss of only one American aircraft.

Dam attacks

In a further attempt to nudge along the tardy armistice negotiations the Far East Air Force decided to knock out the most important North Korean irrigation dams. This would not only destroy a year's supply of rice, most of which would go to the Communist armies, but local flooding would cut roads and railways. The first attack was against the Toksan dam on 13 May by Thunderjets of the 58th Fighter-Bomber Wing. The results fulfilled all expectations and other dams were added to the target list.

The final act of the war in Korea opened on 28 May when the Communists launched a final attack on the United Nations troops. It was met by ground attack sorties flown by the Fifth Air Force and the US Navy's carrier task force, as well as radar-directed attacks on enemy supply lines by the B-29s. By 20 July the attack had been held and a further 72,000 Communist troops had become casualties. On 27 July an Armistice was signed and that same day Captain Ralph Parr of the 4th Fighter Interceptor Wing shot down an Ilyushin Il-12 transport, his tenth victory and the last aircraft to be destroyed in the Korean War.

The lessons of the air fighting in Korea are difficult to assess. There is no doubt that air intervention in the ground fighting prevented the defeat of the United Nations forces on more than one occasion. Similarly, the interdiction campaign hampered the Communists's offensive operations for much of the war. In the air the United Nations forces quickly established an ascendancy, which was repeatedly challenged but was never wrested from them. Yet if these conclusions are to be applied to the context of an all-out war, two important reservations must be borne in mind. Firstly, the Communist forces were able to make use of sanctuary areas in China which were immune from air attack. Secondly, the Communists were able to concentrate forces in a manner which would invite the use of nuclear weapons in a major conflict. The Korean War thus offered many lessons in the applications of air power to a limited conventional war. Their relevance in a major European war remain problematical.

Vietnam War 1962-73

The Geneva Protocols of July 1954 divided the former French colony of Indo-China into North and South Vietnam and brought into being the autonomous nations of Laos and Cambodia. Although there was to be a gradual phase-out of French forces, the peace agreements did not affect the US Military Assistance Advisory Group (MAAG) set up in 1950 or the resupply of equipment so long as it did not exceed the mid-1954 level. The United States sponsored creation of a mutually-protective eight-nation Southeast Asia Treaty Organisation (SEATO). Within this organisation the new nations of Laos and Cambodia, as well as 'the free territory under the jurisdiction of the State of Vietnam', could be defended against Communist expansion inimical to the interests of the United States.

Meanwhile, in Saigon a new premier (and later president), Ngo Dinh Diem, proclaimed South Vietnam to be a republic, which was immediately recognised by US President Dwight D. Eisenhower. Diem's intention to create an Army of the Republic of Vietnam (ARVN) was likewise approved by the Eisenhower administration. At the time the Republic of Vietnam was founded its small air force consisted of 4,140 men and a rag-tag assortment of left-over French and American aircraft. The Vietnamese Air Force (VNAF) was then composed of one fighter squadron equipped with Grumman F8F Bearcats, two transport squadrons of Douglas C-47 Skytrains, two liaison squadrons of Cessna L-19 Bird Dogs and one Sikorsky H-19 Chickasaw squadron. French advisors

trained the VNAF until May 1957, at which time US MAAG advisors took over that responsibility.

The 1956 national unification elections called for by the Geneva Protocols were not held because South Vietnam's government, which was not a signatory, argued that the election was unfairly imposed on it and that, in any event, North Vietnam's one-party system would not allow a truly democratic choice. There followed an uneasy peace

Top: the Douglas B-26K served with USAF Special Operations Squadrons.
Above: air commandos in South East Asia.
Right: helicopter warfare became highly developed in the Vietnam conflict

until May 1959. Then, with all their own territory firmly under their control, North Vietnam's leaders pledged to reunify the country through a concentrated military effort. Thereafter, sporadic terrorist efforts in South Vietnam by local Viet Cong guerrillas would be reinforced by direct aid and supplies from North Vietnam.

Increasing USAF involvement

Initially, a transportation group of the regular North Vietnamese Army (NVA) set about reopening the elaborate World War II system of mountain and jungle paths known after the North Vietnamese leader as the Ho Chi Minh Trail. This network would eventually link North Vietnam to its troops, who were supporting local insurgents in Laos, Cambodia and South Vietnam. Ultimately, the Ho Chi Minh Trail became the essential supply link in the protracted war to consolidate Communist gains in south-east Asia.

To meet the increased Communist aggression, the United States stepped up its assistance programme to South Vietnam. In 1959 the MAAG was more than doubled–from 342 men to 685–to provide US Army Special Forces personnel to train ARVN rangers. In September 1960, the VNAF's ageing F8F Bearcat fighters were replaced by Douglas AD-6 Skyraiders. Later, 11 Sikorsky H-34 Choctaw helicopters were provided.

The Kennedy administration increased America's own counter-insurgency efforts and expanded support of the Saigon government. Consequently, the South Vietnamese army was increased, more, newer American aircraft were provided and a combat development and test centre was established in South Vietnam, devoted to learning and improving counter-insurgency tactics and techniques. The US Air Force responded with a programme of its own by setting up the 4400th Combat Crew Training Squadron at Eglin Air Force Base in Florida. By 11 October the first detachment of commando-type assault teams was on its way to Bien Hoa, South Vietnam.

Thus began a process of escalation on both sides. While the United States was expanding its advisory role–training South Vietnamese aviation, ground and naval personnel–the conflict in south-east Asia broadened. In the autumn of 1961 Viet Cong forces displayed their strength by cutting vital roads in South Vietnam, thus leading President Diem to declare a state of emergency. Additional US Air Force reconnaissance aircraft were brought into South Vietnam on a temporary basis, but it was becoming clear that South Vietnam could not depend solely on its own resources. The opening of the Ho Chi Minh Trail brought great quantities of men and *matériel* from North Vietnam, which was clearly receiving direct aid from the Soviet Union and the People's Republic of China. Moreover, the elusive Viet Cong forces could operate with relative impunity from 'safe' bases in neutral Cambodia and Laos.

The latest phase of the decades-long struggle in Indo-China was an unconventional war that demanded an unconventional response from South Vietnam's allies–principally the United States. One answer was the use of the US Army's airmobile concept, which had been under consideration since the Korean War had drawn attention to the need to deploy forces quickly in rapidly changing combat settings. While the American Air Force, Navy and Marine Corps concentrated on their strategic and tactical uses of air power, with the air cavalry the Army developed its airmobile capability to improve deployment of its own airborne troops (previously delivered only by Air Force transport aircraft).

Air advisors

One of the most unusual vessels to tie up at the seaport of Saigon was the small World War II vintage aircraft carrier USNS *Card* (ex-CVE-11), used by the US Military Sealift Command to carry 32 US Army Piasecki H-21 Workhorse helicopters to south-east Asia. In addition to the helicopters, 400 men from the 8th and the 57th Light Helicopter Transportation Companies were aboard the former escort carrier. The Army helicopters represented the first major symbol of American combat power in Vietnam and marked the beginning of a new era in Army air mobility. Less than two weeks after the troop-carrying helicopters arrived in Saigon they performed their first mission 'in country'. Known as Operation Chopper, the mission involved transporting some 1,000 South Vietnamese paratroopers into a suspected Viet Cong headquarters complex just 16km (ten miles) west of the capital. The Army helicopters caught the Communist insurgents by surprise and enabled the paratroopers to sweep in against only slight resistance. It soon became apparent, however, that there would be more to air mobility than simply transporting troops. As subsequently developed, air mobility gained the unified command it needed, specially-trained personnel, hard-hitting firepower and its own form of reconnaissance in its own element.

However, a major problem with the early American involvement in Vietnam was that, since Americans were only advisors, they could not initiate contact with the enemy. With the early helicopter operations, for example, the Americans provided the transportation and the instruction of what to do in the combat situation, but they could not lead armed assaults. Indeed, under combat conditions, American forces were specifically instructed to 'fire back only if fired upon'. As in the Korean War of a decade earlier, American forces involved in Indo-China were continually dogged by politically-motivated restrictions on their capability to prosecute the war. The political justification for such a tight rein was that conflict with either Communist China or with the Soviet Union was to be avoided.

In view of the similarity between US Army helicopter operations and the airborne assault tactics being developed by the US Marine Corps, the Marine involvement in MAAG was expanded. The move was easily accomplished, as the US Marine Corps had been involved in training Vietnamese marines since 1954 and the arrival of Marine Corps helicopters would allow for the deployment of US Army helicopters elsewhere in South Vietnam. It would also meet the growing need for a wider range of operating areas, particularly in the Mekong Delta, where Viet Cong forces endangered river traffic. In January 1962 the US Army's 93rd Light Helicopter Transportation Company was transported aboard USNS *Card* to a point 16km (10 miles) off the coast of Da Nang in the northern portion of South Vietnam. In what could be considered to be the first carrier operation of the Vietnam War, the Army helicopters flew off the flight deck of the onetime aircraft carrier and landed ashore.

Archie's Angels

Marine Corps helicopters later replaced the Army unit at Da Nang, but initially USMC aircraft were deployed farther south. Marine Medium Helicopter Squadron HMM-362 was sent in April to occupy an old Japanese-built landing field outside Soc Trang, south-west of Saigon. Located near the coast, Soc Trang had one of the few hard-surfaced runways in the area. Although HMM-362's primary complement consisted of 24 Sikorsky HUS

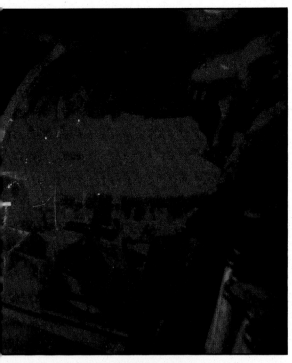

Seahorse helicopters, for this mission the squadron was also equipped with fixed-wing aircraft–three Cessna OE-1 Bird Dog observation aircraft and one Douglas R4D Skytrain. Led by Lieutenant-Colonel Archie J. Clapp, HMM-362 flew from the amphibious assault ship (helicopter carrier) USS *Princeton* (LPH-5) to Soc Trang on the morning of 15 April. The fly-off was both an efficient and inconspicuous way to deliver new *matériel* to South Vietnam. 'Archie's Angels', as the squadron was nicknamed, was soon in place to support ARVN activities in the Mekong Delta region. The unit soon proved its mobility when, on 24 April 1962, 16 USMC helicopters airlifted 591 troops of the 21st ARVN Division to eight landing zones along two canals near Can Tho, the site of a large Viet Cong staging area. During the course of the operation one HMM-362 helicopter was forced down when small arms fire punctured an oil line. An accompanying HUS helicopter retrieved the downed Marine air crew and subsequently returned with a repair crew and a security force to fend off Viet Cong forces while the helicopter was repaired. A short time later, the maintenance crew and the repaired helicopter left the combat zone, demonstrating the US Marines' ability to recover disabled aircraft in an unsecured area during hostile action.

Initially unarmed helicopters were used during military operations in Vietnam, but even though some Viet Cong

Above: leaflets cascade from a Helio U-10 used on psychological warfare sorties from Pleiku in the Central Highlands of South Vietnam.
Above left: the ageing Douglas C-47 was used in a variety of roles during the Vietnam War, the most spectacular being that of the gunship. The AC-47D was armed with three Miniguns, each firing 6,000 rounds per minute.
Left: leaflets are dropped from the cargo hatch of a C-47 over Viet Cong territory in January 1962.
Below: one of the South Vietnamese Air Force's C-47s parked at Tan Son Nhut air base

troops were using antiquated bolt-action rifles, a well-placed or lucky shot was often enough to bring down or damage a helicopter. The US Army at first armed H-21 helicopters with a light machine gun at the door to the aircraft, but that proved to be relatively ineffectual. In mid-1962 the Army's Utility Tactical Transport Helicopter Company was formed and deployed in Vietnam. The unit was equipped with Bell UH-1 Iroquois helicopters, which, when armed with 0·3-calibre machine guns and 2·75 in rocket launchers, were used to protect the larger troop-carrying helicopters. Later versions of the UH-1 were to become one of the symbols of the war: the 'Huey' gunship. Testing under combat conditions, with results analysed by a special Army Concept Team in Saigon, continued into the spring of 1963. This programme led to the improved UH-1B, which was subsequently used to escort Marine Corps as well as Army helicopters in various combat zones.

While the supply of men and *matériel* to South Vietnam gradually increased, and the methods of counter-insurgency improved, political events both inside and outside Vietnam were leading toward radical changes. A military *coup d'état* on 1 November 1963 was followed by a succession of coups and countercoups amounting to nine changes of government in South Vietnam. This eventually led to the flamboyant Air Vice-Marshal Nguyen Cao Ky establishing stable rule through a strong military government in June 1965.

aircraft from Carrier Air Wing 5 of the USS *Ticonderoga* (CVA-14) were conducting a training mission over the Gulf of Tonkin. When the destroyer radioed it was being attacked, four LTV F-8E Crusader jet fighters headed north. Half an hour later they were over USS *Maddox* and Commander R. F. Mohrhardt of Fighter Squadron VF-53 led the F-8s on a run against the enemy vessels.

Mohrhardt later reported: 'Since my section was lowest on fuel, I agreed that my section would attack the trailing PT boat, while the other would work over the lead pair. My wingman and I made our first pass and got off our Zuni missiles. Mine hit in the wake astern and his hit right in front of the PT's bow. As we "bent" around to make a strafing pass, I could see the trailing boat was now dead in the water. Numerous 20mm hits were scored on the strafing runs and, as I pulled off, I saw the boat burning and smoking heavily at the stern and the crew throwing gear and smoke lights over the side, probably to mark their position. In my opinion, our attack sank the third P-4.'

Following the unpremeditated daylight attack on USS *Maddox*, President Johnson warned the North Vietnamese that he would not tolerate infringement of American rights in international waters. He then ordered *Maddox* to be joined in the Tonkin Gulf patrol by a second destroyer, USS *Turner Joy* (DD-951), with further air cover to be provided by the aircraft of the super-carrier USS *Constellation* (CVA-64).

Above: the Lockheed C-130 Hercules was the USAF's standard tactical transport in Vietnam, airlifting troops, supplies and ammunition within the combat zone. The example illustrated is undertaking a leaflet drop in October 1969

Tonkin Gulf Incident

In the absence of decisive battlefield victories, the Vietnamese Communists constantly strove for successful demonstrations of their effectiveness. On 2 May 1964 one of their underwater demolition teams succeeded in sinking the aircraft transport vessel USNS *Card* as it was unloading helicopters in Saigon. Exactly three months later they challenged the US Navy on the high seas. During a routine patrol in the Gulf of Tonkin on 2 August 1964, the destroyer USS *Maddox* (DD-731) was at a point some 45 km (28 miles) off the coast of North Vietnam when the ship's radar showed unusual activity. Three fast moving surface contacts were closing on the ship and, although the destroyer was well into international waters, there was little doubt that it was about to be attacked.

Commander Herbert L. Ogier, the destroyers commanding officer, ordered evasive action and increased speed. The three attackers, later identified as Soviet-built P-4 torpedo boats, continued the pursuit, even after USS *Maddox* fired warning shots. Meanwhile, US Navy

While *Constellation* hastily proceeded from a scheduled stop-over in Hong Kong, the two destroyers returned to the Gulf of Tonkin on 3 August. The following night the two American ships were attacked by five North Vietnamese torpedo boats and several torpedoes were fired at USS *Turner Joy*. Neither American vessel was hit, but *Turner Joy* scored several hits on one of the enemy boats, which then disappeared from all radar screens. In spite of the bad weather that night, aircraft from USS *Ticonderoga* were soon on the scene. Two Douglas A-1 Skyraiders from Attack Squadron VA-52 dropped flares and made strafing runs on the North Vietnamese torpedo boats. The action was soon broken off with no marked success for either side, but reaction to the second incident was swift.

Following the recommendation of Admiral U. S. G. Sharp, Jnr, Commander-in-Chief, Pacific, President Johnson ordered punitive air strikes against the North Vietnamese torpedo boat bases. On 5 August, strike aircraft from *Ticonderoga* and *Constellation* hit PT boat bases in several locations, as well as two oil storage dumps at Vinh. When the raid was in progress, President Johnson announced to the American people that naval forces were making a 'measured response' to the unprovoked attack on US Navy vessels in the Gulf of Tonkin. The raid was entirely successful, but exacted a certain cost. Lieutenant (junior grade) Richard Sather, an A-1 pilot of VA-145, was shot down and killed near the PT boat base at Loc Chao. Lieutenant (junior grade) Everett Alvarez, a

Douglas A-4C Skyhawk pilot, was shot down over Hon Gai and later taken prisoner.

Less than a week later, on 10 August 1964, both houses of the US Congress passed a joint resolution condemning the 'deliberate and systematic campaign of aggression that the Communist regime in North Vietnam had been waging against its neighbours and the nations joined with them'. The resolution empowered the President to 'take all necessary measures to repel any armed attack' and to deter any further aggression. In keeping with this resolution, President Johnson planned retaliatory air strikes by American aircraft if overt acts of Communist aggression were directed at Americans. On Christmas Eve 1964, Viet Cong raiders attacked a hotel used for American officers' quarters in Saigon. On 7 February 1965, a Viet Cong heavy mortar attack was directed at US forces and facilities at Pleiku Airbase and neighbouring Camp Holloway, resulting in the death of eight Americans.

Flaming Dart

The retaliatory plan, called Operation Flaming Dart, was set in motion the same day that Pleiku and Camp Holloway were attacked. Rear Admiral H. L. Miller, Commander of Task Force 77 on station in the Gulf of Tonkin, was ordered to direct air units under his command to targets in North Vietnam. In addition to the aircraft aboard Admiral Miller's flagship, USS *Ranger* (CVA-61), two other carriers were *en route* from the Philippines. Once USS *Hancock* (CVA-19) and USS *Coral Sea* (CVA-43) rendezvoused with *Ranger*, the strike began under the airborne coordination of Commander Warren H. Sells, Commander of Carrier Air Wing 21 aboard *Hancock*. There was poor weather over the targets, but *Coral Sea* launched 20 aircraft and *Hancock* 29 to hit North Vietnamese army barracks and port facilities at Dong Hoi just north of the Demilitarised Zone separating the two Vietnams. At the same time, *Ranger* launched 34 aircraft against the Vit Thuu barracks further inland. US Air Force and VNAF aircraft were to participate in the same raid, but

Above and left: the Fairchild AC-119K gunship, which was developed as a successor to the AC-47D, was armed with four 7·62mm Miniguns, flanked with two 20mm M61 cannon. It went into action over Vietnam in 1969

Left: a USAF A-1E Skyraider drops its bomb-load onto a Viet Cong target in 1965. Nicknamed the 'Spad' by its pilots, the A-1's roles with the USAF included escorting search and rescue helicopters over enemy territory. Inset: an A-1E of the 1st Air Commando, the first USAF unit to take the Skyraider into combat, pictured in 1966

the bad weather of the monsoon season prevented the attack from being carried out.

The American retaliation prompted a further attack by the Communists. On 8 February, Viet Cong forces hit Soc Trang airfield, but inflicted no casualties. Two days later they blew up a US Army enlisted men's barracks at Qui Nhon, killing 23 Americans and seven Vietnamese, and wounding 21 other soldiers. The following day, 11 February, Operation Flaming Dart II was carried out. On orders from Washington, aircraft from the US Air Force and Navy, as well as the VNAF, hit enemy barracks at Chanh Hoa and Vit Thu Lu. Again, however, bad weather hampered the effectiveness of the raid. Because of the low cloud cover, delayed action Snakeye bombs had to be used to allow aircraft time to clear the blast area following the drop. Such low-level operations made the attacking aircraft vulnerable to even small arms fire.

Thus began a long series of raids against the North Vietnamese. The Johnson administration ordered strenuous bombing to impress the enemy with American capabilities and then held off in hopes of receiving some response to bids for peace. However, this approach did not accurately gauge the attitude of North Vietnam's leaders. When the Government in Hanoi did not respond to President Johnson's offer of negotiations, the mood in Washington changed. The administration stopped talking about withdrawing advisors and began considering plans to deploy additional US forces in south-east Asia and to step up direct pressure on North Vietnam.

However, tactical restrictions hampered the effectiveness of the air war over the north. Washington reserved the right to select targets and even chose launch times, irrespective of local weather and operational conditions. As in the Korean War, American forces were continually given limited objectives, rather than a clear strategy for a decisive military victory.

On 7 March 1965, 3,500 US Marines landed at Da Nang to begin a new phase of the war. The Americans would use their superior technology and strength to fight the Communists, while the South Vietnamese concentrated on securing their own country. By July there were 75,000 American combat troops in Vietnam and the number grew monthly until there were more than 510,000 Americans in the country in early 1968.

Bombing North Vietnam

US Air Force and Navy aircraft carried out missions against targets north of the Demilitarised Zone. These operations were called 'Rolling Thunder' raids, since, like thunder, they were to be unpredictable and violent. These raids were also supposed to gradually 'roll' northwards to the capital at Hanoi and American planners felt that the ominous approach of the raids would exert psychological pressure on the North Vietnamese and hamper their ability to funnel supplies to their comrades in the south. The political nature of the war was such, however, that the principal targets of Hanoi and Haiphong were exempted from raids except on special occasions.

As in the case of so many other phases of the war in Vietnam, 'Rolling Thunder' raids were always carried out with the strictest guidance from Washington. Navy and Air Force unit commanders were assigned targets and told the number of sorties to undertake and just what quantities of various types of ordnance to use. They were limited to a primary target or one or two alternatives and if none of them could be hit, aircraft were to dump unexpended bomb-loads. Despite the high speeds involved in these missions, aircrews were required to make positive identification before firing at enemy aircraft, to ensure they were indeed North Vietnamese.

US Air Force and Navy participation in 'Rolling Thunder' raids was coordinated by assigning each service different 'route packages', as the different geographical locations in North Vietnam were called. Elements of the Seventh Air Force generally operated from bases in South Vietnam, while Task Force 77 chose a point in the Gulf of Tonkin codenamed Yankee Station. There were usually at least two aircraft carriers detailed for operations over North Vietnam and one carrier at Dixie Station, south-east of Cam Ranh Bay, operating in the south.

At first American aircraft over North Vietnam encountered limited anti-aircraft fire, but as their raids intensified the level of Communist air defence was raised by North Vietnam's allies. On 5 April 1965 a reconnaissance RF-8 Crusader deployed aboard USS *Coral Sea* returned with the first photographic evidence of the development of surface-to-air missile (SAM) sites in North Vietnam. Within the next few months a pattern of such sites could be seen surrounding Hanoi and the principal port of Haiphong. There was considerable discussion in Washington on how to deal with the proliferation of SAM sites. On one hand there was the fear that a direct attack on the sites might result in the death of Russian civilian technicians and trigger an international incident. On the other hand it was thought that the SAM sites were for defensive purposes only and would not be a factor in the air war so long as Hanoi and Haiphong were not attacked. The question remained unresolved until 24 July, when an Air Force McDonnell F-4C Phantom was destroyed by a SAM. Three days later Washington authorised Air Force retaliatory strikes against two SAM sites north-west of Hanoi. Again, there were restrictions. The Air Force had only that one day, 28 July, to take out the SAM sites and they were forbidden to hit any air bases from which enemy aircraft might oppose them. They achieved their objective, but lost four aircraft in the process.

First MiG kills

A little over a month earlier, the US Navy felt the impact of North Vietnam's growing air defence capability. While on a mission over the north on 17 June, two F-4s from VF-21 deployed aboard USS *Midway* (CVA-41) engaged four MiG-17 aircraft. Commander L. C. Page and his radar intercept officer (RIO), Lieutenant J. C. Smith, spotted the enemy fighters on their radar. After alerting the accompanying F-4–Lieutenant J. E. D. Batson and his RIO, Lieutenant-Commander R. B. Doremus–they prepared for the encounter. The closing speed between the two American and four Vietnamese jet fighters was in the order of 1,000 knots and, as soon as the prominent identification features of the MiG-17s came into view, the two Phantoms launched Sparrow missiles. In an instant two of the oncoming MiGs exploded in clouds of orange and black smoke. The US Navy had bagged the first MiGs of the Vietnam War.

Three days later aircraft from USS *Midway* scored the third MiG kill. Four propeller-driven Douglas A-1 Skyraiders from VA-125 were flying air cover for rescue

Above: a Douglas A-1H Skyraider of VA-176 over the Vietnamese jungle. In October 1966 a pilot from this Squadron, Lieutenant (junior grade) W. T. Patton, flying from USS Intrepid (CVS-11) shot down a North Vietnamese MiG-17 fighter while in combat over North Vietnam

aircraft when two MiG-17s pounced on them. The four Skyraider pilots recognised that the jets had the advantage at altitude, so they headed for the ground. At treetop-level the agile propeller-driven aircraft twisted and turned inside the arcs of the otherwise superior jet fighters. At length, two A-1 pilots–Lieutenant C. B. Johnson and Lieutenant (junior grade) C. W. Hartman–managed to get behind the MiG that had been chasing them. They poured a steady burst of 20 mm gun fire into the MiG-17 and sent it crashing into the jungle.

The aggressive nature of the MiGs that had jumped the flight from VA-125 was indicative of North Vietnam's expanding air defence system. Once MiG bases and SAM sites had been set up to defend Hanoi and Haiphong, additional facilities were established in other locations, where they were fair game for American strikes. When two Douglas A-4E Skyhawks from VA-23 aboard USS *Midway* were lost on the night of 11/12 August, the Navy embarked on an anti-SAM campaign called Operation Iron Hand. Navy aircraft were then equipped with Shrike missiles which could identify and home in on a SAM battery's guidance radar. However, early efforts to locate the highly mobile SAM launching equipment met with little success. Further, in searching for the sites and flying low to avoid SA-2 missiles fired at them, Navy aircraft exposed themselves to conventional anti-aircraft fire. During a morning raid on 17 October, aircraft from Carrier Air Wing 7 aboard USS *Independence* (CVA-62) wiped out a SAM site near Kep airfield, north-east of Hanoi. In succeeding months Navy and Air Force aircraft expended considerable effort to identify and destroy SAM sites.

The air war over North Vietnam took on an almost conventional appearance. Aside from the use of missiles, many of the classic elements of aerial combat were present. On 10 July 1965, for example, two McDonnell F-4Cs from the 45th Tactical Fighter Squadron (Captains K. E. Holcombe and A. C. Clark in one and Captains T. S. Roberts and R. C. Anderson in the other) shot down two MiG-17s. In the south, however, new methods of aerial warfare were being developed by helicopter gunship crews.

The small and versatile Bell UH-1 helicopter had gradually progressed from a utility aircraft to a combat aircraft fitted with armour plating and machine guns. The

US Marine Corps used 'Hueys', as they were affectionately known, at their various locations and the US Navy used Seawolf variants for search and destroy as well as rescue missions launched from LST landing vessels. Certainly the most colourful use of the 'Huey' was made by the Air Cavalry of the US Army. Cavalry units *per se* have not enjoyed much use in modern warfare, in which horses are a liability, but the concept of a fast, highly-mobile and well-armed combat unit is especially applicable to helicopters and that concept was an integral part of the US Army's airmobile programme. If carried out under existing training standards, however, the programme would have called for many more pilot officers than the Army could have assimilated within its command structure. None of the US armed forces had trained enlisted pilots since World War II, so the Army took the middle ground and offered selected enlistees the rank of warrant officer if they qualified as helicopter pilots. Thus, junior commissioned officers could lead helicopter units composed largely of warrant officer pilots.

Air Cavalry in action

In mid-October, regular elements of the North Vietnamese Army assembled in western Pleiku province and nearby neutral Cambodia for a major assault of the Central Highlands of South Vietnam. In the ensuing battle, known as the Ia Drang Valley campaign, Air Cavalry units poured withering machine gun fire into the jungle and transported personnel and supplies throughout the heavy ground fighting. Lieutenant-Colonel H. G. Moore, commander of the 1st Battalion of the 7th Cavalry, later reported: 'I have the highest admiration, praise and respect for the outstanding professionalism and courage of the UH-1D pilots and crews who ran a gauntlet of enemy fire time after time to help us. They never refused to come in; they followed instructions beautifully; they were great.

We in turn called them in when fire was the lightest and tried to have everything ready for each landing to keep them on the ground a minimum time. None were shot down and destroyed, although most of them took hits. Two aircraft were brought in which did not get out. One received enemy fire in the engine and had to land in an open area just off the northern portion of the landing zone; the other clipped a few tree tops with the main rotor upon landing and had to be left. Crews of both aircraft were immediately lifted out by other helicopters. Both downed helicopters were immediately secured by ground troops until they were slung out two days later by CH-47 Chinook helicopters. During the three-day battle these were the only downed helicopters.'

Support for the ground war in South Vietnam also came from the US Air Force, which provided 96 sorties by Boeing B-52 Stratofortress aircraft and 384 tactical air strikes during the Central Highlands campaign alone. The high-altitude B-52s had a devastating psychological effect on enemy ground forces, who neither heard nor saw the aircraft that suddenly rained death and destruction.

Towards the end of 1965 the world's first nuclear-powered aircraft carrier, USS *Enterprise* (CVAN-65) arrived at Yankee Station escorted by the nuclear-powered guided missile frigate USS *Bainbridge* (DLGN-25). On 22 December, aircraft from *Enterprise* and two other carriers – USS *Ticonderoga* and USS *Kitty Hawk* (CVA-63 – were part of a force of more than 100 planes sent to knock out the Uong Bi thermal power plant north-east of Haiphong. The raid was entirely successful, but, even with the ensuing bombing halt, was not enough to move the North Vietnamese to the conference table.

President Johnson announced that bombing would cease at Christmas 1965 and that the ceasefire would continue into the new year. To the North Vietnamese, however, the 37-day respite that followed was a golden

Above: the Cessna A-37A was an adaptation of the USAF's T-37 trainer for counter-insurgency duties. It was evaluated under combat conditions in Vietnam during 1967 and it later served with the South Vietnamese Air Force.
Right: the gunner of a Bell Iroquois of US Navy Light Helicopter Attack Squadron HAL-3 on patrol near Nha Be in the Mekong Delta

opportunity to move men and *matériel* along the Ho Chi Minh Trail into Laos, Cambodia and South Vietnam. It was also a much safer period for North Vietnam's allies to resupply the Communist forces.

The 'Rolling Thunder' raids were resumed on 31 January 1966 with all of the restrictions applied to previous operations. Targets and mission strengths were determined in Washington, not in south-east Asia and a whole range of targets remained off limits – including enemy jet fighter bases. Reduced from punitive to interdiction operations, the 'Rolling Thunder' missions did not prevent the re-supply of Communist forces in South Vietnam. This was particularly evident during the Communists' successful campaign in the A Shau Valley in March. The valley was a major junction along the Ho Chi Minh Trail, from which 2,000 NVA troops easily overran the small US Army Special Forces camp nearby. Helicopters, Douglas AC-47 gunships and Douglas A-1E Skyraiders were called in to halt the enemy advance, but were able to do little more than slow it down.

During the final day of air operations, 10 March, Major D. Wayne Myers' badly-damaged Skyraider was forced to land at the base airstrip, where it subsequently crashed. As NVA troops advanced on Myers' aircraft, Major B. C. Fisher and two wingmen made a series of strafing runs to hold them back. Fisher then landed his A-1E on the rubble-strewn airstrip, taxied over to Myers, who climbed in the back of the aeroplane, and took off amid a hail of enemy gunfire as the North Vietnamese concluded their occupation of the former American position. The NVA was not wrested from the base until two years later. For Major Fisher, however, there was more than the reward of saving a comrade from an uncertain fate. He received America's highest military decoration, the Medal of Honour, and became the first airman of the Vietnam War to receive the award.

As the US Army expanded its use of helicopters, it introduced another unique element into the war, its own 'aircraft carrier'. On 12 April, the 1st Transportation Corps Battalion (Depot) (Seaborne) steamed into Cam Rahn Bay aboard the USNS *Corpus Christi Bay*. Now officially an Army ship, the floating aircraft maintenance facility had been converted from the World War II seaplane tender USS *Albermarle* (AV-5). It was deployed at various points along the South Vietnamese coast, thereby providing badly-needed service facilities to Army heli-

Below: the Bell AH-1G Hueycobra helicopter gunship operated from Da Nang with the US Marine Corps

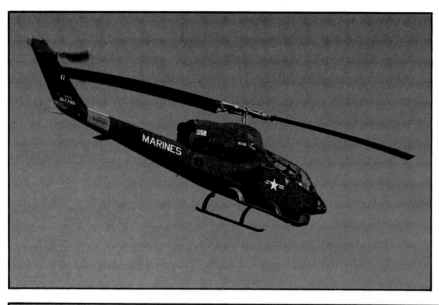

copter units. Mindful of the earlier sinking of the aircraft transport vessel USNS *Card*, the Army employed scuba divers to check the hull periodically for explosives.

Another World War II vessel called to service in the Vietnam War was the aircraft carrier USS *Intrepid* (CVS-11). Assigned to anti-submarine warfare duties since 1962, *Intrepid* returned to the South China Sea on 15 May 1966 with 32 Douglas A-4 Skyhawks and 24 A-1 Skyraiders to launch strikes against many of the same targets her air group had hit in 1945. *Intrepid*'s Carrier Air Wing 10 was not equipped with fighter aircraft, but that did not prevent encounters with enemy aircraft. On 9 October, Lieutenant (junior grade) W. T. Patton of VA-176 was on a mission in his A-1H Skyraider when he was attacked by a MiG-17, which he shot down.

Interdiction campaign

Since the hit-and-run nature of the ground war in South Vietnam made tangible success difficult to define, the key role of the carrier-based air groups was to interdict supplies before they could be used in the south. Washington strategists still hoped to 'dry up' the enemy's resources along the supply routes, but the political restrictions placed on such interdiction missions were confounding and frustrating to American airmen.

That frustration is noted by retired Vice-Admiral William Houser, who was commanding officer of the aircraft carrier USS *Constellation* during what could have been a turning point in the war in the summer of 1966. He recalls: 'We used to see Communist bloc ships and other vessels steaming up the Tonkin Gulf, loaded with trucks and other equipment. We could not stop them, although we clearly had all the elements of power we needed to

Above left: one of the US Army's AH-1Gs undergoing maintenance at Bien Hoa in February 1969. Left: the Douglas EB-66 served in the electronic countermeasures role in Vietnam, disrupting North Vietnamese air defence radars and communications by jamming

interdict them or to turn them back. They then proceeded into Haiphong, which was off limits for bombing. The ships were unloaded on the docks, which were also off limits, where the trucks left one at a time or in small groups. They would hide during the daytime and we would send our aircraft after them at night, which is probably the most hazardous type of bombing. Using flares for illumination, the carrier planes went after the trucks at low altitude and over hilly terrain.

'Constellation's air group lost at least two pilots who probably were not shot down, but who ran into the ground. Reports from the flight indicated there were no preliminary calls that the planes had been hit and were going in. There were just two big flashes on the ground. It was aggravating to have to go after these trucks one at a time at night, when the appropriate thing to do would have been to turn them back when they were still aboard ship in the Tonkin Gulf.'

Admiral Houser also notes that during the concerted attack on North Vietnam's petroleum, oil and lubricants storage and distribution system by Navy and Air Force aircraft, there were some desperate forays toward American ships by enemy PT boats. Those craft were repelled or sunk with no damage to the American ships and, in the case of USS Constellation, photo-intelligence experts identified a number of other boats in camouflage moorings, where most were subsequently destroyed.

The heavy destruction of North Vietnam's petroleum facilities also represented an opportunity not seized by the United States. Admiral Houser observes: 'When the Navy and Air Force airplanes hit the oil storage points in Haiphong and Hanoi, the North Vietnamese were confounded and reeling. They did not know what to expect next. Sending the PT boats out was an act of desperation. Moreover, the Soviet bloc and other ships stopped short of their destination and did not proceed on. In fact, all maritime traffic into Haiphong ceased for many weeks.

'But, instead of taking the element of surprise and moving out with it – by escalating the air war, making a landing or even a feint for a landing – we were allowed to do nothing unusual. In late August and early September the war picked up again, much as it had before the highly

successful air strikes that began at the end of June.'

By December 1966 the US Navy and Air Force raids had badly damaged North Vietnam's above ground petroleum storage sites, but the delay in initiating such a concerted effort, along with the earlier bombing halt, gave the North Vietnamese time to disperse the supplies. Indeed, the Johnson Administration had learned no lessons from its experience for, in the late spring and early summer of 1967, further restrictions were placed on targets that could be attacked in North Vietnam.

As part of this campaign of 'gradualism', certain harbours in North Vietnam were mined to restrict seaborne access to that nation. On 26 February 1967, Commander A. H. Barie, commanding officer of VA-35, led a flight of seven Grumman A-6A Intruders from USS Enterprise to drop mines at the mouths of two important

Above: Strategic Air Command's eight-engined Boeing B-52 strategic bombers operated over North and South Vietnam from Guam and Thailand. Seventeen of these bombers were lost in action, but B-52 tail gunners accounted for two MiG-21 interceptor fighters. Below: a North American F-100 Super Sabre of the 614th TFS, 35 TFG, pictured on a close-support mission

rivers. In March, three new minefields were sown in the mouths of the rivers by A-6s from USS *Kitty Hawk*. It is important to note, however, that no mines were dropped in the deep water ports of Haiphong, Hon Gai and Cam Pha.

Stronger air defences

In March North Vietnamese officials visited the Soviet Union and received well publicised assurances that the Russians would provide 'even more aeroplanes, high-altitude missiles, artillery and infantry weapons' to the Hanoi Government. General Giap responded by sending 37 NVA battalions into an area north of the Demilitarised Zone prior to launching a massive offensive against Quang Tri City on 6 April. US air bases south of the Demilitarised

Zone were a prime target of the offensive and were hotly defended by American air and ground forces. By summer the North Vietnamese offensive was repelled, but the NVA simply shifted their operations to sanctuaries in Cambodia which were safe from American air attacks and which would serve as staging areas for further attacks in the south.

While the US Army and Marine Corps air strength was concentrated on the war in the south, the US Navy and Air Force continued to hit limited targets in North Vietnam. Despite the political limitations placed on the aircrews, the targets they were able to go after suffered severe damage.

Retired Admiral James Holloway III, former Chief of Naval Operations, commanded the carrier USS *Enterprise* during two combat tours of duty on Yankee Station. He notes that during the second tour, 'on 10 May 1967, Carrier Air Wing 9 executed a strike of major importance against the port of Haiphong's thermal power plant. In a spectacular display of precision bombing, the power plant was demolished with 1,000lb and 2,000lb bombs, without causing any damage to the surrounding community. Despite the formidable flak over the target, skilful tactics and adroit flying enabled the *Enterprise* pilots to put their bombs on the target without loss.

'In late May the frequency of attacks into the well-defended heartland of North Vietnam picked up markedly. On one of these attacks, a raid of major proportions against a military installation on the outskirts of Hanoi, our strike group encountered a savage barrage of surface-to-air missiles and two of our planes were lost. The tremendous courage and absolute determination of our pilots was graphically demonstrated when they returned to this same target two days later. They fought their way through SAMs, flak and MiGs, and blasted their ob-

jectives with telling accuracy, leaving columns of flame and smoke towering over the enemy base.

'That same day,' Admiral Holloway recalls, 'another group of *Enterprise* pilots struck Kep airfield, a major MiG base north-east of Hanoi. Undaunted by the clouds of bursting flak so thick as to virtually obscure the target, these battle-hardened veterans pressed home their attacks to level the enemy base facilities and leave a half dozen MiG fighters in flames.'

Although the US Navy had at that time commenced using Walleye glide bombs, television-guided air-to-surface missiles, the high accuracy of the weapons would not have been possible if they had not been brought into the range of highly-effective ground defences. All too often enemy defences found their mark and aircrew members who survived were forced to eject from their aircraft over North Vietnam. There they faced the prospect of being killed by ground troops or hostile civilians or, at best, long confinement under the most harsh and inhumane

Top: the Douglas A-1H (upper) was flown by Air Vice-Marshal Nguyen Ky, South Vietnam's Premier, who led the élite 83rd Special Air Group. The MiG-17 (lower) served with North Vietnamese air defence squadrons. Above: two of the USAF's leading aces pictured with an F-4 at Udorn, Thailand in October 1972. Captain Steve Ritchie (left) and Captain Charles DeBellvue flew with the 432nd Tactical Reconnaissance Wing US Air Force

Below: the US Navy's Grumman A-6A Intruders of VA-196, flying from USS Constellation (CVA-64), drop their bombs on a North Vietnamese target. Bottom: a McDonnell Douglas A-4F Skyhawk attack bomber (upper) of VA-164 embarked on USS Hancock (CVA-19). The AC-47 (lower) was popularly dubbed 'Puff the Magic Dragon' in Vietnam

conditions. Hence, it was vital for both the US Navy and Air Force to deploy search and rescue aircraft that could, if the occasion demanded, penetrate the enemy's defences.

A case in point is the rescue of Lieutenant (junior grade) J. W. Cain, an A-4 pilot with VA-192 who was forced to eject over Haiphong harbour. Cain received constant protection during his entire time in the water. The leader of his air group, Commander Billy Phillips, kept 12 F-8 Crusaders from USS *Ticonderoga*'s VF-191 and VF-194 on the scene, strafing beach installations and distracting the enemy from Lieutenant Cain. This allowed two A-1 Skyraiders from VA-52 to escort a rescue helicopter to the scene. Cain was quickly hauled out of the water and the rescue helicopter departed amid heavy mortar fire from the beach and at least two SAMs.

Battle for Khe Sanh

The aircraft carriers cruised the Tonkin Gulf with impunity. Their defensive screens of ships, missiles and aircraft kept them completely operational while performing their missions on Yankee Station. The major damage to a carrier was inflicted not by enemy action, but by a freak accident. On 29 July 1967, USS *Forrestal* (CVA-59) was a scene of holocaust after a Zuni rocket was inadvertently fired from a McDonnell F-4B parked well aft on the flight deck. The rocket hit the fuel tank of a nearby A-4 and triggered a tremendous fire that put the big supercarrier out of action for seven months and resulted in the loss of 134 lives and 21 aircraft.

Ashore, men and *matériel* were pouring into South Vietnam in record numbers. New aircraft–such as the North American Rockwell OV-10 Bronco and the Grumman OV-1 Mohawk–proved their combat effectiveness as the US continued to buy time for South Vietnamese forces to build up strength and experience. Accordingly, Americans shouldered more and more of the combat responsibilities. During the battle for Quang Ngai, US Marines were engaged in a fierce battle to keep the Viet Cong from overrunning secured positions. At the height of the fighting, Captain S. W. Pless of Marine Observation Squadron VMO-6 landed his helicopter gunship between a large VC force and four wounded American soldiers. He continued to pour rocket and machine gun fire at the enemy while his crewmen brought the wounded men aboard the helicopter. Pless' aircraft was badly overloaded, but he still managed to take off and fight his way clear of the enemy. He was awarded the Medal of Honour.

The year 1967 closed with another unilateral cease-fire

declared by the United States as a peace gesture. Again, the North Vietnamese and Viet Cong used the occasion to strengthen their positions for 1968's battles. This time, however, the Communists had several clear objectives in mind to draw international attention to their ability to thwart American military power. The first move was a squeeze on the US military base at Khe Sanh, a remote outpost off the Ho Chi Minh Trail in the north-west corner of South Vietnam. The Communists' intention was clearly to repeat their decisive defeat of the French at Dien Bien Phu by concentrating their forces at Khe Sanh and strangling the base. Unlike the 1954 battle, however, the Communists had to face an effective air resupply system and the combined firepower of land-based US Air Force units and carrier-based US Navy squadrons. The US Government was determined that Khe Sanh would not fall and, in addition to heavy support for the beleaguered troops, raids on North Vietnam were resumed.

As the battle for Khe Sanh was raging, however, another Communist-inspired incident put new pressure on the American Government. On 26 February 1968, North Korean gunboats seized the intelligence ship USS *Pueblo* (AGER-2) and captured the crew. Retaliation for this breach of international law could have opened a second front in Asia for the Americans, who were already heavily committed to the fighting in Vietnam. Hence, the release of the *Pueblo* crew would have to be negotiated.

The Tet offensive

As if to emphasise America's commitment, the North Vietnamese launched their strongest offensive on the morning of 31 January. During the cease-fire for the Tet (Buddhist new year) celebrations, Viet Cong and North Vietnamese troops had sneaked into Saigon and other key points in readiness for the series of well-orchestrated attacks on American and South Vietnamese installations. In Saigon, for example, the Viet Cong made an earnest attempt to take over Tan Son Nhut airfield and the US Embassy building. Ground communication was so effectively blocked that US Air Force fighters could not be scrambled to aid the defenders. Only individual US Army helicopters, launched on the initiative of their pilots, succeeded in bringing strong aerial firepower to bear on the insurgents. Both the Tet offensive and the squeeze on Khe Sanh failed to produce decisive Communist victories. However, it was demonstrated that, despite heavy losses and constant pounding received, the North Vietnamese could still mount boldly impressive attacks. The American public viewed this grim reality of the Vietnam War in nightly television news broadcasts that were independently

produced and uncensored. In that portrayal, there seemed to be no end to the carnage and the reasons for American involvement became murkier, thereby fuelling the anti-war movement at home.

On 31 March 1968, President Johnson announced a halt to all bombing north of the 20th parallel and his decision not to seek re-election. In this way he hoped to impress North Vietnam's leaders with his non-political motives for wanting peace. However, they were more impressed–and encouraged–by the anti-war movement in the United States. Television coverage of the anti-war demonstrations cast an even darker shadow on reports from the battle zones, where success was all too often measured in tons of ordnance expended and body counts of enemy casualties. The Johnson announcement did lead to the start of peace talks that began in Paris in May.

Kinnear II, who commanded Attack Carrier Air Wing 2 aboard USS *Ranger*. He led missions in A-4, A-6, LTV A-7 and F-4 aircraft and was awarded the Distinguished Flying Cross and three Gold Stars.

The citation for Commander Kinnear's fourth DFC award notes that 'on 7, 8 and 9 May 1968 (he) led six separate armed reconnaissance and co-ordinated attacks against the Xom Trong Hoi barracks and storage complex in North Vietnam. Through (his) personal and daring visual reconnaissance while under accurate anti-aircraft fire a large storage complex was initially located. He personally planned and led the successful strikes that neutralised enemy defences and virtually annihilated this large enemy storage area. Repeatedly exposing himself to heavy anti-aircraft fire, he personally destroyed a bridge, (and) two barges, caused 10 secondary explosions and silenced a large 37 mm anti-aircraft gun site with a devastating direct hit. He led the final highly successful strike against the complex which left fires and explosions erupting that were clearly visible from 40 miles.'

Commander Kinnear was fortunate to get back to his ship. Not so lucky during the 19 June raid on North Vietnam was the F-4B crew of Lieutenant-Commander J. W. Holtzclaw and Lieutenant-Commander J. A. Burns, both of VF-33. They were shot down south of Hanoi and were about to be captured by NVA troops when an armed Kaman UH-2A Seasprite helicopter based aboard the guided missile frigate USS *Preble* (DLG-15) arrived on the scene. The pilot, Lieutenant C. E. Lassen, and his crew fought a running battle with the NVA while they sought a suitable landing spot to pick up the downed Phantom crew. Despite intensive groundfire and at least two SAMs directed at the rescue craft, Lassen picked up Holtzclaw and Burns, and fought his way back to the coast and over the water to the USS *Jouett* (DLG-29). Lassen's exploits earned him the Medal of Honour.

Laos and Cambodia

On 1 November, President Johnson ordered a halt to all bombing north of the Demilitarised Zone, but a divided American electorate did not support his party's platform on Vietnam peace moves. A few days later, Richard Nixon was elected president by a slim majority and announced plans to wind down American troop involvement in Vietnam. Nixon kept his promise and, by year's end 1969, some 69,000 American troops were out of Vietnam. However, he also responded to renewed Viet Cong attacks on Saigon by ordering B-52s to bomb their sanctuaries in Cambodia. This was done clandestinely to maintain the neutral facade of the Sihanouk government

Above and below: USS Forrestal (CVA-59) was swept by an accidental fire on 29 July 1969, off North Vietnam.
Above left: a McDonnell Douglas F-4 Phantom II of VF-154 is towed across the flight deck of USS Ranger.
Top: VF-96's F-4s were successful in air-to-air combat.
Insignia: VF-74 flew F-4s and VA-65 was an A-6 unit (left)

However, the talks soon became bogged down in delays initiated by the North Vietnamese. Military pressure, within the restrictions of the bombing halt, was the only means the US had to induce the North Vietnamese to get the peace talks moving, but the pressure had to be carefully measured, since it was feared too much military action would drive the Communists from the talks.

The difficulties facing American airmen at that time can be seen in the combat experiences of Commander George

in Cambodia. When massive bombing failed to deter the Communists' use of Cambodia, on 24 April 1970, USAF and VNAF aircraft launched tactical strikes into Cambodia as the prelude to a 60-day search-and-destroy mission to eliminate Viet Cong strongholds. This led to open strife between Khmer Rouge (Cambodian Communist) forces and the forces led by Lieutenant-General Lon Nol, who overthrew the government of Prince Norodom Sihanouk. Thus, the Indo-China War widened and American air units began operating openly in support of missions in Cambodia.

The death of Ho Chi Minh on 3 September 1969 did not alter the Paris peace talks, which continued to drag on without result. At North Vietnamese insistence, the National Liberation Front (NLF) was admitted to the talks, but did nothing to curb the Viet Cong forces still fighting in South Vietnam. This stance continued to frustrate the Nixon administration, which, by April 1970, had withdrawn 115,000 troops and promised to pull out another 150,000 over the following 12 months.

The reduction in American troops was balanced as much as possible by supply of equipment for the ARVN forces. When USAF elements were withdrawn in 1970, the VNAF stood at an all-time high of nine tactical wings with 40,000 personnel and a greatly expanded training programme. The VNAF had nearly 700 aircraft, including A-1 Skyraiders, Cessna A-37 Dragonflys, Northrop F-5s, AC-47 gunships, Cessna O-1s and Fairchild C-119s. As the VNAF refined its capabilities, it was continually reinforced by USAF, USMC, US Army and US Navy aircraft, the latter operating from aircraft carriers.

The heavy fighting in South Vietnam, Cambodia and subsequently Laos provided the North Vietnamese with a welcome respite from the heavy raids that had devastated their petroleum and supply facilities. Hence, when ARVN forces crossed into Laos on 30 January 1971 to attack a key point of the Ho Chi Minh Trail, the NVA could respond strongly with tanks, artillery and anti-aircraft weapons. Again, B-52 strikes provided the edge of superiority needed by the ARVN forces, but the South Vietnamese were eventually forced to withdraw from Laos without having achieved their objective.

Meanwhile, American air power was called on to make selective strikes at North Vietnamese targets in response to attacks on unarmed reconnaissance aircraft assigned to monitor NVA activities in the north. In February 1971, stepped up strikes were launched against SAM sites and their support units. By August, petroleum storage areas were on the mission roster and in September a major raid was directed against the Dong Hoi area north of the Demilitarised Zone.

As the bombing halt drew to a close, the NVAF was ready for the new challenge. Its older MiG-17 fighters had been augmented by newer and more powerful MiG-19 and MiG-21 interceptors. The NVAF fighter pilots grew bolder and became more successful in attacking American aircraft, which were still limited by the restrictions against pursuing MiGs back to their bases. That restriction was lifted in November 1971.

Operation Linebacker

With the massive NVA assault beginning on 30 March 1972, the Nixon administration looked to a change in tactics. It suspended the Paris peace talks on 8 May and reintroduced vigorous action against North Vietnam. This time there was a naval blockade of northern ports and minefields were sown in the harbours near Haiphong and other principal ports. Operation Linebacker was the code-

name for massive air strikes against old and new targets in North Vietnam, including those in the capital Hanoi. Even a petroleum pipeline from China was hit on the North Vietnamese side.

Clearly on the offensive, American air units tackled the rejuvenated NVAF and shot down impressive numbers of their aircraft. On 8 May 1972, Lieutenant Randy Cunningham and Lieutenant (junior grade) Willie Driscoll, of VF-96 deployed aboard USS *Constellation*, scored their second kill, a MiG-17. Two days later, in one of the epic dogfights of the Vietnam War, Cunningham and Driscoll shot down three MiG-17s to become the first air aces of that conflict. USAF Captain Richard S. Ritchie of the 555th Tactical Fighter Squadron equalled the score in an F-4C on 28 August.

At this time the North Vietnamese were again trying to influence American politics, hoping to bring down the Nixon administration, which was then reacting to the first indication of the Watergate scandal. When their military moves failed, the North Vietnamese became more conciliatory at the Paris peace talks. That led to a halt of bombing north of the 20th parallel, commencing on 23 October. The following month President Nixon was re-elected by the greatest majority in American history and proceeded to bring 'peace with honour'.

When it became apparent that the Hanoi Government was about to renew its offensive in South Vietnam, the

Above: a USAF F-4 breaks away from a Boeing KC-135 tanker aircraft after a refuelling rendezvous en route to North Vietnam. Above right: a Viet Cong position is attacked by one of VF-96's F-4Bs in 1965. This fighter squadron produced the US Navy's only air aces of the conflict. Right: on 11 August 1967, Col Bob White led an attack by F-105s of the 355th and 388th Tactical Fighter Wings on Hanoi's Doumer Bridge. Keith Ferris's painting emphasises the intense anti-aircraft barrage put up by the defenders

US Government responded with the strongest aerial campaign ever launched against the North Vietnamese. Operation Linebacker II from 18 to 29 December was a strong, well-co-ordinated aerial assault on North Vietnam. USAF and US Navy aircraft hit MiG bases, SAM sites, petroleum storage facilities and virtually every moving military target in sight. USAF Captain David R. Rusch, then a Boeing KC-135 pilot with the 99th Air Refuelling Squadron based at U Tapao airbase in Thailand, flew in support of the final air operations of the war. He recalls that, except for the 24 hours of Christmas Day, there was constant air activity over North Vietnam during the Linebacker raids.

Circling the Tonkin Gulf, Captain Rusch had this view of the second night's raid: 'The B-52s came in high over the gulf as the navy aircraft went down after anti-aircraft artillery sites, which opened fire in return as they were attacked. Then came the SAM calls over the radio and attack planes went in to hit the missile launchers. I saw the B-52s begin their bomb run when, suddenly, the whole sky lit up. A B-52 had taken a direct hit by a SAM. Although the B-52s were protected by fighters and had their own superb electronic jamming equipment, the North Vietnamese found a way to determine the bombers' altitude. One or two MiGs would make a quick run through the formation, not shooting at anyone, but just up there to determine the altitude, which he would radio to the ground. Then, the North Vietnamese would fire several missiles timed to go off at about that altitude and hope for a lucky hit, which they occasionally scored'.

Despite the losses, the Linebacker II raids demonstrated beyond a doubt the American ability to wipe out enemy defences. The much-maligned General Dynamics F-111 proved to be an excellent SAM suppressor and was aided by Navy A-6 all-weather aircraft in softening up the paths for the big bombers. Some 1,000 Russian-built SAMs were fired during the 11-day intensive period.

The fall of Saigon

The North Vietnamese made further concessions at the Paris peace talks and the bombing was halted. American involvement in the war then drew to a close. The aircraft carrier USS *Midway*, which had launched the fighters that had scored the first MiG kill of the war, appropriately accounted for the last. On 12 January 1973, Lieutenants Vic Kowalski and Jim Wise in an F-4B of VF-161 bagged a MiG-17. Eleven days later the cease-fire went into effect.

In February, American transport aircraft began bringing home the prisoners of war who had been released by the North Vietnamese under the cease-fire terms. They bore final testimony to the harsh system that relentlessly sustained the ruinous war effort for over a decade. One prisoner, Captain (now Vice-Admiral) James B. Stockdale, was permanently crippled in brutal response to his refusal to co-operate with his captors. A source of inspiration for all of the residents of the notorious 'Hanoi Hilton' prison camp, Captain Stockdale was subsequently awarded the Medal of Honour in recognition of more than three years' defiance of his gaolers.

After the Americans left Vietnam there was a short period of peace. Then, in clear violation of the Paris agreement, the North Vietnamese made the final push. In April 1975 they overwhelmed ARVN forces and swiftly brought the whole country under their control. American air units made a humanitarian air lift of some non-Communists, but it was clearly impossible to rescue the thousands of people who wished to flee Vietnam. At the end, American aircraft carriers were offshore to recover rescue helicopters and, without warning, some VNAF pilots who had escaped with their US-supplied helicopters and even fixed-wing aircraft and then headed for the freedom represented by the carriers. Back in Saigon, which was soon renamed Ho Chi Minh City, the victors had an impressive stockpile of captured American arms, aircraft and equipment.

Right: the Republic F-105 Thunderchief was highly successful as a fighter-bomber during the Vietnam war. It played a leading part in air attacks on the bottlenecks in North Vietnamese communications and supply routes to the South.
Below: the 1975 North Vietnamese invasion forced many South Vietnamese to flee. This Cessna O-1 made an unscheduled landing aboard the carrier USS Midway (CVA-41)

Six Day War 1967

During the thirty years which followed her emergence as an independent state in 1948, Israel fought four full-scale wars with her Arab neighbours. The Six Day War undoubtedly marked the peak of Israel's military fortunes during this protracted period of tension and her swift and spectacular defeat of the Arab forces in June 1967 was due in no small measure to her masterly use of air power.

The Israeli air force came into being in 1948 with a miscellaneous collection of combat aircraft from many sources, which included Avia S 199s, (derivatives of the Messerschmitt Bf 109) from Czechoslovakia, Boeing B-17 Flying Fortresses from the United States and Supermarine Spitfires and de Havilland Mosquitoes from Britain. For the first nine months of its existence, the new country was at war with Egypt, Syria, Iraq, Jordan and the Lebanon, the embyro Israeli air arm seeing action in defence of Tel Aviv and supporting ground troops.

The contending air forces

In 1956 Israel went onto the offensive against Egypt in Sinai, the Egyptian air force being effectively neutralised by Anglo-French air action as a prelude to their military occupation of the Suez Canal. As a precaution against attacks on Israeli towns by Egypt's Russian-supplied Ilyushin Il-28 bombers, two squadrons of Dassault Mystère IV fighters of the French air force were transferred to Israel. The fighting in Sinai and Suez was halted

by United Nations action and the victors were forced by international pressure to evacuate occupied territory. However, the links forged between France and Israel were to be strengthened over the following decade and, when Israel next went to war, her air force's combat squadrons were exclusively equipped with French warplanes. Similarly, the Soviet Union continued to provide Egypt with modern combat types.

On the eve of the Six Day War the most important warplane serving with the Israeli air force was undoubtedly the Dassault Mirage IIICJ, 72 of which had been supplied to equip three squadrons. Although it was primarily regarded as an air superiority fighter able to meet the Arab air forces' MiG-21s on equal terms, the Mirage III had a secondary role as a ground-attack fighter carrying combinations of bombs, rockets and napalm. However, ground-attack sorties were more usually the task of the older Dassault types in the Israeli inventory–Ouragans, Mystère IVAs and Super Mystère B2s.

For long-range sorties deep into Egyptian territory, France had supplied Israel with 25 twin-engined Sud Vautour light bombers. Lastly, a proportion of the Israeli air force's Potez Magister jet trainers were allotted to light-attack squadrons for battlefield support work. Carrying 110lb bombs or 88mm rockets and machine gun-armed, they fought over all the war fronts.

Israel's air transport force comprised some 50 fixed-

Above left: the Egyptian air force flew subsonic MiG-17 fighters on ground-attack sorties during the Six Day War. The type was also flown by Syria, Iraq and Algeria

wing and helicopter types of French and American origin. Twin-engined Nord Noratlas tactical transports served with one squadron in the air supply and paratroop-dropping roles, while a second unit flew elderly Boeing Stratocruisers and Douglas C-47s. Helicopter transport for ground forces and casualty evacuation from forward areas was performed by Sud Super Frelon and Sikorsky S-58 helicopters.

In all, the Israeli air force could muster some 350 air-

Below: a map showing the routes taken by Israeli fighter-bombers during their initial attack against Egyptian airfields on 5 June 1967.
Below right: the burned-out remains of three Egyptian MiG-21 fighters

Il-28 and two with the more modern Tupolev Tu-16, a force totalling some 70 bombers.

Three of Egypt's Arab allies were also primarily equipped with Soviet warplanes. Syria, Iraq and Algeria could muster between them more than 300 combat aircraft, predominantly MiG-17s, MiG-21s and Ilyushin Il-28s. Jordan's small air force comprised eight de Havilland Vampires and 21 Hawker Hunters, with Lockheed F-104A Starfighter interceptors being phased into service,

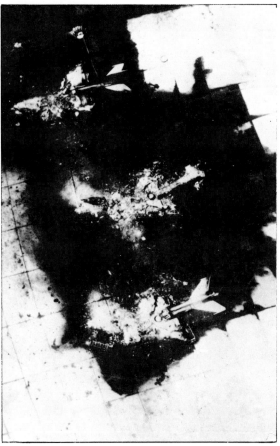

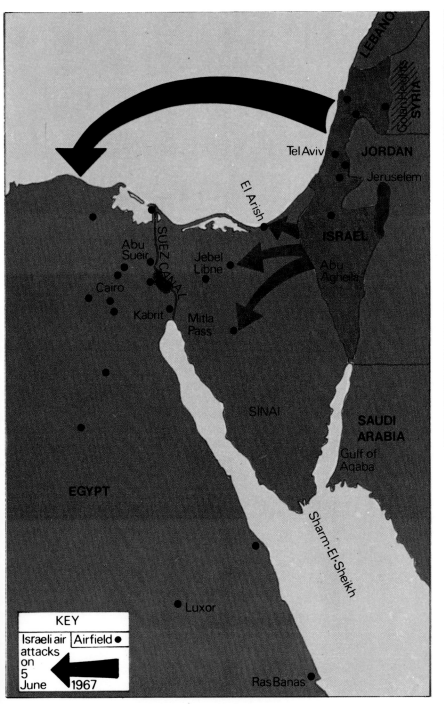

KEY

Israeli air attacks on 5 June 1967	Airfield ●

craft to oppose an Arab force of more than 800 combat aircraft. With some 450 warplanes, the Egyptian air force alone appeared to be more than a match for the Israelis. Six Egyptian squadrons flew MiG-21 Mach 2 interceptors and a further four had the earlier MiG-19. The ground-attack force included one squadron flying the Sukhoi Su-7 and five with older MiG-17 and MiG-15 fighters. Of particular concern to Israel was Egypt's bomber force, which constituted a serious threat to Israel's population centres. Three squadrons were equipped with the Ilyushin

but not then operational. The Arabs' order of battle was completed by a single squadron of Hunters operated by the Lebanon.

If wars were won by superior strength alone, then the outcome of an Arab-Israeli clash would have been a foregone conclusion. However, such factors as morale, training, tactical skill and readiness were of equal significance and Israel was to exploit her qualitative advantages to the full in an audacious attempt to neutralise Arab air power at the outset. On 17 May 1967 the United Nations Secretary General, U. Thant, announced that his peacekeeping forces were to withdraw from the Egyptian/Israeli frontier in response to pressure from Egypt. Five days later Egypt closed the Gulf of Aqaba to Israeli shipping and the die was cast for war.

Complete tactical surprise

Neither the Soviet Union nor the United States wished to see a conflict in the Middle East which could get out of hand and bring about a confrontation between the super powers. Both had sizeable naval forces in the Mediterranean – 20 Soviet ships and the US Sixth Fleet of two aircraft carriers and 50 other vessels – but in the event, save for one incident which has never been satisfactorily explained, these forces remained on the sidelines.

Israel opened hostilities with Egypt on the morning of 5 June 1967 with an attack which has become a classic

example of tactical surprise. The target was Egypt's air force and the intention was to catch it on its airfields and to wipe it out on the ground. The timing of the initial attacks exemplifies the meticulous planning of the Israeli air staff. It was decided that 0745 hours Israeli time would catch the Egyptian air force off its guard, as by this time its dawn air patrols would have landed and the readiness state of fighter aircraft on the ground would have been relaxed. Furthermore, as Cairo time was an hour ahead of Israeli's, the attack would find many senior officers on their way to their headquarters, thus increasing the difficulties of a timely Egyptian reaction to the crucial first bombing runs.

Egypt's forward airfields in Sinai were the target of Mystères and Ouragans flying direct from their bases. The fighter-bombers assigned to hit airfields in the Suez Canal Zone and the Nile Delta swept out over the Mediterranean at low altitude and then swung in over the Egyptian coast – flying into the eye of the sun – to approach their targets from the north-west.

The first priority of the attacking force was to put the enemy runways out of commission. A bomb specially designed by the French was used to crater the concrete runways. Weighing 544 kg (1,200 lb) – of which 363 kg (800 lb) was explosive warhead – the bomb was fitted with two sets of rockets, one of which retarded the weapon's forward momentum immediately after release; a drogue then deployed to stabilise its downward flight and finally the second set of rockets drove it into the runway surface where the warhead detonated.

Delayed-action fuses on a proportion of the bombs

ensured that the task of clearing runways and filling in craters would be a protracted one. In the meanwhile, the grounded Egyptian warplanes were at the mercy of Israeli aircraft, which remained over the target airfields in relays of four for some two hours, at the end of which the Egyptian air force had virtually ceased to exist as a coherent fighting force.

Attacking with fragmentation bombs, rockets and cannon, the Israeli fighter-bombers found many easy targets among warplanes neatly parked in rows along their hardstandings. Eight formations of MiGs were actually surprised while taxiing to their runways. By the end of the day Israeli claims totalled 240 Egyptian aircraft destroyed.

The pattern of the initial onslaught was varied in two areas. Two of the airfields in Sinai – El Arish and Jebel Libne – were spared the destruction of their runways as the Israelis were confident that their ground forces would soon overrun the area and they could put these airfields to good use. In southern Egypt the airfields at Luxor and Ras Banas were beyond the range of the fighter-bombers and became the target of Vautour bombers flying down the Gulf of Aqaba and across the Red Sea. The Egyptian bomber force, especially the Tupolev Tu-16s based in the Cairo area, also received special attention; not one of the

Above: the Israelis' most modern fighter aircraft in 1967 was the French Dassault Mirage III. Below: the MiG-21 was the Mirage's principal opponent, although many MiGs were destroyed on the ground. Right: older fighters were relegated to the fighter-bomber role. Egyptian MiG-17s are pictured attacking an Israeli military convoy near the Suez Canal

Tu-16s survived.

One Egyptian aircraft which was in the air during the Israeli air assault was a twin-engined Ilyushin Il-14 transport carrying Egypt's Chief of Staff, General Amer and bound for Kabrit in the Canal Zone. The aircraft was warned away from its destination in time to avoid interception, but while searching along the Canal for an airfield to land on, the General had a grandstand view of the destruction of his air force.

Army support work

Few air-to-air combats took place, a notable exception being a clash between 16 Mirages and 20 MiG-21s over Abu Sueir during which four MiGs fell to the Israelis' fire. Egypt's allies became the target for attack later on 5 June, when airfields in Jordan, Syria and Iraq were bombed and 68 victories were claimed on these fronts.

With Arab air power effectively neutralised, the Israeli air force concentrated on the support of ground forces. However, air defence of the homeland and air cover for the armies could not be ignored, a fact emphasised by the appearance of Algerian MiG-21s over Sinai on the second day of the conflict. The advance into Sinai was ably supported by air attacks. Potez Magister light-attack aircraft proved unexpectedly effective and their successes on the first day alone included the destruction of 40 tanks, three radar stations, an ammunition train and many supply vehicles.

Helicopter assaults in enemy rear areas were also launched to good effect, notably during the fighting around Abu Agheila. Other notable contributions which the air forces made to the ground fighting in Sinai were the wholesale destruction of armour and vehicles retreating through the Mitla Pass bottleneck and the use of airborne and helicopter-borne troops in the capture of Sharm-el-Sheikh – the key to the strategically-important Straits of Tiran.

There was little call for naval air support during the conflict, but one incident convincingly demonstrated the Israeli air force's capability in this role. This was the attack on the American surveillance ship USS *Liberty* on 8 June, which resulted in the deaths of 34 American seamen and the wounding of many more. Aircraft from USS *America* were dispatched to assist the *Liberty*, but no clashes between Israeli and US Navy fighters took place. It has been suggested that the surveillance ship was acting in support of the Polaris-armed nuclear submarine *Andrew Jackson*, which was tasked with the destruction of Israeli missiles if their use against Egyptian cities was threatened.

The air war against Jordan was a small-scale repetition of that against Egypt. Firstly, the small Jordanian air arm was eliminated and attention then switched to enemy ground forces. However, it was against the well-fortified Syrian positions on the Golan Heights that the Israeli air force fought its hardest ground-support battles. There the Israelis reportedly encountered the SA-2 Guideline surface-to-air missile for the first time in combat – a foretaste of the intense ground-to-air defences which they were to encounter in their fourth war with the Arabs.

At the end of six days of fighting, a United Nations request for a ceasefire brought the war to a close. Israel was in possession of the Sinai peninsula, the west bank of the Jordan and the city of Jerusalem, and in Syria, the Golan Heights – all gains of tremendous strategical and symbolic importance to which air power had contributed. The lessons of defeat were well-learned by the Arabs and when next they went to war with Israel in October 1973 it was beneath the protection of a barrage of anti-aircraft guns and surface-to-air missiles.

Yom Kippur 1973

Unlike the Six Day War of June 1967, the Yom Kippur War of October 1973 found Israel unprepared. Under pressure from the United States which was responsible for the supply of the majority of her military equipment, Israel was unwilling to appear as the aggressor in the eyes of the world. In addition, Israeli and world attention had been momentarily diverted to the Palestinian attack on Soviet emigrants in Austria at just the moment that the Arab ground forces were being assembled for the attacks across the Suez Canal and against the Golan Heights on the Syrian border.

The Yom Kippur War presented another vital difference which the Arab world was determined to exploit – that it was fighting, not as an aggressor but as liberator of Arab territories, unreasonably occupied by Israel for seven

Above and below: the Israeli air force's ability to make the maximum use of its existing equipment is typified by its use of the Potez CM170 Magister trainer in the light attack role. Flown by reserve pilots, Magisters proved effective in attacks on vehicles and fortified positions using bombs, rockets and machine gun fire. A prodigious array of stores is illustrated

years. There had, moreover, occurred a growing tally of incidents in which Israeli forces had provoked Arab units into combat, and often to their destruction; the latest such event had occurred on 13 September when eight Syrian jet fighters had been shot down at Latakia.

Obsolescent equipment

Although no one could be blind to the efficiency and sophistication of the Israeli forces, the Arab governments obviously felt that their own continuous heavy build-up of Russian-supplied equipment of apparently modern concept would provide parity in quality and superiority in numbers. Indeed the Egyptian and Syrian air forces together fielded almost 1,000 fighters, fighter-bombers, bombers, transports and helicopters, including 260 MiG-21s and 175 Sukhoi Su-7s. Against them were ranged fewer than 500 Israeli first-line aircraft, of which 150 were McDonnell Douglas A-4 Skyhawks and 140 McDonnell Douglas F-4 Phantoms. Clearly the Arabs grossly over-rated the MiG-21 which, though an efficient point-defence interceptor, carried a puny punch as a ground-support fighter-bomber. On the other hand, the F-4 Phantom – unquestionably the world's most accomplished and versatile fighter at the time – could lift up to 7,260 kg (16,000 lb) of sophisticated ordnance. This weight was four times the load of an Su-7, seven times that of the MiG-21, and more than ten times that of the principal Arab close-support fighter, the ancient MiG-17.

Both sides were guilty of making exaggerated claims but, had Israeli claims been substantiated by fact, the Arab air forces would have ceased to exist long before the end of the 19-day conflict, while according to broadcast losses the Heyl Ha'Avir or Israeli Air Force (IAF) seemed capable of fighting for ever.

Independent intelligence

The Americans, in whose interests an Israeli victory lay and who were concerned to witness the efficacy of their equipment in combat, maintained reconnaissance cover at extreme altitude with Lockheed SR-71A aircraft during the war and achieved more realistic and less prejudiced intelligence results than either of the warring opponents. Their figures for the losses suffered were put at 242 Egyptian, 179 Syrian and 21 Iraqi aircraft, compared with 114 Israeli aircraft lost. At any rate, they regarded the Israeli losses sufficiently worrying to mount an impressive airlift of replacement arms and new electronic countermeasures (ECM) equipment. American-supplied reinforcements included at least 48 F-4s and about 80 A-4s. While Eastern Bloc nations did attempt some reinforcement of the Arab forces, President Sadat, in eventually accepting cease-fire terms, complained that he could no longer fight Israel and America at the same time.

Although the war was fought simultaneously by Syria on Israel's northern border and by Egypt across the Suez Canal, it was the latter campaign that featured the bitterest fighting, the most air activity and, eventually, proved the key to the war's conclusion. The Latakia incident provoked Syria's President Assad to conspire with President Sadat to commence preparations for a co-ordinated surprise attack on Israel. The chosen day for the assault was 6 October, the Day of Atonement – Yom Kippur – for the Israelis. While the latter lived in a false sense of security dating from their victorious Six Day War, the Egyptians planned their assault across the Suez Canal on the formidable Bar Lev fortifications lining the eastern bank with secrecy and ingenuity; the aim of the Arab nations was to rid Sinai and the Golan Heights of the Israeli forces of occupation.

Element of surprise

On Friday, 5 October, as massed Egyptian forces were spotted moving up to the Suez Canal, the Israelis suddenly recognised their danger and frantically ordered their forces on to the alert. At 1400 hours in the afternoon of the following day, 1,000 Egyptian guns thundered a barrage as the infantry quickly crossed the canal at four points under its cover. The previous night Egyptian commandos had secretly crossed to the eastern bank and

Above: a Sukhoi Su-7 of the Egyptian air force in combat with an Israeli Dassault Mirage III. Su-7 ground attack fighters were extensively used by the Arab air forces in the Yom Kippur War and suffered heavy losses. They were especially vulnerable to groundfire and far less manoeuvrable than the smaller and faster Mirage interceptors, which almost invariably emerged victors

sealed the Israeli flame-discharger nozzles with liquid cement, rendering them impotent.

The Egyptians held the initiative from the outset in the air as they did on the ground, depending for the defence of the west bank upon an impressive belt of surface-to-air missiles (SAMs) and radar-controlled 23 mm flak, and throwing forward their ground-support aircraft against such targets as Bir Gifgâfa, the main Israeli command base in Sinai, and el Tasa, the forward Bar Lev brigade headquarters. Such was the confusion created by the Egyptian *blitz* tactics that the IAF did not respond for two hours, by which time Egyptian forces were crossing the canal in considerable strength.

Losses on this first day were estimated at 11 Israeli aircraft, mostly shot down by SAMs and flak, and ten

Egyptian aircraft, of which about seven were downed by Phantoms and three by Hawk missiles defending Bir Gifgâfa. The Egyptians also attempted to bomb Tel Aviv with Tupolev Tu-16s, launching a Kelt stand-off bomb which was shot down by an IAF Phantom. By the evening of this first day, on which 200 Egyptian aircraft were thrown into the battle, the attacking armies had penetrated the Bar Lev line and their tanks were fanning out across Sinai.

Sunday, 7 October witnessed some of the heaviest fighting of the whole war on the ground, at sea and in the air. Stung by the weight of Egyptian air attacks on the previous day, the IAF now countered with attacks on the SAM sites and enemy airfields, losing about six A-4s in doing so. However, little damage was caused to Egypt's well-dispersed and concrete-protected air bases, as much had been learned from the devastating pre-emptive Israeli air strikes in the opening hours of the Six Day War. While Egyptian helicopters brought assault forces into the Sinai combat areas, 36 MiG-17s and Su-7s were lost to the defences during attacks on Israeli air bases.

Extravagant claims

The following day it was the Egyptians' turn to attempt to destroy the Israeli ground-to-air missile sites, striking installations at Baluza, Judi and Samarah, and bases at

Bir Thamada, Mulayhis, Umm Khisheib and Umm Marjam in Sinai. Both sides made extravagant claims of aircraft destroyed but it seems that about 15 Israeli A-4s, F-4s and Dassault Mirages were shot down, mostly by groundfire, in addition to about four helicopters destroyed on the ground at Bir Thamada. Egyptian losses were said to be roughly the same, seven MiG-17s having fallen to Raytheon Hawk missiles.

While the Israeli ground forces suffered a major defeat in Sinai on the 9th, with the destruction of the 190th Tank Brigade, their A-4s and F-4s made vain attempts to attack the Nile Delta airfields at Mansurah and Qadmiyah, but were frustrated by the Egyptian missile defences which evidently destroyed about 16 of the attackers. By now Egypt, Syria and Israel were seeking to support their victory claims by displaying captured enemy pilots.

On Wednesday the 10th the Israeli Air Force continued to attack the Egyptian missile screen which was now being deepened as a belt of SAMs was established on the east bank of the Suez Canal. These attacks, and others on forward airfields and the bridges over the canal met with only limited success and were accompanied by the loss of about a dozen IAF aircraft, including four helicopters. The Israelis had by now checked the Egyptian advance into Sinai and were content for the time being to hold a line some 19–24 km (12–15 miles) east of the canal.

Left: the Israeli Chief of Staff, Lt Gen David Elazar, watches the progress of the battle over the Suez Canal from a helicopter on 19 October 1973. By this stage of the war Israel had lost over a hundred warplanes in combat

American airlift

By 12 October independent observers estimated that Egypt had thus far suffered the loss of 82 fighters and fighter-bombers, plus 17 helicopters, and the Syrians 80 fighters and fighter-bombers, plus seven helicopters, a total of 186 aircraft. The same sources estimated IAF losses at 94 aircraft, including sixteen helicopters. The following day Israel made an extraordinary revelation – that the nation possessed war material for no more than four further days of warfare. Whether or not this was just one more ploy in Israel's campaign to win American succour, it certainly had the desired effect when the Americans decided to commence airlifting huge quantities of replacement equipment, as well as highly-sophisticated ECM items. Numerous IAF jet aircraft were by now being repaired at home factories, having suffered serious damage from heat-seeking SA-7 Strella missiles, and US counter-measures equipment was provided to lend immunity from these weapons.

Day Nine, 14 October, was a critical point in the battle for Sinai. Egyptian armoured units made strenuous attempts to force the passes of Khatmia and Mitla, but encountered such determined opposition that a major tank battle developed, which cost Egypt the loss of at least one hundred tanks, and Israel almost as many. More important, it prompted Egypt to rush large numbers of

Above: the MiG-17 shared ground attack duties with the Su-7 in the Egyptian and Syrian air forces, both air arms having over 100 MiG-17s on strength at the outbreak of hostilities. Left: according to Israeli sources, Arab air losses totalled 248 Egyptian and 221 Syrian aircraft between 6 and 24 October. A MiG-17 is illustrated

tanks across the canal which it had been holding back in readiness for an anticipated Israeli airborne assault on the west bank.

The significance of Egypt's denuding her west bank reserves was felt two days later when an Israeli column not only battered its way to the canal in the south, but in the dead of night managed to send some tanks across to the west bank. Within hours, before the Egyptian air force reacted to this threat, a small but well-defined bridgehead had been established. From this point on, despite tre-mendous losses, the initiative on the Sinai front passed almost exclusively to the Israelis who, the following day received 24 replacement F-4s and a large number of Shrike air-to-ground radar-homing missiles from America.

Israeli bridgehead

On 18 October, the Israeli west bank pocket was con-solidated with the construction of a bridge over the canal. At last the Egyptians woke to the real danger of the bridge-head and attempted to destroy it. The Israelis had, how-ever, overrun the SAM sites in the immediate vicinity and were able to give effective air cover to their troops so that, when Egyptian Su-7s attempted to attack the bridgehead under MiG-21 top cover, vicious air battles developed with IAF Phantoms and Mirages, from which the Egyptians certainly emerged second best.

The next four days brought catastrophe to the Egyptians, with the Israelis on a veritable rampage west of the canal. On the 19th, the Egyptians lost about 20 aircraft, the next day a further ten, followed by about 15 on the 21st. By the evening of the 22nd, Israeli forces controlled the Egyptian airfields at Fayid, Kabrit and Kasfareet, and were threatening the important air base at Abu Sueir. Large numbers of Egyptian SAMs had been destroyed or captured so that the much-vaunted missile screen was no longer able to protect the rear areas.

The inevitable cease-fire, agreed by President Sadat, whose Third Army faced encirclement and annihilation by sophisticated American weaponry should have come into effect of 22 October. However, fighting, in the air and on the ground, flared up time and again for a further two days.

The Syrian Front
In the north the pattern of the war ran much the same as in the south, with initial success attending Syrian forces in their assault on the Israeli-occupied Golan Heights, and Mount Hermon fell to helicopter-borne assault troops on the first day. However, the Syrians failed to move their SAMs forward quickly enough to protect their ground forces from heavy air attacks by IAF Skyhawks.

As in the south, the Israelis now recognised the importance of the Syrian SAM screen, and set about an all-out attempt to destroy the sites and missile vehicles. During the first five days, air losses on both sides mounted quickly, though it was noticeable that most IAF losses were incurred over the ground battle area, suggesting that Syria's rear areas were less well protected by SAMs. A number of crippling strikes against targets at Damascus, Homs, Latakia, Minat al Bayda, Qatinah and Tartus were achieved by the IAF with little loss.

Despite the severity of the fighting in Sinai, and the obvious difficulty experienced by Israel in fighting on two fronts, it was in the north that Israel first made significant headway against the Arabs on the ground. On 11 October, the Syrians began a withdrawal from the Golan Heights (though Syrian and Moroccan troops held firm on Mount Hermon), the reason for this evidently being the enforced withdrawal of Syrian air cover (both missiles and fighters) from the battlefield to give protection to the towns and factories in the rear as well as airfields.

By 16 October, the Israelis had come up against the Saasa defence line and were checked. Five days later they attempted to assault Mount Hermon using about 200 helicopter-borne troops and some 80 paratroops. The battle on and over this key point continued up to and beyond the so-called cease-fire, as both sides threw in airborne troops under cover provided by their respective air forces.

On the last day of fighting, in a show of strength and backed by the newly-delivered American ECM equipment, the IAF launched a number of 'strategic' raids against Syria's industrial plants, including a devastating raid by 60 aircraft – many of them bomb-carrying Phantoms – on a large Damascus oil installation. About ten aircraft were lost by each side.

Seven years earlier, Israel won the Six Day War by use of pre-emptive surprise and superior air power. To guard against a repetition, the Arab nations had acquired large quantities of SAMs from Russia, while their air forces –

almost totally destroyed in 1967 – were rebuilt from scratch. Nevertheless, both Egypt and Syria failed to acquire really modern aircraft and the combat aircraft were still much the same as in the previous war. Moreover, as before, the Arabs again fielded a roughly two-to-one numerical superiority. By adopting the Israeli surprise and *blitz* tactics at the outset, the Arabs certainly looked set to achieve their aims quickly, and there is no doubt that after about five days of catastrophic setbacks the Israelis' situation seemed desperate.

The key to the air war, and therefore almost certainly to the final outcome of the whole conflict, was undoubtedly the Arabs' missile network. The brilliant plans followed by the IAF to attack the missile sites, irrespective of losses, certainly prevented their effective use in defence of the ground forces. Although the SAM network was never totally destroyed, it was rendered almost impotent by the arrival of American countermeasures equipment. Perhaps it is significant that while the United States was prepared to release quantities of very modern aircraft and equipment to safeguard Israel's survival, the Soviet Union was evidently reluctant (or unable) to supply to the Arab nations similar *matériel*.

Below: Egyptian surface-to-air and anti-tank missiles made important contributions to that country's early successes against Israeli forces. AT-1 Snapper anti-tank missiles are pictured. Bottom: high level attack was guarded against by Egyptian SA-2 Guideline missiles, a captured example of which is being recovered for Israeli evaluation and testing

Above: the Lockheed C-130 Hercules formed the backbone of the Israeli's transport and logistic support units.
Right: the IAI-built Magisters of the Israeli air force's training wing, based at Hatzerim, were operated with success in the light attack role.
Below right: the Sikorsky S-65C-3, together with the Aérospatiale SA 321K Super Frelon, gave the Israeli's a potent battlefield heavy transport and assault component. The S-65C-3 in assault configuration can carry up to 25 troops

Friedrichshafen Raid 1914

With the outbreak of hostilities in August 1914, the British Admiralty, highly conscious of the potential menace of Germany's airship fleet, immediately considered plans for possible aerial destruction of the known Zeppelin bases. In doing so, it might be said that the naval high command instigated the practical concept of strategic

bombing in its simplest form. Deciding to concentrate on the large airship shed complex at Friedrichshafen on the shores of Lake Constance, the Admiralty appointed Lieutenant Noel Pemberton-Billing RNVR to prepare all necessary equipment and personnel for an aerial attack on this objective. Billing left England on 21 October 1914 and

The Avro 504 was the best aircraft available to the British in 1914 for the Friedrichshafen raid, the first 'strategic' bombing raid by British aircraft

arrived at Belfort Fortress in Belgium three days later, where he first obtained permission to utilise the parade ground field within the fortress as the base for such a raid. Then, aided by Belgian and French intelligence reports, he mapped out the proposed method and route for the sortie. This involved a flight of approximately 200 km (125 miles) to Friedrichshafen, deliberately skirting the northern border with Switzerland in order to avoid any possible breach of neutrality.

The Raid
On 28 October Billing returned to England to assemble the raiding force. Four 80 hp Gnome-engined Avro 504 biplanes were selected – Nos 179, 873, 874 and 875 – and four pilots: Squadron Commander E. F. Briggs, Flight Commander J. T. Babington, Flight Lieutenant S. V. Sippe and Flight Sub-Lieutenant R. P. Cannon. Together with 11 naval air mechanics, these pilots formed, in Manchester, a new unit, commanded by Squadron Commander P. Shepherd. The unit moved *en bloc* to Belfort on 13 November and, by the afternoon of the following day, all four Avros had been reassembled, tested and were ready for operations. Bad weather conditions prevented any flying for a week but, on Saturday 21 November, conditions improved considerably and the raid was declared 'on'.

At 0930 hours on the morning of the 21st the four Avros were lined up on the airfield, each loaded with four 20 lb Hales bombs and engines were run up. The Avros left Belfort at five minute intervals, with Briggs taking off first (in No 873), then John Babington (875), followed by Sippe (874). Cannon (179) failed to become airborne and had to abandon the sortie. The three airborne bombers made their way independently to the target and Briggs was the first to attack, arriving over Friedrichshafen at about 1145 hours. Sweeping in low at 150 m (500 ft),

Briggs ran a gauntlet of concentrated rifle and machine gun fire as he released his bombs over the huge airship hangars. Then, wounded in the head and his aircraft with a ruptured petrol tank, he was forced to land. He was then subjected to rough handling by enraged civilians but was 'rescued' by the military and taken to Weingarten hospital. He was subsequently imprisoned in Ingelstadt, but eventually escaped in April 1917 and returned to England.

Next to arrive was Sidney Sippe, whose subsequent raid report read, in part: '11.55 am When half a mile from the sheds put machine into dive, and came down to 700 ft. Observed men lined up to right of shed, number estimated 300–500. Dropped one bomb in enclosure to put gunners off aim, and, when in correct position, two into works and shed. The fourth bomb failed to release. During this time very heavy fire, mitrailleuse and rifle, was being kept up, and shells were being very rapidly fired. Dived and flew north out of range of guns, then turned back to waterside shed to try and release fourth bomb. Bomb would not release; was fired on by two machine guns (probably mitrailleuse), dived down to surface of lake and made good my escape.' Sippe eventually landed back at Belfort at 1350 hours, but the third Avro piloted by Babington, after attacking the sheds, was forced to land just 56 km (35 miles) short of base, though without harm or damage.

Aftermath
Of the 11 bombs actually dropped, one blew out a window of a small airship shed which housed the L.7, but, despite Allied claims at that time, the L.7 was not touched. At least one of the bombs hit a nearby gas works, resulting in a gigantic explosion which shook the surrounding countryside. Though relatively little damage had been suffered by the airship base itself, the German authorities immediately went to great lengths to protect Friedrichshafen against any further attacks. A vast network con-

The three Avro 504s which carried out the raid on Friedrichshafen preparing to take off. A fourth did not leave the ground. The aircraft farthest from the camera is Sippe's, the only one to return intact. No 873 is Briggs' and No 875 Babington's. Although the raid did negligible damage, in proving such operations were possible it alerted the military authorities on both sides to the developing power of aircraft

Above: Flight Lieutenant Sidney Sippe piloted the third Avro 504 to take off from Belfort for the 200 km (125 mile) flight to Friedrichshafen on 21 November 1914.
Below: the Avro 504s which took part in the raid were powered by the 80 hp Gnome rotary and each carried a bomb-load of four 20 lb Hales bombs

struction was built over the sheds, military guards were doubled, a large increase was made in anti-aircraft guns and searchlights and two additional gunboats were stationed near the floating hangar on the lake. In the event Friedrichshafen was not attacked again by the Allies, but the extra military equipment and personnel remained throughout the war.

Immediately after Sippe and Babington returned to Belfort, both men were personally decorated with the Légion d'Honneur by General Thevenet, Governor of Belfort Fortress. In the 1915 New Year's Honours List, Briggs, Babington and Sippe were each invested as Companions of the Distinguished Service Order (DSO). Having completed their specific task, the remaining three Avro machines were then dismantled, crated, packed onto a special train and returned to England, arriving there on 26 November 1914.

One outcome of the raid was a diplomatic note of protest to London from the Swiss Government. Sidney Sippe's report clearly indicated that *en route* to Friedrichshafen he had, at one point, flown over Swiss territory; this breach of neutrality was questioned officially. The British Foreign Office's reply pointed out that the original orders for the sortie had specifically precluded any such possible violation of neutral zones. It also added discreetly that in any case the question of 'territory in the air' had not been resolved by the 1910 International Congress and that therefore there was no breach of international law.

Of the three pilots who undertook this pioneer bombing sortie, Briggs eventually retired from the RAF in February 1930 as a Group Captain, DSO, OBE. Sippe rose to the rank of Major, while John Babington remained in the RAF until World War II, ultimately attaining the rank of Air Marshal.

Tondern Raid 1918

With the outbreak of World War I, the chief aerial menace feared by British authorities was undoubtedly the German rigid airship. The Admiralty in particular was highly conscious of the potential threat of these air giants, and with its responsibilities for the aerial defence of the United Kingdom it adopted the policy of using offence as the best form of defence. Thus from the start of hostilities the tiny Royal Naval Air Service sought means and methods of attacking the airship bases along the north-western coastal zones of Europe. One such base was Tondern in Schleswig-Holstein, opposite the island of Sylt. Built during the winter of 1914–15, Tondern berthed its first airship on 23 March 1915 and in the following years housed at least 15 such craft at some period.

Speculative attack

The first serious attempt to bomb Tondern could not be undertaken until early 1916, when HMS *Vindex*, carrying three Short and two Sopwith Baby floatplanes aboard, arrived off the coast on 25 March. Launching all five aircraft in the early morning, the pilots had been briefed to find and bomb an airship shed 'believed to be at Hoyer'. No sheds were visible at Hoyer, but one pilot overflew the nearby Tondern base and immediately attempted a low-level attack. His bombs failed to leave their racks however, and he returned to report the precise location of the target. Three of the remaining four seaplanes fell into enemy hands. A second raid was planned for early April 1916, but of the 11 aircraft which attempted to set out only one ever reached Tondern. Two 65 lb bombs were dropped without doing any damage, although the airship L7 was in residence at the time.

It was to be two years before any further attempt was made to eliminate the Tondern base. The limitations of contemporary aircraft in operational range excluded any land-based bombers, while the state of progress in ship-borne aircraft was such that any venture of this nature was impractical. In the spring of 1918, however, the possibility was revived. Several vessels had been modified in the interim to accept aircraft; one of these was the cruiser HMS *Furious* which, by 1918 had been drastically modified to have a 90 m (300 ft) flight deck. A scheme for *Furious* to carry two special flights of Sopwith 2F1 Ship's Camels was officially approved, special training for the sortie being undertaken at Turnhouse, near Edinburgh. At the end of June, both flights and their pilots were taken aboard *Furious*, which sailed from Rosyth on 27 June. Within 48 hours, however, atrocious weather conditions forced a postponement of the operation and *Furious* returned to port with her aircraft.

A second attempt was made on 17 July, only to run into violent thunderstorms next day. At dawn on 19 July, *Furious* and her escorts were stationed 128 km (80 miles) north-west of Tondern. Of the eight Camels aboard, seven were prepared for the raid in two 'waves', each Camel loaded with two 50 lb bombs. In the first wave of three Camels were Captains W. D. Jackson, W. F. Dickson and Lt N. E. Williams, while the second wave quartet was piloted by Captains B. A. Smart, T. K. Thyne and Lts S. Dawson and W. A. Yeulett. The first trio took off at 0314 hours, followed some ten minutes later by the other four Camels. *En route* to the target Smart's rear echelon was soon reduced to three aircraft when Thyne was forced to ditch in the sea with engine trouble.

Inadequate defences

At Tondern, few personnel were awake when, at 0432 hours, a sentry at Scherrebeck, south-east of the airfield, telephoned to report three unidentified aircraft approaching. The few gun crews available were hastily called, but there were no other defences; the airfield's five Albatros D III fighters provided for just such an event had been withdrawn on 6 March for more active service elsewhere. Three minutes after the alert the leading Camel trio swept in to attack. William Dickson's report gives an account of what followed; 'I saw a low shed, very solidly built and looking semi-underground. It was about the same size as the large Zeppelin shed at East Fortune. No chimneys or outbuildings could be observed round it, so I decided to drop one bomb on it, which I did from a height of 700 feet, hitting it in the middle. I observed no signs of fire but many clouds of smoke.

Above: a Sopwith 2F1 Ship's Camel which took part in the Tondern raid.
Opposite above: a Sopwith Pup fitted with a skid undercarriage lands on the flight deck of HMS Furious in 1918. Landings were hazardous during the early years of carrier operations.
Opposite: Sopwith 2F1 Ship's Camels embarked on HMS Furious, the first through-deck aircraft carrier. Seven such aircraft were flown off HMS Furious on 19 July 1918 to bomb the Tondern Zeppelin sheds

'Immediately after this I saw Captain Jackson at about 3,000 feet above me and a good distance to the east coming down in a dive, with Lieutenant Williams about half a mile astern of him. I climbed a little and joined in with them and then observed two very large sheds . . . and also a smaller one. These were at least five miles north of the town . . . There was absolutely no sign of life until Jackson began diving on the shed when a battery on the Tondern-Hoyer road opened fire; besides this no other battery opened fire during our bombing. Captain Jackson dived right on the northern-most shed and dropped two bombs, one a direct hit in the middle and the other slightly to the side of one shed. I then dropped my remaining bomb, and Williams two more. Hits were observed. The shed then burst into flames, and an enormous conflagration took place rising to at least 1,000 feet, the whole of the shed being completely engulfed. After dropping Jackson went straight on, Williams to the left, and I to the right. Two or more batteries then opened fire on us but the shooting was not good. This is the last I saw of the other two.'

Ditching and internment

This initial attack saw three bombs penetrate the large hangar housing the airships L54 and L60, both of which were totally destroyed by fire. Another bomb hit a smaller hangar, damaging the captive balloon inside. About ten minutes later Smart and his two companions arrived over Tondern and concentrated on the apparently undamaged smaller hangar, setting it afire with two bombs, while four other bombs fell nearby. One Camel lost a wheel during the attack but all three left the target safely.

The return journey of each of the six Camels became a series of good luck, misfortune and tragedy. Dickson managed to reach the naval force, landed in the sea near HMS *Violent* and was rescued from his sinking Camel. Smart headed for the pre-arranged rendezvous with his companions at Brede, circled for a while, then set off alone to regain the naval formation. He too eventually alighted alongside *Violent*, but only after a final 20 minutes of anxious flying with little petrol just above the waves. Of the remaining four Camels, nothing was seen. Yeulett was forced to ditch and was drowned before any rescue was possible; Jackson force-landed in Denmark and deliberately burned his aircraft, while Williams and Dawson were both interned in Denmark after forced-landings. The latter three all had insufficient fuel to complete their intended round trips. Thyne, the pilot who had originally been forced to ditch with a recalcitrant engine, had already been recovered safely by one of the escort destroyers.

The balance sheet

The effect of their surprise raid was more widespread than the pilots realised. In terms of specific casualties and damage, they had destroyed two of Germany's latest airships, injured four groundcrewmen and severely damaged the main hangars at Tondern. Indeed, from then until the end of the war Tondern became simply an emergency landing ground and no longer operational as an airship base. The larger effect, however, was to spread anxiety and deep concern throughout the German Naval Airship Division, which lived in constant fear of a similar attack on its other airship bases.

The whole operation had been the first-ever attack by seaborne aircraft against a major land target and as such pioneered a tactic which was to have devastating effects in maritime aviation warfare little more than two decades later. Yet the carrier *Furious* did not repeat the feat in 1918. Though able to fly off aircraft, its upper deck layout made

landings highly dangerous for pilots. The vessel reverted to being a carrier for non-rigid airships and in November 1919 was put into reserve at Rosyth. She was re-commissioned in new, flush-deck guise in 1925 and served with success in World War II. Camel pilot William Dickson transferred from the Royal Navy to the newly-created Royal Air Force for a permanent career, and eventually rose to become Marshal of the RAF and Chief of the Air Staff from January 1953 to January 1956.

Below: a painting by C. Pears of HMS Furious as she appeared in 1918. Centre: the large Tondern airship shed ablaze after the raid on 19 July 1918. Bottom: Zeppelins L54 and L60 (pictured) were destroyed as a result

Kabul Airlift 1928-29

In October 1922 the first example of a new aeroplane design, the Vickers Vernon, was completed. Derived from the Vickers Vimy, the Vernon was the RAF's first aeroplane designed as a troop transport, though this title was later changed to bomber transport. Issued to Nos 45 and 70 Squadrons in Iraq, production versions of the Vernon served for several years in the mid-1920s in the Middle East. Among their little-known achievements were two mercy operations which virtually set a pattern for all future air transport within the RAF.

On 5 September 1922 two Vernons, along with 24 DH9As and three Bristol F2bs, comprised a hastily-assembled force to evacuate a total of 67 British subjects and a large quantity of arms, ammunition and other stores, from Kirkuk during a rebellion by local tribesmen. In the following 15 months Vernons were also instrumental in evacuating a total of 161 sick and wounded Servicemen from outlying stations to base hospital in Baghdad. Other proof of the future potential of large air transport machines was the inauguration of the Baghdad-Cairo air mail service by Vernons of Nos 45 and 70 Squadrons – a vital link in the proposed chain of communications linking the countries of the British Empire.

Revolt in Afghanistan

By late 1926 the Vickers Victoria was replacing the Vickers Vernon in service. Nominally capable of lifting twice a Vernon's load, carrying a two-man crew and 22 fully-kitted troops, the Victoria undertook a number of long-distance pioneering Service flights in the following two years. However, it will always be associated in RAF history with what has since come to be known as the world's first major airlift – the Kabul evacuation.

In Afghanistan the British Legation, first established there in 1919, found itself unwittingly in the centre of a massive civil war caused by tribesmen attempting to oust the Afghan king Amanullah and his royalist forces. For a number of years the king had advocated drastic modernisation of his country and subjects, including the introduction of European dress for his court and, more seriously, the emancipation of Afghan women. Such reforms infuriated his Islamic subjects, who, led by the Shinwari tribe, finally declared open revolt against Amanullah and, by late 1928, laid siege to the capital city Kabul. The British Legation, situated 5·6 km (3·5 miles) outside the city, stood between the opposing factions and quickly came under fire from both heavy guns and thousands of rifles on both sides.

Airlift requested

The British Envoy Extraordinary at Kabul, Sir Francis Humphrys – himself an ex-RAF pilot – realised that the

Above right: a painting by Brian Witham, 'The Evacuation of Kabul', depicting Vickers Victorias escorted by a Westland Wapiti over India's North-West Frontier. Right: evacuees from Kabul disembarking from a Victoria at Risalpur. The RAF evacuated 586 people in two months

only safe method of evacuating the several hundred British and foreign subjects in his and other legations was by air, using the nearby Afghan Air Force base of Sherpur. Accordingly, on 5 December, Humphrys signalled the air commander in India, Air Vice-Marshal Sir Geoffrey Salmond, requesting airlift facilities. This put Salmond in a difficult situation. His only readily-available aircraft were the DH9As of Nos 27 and 60 Squadrons, plus some Bristol F2bs, and two Westland Wapitis, the latter undergoing tropical trials in India. The nearest RAF large transport aircraft were the Victorias of No 70 Squadron based at Hinaidi, Iraq, some 4,500 km (2,800 miles) from northern India. Salmond requested the Air Ministry to have No 70 Squadron detached to India for the Kabul operation. Meanwhile, he issued orders for the DH9A squadrons to have their 'Ninaks' stripped of all war equipment and be prepared for initial evacuation of the Legation's personnel.

In an attempt to provide the Legation with some form of communication – all land lines were out of action – one DH9A of No 27 Squadron, piloted by Flying Officer C. W. L. Trusk with Leading Aircraftman G. A. Donaldson as passenger, flew low over the Legation and dropped a Popham Panel ground-to-air signalling device. The DH9A was hit by rifle fire and forced to land hastily at Sherpur airstrip. Two days later the two men managed to gain entry to the Legation, where they remained throughout the subsequent operation. At Risalpur, main base for the Kabul operations, Squadron Leader R. S. Maxwell of No 70 Squadron made the first evacuation flight in a Victoria on 23 December, landing at Sherpur that day and taking off again for Peshawar with 23 women and children. This was the first of 19 such trips to be flown by Maxwell, lifting a total of 218 people. He was accompanied on the 23rd by three DH9As and a Wapiti. On 24 and 26 December, the single Victoria and 16 DH9As evacuated a further 51 women and children.

Sub-zero temperatures

On Christmas Day reinforcement, in the shape of a Handley Page Hinaidi transport, arrived from Iraq, while four days later two more Victorias from No 70 Squadron arrived in India. By 1 January, utilising every available aircraft, the last of the women and children had been safely retrieved from Sherpur. On 10 January, however,

the rebel tribes advanced on Kabul again and four days later King Amanullah abdicated in favour of his brother Inayatullah – who promptly fled to Kandahar on 18 January. The rebels' leader, Bacha-i-Saqao, immediately assumed kingship, and on the same day Sir Francis Humphrys decided to close the Legation. Permission was obtained from the new king for aircraft to land daily at Sherpur to complete the total evacuation of non-Afghans.

For the next four weeks the lumbering Victorias – five more arrived between 8 and 15 February – with their faithful DH9A companions continued to fly through the menacing mountains along Afghanistan's border in one of the worst winters ever experienced on the North-West Frontier of India. In temperatures as low as minus 20 degrees centigrade the crews in their open cockpits endured snow, ice and freezing conditions – at one period Sherpur airstrip was covered in 17 inches of snow. Finally, on 25 February, seven Victorias landed at Sherpur to take out the last Legation personnel, the last to leave being Humphrys, Trusk and Donaldson. In 84 flights the airmen had covered a total of 92,437 km (57,438 miles) and flown out over 41 tons, including 586 people. This, the first major airlift in RAF history, was accomplished without a single serious casualty, although several aircraft had been damaged due to various reasons. Subsequently the award of an Air Force Cross was made to five of the pilots involved, while LAC Donaldson, who had been responsible for setting up and maintaining wireless communication at the besieged Legation throughout the two perilous months, was awarded an Air Force Medal.

Taranto 1940

The situation existing in the Mediterranean immediately following Italy s entry to World War II in June 1940 was decidedly unfavourable for the Royal Navy. Hitherto Allied shipping had sailed from the Suez Canal to Gibraltar, being adequately protected by such naval forces which existed at Alexandria, Malta and Gibraltar, with assistance from the French navy. The collapse of France, the presence of a powerful Italian fleet–together with the immediate need to reinforce Malta and the British land forces facing the Italians in the Western Desert–appeared likely to overtax the resources of a Royal Navy necessarily deployed over the entire globe.

War in the Mediterranean

The Royal Navy gradually managed to strengthen its forces at Alexandria and Admiral Sir Andrew Cunningham

lost no time in attempting to bring the Italian fleet to action. However, although the Italians possessed a greater strength in terms of numbers of warships, they proved less than eager to accommodate the British admiral's plans. The Italians possessed no aircraft carriers, depending solely on shore-based aircraft for support, while the Royal Navy could usually call upon at least three carriers in the Mediterranean at any one time.

Nevertheless the mere presence of an Italian battlefleet represented a continuing threat to the safety of Allied convoys. Although three such convoys reached Malta during October and early November under cover of the Mediterranean Fleet, the unprovoked Italian attack on Greece created further commitments for Allied shipping. not least in the British attempt to establish a forward base at Suda Bay in Crete.

Fairey Swordfish from HMS Illustrious attacked Italian warships in Taranto harbour on the night of 11/12 November 1941, and, achieving complete surprise, put out of actions three of Italy's six capital ships. This single action removed the threat of Italian naval intervention in the Royal Navy's operations in the Mediterranean

It was now that Admiral Cunningham determined to use his sea-borne torpedo bombers in a long-cherished plan to attack the Italian navy in its base at Taranto. This attack was planned as a prelude to passing a number of important troopships and merchant convoys from Gibraltar to Alexandria during November.

Malta's recce flight

With three carriers, four battleships and battlecruisers and numerous cruisers and destroyers now based at Gibraltar and Alexandria, the stage was set for a decisive attack to take place on 21 October–the anniversary of the Battle of Trafalgar. It was intended that 30 Fairey Swordfish torpedo bombers of Nos 813, 815, 819 and 824 Squadrons of the Fleet Air Arm would be launched from the carriers HMS *Eagle* and *Illustrious*.

However *Eagle* was suffering defects following near misses from Italian bombers and it was decided to transfer a few of her aircraft and aircrew to *Illustrious* for the attack. Flying his flag aboard *Illustrious* was Rear Admiral Lumley Lyster, a World War I pilot who had served with a squadron of the Royal Naval Air Service at Taranto more than 20 years previously and who, in 1938, conceived the idea of an air attack on the naval base. He had, moreover, trained some Swordfish pilots in night attacks while serving in the Mediterranean at that time; some of these pilots were now with him in *Illustrious*.

While the carrier's crewmen were fitting extra fuel tanks in the Swordfish, however, a serious fire broke out in the hangar which destroyed two aircraft and damaged five others. The attack, codenamed Operation Judgement, was thus delayed until 11 November.

As a preliminary however, the Royal Air Force was asked to carry out a detailed reconnaissance of Taranto harbour. A Martin Maryland of No 431 (General Reconnaissance) Flight took off in appalling weather from Luqa, Malta on 10 November to perform what was to be regarded as one of the truly remarkable reconnaissance sorties by the RAF during World War II.

The pilot of the Maryland was Pilot Officer Adrian Warburton, who, with Sergeants John Spire as navigator and Paddy Moran as gunner, set course for Calabria, flying just above wavetop height. Warburton warned his crew that he proposed to remain inside Taranto harbour until they had located and plotted every enemy vessel.

The Italians were taken by surprise by the low-flying Maryland. The customary balloon barrage had not been flown, and Warburton flew twice round the harbour at low altitude before the flak opened up. Spires furiously pencilled the names of the Italian warships, while Warburton operated the camera. As the intensity of ground fire increased, the pilot withdrew for a spell but decided to make one more run round the ships in order to make sure he had gained a complete picture of the port.

Despite the attentions of an Italian fighter, the Maryland pilot returned safely to Malta where his photographs and notes were quickly processed and flown to HMS *Illustrious*. They showed no fewer than five battleships, 14 cruisers and 27 destroyers moored in Taranto harbour. Late that evening an RAF flying boat crew reported that a sixth Italian battleship had entered the port.

Surprise attack

Now in possession of detailed information about the target, Captain D. W. Boyd, commanding *Illustrious*, could signal Admiral Cunningham his confidence in the planned attack. Accordingly two waves of Swordfish were launched on the evening of 11 November. The first wave of twelve aircraft–six armed with torpedoes, four with bombs and two with bombs and flares–led by Lieutenant-Commander Kenneth Williamson flew off at 2040 hours. The second wave of nine aircraft–five with torpedoes, two

A Fairey Swordfish being loaded with an 18 in torpedo. Eleven of the 21 Swordfish flown off HMS Illustrious to attack Taranto on the night of 11/12 November 1940 carried torpedoes set to detonate either on contact or by magnetic proximity to a hull

A Fairey Swordfish Mk II serving with No 824 Squadron, Fleet Air Arm. Swordfish from HMS Illustrious and aircraft and crews transferred from HMS Eagle carried out the attack on Taranto. Apart from 11 torpedo-carrying Swordfish, six carried bombs for use against shore installations, two had flares to mark targets and two had both bombs and flares

with bombs and two with bombs and flares–led by Lt-Cdr John Hale took off at 2130 hours from a position 275 kilometres (170 miles) south-east of Taranto.

Slightly less heavily loaded with fuel, the second wave was only ten minutes behind when Williamson's Swordfish swept into Taranto, taking the defences almost completely by surprise. The previous day's storms had destroyed much of the balloon barrage, while the Italians had decided against fixed anti-torpedo nets as, it was said, they hampered the movement of ships. Despite attempts to achieve a blackout at the port, the naval pilots had been given such accurate dispositions of the Italian ships that, by the light of their own flares, they quickly sank the new battleship *Littorio*–a 35,000 ton ship only completed three months earlier–with three torpedoes at her moorings. Two older 23,600 ton battleships, *Conte di Cavour* and *Caio Duilio*, were badly damaged, the former never to sail again. At a single stroke three of Italy's six capital ships had been put out of action. In the inner harbour a heavy cruiser and a destroyer were also hit.

The leading Swordfish of Lt-Cdr Williamson himself was shot down–he and his crewman being taken prisoner–and an aircraft of Hale's second wave also failed to return, its crew being killed; another of the attacking aircraft failed to drop its weapon.

Aftermath

In a single night the balance of power in the Central Mediterranean had swung back in Cunningham's favour and the British maritime power in the theatre was re-asserted. Had that shift in fortune not occurred, the risks attending the British reinforcement of Greece by sea would in all probability have been too great. Indeed only the intervention by the Luftwaffe to rescue the Italians from a disastrous stalemate in the Balkans eventually forced the British out of Greece and Crete, with heavy losses among Royal Naval ships.

One interesting postscript to the Taranto attack was afforded by Japan's recall from London at that time of her naval attaché, Commander Minoru Genda. He was subsequently ordered to carry out the staff planning for a surprise attack on the American Pacific Fleet at Pearl Harbour, and there is little doubt that the Royal Navy's attack on Taranto served as a closely-studied prototype on which his plans were based.

Below: a painting by Bagley depicting the Fleet Air Arm's attack on Taranto. The barrage of Italian anti-aircraft fire was intense, but only two Swordfish were lost, including the aircraft of Lt-Cdr Williamson

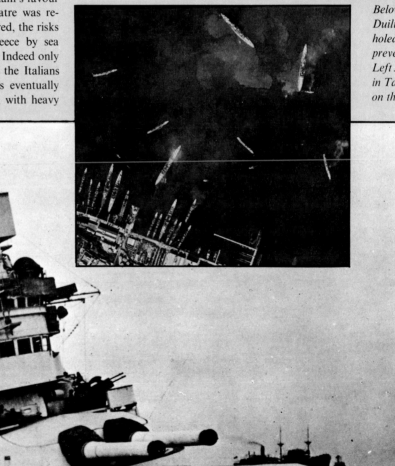

Below: the battleship Duilio with her hull badly holed had to be beached to prevent her sinking.
Left: damaged cruisers lie in Taranto's inner harbour on the day after the raid

Darwin 1942-43

At Darwin, North-West Australia, the Japanese delivered their most devastating air attack since Pearl Harbour. Escorted by two battleships, five cruisers and about 20 smaller warships, four aircraft carriers of the Japanese 1st and 2nd Carrier Divisions entered the Arafura Sea from the Banda Sea under cover of darkness. Early in the morning of 19 February 1942, when about 200 kilometres (130 miles) from Australia's northern coast, the carriers turned into wind to fly off their aircraft – 27 Nakajima B5N2 Kate attack bombers and 27 Aichi D3A Val dive-bombers, escorted by three groups of nine Mitsubishi A6M Zero fighters. Their task was to neutralise Darwin as a base during the invasion of Timor.

Unprepared defences

The rapid advance of the Japanese down the Malayan archipelago had alerted the Commonwealth to the dangers of invasion; but, while Darwin was a hive of maritime activity, it was curiously unprepared for air attack. There had already been warnings and Japanese reconnaissance aircraft had been observed. However, when, on that fateful morning, observers on Bathurst Island radioed to Darwin that a large formation of aircraft was approaching, it was assumed to be a patrol of American P-40 Warhawks. In fact, five Warhawks on local patrol were the first to encounter the enemy and the Zeros promptly shot three of them down into the sea. Other Zeros were by then swooping low to attack shipping while Kates, in almost perfect formation at 4,200 m (14,000 ft), started pattern bombing the shipping moored in the harbour.

The 16 3·7 in and two 3 in anti-aircraft guns of the

The Spitfire Mk VC of Sqn Ldr E. M. Gibbs, CO of No 54 Sqn, is pushed under camouflage nets at Night Cliff, Darwin on 22 June 1943. The RAF Spitfire Wing, supported by a radar early warning system, effectively countered Japanese raids on Darwin in 1943. They made heavy but successful intercepted raids in March, May and June, but from 20/21 August made a few night raids only

Left: a Spitfire Mk VC of No 54 Sqn pictured in a camouflaged dispersal bay before take-off at Night Cliff on 22 June 1943. Below: a No 54 Sqn Spitfire Mk VC undergoing maintenance at Night Cliff on 22 June 1943. No 54 Sqn, RAF and Nos 452 and 457 (Australian) Sqns, RAF formed No 1 Fighter Wing, RAF, commanded by Wing Commander C. R. 'Killer' Caldwell, the top-scoring Australian fighter pilot. The Wing became operational in February 1943 and was engaged in repulsing a steady number of Japanese air raids on Northern Australia and on convoy patrols until going onto the offensive in 1944

harbour defences lacked experienced gunners. Keeping formation, the Kates circled round to make a second run over the harbour while Vals and Zeros bombed and strafed individual ships.

Largest of the ships in harbour, the 10,000-ton SS *Meigs*, attracted the most attention and, after being repeatedly hit, it was set on fire. The 6,900-ton tanker *British Motorist* was sunk, as was the merchantman SS *Zealandia*. In spite of getting quickly under way to try to evade the bombs, the destroyer USS *Peary* received three direct hits and was burnt out. Rescue work was hampered when the hospital ship *Marunda* also received hits. Billowing smoke, drifting across the harbour, evidently saved the Qantas Empire flying boat *Camilla*, which was moored in the harbour, but some US Navy Catalinas were destroyed on the water. Part of a wharf was blasted away, hurling a railway locomotive into the water, killing over 20 dockers and cutting off survivors from the shore, and buildings along the waterfront, including the telegraph office, were wrecked.

Five American-flown Warhawks, refuelling at the time, were then the only fighters available to the defences; one of them was destroyed before it left the ground and the others before they could gain combat height. This left no fighter cover at all for the second attack, which came at mid-day. This time the attackers were in two formations, each of 27 land-based Mitsubishi G4M Betty bombers of the Japanese Navy, operating from Kendari in the Celebes, with the Darwin military airfield as their prime target. Hangars, barrack blocks, stores and vehicles were wrecked and six Royal Australian Air Force Hudsons were destroyed, together with a United States Army Air Force Liberator in transit and three Beechcraft light transport aircraft.

Panic ensued; rumour spread of Japanese invasion and an order to evacuate the pitted airfield for clear ground a mile away became garbled in relaying. Some servicemen joined civilians in departing from the area. During the lull between raids the 6,000-ton MV *Neptuna*, berthed at a wharf, had blown up with 200 depth charges in her hold, creating havoc in the harbour. In all, there were hundreds

Left: billowing smoke over the 6,000-ton Neptuna between raids on Darwin. She blew up with 200 depth charges in her hold

of casualties, including nearly 250 dead. Because of the confusion and the different forces involved, casualty figures were never precisely assessed. Neither have the raiders' losses been confirmed; the Japanese admitted 15 aircraft lost, but the Allies could only confirm claims for five aircraft destroyed.

No 1 Fighter Wing

The military situation was taken quickly in hand and a court of inquiry found shortcomings in leadership, training and administration. A warning radar, installed but not ready for operation that February, was brought into use in March. Defence of the area was co-ordinated under General Sir Edmund Herring, recalled from the Middle East, and an air headquarters was established near the district headquarters 29 kilometres (18 miles) south of Darwin. More Warhawks were supplied and two forward airfields were quickly built by the US 808th Airfield Construction Squadron by adapting sections of the highway as runways and providing adjacent camp and equipment areas. Another radar station was erected to the north-west and the Royal Australian Navy put a patrol ship on picket duty to the north.

Attacks on the Darwin area continued by land-based aircraft during March and April, but on a much reduced scale, and there was little damage apart from one hit on an oil tank. Due to the defence measures taken, 17 enemy bombers and 11 fighters were destroyed up to 25 April, when the Japanese made a determined attack which proved something of a turning point in Australia's fortunes of war. Approaching from the direction of Bathurst Island, giving ample warning, the 24 bombers were met by twice their number of Warhawks, which destroyed 11 of the attackers without loss.

The Australian Government requested Spitfires from Britain to secure the area and Prime Minister Winston Churchill agreed at the end of May to dispatch three squadrons; Nos 452 and 457 (Australian) Squadrons formed in Britain, and No 54 Squadron RAF. The Spitfires were diverted *en route* to meet the desperate needs of the RAF in the Middle East and another convoy

The interior of 13 Squadron's hangar on 25 June 1942 after a Japanese raid on Darwin. At this time Northern Australia was defended by USAAF Warhawk fighters

had to be dispatched, delaying deployment in the Darwin area until 1943. However by January that year over 100 Spitfire Vs had reached the Commonwealth under the British Government's agreement to maintain No 1 Fighter Wing RAAF, composed of the three squadrons at a strength of 16 Spitfires per squadron, with a wastage replacement rate of five aircraft per squadron per month.

Spitfires in action

Under the command of Wing Commander C. R. Caldwell, 54 Squadron was deployed at Darwin and 452 and 457 were stationed at Strauss and Livingstone respectively, to the south. The first Spitfire victory went to Flt Lt R. W. Foster of 54 Squadron, who intercepted a Mitsubishi Ki-46 Dinah of the Japanese Army Air Force and shot it down 56 kilometres (35 miles) off Cape Van Diemen on 6 February 1943. The first major clash with the Spitfires came on 2 March when 16 Japanese aircraft attacked the airfield of Coomalie, south of the Darwin defences. Two Zeros and a Kate fell to the fighters. A more determined attack on the 15th led to dogfighting, when the Spitfire wing intercepted the raiders over Darwin itself. Seven of the enemy were shot down for the loss of four Spitfires, the only fatal casualty being Sqn Ldr R. E. Thorold-Smith, the commanding officer of 452 Squadron.

At times the whole wing rose to counter attacks and the airmen were being constantly alerted. There was considerable wear on Merlin engines, causing a reduction in performance which was vital as the Spitfire V's normal 587 km/h (365 mph) maximum speed was only marginally superior to that of the Zeros. Engine failures often meant a descent into the grim isolation of the outback. This happened on Sunday 2 May when 18 bombers escorted by 27 fighters made a direct attack on Darwin. It says much for the improved defence system that the Bathurst radar gave 49 minutes warning of the impending attack. Within five minutes all off-duty Spitfire pilots had been alerted and 15 minutes later all three squadrons were ordered up to gain height for the expected encounter. Even so, the Japanese had the advantage of height and an approach from the direction of the sun, forcing Caldwell to wait until they had dropped their bombs and turned away.

The heavy anti-aircraft guns, expending over 200 rounds on the raiders, accurately judged their height, but aimed badly. However, the bombers, misled by photo-graphic intelligence, pattern-bombed the old airfield, killing a soldier, but otherwise causing little damage apart from cutting electricity and telephone wires. Instead of flying an immediate reciprocal course to return, the bombers made only a 90 degree turn and flew for about 50 km (30 miles) over Australian territory before heading out to sea over Fog Bay, where the Spitfires delivered their main attack. Five Spitfires were lost but three of their pilots were rescued from the sea. Eight Spitfires made forced landings, three with engine failure and the rest short of fuel. Although they had shot down several enemy fighters, the enemy bombers had been well protected and only one was shot down by the defenders.

Allied bombers counter-attack

Australian intelligence judged correctly that the raiders, the Japanese 202nd Air Corps, came from Penfui near Koepang in Timor. That same day a flight of Beaufighters of No 31 Squadron RAAF set out from Coomalie to raid their airfield, catching Zeros taxying on the runways. At night the Mitchells of No 18 (Dutch) Squadron, based at Bachelor, followed up the raid. Confidence in the Spitfire wing was soon restored after a similar Japanese attack on 18 June. This time nine bombers and five fighters were destroyed and many others damaged for a loss of two Spitfires. Again No 18 Squadron raided Penfui at night, joined by Hudsons of No 2 Squadron RAAF and Cata-linas of the US Navy's 101st Squadron. B-24 Liberators of the USAAF 380th Bombardment Group were moving into the area to make attacks on Japanese bases over a wide area, including Penfui. The Liberator bases then became a prime Japanese target, involving the Darwin air defences in their protection.

Later in 1943 the Japanese attempted night attacks, but by the end of the year these attempts were abandoned. During 1944 Japanese aircraft rarely ventured across the Timor Sea and the Japanese Army, assembled in Timor for the invasion of Australia, was dispersed. Two of the original RAAF Spitfire squadrons moved to a more active theatre and were replaced by Nos 548 and 549 Squadrons RAAF, while No 54 Sqn RAF remained in the area and converted to Mk VIII Spitfires and trained in night fighting. However, the Japanese were by then in no position to challenge the Australian defences, either by day or by night.

Augsburg Raid 1942

On Christmas Eve 1941 three brand-new Avro Lancasters arrived at RAF Waddington in Lincolnshire, thereby becoming the first of several thousand examples of that magnificent four-engined 'heavy' to serve with the squadrons of Bomber Command. It was an event of great significance in the annals of the RAF.

The recipient of this Christmas present was No. 44 (Rhodesia) Squadron, flying Handley Page Hampdens, twin-engined bombers, which had variously been dubbed 'Flying Suitcases', 'Flying Tadpoles' or 'Flying Pan-handles' because of their unique fuselage shape and which by that time were virtually obsolete. The squadron had incorporated the word 'Rhodesia' in its title since the previous September in recognition of that country's generous donations to the war effort–a particularly appropriate idea as about a quarter of No. 44's personnel were Rhodesian at the time. The association is preserved to this day in the squadron's badge which features an African elephant. (At the time of writing No. 44 flies Vulcan bombers–another product of the famous old Avro Company, which is now known as Hawker Siddeley Aviation, Manchester).

Coinciding with the introduction of the Lancaster into squadron service was the arrival at Bomber Command Headquarters, at High Wycombe in Buckinghamshire, of a new AOC-in-C, Air Marshal Arthur Harris. Known to his close friends as Bert, and to the 'bomber boys' generally as 'Butch', he became Bomber Command's most famous wartime leader and remained at its helm until victory came. (He, incidentally, spent much of his youth in Rhodesia before World War I).

When Harris took over, in February 1942, the outlook for Bomber Command was in many ways infinitely more favourable than it had been when his predecessor's term of office began in October 1940. Substantial numbers of four-engined heavies–principally Stirlings and Hali-faxes–were already in service, together with the first of the revolutionary radar navigational aids and what was to become an extensive armoury of bigger and better bombs. Bomber Command's *raison d'être* was the strategic bombing of Germany, but from the earliest days of the war much of its effort had frequently been diverted to other tasks, notably in connection with the war at sea, and this problem remained for Harris to face.

Target–U-boat bases

The German U-boat bases figured among the bombers' targets and in 1941 the enemy took steps to safeguard five of them–Lorient, Brest, St Nazaire, Bordeaux and La Pallice–by building bomb-proof U-boat pens. By the spring of 1942 these were already armoured with several feet of concrete which no existing bombs could penetrate, so during that year Bomber Command's main effort against the U-boats took the form of raids on the sub-marine construction yards in German North Sea and Baltic ports, including Bremen, Hamburg, Kiel, Emden and Rostock.

As part of this contribution to the war at sea, Harris laid on a daylight long-distance raid by Lancasters into southern Germany very soon after he took over at High Wycombe. The target was the MAN factory (full name Maschinenfabrik Augsburg-Nurnberg Aktiengesellschaft) on the outskirts of the manufacturing town of Augsburg, in southern Bavaria. This was the largest diesel-engine factory in Germany, its output including the specialised marine engines which gave motive power to U-boats when on the surface. The manufacture of such engines was thought to be the bottleneck of the entire U-boat industry

An Avro Lancaster B Mk I of No 44 Sqn, the unit which, with No 97 Sqn, made the daylight bombing raid on the MAN factory near Augsburg on 17 April 1942. On the outward route across North East France the Squadron was intercepted by French-based Luftwaffe fighters and lost several of its Lancasters. Three more aircraft were lost on the homeward route. Sqn Ldr Nettleton was awarded the VC for his part in leading the raid. This raid, with its unacceptable loss rate, was instrumental in convincing RAF Bomber Command that daylight bomber operations over Europe were not viable

Reconnaissance shot of the area around the MAN works and the specific target points

at that time and, to Harris, the target thus seemed to be of major importance. In addition to contributing to the Battle of the Atlantic, the operation was seen as a means of testing the work capacities of the new Lancaster, maintaining pressure against the German fighter force in France, and compelling the enemy to disperse his defences. Its objectives were, therefore, four-fold.

The operation involved a round trip of 1,250 miles, most of it over enemy territory, and was among the most daring raids ever undertaken by Bomber Command. From the point of view of long range navigation and precision bombing, it was also one of the most ambitious tasks ever

tackled. Fourteen Lancaster crews, seven each from Nos. 44 and 97 Squadrons, were selected for special training, the seventh crew in each unit acting as a reserve. The big day was to be 17 April, and a few days beforehand, the two squadrons were told to make long-distance formation flights–independently at this stage–to obtain endurance data on the Lancaster. This was a blind, but the crews guessed that an important daylight operation was in the offing and when, on 15 April, both squadrons were sent out on a long cross-country flight at low level over England and Scotland, their theories were considerably strengthened. After flying south and round Selsey Bill, they proceeded up to Lanark, across to Falkirk and up to Inverness, making a dummy attack just outside the town before returning to their bases after a round trip of more than 1,000 miles.

On 16 April the crews were told that the mission for which they had been preparing would probably be flown next day. Rumour about the possible target had, of course, been rife for some time, but the crews were still kept guessing and, furthermore, were confined to camp with strict instructions to make no telephone calls to their wives nor to any other persons outside and to keep right off alcoholic drink.

On the following morning the operation orders were circulated at Waddington and Woodhall Spa, and at 11 o'clock briefing began at each of the two bases simultaneously. The crews were surprised when the target was Augsburg, deep in southern Germany, at the other side of the Danube. Briefing was very thorough. The precise target was a single building, the engine assembly shop, which lay in the midst of the MAN factory complex, and the crews had to study numerous photographs and plans, as well as a pencil sketch of the factory drawn in perspective to show them exactly how it would look at low level.

Low-level attack

The outward journey was to be made in formation at the lowest possible altitude; the attack would also be delivered from low level, each Lancaster dropping a salvo of four 1,000 lb general purpose high-explosive bombs fused with a delay action of eleven seconds. The bombers were to make the return trip individually, and because much of it would be in darkness, they could fly at the higher altitude more usual for night bombers.

By flying at low level on the way out it was hoped that the Lancasters would elude the enemy's early warning radar until the last possible moment and make attacks by any enemy fighters which might intercept them more difficult. No fighter escort was provided, but 30 Boston light bombers of No. 2 Group and over 500 fighters were scheduled to sweep over northern France and make diversionary attacks on targets in the Calais-Cherbourg-Rouen area. Unfortunately this diversion did not go according to plan; it had the effect of stirring up a hornet's nest and putting the Luftwaffe on the alert.

While the Lancasters were warming up, one of No. 97 Squadron's aircraft became unserviceable, so that unit's reserve Lanc' kept its engines running and at 3 o'clock took off with the others. Rendezvousing over Selsey Bill, the 44 and 97 Squadron forces formed up in two sections, sub-divided into 'vics' of three, flying within sight of each other. Sqn Ldr Nettleton was leading the first (44 Squadron) section, and it seemed to Sqn Ldr J. S. Sherwood, leading the 97 Squadron section, that Nettleton was taking a course slightly north of the prescribed track. Sherwood's navigator agreed with him, whereupon he decided to steer his own course.

When the French coast came into view the two sections were already several miles apart, with Nettleton's well to the north and still in the lead. Nettleton now took his formation down to somewhere between 25 and 30 feet and with each 'vic' keeping tight formation the six Lancs began contour-chasing across the springtime French countryside. Nettleton's formation had almost reached Sens, the second turning point on the route, when about 20 or 30 Messerschmitt Bf 109s appeared. They were apparently flying in two formations and they immediately attacked.

Sketch of the MAN works given to the crews at the briefing for the raid

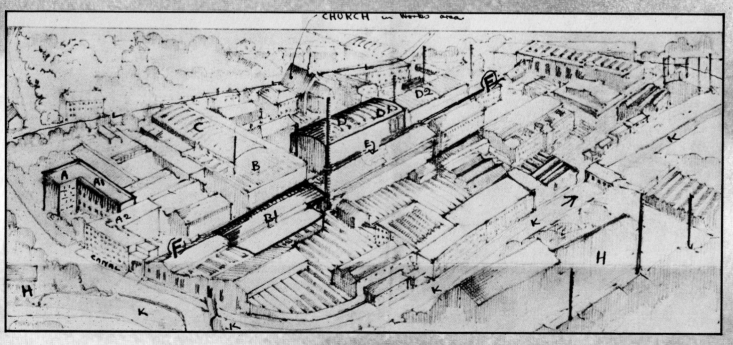

Above: the rear fuselage of a brand-new Lancaster I, showing the tail turret with four ·303 in Browning machine guns and the mid-upper turret with two ·303 Brownings.

At first Nettleton saw only two or three fighters about 1,000 feet above the Lancasters, but almost instantly there seemed to be fighters all round him. 'A fierce running fight developed,' he said afterwards. 'It was our job to pierce straight through to our target, so we kept the tightest possible formation, wing-tip to wing-tip, so as to support each other by combined fire. We went roaring over the countryside, lifting over hills and skimming down the valleys. Fighter after fighter attacked us from astern. Their cannon shells were bursting ahead of us. We were continually firing at them from our power-operated turrets. We rushed over the roofs of a village, and I saw the cannon shells which had missed us crashing into the houses, blowing holes in the walls and smashing the gables and roofs.'

The battle lasted fifteen minutes or so, and four of the Lancasters were shot down before the enemy fighters broke off the engagement and turned away–probably because they had run out of ammunition or were getting short of

fuel. The fighters had first concentrated on the rear 'vic' of Lancasters, and having disposed of these three aircraft, attacked Nettleton's 'vic' and shot down the aircraft captained by Sergeant Rhodes.

Accompanied by the one remaining Lancaster of his section of six–the captain of this machine was Flight Lieutenant Garwell–Nettleton flew on across France, skirted the border of Switzerland and Germany and continued across southern Germany in the afternoon sun until he sighted the River Lech, which he followed to his target. By now the sirens were sounding in this remote part of Germany and the big Augsburg factory was alerted. Coming over the brow of a hill on to the target the two Lancasters were met by low-angle light flak. In fact the bombers were so low that the Germans were even shooting into their own buildings.

Belly landing

The factory was in a fork made by the River Wertach and a canal, and the engine shops rose up exactly ahead of them. Nettleton had to gain height to clear their roofs as he delivered his attack, which was immediately followed by Garwell's. But Garwell's luck ran out, for no sooner had he released his bombs than his aircraft was hit by flak and set on fire. Nettleton saw it turn away to make a belly landing in a field about two miles west of Augsburg. He turned his Lancaster and was also able to watch the target; the delayed action bombs exploded and threw dust and debris high into the air. Nettleton set course for home just as the light was beginning to fail. Until it was dark he flew on just above the ground, then climbed to a normal height and got home without further incident.

The second formation of six, led by Squadron Leader Sherwood, encountered no fighters. At the time that Nettleton's formation had been attacked Sherwood's formation had glimpsed several aircraft crashing in

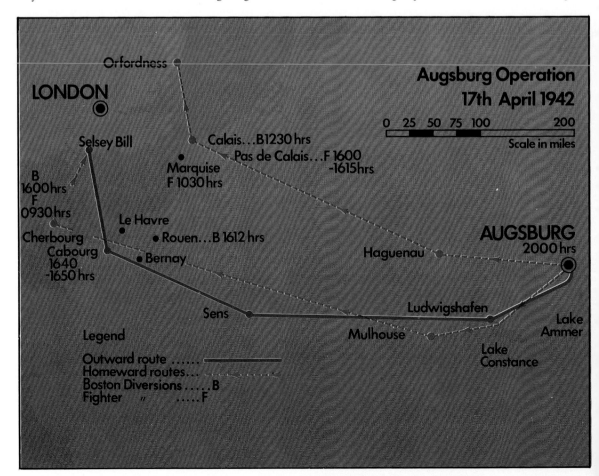

HOLE

C

X

B1

GUIDE PRINT

Reconnaissance photograph taken after the raid. The annotations were explained thus, at the time: 'C–the main diesel engine assembly shop, severely damaged, showing a hole 80 ft wide in its roof. B1–a crank grinding shop which has been demolished. X–an area adjoining the shop in B1 is severely damaged and in this area there is another crank grinding shop'

John Dering Nettleton, VC, leader of the Augsburg raid, pictured here in 1943 as a Wing Commander

flames on the horizon to the north, but they did not connect this with their own raid. At one stage they also saw a lone German army co-operation aircraft; it approached them and then made off quickly. Just inside Germany Flight Lieutenant Deverill spotted an SS guard and watched him run into a building, probably to report the Lancasters' presence by telephone. The bombers also passed over a squad of German soldiers doing physical training exercises. Their physical jerks were enlivened by a burst of fire from one of the rear gunners and, as Sherwood later remarked, 'the speed with which they took cover did great credit to their instructor.' Crossing Lake Constance they saw a small white ferry boat chugging along and a German officer standing defiantly in the stern fired at them with his Luger.

They reached the target shortly after 8 o'clock and saw Nettleton and Garwell dropping their bombs. They flew straight in through the hail of gunfire to which a solitary German on the top of the main building was contributing with his machine gun. He was shot off the roof by one of the Lancaster rear gunners. When still three miles away the Lancaster piloted by Warrant Officer Mycock was hit and the port wing caught fire. He could have turned away and made a forced landing, but he flew on, dropped his bombs accurately on the target and then, with his aircraft enveloped in flames, crashed to earth. The formation leader, Squadron Leader Sherwood, dropped his bombs; then his aircraft, too, was set on fire and was last seen burning on the ground ten miles from Augsburg, though he survived. Another Lancaster flew so low over the MAN works that it passed between two chimneys.

More hits

Flight Lieutenant Deverill's Lancaster, which had been hit in the starboard wing as it approached the target, was hit again over it and a fire started inside the fuselage.

However, the blaze was extinguished by the wireless operator just as the bomb aimer released the bombs. As it turned away the Lancaster's port outer engine stopped but was successfully re-started on the way home. Squadron Leader Hallows' aircraft was hit in the starboard wing as it flew over the assembly shop, but his bombs fell on target.

Only five of the total force of 12 Lancasters returned, but eight of the 12 had bombed the target. Reconnaissance photographs revealed that the main diesel engine assembly shop as well as some other buildings in the factory complex had been hit and damaged, but the full results were not learned until after the war. It transpired that five of the delayed-action bombs which the Lancaster crews had braved such dangers to drop accurately on the factory had failed to explode. The others caused substantial damage to a forging shop and a machine tool shop. Eight machine tools were completely destroyed, 16 heavily damaged and 53 lightly, out of a total of 2,700; five cranes were completely destroyed and six heavily damaged out of 558. The effect on production was slight, particularly since at least five of the MAN factory's licencees were building U-boat diesel engines at that time. In all, 85 aircrew took part in the raid and 49 of them failed to return. Squadron Leader Nettleton's part in the operation was recognised by the award of the Victoria Cross. Early in 1943 he was promoted to wing commander and given command of a squadron, but on the night of 12-13 July he lost his life during a raid on Turin.

Winston Churchill, when referring to the Augsburg raid at the time, said 'No life was lost in vain'; but had the facts then been known, the raid could only have been described as a gallant failure. Even so, it was immediately obvious that without long-range fighter cover it was generally impracticable for heavy bombers to make daylight raids against German targets.

Thousand Bomber Raids 1942

In the latter half of 1941, RAF Bomber Command operational research experts made a specially-commissioned comprehensive study of target photographs, following a move to equip a large proportion of the night bomber force with cameras capable of taking target pictures at the moment of bomb release. Their findings amply confirmed the long-held fears that very few bombers ever got close to their specified aiming points. Consequently, the story began to circulate that Bomber Command's strategic night offensive was a failure and the War Office and the Admiralty renewed their efforts to have the Command reduced in size.

Target-finding raid

The bomber crews urgently needed scientific aids to navigation and target-finding if they were to find the small military targets listed for attack by the Air Ministry. Thus Bomber Command advocated the new policy of using incendiary bombs against large industrial centres, with the emphasis on damage by fire. In March 1942 the introduc-

Left: notable in being the RAF's first four-engined 'heavy', the Short Stirling joined Bomber Command's operational strength in August 1940, flying its last raid in September 1944. Right: forty aircraft of the total force dispatched by Air Marshal Harris failed to return, a phenomenally low loss rate of some 3·8 per cent. Below: Short Stirlings of No 7 Squadron, the first unit to receive the type. The Squadron participated in all three Thousand Bomber Raids mounted in May/June 1942

tion into operational service of the semi-radar device known as 'Gee' at last went a considerable way towards overcoming the basic problem of all-weather navigation, for it provided navigators with a fairly accurate position fix within ranges of up to 640 km (400 miles) from the ground transmitters. However, the hopes originally held by the scientists that it would prove accurate enough for blind bombing, or at least blind releasing of flares, were seen to have been unduly optimistic.

The forceful and charismatic Air Marshal A. T. (later, Sir Arthur) Harris was appointed C-in-C of Bomber Command in February 1942. He inherited Gee – which was then being installed in the bombers and was still untried over enemy territory – from his predecessor, Air Marshal Sir Richard Pierse, who had been responsible for instigating the previously-mentioned survey of the Command's bombing results. Harris, during his first six months of office, had at his disposal an average of only 250 serviceable medium bombers (Handley Page Hampdens, Vickers Wellingtons and Armstrong-Whitworth Whitleys) and 50 serviceable heavy bombers (Handley-Page Halifaxes, Avro Lancasters and Manchesters and Short Stirlings). A few concentrated Gee-assisted raids mounted against the Baltic ports of Lübeck and Rostock in March and April 1942 proved the most damaging attacks made up to that time. Both these towns were in fact beyond the range of Gee, but the new 'navaid' set the bombers on the correct course and, as both towns were on the coast, they were relatively easy to find.

Encouraged by these results, Harris determined to stage, at the earliest opportunity, an attack by no less than a thousand bombers on one of Germany's really large industrial centres. It was an enormous gamble and, on the face of it, an impossible venture. Harris reasoned, however, that its success might produce results so impressive that it would constitute the turning point in the fortunes of Bomber Command. Hitherto, the largest force dispatched by Bomber Command against a single target had been 235 aircraft on the occasion of the aforementioned Lübeck raid, and to execute his projected scheme, Harris proposed to employ not only the entire front-line strength of medium and heavy bombers, but also a high proportion of the aircraft used by the Operational Training Units and Heavy Conversion Units. The balance, he reckoned at first, would have to come from other commands.

Objective Cologne

Both the Air Staff and the Prime Minister were enthusiastic about the scheme, and Churchill indicated that he was prepared for a loss of 100 aircraft. There followed a period of intensive preparation for the big venture, which was given the code-name Operation Millennium. Work was hastened on all aircraft in the repair sections and arrangements made for scratch crews to be raised for the reserves. All leave was cancelled and many of the station, group and command staffs volunteered to fly on the raid; indeed aircrew left sick quarters to help fill vacancies. Appeals from Harris brought a promise from Coastal Command of the use of 250 aircraft, including some which had been detached from Bomber Command earlier in the year to assist in the Battle of the Atlantic; Training Command promised to contribute about 30 Wellingtons. In the event, Admiralty pressure compelled Coastal Command to withdraw its offer completely, and of the aircraft promised by Flying Training Command only four Wellingtons materialised. Fortunately, the response from Harris's own operational and training groups proved so overwhelming that he was able to raise 1,042 aircraft, which, together with Flying Training Command's token contribution, gave him a force of 1,046 bombers.

Due to the size of the force and the inexperience of many of the crews, the target had to be one close to Germany's western frontier and, furthermore, easily

Below: a Handley Page Hampden Mark I bomber serving with No 408 (Goose) Squadron Royal Canadian Air Force, one of the Bomber Command units taking part in Operation Millenium. In all, 1,046 aircraft took part.
Bottom: the bomb-scarred city of Cologne and its cathedral, painted by a British war artist. On the night of 30/31 May the RAF dropped 1,455 tons of bombs on the city

identifiable. It was also necessary for the raid to be made in bright moonlight. Hamburg and Cologne were the two obvious possibilities, the final choice depending entirely on the weather. The raid was tentatively scheduled for the night of 27/28 May, two nights before full moon, and the bomb-loads were to be predominantly incendiary. However, where high explosives had to be carried to make up economical loads, they were to consist of the largest possible bombs. The bomber force was to fly for the first time ever in a carefully-planned stream, which would, it was hoped, overwhelm the German night fighter defences.

Cologne was chosen as the target and the assault was to take place within 90 minutes, giving a planned density of about eleven bombers per minute. The first fifteen minutes of the assault were allocated to aircraft of Nos 1 and 3 Groups equipped with Gee–about 100 in all–and they carried the greatest proportion of incendiary bombs. The last fifteen minutes were given over to the heavy bombers of Nos 4 and 5 Groups. In between came the main body of the force, including the non-Gee-equipped aircraft of Nos 1 and 3 Groups. In order to achieve an even coverage of the target area three separate aiming points in Cologne were allotted to various parts of the force. Aircraft unable to find Cologne were ordered to bomb any built-up area in the Ruhr, preferably Essen.

Adverse weather conditions

On the night that had been provisionally fixed for the raid, thundery conditions and heavy cloud over the continent caused a postponement, the same happening on the following night. The weather was now causing concern; the vast armada could not stand by indefinitely and the moon would soon be on the wane. On 30 May, good weather was promised at home bases, but over Germany thundery clouds still persisted; only the Rhineland offered any hope of a successful attack. Thus at midday Harris, seizing the chance of landing the bombers back again in clear weather and accepting the risk that the target would be covered in

cloud, decided to strike that night against Cologne.

Accordingly, as dusk fell, the bombers took off from 52 airfields and set course for the target–the third largest city in Germany. Wellingtons, Whitleys and Hampdens made up the bulk of the force, numbering 708 in all, the remaining 338 aircraft being Stirlings, Halifaxes and Manchesters plus a sprinkling of the new Lancasters. While the bomber stream headed across the North Sea, fifty Bristol Blenheims of No 2 Group, Bomber Command and Army Co-operation Command, plus Douglas Bostons and Havocs and long-range Hawker Hurricanes–38 aircraft in all–from Fighter Command took off for their part in the operation. Intruding over enemy airfields in France, Belgium, Holland and western Germany, they were active until the attack on Cologne had ended.

On the way across the North Sea the bomber stream encountered thick cloud, but this began to break up across Holland and there were only small wisps of cirrus over Cologne. The timing of the attack was, on the whole, fairly accurate and, although the first bombs went down at 0038 hours, which was seventeen minutes early, and the last at 0310 hours, which was forty-five minutes late, only 38 of the 898 aircraft claiming attack bombed outside the limit of ninety minutes. Gee took the first wave near enough for the crews to identify the target visually in the bright moonlight and those who followed were guided by considerable fires. Fighters and flak were active and although some of the crews thought the flak was unusually weak, this impression was probably created because the guns and searchlights tended to concentrate on single aircraft. The bombers dropped 1,455 tons of bombs on the city, two-thirds of this total being incendiaries.

Subsequent daylight reconnaissance fully confirmed that the raid had been an outstanding success. Over 240 hectares (600 acres) of Cologne, half of it in the centre of the city, had been completely destroyed. This was almost equal to the total destruction so far caused by Bomber Command's raids on Germany. That much damage was caused to industrial property is confirmed by German police records, which add that 486 people were killed, 5,027 injured, and 140,000 had to be evacuated. Nine days after the attack, Cologne was still cut off from communication with the rest of Germany. Bomber Command had at last won a major victory against a significant target.

Furthermore, this victory had been achieved without insupportable losses. Forty aircraft of the 1,046–3·8 per cent–failed to return and, in addition, 116 suffered damage–twelve so badly that they were beyond repair.

One of the missing bombers was captained by Flying Officer L. T. Manser, a pilot of No 50 Squadron. His Manchester was caught in searchlights and intense flak, but he pressed on to bomb the target. On the return journey his aircraft was set on fire. The blaze was extinguished, but the machine lost height and a crash became inevitable. Manser ordered his crew to bale out while he remained at the controls to keep the aircraft steady. He was still at the controls when the Manchester plunged down and burst into flames. His self-sacrifice was later made known when the men he died to save could communicate and in October 1942 he was posthumously awarded the Victoria Cross.

Operation Millennium's amazing success won widespread acclaim in Britain and America. The enemies of the policy of air attack on Germany were silenced and enthusiasm for the air offensive was rekindled. Churchill took action which ensured that the necessary priorities were assigned to meet the needs of Bomber Command.

Harris quickly mounted two further thousand bomber raids against Essen and Bremen–on 1/2 June and 25/26 June respectively–but, although these failed due to the presence of cloud over the targets, the resounding success of the earlier Cologne attack ensured that Bomber Command remained well and truly on the map.

Right: a captured RAF airman is questioned by Luftwaffe interrogators. Below right: the burned-out remains of a Vickers Wellington which fell victim to the German flak defences

Ploesti Raids 1942-43

During World War II the name of a town in southern Romania, Ploesti, became synonymous with oil. When Hitler's armies invaded Russia in 1941, a major objective was to secure the Romanian oil fields whose output would be essential to the German war effort. A year later Germany was drawing 60 per cent of her natural oil from Ploesti, which was a third of the total consumption of oil products from all sources. Soon this would include nearly half the vital high-octane aviation fuel. As Allied control of the oceans tightened, preventing overseas oil reaching Germany, dependence upon Ploesti increased.

The vast complex of refineries at Ploesti afforded a good target for aerial attack. However, there were two major

The first Ploesti raid on 11/12 June 1942 was coded Halpro. The 1 August 1943 raid was coded Tidal Wave. The Crotone raid on 29 March 1943, conceived by Norman Appold, tested low-level bombing prior to Tidal Wave

obstacles; it was beyond the range of most Allied bombers and its location, deep within the enemy occupied Balkans, would give the defences ample time to deal with a daylight bombing force. Nevertheless, American war planners developed a particular interest in the strategic importance of Ploesti and when a small force of Consolidated B-24 Liberators arrived in the Middle East in June 1942 *en route* to China, the opportunity was taken to fly a mission to Ploesti, principally as a gesture of support to the hard-pressed Russians. The Liberator was then the only bomber in service with sufficient range to make the 3,540 km (2,200 mile) round trip from Egypt. Even then this could only be accomplished with extra fuel tanks in the bomb-bays, thus reducing the bomb-load of each aircraft to 1,360 kg (3,000 lb).

To better the chances of evading interceptors, the flight to the target was made in darkness on the night of 11/12 June 1942, arriving over Ploesti at dawn and violat-

Above: Col John ' Kill Kane, CO of the 98th Bomb Group, was awa the Medal of Honour f his part in the Tidal W raid on 1 August 1943. Right: a Consolidated over the Astro Roman refinery, the priority target bombed by Kan Group on 1 August, sh the low level at which raid was flown

APPOLD'S RAID ON CROTONE

HALPRO

TIDAL WAVE
118 MILES TO ONE INCH

ing neutral Turkey's airspace to make good an escape and land in Iraq. However, the 13 B-24s involved found cloud over Romania and little, if any, damage was done to the refineries. No opposition was encountered but poor navigation resulted in only seven bombers reaching Iraq; the other six force-landed in Turkey and Syria. Thereafter the Allies were too busy with the critical Middle East situation to engage in further action against Ploesti. As a result of this raid, the Germans, aware of Allied attentions and capabilities, bolstered the defences around the oil refineries to deter any further acts of aggression from the air forces of their adversaries.

Ploesti continued to loom large in the schemes of American air strategists and in 1943 a plan was devised to launch a massive attack against the refineries. Only two groups of Liberators–the 98th and 376th Bomb Groups–were operating in the Middle East under the US Ninth Air Force, so the three Eighth Air Force groups–44th, 93rd and 389th–were temporarily transferred from England to raise the potential strength of the strike force to 200 heavy bomber aircraft.

The mission was to be flown in daylight to give the best opportunity of hitting the seven individual targets accurately; three groups were assigned a refinery each and the 44th and 93rd Groups divided their formations to attack two each. To minimise loss, the decision was taken to fly the mission at very low level in the hope of eluding radar detection and gaining the element of surprise. The planned route was not direct but crossed Albania and southern Yugoslavia before veering east across Bulgaria and finally sweeping in on the target from the north-west; withdrawal was to be across the Aegean Sea.

Faulty navigation

This daring operation was finally launched on 1 August 1943 with 179 B-24s taking off between 0400 and 0500 hours from bases in the Benghazi area of Libya. One aircraft crashed shortly after becoming airborne and another, from the 376th Bomb Group, went out of control near Corfu and did not recover before hitting the sea. This was the lead aircraft of the lead group and its loss caused such confusion that the 376th Bomb Group failed to make a scheduled change in course. In consequence the 376th, with the 93rd following, became separated from the trailing groups when the third group in line, the 98th, made the correct turn and did not follow the leading Bomb Groups.

The strike force, now in two distinct formations, continued toward Romania with the 376th reaching the area of the Initial Point for turn to the target shortly after

Right: a painting by Standley Dersh depicting Consolidated B-24s over the Ploesti oil refineries. Below: a North African-based B-24, a veteran of the Ploesti raids, is prepared for a ferry flight to the USA. The map on the fuselage side shows missions it has flown, including Ploesti

1110 hours. Unfortunately, the lead group made its turn for the target over the wrong landmark and, with the 93rd in trail, bore down on Bucharest, not Ploesti, at a height of 150m (500ft). The leader of the 93rd, Colonel Addison Baker, saw the refineries off to the left and, realising that the 376th had missed the target, turned his group into the attack. They were met by intense anti-aircraft fire from the alerted defences, Baker's aircraft being one of eight shot down from his group. The 376th Bomb Group, discovering its error, also turned for Ploesti where most aircraft attacked targets of opportunity.

Meanwhile the three other groups were approaching their targets only to find a hail of flak ahead. The 98th Bomb Group found that its briefed refinery had already been attacked by part of the 93rd and was burning. The anti-aircraft fire was so intense that no less than 13 of the 98th's force of 41 Liberators went down in the target area and five more were later lost to fighter attack. Part of the 44th Bomb Group also met murderous ground fire and lost seven aircraft out of 16 over the target. The 389th, least experienced unit of the strike force, successfully located and attacked its assigned refinery at Campini, losing four bombers to flak. All told 33 Liberators had fallen victim of the enemy gunners, the large, comparatively slow aircraft being very vulnerable at such low altitude. Another eight Liberators were lost to fighter interception and seven force-landed in Turkey, two had collided during the return flight and another ditched in the sea off Turkey. Out of the 179 aircraft dispatched, 165 attacked their targets, 52 were lost and 58 damaged. The strike force had paid a high price for its persistence.

*Right: damage inflicted by the US Air Force on the Romana Americana oil refinery, which was the third largest–and the most bombed–in Romania.
Left: an oblique view of the Romana Americana oil refinery, with the main installations annotated–
1: the distillation unit
2: the boiler houses
3: the distillation and cracking towers*

Considerable damage

While the mission did not achieve its desired aim of destroying 90 per cent of the refinery capacity at Ploesti, due principally to the errors and misfortunes on the route to the objective, it did cause considerable destruction, putting two refineries completely out of commission. Installations were severely damaged at other sites which had been attacked and it was eight months before production returned to the level existing before the raid. The low-level Ploesti mission was undoubtedly the most famous and costly operation ever undertaken by USAAF Liberator crews. Many incidents of great bravery were reported and the award of five Medals of Honour was unique in the annals of US Air Force history. Three of these were posthumous: Colonel Baker and his pilot Major John Jerstad, and Lt Lloyd Hughes, pilot of a 389th aircraft who continued on his bombing run after his Liberator had been badly damaged. This highest American award for bravery also went to Colonel John Kane, leader of the 98th Bomb Group, and Colonel Leon Johnson who commanded the 44th.

Ploesti was not subjected to another American air attack until April 1944, when the distance the heavy bombers had to fly to reach it had been almost halved by the acquisition of airfields in the Foggia area of Italy. The US Fifteenth Air Force was based there with an operational brief to carry the Allied Combined Bomber Offensive to strategic targets which could not be reached from Britain. At this date the enemy's oil industry was not a first priority target for the Combined Bomber Offensive, although USAAF leaders believed it should be. Thus the bombs that fell in the Ploesti refinery area on 5 April were officially 'spillage' from the authorised attack on the marshalling yards, a mission in the campaign to disrupt German rail communications in the Balkans to assist the Russian advance.

The importance of Ploesti to the Germans was evident from the strong reaction which missions to this target provoked. Four more missions, ostensibly to the marshalling yards, were flown by the Fifteenth Air Force during April and May. Then, on 18 May, the first authorised attack was made on the oil refineries by 206 heavy bombers. Flak defences had been increased to such a point that it was estimated that Ploesti was the third most heavily-defended target in Europe. To add to the difficulties of the American bombers, the Germans had devised a most effective smoke screen system.

On 10 June 1944 another tactic was tried against Ploesti. Using two groups of long-range Lockheed P-38 Lightnings, one with each aircraft carrying a 1,000lb bomb, a surprise, low-level, dive-bombing attack was carried out on a major refinery. The opposition encountered was considerable and, although the P-38s caused fires at their target, 24 aircraft failed to return.

The conventional high-level bombings of Ploesti continued throughout June and July and by mid-August these raids had resulted in production being cut to a fifth of its capacity. Royal Air Force Liberators, Handley Page Halifaxes and Vickers Wellingtons operating from Italy joined in the campaign by making night attacks on the refineries. The last American heavy bomber raid was flown on 19 August and proved to be the only one in which the Fifteenth Air Force did not suffer losses. In all, 19 missions had been flown to Ploesti by the B-17s and B-24s since 5 April 1944, during which 223 had been lost. The total number of aircraft bombing during this period was 5,479 and 13,469 tons of bombs were dropped. The RAF night effort added a few hundred tons for a loss of four bombers. Russian ground forces overran the Ploesti area at the end of August, making further raids unnecessary; thereafter synthetic oil became the mainstay of the crumbling Nazi regime.

Stalingrad Airlift 1942-43

The destruction of the German Sixth Army at Stalingrad in January 1943, involving the loss of more than three-quarters of a million men after five months of hideous carnage, marked the turning point of the Russo-German campaign that had started twenty months previously as Operation Barbarossa. With the British victory at El Alamein in North Africa, this defeat represented the turn in Allied fortunes in World War II.

As far back as July 1942 the German advance by Field Marshal Wilhelm List's Army Group A was smashing forward from the Eastern Ukraine with Friedrich von Paulus' Sixth Army aimed directly at Stalingrad, a city of half a million inhabitants on the west bank of the Volga river. On von Paulus' left flank was the Fourth Panzer Army and on the right Paul von Kleist's First Army. However, so intent was Hitler on seizing the Caucasus oilfields that in September he diverted the Fourth Panzer Army south to the Caucasus, effectively leaving the German left flank 'in the air'.

Overstretched supply lines

It was during September that the Sixth Army reached the outskirts of Stalingrad, meeting the full strength and determination of the Russians to hold the city at any cost. At once the battle degenerated into a desperate street-by-street, house-by-house and room-by-room struggle and, in the course of a single night raid by supporting German bombers, more than 40,000 Russian civilians were killed.

Against a steady build-up of Russian reserves the Germans now felt the full effect of overstretched supply lines. Tanks and guns were destroyed, never to be replaced; food and ammunition were soon to run short and the Russian winter was to find the Wehrmacht quite inadequately clothed and shod. Nonetheless, as the Germans forced the defenders closer to the west bank of the Volga it seemed just possible that the Russians would be trapped by mid-October with no chance of escaping across the swollen river.

By the end of that month, although the Russians continued to hold a narrow fringe of ruined buildings on the Volga's west bank and had been reinforced by a Guards Regiment, von Paulus recognised the threat of his own encirclement. The Soviet commanders, Zhukov and Vasilevsky, were building up their forces against the Fourth Panzer Army in the South as well as the weakly-held northern flank.

On 19 November the Russian attack burst on the flanks, and by the 22nd had all but cut the German supply corridor to the west of Stalingrad. Despite appeals by von Paulus to Hitler to be allowed to extricate his army, the Sixth Army was ordered to fight on and complete the capture of the city. The next day the trap was snapped shut at Kalach and a quarter of a million Germans and Romanians were caught in a pocket 48 km (30 miles) long and an average of 19 km (12 miles) wide. In the east of this area lay the rubble and ruins of the Russian city, in the west was frozen steppe on which lay two fairly modern aerodromes and six small landing grounds. To add to von Paulus' plight, the Fourth Panzer Army failed to break through to relieve him from the south;

Below: a victorious Soviet fighter pilot pictured during the battle for Stalingrad. The ascendancy of the Russian fighter force was one of the factors which led to the defeat of the German Sixth Army

the Sixth Army seemed doomed to annihilation.

As Erich von Manstein's newly-formed Army Group Don tried in vain to re-open the supply corridor from the west on the 24th, Reichsmarschall Hermann Goering undertook to supply the encircled Army by air with 500 tons of supplies daily, it being estimated that 300 tons was the bare minimum required for survival. His undertaking was clearly prompted by memory of a remarkable airlift at Demyansk the previous spring when a total of 24,300 tons of supplies was airlifted to six encircled German divisions.

However, conditions were now very different. To begin with, the Demyansk operation had cost the Luftwaffe 262 aircraft and more than 200 experienced transport pilots— losses which had not been made good. Secondly, the springtime conditions at Demyansk were vastly different from Stalingrad's winter, while the Soviet air force was now considerably stronger, especially in fighter aircraft.

Into the Cauldron

At the beginning of the airlift to Stalingrad there were no more than five *kampfgruppen zur besonderen verwendung* (KGrzbV) in the southern sector of the Russian front, equipped with about 90 Junkers Ju 52/3m transports, of which not more than 60 were serviceable at one time. It was immediately obvious that these aircraft were insufficient to carry the required tonnage and during the first two days they delivered only 65 tons to the Stalingrad airfield at Pitomnik. Within a week six more Ju 52/3m *gruppen* and six equipped with 176 Heinkel He 111s had been rushed to the area and on 30 November 100 tons of supplies reached Stalingrad by air in one day for the first time during the airlift.

Henceforth the vast proportion of supplies was carried by Ju 52s and He 111s into the Kessel (Cauldron), as the inferno of Stalingrad was now named. Additionally, some 60 aged Junkers Ju 86s of KGrzbV 21 and KGrzbV 22

Right: wounded German troops were evacuated by the Luftwaffe transports during their flights out of Stalingrad. Despite hopes of sustaining the garrison by airlifted supplies, the Sixth Army was reduced to starvation at the time of its surrender in January 1943. Below: a newspaper headline announces the German occupation of Stalingrad – a triumph that was soon to turn to defeat

were pressed into service, but during the next two months more than 40 of these succumbed to the Russian winter and to enemy fighters. Following Goering's undertaking, General von Richthofen appointed Oberst Dr Ernst Kühl as Lufttransportführer 1 in command of all units flying Heinkel He 111 converted transports. They included I and II/KG 55 at Morosovskaya, all *gruppen* of KG 27 under Oberstleutnant Hans-Henning von Beust at Millerovo and I/KG 100, KGrzbV 5 and KGrzbV 20 operating from Morosovskaya.

Air operations continued to gain momentum during the first half of December and gradually the daily tonnage increased. At the same time the returning transports flew out hundreds of wounded soldiers from the pocket. However, the Russian pressure on the encircled Army was growing inexorably, with repeated barrages by guns and Katyusha rockets. At this time von Manstein abandoned his attempts to relieve the Sixth Army and turned his attention to keeping open the escape route for the Axis forces now endangered in the Caucasus.

On 23 December thick fog concealed a Russian armoured thrust towards the airfield at Morosovskaya, making it unusable and forcing Kühl to disperse his aircraft to Novocherkassk. However, at the last moment the skies cleared and allowed the Stukas of Schlachtgeschwader 1 and Stukageschwader 2 to attack and repulse the enemy armour.

Winter arrives

The respite was only shortlived and the bad weather returned, coinciding with the Russians' introduction of the KV-1 and T-34 tanks for the first time. These proved superior in firepower and armour to the remaining German PzKw III and IV tanks as well as being virtually immune to attack by 30mm guns from the air.

On Christmas Eve, freezing fog masked a Soviet attack on the German-held airfield at Tazinskaya and as shells started falling all over the field 108 Ju 52/3ms and Ju 86s scrambled into the air in appalling visibility and struggled to land at Novocherkassk and Rostov. Such was the dire

need to preserve these transports that one aircraft was flown from Tazinskaya to Novocherkassk by Hauptmann Lorenz, who had never before flown an aeroplane.

Novocherkassk again came under Russian attack on Christmas Day and the transport aircraft were withdrawn to Sal'sk. The New Year brought new measures to assist the airlift. No longer able to fly the transports into the pocket individually by day owing to the depredations of Russian fighters, the Germans adopted large formations closely escorted by fighters, most often those of Hannes Trautloft's Jagdgeschwader 52, as well as attempting night supply flights – the latter rendered almost suicidal by frequent storms and drifting snow on the congested landing grounds. Fresh units now joined the airlift as 7 Staffel, Transportgeschwader 4, arrived with a dozen Gotha Go 244 powered gliders. On 9 January 1 and 3 Staffeln, Kampfgeschwader 40, brought 18 Focke Wulf Fw 200 Condors from Stalino to the southern front where they formed KGrzbV 200 under Major Hans-Jürgen Williers; these big aircraft were flown into Pitomnik (the only airfield with adequate landing run) but after a week, when it fell to the Russians, they were forced to drop their stores by parachute to the trapped army.

About 30 Heinkel He 177A-3s of I/KG 50, which was undergoing winter training at Zaporozh'ye, were rushed to the Stalingrad area where the unit was temporarily redesignated Fernkampfgruppe 2. Teething troubles were, however, still being experienced with these aircraft and after only a dozen supply missions – during which seven Heinkels were destroyed following engine fires – the unit was withdrawn. On 1 January 30 more He 111s of III/KG 55 joined Lufttransportführer 1 and the following day a new unit was created. This was the Viermotorige Lufttransportstaffel 290 (LTS 290), established at Tempelhof/Berlin under Hauptmann Heinz Braun with the Junkers Ju 90V4, six Ju 90B-1s, the Ju 290V1, a Ju 290A-1, the Ju 252V5 and an Fw 200B. Operating directly under the control of the Luftwaffe high command, these large transports flew a number of supply sorties to Stalingrad, losing the Ju 290V1 in a take-off crash on 13 January.

Appalling losses

As already mentioned, Pitomnik airfield finally fell to the Russians on 16 January and the Heinkel He 111s were diverted to Gumrak. On the same day the Ju 52/3ms were forced to move from Sal'sk to Sverevo, where, within 24 hours, they were caught on the ground by a Russian bombing raid, losing no fewer than 52 of their number.

By 21 January the Stalingrad perimeter extended over an area of no more than six miles by four. That night Gumrak airfield was rendered unusable owing to Russian shellfire and the He 111s took off for the last time. Hitler persisted in his refusal to allow von Paulus to capitulate, but the transports had evacuated no fewer than 40,000 wounded and continued to drop supplies to the ragged, starved and exhausted survivors. By 28 January supplies of morphine were exhausted and that day a shattering mortar barrage caused more than 10,000 further casualties.

Two days later, on the tenth Anniversary of the Third Reich, Hitler promoted von Paulus to field marshal in the hope that he would recall that no German field marshal had ever allowed himself to be captured alive. However, despite all efforts in the air by the Luftwaffe, the German commander gave himself up to a Russian tank officer on 31 January and formally surrendered the 110,000 survivors of his army to General Shumilov. Sporadic resistance continued for two more days by isolated parties of Germans, but on 3 February Leutnant Kuntz, an He 111

pilot of I/KG 100 made the final sortie over the city of Stalingrad, his supplies falling only among the frozen corpses of a once-victorious army.

The Stalingrad airlift delivered less than 20,000 tons of food and ammunition to the trapped German soldiers in just ten weeks at a cost of more than 470 aircraft, including no fewer than 165 He 111s, vital bombers that Germany could ill-afford to lose. Moreover, the drastic loss of transport aircraft at Stalingrad was to be keenly felt five months later when another German army faced annihilation or surrender in the warmer clime of Tunisia.

Right: Junkers Ju 87Ds flying over Stalingrad in 1942. The Ju 87 was used against Russian armour in the area but fighter opposition and winter made Luftwaffe close-support operations particularly hazardous. Below and bottom: Stalingrad, devastated by aerial and artillery bombardment was finally surrendered on 31 January 1943

Dams Raid 1943

It is doubtful whether any other individual unit of the RAF has ever received even a proportion of the publicity and acclaim accorded to 617 Squadron from its inception up to the present day. Formed specifically–and uniquely–to undertake a single vital operation, 617's history has always been associated with aerial bombing in its most precise form; indeed its original aircrew members included an unusually high proportion of the most experienced and skilled bomber men of the RAF.

The origin of the Squadron can be traced to the genius of a softly-spoken civilian aeronautical engineer and designer named Barnes Wallis, whose brilliant vision initiated a wide variety of ideas and inventions. One such idea concerned the basic sources of Germany's industrial power: coal-mines, oil dumps and wells, and the massive water dams which served the sprawling industrial complex of the Ruhr. Destruction of these obvious targets was impossible to achieve with the aircraft and armament available to the RAF during the early years of World War II. Acutely aware of this inability, Wallis proceeded

The 200 ft-wide breach in the Möhne Dam wall which resulted from attacks by five Lancasters of No 617 Squadron with Barnes Wallis's special bouncing bomb on the night of 16/17 May–Operation Chastise

with the research and calculations necessary to develop a weapon which could destroy such targets. His first results showed the need for a bomb weighing 31,750 kg (70,000 lb)–4,500 kg (10,000 lb) heavier than the gross weight of the RAF's latest bomber (in 1942), which was the Avro Lancaster.

The Wallis bomb

Understandably sceptical of Barnes Wallis's apparently impracticable notions, Air Ministry officialdom refused to sanction any development of monster bombs. Wallis then turned his thoughts to other means of achieving the objective, concentrating on ways and means of destroying the principal dams. He quickly realised that the only solution was to get a bomb into contact with the dam face, relying on shock waves from the explosion to cause the collapse of the dam wall structure. If this could be done, an explosive charge as small as 2,720 kg (6,000 lb) of RDX explosive would be sufficient for the task, according to Wallis's calculations.

A series of proving tests of this theory was undertaken in August 1942 at the Nant-y-gro Dam of the Rhayader Lake in Radnorshire, Wales, and proved highly successful in destroying the dam. As a result of this success, authority was given for six half-size prototype bombs to be made and dropped from a Wellington bomber. These bombs were spherical in shape and had to be dropped from very low altitude on approach across the water. On contact with the water the spherical bombs would then ricochet along the surface until they reached the dam, thereby avoiding (or, if necessary, breaking through) any anti-torpedo defence nets in the lake.

Further experiments confirmed that the best results would be obtained if a certain amount of backspin was imparted to the bomb prior to release from the aircraft. On reaching the dam, the bomb would thus bounce back and then approach the dam again, finally rolling down the wall until it reached a pre-set explosion depth of 9m (30ft). Five dropping tests were flown between 4 and 15 December 1942 by J. 'Mutt' Summers, Vickers' chief test pilot, and these eventually proved the feasibility of the concept. The decision to instal the weapon in an Avro Lancaster was not made until 26 February 1943. Immediately the aircraft's designers went ahead with necessary modifications to the Lancaster's bomb-bay while the Vickers company proceeded with detail design of the final weapon.

Production considerations dictated that the weapon should become a cylindrical container 1·52m (60in) long by 1·27m (50in) diameter, with three hydrostatic pistols set to detonate the main explosive charge at 9m (30ft) water depth. Of its gross weight of 4,200kg (9,250lb), 3,000kg (6,600lb) was main charge explosive (RDX). The bomb was carried in a modified Lancaster bay, slung between two V-shaped arms. Each end of the bomb casing had a hollow circular track 508mm (20in) in diameter, mating with disc wheels of similar diameter on the aircraft's calliper arms. The apparatus was connected by belt-drive to a hydraulic motor in the fuselage and imparted the pre-release back-spin to the bomb (of some 500rpm) from about ten minutes before release. A total of 20 Lancasters was quickly modified to carry the Wallis bomb. Speed was essential in view of the need to carry out any operations against the dams before the end of May

Right: the impressively-detailed target model used to brief crews for the Dams Raid. Starting on 27 March 1943, the hand-picked crews of No 617 Squadron trained intensively in low-level flying and bombing techniques

1943, when the water levels would be at their highest; moreover, the necessity for a moonlit night for the actual operation further reduced the options to the middle of May as the latest feasible period.

Hand-picked crews

Long-standing special committees within the Air Ministry had previously selected specific German dams as the most likely objectives for future attention–particularly the Möhne, Eder, Sorpe, Lister, Schwelme and Ennepe dams –but had lacked the practical means of attacking such targets. Now, with the availability of Wallis's weapon (albeit still not fully proven), yet another special committee was appointed on 8 March 1943 to deal with the projected attack on the dams. Despite the firmly recorded objections of Sir Arthur Harris, AOC-in-C, Bomber Command, to any form of *corps d'élite* within Bomber Command–as witnessed by his initial opposition to the

formation of the Path Finder Force in the previous year – he now decided to form a new squadron specifically to undertake the proposed dams raid. The original official directive for this was dated 17 March 1943 and 617 Squadron officially came into being at Scampton, near Lincoln, four days later, although on that date it was still referred to as 'X' Squadron, because its number had not been finally approved.

The AOC No 5 Group, Sir Ralph Cochrane, selected Wing Commander Guy Penrose Gibson DSO DFC (then CO of No 106 Squadron) as commander of the new unit. Gibson, a pre-war pilot with the RAF, had by then completed three tours of operations – two on bombers and one on night-fighters – totalling 170 operational sorties. The last of these was flown on the night of 11 March 1943 and Gibson was about to proceed on leave the following day when he was notified that his leave was cancelled. He was posted to 5 Group Headquarters with effect from 13 March, where the AOC asked him to undertake 'just one more operation'. Although not told the nature of the sortie, Gibson agreed to Cochrane's request.

Gibson was immediately given a completely free hand to select the crews for his new command – a hitherto unknown privilege – and proceeded to choose the most experienced men of each aircrew category from various operational squadrons. Nearly all of them were men well into their second tour of bomber operations and veterans of Bomber Command. Still unaware of the final objective, Gibson was instructed to train his men in very low-level flying and bombing techniques, beginning on 27 March. The crews' specific terms of reference were to be able to release a bomb from an altitude of exactly 18 m (60 ft) above the water, at a speed not in excess of 400 km/h (250 mph), at a distance of between 400 and 450 yards from the target – precise limits never before attempted.

At last, on 15 May, Guy Gibson conducted the actual briefing for the dams raid, which was to take place on the night of 16 May. In all, 21 complete crews had been trained for the operation, with 20 Lancasters standing by. In the event two crews were withdrawn through illness and one Lancaster did not participate.

The Dams Raid

Just before 9.30 pm on 16 May the first Lancaster was airborne from Scampton. It was one of the second wave formation, intended to attack the Sorpe dam. The formation left without its leader, Flight Lieutenant 'Joe' McCarthy, an American citizen serving in the RAF, who had been delayed at take-off. Meanwhile, Guy Gibson led his nine Lancasters off, heading first for the Möhne dam. The remaining five Lancasters, a mobile 'reserve', did not leave until nearly three hours later.

Above: one of the Avro Lancaster B Mk IIIs specially modified for the Dams Raid. The cylindrical Wallis bomb weighed 4,200 kg (9,250 lb).
Right: the Möhne Dam before and after the raid

Gibson's formation lost one aircraft on the outward route, but the remaining eight bombers arrived at the Möhne dam intact. Gibson made the initial run-in, then circled, issuing instructions to his men over the specially-fitted VHF radio sets carried in each Lancaster. Four more Lancasters released their Wallis bombs in turn against the dam without apparent effect, one crew (captained by Flight Lieutenant John Hopgood) being lost to the flak defences. As the sixth Lancaster obeyed Gibson's order to start its attack, the dam wall crumbled and released its gigantic waters in a torrent of destruction. Leading the three remaining bomb-laden Lancasters to their secondary objective, the Eder dam, Gibson once more directed the attack and the third run-in, by Flight Lieutenant Les Knight's Lancaster, finally broke the dam wall.

One Lancaster in the Sorpe wave scraped its bomb off when the aircraft 'bounced' off the surface of the Zuider Zee east of Texel and had to abort the mission. A second was hit by light flak which destroyed the aircraft's radio system and forced it to turn back as well. Two other Lancasters in this wave disappeared without trace. Only the tardy McCarthy, who should have been in the lead, reached the Sorpe dam, where his lone attack only crumbled the earth crust on the crest of the dam wall, leaving its concrete core intact. Three Lancasters of the reserve wave were then detailed to back up McCarthy's partial success. Only one succeeded in attacking and its bomb failed to complete the destruction of the dam wall. Of the other two, one disappeared and the other failed to locate the target. The remaining pair of Lancasters from the mobile reserve wave were dispatched to bomb the Lister and Schwelme dams. The latter target was attacked without apparent success and the attack on the former resulted in the loss of yet another crew, with no evidence as to the cause of its loss.

Of the 19 Lancasters, which set out with their 133 aircrew, eight failed to return. Of the survivors, 33 men were decorated for their courage, while the leader of this unique operation, Guy Gibson, was awarded a Victoria Cross. It was the largest number of gallantry awards ever made to any single RAF unit for an individual feat of arms.

Precision operations
Although 617 Squadron had lost almost half of its aircrew in this one operation, 'Butch' Harris decided to retain the Squadron as a special unit for specific precision operations. Guy Gibson was replaced as unit commander by Squadron Leader G. W. Holden DSO DFC, but the Squadron did not fly operationally again until mid-July 1943, when it participated in the 'shuttle service' attacks by Bomber Command against Italian transportation targets. At the end of August, the Squadron moved base to Coningsby, Lincolnshire, from where, on the night of 14/15 August, it attempted to destroy the Dortmund-Ems canal with 12,000lb HC bombs. Of the eight Lancasters dispatched, only three returned. On the following night, 617 was again airborne, this time attacking the Anthéor Viaduct on the Franco-Italian border, led now by Squadron Leader H. B. 'Mick' Martin DSO DFC. The raid did not achieve the destruction of the viaduct. On 10 November 1943, command of 617 passed into the capable hands of Wing Commander G. L. Cheshire DSO DFC, who had willingly dropped a rank in order to return to the operational scene.

Throughout its early months of operations, 617 had (apart from the unique tactics of the Dams Raid) employed high-level bombing techniques, with dismal results. In Leonard Cheshire, however, the squadron had a leader who

openly preached the value of low-level bombing and target-marking. He exemplified these tactics superbly on the night of 8 February 1944 in a highly successful precision attack on the Gnome-Rhône aero-engine factory at Limoges, France. Further near-disastrous attempts to bomb the Anthéor Viaduct from high level merely confirmed Cheshire's views and 617 Squadron was given permission to create its own low-level marking component. For this Cheshire was given a Mosquito bomber and he flew it on its first marking operation on the night of 5/6 April 1944.

Based at Woodhall Spa, Lincs, from 9 January 1944, 617 Squadron began a run of increasingly-successful precision attacks on German targets. Cheshire provided the driving force and brought the art of initial target-marking and raid-direction to a high peak of efficiency. In attacking such varied targets as German troop concentrations, V2 missile sites, railway tunnels, E-boat pens and main cities, Cheshire continued to lead 617 on every sortie, until his final mission (his 100th of the war) on 6 July 1944, after which he was taken off operations and awarded the unit's second Victoria Cross. The third member of 617 Squadron to wear the ribbon of the VC at this period was Flight Lieutenant W. Reid VC, who had actually won the award on 3 November 1943 while serving with 61 Squadron.

Tallboys and Grand Slams
Cheshire was succeeded as CO of 617 by Wing Commander J. B. 'Willie' Tait DSO DFC, who led the unit on many of the ensuing attacks against German-occupied ports and naval bases, using the Wallis-designed 12,000lb Tallboy DP (Deep Penetration) bomb. It was with this latest product of Wallis's fertile brain that Tait and his men (accompanied by 9 Squadron) were detached temporarily to Russia in late 1944. Their target was the German capital ship *Tirpitz*, which was badly damaged during an attack on 15 September by the two squadrons. In a second raid in conjunction with 9 Squadron on 12 November from Lossiemouth, Scotland, the *Tirpitz* was

finally sunk. Shortly afterwards, Tait was rested from operations, having been awarded a record quadruple DSO and double DFC at that time.

Tait's place as 617's commander was taken by Group Captain Johnny Fauquier, a Canadian ex-bush pilot, who, like Cheshire, eagerly relinquished higher rank in order to fly on operations again. The squadron's targets continued to be mainly naval, including U-boat pens, but on 14 March 1945 a 617 modified Lancaster, piloted by Squadron Leader C. C. Calder, dropped the first example of Barnes Wallis's mighty 22,000 lb Grand Slam bombs on a viaduct at Bielefeld with huge success. No 617's final war operation came on 25 April 1945, when eight crews bombed Hitler's personal retreat at Berchtesgaden.

In peacetime 617 Squadron remained a part of the postwar RAF, re-equipping with Avro Lincolns in late 1946 when based at Binbrook, Lincs. At the start of 1952 it received its first jet aircraft – English Electric Canberras – but it was disbanded on 15 December 1955. Three years later, on 1 May 1958, the 'Dam-busters' were reformed at their wartime base, Scampton, equipped with Avro Vulcan bombers as part of Bomber Command's new V-force. In September 1961 617 Squadron was further re-equipped with Vulcan B2 aircraft, becoming the first Squadron to be equipped with the Blue Steel stand-off bomb.

The Squadron established a unique string of 'firsts' in RAF history, even to the extent of having the reigning sovereign (King George VI) make the final selection of the design and motto for the official squadron badge; its motto 'Après moi le Déluge' was the first French motto to be adopted by the RAF. It is also the youngest squadron ever to be awarded a Squadron Standard (on 14 May 1959), an honour normally reserved until a unit has completed 25 years' service. If these were not enough, the Squadron also has its own march, the *Dam-Busters' March*, composed by Eric Coates for the film of the legendary dam-busting mission made in 1955, mainly at Scampton, the Squadron's birth-place.

Opposite: part of the flood damage caused by the breaching of the Möhne Dam.
Left: Sir Arthur Harris, AOC Bomber Command (left) and No 5 Group's commander Sir Ralph Cochrane look on as Guy Gibson's crew is debriefed after the Dams Raid.
Below left: No 617 Squadron's finest exploit was celebrated by the 1955 film The Dambusters

D · Michael **REDGRAVE** IN

THE DAM BUSTERS

SYDNEY · PATRICK BARR · ERNEST CLARK AND **DEREK FARR**

SCREENPLAY BY R. C. SHERRIFF
DIRECTED BY MICHAEL ANDERSON
Distributed by Associated British-Pathé

Schweinfurt Raids 1943

The concept of strategic bombing–the destruction of an enemy's war industry through aerial attack–originated during World War I but was not truly put to the test until the latter years of World War II. The two powers that made major efforts to develop strategic strike forces were Britain and the United States, but they did so along quite different lines. The Royal Air Force concentrated on weapons and equipment for use under cover of darkness, believing that daylight operations would render heavy bombers too vulnerable to enemy interceptors. On the other hand, the US Army Air Corps–later Army Air Force –planned to operate by day, as it was only then that accurate bombing could really be achieved. For its bombers to survive in daylight against enemy defences, the four-engined Boeing B-17 Fortresses and Consolidated B-24 Liberators were heavily armed with machine guns and flown in massed formations to confront interceptors with formidable firepower. The development of turbo-supercharged engines allowed the American bombers to operate at the then very high optimum altitude of 7,600 m (25,000 ft) and, by using a Norden precision bomb-sight, great accuracy could be obtained in target strikes.

The USAAF campaign of daylight strategic bombing was principally carried out by the Eighth Air Force in England. Early missions showed promise that the Fortresses and Liberators could carry out attacks on targets in Germany and occupied territories without prohibitive losses. The

Right: Eighth Air Force groundcrew collect machine gun cartridges from a Boeing B-17 after a raid on Germany.
Below: a German fighter is shot down by B-17s on their first mission to Schweinfurt on 17 August 1943.
Left: A Boeing B17G of the 381st Bomb Group, US Eighth Air Force, which sustained the highest losses of any group on the first raid

real test did not come until the summer of 1943 when the Eighth Air Force had received sufficient B-17 groups to conduct far-ranging missions into Germany, chiefly against the enemy's aircraft industry. At this time the Luftwaffe, aware that early attempts to turn back the USAAF formations by fighter interception had not met with much success, made strenuous efforts to bolster its fighter forces for the defence of the Reich and to evolve better tactics.

Strategic experts in the Allied camp held that one of the most profitable target systems to attack would be the German bearing industry which, vital to the manufacture of all military vehicles and aircraft, was concentrated in a few locations, chiefly around Schweinfurt, a town in south central Germany. Successful destruction of the major bearing plants could cause a critical situation in German war production. A major obstacle to launching such an attack was the distance involved – a 1,450km (900 mile) round trip from England, with the bombers in hostile skies for six hours where heavy losses could be expected. A plan was devised whereby two separate forces would be sent into Germany; the first would attack the Regensburg fighter factory near the Austrian border and then turn south across Italy and the Mediterranean to land in Allied North Africa. The second force, flying a similar penetration course and ten minutes behind the Regensburg

bombers, would hit Schweinfurt. In this way it was hoped to divide and confuse the enemy defence whose interceptors had limited flight duration. Good visibility over the target area was an essential requirement if good bombing was to be achieved and such weather was finally predicted for 17 August 1943 when the mission was flown.

Delayed departure

Matters did not go well from the outset for dawn found a thick ground fog over much of the eastern part of England, making take-off dangerous. Eventually the 4th Wing's B-17s – which were to fly to Regensburg – had to be dispatched to ensure their arrival over Africa in daylight. Their bases were near the east coast where the fog had thinned, but it persisted further inland delaying departure of the 1st Wing force for Schweinfurt. The timing of the two forces was planned so that enemy fighters attacking the first would not have time to refuel to meet the second and thus some of the anticipated opposition would be dissipated. With the delay this advantage was lost and the 1st Wing bombers were held until American fighters that had given the Regensburg force penetration cover to the German border had had time to return and refuel.

The Schweinfurt bombers eventually departed three-and-a-half hours behind those attacking Regensburg and consisted of 230 B-17s in four combat formations. The

Below: B-17s of a depleted formation bomb Schweinfurt on 17 August 1943. The results of the bombing were unsatisfactory and losses were heavy. The timing of the mission became dislocated, the escort was inadequate and the weight of the bomber force was further dissipated by prolonged fighter attacks. Right: bombs strike the bearing complex at Schweinfurt during a daylight raid on 13 April 1944 by USAAF bombers

results were achieved with three of the five plants at Schweinfurt receiving heavy damage. There was no let-up in the Luftwaffe attacks on the return journey and vicious assaults were made on the leading elements of the 3rd Division. Late in the afternoon the first Fortresses began to reach England and soon it was known that the cost of the raid had been 60 B-17s missing in action, five more had crashed in England and 133 were damaged, some so badly that repairs were not economically worthwhile. A total of 600 men was missing and there were five dead and 43 wounded on returning bombers. Against this terrible loss was the claimed destruction of 288 enemy fighters and the laying waste of three bearing factories. The claims of enemy aircraft were obviously exaggerated through the confused nature of the air battle (actual losses were about 50 fighters), but the bombing could be verified by photographic reconnaissance. The attack cost the Germans a 50 per cent fall in bearing production and it was six months before production returned to the pre-raid level. However, despite this achievement, the USAAF day bombers had taken what was to be the highest percentage loss to a major task force during their campaign and, coming after a week of similarly costly raids, this convinced most dedicated supporters of the self-defence bomber mission that such tactics were no longer tenable.

Diminishing importance

Although the 14 October raid had considerable success, a follow-up attack could have had a more telling effect on the German war economy. The bearing complex was not attacked again until the following February and by this time the Germans had had time to disperse their bearing production to a number of smaller sites. While another 14 bombing raids were made on the Schweinfurt plants during the war, none caused so much disruption to the supply of ball-bearings as the first two strikes.

The third attack on Schweinfurt, carried out by 238 B-17s of the 1st Division, took place on 24 February 1944. Only 11 Fortresses were lost but the formation had the benefit of long-range fighter support. RAF Bomber Command visited the scene that night and 663 Avro Lancasters and Handley Page Halifaxes unloaded over 2,000 tons of bombs over the factory complex. Heavy attacks by Eighth Air Force bombers were carried out on 21 July and 9 October 1944, only by this date Schweinfurt was no longer of major importance to the German bearing industry – a fact not then fully appreciated by Allied intelligence. Further attacks were carried out, the last by medium bombers of the Ninth Air Force in April 1945.

The Schweinfurt raids resulted in a reappraisal of the whole concept of US Army Air Force strategic bombing. It was evident that success depended upon gaining air superiority over Germany. This belated conclusion hastened the introduction of the North American P-51 escort fighter which was capable of missions to Berlin. Secondly, the Allied air commanders were effectively convinced that targets should be repeatedly attacked in a more co-ordinated, massive and continuous campaign.

When an American armoured column captured Schweinfurt at the end of hostilities the Nazi flag flying in the town was sent to the Eighth Air Force in England to be donated to the unit that had suffered most grievously over this infamous target. The flag was given to the 305th Bomb Group which had lost 14 bombers on the second raid. While the bombing of the German bearing industry failed to realise the hopes of the strategic planners, the name Schweinfurt has become famous in popular history as the epic mission of the Eighth Air Force.

first fighter attacks were encountered soon after crossing the Belgian coast and these continued intermittently to the target and back to the coast, some 200 enemy fighters being involved. Attacks were concentrated on the leading elements from which 21 of the 36 B-17s lost by the whole force were shot down. The disruption of the leading formation had the effect of causing some of the bombing to be off target although a considerable number of hits was obtained on factory buildings. Although claimed as a success by the American authorities, later examination of reconnaissance photographs showed the damage at Schweinfurt to be far from the crippling blow required.

Second attempt

A return mission to Schweinfurt was planned using the whole Eighth Air Force bomber establishment to ensure maximum destruction within the target area. Other commitments and poor weather delayed this raid until 14 October 1943 when 420 B-17s and B-24s were scheduled. The number would have been higher but for heavy attrition during recent missions. Weather over home bases again interfered and the small B-24 formation was unable to assemble on time and therefore flew a feint over the North Sea. Even the Fortresses were fewer than planned with a total of 291 departing England in two divisional forces.

The 1st Division took what was a more or less direct route and the trailing 3rd Division followed a zig-zag course to deceive the enemy into believing it was heading for a different target. This was successful, for the 3rd Division encountered little concentrated fighter activity until it had bombed the target and was on its way home. The 1st Division was not so fortunate, coming under continuous fighter attack as soon as the US escort had withdrawn. Confusion during the assembly in poor weather over England had resulted in some combat wings being scattered and it was on these that the enemy concentrated his forces. The 305th Bomb Group was almost annihilated, only three of its B-17s surviving. From the combat wing in which this Group was flying, half the strength dispatched had been lost by the time the target was reached. Despite the intensity of the opposition, good bombing

Battle of Berlin 1943-44

The Commander-in-Chief RAF Bomber Command, Air Chief Marshal Sir Arthur Harris, had a theory that devastating the German capital would produce a blow that would shorten the war. In a minute to Winston Churchill on 3 November 1943 he had stated 'We can wreck Berlin from end to end if the USAAF will come in on it. It will cost between 400–500 aircraft. It will cost Germany the war'.

Harris had been pressed earlier to attack the German capital as a retaliatory measure, but had chosen to concentrate on destroying the industrial capacity of the Ruhr and the Baltic ports. Berlin was deep in the Reich, beyond the range of 'Oboe' and 'Gee', the British navigational aids. Nevertheless, it had been attacked from time to time. Now the effectiveness of his force had greatly increased, not only in aircraft but in techniques. In July 'Window', strips of tinfoil to disrupt enemy radar, had been used in a Hamburg attack so devastating that Harris had confidence in destroying the larger areas of Berlin in a series of raids. Since then, new techniques had been introduced: 'spoof raids' or simulated attacks on cities to divert enemy fighters, and the 'Airborne Cigar' which disrupted communication between those fighters and their controllers,

together with the introduction of German-speaking personnel transmitting false directions.

Three attacks had been delivered against the German capital in August 1943 causing widespread evacuation of non-essential personnel for a loss of 126 aircraft. Bomber Command's reasons for intensifying these raids were contained in the following statement:

'The destruction of Berlin without a much heavier weight of attack than Bomber Command alone can produce is an extremely difficult problem. It is the target which above all the Luftwaffe has to defend, and no chances will be taken with it even if this involves lesser places like Stettin and Hanover being relatively lightly protected. The penetration of enemy-held territory to reach it is large. Finally its sheer size–18,000 acres of closely built-up area as compared with 8,380 at Hamburg–means that no noticeable impression can be made on it except by a large force'.

The Battle opens

The time for an all-out assault, Harris judged, was right. German morale was low. The war against Russia was not going well; in the south, Italy, an ally in the summer, had

turned enemy in the autumn, and from the west came the nightly visitations upon German cities by the RAF and day attacks by the USAAF. By a blow to the heart of the Reich, namely the capital Berlin, German morale might well collapse. That was the theory.

The first of the series of blows against Berlin, on the night of 18/19 March, was two-pronged, with 444 aircraft directed to Berlin and 395 crews briefed for Mannheim. This attack had the desired effect of splitting and confusing the defences; losses of nine aircraft were the lowest of all the Berlin attacks. But the attack could not be called a success. There was heavy cloud over the target and the aiming points had to be marked 'blind' by the Path Finder Force using H2S radar. The Mark III version of this radar, recently rushed into service, was only marginally better than the Mk II with which crews were more familiar. Just how effective this attack was could not be assessed, as the town was hidden under a blanket of cloud, making

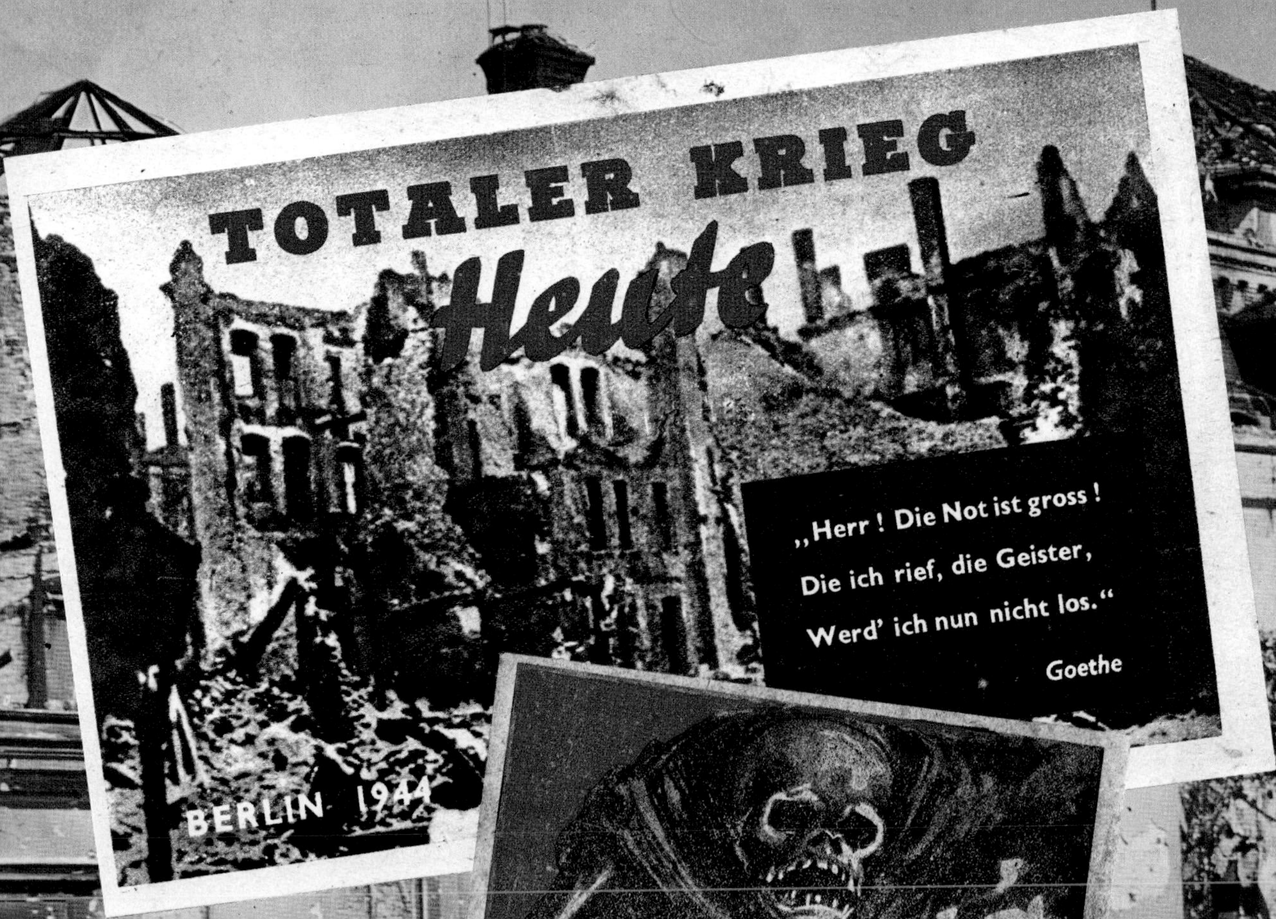

TOTALER KRIEG
Heute

"Herr! Die Not ist gross!
Die ich rief, die Geister,
Werd' ich nun nicht los."
Goethe

BERLIN 1944

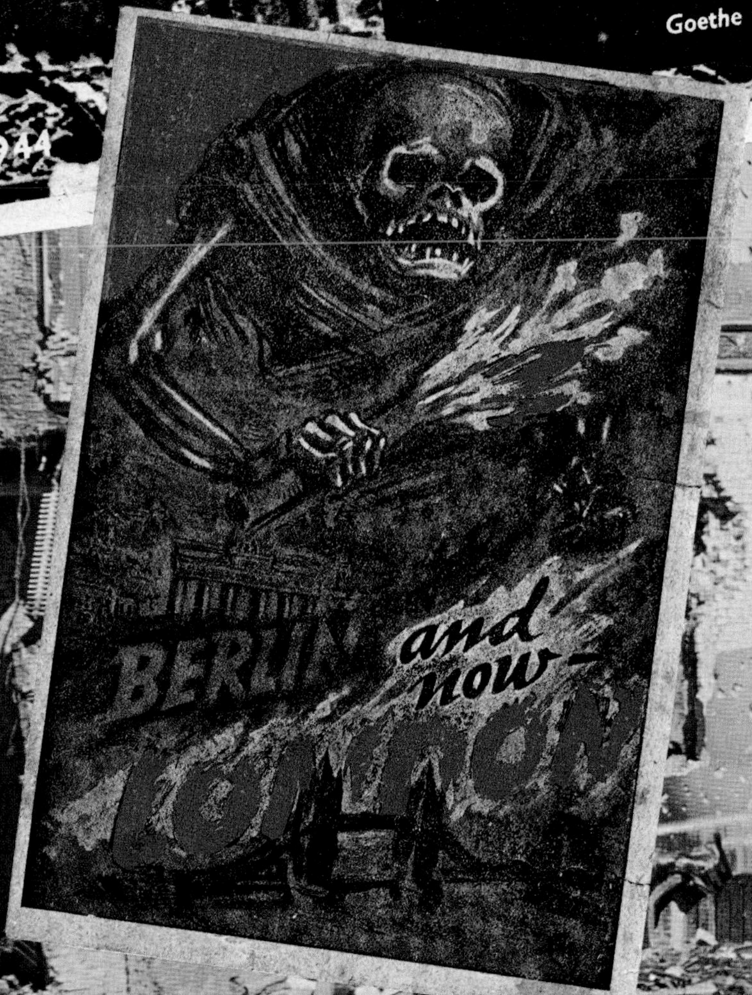

BERLIN and now—

photographic reconnaissance impossible.

Four nights later Harris ordered the largest attack that Berlin had experienced, by 764 aircraft, including 121 of Path Finder Force – the largest number of these aircraft ever to operate. Also creating a precedent that night was KB700, the first Canadian-built Lancaster to operate.

While the numbers of aircraft attacking may not seem impressive in view of the 1,000-bomber raids of 1942, it should be appreciated that on those occasions operational training aircraft had participated. Moreover, while the bulk of aircraft then were twin-engined Wellingtons, Whitleys and Hampdens, the force was now one consisting mainly of four-engined heavy bombers.

The bomber force

During the Battle of Berlin period, Bomber Command was divided into Nos 1, 3, 4, 5, 6 (Canadian) and 8 (Path Finder) Groups, each controlling station in Eastern England maintaining from one to three squadrons according to size and facilities. In all, in late 1944, there were 61 squadrons available for operations with a total of 1,360 aircraft.

Of the four-engined heavy bomber squadrons there were 35 of Lancasters, 19 of Halifaxes and six of Stirlings; statistics had shown a loss rate of one per 132, 56 and 41 tons dropped by each respective type and so the policy of re-equipping Stirling units with Lancasters continued during the Battle. The Halifax, by the same token, was also much inferior to the Lancaster, but the disparity was lessened by the introduction of the Mk III, with which Halifax squadrons were re-equipping during the Battle. There were also six squadrons of Mosquito light bombers for nuisance raids or specific target attacks and finally, the front-line at this time included No 300 (Polish) Squadron still flying Wellingtons. These aircraft were not suited for Berlin attacks, involving as they did a flight of 600 miles without diversionary routes to confuse the defences. In addition to the main force there were eight special duty and support squadrons operated by the Command which were brought under the control of No 100 (Special Duties) Group formed in December.

The raid on 22/23 November was repeated the following night at half strength and two nights later the target was switched to Frankfurt. However, on the fourth Berlin attack on 26 November there were clear skies and fires were seen still smouldering from earlier attacks. This time the Pathfinders' indicators could be seen clearly on the ground and much industrial damage resulted, in particular to the gun shops of Rheinmetall Borsig. While 450 aircraft made for the capital, 178 had set out to cause a diversion at Stuttgart.

A very high percentage of the bombers attacking had been Lancasters. Of the 458 bombers winging their way to Berlin on the fifth attack, all were Lancasters except for 15 Handley Page Halifaxes of No 35 Squadron operating with Path Finder Force.

A Berlin attack was called the very next night, but later the target was changed to Leipzig. The bombers set out as if making for the capital, and Mosquitos dropping 'Window' all the way there fooled the defences into sending the bulk of the fighters to Berlin.

Harris changes tactics

Harris was concerned about the result of his attacks; the dull winter weather was still hampering aerial reconnaissance. Attacks could not be made when morning mist

Above right: Avro Lancaster IIIs of 619 Squadron in February 1944. The unit operated from Woodhall Spa, Lincs, as members of the Path Finder Force

Above: Bomber Command aircrew photographed on 21 January 1944. That evening the RAF raided Berlin in force, starting fires that were still burning the following night

threatened to shroud the airfields on return, or during 8–14 December when the full moon would help the enemy fighters. Losses had risen to 40 aircraft on the last raid and Harris waited until 16 December before ordering the next, when new tactics were tried. Mosquito fighters set out with the bombers to combat their enemy counterparts. That night Beaufighters operated in this role for the first time, and their 12 sorties in the Battle were the only Bomber Command Beaufighter sorties of the war.

At this stage another battle commenced, 'Operation Crossbow', directed against the German V-bomb weapons. The launching sites across the Channel were already under attack by Allied fighter-bombers and medium bombers; now Bomber Command was ordered to add its weight with daylight attacks. Inevitably, this added task lengthened the Battle; crews could not operate night and day. As it was, they were under considerable strain, being frequently warned and briefed for attacks cancelled at the last minute due to weather conditions. Nevertheless, over 650 aircraft set out that night for Frankfurt, while 54 made for

Mannheim as a diversion – which failed, for the Frankfurt force lost 40 aircraft.

At last, after days of overcast weather preventing reconnaissance, photographic cover of the target was brought back. The bombing had been accurate. The principal districts affected were Charlottenburg (a largely residential area but industrial to the north), Mitte (government and commercial offices, industrial and residential buildings) and Tiergarten (embassies, legations and residential district). There was damage to nearly a hundred industrial premises that British Intelligence knew by name. The Lehrter and Potsdamer passenger stations had been gutted and the Stettiner and Wriezener stations seriously damaged.

On the other hand, some of the bombing was widespread. Just as Harris laid on 'spoof raids' to fool the defending fighters, so the defences tried to fool the attacking bombers. Decoy sites had been constructed around Berlin; one in particular, 15 miles to the west of the capital, stretched for eight miles. The Germans simulated British target markers and bomb flashes over the area, started ground fires and used searchlights and anti-aircraft fire to lure the bombers to the false targets.

Bomber Command's final major efforts in 1943 were directed against the German capital and the new year started with two attacks in quick succession. Then came a lull for Berlin, but not for Bomber Command crews who visited Stettin and Brunswick. Mosquitos were out frequently over German towns, including the capital, on what were loosely called 'nuisance raids' – but their 4,000lb bombs were somewhat more than a nuisance.

Heavy RAF losses

It was back in strength to the 'Big City', as it was known to crews, on the evening of 21 January; Mosquito crews, adding a few 4,000lb bombs the next night, reported fires still burning. A week later Mosquitos were over in the evening, followed by the main force in the early hours. Although Stirlings were not now sent to distant targets like Berlin, they played their part. That night 63 Stirlings, sent to lay mines in Kiel harbour, made an approach as if heading for Berlin. This drew up the fighters which, as planned, ran short of fuel at the time the main stream moved towards the capital.

The Battle was reaching a climax. Again the bombers set out the following night and repeated the raid two nights later. It was a great strain for crews, long hours in cramped positions at sub-zero temperatures – some were even frost-

bite casulaties. The damage being caused now was less, as so much of the city had already been devastated. German morale was sustained to a degree by the bomber losses. Their propaganda made much of the fact that well over 100 four-engined bombers had been shot down in four nights. As with the Hamburg raid that provoked the Baedeker raids, the attacks on the capital, led to a small series of attacks, this time on London, in what became known as the 'Baby Blitz'.

During February Bomber Command turned to other targets in general; Augsburg, Leipzig, Stuttgart and Schweinfurt suffering in turn. These were partly in conjunction with an Allied plan to smash the German aircraft industry. In mid-February Harris delivered the heaviest attack of the Battle when 891 bombers set out.

US daylight raids

Now the Americans came on the scene with daylight attacks. They had been briefed to attack the capital as a follow-up to the second raid of the Battle, but that was cancelled; then came the decision to concentrate on the German aircraft industry. So, in daylight on 4 March, 502 B-17 Fortresses of the Eighth Air Force formated over East Anglia and set out for their first attack on Berlin. Abnormally high thick cloud caused a recall; on this occasion it was unheeded by one combat wing of 30 Fortresses which dropped their bombs through thick cloud on the south-western suburbs.

The Germans anticipated rightly that the Eighth Air Force would try again and disposed their fighters accordingly. They had but two days to wait; then 730 B-17 Fortresses and B-24 Liberators took off for the capital escorted by 796 fighters – P-38 Lightnings, P-47 Thunderbolts and P-51 Mustangs of the Eighth and Ninth Air Forces and Mustangs of the RAF. The bombers were spread in a 60-mile column advancing towards Berlin when squadrons of FW190s and Bf109s took off to attack. As they neared their quarry the German defence controller realised that the escort had concentrated in the front and rear, exposing the flanks in the centre. Alerted to this situation, the fighters shot down 31 bombers in quick succession. The remaining bombers had to face the Berlin flak and fighters on the return leg. The Germans claimed 140 bombers destroyed, but in reality 69 were lost and 120 others returned with major damage and casualties – the 350th Squadron, with ten losses, being practically wiped out. Berlin's suburbs had suffered, but the primary industrial targets had remained untouched.

The balance sheet

The crews landing from the raid in which their Force had suffered one of its greatest losses of the war were briefed for a return to Berlin with just one day's rest. In spite of all the losses and damage, 600 set out two days later – this time in clear skies. The Erkner bearing plant and many other establishments were wrecked for the loss of 39 bombers. Berlin was yet again the target the next day. Cloud had returned over the city and bombing was by radar; the fighter controller, realising that there was nothing to fear from precision bombing, left it to the gunners who made an accurate claim of nine heavy bombers shot down. Three were lost additionally from other causes.

Bad weather over central Germany gave Berlin a temporary immunity from attack until 22 March, when the Americans made their fifth and last attack of the Battle. Cloud hindered the bombing accuracy but it also hampered the fighters.

RAF Bomber Command, meanwhile, had been continuing attacks on German cities, causing a mass exodus from Frankfurt. Harris realised that with the invasion of the Continent planned, he would be directed to switch targets. He made his last attack of the Battle on the night of 24 March 1944, with differing results. Cloud varied and some crews saw clearly the ground markers laid by the Pathfinders, but one marker flare above the cloud drifted miles away. The guns were particularly vicious that night and fighters had nearly 20 successes, making this last raid of the Battle the most costly; 95 aircraft were lost or wrecked on return.

The Battle of Berlin was over, but the bombing went on. Berlin had not been totally destroyed by high explosive and incendiaries; indeed, aircraft production had increased through wide dispersal. The Allies had lost thousands of trained aircrew and nearly 1,000 heavy bombers. The overall effect of the Battle of Berlin, however can never be accurately assessed in terms of statistics alone. It had forced Germany into providing increased anti-aircraft defences at a time when steel was desperately needed for armour; it had weakened the Luftwaffe, in particular by its toll of trained pilots. At the end of the Battle, Bomber Command and the Eighth Air Force were still able to sustain the same weight of attack; the Luftwaffe could barely mount even token retaliation.

A stick of bombs drops on Templehof, Berlin, during a daylight raid by the US 8th Air Force

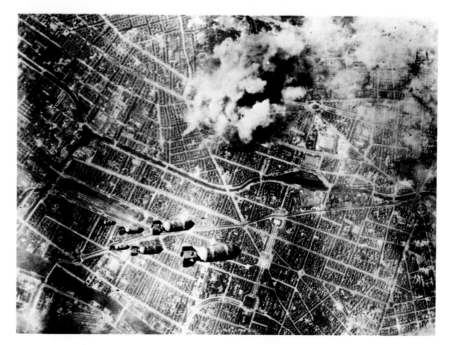

Amiens Raid 1944

In February 1944 a small group of de Havilland Mosquito bombers set out from England with full bomb loads on a unique mission – to *save* lives. The sortie was specific in its intention – to initiate a break-out from Amiens gaol of some 700 French Resistance workers, many of whom were on the eve of execution by their German gaolers for their part in fighting against the Nazi occupation of their homeland, France.

The Mosquitoes' part was to bomb the outer walls of the prison, and to demolish certain internal buildings usually occupied by German guards and staff. Absolute pin-point precision in such bombing was vital – a few

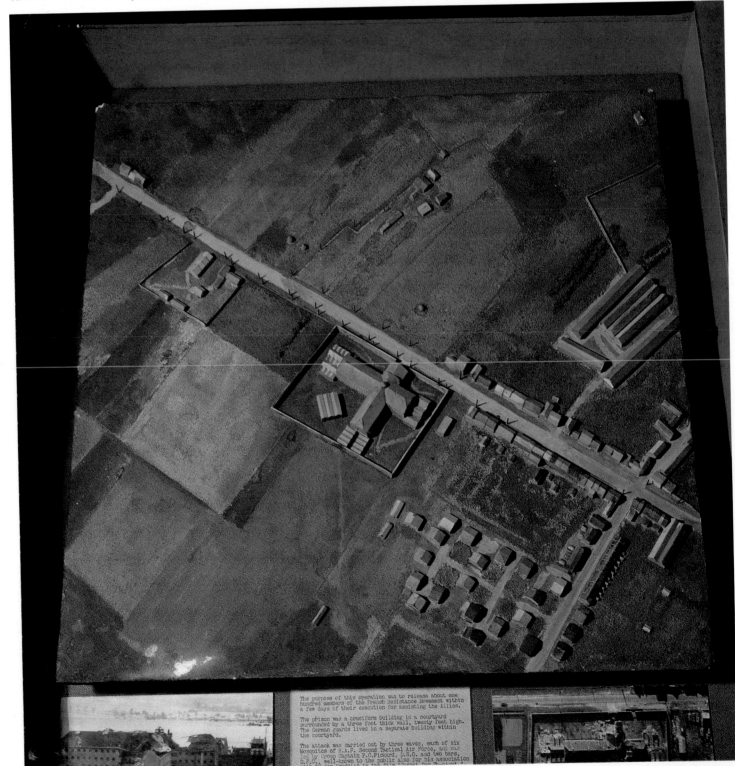

The purpose of this operation was to release about one hundred members of the French Resistance Movement within a few days of their execution for assisting the Allies.

The prison was a cruciform building in a courtyard surrounded by a three foot thick wall, twenty feet high. The German guards lived in a separate building within the courtyard.

The attack was carried out by three waves, each of six Mosquitos of R.A.F. Second Tactical Air Force, and was led by Group Captain P.C.Pickard, D.S.O. and two bars, D.F.C., well-known to the public also for his association

Above: Group Captain
P. C. Pickard (left), who
led the Amiens raid, and
his navigator, Flt Lt W.
Broadley, both of whom
were killed on the raid
when Pickard remained
behind to observe the
effects of the bombing and
was shot down by a Focke
Wulf Fw 190.
Left: the scale model of
the Amiens gaol (centre)
used to brief the DH
Mosquito pilots of No 140
Wing, RAF who carried out
the precision bombing of
the gaol to enable French
resistance workers,
imprisoned there by the
Gestapo, to escape. The
model is preserved in the
Imperial War Museum,
London

inches or seconds in miscalculation by the Mosquito crews would mean the difference between possible freedom or wholesale slaughter for the French patriots. The mission was initially requested by the French Maquis; a desperate last-ditch attempt to save their countrymen from certain death at the hands of the Gestapo. On receiving their extraordinary request, the RAF had deep reservations about the feasibility of such precise bombing, apart from the inevitable possibility of killing the very people it was intended to save. It meant placing bombs almost as if by hand in specific sections of the prison structure to facilitate the final escape. It meant low-level run-ins no higher than *15 feet*, pinpoint bombing, and then an immediate climb to clear the 60-feet high prison walls. Above all, it meant absolute precision in timing between individual Mosquitoes on the bombing run-in. And the whole mission, code-named 'Jericho', could only be done once.

The task was given to No. 140 Wing, 2 Group, RAF, and despite the many obvious risks involved, each crew member at the initial briefing wanted to go on the raid. After several postponements due to impossible flying conditions, the Mosquito crews were finally called for early briefing on the morning of 18 February 1944. Three formations of six Mosquitoes, each crewed by the most experienced men from 21, 464 and 487 Squadrons were detailed for the operation. A single Mosquito from the Film Production Unit would follow these to record results. The first wave was to comprise two 'vics' of three Mosquitoes from the New Zealand unit, 487 Squadron, followed by two 'vics' from the Australian 464. 21 Squadron's aircraft were to be held in reserve to complete any

unfinished part of the bombing.

Inseparable planners

Master-minding the operation in the air was the responsibility of a tall, blonde-haired Group Captain with four years of almost continuous operations behind him; Percy Charles Pickard, DSO, DFC. The whole navigational plot was in the worthy hands of Pickard's inseparable friend and navigator, Flight Lieutenant J. A. 'Bill' Broadley, DSO, DFC, DFM. It was to be their ultimate operation together, for both found death and immortality at Amiens. The photo' Mosquito, DZ414, 'O-Orange', piloted by Tony Wickham, was to follow the second wave of bombers over the prison, while Pickard was to circuit the area and decide if 21 Squadron's third wave was needed.

The fighter escort, a dozen Hawker Typhoons of 198 Squadron, was detailed to prevent any Luftwaffe interference. The New Zealanders' job was to breach the prison's outer wall in two places at ground level and the Australians were to rupture the main prison block inside the compound by destroying the German guards' annexe. Only three minutes maximum could be allowed between these two attacks. Each Mosquito was to be loaded with two 500lb HE bombs, fused with 11-second delay detonators.

For two hours the crews studied a replica model of the prison and its surrounds, calculating angles, heights, obstacles, known gun-posts, run-out routes. Each of the first two waves were told explicitly that once they had bombed they were to set course for home immediately.

The first wave of Mosquitoes struck Amiens gaol, scoring hits on buildings beside the road. As the attack continued, devastation mounted. 'The air was thick with smoke but of all the bombs dropped . . . only one went astray'. Circling the target, Pickard saw that the prison walls had been breached and called off the final wave of Mosquitoes from 21 Squadron. Bottom: a de Havilland Mosquito FB Mk VI of 487 Squadron which spearheaded the attack

The crews dispersed to their aircraft and by 10.30 am all 19 Mosquitoes were parked, ready, at the end of Hunsdon airfield's main runway, waiting for the 11 am take-off.

'Give everything'

The raid was scheduled to start over the gaol at precisely 12.03 pm; the time detailed for the New Zealanders to make their drop. Flying Officer N. M. Sparks, a skipper in the first vic, takes up the story: 'We were determined to give everything we could to this job. I remember Group Captain Pickard putting into words what we were all beginning to feel when he said, "Well boys, this is a death-or-glory show. If it succeeds it will be one of the most worthwhile ops of the war. If you never do anything else you can still count this as the finest job you could ever have done". So we went outside and looked at the weather again. It was terrible! Snow was still falling, sweeping in gusts that now and again hid the end of the runway from sight. If this had been an ordinary operation it would pretty certainly have been scrubbed .... We got into our aircraft, warmed up the engines, and sat there thinking it was no kind of weather to go flying in, but knowing somehow we must. When we saw the Group Captain drive up in his car and get into his Mosquito, we knew for certain the show was on. The 18 aircraft took off quickly, one after another, at about 11 in the morning – we were going to hit the prison when the guards were at lunch.'

Of those 18, two from 21 Squadron and two more from 464 detached and returned to base because of weather condition problems. F.O. Sparks continues the story: 'By the time I got to 100 feet I could not see a thing except that grey soupy mist and snow and rain beating against the perspex window. There was no hope of either getting into formation or staying in it, and I headed straight for the Channel coast. Two miles out from the coast the weather was beautifully clear, and it was only a matter of minutes before we were over France. We skimmed across the coast at deck level, swept round the north of Amiens and then split up for the attack.'

'Like a Hendon demonstration'

'My own aircraft, with our Wing Commander's and one other, stayed together to make the first run-in; our job was to blast a hole in the eastern wall. We picked up the straight road that runs from Albert to Amiens, and that led us straight to the prison. I'll never forget that road – long, straight and covered with snow. It was lined with tall poplars and the three of us were flying so low that I had to keep my aircraft tilted at an angle to avoid hitting the tops of trees with my wing. It was then, as I flew with one eye on those poplars and the other watching the road ahead, that I was reminded we had a fighter escort. A Typhoon came belting across right in front of me and I nearly jumped out of my seat. The poplars suddenly petered out and there, a mile ahead, was the prison. It looked just like the briefing model and we were almost on top of it within a few seconds.

'We hugged the ground as low as possible and at the lowest possible speed; we pitched our bombs towards the base of the wall, fairly scraped over it – and our part of the job was over. There wasn't time to stay and watch results. We had to get straight out and let the others come in. When we turned away we could see the second New Zealand section make their attack and follow out behind us.'

Wing Commander I. S. 'Black' Smith, DFC, leading that first vic of Mosquitoes, commented afterwards, 'My section went right in for the corner of the east walls, while the others drew off a few miles and made their run-in

on the north wall. Navigation was perfect and I've never done a better flight. It was like a Hendon demonstration. We flew as low and as slowly as possible, aiming to drop our bombs right at the foot of the wall. Even so our bombs went across the first wall, across the courtyard, and exploded on the wall at the other side. I dropped my own bombs from a height of 10 feet, pulling hard on the stick. The air was thick with smoke but of all the bombs dropped by both my section and the other, only one went astray.'

Skidding bombs in

As soon as the New Zealanders had cleared the target, Wing Commander R. W. 'Bob' Iredale, DFC, led in his Australians to complete the second phase – demolition of the guards' annexe. Flying so low that they had to lift over the outer wall and immediately skid their bombs in, the Australians flew straight through thick smoke and debris thrown up by the preceding New Zealanders' bombs.

Meanwhile, circling the target, Pickard saw that the job had been successfully accomplished. Gaping holes in the outer walls were disgorging escaping prisoners; tiny black ant-like figures starkly contrasted against the snow landscape. Accordingly, he gave the order for 21 Squadron to return to base – their bombs were not needed. At the same time, Wickham, in his photo' Mosquito started his first pass over the prison. 'We could see, the first time we flew over the objective, that the operation had been a complete success. Both ends of the prison had been completely demolished, and the surrounding wall broken down in many places. We could see a large number of prisoners escaping along the road. The cameras fixed in the plane were steadily recording it all, and the photographer was crouched in the nose taking picture after picture as fast as he could. He was so enthusiastic that he got us to stay over the objective longer than I considered healthy.'

Losses and success

Smoothly as the whole operation had gone it was not without loss. Squadron Leader I. R. McRitchie, leader of the second Australian vic, was re-forming near Albert when flak riddled his Mosquito MM404, wounding him and killing his navigator, Flight Lieutenant R. W. Sampson. With instinctive superlative skill McRitchie crash-landed at over 200 mph and survived to become a prisoner of war. By then several Focke Wulf Fw 190 fighters had appeared on the scene, but the force leader Pickard was absorbed in ascertaining the fate of McRitchie. Flying low over the crashed Mosquito, Pickard failed to notice two Fw 190s on his tail. These opened fire and Pickard's aircraft, HX922, 'F-Freddie', flicked over on to its back and dived straight into the ground. Three other Mosquitoes sustained serious damage but returned to England.

The raid had succeeded admirably in its objectives. Of the 700 or more prisoners in Amiens gaol that day, 258 escaped, including 12 who were marked for execution by firing squad the following day. Others who had escaped were recaptured or killed in the action; some of the latter by the German guards. Of the German prison staff about 50 were killed by the bombing. Today the actual model used for briefing 140 Wing's crews, along with a door lock from one of the prison cells from which a prisoner escaped successfully, can be seen in the galleries of the Imperial War Museum in London. In Amiens there is a memorial, erected in 1945, to the memory of Percy Pickard and 'Bill' Broadley – leaders of one of the war's most brilliant Mosquito operations.

Nuremburg Raid 1944

A green light winked across the sprawling Yorkshire bomber base of Burn, close to the Selby Canal; as it did so, a heavily-laden Halifax Mk III of No 578 Squadron rolled slowly forward, gathered speed and roared down the runway bound for Germany. Pilot Officer Cyril Barton and his crew were among several from No 578 Squadron who were now, on the penultimate night of March 1944, scheduled to participate in a heavy RAF Bomber Command attack on the vital industrial centre and railway junction at Nuremburg. *Excalibur* was the name of Barton's Halifax, the emblem painted on its nose depicting a hand emerging from the base of a cloud and brandishing the legendary sword of King Arthur. Bomber Command, in concert with the US Eighth Air Force flying daylight raids, was pressing on relentlessly with its round-the-clock offensive against industrial Germany and, in its unshakable resolve, was accepting casualties greater than any other arm of Britain's fighting services. This particular night was to prove the worst that it ever had to endure.

Vengeful sword

A total of 795 aircraft of Bomber Command (including 110 from the Path Finder Force) was dispatched against the Bavarian city, which lay deep within enemy territory and, as they took off from eastern England, neither Barton's crew nor any other was aware that, on this occasion, the vengeful sword was to be firmly in the enemy's hand. Things went badly from the very start: for some incomprehensible reason, the bombers were given an outward route which involved flying first to the vicinity of Charleroi in Belgium, then due east for nearly 400 km (250 miles) to Fulda, near Frankfurt, whence they were to make their final run-in to Nuremburg from a north-north-westerly direction.

A zig-zag route was normally employed on bombing missions, but this mission's long direct approach leg took the force close to the positions of two known German night fighter beacons. Furthermore, the raid planners adjudged weather conditions over the North Sea too bad to make any extensive diversionary operations; such diversions had long been a major factor in reducing losses. Earlier in March 1944, for example, when attacks were being made on Frankfurt, diversions over the North Sea had completely misled enemy fighters.

The German night fighter crews were soon to have their revenge. The high cloud, which was expected to afford the bombers adequate concealment along the route, dispersed before they had made a landfall on the Belgian coast and left them exposed in the light of a half moon. At the same time, transmissions from the bombers' H2S 'magic eye' radar apparatus had been picked up by German ground direction-finding stations, thus enabling

Below: the scene in the briefing room prior to the Nuremburg Raid on the night of 30 March 1944. The skies over Belgium were clear and the bombers and their vapour trails were easily seen in the moonlight by the German night fighters

the enemy to plot accurately the bombers' flight path. Thenceforth a firm grip was kept on the bomber force's movements and, judging correctly that a force of some 50 Halifaxes engaged in laying mines in the Heligoland Bight could be neglected and that attacks being made by Mosquitoes on objectives in Holland and the Ruhr were also intended as diversions, the enemy concentrated night fighters in the vicinity of the two aforementioned radio beacons.

As the Halifaxes and Lancasters thundered across Germany they left dense condensation trails in their wake, although they were below the height at which these tell-tale ribbons were usually produced. Being a clear night, the glow of the half-full moon gave the contrails a phosphorescent quality and many a crew-member in the bomber force must have viewed them with distinct apprehension. Yet another hazard was that, even before reaching the 400 km (250 mile) leg due east, the bomber stream had begun to lose cohesion due to unexpected winds. It was soon spread over a broad belt north of the true track and it was in this form that it eventually flew right into the swarm of night fighters which were milling round the first radio beacon, whose code-name was Ida. A running battle was fought over a distance of nearly 400 km (250 miles) from Aachen eastwards past the second beacon (code-named Otto) and then southwards, with increasing numbers of fighters joining in as the enemy correctly divined the target.

Easy prey

Exposed in the moonlight and often silhouetted against lower clouds, the bombers were easy prey and, as the fighters struck, many of them fell in flames, one after another. Night fighter *gruppen* from bases all over Germany joined in the slaughter and, as one *oberleutnant*, Fritz Brandt, reported afterwards 'It was possible to

Opposite: the nose artwork of Handley Page Halifax B Mk III, LV 907, 'Friday the Thirteenth' carried unlucky omens and a motto apt to the Nuremburg raid. Despite superstition, it flew 128 operational sorties including the Nuremburg raid, which was considerably above the average. On the Nuremburg raid 94 out of 795 bombers failed to return, Bomber Command's heaviest loss on a single operation.
Left: Pilot Officer Cyril Barton was awarded a posthumous Victoria Cross for battling against impossible odds to complete his mission during the Nuremburg Raid.
Below: a map showing diversionary raids and the path of the bomber stream. The latter's course took the bombers near to two known German night fighter assembly beacons

plot your course to the target by the number of wrecked aircraft which we could see the next day. They ran in a smouldering line across half Germany.'

Seventy-five Lancasters and Halifaxes of the Royal Australian Air Force were among the bomber force which set out on the raid; at least 20 were intercepted, although most of them managed to ecape by skilful flying or spirited return fire. One Lancaster pilot of No 467 (RAAF) Squadron counted 30 burning aircraft between Aachen and Nuremburg and it is probable that at least 50 machines from the total Bomber Command force were shot down before reaching the target. Up to this point set-backs had been due to factors over which the force had little control, but even those bombers which had fought through to Nuremburg found that their difficulties were by no means at an end.

The pathfinders were 47 minutes late and the city itself was hidden by cloud. The first bombs had been due to fall at 0110 hours but, for some time after this, hundreds of bombers milled round the target area anxiously seeking the pathfinders' flares. Several collisions were narrowly averted and soon some aircraft started to bomb independently. One Lancaster of No 460 (RAAF) Squadron eventually bombed a searchlight position already a target for other aircraft, only to see the first pathfinder markers go down 32km (20 miles) to the north-east. Impatient crews were releasing their bombs everywhere and those without H2S, which were thus relying on the incorrectly-forecast winds, bombed places as far distant as Schweinfurt, 40km (25 miles) away.

Worst fears confirmed

The only evidence that bombs fell on Nuremburg came from German radio reports; RAF crew reports were so pessimistic that Bomber Command's C-in-C, 'Bert' Harris, did not even request Photographic Reconnaissance Unit cover. After the war, Bomber Command's fears were largely confirmed when the captured War Diary of the Luftwaffe First Fighter Corps revealed that most of the damage done at Nuremburg involved residential areas, with only slight damage to industry.

By the time the bombers set course for home they were so widely dispersed that the German night fighter force lost contact almost completely. However, they now became ideal targets for the flak batteries and at least 14 of them are thought to have been claimed by the guns.

Still among the bomber force at this stage was the Halifax flown by Pilot Officer Cyril Barton, but it was now very much a lame duck. Barton's problems had begun on the outward trip, when he was still some 113km (70 miles) from Nuremburg; a Junkers Ju 88 had fired on his aircraft and wrecked the intercom. A Messerschmitt Me 210 had joined the combat, damaging one of the Halifax's engines and the Halifax's machine guns were out of action. The attacks had continued almost non-stop as the bomber struggled on and, in the confusion at the height of the battle, a hand signal had been misinterpreted and the navigator, bomb aimer and wireless operator had baled out.

Barton's aircraft was now badly damaged, some of his crew had gone and he could not communicate with the remainder. He had realised that if he continued his mission he would be at the mercy of hostile fighters when silhouetted against the fires in the target area. If he survived, he knew he would have to make a four-and-a-half-hour journey home on three engines across heavily-defended territory. Despite everything, Barton pressed on, reached Nuremburg and released the bombs himself before turning

for home. At this juncture, the propeller of the damaged engine, which was vibrating badly, flew off and Barton discovered that two of the fuel tanks were leaking, He nevertheless struggled on and, despite strong headwinds, managed to avoid the worst of the ground defences.

He eventually crossed the English coast only 145km (90 miles) north of base with the bomber's fuel almost exhausted. Before a suitable landing place could be found, the remaining port engine stopped. With two dead engines on the same wing, the damaged Halifax was almost uncontrollable and, as it was now too low to be abandoned, Barton ordered the three remaining members of his crew to take up their crash stations, the starboard outer engine also stopping as he did so. With only one engine remaining, he made a desperate attempt to avoid some houses. The Halifax crashed and broke up on a slag heap at Ryhope Colliery, near Sunderland, County Durham.

Unsurpassed courage

Barton was killed, but his three comrades survived to tell the story of his gallantry and in June 1944 he was posthumously awarded the Victoria Cross. Barton had previously taken part in four attacks on Berlin and 14 other operational missions. On one of these, two members of his crew were wounded during a determined effort to locate the target despite appalling weather conditions. 'In gallantly completing his last mission in the face of impossible odds', ran the closing sentence of the official citation concerning his VC award, 'this officer displayed unsur-

Below: staff in a control tower anxiously await the return of the bomber crews. Of the 795 aircraft dispatched to Nuremburg, including 110 pathfinders, 94 failed to return and 12 were destroyed on landing. Right: an air crew are debriefed following their return. Many of the aircraft bombed places up to 40km (25 miles) away from the target, due to incorrectly-forecast winds and a 45-minute delay in the arrival of the pathfinders. Below right and bottom: devastated areas of Nuremburg photographed after the war. Ironically the raid in March 1944 contributed little to this damage, despite the severe losses of the attackers

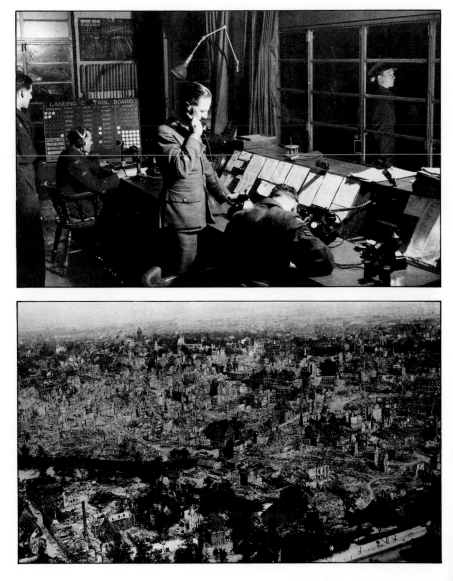

passed courage and devotion to duty.

Another bomber which survived the raid was a Halifax Mk III of No 424 (RCAF) Squadron piloted by Flying Officer F. F. Hamilton DFM. The bomber was suddenly engaged by a fighter and before evasive action could be taken it was repeatedly hit by cannon and machine gun fire. The controls to the starboard engines were fused and one of the engines caught fire, while the constant-speed unit was damaged. Considerable height was lost before Hamilton regained control. The engine fire was extinguished, but the aircraft was vibrating violently and the situation was serious. At this stage the propeller of one of the damaged engines flew off. The bomber became steadier and Hamilton nursed it safely back to base. The Halifax was twice attacked by fighters on the homeward flight, but they were driven off.

For Bomber Command, the cost of the Nuremburg raid was stupendous: of the 795 aircraft dispatched, 94 failed to return, 12 were totally destroyed after returning and another 59 were damaged. This represented a loss rate over the target and *en route* of 11·8 per cent and a total casualty rate of 20·8 per cent. Bomber Command had suffered what proved to be the most severe blow in its history and the raid halted the Command's long-employed tactics of massed and concentrated attack against major targets. They were not resumed until the situation in the skies over Germany had been radically altered and, in the meantime, Bomber Command's main effort was focused on targets in France in preparation for and, after D-day.

Battle of the V-Weapons 1944

The German experimental station at Peenemünde, planned in 1935, was opened in April 1937. Here, on a tongue of land jutting out into the Baltic, 96 km (60 miles) north-west of Stettin, a team of scientists headed by Werner von Braun devised rocket weapons under the direction of General Walter Dornberger. Von Braun's main interest was space exploration, fostered at first as a matter of national prestige, but when war came rockets were seen by the Nazis as possible long-range artillery. Early experiments had limited success until the A-4 type gyroscopically-stabilised, finned rocket reached a height of 85 km (53 miles) on 3 October 1942.

When a pulse-jet-powered flying bomb was projected by Argus Motorenwerke, and developed by Fieseler as

Above: a V-1 falls near Piccadilly, London. The course of a V-1 was set on its gyroscopic compass and its range determined by measuring its fuel. When the fuel ran out, the engine cut, and the V-1 descended. Each carried a ton of high explosive.
Left: trains carrying V-2s destroyed near Kleinbodungen one of the largest V-2 manufacturing plants in Germany, surveyed by a US soldier. The German V-weapon offensive was halted by repeated attacks by Allied fighter-bombers and bombers upon launching bases, transports and factories, and finally when the launching sites in North-east France and the Netherlands were overrun by Allied troops

A Hawker Tempest Mk V closes upon its prey, a V1 flying bomb, over Southern England. Only the the fastest fighters, such as the Tempest, North American P-51, Republic P-47 and Supermarine Spitfire Mk XIV could be used to intercept the fast-flying V1s

their Fi 103, it was sent to Peenemünde for proving as the FZG76 (Fernzielgerät or long-range target apparatus). Early experimental fuselages of December 1942 were air-launched from a Focke Wulf Fw 200 and in July 1943 a 246 km (153 miles) ground-launched flight with good accuracy encouraged further development. It was this bomb that the Germans called their V1 (Vergeltungswaffe 1 or reprisal weapon 1) and placed it in large-scale production at the Volkswagen works at Fallersleben.

Trial launches

To operate the V1, a new unit, designated Flak Regiment 155W, was formed under Colonel M. Wachtel. Trial launches were started at Zempin, a village near Peenemünde, before moving to Northern France where sites for the storage and launching of flying bombs were being prepared. Plans were made to launch the V1 attack late in 1943 with 1,000 missiles a day dispatched from a series of small sites holding 20 and large sites with storage space for 250.

As early as November 1939 British intelligence had been warned of rocket experiments at Peenemünde in a document delivered to the British Embassy in Oslo. Interrogation of German prisoners and escaped Polish nationals gave credence to reports of German experiments with long-range missiles. Photographic reconnaissance failed to attain any significant evidence until, quite by chance during a sortie in a Spitfire on 15 May 1942 to Swinemünde, Flight Lieutenant D. W. Steventon detected an airfield and activity near the mouth of the River Peene and set his cameras in motion. From then on the area was kept under periodic surveillance.

As a result of the intelligence collected, Air Marshal

Left: the RAF Bomber Command night attack on the Peenemünde experimental station on 17/18 August 1943 seriously disrupted V1 testing. Centre: a V1 seen after launching. Numbers of V1s were also air-launched from Heinkel He 111s. Bottom: a painting by L. Cole depicts a V1 shot down by anti-aircraft fire while another flies on. About half the V1s successfully launched were brought down

Harris ordered Operation Hydra, in which a force of 600 bombers made an attack on Peenemünde on the night of 17/18 August, in full moon to permit accurate location of the dispersed buildings set in woodland. Because the target route was similar to that of recent Berlin raids, a diversionary attack on the German capital was carried out that night by de Havilland Mosquitoes. A few aircraft were forced to abort and 597 heavy bombers set out. The recently-introduced master bomber technique was used and its success was enhanced by an early identification of the target area before the smoke screen defences had time to take effect. Among the 27 buildings completely destroyed was the senior officers mess and a key scientist was killed. By the time the bombers were returning, however, the German fighter controller had deployed his night fighters and in the bright moonlight some 30 bombers were shot down; a total of 41 was lost.

The raid seriously affected V-weapon proving, but building work continued on the launching sites in France. Soon photo-reconnaissance of Northern France revealed a series of ski-shaped erections, confirmed by intelligence from French resistance at some 80 locations, all placed at a distance of 217km (135 miles) from London. Photographic interpreters, among whom was Constance Babington Smith of the Women's Auxiliary Air Force, detected a small type of aircraft at some of the sites; both the aircraft and the site shapes linked with photographs taken over Peenemünde. The signs were ominous and defensive measures were planned under the code-name 'Crossbow', the code-word 'Diver' being allotted to the V1 weapon itself.

'Noball' targets

Attacks by RAF heavy bombers and Martin Marauder medium bombers of the US Ninth Air Force on the launching and supply sites, code-named 'Noball' targets, started on 20 December 1943 and, from Christmas Eve onwards, were joined by 'heavies' of the US Eighth Air Force. Between April and June, RAF Bomber Command, committed both to invasion preparation and support work and maintaining its offensive against German towns, devoted thirteen per cent of its total effort against flying bomb supply and launching sites, suffering the loss of 38 aircraft.

A week after D-day, in the early hours of 13 June 1944, the first V1 rockets were launched against south-east England. Observer Corps M2 post members made the first 'Diver' sighting, while other less well-informed individuals reported objects coming in over the sea trailing flames and sounding like two-stroke motorcycles. The first of the four V1s crossing the coast fell at Swanscombe, Kent, while one reached London to hit a railway bridge at Bethnal Green, killing six people. Then came a short lull, due to German inability to sustain the attack. However, two nights later the onslaught began in earnest. Immediately Air Marshal Sir Roderic Hill, commanding Air Defence Great Britain, put his anti-Diver plans into operation. Barrage balloon squadrons were re-deployed to form a screen to the south of London stretching from

Leatherhead in Surrey to Gravesend in Kent. Further south, anti-aircraft batteries took up new positions along the North Downs, while along the coastal strip and out to sea fighters had free range.

For the fighters, tackling pilotless aircraft flying up to 644 km/h (400 mph) posed new problems. Spitfire Mark XIVs and Tempest Mark Vs of the six squadrons initially allotted to the anti-Diver role were modified to achieve extra speed; armour was removed since there was no retaliatory fire, and, in some cases, paint was removed and surfaces were polished to reduce drag. To close in, fire and destroy the V1, meant pilots risking destruction in the explosion. Causing bombs to fall short of the metropolis by other means and explode in the sea or rural areas was also effective. With this in mind on 23 June, a Spitfire pilot tipped a V1 over by drawing level and edging nearer to flip its wing with his own wingtip. Four days later a Tempest, with the advantage of height to aid its speed, overtook a V1, causing it to dive out of control in the air turbulence of the Tempest's slipstream. Soon pilots were using all three methods and Spitfire Marks IX and XII, Hawker Typhoon day fighters and Mosquito night

fighters joined the fray.

In spite of the defences' joint endeavours, about half the 'Doodle-bugs', as the V1s were colloquially known to the public, succeeded in reaching London. They wrought terrible havoc; the bombs, set on course from their launching ramp, came down when their carefully-measured fuel gave out. Diving to earth, their 850 kg warhead of Trialen exploded on contact, reducing buildings in the immediate vicinity to rubble and causing damage over a wide radius. By mid-July, some 4,000 civilians had been killed by the weapons and many others injured.

Anti-aircraft defences

A desperate measure was taken on 17 July, effecting a change of defence planning and another massive redeployment. The bulk of the guns of General Sir Frederick Pile's Anti-Aircraft Command were moved to the coast, giving better visual approach conditions and uncluttered radar responses. Some of the defences had been placed to shield Bristol from attack from launching sites in the Cherbourg area but, as the Allies overran the latter area, an even greater density of guns could be ranged between St

Top left: a Supermarine Spitfire employs one of the methods of destroying a V1 – putting it out of control by tipping its wing to upset its gyroscope.
Top: a V1 launch site (marked A), in the Pas de Calais, following an Allied attack. B to E indicate where V1s crashed on launching.
Above: a painting by J. B. Stafford-Baker depicts a V2 transport train destroyed near Oyle by Second Tactical Air Force aircraft.
Above left: a technician makes an adjustment to a V2 before it is launched against Britain

Margaret's Bay, Kent, and Beachy Head, Sussex. Soon the guns, using proximity fuses, were shooting down more V1s than the fighters.

With their fiery tails, V1s were easy to locate in the dark and the fighter offensive, directed in lanes to avoid the areas of massed guns, continued day and night. A flight of North American Mustang Mk IIIs of No 316 (Polish) Squadron were assigned to the anti-Diver task and proved so effective that a Mustang wing of the Second Tactical Air Force was brought in. The first of the RAF's jet units, No 616 Squadron, became operational from 14 July and their Gloster Meteor Mk Is shot down 13 V1s. Mosquito squadrons were also placed on anti-Diver patrols; Sqn Ldr Francis R. L. Mellersh of No 98 Squadron achieved the record of nine V1 kills in a single sortie. Several pilots lost their lives firing on V1s, among them Commandant Jean-Marie Maridor DFC serving with No 91 Squadron RAF; he died in the explosion of his 11th kill.

During the evening of 2 August 1944 a squadron of P-51D Mustangs of the 4th Fighter Group USAAF attacked a train detected in a siding at Remy, while another squadron of the Group provided top cover. After strafing the heavily-camouflaged wagons there was an explosion so mighty that even the top cover aircraft rocked in its blast. Haystacks many fields away were set on fire and buildings in distant villages were damaged as a flying bomb supply train disintegrated.

From July to September, Bomber Command dropped 44,335 tons of bombs on V-weapon targets, representing twenty-five per cent of its total effort. The US Eighth Air Force made daylight attacks on Peenemünde and made 16,272 sorties against Noball targets, losing 63 B-17s and B-24s. Their Noball attack was made on 30 August but the Ninth Air Force, based on the Continent, continued their attacks into 1945.

The turning point was reached on the night of 27/28 August when, out of 97 V1s launched, only 10 slipped through to London. Then the Allied advance along the French coast caused launchings from France to cease from 2 September. Up to that time the fighters claimed 1,900 V1s destroyed, the guns 1,560 and the balloons 278. The lull was only temporary, however, for Germany continued the offensive by air-launching V1s from Heinkel He 111s operating from Dutch bases from the night of 4/5 September and from German bases in mid-September.

V2 rocket

However, by that time a more serious attack was developing for which there was no defence. After some 250 A-4 rockets had been built at Peenemünde they were put into large-scale production at a plant in the Harz Mountains as Hitler's revenge weapon, the V2 rocket. The concrete structures in France, planned as launching sites, had attracted so much attention from the Western Allies that long, mobile trailers were made to launch the 14m (46ft) rockets, with ramps to raise the rocket for launching, controlled by an attendant armoured vehicle. Final development work was transferred to Poland and rocket debris was soon in the hands of Polish partisans, who contacted British intelligence. A Douglas Dakota fitted with long-range fuel tanks, of No 267 Squadron, RAF based at Brindisi in Italy, made three trips to a secret landing ground in Poland and brought back rocket and flying bomb parts for scientific analysis.

At 1843 hours on 8 September the first two V2 rockets reached Britain. They fell simultaneously, one harmlessly

at Epping and the other at Chiswick causing 13 casualties. The launching sites were traced to The Hague district of Holland and both intruder raids and armed reconnaissance flights were made from Britain. Allied Expeditionary Force fighters based on the continent added their weight to strafing attacks, particularly along the supply lines. Due to Allied advances the launching positions were withdrawn to Friesland and directed towards Norwich. After the Allied check at Arnhem, however, sites were again moved

forward to The Hague to bring London within the 320 km (200 mile) range capability of the rockets. These reached a maximum speed of 5,580 km/h (3,467 mph), levelled off and descended vertically at such speed that there was virtually no warning. Their 975 kg (2,145 lb) warheads, composed mainly of amatol, caused large craters. One hit a large store by New Cross Gate station in south-east London on 25 November, killing 160 people and seriously injuring over a hundred more. Later, a hit on a block of flats at Stepney killed 134 people outright.

Sporadic attacks by air-launched V1s continued, the most determined effort being made the night before Christmas Eve when Heinkel He 111s crossed the coast to direct 30 V1s to Manchester; only one reached the target area. Among the defensive measures taken was a new gun strip along the East Anglian coast with offshore patrols carried out by Mosquitoes. The last air-launch against Britain was made on 7 January 1945, but this was not the last of the bombs. Three launching sites were made in Holland for use with increased-range V1s and of the 125 launched, 13 reached London. The majority were claimed by Anti-aircraft Command, naval gunners on warships accounting for two.

Because of the difficulties in reaching London, the Germans turned the weight of their V-weapon attacks against Antwerp in an effort to stop the Allies using the port facilities. By this time there was a quick reaction by Allied Expeditionary Air Forces fighters, from a watch kept on V2 launchings; furthermore rocket fuel was becoming scarce due to continuous pounding by Allied aircraft along railways, roads and canals.

The last V2 to reach Britain fell at Orpington, Kent on 27 March. By that time 517 had fallen on London, 537 in other parts of the country and 58 were reported exploded at sea; others had exploded in the air. Two days later the last of some 9,000 V1s operationally launched reached England. Many had failed on launching sites or disappeared into the sea. The United Kingdom defences reported 6,725 approaching and recorded 5,233 coming overland. Altogether the V-weapons which fell on Britain killed 8,994 people and injured 24,504.

A V2 captured by Allied forces in France is pictured on display in Trafalgar Square in 1945. The British were defenceless against the V2 which approached from great height and faster than the speed of sound. However, too few were launched to produce the devastation and panic hoped for by Adolf Hitler

Normandy Invasion 1944

For months preparations had been going on for Operation Overlord, the invasion and liberation of Europe. The photographing of the beaches and bombing of coastal radars and defences had been widely spread to give no hint of where penetration was planned. Indeed, a greater bomb-load was devoted to the Pas de Calais area to mislead the enemy into thinking that the shortest route to the Continent would be taken.

A massive air umbrella for the landings was planned, code-named Operation Neptune, with a series of smaller operations co-ordinated within the master plan. Directly supporting the land forces was the Allied Expeditionary Air Force (AEAF), with IX Fighter, IX Bomber and IX and XIX Tactical Air Commands of the US Ninth Air Force, together with the British and Commonwealth squadrons of the Second Tactical Air Force (2TAF), which would give close cover during the landings and move later to the Continent as ground was gained and airstrips made. Commanded by Air Chief Marshal Sir Trafford Leigh-Mallory, AEAF also included the British-based IX Troop Carrier Command of the Ninth Air Force and Nos 38 and 46 (Transport) Groups RAF, which would provide the respective airlifts for the US and British airborne troops securing the flanks of the landing areas. Also temporarily under AEAF was RAF Fighter Command, known at this period of the war as Air Defence of Great Britain, to meet the retaliation expected from the Luftwaffe against the invasion ports.

Special aircraft markings

To avoid mis-identification during the operation, it was decreed that AEAF aircraft would bear conspicuous white and black striping around wings and fuselage. Since this compromised camouflage, the instruction to paint

In the vanguard of the Normandy landings were the airborne troops of the US Army's 82nd and 101st Airborne Divisions. Two paratroopers of the Screaming Eagles, as the 101st Division was named, don their warpaint before boarding a Douglas C-47 Skytrain transport

Middlesex, with a sub-station at Ventnor on the Isle of Wight. The control and reporting techniques developed by Fighter Command were now to control the greatest concentration of air power the world had known.

RAF Bomber Command had latterly been adding its weight to disrupting the railway system in northern France and attacking military centres and coastal defences. On the evening before D-day most crews, except for those of 31 DH Mosquitoes detailed to attack Osnabrück, were briefed to attack coastal targets that night and so became the first Allied aircraft to operate on D-day. There was a full moon but some cloud, as Mosquitoes equipped with Oboe blind bombing equipment dropped their red target markers at La Pernelle, St Martin, Hougate, Ouistreham and Pointe du Hoe, sites of coastal batteries between Rouen and Cherbourg. Cloud increased during the attacks and only a few bombs hit their targets, but several cliff falls were started, destroying some minor defence points. One hundred Avro Lancasters, detailed to bomb an important coastal battery at Merville, ten minutes before airborne troops landed to capture it, missed the target altogether. Flak claimed a Handley Page Halifax over Mont Fleury, two others were seen to go down in combat over Caen and Lisieux and three other bombers were missing. One Halifax crashed on landing and another was destroyed in a taxying accident.

Beach-head bombing

As daylight approached the pounding role was taken over by the mighty US Eighth Air Force. The American bombers, 659 Boeing B-17 Fortresses and 543 Consolidated B-24 Liberators, formed up in the early hours over the Midlands and flew south in planned air corridors to cross the coast between Selsey Bill and Beachy Head. After flying straight across the Channel and reaching the Normandy coast from 0600 hours, the American bombers flying in three main streams deposited over 3,000 tons of bombs along the beach defences. Turning right across the Cherbourg peninsula after bombing, the bombers skirted the Channel Islands, before re-entering British airspace over Portland Bill. There was no close fighter escort, but 1,347 of the Eighth's fighters – Lockheed P-38

Above: a North American Mustang tactical reconnaissance fighter overflies landing craft in Eric Aldwinckle's painting 'Invasion Pattern, Normandy'.
Below: this Lockheed P-38 Lightning, parked on a beach-head landing strip, displays the distinctive D-day stripe markings

these markings was delayed until the evening of 3 June, to take effect the next day, but aircraft so marked were not to approach enemy coasts until D-day, planned for 5 June. However, adverse meteorological reports caused postponement by one day.

Bombers of the strategic air forces were not affected by the marking regulation, although they were employed tactically on D-day to bring maximum air power to bear. Units of AEAF had earlier made provision for an unprecedented four sorties per day. Since over 10,000 aircraft were involved, a special Combined Control Centre was set up at No 11 Group Headquarters, Uxbridge,

Lightnings, Republic P-47 Thunderbolts and North American P-51 Mustangs – were out sweeping over France from the Seine to the Loire, attacking enemy airfields. That attack was the best method of defence was borne out by the losses; only one B-24 was destroyed by enemy action, although two others were lost in a collision. Three times later in the day the heavies attacked further inland, making a total of 2,362 USAAF heavy bomber sorties for the day. This figure included three sorties by Fortresses dropping leaflets at Thury Harcourt, St Lo and Caen to warn French civilians of danger areas.

Medium bombers – Martin B-26 Marauders and Douglas A-20 Havocs of US IX Bomber Command, and Douglas Bostons, North American Mitchells and Mosquitoes of 2TAF – intermittently bombed coastal targets from 0343 hours in direct support of the troops approaching French soil. One of the greatest benefits from these attacks was the premature exploding of minefields. Meanwhile American P-38 Lightnings flew as close fighter escort flanking the shipping lanes. With their twin-boom fuselages it was thought that they were the fighter type least likely to be victims of mis-identification.

Airborne landings

While the bombers pounded the beaches, the airborne landing phase of Operation Neptune was being enacted. Basically the task of these forces was to seal off the assault area and protect its flanks by seizing strongpoints and destroying bridges to prevent German reinforcements reaching the area. It was six minutes to midnight when the first of the American transports of IX Troop Carrier Command took off from their bases in the Midlands and South-West England. The majority of their 770 Douglas C-47 Skytrains (Dakotas in British service), lifting the American 82nd and 101st Airborne Divisions, formed up in the dark.

The two divisions were to take up position across the Cotentin peninsula, the 101st dropping first from 0130 hours in the van of the invasion forces. Unfortunately due to navigational errors and increasing cloud, the 6,600 troops were widely scattered with only 1,100 deposited in their assigned landing area; furthermore, over half

their equipment was lost. The 82nd, dropping from 0230 hours, was also scattered and one battalion, meeting enemy opposition, was completely wiped out. Fortunately the Germans were equally confused by the apparent lack of concentration and the Americans quickly re-grouped. Most of the equipment of the initial wave was carried in 102 gliders – American Waco CG-4A Hadrians and British Airspeed Horsas. As part of the Ninth Air Force, the transports enjoyed the protection of their own fighters, but, again, the policy was to beard the enemy fighters in their own dens, rather than provide close escort for the transports returning after daybreak.

Top: barrage balloons float over the invasion fleet in anticipation of heavy German air attacks. In the event, the Luftwaffe's response to the Allied landings was minimal. Above: one of the US Ninth Air Force's Republic P-47 Thunderbolts crash-landed on a battle-scarred beach

Six pathfinding Armstrong Whitworth Albemarles taking off from Harwell, Berkshire, at 2303 hours on 5 June, heralded the British airborne forces. They were due over their three dropping zones at 0200 hours on D-day to drop troops who set up signalling beacons and illuminations to guide in following parachute and glider troops. Air Vice-Marshal L. N. Hollinghurst, who had planned this airborne landing phase, Operation Tonga, flew as passenger in one of the aircraft. Unfortunately one pilot mistook a dropping zone and the troops, unaware of the error, set up their beacons causing some of the following aircraft to be mis-directed. Another zone, correctly identified from the air, proved to be unsuitable due to partially-flooded ground, rendering the beacons ineffectual and hampering movement.

Albemarles carrying glider-borne troops inland in the Caen area to seize bridges carried bombs to attack a powder factory near Caen, in an effort to disguise the troop carrying as a bombing operation. In spite of 68 coastal observation posts in the area, almost complete surprise was achieved and some of the earliest prisoners taken were three men of Fluko (Flugwachkommando, the German Observer Corps) No 60 post at St Aubin.

Troops in three Horsa gliders towed by Albemarles were given the special task of silencing the guns of the Merville coastal battery menacing the beaches. They were to land in the battery area, assault the gun crews and blow up the guns. Unfortunately the tow rope of one glider broke over England and both the other two were damaged by flak over the French coast. Smoke from bombing, which had taken place minutes earlier, obscured the pilots' view and one of the two landed some distance away, but the other landed just outside the battery perimeter. In spite of these handicaps, the operation succeeded and the battery was silenced by 0445 hours.

Successful deception

The Germans, although expecting the invasion, failed to find out where the Allies intended to land. Operation Taxable, performed by RAF Bomber Command, was designed to mislead on this score. Since the actual blow would fall in Normandy, that attack had to be made to appear a feint. To give credence to the ruse that the chief blow would fall in the Pas de Calais area to the north, at the narrowest point of the Channel, the Lancasters of the famous Dam-busters (No 617 Squadron) were given this exacting task. Each Lancaster had five extra crew members: a co-pilot and co-navigator to ensure a rigid adherence to pattern flying for 3 hours 30 minutes and three dispatchers to dispense the metallised strips code-named Window through the flare chute at four-second intervals. While a small token convoy steamed towards the enemy coast, the Lancasters weaved a counter-marching pattern overhead, edging towards the French coast at convoy speed dropping Window. The desired effect on enemy radar screens, suggesting a large surface convoy approaching the Seine Estuary, was so well achieved that radar-predicted guns eventually opened fire on non-existent ships. Meanwhile, Short Stirlings dropped Window to the west of the landings, to confuse the Germans further and draw attention from American transports.

Operation Titanic, another part of the deception plan, involved over a hundred RAF Lancasters, Halifaxes, Stirlings, Fortresses and Mosquitoes. Enemy radio was jammed by airborne transmitters, dummy parachutists were dropped over a wide area from Stirlings as well as small parties of Special Air Service (SAS) troops. Another small party of SAS was dropped in Brittany to cut

railway lines. These measures, together with the fighter sweeps of Air Defence Great Britain concentrating on the Pas de Calais area, were instrumental in backing Hitler's own belief that the invasion would come directly across the Dover Straits. As a result, enemy armour which might have been ordered to the vulnerable bridgehead area was held back for some days by the Germans.

Naval co-operation

Naval intelligence estimated the presence of five destroyers, five torpedo boats and 50 E-boats deployed between Ijmuiden in the Netherlands and Cherbourg, all of which could menace the Allied armada crossing the Channel and the following supplies. It had been arranged that from the moment Overlord was signalled, Coastal Command would intensify patrolling to block the Channel either side of the Allied shipping lanes. Three German destroyers dispatched to the assault area were spotted, tracked and attacked. Bristol Beaufighters of the Wick Wing, operating temporarily in the south, attacked the destroyers with rockets and cannon fire, protected by a Mosquito escort. A subsequent torpedo attack, made by Beaufighters in moonlight, scored hits but did not achieve any sinkings and the warships were later dealt with by the Navy.

An Air Spotting Pool was established at Lee-on-Solent, Hampshire, to report fall of shot for the naval escorts bombarding the coast defences. This consisted of four Fleet Air Arm squadrons flying Supermarine Spitfires and Supermarine Seafires, two RAF Spitfire squadrons and VCS-7, the only US Navy squadron to fly Spitfires. The American squadron had been quickly formed from pilots of floatplane and scouting flights using borrowed Spitfires to scout for the Western Naval Task Force, which was composed mainly of American ships.

The Luftwaffe's response to the Allied landings was barely perceptible. Allied intelligence had put the strength of Luftflotte 3 in France at some 800 aircraft, of which some 600 could be used to oppose the landings by bombing or strafing, but postwar research revealed that the estimate was high. In the event, the Luftwaffe flew less than 100 sorties during daylight, most of them by fighters. Four Junkers Ju 88s, attempting to attack shipping were shot down and a Focke Wulf Fw 190, before crashing into the sea, damaged HMS *Bulolo*, the local air control ship stationed offshore. It was planned that an RAF Base

Defence Sector Control Unit would organise defensive operations in the beach-head area. However, heavy machine-gun fire prevented the unit landing in the morning and in the afternoon most of their vehicles stalled when they disgorged from landing craft into deep water, rendering the unit inoperative for some days.

German activity increased after nightfall, when long-range bombers and torpedo bombers attacked the beach-head. By that time anti-aircraft defences had been established ashore and ships offshore added to the barrage. Furthermore, German flak crews, conditioned to overwhelming Allied air power, attacked their own aircraft, but this also happened on the Allied side.

During the evening, with a beach-head established, the reinforcement plans were set in motion. Operation Mallard concerned the airlifting of the remainder of the 6th Airborne Division. The transport aircraft this time acted mainly as tugs for the 226 Horsa gliders, carrying men, jeeps and trailers, and 30 General Aircraft Hamilcar gliders conveying armour and artillery. This time there was less cloud and all but ten gliders had landed in their designated zones by 2130 hours. Two gliders ditched in the Channel and another disappeared without trace; but the others, with broken tow-lines, landed in England or in France within the beach-head area. The only loss to enemy action was a Dakota glider-tug.

Re-supply was also necessary and 50 Dakotas set out with 116 tons of ammunition, food and equipment in Operation Rob Roy. As the Dakotas approached low from seawards on their supply mission, they were mistaken for a further wave of German bombers that had just attacked the shipping. Heavy anti-aircraft fire caused the formation to scatter, forcing some aircraft to return damaged. One ditched in the Channel and five others were missing. Less than a quarter of the supplies were delivered.

Altogether during the 24-hours of 6 June 1944, 9,210 AEAF aircraft had participated, backed by strategic bombers, naval and coastal aircraft. Other aircraft, including nearly a hundred in the air-sea rescue role, were on standby. In fact a Halifax had ditched 480 km (300 miles) off Lands End and a dramatic long distance rescue operation was being mounted – but that task involved but a very few of the 14,674 sorties flown by the Allied Air Forces that day in the Channel area.

Opposite: Albert Richards' painting 'Crashed Gliders. The Landing Zone at Ransville' shows British Airspeed Horsas used in the airborne landing phase of Overlord. Below: the break-out from the Normandy beach-head was spearheaded by rocket-firing Hawker Typhoons of the Second Tactical Air Force, depicted in Frank Wootton's painting

Arnhem 1944

'There can have been few episodes more glorious than the epic of Arnhem, and those that follow will find it hard to live up to the high standards that you have set.'

This was the message, in part, of Field Marshal Montgomery to men who had taken part in what was to have been a glorious Allied example of combined air and ground attacks but which turned out to be an example of tactical misappreciation, failure of communication between air and land forces and a breakdown of intelligence.

Essentially the Battle of Arnhem in September 1944 was part of a wider attack by troops and aircraft of the 1st Allied Airborne Army (under the command of Lieut-Gen L. H. Brereton) and its 1st Airborne Division (Maj-Gen R. E. Urquhart), including the Polish Brigade, the 82nd US Division and the 101st US Division, plus the 52nd Lowlanders, the RAF's 38 and 46 Groups, and the US IX Troop Carrier Command. Their objective was to combine with ground forces in attacking and seizing not only Arnhem but also Eindhoven, Grave, Nijmegen and – principally – the bridges over the Rhine, Waal and Neder Rijn rivers and to open a corridor to the Zuiderzee. The ground thrust was to be by XXX Corps, XII and VIII Corps, the first, commanded by Lieut-Gen Brian Horrocks, providing the central and all-important drive, assuming the success of the airborne attack.

Montgomery's plan
Operation 'Market Garden', as it was code-named, was

Below: Waco Hadrians towed by Douglas C-47s pass near Eindhoven on their way to reinforce the 1st Airborne Army.
Right: paratroops could be tactically decisive but they could only fight unsupported for a limited time

essentially devised by Montgomery and involved the closest co-operation between ground and air forces of British, Polish and American units. Perhaps inevitably, there were differences as to how these forces could best be deployed and there was no direct link between the Corps headquarters and the tactical air forces whose commitment was vital. If successful, according to 'Monty', the thrust would provide an 'open road' to Berlin, yet no strategic reserves to provide the necessary back-up were planned. Finally, though Allied bombers on missions to Germany had noted an increase in flak from the Arnhem area, intelligence services failed to warn of the strengthening of artillery in the area and the presence of II Panzer Corps.

The aerial part of the attack, which concerns us here, began on 17 September 1944 and involved 519 aircraft with troops of 1st Airborne Division, including the Polish Brigade, 530 for the 82nd Division and 494 for the 101st Division.

All the US aircraft were Douglas C-47s from IX Troop Carrier Command, while the British force was made up by 149 American and 130 RAF C-47s and some 240 converted RAF bombers. These included Handley Page Halifaxes, mainly for towing the gliders, Short Stirlings and a few Armstrong Whitworth Albemarles, which had been used successfully to drop paratroops into Normandy earlier that year. Fighter cover came mainly from Spitfires and Hawker Tempests and more than 1,200 fighters were used in the operation.

The airborne attack depended on the use of gliders, though this, too, was a matter of differing opinions. In total some 2,800 gliders were used, mostly by the British

On the way to the DZ: soldiers with their weapons, their kit packed in leg bags or under smocks, to prevent it catching in the parachute harness

forces, whose commanders favoured the Airspeed Horsa, which could carry up to 29 fully-armed soldiers, and the giant Hamilcar, used mainly for heavy equipment.

American gliders were the Waco CG-4A, smaller than the Horsa and capable of carrying some 15 fully-equipped paratroops. US commanders favoured using the C-47, which could carry at least 19 troops. Thus it was decided that the RAF would tow gliders and the Americans drop most of their paratroops, using the Wacos only sparingly.

Right: groundcrewmen of the USAAF watch C-47s form up over their airfield en route to the Arnhem dropzone. American transport aircraft carried British paratroops in the Arnhem operation, as well as the US 82nd and 101st Airborne Divisions

The 101st was to commit one parachute regiment in the Weghel area, south-west of Grave and use the remainder to establish an air-head north west of Zon, above Eindhoven, sending out detachments to the north and south to secure the bridges. Meanwhile the 82nd was to drop two parachute regiments plus divisional troops and 50 glider-loads of guns and equipment on the slopes of Groesbeek heights, the remaining regiment jumping north of Maas and east of Grave. The RAF had accepted a zone south of the Rhine, close to the Arnhem-Nijmegen road, as the DZ (dropping zone) for 1st Division and LZs (landing zones) north-west of the river for gliders. There were to be three main lifts, on the 17th, 18th and 19th, the

first taking about two-thirds of the airborne divisions and the others bringing in reserves and supplies.

The first lift began at 1430 hours on 17 September from seven British and 17 US airfields in England. The smaller force of 494 C-47s and 70 Wacos of 101st Division flew a southerly course to Gheel and wheeled left to approach the DZs and LZs near Eindhoven. The larger force of 1st Airborne and 82nd Division went north over the Dutch coast and then eastwards before splitting over s'Hertogen, the 82nd Division heading towards Grave and Nijmegen and the 1st for Arnhem.

Initial surprise

The RAF had insisted on air planning which would provide maximum safe landings and, as Maurice Tugwell records in his book *Airborne to Battle:* 'They believed it to be their duty to deliver the soldiers alive and consequently wished to frame the landing plan around a compact, safe area.' They were concerned to avoid heavy concentrations of flak, for the sake of the troops, yet pilots had no qualms on their own behalf about flak.

Of Lift One, 35 C-47s and 16 Wacos were destroyed but not one troop carrier on the Arnhem lift was destroyed by enemy action, though 12 gliders either force-landed or ditched for various reasons.

Initial surprise at Arnhem was complete, even after a pathfinder force had been dropped at midday from 12 Stirlings to mark the DZs and LZs. But a Waco crashed not far from the headquarters of Colonel-General Kurt Student, commander of a new German army (the 1st Parachute) near s'Hertogen. On the body of one of the officers the Germans found a set of operation orders and

Above: paratroops under training drop from an Armstrong Whitworth Whitley of 1 Parachute Training School.
Left: a Short Stirling glider tug tows off an Airspeed Horsa

Student later acknowledged that they proved of supreme importance. Within an hour of the attack starting he was in a position to counter-attack. The II SS Panzer Corps at Doetinchen and the 9 Panzer Division at Deelen went rapidly into action as the Irish Guards led Horrocks' XXX Corps towards Arnhem and 200 RAF rocket-equipped Typhoon fighter-bombers of 83 Group attacked anti-tank positions ahead of them.

Gradually, over the succeeding days, the plans began to fall apart as the weather worsened and the troops at Arnhem met fierce resistance. Luftwaffe fighters – mainly Focke-Wulfe Fw 190s and Messerschmitt Bf 109s – inflicted heavy casualties on gliders and C-47s. During the

first four days more than 4,000 aircraft and 2,800 glider sorties were flown. RAF transport aircraft braved concentrated flak to deliver supplies and 55 were lost.

On 21 September it was suggested that a grass airfield could be opened up near Grave for C-47s to evacuate casualties and bring in supplies but clearance for the project was not forthcoming from the RAF for two days. On the 25th the strip handled 209 landings and take-offs without accident, yet next day there were no further landings because 83 Group claimed the strip for its fighter-bombers. The battle report of 1st Airborne Corps recorded: 'It is of interest to note that at no time did 83 Group or 2nd Tactical Air Force communicate with or

visit Airborne Corps, nor did they reply to Corps offers to make them a fighter strip or strips.'

The RAF's 83 Group came in for further criticism in that report, which claimed that its air support had been 'negligible' until 23 September. Partly, however, this was due to bad weather but mainly to the fact that they were forbidden to fly over the battle area during any time allocated for the delivery by air of troops or supplies! This, in fact, covered most daylight hours.

By the fifth day of the battle at Arnhem Urquhart knew that the situation was virtually hopeless and that it was a matter of those troops caught in and around the town hanging on. They were able to hold the bridge for a time but the armoured divisions could not break through and the bad weather prevented many of the supplies reaching them.

The 1st Airborne Division was ordered to pull back to the left bank of the Neder Rijn. On the night of 25-26 September 2,163 men crossed the river. They were the remnants of 8,900 officers and men and 1,100 glider pilots who had fought side by side. The Polish Brigade lost 1,000 and the 82nd and 101st 1,669 and 2,074 killed, missing and wounded. About one-third of the original force of 34,876 men were lost in this 'epic' which became a failure.

Above: men of the Headquarters Group, 1st Airborne Division artillery unloading equipment from the first two Airspeed Horsa gliders to land at Arnhem. On the first lift to Arnhem on 17 September 320 Horsas were used, and 296 on the second lift the following day.

Right: gliders on landing zone 'Z', some of which have crashed on landing. Several have been broken in half for unloading

Hiroshima and Nagasaki 1945

Colonel Paul Tibbets, the pilot of the Boeing B-29
Superfortress which dropped the Hiroshima atomic bomb,
waves from the cabin before taking off for the target

On 6 August 1945 an estimated 80,000 persons lost their lives and the greater part of a city was devastated as the result of a single explosion of unprecedented magnitude. Three days later 35,000 people were killed by a similarly powerful and destructive blast unleashed over another Japanese city. The use of the first atomic weapon had brought a terrifying new dimension to warfare and ensured that the names of Hiroshima and Nagasaki would always be synonymous with the catastrophic horror resulting from this type of explosion.

The Manhattan Project

The development of the atomic bomb can be traced to a letter that the great physicist Albert Einstein sent to President Roosevelt in the autumn of 1939. He warned that Nazi Germany's research into nuclear fission might result in the construction of an extremely powerful bomb. The President was eventually persuaded to arrange for a United States scientific investigation into the building of such a weapon to counter similar work by the potential enemy. Britain had already embarked on such a programme and there was co-operation and eventual agreement to concentrate the practical development of the weapon in the United States.

Under the code name 'Manhattan Project', work accelerated after America was brought into the war in December 1941. The whole operation was shrouded in great secrecy and many scientists at the principal site, Los Alamos in the New Mexico desert, were virtually prisoners during its crucial stages. Some two billion US dollars were used to fund the project which had top priority for all requirements. Under the scientific direction of Robert Oppenheimer work had progressed to a point where the construction of two types of bomb, using the fissionable materials uranium 235 and plutonium, was under way by the summer of 1944. At that time the overall director of the 'Manhattan Project', Brigadier General Leslie R. Groves, arranged for a special unit to be set up and trained to deliver the bombs.

The weight of the bomb was expected to be some 4,500 kg (10,000 lb) and the only practical delivery aircraft available was the Boeing B-29 Superfortress. The decision was taken to separate a squadron from one of the new B-29 groups being trained for combat and the 393rd Bomb Squadron of the 504th Bomb Group at Fairmont Field, Nebraska, was selected. In September 1944 the squadron was separated from the parent group and moved with its complement of 15 B-29s to the isolated base at Wendover in Utah. There ground units were assigned to give it direct support. Colonel Paul W. Tibbets Jnr took command and started training the 393rd for its special mission. Tibbets was at that time the only member of the squadron who knew exactly what their mission was, he having been specially selected for the task. Tibbets piloted the first 8th Air Force B-17 to penetrate Hitler's Festung Europa (Fortress Europe) and completed a tour of operations with the 97th Bomb Group in North Africa. On return to the United States he was involved in the flight development programme of the B-29, testing and instructing.

In his new command Tibbets gathered a few of the men whose particular expertise had impressed him in previous assignments. They included Captain Robert Lewis, an outstanding B-29 pilot, Major Tom Ferebee, who had been Tibbets' bombardier in North Africa, and Captain Theodore van Kirk, his navigator during combat missions over Europe. These men and others he formed into what he regarded as his personal crew, with whom he intended to drop the first atomic bomb.

*Left: the funeral pyre of Hiroshima on 5 August 1945. The atomic explosion impelled a mushroom cloud of smoke and debris to 18,000m (60,000ft) above the city.
Above right: the devastation at Hiroshima was utter for 13 sq km (5 sq miles). In this area thousands of people were killed. Many more died from exposure to radiation.
Right: two scenes of the aftermath of the atomic explosion at Nagasaki, 9 August 1945*

Special mission training
It was not long before most men in the 393rd realised that their special mission was to involve some new weapon. Tibbets had been given basic details of the weapon's size and weight and how it would have to be delivered. Training flights were flown by individual aircraft dropping 4,500 kg (10,000 lb) practice bombs from 9,000 m (30,000ft). Tibbets was told that it was imperative to get the aircraft as far away from the target area as possible before the bomb exploded. Consequently, after releasing the practice missiles a sharp diving turn was made, so that the bomber was 8 km (five miles) away when the bomb detonated.

A specialised ordnance squadron was added to the 393rd's supporting units and on 17 December 1944 the 509th Composite Group was activated under Tibbets' command at Wendover. An additional unit formed at the same time was the 320th Troop Carrier Squadron, equipped with Douglas C-54 transports. This further enhanced the strict security imposed by making it unnecessary to employ outside carriers for the personnel and equipment flown between Wendover and various sites involved in the project.

With work on the first two atomic weapons almost complete at the end of April 1945, the 509th Group started to move to North Field, Tinian, in the Mariana Islands. The 21st Bomber Command was already based there, carrying out conventional bombing operations against Japan, some 2,400 km (1,500 miles) away. A specially-fenced compound was home for the 509th and its aircraft–new Martin-built B-29s–were under constant guard. These measures understandably aroused considerable speculation among the personnel of the other bomb groups at North Field as to the purpose of this strange organisation. The 509th Group flew practice missions with live bombs against Rota, an island 80km (50 miles) south of Tinian, where a Japanese garrison had been bypassed in the United States' island-hopping campaign in the Pacific Theatre.

Target selection
A target list for the first atomic attack had been prepared. Originally Kyoto, Hiroshima, Yokohama and Kokura

were selected as suitable large areas of population. Kyoto, a city of historic and cultural significance, was deleted–at the insistence of Henry Stimson, the venerable US Secretary of War–and Niigata substituted. These places were then notified as forbidden targets for conventional bombing raids. Later Yokohama was considered too important a port to leave for an untried weapon and this city was removed from the target list and Nagasaki added. Hiroshima emerged as the primary target, as it had very distinctive landmarks and thus was easily identified from 9,000 m (30,000ft). It was also believed to be the only one

Opposite: a nuclear test in New Mexico. For over 20 years since 1945 jet-propelled heavy bombers of the U.S., U.K. and U.S.S.R. maintained the deterrent policy of peace through fear of an atomic attack. Today this role has largely, though not completely, been taken over by intercontinental nuclear missiles, based on land or submarines.

of the four targets which did not house a large Allied prisoner of war camp.

The uranium 235 bomb, known as 'Little Boy', was to be used on the first drop and scientists were confident that this would function without a test explosion. 'Fat Man', the plutonium bomb, had a complicated detonation system and a test was declared necessary. This was successfully carried out in the Alamogordo desert, New Mexico, on 16 July 1945.

The 393rd Bomb Squadron began high level operations over Japan, commencing on 20 July. Small numbers of aircraft (two to six) conducted much the same tactics as devised for atomic attack, but dropped conventional bombs. This was to accustom the Japanese defences to such penetrations of their airspace, so that when the real attack was launched they would not suspect anything unusual. As a further measure to avert suspicion which might lead the enemy to single out these sorties for attack, the 393rd's aircraft had the identity marking (an arrow-head in a circle) removed from their tails and markings of other groups in the 20th Air Force substituted. In any event, interference from flak or fighters was not envisaged at the high altitudes involved.

By early August the 'Little Boy' had arrived on Tinian and, following the rejection of Allied surrender terms, the decision was taken by President Truman and his advisors to use the weapon. A special pit was constructed at the 509th Group's site on North Field into which 'Little Boy' was lowered and the B-29 to be used–serialled 44-86292–positioned over it. The weapon was approximately 3m (10ft) long and 70cm (28in) in diameter and weighed something over 4,100kg (9,000lb). The fissionable material weighed only 10kg (22lb), most of the weight being concentrated in a device which brought the two masses of uranium 235 together and caused the explosion. A conventional explosive charge achieved this by blasting one part of the fissionable material into the other in a mechanism which was not unlike a gun barrel.

Atomic warfare

Seven B-29s were involved in the operation launched on 6 August 1945. One flew to the island of Iwo Jima on the route to Japan to act as a standby in case the bomb-carrying aircraft developed trouble. Three B-29s were to fly ahead to Hiroshima and the alternative targets Kokura and Nagasaki, where weather reports would be radioed to the attack bomber. Two other aircraft would accompany the bomb carrier–which Tibbets had named *Enola Gay* after his mother–one to drop scientific sensing devices and the second to make a photographic record.

Enola Gay took off at 0245 hours local time, with Tibbets at the controls and Bob Lewis as co-pilot. Ferebee was bombardier and van Kirk the navigator. The bomb

was armed in flight by Captain William Parsons USN, who had been specially trained at Los Alamos for this task. The flight went according to plan and at approximately 0815 hours (Japanese time) the bomb was released and exploded at 600m (1,900ft) above the ground. Tibbets had executed his diving turn and his aircraft was about nine kilometres (six miles) away when the explosion occurred, but the B-29 encountered two severe shock waves. The fireball was seen as far as 400km (250 miles) away and the mushroom-shaped cloud rose to an estimated 18,000m (60,000ft) above the devastation. Over 129,000 casualties were caused and over 60,000 buildings were considered destroyed by a blast of 20 kilotons (equivalent to that of 20,000 tons of TNT).

Despite the holocaust at Hiroshima, there was still no sign of the Japanese acceptance of Allied surrender terms and the decision was made to drop a second bomb. This was the plutonium device known as 'Fat Man', which, because of its girth, could only just be accommodated in the B-29's bomb-bay. Tibbets selected Major Charles W. Sweeney, commander of the 393rd Bomb Squadron, to carry out the second mission. The aircraft involved was 44-27297, named *Bock's Car*. The mission was flown on 9 August with take-off from North Field, Tinian, at 0230 hours. The target was to be Kokura, but upon arrival cloud had gathered and made it impossible for the bombardier of *Bock's Car* to locate the aiming point. Frustrated, Sweeney turned for the secondary target, Nagasaki, some 150km (95 miles) away. Here too it seemed that cloud would prevent bombing, but, just as Sweeney was considering abandoning the mission, a clear patch allowed the bombardier to make his sighting. Release was made at 1050 hours (Japanese time) at an altitude of 8,800m (28,900ft). 'Fat Man' exploded as planned, although the devastation and loss of life was not so great as at Hiroshima because the undulating land on which the city was built tended to limit damage from blast. Casualties amounted to 95,000, of which 35,000 were deaths. The extra time spent in trying to sight on the target had made unforeseen demands on fuel supplies in Sweeney's aircraft and an accompanying B-29, so that both aircraft had to land on the island of Okinawa before continuing their journey back to Tinian.

The second atomic attack and Russia's entry into the war against Japan next day were crucial factors in persuading Japan's leaders to accept the surrender terms. The morality of dropping the two atomic bombs has since been an oft-debated subject. The fact remains that the decision to use them brought about an early end to hostilities and made the planned invasion of Japan unnecessary. Such an invasion, it was estimated, would have cost the lives of over a million Allied combatants and perhaps four million Japanese would have been killed.

The Boeing B-29 Super-fortress named 'Bock's Car' which dropped the atomic bomb on Nagasaki on 9 August 1945. The B-29 was the only aircraft available which had the capability of carrying the heavy atomic bombs over the distance demanded. Even so, both 'Bock's Car' and 'Enola Gay' were considerably overloaded at take-off

Index

Acknowledgments

Illustrations were supplied by Air Portraits, Auckland Collection, Australian War Memorial, Aviation Photographs International, Bapty, Bell Helicopter Co, G. Bingham, Blitz Publications, K. Brookes, A. Brown, C. Brown, Bundesarchiv, Canadian War Museum, F. Cheesman, Emy Conrad, D. Copsey, Crown Copyright, Deutches Museum, G. Finch, E. Gee, J. Gilbert, J. Goulding, Grosset and Dunlap, Grumman International, C. Harrison, J. Heritage, M. Hooks, Robert Hunt Library, Imperial War Museum, A. Imrie, J. Jahr, J. Jorgensen, G. W. Kaelia, P. Kilduff, D. Kingston, Lockheed, P. March, F. Mason, Ministry of Defence, National Defence H.Q. of Canada, Novosti, D. Oliver, Public Archives of Canada, RAF Museum, B. Robertson, Rolls Royce Ltd, C. Shores, Sikorsky Aircraft, M. Turner, U.S. Airforce, U.S. Army, U.S. Marine Corps, U.S. National Archives, U.S. Navy, B. Withan, Wojskowa Agencja Fotograficzna, H. Woodman, F. Wooton.